The Distribute Emergency Management and Homeland Security

The Distributed Functions of Emergency Management and Homeland Security outlines the roles and responsibilities of various individuals and agencies involved in emergency management and other aspects of homeland security. Each chapter focuses on the duties and actions of a range of public servants in various departments and the organizations that they represent.

Rather than presenting a theoretical exploration alone, the book examines the practical knowledge and hands-on skills related to various functions and how decisions and actions play into the larger framework of safety and security in the public, private, and non-profit sectors. Every professional has a unique and integral duty to perform, whether it be in relation to prevention, mitigation, preparedness, response, or recovery operations. Personnel that frequently come to mind in such scenarios include emergency managers, geographers and land-use planners, EMTs and paramedics, firefighters, police officers, public health officials, nurses, public administrators, and public information officers. And while these individuals are integral to emergency management and homeland security, there are other professionals that also perform essential duties that – while they aren't first-to-mind – are vital to efforts relating to terrorism and disasters. This includes pilots in the aviation sector, the military, attorneys, psychologists, and forensic professionals serving in pathology, DNA, and dentistry roles.

The chapters of this book provide a holistic rendering of the emergency management and homeland security landscape which covers all of these various professional capabilities and contributions. This includes how current functions are coordinated as well as how future efforts might change relative to a more proactive, all-hazards, and holistic approach. As such, the book will be a useful resource for students and practitioners to understand the dynamic professions – and various disciplines and fields – that impact disasters and terrorism preparedness and response capabilities.

David A. McEntire is a professor in both the Emergency Services and Criminal Justice Departments at Utah Valley University, USA. He teaches emergency management and national security. His expertise is in emergency management theory, vulnerability reduction, community preparedness, response coordination, terrorism, and homeland security. He has received a number of grants that have allowed him to conduct research on disasters and emergency management systems in Australia, California, Canada, Costa Rica, Dominican Republic, Haiti, New York, New Zealand, Texas, and Utah. Dr McEntire has written five books and published over 140 articles. He has presented his research in both domestic and international conferences. He is the recipient of FEMA's Dr B. Wayne Blanchard Award for Academic Excellence and the Scholarship of Teaching and Learning Award from the University of Central Florida.

The Distributed Functions of Emergency Management and Homeland Security

An Assessment of Professions Involved in Response to Disasters and Terrorist Attacks

Edited by

David A. McEntire
With special contributions by Barbara Burr

CRC Press
Taylor & Francis Group
Boca Raton London New York

CRC Press is an imprint of the
Taylor & Francis Group, an **informa** business

Designed cover image: Shutterstock

First edition published 2023

by CRC Press
6000 Broken Sound Parkway NW, Suite 300, Boca Raton, FL 33487-2742

and by CRC Press
4 Park Square, Milton Park, Abingdon, Oxon, OX14 4RN
CRC Press is an imprint of Taylor & Francis Group, LLC

ISBN: 978-1-032-39645-3 (hbk)
ISBN: 978-1-032-39644-6 (pbk)
ISBN: 978-1-003-35072-9 (ebk)

DOI: 10.4324/9781003350729

Typeset in Sabon
by Deanta Global Publishing Services, Chennai, India

Dedicated to disaster and homeland professionals everywhere – to the heroes both visible and unsung.

Contents

Contributors

Abraham David Benavides is an associate professor in the Department of Public Administration at the University of North Texas, USA. He has been at UNT for 19 years. He received his Doctorate's Degree from Cleveland State University, USA, his Master's Degree in Public Administration from Brigham Young University, USA, and his Bachelor's Degree from George Washington University, USA. His research interests include local government, human resources, cultural competency, ethics and leadership, age-friendly policies, and human service issues. He has over 50 publications including academic journal articles, book chapters, book reviews, and professional reports. Benavides has given a number of national and international presentations on various topics, is a former department chair in the Department of Public Administration at UNT, and a former accreditation compliance officer for Summit County, Ohio.

Dave Bergner retired as Public Works Superintendent after nearly 21 years with the City of Overland Park, Kansas. Prior to that he was with the City of Kansas City, Missouri, for 15 years, lastly as Traffic Operations Manager. During his career, he was extensively involved in response to numerous traffic incidents, natural disasters, planned special events, and other critical situations. He is the Chair of the Transportation Research Board's Maintenance and Operations Personnel (TRB) committee and a member of the Operations Resilience and Emergency Response committees. Dave has authored articles and papers on public works' role in emergency management and traffic incident management and presented at APWA, American Society of Civil Engineers, American Society for Public Administration, IMSA, International Road Federation, Institute of Traffic Engineers, PIARC World Road Congress, Society of American Military Engineers, and TRB. Dave has a Master's in Management and holds the APWA designations of Public Works Leadership Fellow and Certified Public Works Professional-Manager.

Rodger Broomé is a humanistic-existential psychologist specializing in emergency and crisis psychology at the Department of Emergency Services, Utah Valley University, USA. He is a retired and experienced public safety leader having worked in fire, emergency medical services, and law enforcement. Rodger is a psychological researcher and expert in scientific phenomenological research, having published on public safety psychology and research epistemology. His research approach and theoretical perspectives re-humanize the badge through the lived experiences of firefighters, police officers, and emergency medical professionals that stand trained and ready in protection of their communities.

Peter Burke began his fire service career as a junior firefighter in Swansea, Massachusetts. In 2017 he was appointed as the Fire Chief of the Hyannis Fire Department. Burke is an instructor at the Massachusetts Firefighting Academy and has taught extensively in the recruit, technical rescue, hazardous materials, and rapid intervention programs. He is an adjunct professor at Cape Cod Community College. He holds a Bachelor's Degree in Fire Science from Providence College, USA, and a Master's Degree in Emergency management from the Massachusetts Maritime Academy, USA, where he was the recipient of the Jerry S. Parr award for excellence. Burke is a graduate of the Chief Fire Officer Program jointly conducted by the Firefighting Academy and UMASS Boston's Collins Institute. He is also a graduate of the Harvard Kennedy School Leadership in Homeland Security Program and the Suffolk University Local Government Leadership and Management certificate program.

Barbara Burr is an assistant dean in the College of Health and Public Service at Utah Valley University, USA. Prior to joining UVU, she worked at the University of Utah, USA, School of Dentistry as the Director of Student Affairs. Before relocating to Utah from southern California, Barbara worked for the University of Southern California, USA, in several capacities, including as the Clinical Education Administrator for the USC Primary Care Physician Assistant Program, Program Manager for External Programs & Continuing Education at the School of Pharmacy, and the Healthcare Administrator for the USC+LAC Maternal-Child & Adolescent Infectious Disease Management and Research Center. Barbara has worked in healthcare management and administration for the past 30+ years, both in the private sector and higher education. She has a Bachelor of Science in Sociology from Brigham Young University, USA, and a Master of Health Administration from the University of La Verne, USA, as well as Certificates in Management, Project Management, and Human Resource Management from USC. She has also earned professional certification through the Society for Human Resource Management.

Tina Bynum is an author, researcher, educator, and consultant in the homeland security and emergency management enterprise. Dr. Bynum is the Associate Dean of Law, Public Safety, and Social Sciences with Pikes Peak State College and an Associate Editor with the Journal of Homeland Security & Emergency Management. She also serves as an emergency management program assessor with the Emergency Management Accreditation Program (EMAP). Bynum holds a Doctor of Management – Homeland Security from Colorado Technical University, and a Master of Public Administration and a Bachelor's Degree in Psychology from the University of Colorado, USA. Bynum previously served as the University Program Director for the College of Security Studies at Colorado Technical University, the Associate Director of Operations and Educational Programs at the Center for Homeland Security at the University of Colorado Colorado Springs, and the Associate Director for the CU-Trauma, Health, and Hazards Center at the University of Colorado Colorado Springs. Bynum develops and teaches courses in criminal justice, emergency and fire management services, public administration, and homeland security. A retired firefighter and emergency medical technician, she also volunteers as a senior emergency exercise planner for her community.

Andrew Byrnes retired as a Special Operations Battalion Chief from the Orem Fire Department in Utah. He was a sworn law enforcement officer for 18 years and Paramedic for 16 years. He is currently a professor in the Emergency Services Department at Utah Valley University (UVU), USA. He is the Director of the Firefighter Recruit Candidate Academy program at UVU for entry-level firefighters. Byrnes is a course designer and instructor for the National Fire Academy in Emmitsburg, Maryland, specializing in Hazmat/WMD Response, Chemistry, and Advanced Science. He has reviewed and contributed to several textbooks related to Hazmat/WMD chemistry and response and is a frequent course reviewer, researcher, and subject matter expert in the areas of hazmat, firefighting, leadership, and management. He is a current member of the NFPA 470

Technical Committee for Hazardous Materials. He graduated from the National Fire Academy's Executive Fire Officer Program and holds an Associate degree in Fire Science, a Bachelor's degree in Public Emergency Services Management, and a Master's degree in Education from Utah State University, USA.

Joy Cole is a nurse educator who promotes the ongoing development of the nursing profession and the educational process. As a registered nurse, Cole's experience spans decades and includes direct patient care, education of both undergraduate and graduate-level nursing professionals, and service to community members to promote wellness and compassionate inclusion. She holds a Doctor of Philosophy degree in Nursing Education from the University of Northern Colorado, USA.

John R. Fisher is a professor and chair of the Department of Emergency Services at Utah Valley University (UVU), USA. Before coming to UVU, he taught management and communications at Northwest Missouri State University, USA, Boise State University, USA, Athabasca University, USA, and the University of Alberta, Canada. John began his career as a newspaper reporter/photographer, reporting the court and police beats and covering emergency services. For eight years he was a public administrator in the Alberta government, working in policy analysis, public information, and legislative affairs. He has a Bachelor's and a Master's from Brigham Young University, USA, and a Doctorate Degree from the University of Alberta. His principal areas of research are mass media coverage of disaster public policy, disaster preparedness and community resilience, and applied learning online for adult learners. He was a Fulbright Scholar in Kosovo at the Kosovo Academy of Public Safety in 2018–2019.

Mike Gutierrez is an assistant professor in the Department of Emergency Management and Homeland Security at Massachusetts Maritime Academy. In addition, Gutierrez serves as an adjunct professor for NOVA Southeastern University, USA, within the Department of Disaster and Emergency Management, and for Lamar University, USA, within the Master of Public Administration Program. Gutierrez holds a Bachelor's, Master's, and Doctorate Degree from the University of North Texas, USA. He currently serves as a Council Member on the Southeastern Regional Homeland Security Advisory Council. Gutierrez's prior experiences include serving as an Army Ranger with the 1st Battalion 75th Ranger Regiment, as a Texas law enforcement officer, president of a municipal development district, and as co-chair for the planning and zoning commission.

Steve K. Holley is an assistant professor in the Emergency Services Department at Utah Valley University, USA, with a concentration in Emergency Medical Services. He earned a Bachelor's from Idaho State University, USA, and an Associate of Arts degree from Ricks College, USA, both in Economics. He also holds a Master of Public Administration degree, with an emphasis in Public Finance and Budgeting, and a Master of Arts in Political Science from Idaho State University as well. Steve recently served as the EMS Director of a hospital-based, ALS ambulance service in a rural resort area. Prior to that, he was a Flight Paramedic at a rotor-wing base for the U.S. Navy. He was trained to the Firefighter II level, HAZMAT Operations and as a Fire Marshal/Inspector as well. Holley is a National Registry Paramedic, a University of Maryland-Baltimore Critical Care Paramedic, and a BCCTPC Flight Paramedic-Certified. He is a member of the U.S. Navy Reserves, and assisted the Army National Guard with wildland firefighting. He is presently pursuing a degree in Educational Administration at Idaho State University.

Amie Houghton serves as the program director of the Forensic Investigation emphasis at Utah Valley University, USA. She has an extensive background in crime scene investigation, analysis, and reconstruction, which she obtained from over a decade of working in federal law enforcement. Prior to her appointment at UVU, Amie was a Special Agent with the Naval Criminal Investigative Service (NCIS). During her 11 years of experience with NCIS, she conducted felony-level criminal investigations for the Department of the Navy (DoN) within the US and overseas, including Afghanistan. She worked homicide, suicide, natural death cases, property crime, and adult and child sexual assault. In 2013, she joined a specialized unit within NCIS, Office of Forensic Support (OFS), where she served as forensic consultant for Marine West, Camp Pendleton, California. In this capacity she supported all Marine Corps bases in the western US with consultation on major or complex crime scene investigations/analysis. In 2015, she was promoted to Supervisory Special Agent for the Pacific Region in the OFS. She supervised Forensic Consultants who provided support in the western US and Far East regions for the DoN.

Dale Maughan is an associate professor at Utah Valley University, USA, where he currently serves as Chair of the Department of Nursing. Prior to his full-time appointment in Nursing, he was a part-time faculty member teaching in the Paramedic Program at Utah Valley University for 12 years. Dale received a Bachelor of Science in Nursing and a Master of Science in Health from Brigham Young University, USA. He has completed a Doctorate in Health Promotion and Education from the University of Utah, USA, and a Master of Science in Nursing from Utah Valley University. Dale's work experience includes 39 years in nursing, most of which were spent in the Emergency Department in various capacities. For a little over 13 years he also worked in emergency medical services as a firefighter-paramedic for Provo City in Provo, Utah.

David A. McEntire is a professor in both the Emergency Services and Criminal Justice Departments at Utah Valley University, USA. He teaches emergency management and national security. His expertise is in emergency management theory, vulnerability reduction, community preparedness, response coordination, terrorism, and homeland security. He has received a number of grants that have allowed him to conduct research on disasters and emergency management systems in Australia, California, Canada, Costa Rica, Dominican Republic, Haiti, New York, New Zealand, Texas, and Utah. McEntire has written five books and published over 140 articles. He has presented his research in both domestic and international conferences. He is the recipient of FEMA's Dr B. Wayne Blanchard Award for Academic Excellence and the Scholarship of Teaching and Learning Award from the University of Central Florida.

Margaret Mittelman is a professor in the Department of Emergency Services at Utah Valley University, USA. She has worked in the capacity of teaching Emergency Management as well as for 20+ years was the Program Coordinator for the Emergency Medical Technician (EMT) & Advanced EMT for the university. During her tenure she, along with adjuncts and students created the Utah Valley Emergency Response Team (ERT) – the EMS Response unit for main campus faculty, staff, and students in Orem, Utah. From 1993 to 2015 Margaret was the Proctor for the Emergency Service Psychomotor Exam for the Bureau of EMS in Utah. As a paramedic she has worked with Payson EMS and continues to do their training, Levan EMS as their training officer, and many other Utah EMS agencies, training as well as teaching at EMS conferences across the nation. She has reviewed and contributed to EMS-related textbooks for emergency medicine as well as a few peer-reviewed journals. Margaret holds an Associate in General Studies, a Bachelor's in Behavioral Science, a Bachelor's in Emergency Management, and a Master's in Educational Technology from Utah State University, USA.

Jackson Roberts studies National Security at Utah Valley University (UVU), USA. He has joined UVU's Reserve Officer Training Corps (ROTC) to commission as a 2nd lieutenant in one of Utah's Military Intelligence battalions, where he specializes in Signals Intelligence (SIGINT), translating from any of the three foreign languages he knows into English and working closely with other government agencies. He intends to make a career within Military Intelligence.

Eric J. Russell is an associate professor with Utah Valley University, USA, in the Department of Emergency Services. His writings and research focus on the influence and impact of servant leadership on emergency services organizations and individual responders as well as homeland security education. He is the author of more than 80 peer-reviewed and trade publications as well as two books. Eric retired early as a Captain from the Department of Defense/USAF Fire and Emergency Services with combined active duty military and DoD service.

Lorin Schroeder is currently an independent emergency management consultant. He has over 30 years of experience including firefighting/EMS, law enforcement, and health care. For the past 20+ years he has been an emergency manager for trauma level I and II hospitals in Colorado Springs, Colorado. He is a FEMA and Colorado State–certified ICS instructor and a FEMA instructor for HazMat for First Responders. He holds numerous FEMA IS certifications and is completing his capstone project for Master Exercise Practitioner (MEP). Recently he has supported COVID-19 response for healthcare and government agencies in Missouri, New York City, Austin, Texas, and Florida. He currently holds a National Healthcare Disaster Certification (NHDP-BC™) with the American Nurses Credentialing Center (ANCC). He has a Bachelor of Arts degree in Leadership and Ethics from Nazarene Bible College, USA, and is pursuing a Master of Business Administration in Healthcare Management with Western Governors University, USA.

Laura K. Siebeneck is a professor in the Department of Emergency Management and Disaster Science at the University of North Texas, USA. She earned her Doctorate Degree in Geography from the University of Utah, USA, in 2010. Her research and teaching interests include evacuation and return-entry processes, disaster displacement, hazard risk perception and communication, and emergency management. Siebeneck has published her work in various journals such as *Natural Hazards*, *Natural Hazards Review*, and *Risk Analysis* and she has received funding from the National Science Foundation to support her research endeavors. She is the recipient of the 2021 UNT Teacher-Scholar Award and the 2021 FEMA Higher Education Program's Scholarship of Teaching and Learning Award.

Arthur J. Simental is a Homeland Security & Emergency Management adjunct instructor for the College of Security Studies at Colorado Technical University, USA. Mr. Simental is also the Director of Emergency Management for the University of Colorado Colorado Springs and the Founder of Simental Industries Ltd. a Homeland Security consulting firm and disaster research collaborative. Mr. Simental is also a former Public Health Advisor for the Centers for Disease Control and Prevention, and has over 14 years of service in government, homeland security and emergency management, and emergency services. Serving at the local, county, regional, state, and federal level, and in the private and non-profit sectors in homeland security, emergency management, healthcare and public health emergency preparedness, space and defense, security, education, and critical infrastructure. Simental earned a Master of Science in Homeland Security, Emergency Management, and Public Health from Colorado Technical University. Simental is also an academician and researcher on various topics spanning homeland security, emergency management, disaster resilience, climate adaptation, space technology and innovations, and systems science.

Michael L. Smidt teaches Criminal Justice and National Security Studies courses at Utah Valley University, USA. Prior to coming to Utah Valley University, Mike retired as a Colonel from the U.S. Army. He started out as a paratrooper in the infantry, volunteered for Special Forces, and eventually became a Judge Advocate. Mike's last three assignments were at U.S. Strategic Command, U.S. Northern Command, and U.S. Special Operations Command. His research interests are primarily in national security law and the law of armed conflict. His awards include the Defense Superior Service Medal with oak leaf cluster, Bronze Star Medal with oak leaf cluster, Defense Meritorious Service Medal, Master Parachutist Badge, and Special Forces Tab. He also worked as a police officer for the City of San Diego for three years.

Allison Swenson is an associate professor at Utah Valley University, USA. Allison earned a bachelor's in nursing and a master's in nursing education from Utah Valley University. She is currently working toward a doctoral degree as a DNP-FNP from Idaho State University. Allison's work experience includes 25 years in nursing working as a pediatric nurse, a float nurse, a clinical educator, and now teaching full time in higher education. Allison has been at Utah Valley University since 2010 teaching nursing courses in the ASN program.

Jack Troutt is an assistant professor at the School of Aviation Science, Utah Valley University, USA. He attended Oklahoma State University, USA, where he graduated Cum Laude with a bachelor's degree in aviation management. Upon graduation he commissioned as a Second Lieutenant in the United States Air Force through OSU's Air Force ROTC program. Upon leaving the Air Force, he worked at Omni Air International in Tulsa, Oklahoma, holding positions such as Maintenance Programs Administrator and Manager of Operations Training. While working at Omni Air, he completed both his Master's and Doctorate in Aviation Sciences. Starting the Fall of 2013, he taught as an adjunct at OSU-Tulsa, before becoming a full-time faculty for Utah Valley University, USA, in August of 2018 as an assistant professor.

Heriberto Urby, Jr. retired from the Emergency Management Program at Western Illinois University, USA. Urby previously taught at Texas A&M International University, served as a Teaching Fellow III at the University of North Texas, and as adjunct professor and lecturer at Texas Woman's University, University of Texas at Arlington, USA, and Sul Ross State University, USA. He earned his Juris Doctor Degree from Texas Southern University Thurgood Marshall School of Law, USA, and his Doctor of Philosophy in Public Administration and Management from the University of North Texas, USA. Urby, an attorney for over 40 years, has research/writing experience in Peru, Paraguay, Costa Rica, and Mexico on Latin American emergency management systems (chapters contained in the McEntire *Comparative Emergency Management Systems* e-book). Urby has presented at local, state, and national venues, and has produced a number of seminal and other peer-reviewed publications (including the *Journal of Homeland Security* *and Emergency Management, Journal of Emergency Management, Law Enforcement Executive Forum,* and *The Conversation – Canada).*

Edward J. Valla teaches Emergency Management and Homeland Security courses at the Massachusetts Maritime Academy, USA. He has also taught terrorism, intelligence, and related national security courses as an adjunct professor at Bridgewater State University, USA; the University of Massachusetts, Lowell, USA;, Endicott College, USA; and the National Defense Intelligence College, USA. Prior to joining Massachusetts Maritime Academy in 2016, Valla served as a career intelligence analyst with the FBI's Boston Division where his main areas of expertise were international and domestic terrorism. His main research interests are intelligence analysis, international terrorism, the history of terrorism, and domestic terrorism. Valla retired from the U.S. Army Reserve at the rank of Major after a 20-year career as an intelligence officer.

Brian D. Williams is an assistant professor and serves as the Director for the Master of Public Administration program and for the Center of Public Policy Studies housed in the Department of Political Science at Lamar University in Beaumont, USA. He holds a Doctorate Degree in Public Administration and Management with a specialization in Emergency Management from the University of North Texas, USA. Williams served over 22 years in the military before attaining his doctorate and has managed public safety and emergency management operations during combat operations in Iraq. His research interests include the emergency management knowledge gap, the practical theory of vulnerability, state and local relations in emergency management, and disaster policy.

Rachel Wolfe is a graduate of the Masters of Science program in the Department of Emergency Management and Disaster Science at the University of North Texas, USA. Her research interests include individual housing recovery and natural hazard mitigation strategies. Her thesis work examines household recovery practices in the New Jersey area following Hurricane Sandy.

Kathleen Young is an associate professor at Utah Valley University, USA, teaching dental hygiene. Prior to beginning teaching she had over 25 years of clinical experience. She worked in California, Alaska, and Utah as a clinical dental hygienist. She completed her dental hygiene training at Cabrillo College in California, USA, her Bachelor of Dental Hygiene at Utah Valley University, and her Masters in Instructional Technology and Learning Science at Utah State University, USA. Kathleen is actively involved in her professional organization and has served at the state level as President. She is also on the Department of Public Licensing Board (DOPL) for the Dental and Dental Hygiene Board. Kathleen is a fellow of the Higher Education Academy.

Elyse Zavar is an associate professor in the Department of Emergency Management & Disaster Science at the University of North Texas, USA. She earned her Doctorate Degree in Environmental Geography from Texas State University, USA. Her research focuses on hazard mitigation, long-term community recovery, and disaster commemoration practices. Buyout programs are of particular interest to her, especially commemoration practices following household relocation and the use and management of post-buyout open space. Zavar is a 2020 National Academies of Sciences, Engineering & Medicine Gulf Research Program Early-Career Research Fellow.

Foreword

The scale and intensity of disasters globally are on the increase. Accompanying this augmented risk is the devastation of communities in terms of lives lost, injuries, property damage, and environmental destruction. According to experts, there is a growing concern that the impacts of disasters on society will continue to increase, especially due to climate change, global political unrest, world-wide pandemics, etc. One way to ameliorate the destruction caused by disasters, including terrorist attacks, is for communities to have sound mitigation, preparedness, response, and recovery systems in place. As society grapples with how to effectively deal with disaster impacts, there is an urgent need to explore new ways to improve our current emergency management and homeland security system.

Emergency managers play an important role in helping communities to mitigate the impacts of disasters and terrorist attacks. As such, many emergency management books and articles written by academics and practitioners have emphasized the important role emergency managers play in helping communities become more resilient to disasters and terrorist attacks. However, an often neglected point is the role that other professions play in the emergency management system. Indeed, professions such as public health, geography, engineering, forensic pathology, information technology, nursing, public administration, among others, are just as important in any emergency management and homeland security system. This is the essence of the "distributed functions of emergency management," a concept that is also supported by the "whole community approach" of the Federal Emergency Management Agency (FEMA) as well as the "collaborative" principle of emergency management. Consequently, the main essence of this excellent edited book is that it shines light on the other professions and disciplines that hitherto have not received the recognition they deserve in helping to promote community resilience to disasters and terrorist attacks.

This volume features exciting chapters that explore the concept of distributed functions of emergency management through the perspectives of brilliant academics and practitioners from diverse disciplines and professions related to disasters and terrorist attacks. Moreover, the authors provide excellent arguments and concrete evidence in support of the important roles others aside from emergency managers play in helping communities confront the myriad challenges posed by disasters and terrorist attacks, globally. In addition, the edited book demonstrates the interdependence of professions related to disasters and terrorist attacks, arguing that these professions typically experience similar challenges from disasters and terrorist attacks. Furthermore, the book reveals that these professions are generally interested in crafting solutions to reduce the impacts of disasters and terrorist attacks on society. Indeed, the interdependency of professions provides an opportunity to share resources, expertise, and information needed to ameliorate disaster impacts or prevent terrorist attacks. Another commendable feature of this edited book is that it identifies several problems inherent in addressing disasters and terrorist attacks and discusses potential solutions to address the challenges we face. In addition, the edited book outlines ways to take advantage of future opportunities to enhance societal responses to future disasters and terrorist attacks.

This book will be useful to disciplines related to disasters and terrorist attacks. Graduate programs in emergency management, homeland security, fire science, disaster science, geography, public health, public administration, etc. will benefit immensely from this book. The chapters focusing specifically on different disciplines will provide important insights on the role of each discipline in addressing the challenges posed by disasters and terrorist attacks as well as how they can improve the collaboration with emergency management and homeland security agencies. The layout of the edited book is simple and logical, which makes it an enjoyable read. Also, the book contains several questions that help to promote deep conversations on emergency management and homeland security.

In sum, this collection of excellent chapters is a must read for those interested in broadening their knowledge and expertise on ways to improve society's ability to address current and future challenges from disasters and terrorist attacks through a new perspective known as distributed functions of emergency management.

Abdul-Akeem Sadiq, PhD
Professor and Public Administration/Public Policy Academic Program Coordinator
School of Public Administration
University of Central Florida
Orlando, Florida, USA

Preface

Disasters in our modern era are copious, complex, and consequential. These increasingly prevalent events are triggered by diverse hazards (e.g., Winter Storm Uri, COVID-19, Colonial Pipeline attack). They are exacerbated by human vulnerability and complicated by social processes, the built environment, and our aging infrastructure. The impacts are far reaching and endure long after the initial response occurs.

The unique, dynamic, and sometimes (or frequently?) unpredictable nature of disasters creates a situation where it is impossible for designated emergency managers to solve these convoluted problems alone. They must increasingly work with and rely on a myriad of professionals in the public, private, and non-profit sectors. With this in mind, the following book is based on the concept of the "distributed functions of emergency management."

I first heard this term while attending the FEMA Higher Education Symposium several years ago. Jessica Jensen (a well-known scholar at North Dakota State University) mentioned in a presentation or a personal conversation that multiple actors and agencies are involved in mitigation, preparedness, response, and recovery operations. Therefore, emergency managers must do more to harness the knowledge, skills, and abilities of others who can help reduce and react to disasters.

The following book, which is comprised of diverse chapters written by bright scholars and experienced practitioners, explores a number of professions that are related to disasters and terrorist attacks. It mentions their important roles in emergency management and homeland security, and explores vital recommendations to address current problems and take advantage of future opportunities.

It is hoped that this book might add to our understanding of disasters and terrorist attacks, and help advance emergency management and homeland security functions – regardless of where they are being practiced and who is involved in their implementation.

CHAPTER 1

Disasters, Terrorist Attacks, and the Whole Community:

A Preview of Professionals Involved in the Distributed Functions of Emergency Management and Homeland Security

Joy Cole and David A. McEntire

INTRODUCTION

When one considers disasters and terrorist attacks, it is logical to reflect on the important role of emergency managers and other specific personnel associated with homeland security. While professionals in these areas are indeed increasingly important and even indispensable, there are many others that anticipate and react to events that produce injuries, death, damage, and disruption. In 2007, Lou Canton asserted that this reality reflects a "distributed function." What he was suggesting is that emergency management functions – mitigation, preparedness, response, and recovery – are fulfilled by many individuals and organizations and not just the emergency manager (Canton 2007).

In 2012, the Federal Emergency Management Agency (FEMA) Higher Education Report on the discipline of emergency management followed up on the fact that there are more individuals and agencies involved in dealing with disasters and terrorist attacks than local emergency managers or those working in FEMA and the Department of Homeland Security (DHS). Jessica Jensen and her colleagues (2012, p. 2) reiterated that there are "a host of other professions (e.g., public administration, law, natural resources and environmental management, business administration, non-profit administration, social work, public health practice, hospital administration, and engineering) that undertake a diverse array of EM related tasks and activities before, during, and after events occur." Their report emphasized that such professionals span all levels of government and emanate from the private and non-profit sectors. Each one plays a vital role in determining the success of emergency management. A few years later, Jensen and her colleagues elaborated again on this notion and declared that "the governmental and nongovernmental organizations that do the actual work associated with the vast majority of 'emergency management' activities are many and diverse" (2014, p. 177).

Keeping this assertion about the "distributed functions" of emergency management and homeland security in mind, the following book covers the functional responsibilities

DOI: 10.4324/9781003350729-1

1

of a variety of individuals and their respective professions. This preliminary chapter first explores concerns about the apparent rise in the frequency and severity of disasters and terrorist attacks. It then reviews the nature and importance of the Whole Community concept and explains why an all-hands-on-deck approach is warranted. This initial chapter then gives a preview of each subsequent chapter, paying attention to the foundation of emergency management along with other important professions – whether they be fully or insufficiently recognized as essential partners in our endeavor to prevent and react effectively to disasters and terrorist attacks. The chapter concludes with some overall thoughts about the importance of promoting inclusion of representatives from a vast array of professions as an essential element when mounting a Whole Community response to ongoing and future disasters.

DISASTERS AND TERRORIST ATTACKS ON THE RISE

The frequency, scope, and repercussions of both natural, technological, and anthropogenic disasters is increasing (Quarantelli, 1992; Lagadec, 2006; Thomas and Lopez, 2015; Institute for Economics and Peace, 2020), and entities promoting safety and security of citizens now face more novel and complex challenges than in the past. Disasters in recent decades and years provide numerous examples of the rationale for broad professional inclusion when planning and enacting response efforts.

Several natural disasters exposed infrastructure weaknesses that compounded both human and financial losses. In 1992, Hurricane Andrew pummeled Miami-Dade County in Florida and destroyed over 25,000 homes. Deficits in design, construction, and inspection of the dwellings contributed to the destruction (Tsikoudakis, 2012). Some of these same, uncorrected issues as well as the lack of proper maintenance also resurfaced after the 2021 collapse of the Champlaine Towers condominiums in Miami. In 1993, flooding from the Mississippi River damaged tens of thousands of homes, waterlogged hundreds of thousands of acres of prime farmland, and disrupted millions of citizens' economic and social foundations. Fiscal damages from the flooding were estimated to range from $12 billion to $16 billion, and post-disaster evaluation pointed to gross mismanagement of the Mississippi basin floodplain as a contributing factor (Galloway, 1995). Hurricane Katrina in 2005 caused over 1,800 casualties and $125 billion in damages partially because members of vulnerable populations inhabited the hardest hit areas that were left unprotected by engineering flaws in the flood protection system (Schwartz, 2007). Likewise, Hurricane Irma revealed the inadequacies of warning and evacuation procedures as floodwaters reached historic heights in the Jacksonville, Florida area (Rautenkranz, 2021).

Human-generated events also highlighted disaster response weaknesses. After the bombing of the Alfred P. Murrah Federal Building in Oklahoma City, Oklahoma, in 1995, the limitations of local disaster response capacity were exposed and included a sometimes disorganized facilitation of volunteer efforts, overloaded communication systems, and inadequate education of first responders related to disaster response logistics. When terrorists attacked the Twin Towers in New York City in 2001, the impact on the central business district caused colossal damage and resulting economic hardships. Within the rubble, many human remains were left and required identification by forensic scientists (McEntire, Robinson, and Weber, 2003). Rioting and looting following racially charged social events in 2020 showed that those specifically charged with protecting the public can aggravate or ameliorate volatile public sentiment (Institute for Constitutional Advocacy and Protection, 2021). Despite multiple smaller precursor events, the cyberattack on the Colonial Pipeline revealed immense vulnerabilities of the computer networks supporting our society (McEntire, 2022a). Likewise, the COVID-19 pandemic that continues to have a devastating impact on millions of people exposed the biologic threat (McEntire, 2022b).

Each of the disasters highlighted above supports the premise that an improved approach to disaster response should be multifaceted and include experts from many professional arenas. The contributions of engineers, geographers, and land managers could have reduced the effects of the hurricanes and flooding events. Rescuers, debris removal experts, odontologists, forensics specialists, and social workers could have provided much-needed post-disaster relief following destructive episodes that resulted in trapped victims, uprooted communities, and traumatized societies. The expertise of nurses, public health officials, lawyers, and psychologists are currently in high demand as officials scramble to meet the ever-changing challenges of an evolving pandemic. Soliciting input from a variety of experts serves to enrich the knowledge base available to guide improved disaster management efforts.

After the 2001 World Trade Center terror attack highlighted inefficiencies in the response to a major disaster, the Homeland Security Act was signed into law by President George W. Bush. One provision of the law included the absorption of the Federal Emergency Management Association into the Department of Homeland Security. This entity bore the responsibility of disaster response coordination at a national level, but the highly publicized and delayed response to Hurricane Katrina in 2005 revealed weaknesses in response systems developed under the DHS.

In the past, mitigation measures were almost non-existent and technology did not support the instant notification of hazards to the public. Individual communities dealt with unanticipated disasters in a haphazard way. Conversely, modern citizens now expect an efficient, effective, coordinated response from government at all levels. Such action requires the expertise of individuals from numerous professions who can address their roles during the mitigation, planning, response and recovery phases of disaster.

THE IMPORTANCE OF THE WHOLE COMMUNITY CONCEPT

Recognizing the broad and far-reaching causes and consequences of disasters, Craig Fugate, the FEMA Administrator in 2011, stressed the imperfections associated with only applying a government-centric approach. He said, "Government can and will continue to serve disaster survivors. However, we fully recognize that a government-centric approach to disaster management will not be enough to meet the challenges posed by a catastrophic incident. That is why we must fully engage our entire societal capacity" (Fugate, 2011). Fugate's comments contributed to the initiation of an emergency management dialogue focused on using a "Whole Community" approach.

The "Whole Community" philosophy stresses the importance of involving all types of individuals in the solution to the unique problems related to disasters and terrorist attacks. In addition, this perspective – the conducting of the business of emergency management – must occur not only with emergency management practitioners, but also with government officials, community leaders, and others in the private and non-profit sectors. The belief is that the pooling of all types of human capital fosters a more effective and efficient system that is also individualized to the needs and capacities of each community.

Three guiding principles of the Whole Community approach emerged during its development of this concept:

- Understand and meet the actual needs of the community.
- Engage and empower all parts of the community.
- Strengthen what works well in a community on a daily basis (FEMA, 2011).

Through further research and discussion, Whole Community dialogue participants identified six strategic themes that support the three principles and provide action pathways for their implementation. These include:

- Understand community complexity.
- Recognize community capabilities and needs.
- Foster relationships with community leaders.
- Build and maintain partnerships.
- Empower local action.
- Leverage and strengthen social infrastructure, networks, and assets (FEMA, 2011).

Because of the advantages of these principles and action pathways, FEMA cites several benefits of the Whole Community approach including "shared understanding of community needs and capabilities; greater empowerment and integration of resources from across the community; stronger social infrastructure; establishment of relationships that facilitate more effective prevention, protection, mitigation, response, and recovery activities; increased individual and collective preparedness; and greater resiliency at both the community and national levels" (FEMA, 2011). For these reasons, it is more important than ever to understand the contributions of each of the professionals involved in dealing with disasters and terrorist attacks.

PREVIEW OF THE BOOK

To successfully implement the Whole Community approach, further understanding of the contributions of various professionals along with their potential strengths and weaknesses will be required. Drawing upon the knowledge of experts from the emergency management profession, foundational and closely related professions, recently recognized professions and insufficiently recognized professions, the information in the following chapters serves to extend and enhance the ongoing dialogue whose focus is effective and efficient disaster mitigation and response. Each of the authors was asked to discuss the history of their identified profession, explore its relation to disasters and terrorism, explain the role of the profession in emergency management and homeland security, identify current challenges, and provide recommendations for the future. Collectively, the authors' contributions offer a unique insight into the role and capacity of varied professions. To help guide the discussion, the book will first discuss lessons learned from the emergency management profession and then identify other foundational professions as well as others that have been insufficiently recognized.

The Emergency Management Profession

Emergency management stands as the most widely recognized profession associated with disasters and terrorist attacks. Brian D. Williams, who teaches in the Department of Political Science at Lamar University, discusses how emergency management directors prepare response plans and protocols to be used when disaster strikes and then act as leaders and facilitators of efforts during both ongoing disasters and their aftermath. The addition of decentralized government entities whose efforts must be coordinated amid an ever-shifting political climate results in the role of emergency managers becoming increasingly complex, nuanced, and dynamic.

Recognition of emergency management as a vital element of disaster response evolved as local officials initially distrusted outside influence but later became overwhelmed, and appreciated the contributions of those with broad, applicable experience. Fiduciary responsibility weighs heavily in the role of emergency managers as they must navigate local authorities' access to federal emergency funding along with leveraging available financial and physical resources at the location of a disaster. Moreover, as the recognized experts in disaster response, emergency management professionals must stand in constant readiness despite the inherently unpredictable nature of emergencies.

Foundational and Closely Related Professions

Geographers and land use managers, fire fighters, law enforcement officers, and emergency medical care providers serve as foundational elements in disaster response planning and implementation. Because of their high-profile responsibilities, these professionals serve as the public face of disaster response. Each of these groups contributes specialized knowledge and skills essential to an effective disaster response.

Physical, human, and environmental geography directly influence the development and implementation of disaster response plans. Through early identification of potentially hazardous risks, geographers and land use experts provide significant insight into the feasibility of enacting response plans in a specific area. During acute disaster response, geographers may serve in a coordinative capacity by identifying risk factors particularized to a specific area or population. Laura Siebeneck, Elyse Zavar, and Rachel Wolfe hail from the Department of Emergency Management and Disaster Response at the University of North Texas. They offer commentary regarding the role of geographers in disaster response.

Once considered a reactionary unit, contemporary firefighters face an expectation to prepare in advance for any emergency. Andrew Byrnes, from the Department of Emergency Services at Utah Valley University, addresses fiscal challenges faced by firefighters and the expectation for members of the firefighting profession to continually respond to disasters through innovation and evidence-based strategies. The capacity of firefighters to adapt to change directly influences their effectiveness during disaster response and, thus, ongoing strategic planning must be employed to identify and address current issues that affect the profession.

Mike Gutierrez and Ed Valla from the Department of Emergency Management and Homeland Security at Massachusetts Maritime Academy, highlight the many roles law enforcement professionals fill in disaster response beyond those of safety and security. The flexibility required to switch professional hats demands physical and financial resources dedicated to education and preparation. Within the current climate of fluctuating respect for law enforcement, funding for the profession faces instability and threatens the capacity for coordinated disaster response training that facilitates effective response actions.

Emergency medical care includes human injury response at incident sites and during transport to medical facilities. Peter Burke, Steve Holley, and Margaret Mittleman – faculty members in Emergency Medical Services at Utah Valley University – share their combined experience to examine the niche of emergency medical services related to disaster response. Whether sponsored by local governments, healthcare facilities, or private entities, emergency medical service professionals bear the responsibility of providing acute life-saving services as well as participating in numerous other roles in a community. The revenue-generating capacity of emergency medical services introduces an additional level of complexity to their operation and results in some dissonance when addressing responsibilities in public safety, health care, and public health.

Recently Recognized Professions

In recent years, the professions of Public Administration and Public Health have gained elevated visibility as key participants in disaster response activities. The global COVID-19 pandemic and its associated challenges highlighted both the successes and opportunities for improvement in the two professions. Concurrently, climate change consequences, infrastructure failures, migration crises associated with global political unrest, and various economic challenges pushed these professionals to the forefront of conversations related to disaster response.

Public administration professionals facilitate the will of the people through elected officials and appointees. Abraham David Benavides, from the Department of Public Administration at the University of North Texas, discusses how public administration, as an overarching profession, encompasses many other disaster response entities and seeks to balance the needs of community members with available resources. While unknown disasters and novel tragedies are to be expected in the future, public administrators maintain a focus of supporting government-led responses at all levels to promote recovery and rebuilding efforts.

John R. Fisher, from the Department of Emergency services at Utah Valley University, discusses the evolution of the role of public information officers and details the critical components of their functions in disaster response. With a focus on disseminating life-protecting instruction to the public that is both accurate and timely, this chapter reviews the influence of social media in sharing information. The public information officer role requires ongoing planning, relationship building, and rehearsal so that citizens know where to turn for information during crises.

Non-profit managers have also been an important component of emergency management, particularly as it relates to volunteer management and the long-term recovery of victims. Tina Bynum (Emergency Service Administration Department at Pikes Peak Community College), Heriberto Urby (Department of Emergency Management, Western Illinois University), and Arthur J. Simental (College of Security Studies, Colorado Technical University) differentiate between for-profit and non-profit organizations, and they trace an increasingly important role for these professionals in all aspects related to disasters and emergency management. They remind us that these individuals are involved in humanitarian operations such as the one witnessed during the Russian invasion of

Ukraine. These authors also suggest that non-profit managers must become more focused on environmental and social justice causes as well as emotional support.

Because of the 9/11 terrorist attacks, Homeland Security professionals are now seen as indispensable partners in emergency management and homeland security. Nevertheless, the chapter by Jackson Roberts and David A. McEntire, a student and professor, respectively, at Utah Valley University, illustrates that the creation of the Department of Homeland Security has not been without its challenges – particularly for those involved in FEMA and emergency management. The chapter reveals changes that have been made after the poor response to Hurricane Katrina and suggests that more attention is required to enhance the security of our nation in many sectors of the economy.

The work of public health professionals reached new heights in recent years. Managing perceptions of public health initiatives; facilitating primary, secondary, and tertiary health promotion activities; and disseminating novel and dynamic information during a politicized crisis challenged professionals in this field. Arthur J. Simental, from the College of Security Studies, Colorado Technical University, Tina Bynum, from the Emergency Service Administration Department at Pikes Peak Community College, and Lorin Schroeder from Hagerty Consulting share their expert insights related to ongoing public health issues and expected challenges in the future.

Rodger Broomé and Eric Russell, from the Department of Emergency Services at Utah Valley University, draw upon their combined experiences in emergency services to discuss psychological impacts associated with disaster response. While acknowledging the stigma associated with a medical model of psychology, the authors document the devastating mental health effects of disasters. Additionally, they offer recommendations for advance systemic preparation to address the psychological impact of catastrophic events.

Insufficiently Recognized Professions

While the previously mentioned professions may carry the greatest disaster response workload, other auxiliary professions lend critical service that makes effective disaster response possible. Experts from nine professions provide specialized information describing their history, current disaster response capacity, and both current and future challenges. Each of the chapters contains descriptions of the specialized actions for the professions and serves to provide a more complete description of disaster response professions.

Drawing from many years of aviation experience in multiple environments, Jack Edwin Troutt III, from the Utah Valley University Department of Aviation Services, describes the responsibilities of pilots related to disaster response. The "need for speed" characterizes the contributions from aviators as they conduct search-and-rescue operations, transport supplies and food to areas affected by disasters, and offer direct firefighting support by dropping water and retardant on large fires. The dangers associated with aviation as a perpetrator of disasters are also discussed with special attention given to preventative measures in place to reduce such incidents.

In a detour from the commonly recognized peacekeeping activities associated with members of the military, Michael L. Smidt, from the Department of Criminal Justice and National Securities Studies at Utah Valley University, presents the complicated challenges faced by these professionals when performing duties related to disaster response. While resources in the military are plentiful, their use may be curtailed by governing bodies. Conversely, Smidt describes the enormous capacity of military professionals to provide critical, expert human power as a tool in disaster response.

Heriberto Urby, who retired from the School of Law Enforcement and Justice Administration at Western Illinois University, offers important information regarding potential litigation threats that arise during disasters. The information in this chapter reveals the need for more research and education focusing on avoidance of litigation through provision of expert advice related to disaster prevention, response, and recovery. Dr Urby presents the case for disaster response stakeholders to collaborate closely with legal experts as they plan and implement their activities.

Arthur J. Simental and Lorin Schroeder (two instructors and consultants in Colorado) cover the underappreciated responsibilities of hospital and other medical personnel who provide services that enhance, sustain, or restore the health of individuals and their communities. After reviewing the appearance of this new professional responsibility, these authors explore many of the challenges associated with responding to COVID-19 and organizational structure: surge capacity, ethical decision making, and training and implementation of the Incident Command System (ICS) and the National Incident Management System (NIMS).

Three seasoned nurses who are faculty members at Utah Valley University – Dale Maughan, Allison Swenson, and Joy Cole – detail the storied history of nursing, a profession born of the need to respond to calamities. Additionally, these professionals explain the many roles that nurses assume during disasters and discuss challenges in meeting these expectations. Finally, the trio offers insight into possible solutions intended to make their disaster-related service more effective.

Two subsequent chapters that focus on forensics – from the perspective of both the technologist and the pathologist – highlight the specialized skills associated with evidence gathering and evaluation during and after a disaster. Amie B. Houghton, from the Utah Valley University Forensic Science Program, provides expert knowledge about the nuances associated with forensic activities during disaster response. A discussion of the glamorized media portrayal of forensic science reveals a much more methodical, time-consuming description of forensic activities related to disaster response.

Another profession-focused chapter, authored by Kathleen Young, from the Dental Hygiene Department at Utah Valley University, exposes the vital importance of dentistry as a function of victim identification following disasters. Young offers a description of processes that help in revealing or confirming the identity of victims using dental records. Additionally, the chapter contains recommendations for using dental experts more effectively and for providing education to dental hygienists in preparation for performing forensic odontology.

The following chapter covers the subject of Public Works. Written by Dave Bergner, a well-known expert and consultant in this area, this section of the book indicates that public works is closely related to engineering and has broad functional responsibility in emergency management. However, public works professionals often deal with transportation issues after a disaster. And, Bergner reminds us that our aging infrastructure must sooner or later be addressed by public works professionals if we are to reverse the trend of increased disasters in this area.

The penultimate chapter on Information Technology by Jackson Roberts and David A. McEntire asserts that information technologists have not historically been considered as important partners in emergency management. However, the increased reliance on technology – including benefits and drawbacks – is making this profession indispensable for effective operations before and after disasters. In addition, the fact that we are having – and will continue to have – more cyberattacks mandates increased involvement of these individuals in future emergency management planning.

Finally, a closing chapter by David McEntire, a professor in the Emergency Services Department at Utah Valley University, summarizes the information, controversies, and recommendations offered by the chapter authors. The consolidating theme of multi-faceted contributions from diverse professions provides the reader with thought-provoking insights and propounds the need for greater interprofessional cooperation and collaboration as a vital step in efforts to maintain and improve disaster response efforts.

CONCLUSION

Because the scope, severity, and complexity of disasters and terrorist attacks continue to expand, the lens with which emergency management and homeland security contributions is viewed must also expand. Upticks in the severity of weather-related calamities, increased sophistication of human-generated disasters, and greater public expectations for coordinated, effective emergency management and homeland security programs demand a refreshed approach that recognizes and uses the expertise available from representatives of many professions. The Whole Community approach aligns well with this idea and offers a framework for a more profession-inclusive strategy to guide disaster response.

While a cursory view of the potential for greater collaborative efforts reveals the value of interprofessional engagement in disaster response, a greater understanding of the contributory capacity of varied professions is needed. Each chapter of this book provides an "insider view" of the potential for professionals from many areas to join the disaster response dialogue and bring the vision of a Whole Community perspective to fruition. We hope this book will (1) help to advance knowledge of those who are involved in preventing and responding to disasters and terrorist attacks, and (2) illuminate ways that professionals from diverse backgrounds can work together to minimize risk and react in the most effective manner possible.

REFERENCES

Canton, L. (2007). *Emergency Management: Strategies and Concepts for Effective Programs*. Hoboken, NJ: John Wiley and Sons.

FEMA. (2011). A Whole Community Approach to Emergency Management: Principles, Themes, and Pathways for Action. FDOC 104-008-1. https://www.fema.gov/sites/default/files/2020-07/whole_community_dec2011_2.pdf.

Fugate, Craig. (2011). "Catastrophic Preparedness: How Ready is FEMA for the Next Bit Disaster?" Testimony of Craig Fugate, Administrator, Federal Emergency Management Agency, Before the U.S. Senate, Homeland Security and Governmental Affairs Committee. https://www.dhs.gov/news/2011/03/17/testimony-craig-fugate-administrator-federal-emergency-management-agency.

Galloway, Gerald E., Jr. (1995). "New Directions in Floodplain Management." *Journal of the American Water Resources Association* 31(3): 351–357.

Institute for Constitutional Advocacy and Protections (ICAP). (2021). *Protests and Public Safety: A Guide for Cities and Citizens*. https://consitutionalprotestguide.org/.

Institute for Economics & Peace. (2020). "Ecological Threat Register 2020: Understanding Ecological Threats, Resilience and Peace." https://www.visionofhumanity.org/wp -content/uploads/2020/10/ETR_2020_web-1.pdf.

Jensen, Jessica, Bundy, Sarah, Thomas, Brian and Yakubu, Mariama. (2014). "The County Emergency Manager's Role in Recovery." *International Journal of Mass Emergencies and Disasters* 32(1): 157–193.

Jensen, Jessica, Feldemann-Jensen, Shirley, Kushma, Jane, McEntire, David and Rubin, Claire. (2012). *Report of the Disciplinary Purview of Emergency Management Focus Group Held September 10–11, 2012*. Emmitsburg, MD: Federal Emergency Management Agency.

Lagadec, Patrick. (2006). "Crisis Management in the Twenty-First Century: 'Unthinkable' Events in 'Inconceivable' Contexts." In Havidan Rodriguez, Enrico L. Quarantelli and Russell R. Dynes. *Handbook of Disaster Research*. New York: Springer, pp. 489–507.

McEntire, David A. (2022a). "An Assessment of Crisis Communication During the Covid-19 Pandemic." *Journal of Homeland Security and Emergency Management* 19(3): 347–9.

McEntire, David A. (2022b). "Cyber-Attacks and Their Implications for Emergency Management." *Journal of Emergency Management* 20(1): 1–2.

McEntire, David A., Robinson, Robie and Weber, Richard. (2003). "Business Responses to the World Trade Center Disaster: Corporate Roles, Functions and Interaction with the Public Sector." Chapter 18 in *Beyond September 11th: An Account of Post-disaster Research*, pp. 431–258. Special Publication #39. Natural Hazards Research and Applications Information Center, University of Colorado, Boulder, CO (Invited).

Rautenkranz, Lauren. (2021). "Hurricane Irma: A Look Back at the Storm's Path and Intensity Four Years Later." September 10, 2021. https://www.firstcoast- news.com/article/news/hurricane-preparedness/hurricane-irma-a-look-back-at -the-storms-path-and-intensity-four-years-later/77-7bd640be-be52c-449e-abdb -b05371f3c72e.

Schwartz, John. (2007). "Engineers Faulted on Hurricane System." *The New York Times*. July 11, 2007. https://www.nytimes.com/2007/07/11/us/nationalspecial/11corps .html.

Thomas, Vinod and Lopez, Ramon. (2015). "Global Increase in Climate-Related Disasters." *Asian Development Bank Economics Working Paper Series No. 466*. https://papers.ssrn.com/sol3/papers.cfm?abstract_id=2709331.

Tsikoudakis, Mike. (2012). "Hurricane Andrew Prompted Better Building Code Requirements." *Risk Management*. August 19, 2012. https://www.businessinsur- ance.com/article/00010101/NEWS06/30819985/Hurricane-Andrew-promoted -better-building-code-requirements.

Quarantelli, E.L. (1992). "The Environmental Disasters of the Future Will Be More and Worse, but the Prospect Is Not Hopeless." *Disaster Prevention and Management* 2(1): 11–25.

CHAPTER 2

The Role of the Emergency Manager in Disaster and Homeland Security:
Navigating the Challenges of Intergovernmental Relationships through Networks

Brian D. Williams

INTRODUCTION

The contemporary local emergency management system operates within a highly decentralized federal system where intergovernmental, intersectoral, and intercommunity elements strive to reduce the impact of hazards as well as to normalize life when disaster strikes (Averch and Dluhy, 1997; Mileti, 1999; Sylves, 2008). At the core of this system is the emergency manager who must daily navigate the politics of disaster in order to coordinate an effective mitigation and preparedness strategy to reduce risk and hazard impacts as well as oversee an effective response and recovery effort to restore normality in the wake of disaster.

It is true that many professions contribute to emergency management, including the military, law enforcement, health care, fire and rescue, maritime, public health, and aviation. However, it is the role of the emergency manager to serve at the core of the emergency management system and harness crucial networks and a conglomerate of skills from others who are involved in disasters and homeland security. This will undoubtedly help the emergency manager coordinate all functions of preparedness, response, recovery, and mitigation efforts at the local level, where society most keenly feels the impact of disasters or terrorist attacks.

But this integration does not happen by itself. Dombrowsky (1998) reminds us about the foolishness and madness that ensue when we attempt to influence a system without an understanding of its intricate inner workings, and this is especially true for those integral systems that reduce risk and hazard impact to avert disaster. As a gesture toward avoiding that madness, this chapter explores the role of the emergency manager in disaster and terrorism. First, it discusses the history of the emergency manager as part of the

DOI: 10.4324/9781003350729-2

formal and informal system of emergency management. Next, it explores the emergency manager's role in disaster and terrorism and then how that role relates to the intergovernmental relationship of emergency management and homeland security. The chapter will culminate in some of the current challenges that emergency managers face as well as recommendations to address the future needs of emergency managers.

HISTORY OF THE EMERGENCY MANAGER

From one widely shared view, emergency management and, subsequently, the role of the emergency manager originated in the ancient world where communities of many cultures, through many generations, created and disseminated folklore to explain catastrophic events and their consequential disasters (Drabek, 1991). These mythologies accounted for what we understand as natural events – floods, volcanoes, earthquakes – by explaining them as consequences of angering the gods. Shamans, priests, and oracles may have been the first examples of emergency managers in existence, in that they led communities in a search for explanation. Those searches and stories led to efforts of mitigation where people came together to appease the gods to avert future disaster.

In their discussion of the profession's history, Phillips, Neal, and Webb (2017) draw on the Dynes (2003) analogy of Noah – a biblical figure – as an ancient emergency manager. Noah prepared for a flood of epic proportions by coordinating multiple populations to engage in survival and mitigation efforts, though none heeded the warning. If there is a bit of humor in making these connections, there is also truth. Emergency managers have always been people with special skill sets and access to networks that enable them to communicate and coordinate among systems to prepare for and mitigate disaster.

Before World War II, the United States was very reactive to disaster. Butler (2012) reveals that this reactive nature is due to a lack of federal responsibility for addressing disaster. Legislation was directed at specific events in the wake of the event. This resulted from an ideology that communities had a moral responsibility to provide assistance in the event of a disaster (Platt, 1999). Examples include the 1900 hurricane in Galveston, Texas, the 1906 earthquake in San Francisco, and the flu pandemic of 1918–1919.

In the first half of the 20th century, preparedness for and mitigation of natural hazards were relegated to local-level emergency managers as Cold War fears of nuclear attack caused the prioritization at the national level of military concerns and civil defense (Kreps, 1984; Webb, 2007). Compounding this issue was the fact that into the 1950s, the guiding theory in the emerging profession was that upon learning of a threat, the public a) would be helpless and dependent upon government, b) would collectively panic, and c) would socially devolve into looting and other criminal behavior (Dynes, 1993). These political circumstances and societal misconceptions led to the idea that conflict and division among the public would need to be dealt with by force, and those kinds of responses would bring about practical concerns for protecting the civil rights and general well-being of citizens and communities.

Disaster studies subsequently provided empirical evidence that dispels the pre-1950s assumptions that emergency managers had about human behavior. The federal government began providing funding and direction for the content and focus of disaster studies. The practices that would emerge from this research into post-World War II emergency management served both natural threat response and civil defense planning. Studies like these that looked at natural disaster response have also served as proxies for understanding how people may respond to unexpected military attacks (Fritz, 1961; Webb, 2007) and have shown that in reality, disaster minimizes conflict and creates unity (at least initially) through a consensus on value priorities where antisocial and conflict behavior, while they may occur in isolated cases, are not the norm (Dynes, 1970).

It was this new lens on the study of natural disasters – as proxies for civil defense – that marked a shift, from the 1950s through the 1990s, from a federal emergency system that concentrated only on civil defense to one that would take a similar role in natural events. Congress did enact the Civil Defense Act of 1950. However, it also passed the 1950 Disaster Relief Act, the Disaster Relief Act of 1974, and the Stafford Act of 1988 to legislate the federal government's ability to provide ad hoc support and resources for local government disaster response without having to create federal legislation for specific types of events. The creation of the Federal Emergency Management Agency (FEMA) in 1979 set up a one-stop shop for all things emergency management at the federal level. FEMA has also since served as a mechanism to further the profession of emergency management and the role of the emergency manager.

Hoetmer (1991) proposes that one reason federal government exists is to organize a response when local governments become overwhelmed. While FEMA has continued to coordinate and provide the needed resources for local government before, during, and after an event, it was not until the early 1990s, when James Witt assumed FEMA directorship, that the profession of emergency management and the role of the emergency manager became a top priority for the federal government under the Clinton Administration (Phillips, Neal, and Webb, 2017). Director Witt gained emergency manager experience from his time as an Arkansas county judge and as Arkansas Emergency Manager under then Governor Clinton. Into the early 2000s, FEMA bolstered the emergency manager as a coordinator and operations manager to mitigate the hazard effects on communities and the resulting vulnerability.

Turn-of-the-century events like Hurricane Andrew in 1992, the 9/11 terrorist attacks in 2001, and Hurricane Katrina in 2005, among others, have brought FEMA under close scrutiny and resulted in federal policy to address actual and perceived failures. For example, the Disaster Mitigation Act of 2000 provides incentives for states to engage in mitigation efforts, and the National Response Plan attempted to create a comprehensive framework for all disciplines and all hazards but was replaced by the National Response Framework to create a national guide for response. As a result of these events, FEMA lost its Cabinet position and became part of the Department of Homeland Security with reduced authority, but the Post-Katrina Emergency Management Reform Act in 2006 returned authority to FEMA to address the failures that occurred during Hurricane Katrina. These events and the resulting policies have clarified the ongoing need for effective emergency managers at all levels of government.

As can be seen, the concept of the emergency manager has always existed in the United States, though not always in an official position. The emergency manager, as a coordinating hub, has evolved in the United States as federal entities have come to understand the need to coordinate an intergovernmental relationship for the good of all. Just as the history of emergency management in the United States was instigated by the possibility of nuclear attack, the relationship of the emergency manager to disaster and terrorism can be understood by examining the nature of focusing events and disaster policy in the United States.

EMERGENCY MANAGER RELATIONSHIP TO DISASTER AND TERRORISM

Emergency managers are closely associated with disasters and terrorism, and must learn early in their careers to navigate the political environment of disaster policy and intergovernmental relations. Historically, their role has been determined and re-determined by shifting positions on the hierarchy of governmental authority during disaster response. For instance, the political environment has produced a conflict between the disaster and terrorism focus that has shifted from natural disasters to terrorism and back to natural disasters with attempts to incorporate an all-hazards approach. This section looks at how focusing events such as the SoCal Fires, the 2001 World Trade Center attacks, and Hurricane Katrina have influenced the practice of emergency management due to the Incident Command System (ICS), the National Incident Management System (NIMS), and the emergence of the Department of Homeland Security (DHS) and its impact on FEMA.

National implementation of the Incident Command System in emergency management helped transform the federal perspective as emergency management evolved in the late 1970s as a result of major fires and a lack of standardized response equipment and policy in California. ICS is a management tool and strategy that provides response efforts with a command-and-control aspect in order to increase effective response to an event (Buck, Trainor, and Aguirre, 2006; McEntire, 2015). ICS initially served the firefighting community from the early 1970s after communication failures during the southern California wildfires of the late 1960s. The goal of the Wildland Fire ICS was to standardize communication and equipment across firefighting organizations to reduce confusion where multiple organizations were needed to effectively respond in an event that overwhelms a single organization. This has created some tension between centralized/decentralized and standardized/flexible approaches to disasters and terrorist attacks.

The creation of FEMA in 1979 ushered in a true federal system of emergency management (Sylves, 2012). From 1979 until 2001, FEMA operated with a bottom-up intergovernmental approach – as opposed to top-down strategy (Sylves, 2008) – where federal policy provided the laws, expectations, and goals with local emergency managers taking the lead in all matters of emergency management. This bottom-up approach was based on an understanding that local governments (i.e., local emergency managers) should initially lead a disaster response; in other words, a grassroots, community-based approach was the standard, and federal assets would be engaged only when local and state assets were unable to cope with the effects of an event.

Through 2001, FEMA and local emergency managers increasingly concentrated on natural events such as the 1989 Loma Prieta earthquake. During the response to that particular event, the grassroots, bottom-up approach came under attack as local officials were perceived to have provided inaccurate information that prevented a smooth process of state and federal response (Schneider, 1992). The public had been preconditioned to the pre-established, subservient role of local government in a hierarchical intergovernmental structure, so the public began to call for a more controlling federal government. On September 11, 2001, these calls for a more controlling federal government solidified as terrorism took the spotlight away from natural events.

The events of September 11, 2001, clarified the need for a coordination of information and asset functions to address the unique needs that global terrorism had revealed. The structure of FEMA and the federal emergency management system already provided much of this structure; however, rather than allowing FEMA to take oversight of terrorism operations, DHS was created in 2003 (Congress, 2002). As a result, FEMA lost its Cabinet status and was placed under the DHS coordination umbrella. Although one intended function of DHS was to address emergency preparedness and response, previous FEMA initiatives were deprioritized, losing resources and coordination assets. One such initiative was the Hurricane Pam Exercise.

In 2004, FEMA and the State of Louisiana designed the imaginary Hurricane Pam Exercise based on conceivable worst-case scenarios of a hurricane impacting New Orleans (Beriwal, 2006). Unfortunately, the Hurricane Pam Exercise was not given priority under the new DHS structure, and while most elements of the Hurricane Pam scenario were listed as TBD (to be determined), many of the events imagined in that exercise came about in 2005 during Hurricane Katrina. As such, local and state emergency managers were left without vital support and resources during critical periods. The unfolding events brought to light systemic weaknesses in U.S. emergency management federalism and served to bring natural disasters back into focus as public cries continued to demand a more commanding federal government (Birkland, 2006, 2009; Rubin, 2012).

The same year as the Hurricane Pam Exercise, DHS implemented the National Incident Management System. The purpose of NIMS was to create a disaster management strategy with a top-down, unified approach that would bring federal, state, and local resources together for an effective response to any event by mandating the use of the Incident Command System (Jensen and Waugh, 2014). Of course, this top-down approach ran counter to the grassroots, community-based emergency management system to which local emergency managers had become accustomed. While many emergency management professionals today support the use of NIMS and ICS, the new strategy does have its opponents who claim the system is not as flexible as it ought to be and is not easily implemented for all operations such as law enforcement, public health, or social services. However, one overarching function of NIMS is to link federal funding for using ICS and emergency management functions of the Federal Response Plan at the local level and support the emergency manager role. As such, the role of the emergency manager in disaster and terrorism has evolved in a political environment that is reactive to major focusing events.

ROLE IN EMERGENCY MANAGEMENT/HOMELAND SECURITY

Emergency managers are central participants in emergency management and homeland security. Unfortunately, these professions operate under an "intergovernmental paradox." Averch and Dluhy (1997) identified an "intergovernmental paradox," which is an inherent issue in a multi-level emergency management system where local governments are primarily responsible for response, yet their capacity is easily overwhelmed when policy-makers deprioritize local emergency management needs (Mileti, 1999). Emergency managers are placed squarely within this difficult and unavoidable paradox, and they are the connective tissue that provides cohesion and flexible support before and after disasters occur. However, in the 1980s and early 1990s, the role of the emergency manager was not well understood or accepted by local governments (Kreps, 1991). The credibility of the profession grew only as trained and educated emergency managers consistently displayed effective communication, organization, human relations, and control under stress during real-life disasters. Yet because of the intergovernmental paradox, local jurisdictions still needed proof, as of the late 1990s, that the emergency manager role was worthy of investment.

The early 2000s brought multiple shifts in the focus of emergency management, namely 9/11 and Katrina, that illustrated the need to protect from and prepare for both natural and human-induced disasters. Importantly, Waugh and Streib (2006) proposed that due to the extensive unknowable outcomes of disaster and terrorism, the most important aspect of the emergency manager's role was the ability to collaborate with other emergency managers as well as other levels of government and community partners. That study highlighted the exigent need for a professional who could maneuver at the local level but within an intergovernmental emergency management system.

At around the same time, a study by Stehr (2007) clarified a need to shift funding priorities by looking at data from 1999 to 2006 that showed how emergency managers in King County, Washington, allocated their time. Stehr (2007) reported on numerous emergency management activities that included administrative functions, homeland security grants, and mitigation, preparedness, response, and recovery activities. That study found that preparedness assumed the largest portion of time when averaged from 1999 to 2006 with an overall average of 39.7%. However, the effort dedicated to preparedness was reduced substantially from 73.4% in 1999 to 32.9% in 2006. But this dramatic shift occurred because homeland security grant administration did not exist for emergency management in King County, Washington until 2002. In 2006, homeland security grant administration took up a notable percentage of time, 31% on average. The data in the Stehr (2007) study reveal the federal priority given to terrorism, increased fund availability for terrorism protection measures, and the general need for operating funds to support the role of emergency managers in the United States.

This type of influence of focusing events and federal policy on the role of the emergency manager is well documented (for examples, see Birkland, 2006, 2009; Drabek, 1991; McEntire, 2007b, 2016; Mileti, 1999; Phillips, Neal, and Webb, 2017). As such, the monetary incentives provided by emergency management federalism have profoundly influenced the role and focus of the emergency manager at all levels. These monetary incentives seek to modify jurisdictional behavior through the state and local actions required to receive federal funding for mitigation, preparedness, response, and recovery operations. To show these incentives and the process in action, we can look to the State of Texas as an example.

The Texas Department of Emergency Management (TDEM) sets out in TDEM-100 the preparedness standards for emergency management in Texas. TDEM-100 provides specific guidance that outlines the jurisdictional approach and allows for annexed standards for basic, intermediate, and advanced levels of readiness and gives additional direction for specific areas of need (Texas Division of Emergency Management, 2000). These annexes provide the centerpiece to a comprehensive emergency management program (Texas Division of Emergency Management, 2008). State and federal programs use the identified level of readiness to determine funding distribution for federally funded emergency management programs. While the basic plan is a state legal requirement regardless of need, the creation of annexes for all levels of readiness can stipulate access to additional federal funds depending upon the financial and physical needs of a community.

Williams (2017) sought out the perspective of the emergency manager to better understand the emergency manager role in Texas. One year after the events of Hurricane Harvey, he conducted interviews with Texas emergency management professionals. The study revealed that emergency management directors (specifically, city mayors and county judges) depend on the counsel of professional emergency management coordinators to navigate the unpredictable. The study further revealed that the emergency management coordinator carries out the day-to-day affairs of emergency management to ensure that mitigation and preparedness actions for disaster, as well as protective actions for terrorism, are in place for the community.

Emergency management professionals revealed in the Williams (2017) study that they are like symphony conductors. For example, they do not need to know how to play every instrument, but they must know how the symphony functions as parts of a whole and be able to facilitate that functioning for the most beautiful aesthetic. More literally, emergency management coordinators do not need to know how to put out a fire or clean up a chemical spill, yet they do need a network of experts and organizations upon whom they can call to affect the most competent and expeditious response possible.

It is this ability to collaborate and facilitate that Waugh and Streib (2006) propose continues to remain the role of the emergency manager. Williams and Webb (2020) find that emergency managers in Texas reported the need to be able to form a network of peers in order to navigate the political environment of emergency management. One such reported strategy was that emergency managers must acquire buy-in from other departments, elected officials, and the public in order to be able to reduce vulnerability in the communities they serve. Mann and Williams (2020) found that emergency managers who serve a dual function in law enforcement reported the need of a network of informal relationships with other law enforcement organizations and search-and-rescue agencies at the local, state, and federal levels for times when formal communications break down; such networks can serve to mitigate the vulnerability of an effected community.

As described here, Texas provides an example of how the role of the emergency manager functions in the intergovernmental paradox. Their profession is inherently intertwined with and influenced by the political environment and policy decisions that guide local, state, and federal governments as they prepare for, respond to, recover from, mitigate, and protect against natural and human-induced hazards. In a society where the governed have a say in how they will be governed (usually through voting), it is the elected representative and his or her political motivations at all levels that can influence the actions of emergency managers to reach and meet the needs of vulnerable populations.

STRUCTURE/RELATION TO EMERGENCY MANAGEMENT/HOMELAND SECURITY

To this point, the discussion has relied heavily upon the federal role in emergency management along with the influence of federal policy on the evolution of the emergency manager in the United States. However, the emergency manager operates in a structure that is influenced by the political jurisdictions and interests at all levels – local, state, and federal – to address emergency management and homeland security challenges. This broad and decentralized structure of emergency management in the United States tends to function based upon local and state policy. For example, the states of Texas and Louisiana, though they may experience the same hazards, have different operating procedures and emergency management structures.

Texas operates its response to disaster in accordance with Texas Department of Emergency Management (TDEM) guidance. TDEM maintains written standards in TDEM-10. TDEM-10 is the *Local Emergency Management Planning Guide* and outlines local, state, and federal emergency management responsibilities and planning standards in Texas (Texas Division of Emergency Management, 2008). It mandates that all political units, whether county or city, maintain or participate in an emergency management program. TDEM-10 designates that the municipal mayor and the county judge are designated as an emergency management director, who may then designate an emergency management coordinator to provide emergency management plan guidance and implement the plan. However, some jurisdictions may not have a dedicated plan; those areas may coordinate under another jurisdiction's plan to meet federal funding requirements.

The State of Louisiana structures its homeland security and emergency prepared-ness under the Louisiana Homeland Security and Emergency Management Assistance and Disaster Act (Louisiana Disaster Act) – Louisiana Revised Statute Title 29:721-739 (GOHSEP, 2021). Louisiana homeland security and emergency management is struc-tured with nine regional offices, each having a Regional Director that is selected from and by the Parishes, and a Regional Coordinator from the Governor's Office of Homeland Security and Emergency Preparedness. Each of the 64 Parishes (County) have an Office of Homeland Security and Emergency Preparedness staffed by a Parish Representative with the title "Director" to coordinate local efforts for emergency management and homeland security.

As described, the states of Texas and Louisiana are distinct in their structure for emergency management and homeland security. Texas is a decentralized structure with a mandate for local municipality and county assignment of emergency management authority in a director that appoints a coordinator to handle daily operations, as well as creation of or inclusion in a formal emergency management plan that includes home-land security aspects. In contrast, Louisiana's structure is more centralized, starting at the Parish level for coordination to implement regional operations through Parish and Regional Directors with support from state-level appointed coordinators at each regional office. However, the Louisiana Disaster Act does require that municipalities respond to an event when the municipality has the resources available.

All of this means that the structure the emergency manager operates within can vary across the three political jurisdictions: Municipality, County (Parish), and State. However, emergency managers at the state and local level, regardless of the official title they hold (Coordinator or Director) must all consider federal regulations and laws. The differing structures are a result of the political environment that can influence the role of the emergency manager as a coordination hub within this intergovernmental structure. This structure, combined with the role of the emergency manager in an intergovernmen-tal environment, reveals a number of challenges that emergency managers face on a daily basis, some of which have plagued the field throughout the history and evolution of the emergency manager.

CURRENT CHALLENGES

As one respondent noted in the Williams (2017) study, emergency managers are expected to be the best suited professionals to deal with the unexpected. However, when dealing with the unexpected, it can be difficult to acquire buy-in for funding and support for an event that has not happened and may never happen. This is the modern emergency man-ager's continual challenge as they navigate daily the political, social, and economic policy decisions that unfortunately take precedence over protecting against and preparing for future unknowns (Williams and Webb, 2020).

One definition of emergency management says that the profession reduces the impact of hazards to normalize life when disaster strikes. Disaster, whether a result of natural events or terrorism, is felt first at the local level with effects that can vary from commu-nity to community. On any given day, "normal" operating procedure calls for the emer-gency manager to plan for and expect the unimaginable; this is because on any given day, a hazard can instantaneously debilitate an unprepared or underprepared populace. As first responders are trained to respond to specific and localized types of emergencies (like crime or fire), emergency managers are trained to handle this challenge through a broad response when an emergency affects entire populations. For example, a hurricane can suddenly strengthen or shift direction in a short period of time, or a terrorist can unexpectedly decide to attack a less-populated area because it lacks the reinforced externalities that protect larger populations. These larger events definitely involve the emergency manager and many other individuals and organizations in society.

Economic factors pose a challenge as they influence policy decisions, and this often results in a loss of funding for emergency management even when there are foreseeable disasters. The problem of funding springs naturally out of the intergovernmental paradox in which emergency managers operate. For example, decision-makers, such as those mentioned earlier in King County, Washington, may divert a majority of effort and time to homeland security grant administration to combat terrorism because that is where the funds are made available; they can then allow these local funds to be used for other community needs. However, a choice must be made as to where funds will be spent due to the combination of the lack of personnel and the multiple duties that emergency managers are tasked with such as planning, training, and grant-writing for multiple hazards across diverse communities. This may mean, though, that another funding need, say, natural disaster mitigation, is deprioritized as federal funds are focused on protections against terrorism.

Another budgetary or economic policy challenge is educating the public and elected officials so that they understand wherein their communities' vulnerabilities lie. Williams and Webb (2019) found that one way the emergency manager defines vulnerability is a lack of knowledge on the part of the public and local government department heads and elected officials that contributes to the intergovernmental paradox. For example, a majority of people in a community may view a chemical refinery or a nuclear power plant as a primary income source and the reason for a lucrative economic environment. With federal regulations providing funding to protect assets from an external terrorist attack, other areas of need may be overlooked or deprioritized, such as a natural hazard, because of the lack of knowledge of other threats. Thus, the people go about their daily lives among a spider web of pipelines without a thought of the threat that may be posed and that can result in a community vulnerability rather than an individual or specific characteristic vulnerability.

For instance, Terpstra (2011) proposes that a population becomes more vulnerable when certain protective actions are taken that lower the general perception that "bad things can happen." This negative externality of hardening a structure against a natural or human-induced hazard can indeed result in vulnerability if the true problem is not accurately identified. Additionally, the Pavlak (1988) proposal says that sometimes policy "solves the wrong problem." For example, Williams and Webb (2020) found emergency managers to be frustrated with federal policy that authorized the American Red Cross to provide disaster relief services to vulnerable populations based on socioeconomics which did not align with local community needs. For emergency managers, this challenge is made more difficult by the idea that the task of the full-time emergency management agency is not to engage in operations but to coordinate policy goals among vulnerable populations and gather information from vulnerable populations to influence future policy (Comfort, 1988). In other words, if policies are ineffective in any way, they can render the operations of emergency management and the roles of emergency managers less effective.

Another challenge to operating within the budget constraints of the intergovernmental paradox is to operate within the spirit of the law when protocols mandate specific actions but do not take into account the unique needs of the community (Williams and

Webb, 2020). For example, to receive federal funds for recovery operations after a disaster, a municipal jurisdiction may need to shut down all library functions during a normal power outage and either continue to pay the non-working employees or send them home without pay for the day or days effected. If this action is not taken, the municipal jurisdiction may not receive funding during a federally declared disaster. Emergency managers often find themselves having to make these difficult decisions about honoring the spirit of the law even when all or part of the law does not pertain to their community's needs; occasions arise when step two of four may not be necessary, but funding will be lost if that step is not taken.

Comfort (1988) revealed another challenge emergency managers continue to face, which is "creating the appropriate mix of organizational learning, command and control structures, and integrating patterns of communication to achieve effective performance in the dynamic emergency environment" (4–5). In light of the intersection of focusing events that brought emergency management and homeland security together, McEntire (2007a) identified 13 challenges to emergency management and homeland security. These challenges included limited budgets, heavy workloads, political appointees, politics, and a tension between national security and the emergency management all-hazards approach. Many of these challenges remain for emergency managers despite the expanding body of research that has revealed these realities.

RECOMMENDATIONS FOR THE FUTURE

The role of the emergency manager in disaster and homeland security is wrought with frustration as political motivations continue to guide policy decisions that tend to place natural and technical source disaster in competition with terrorism for who gets what and when. McEntire (2007b) proposed that competition for attention between homeland security and emergency management exacerbated the issue and suggested a move to a liability-reducing, capacity-building model for emergency management. To counteract the constantly shifting focus between homeland security and emergency management, as well as the resulting shifts in policy with conflicting goals and objectives, McEntire (2007b) further suggested that emergency managers must network in order to spread the workload and funding across other departments, agencies, and nongovernment organizations.

The idea that the emergency manager's strength lies in powerful networks is not a new one (Williams, 2017; Williams and Webb, 2020). However, while it has often been addressed, it seems yet to be fully understood or realized. The concept of managing networks is a vital aspect that must be a part of the education of future emergency managers. Emergency managers must function effectively, i.e., they must confront difficult, sometimes shocking circumstances in real time to coordinate responses by key people and organizations within a high-impact, high-consequence environment. While real-world experience can help the emergency manager deal with the high stress that disaster can bring, the uncertain nature of the emergency management world requires a vast array of knowledge across multiple types of hazards and different functions that necessitates their being part of a network of peers to facilitate the role they must play in coordinating efforts before, during, and after an event.

A second recommendation is in the Tierney (2014) proposal that social, political, and economic policy issues can actually create vulnerability during a disaster instead of minimizing it. Williams and Webb (2019) agreed that emergency management professionals do indeed encounter this aspect of vulnerability, which is created by political interests. Williams and Webb (2020) propose that emergency managers need to acquire buy-in amid these same confounding political interests that pit homeland security against disaster in policy decisions, which includes the ability to leverage federal and state protocols to address limited budgets, a lack of personnel, and the political environment.

A third recommendation comes as a result of the events of the COVID-19 pandemic in 2020–2021 that highlights the irony of a political environment and showcases the need for emergency management professionals who understand the agenda-setting process in which policy-makers operate. For example, the media has the ability to control the policy agenda at the federal level by controlling the narrative, so Williams and Nelson (2020) proposed that local emergency managers absolutely must have an open and fluid relationship with the media. Keeping the media involved and informed can help reduce its need to create a narrative that does not reflect the realities of the situation. Additionally, COVID-19, like previous health hazards such as Ebola, accentuates the need to include public health officials as a collaboration partner for the emergency manager.

These previous recommendations persist not only in the view of academia but also in the opinion of emergency management practitioners. However, Williams (2021) proposes that emergency managers continue to rely upon personal experience and the experience of their peers along with state and federal regulations and guidance rather than academic research. As emergency management programs continue to proliferate in higher education, academia is in a position to equip emergency managers with the knowledge, skills, and abilities to better understand not only their networking responsibilities but also how to navigate the political and legislative environments. To accomplish this, academia and the professional emergency manager must work to close the knowledge gap through research collaborations and relationship building between institutes of higher education and emergency managers in the surrounding communities.

CONCLUSION

The emergency manager stands at the helm as the central hub and performs the core role of emergency management. Even in jurisdictions that do not have a full-time, professional emergency manager, some key person will be called upon in a given situation to assume this role, and they must be adequately prepared to do so. While emergency management may include medical, military, law enforcement, fire and rescue, maritime, public health, and aviation interventions, it is the emergency manager who provides the daily guidance, communication, and coordination before an event occurs that enables a community to respond and recover when a hazard impacts society. In order to reach and meet the needs of vulnerable populations, the emergency manager must effectively navigate the political and legislative environment that guides the complex intergovernmental structures that must work in partnership during disaster.

The emergency manager of the future will be politically adept and an expert in understanding human behavior, managing that behavior by creating effective networks. Academia has the ability and opportunity to collaborate with emergency managers through professional training and higher education programs. Again, the maestro emerges as our best example of this kind of work, which requires experience in execution, knowledge of all the working parts of the whole, and buy-in from all key players to follow the maestro from rehearsal through performance.

CLASS DISCUSSION AND ESSAY QUESTIONS

1. Emergency management has a long history and a somewhat turbulent relation-ship with civil defense. Explain when emergency management appeared (unof-ficially and officially) and how emergency management has changed over time.
2. Emergency management has been approached from both a bottom-up and top-down perspective. How have local and federal governments influenced the devel-opment of emergency management?
3. Events like 9/11 and Hurricane Katrina have altered, to a large extent, the pri-orities of those working in emergency management. Discuss the impact of these pivotal events on the role of emergency managers in relation to terrorism and natural disasters.
4. What is the "intergovernmental paradox" and how can emergency managers best deal with this challenge when disasters occur?
5. The states of Louisiana and Texas provide different structural arrangements for emergency management. What are the advantages and disadvantages of central-ization and decentralization?
6. Emergency managers may experience excessive workloads with limited person-nel and financial resources. Can networking minimize these challenges? If so, how and why?

REFERENCES

Averch, Harvey, and Milan Dluhy. 1997. "Crisis Decision Making and Management." In *Hurricane Andrew: Ethnicity, Gender, and the Sociology of Disasters*, edited by Walter Gillis Peacock, Betty Hearn Morrow, and Hugh Gladwin, 75–91. Miami, FL: International Hurricane Center-Laboratory for Social and Behavioral Research.

Beriwal, Madhu. 2006. "Preparing for a Catastrophe: The Hurricane Pam Exercise." In *Senate Homeland Security and Governmental Affairs Committee*, edited by United States Congress Senate Committee, Vol 4. 15–20. Washington, DC: HSGAC.

Birkland, Thomas A. 2006. *Lessons of Disaster, Policy Change after Catastrophic Events*. Washington, DC: Georgtown University Press.

Birkland, Thomas A. 2009. "Disasters, Catastrophes, and Policy Failure in the Homeland Security Era." *Review of Policy Research* 26(4):423–438.

Buck, Dick A., Joseph E. Trainor, and Benigno E. Aguirre. 2006. "A Critical Evaluation of the Incident Command System and NIMS." *Journal of Homeland Security and Emergency Management* 3(3): 1–27.

Butler, David. 2012. "Focusing Events in the Early Twentieth Century: A Hurricane, Two Earthquakes, and a Pandemic." In *Emergency Management: The American Experience 1900–2010*, edited by Claire B. Rubin, 13–50. Boca Rotan, FL: CRC Press.

Comfort, Louise K. 1988. "Designing Policy for Action: The Emergency Management System." In *Managing Disaster: Strategies and Policy Perspectives*, edited by Louise K. Comfort, 3–21. Durham, NC: Duke University Press.

Congress, 107th. 2002. "Public Law 107-296," edited by The Department of Homeland Security. Washington, DC: Congressional Record. Accessed on 20 March 2023 at https://www.congress.gov/107/plaws/publ296/PLAW-107publ296.pdf.

Dombrowsky, Wolf R. 1998. "Again and Again: Is a Disaster What We Call a 'Disaster'?" In *What Is a Disaster?: Perspectives on the Question*, edited by Enrico L. Quarantelli, 19–30. New York: Routledge.

Drabek, Thomas E. 1991. "The Evolution of Emergency Management." In *Emergency Management: Principles and Practice for Local Government*, edited by Thomas E. Drabek, and Gerard J. Hoetmer, 3–29. Washington, DC: International City Management Association.

Dynes, Russell R. 1970. *Organized Behavior in Disaster*. Lexington, MA: D. C. Heath.

Dynes, Russell R. 1993. "Disaster Reduction: The Importance of Adequate Assumptions about Social Organization." *Sociological Spectrum* 13(1):175–192.

Dynes, Russell R. 2003. "Noah and Disaster Planning: The Cultural Significance of the Flood Story." *Journal of Contengencies and Crisis Management* 11(4):170–177.

Fritz, C. E. 1961. "Disasters." In *Contemporary Social Problems*, edited by R. K. Merton, and R. A. Nisbet, 651–694. New York: Harcourt.

GOHSEP, Governor's Office of Homeland Security and Emergency Preparedness. 2021. "Louisiana Homeland Security and Emergency Assistance and Disaster Act (Louisiana Disaster Act)". Edited by Governor's Office of Homeland Security & Emergency Preparedness. Baton Rouge, LA: GOHSEP. Accessed on March 20, 2023 at https://gohsep.la.gov/ABOUT/AUTHORITIES/Louisiana-Disaster-Act#:~:text=The%20Louisiana%20Homeland%20Security%20and,from%20natural%20and%20manmade%20disasters.

Hoetmer, Gerard J. 1991. "Introduction." In *Emergency Management: Principles and Practice for Local Government*, edited by Thomas E. Drabek, and Gerard J. Hoetmer, XVII–XXXIV. Washington, DC: International City Management Association.

Jensen, Jessica, and William L. Waugh. 2014. "The United States' Experience with the Incident Command System: What We Think We Know and What We Need to Know More About." *Journal of Contingencies and Crisis Management* 22(1):5–17.

Kreps, Gary A. 1984. "Sociological Inquiry and Disaster Research." *Annual Review of Sociology* 10(1):309–330.

Kreps, Gary A. 1991. "Organizing for Emergency Management." In *Emergency Management: Principles and Practice for Local Government*, edited by Thomas E. Drabek, and Gerard J. Hoetmer, 30–54. Washington, DC: International City Management Association.

Mann, Jim, and Brian D. Williams. 2020. "Policing in the Eye of the Storm." *Journal of Police and Criminal Psychology*. https://doi.org/10.1007/s11896-020-09394-y.

McEntire, David. 2007a. "The Historical Challenges Facing Emergency Management and Homeland Security." *Journal of Emergency Management* 5(4):17–22.

McEntire, David. 2007b. "Local Emergency Management Organizations." In *Handbook of Disaster Research*, edited by Havidan Rodriguez, Enrico L. Quarantelli, and Russell R. Dynes, 168–182. New York: Springer.

McEntire, David. 2015. *Response and Recovery: Strategies and Tactics for Resilience*. 2nd ed. Hoboken, NJ: Wiley.

McEntire, David. 2016. *Disciplines, Disasters and Emergency Management: The Convergence and Divergence of Concepts, Issues and Trends from the Research Literature*. Emmitsburg, MD: Emergency Management Institute.

Mileti, Dennis. 1999. *Disasters by Design: A Reassessment of Natural Hazards in the United States*. Washington, DC: Joseph Henry Press.

Pavlak, Thomas J. 1988. "Structuring Problems for Policy Action." In *Managing Disaster: Strategies and Policy Perspectives*, edited by Louise K. Comfort, 22–38. Durham, NC: Duke University Press.

Phillips, Brenda, David M. Neal, and Gary R. Webb. 2017. *Introduction to Emergency Management*. 2nd ed. Baton Rouge, LA: CRC Press.

Platt, Rutherford H. 1999. *Disasters and Democracy: The Politics of Extreme Natural Events*. Washington, DC: Island Press.

Rubin, Claire B., ed. 2012. *Emergency Mangement: The American Experience 1900–2010*. 2nd ed. Boca Rotan, FL: CRC Press.

Schneider, Saundra K. 1992. "Governmental Response to Disasters: The Conflict Between Bureaucratic Procedures and Emergent Norms." *Public Administration Review* 52(2):135–145.

Stehr, Steven D. 2007. "The Changing Roles and Responsibilities of the Local Emergency Manager: An Emperical Study." *International Journal of Mass Emergencies and Disasters* 25(1):37–55.

Sylves, Richard. 2012. "Federal Emergency Management Comes of Age: 1979–2001." In *Emergency Mangement: The American Experience 1900–2010*, edited by Claire B. Rubin, 115–166. Boca Rotan, FL: CRC Press.

Sylves, Richard T. 2008. *Disaster Policy and Politics*. Washington, DC: CQ Press, a Division of Congressional Quarterly.

Terpstra, Teun. 2011. "Emotions, Trust, and Perceived Risk: Affective and Cognitive Routes to Flood Preparedness Behavior." *Risk Analysis* 31(10):1658–1675.

Texas Division of Emergency Management, Preparedness Section. 2000. "Preparedness Standards for Emergency Management in Texas: TDEM-100," edited by Department of Public Safety. Austin, TX. Accessed on 20 March 2023 at https://tdem.texas.gov/preparedness/local-planning.

Texas Division of Emergency Management, Preparedness Section. 2008. "Local Emergency Management Planning Guide: TDEM-10," edited by Department of Public Safety. Austin, TX. Accessed on 20 March 2023 at https://tdem.texas.gov/preparedness/local-planning.

Tierney, Kathleen. 2014. *The Social Roots of Risk: Producing Disasters, Promoting Resilience*. Stanford, CA: Stanford University Press.

Waugh, William L., and Gregory Streib. 2006. "Collaboration and Leadership for Effective Emergency Management." *Public Administration Review* 66(s1):131–140.

Webb, Gary. 2007. "The Sociology of Disaster." In *21st Century Sociology: A Reference Handbook*, edited by Clifton Bryant, and Dennis Peck, 278–285. Thousand Oaks, CA: Sage.

Williams, Brian D. 2017. "An Investigation of the Impact of Social Vulnerability Research on the Practice of Emergency Management." Ph.D. Dissertation, Public Administration. University of North Texas.

Williams, Brian D. 2021. "Understanding Where Emergency Management Gets the Knowledge to Solve the Problems They Face: Where Are We More Than 20 Years after the IJMED Special Edition Calls on Closing the Gap?" *International Journal of Mass Emergencies and Disasters* 39(3): 417–433.

Williams, Brian D., and James P. Nelson. 2020. "Media, Governance and Ebola: What Local Government Needs to Understand about Media Influence of Response Operations When the Improbable Becomes Reality." *Journal of Homeland Security and Emergency Management* 1 (ahead of print). https://doi.org/10.1515/jhsem-2017-0074.

Williams, Brian D., and Gary R. Webb. 2019. "Social Vulnerability and Disaster: Understanding the Perspectives of Practitioners." *Disasters* 45(2):278–295. https://doi.org/10.1111/disa.12422.

Williams, Brian D., and Gary R. Webb. 2020. "Vulnerability and Disaster: Practitioner Strategies for Addressing the Needs of Vulnerable Populations." *Journal of Homeland Security and Emergency Management* 1 (ahead of print). https://doi.org/10.1515/jhsem-2018-0063.

CHAPTER 3

The Roles of Geographers and Land Use Managers in Emergency Management:
Contributions Relating to the Space and Place of Hazards, Disasters, and Terrorist Attacks

Laura Siebeneck, Elyse Zavar, and Rachel Wolfe

INTRODUCTION

Geographers, land use managers, and members of allied fields assume important roles in hazard and emergency management. Geographers engage in hazard management by identifying and mitigating potential hazards that pose risk to a community. Furthermore, they participate in emergency management by coordinating resources and identifying responsibilities related to crises, including disasters. Geographers assume diverse roles within these two areas due in part to the diversity of the geographic discipline. This discipline encompasses a range of scholarship including the study of the inhabitants of Earth, how they move across the globe, and their relationships to each other; all of which inform how disasters are managed. As noted geographer Yi-Fu Tuan (1991, p. 99) explained, "Geography is the study of earth as the home of people." The field is often divided into three general branches of foci: physical, human, and environmental geography. Physical geographers study the physical features on Earth's landscape and the processes associated with creating these landforms (Holt-Jensen, 2009). Subject topics within physical geography span such features as flora, fauna, soils, glaciers, rivers, oceans, weather, and climate. Human geographers focus on people and a myriad of social phenomena as represented by the subfields of social, cultural, political, historical, and economic geography. Some topics examined in this area include population, migration, trade, transportation, nationalism, state-building, and urban development. Environmental geographers integrate concepts and topics from both physical and human geography to examine interactions between physical and human systems (Holt-Jensen, 2009). Environmental geography is characterized by the management of resources (e.g., water, minerals, flora) or hazards (e.g., earthquake, flood, fire) (Burton et al., 1993). Land use, urban planning, and forms of land management draw on the skill sets and training offered in environmental geography.

DOI: 10.4324/9781003350729-3

Spanning these three branches are the spatial technologies utilized in research and practice. These technologies include Geographic Information Systems (GIS) and remote sensing. Geographers from each branch engage with the spatial technologies to examine, analyze, and evaluate their topics of study. Given that geographers often address questions related to location, the field contributes to the advancement and applications of spatial technologies in many areas of inquiry such as emergency management, urban planning, logistics, transportation planning, and land use planning. That said, the current range of training, skill sets, and areas of focus within geography contribute vital skills to hazard and emergency management.

As the Royal Geographical Society (2021) notes, "Geography is unique in bridging the social sciences and natural sciences." The discipline spans topic areas, methodologies, epistemologies, and ontologies; this diversity has produced numerous attempts to define and move the discipline toward specific aims and goals (Livingstone, 1992). One of the strengths of the field is often one of its most cited criticisms: geography is a pluralistic field that draws on many other areas of study to examine spatial relationships (Fenneman, 1919; Liu et al., 2017). Due in part to the breadth of the field, geography is a discipline of self-reflection. In the United States, geography graduate programs educate students not only on the theoretical underpinnings of the discipline, but also on how scholars grapple(d) with defining the discipline. The evolution of geography as an academic field of study has required engagement with questions related to whether the discipline can persist given there is no one agreed-upon ontology or epistemology guiding it. Yet for many within the field, it is this tension and diversity that serves as the discipline's greatest strength: the ability to bridge across the social and physical sciences. This is particularly true for studying hazards, those elements that pose risk to social and physical systems, and disasters, the events that disrupt those systems from a geographic perspective.

The most direct contributions to the emergency management profession come from the subfield of hazards geography, which has simultaneously shaped the theoretical understanding of disaster science while providing applied skill sets to disaster management practitioners. As hazard geographer Harlan Barrows (1923) argued, "Geographers study the 'adjustment of [hu]man[s] to [their] natural surroundings.'" Yet, as examined in this chapter, geographers engaged in research and practice from across the breadth of the discipline contribute to the emergency management and homeland security professions. In this chapter, we briefly review the origins of geography; identify contributions of geographers to the fields of disasters and terrorism; discuss professional roles of geographers within disaster management; consider challenges within the field; and spotlight the future growth of the discipline within the emergency management and homeland security context.

ORIGINS OF GEOGRAPHY

The exact origins of geographic study and the profession are unknown; however, throughout history the question of *where* has sparked the interest of scholars and civilizations. As early as 2,000 years ago, Strabo, Herodotus, and Ptolemy created some of the first known maps illustrating spatial relationships and proximities among various cities, peoples, and physical landscapes. Within the past 1,000 years, scholars such as Al Idrisi, Al Muqaddasi, and Alexander Von Humboldt compiled and recorded detailed descriptions of the different cultures, places, climates, and resources of their times.

Though not explicitly called "geographers," the professions that overlapped with and advanced early geographic inquiry included titles such as cartographer, explorer, astronomer, and mathematician. For example, Eratosthenes, a renowned mathematician, poet, and geographer, is credited with inventing the concept of latitude and longitude as a means of mapping and describing location. Ptolemy, a mathematician and astronomer, built upon this concept and proposed that curved parallel lines better project the size and area of mapped land masses. Twelfth-century Arab geographer Al Idrisi created an atlas where he mapped parts of Africa, Asia, Europe, and the Mediterranean Sea and described the climate of these areas (National Geographic Resource Library, n.d.).

As cartographers, explorers, and navigators charted and mapped Earth's features, other fields contributed to the theoretical underpinnings of the future discipline of geography. Specifically, the work of philosopher Immanuel Kant laid the foundation for the discipline's existence (Hartshorne, 1939). In a series of 18th-century lectures, Kant argued that there are two fundamental ways to classify phenomena: (1) by their features as performed in fields like biology or (2) by their temporal or spatial organization as utilized in history and geography, respectively (Holt-Jensen, 2009). Kant's depiction of geography as a way to study the features of the same place influenced 18th-century scholars including Alexander Von Humboldt, who contributed to the development of physical geography through his study and descriptions of Earth's physical features, and Carl Ritter, who advanced human geography through his systematic approach of comparing regions of the world (Holt-Jensen, 2009).

It was not until the 19th century that geography emerged as a formal academic discipline. The creation of academic departments at European universities led to even greater advancements in geographic understanding. Many early graduates of these programs found employment as professors and instructors, cartographers and surveyors, librarians, and federal government employees (Monk, 2017). Interest within the field continued to grow and by 1885, almost 100 different geographical societies existed globally with a total membership estimated at over 50,000 people (Freeman, 1961).

U.S. geographers played significant roles in mapping the country and recording locations and descriptions of physical features such as rivers, mountains, and valleys. During the Revolutionary War, Robert Erskine, a land surveyor and engineer, was appointed "Geographer and Surveyor General of the Continental Army" by General George Washington. In this role, Erskine and a team of land surveyors provided maps that informed tactical decisions made throughout the war (National Geospatial-Intelligence Agency, n.d). Also during this time, one of the earliest roles of the U.S. Navy was to produce and expand geographic knowledge of the nation's coastlines. Surveyors and cartographers were instrumental in mapping the coastlines and providing military leaders with geographic information necessary to strategize the naval battles fought during the Revolutionary War (Chester, 1904). The interest in exploring and documenting coastlines both at home and abroad continued into the early 20th century. A 1904 National Geographic article by U.S. Rear Admiral C.M. Chester highlights the work of geographers during the early 1900s. Naval Officer William Slacum conducted research along the western United States coastline, gathering information about its physical geography, people, and politics. Rear Admiral Charles Wilkes recorded the geography of Antarctica and documented 280 islands in the Antarctic Ocean. Additionally, geographers surveyed and mapped the Panama Isthmus, as the United States had interest in determining the feasibility of constructing a canal connecting the Atlantic and Pacific Oceans.

Following the first aerial photograph taken by balloon in 1858 by Gaspard-Felix Tournalan, geographers and photographers began regularly capturing imagery of Earth's surface from above. The popularity of aerial imagery increased over the following decades and during World War I, these images aided military reconnaissance missions. During World War II, geographers with cartography and aerial photograph interpretation skills were again in high demand. As described by Barnes (2016), political geographers with expertise about other countries, politics, and cultures served as spies. Other geographers worked as military intelligence officers. Additionally, universities provided courses to military personnel in order to increase their knowledge and language proficiency of countries to which they were to be deployed. Like their American counterparts, Maddrell (2008) notes that some women geographers served as lecturers in British universities during World War II and provided soldiers with training on how to map and survey landscapes, while others supported the war effort as cartographers and aerial photograph interpreters.

As the geographic discipline and profession continued to evolve after World War II, the field sought to address the question of "What is geography?" In defining the discipline, geographer William Pattison (1964) identified four traditions within the "geographic enterprise": (1) spatial, (2) area studies, (3) man-land, and (4) earth science. The *spatial tradition* addresses questions that enhance fundamental understanding of "geometry and movement" across space. Geographers' specializations within this tradition include migration studies, transportation, and business geography. This first tradition also encompasses the development and application of modern-day geographic tools such as GIS, remote sensing and aerial imagery analysis, spatial analysis, and cartography. Next, geographers representing the *area studies tradition* seek to understand "the nature of places, their character and their differentiation" as well as "characterizing a place, be it neighborhood or nation-state" (Pattison, 1964, p. 213). In an academic setting, this may include knowledge within world geography, regional studies, and international studies. Geographers emerging from the *man-land tradition*, now referred to as the human-environment tradition, aim to understand interactions between humans and their natural and built environments. It is within this tradition that hazards geography and land use management emerged. Finally, geographers of the *earth science tradition* focus on understanding the physical Earth systems. Within this tradition, geographers study a myriad of processes within the lithosphere, cryosphere, atmosphere, and biosphere.

Today, careers in Geography span the public, private, and non-profit sectors. The American Association of Geographers (AAG) regularly updates and publicizes information about geographic occupations. Geography as a discipline is broad in scope and as a result, many with geography degrees have professional job titles other than "geographer." Drawing from a projected job growth report by the Bureau of Labor Statistics in 2018, the AAG (2020) spotlighted geography jobs that are expected to be in high demand over the next decade. These titles include Geospatial Information Scientists and Technologists, Geographic Information Systems Technicians, Remote Sensing Technicians, Urban and Regional Planners, Environmental Scientists and Specialists, and Climate Change Analysts. Because of the diversity of career paths and titles, the training for careers in geography varies. Many entry-level positions in the field require candidates to earn either a two- or four-year degree and often desire experience with GIS, remote sensing, cartography, spatial modeling, or planning/land use management. The next section introduces how the profession of geography informs modern-day management of disasters and terrorism as well as the fields of emergency management and homeland security.

GEOGRAPHY'S RELATION TO DISASTERS AND TERRORISM

Given that disasters emanate from hazards and disrupt social and physical systems, geographers contribute to a wide range of disaster management and counter-terrorism activities. During the disaster response phase, emergency managers and related professionals increasingly utilize geographic information to understand the nature of the threats, allocate resources, and inform other response-related decisions. One example of this is the

Geographic Information Systems Specialists who work with wildfire incident command teams on-site during wildfires to provide mapping and visualizations of the incident site (e.g., topographic maps, fire perimeter maps, location of roads) as well as modeling and forecasting wildfire behavior, which is valuable information when making tactical and protective action decisions during these events. Additionally, volunteered geographic information (VGI) or spatial information gathered through open-source platforms such as GeoCommons, OpenStreetMap, and Ushahidi (Goodchild, 2007; Zook et al., 2010; Parr, 2015) have helped first responders and other community officials know where various resources are needed during disaster response and recovery. For example, Ushahidi was deployed during the 2010 earthquake in Haiti. Through the use of Twitter hashtags and emails sent by individuals within the disaster-impacted communities, locational information attached to short text messages allowed for information to be shared and organized about various resource needs, locations of individuals that needed to be rescued from collapsed buildings, and locations of fatalities (Zook et al., 2010). Similarly, collaborative mapping in OpenStreetMap drew on volunteers from across the globe to assist local relief workers on the ground in response to the 2015 Nepalese earthquake (Parr, 2015).

Geographers increasingly contributed to surveillance and intervention activities in response to terrorism threats and incidents following the September 11th terrorist attacks in 2001. As described by Medina and Hepner (2013), geospatial data and geographical information systems are essential in the analysis of spatial patterns and oftentimes generate new knowledge and insights in the form of maps and other spatial visualizations. Just as geographers working within emergency management are influenced by the four traditions of geography, those working within counter-terrorism are also guided/influenced by this foundational knowledge. For example, within the area studies tradition, geographers focus on how history, culture, and current events shape and influence the presence and extent of terrorist activities. Geographers from the human-environment tradition offer insights into how environmental phenomena such as hazards, droughts, war, and famine influence and sometimes exacerbate conflict and migration. Likewise, those trained in the spatial tradition approach and analyze spatial patterns in the geographic distribution of terrorism activity including space, targets, networks, and location of safe havens. Geographic methodology, such as spatial analysis and platforms like GIS and remote sensing software, is instrumental in the examination of geographic patterns in types of attacks, types of locations (e.g., public place, utilities, place of worship, communication infrastructure), targets, and the extent to which attacks cluster or are dispersed (Siebeneck et al., 2009; Nunn, 2007). The ability to visualize geospatial information has been particularly valuable in preparing for potential terrorist attacks. For example, following the deadly 2008 terrorist attacks on the Taj Mahal Hotel in Mumbai, India, members of the New York City Police Department (NYPD) sent personnel to the site of the attack to gather information about the incident, interview first responders, and gather any data that could be useful in preparing for potential future attacks in New York City. As described by NYPD Police Commissioner Raymond R. Kelly in his testimony to the House of Representatives Committee on Homeland Security in 2009, the NYPD learned that the terrorists who carried out the attack on the hotel had information and diagrams of the layout of the hotel and knowledge of the location of various stairwells and doors throughout the building. However, responding officers to this event did not have immediate access to this knowledge, which hindered their ability to respond. Based on this international incident, Commissioner Kelly and the NYPD initiated a project to map and diagram various hotels and landmarks throughout the city, noting key details that would aid in a safer and more successful response to a terrorist attack on these types of facilities and locations. This information was then utilized in the development of various training and security exercises aimed at improving the efficiency and efficacy of the city's response to any future attacks (House Hearing, 111th Congress, 2009). In order to recognize the role of geography in managing disasters and terrorism, the next section explains the origins of hazards geography as related to emergency management and homeland security.

GEOGRAPHY'S RELATIONSHIP TO EMERGENCY MANAGEMENT AND HOMELAND SECURITY

While professionals from all areas of geography contribute to emergency management and homeland security today, the initial involvement of geographers reflects early scholarship on human-environment interactions. Much of this research emerged from the University of Chicago, home to the first geography department in the United States, established in 1903. It was there that Harlan Barrows, a pioneer in the field of geography, began his career as one of the program's first geography students; eventually he served as chair of the department (Colby and White, 1961). A lecturer in historical geography, Barrows embraced the multidisciplinary nature of geography and took inspiration from ecologists, historians, and other prominent geographers of the day (Koelsch, 1969). Barrows was one of the first to analyze historical geography through an ecology-influenced lens. Rather than the environment exerting immovable influence on human development, he instead proposed that humans interact with their environment over the course of development. This line of thought challenged dominant perspectives and greatly advanced human-environment interactions as a tradition within geographic study.

Building on Barrows' research, Gilbert White became a leader in natural hazards geography with his groundbreaking dissertation *Human Adjustment to Floods*. In his dissertation he wrote, "[f]loods are acts of God, but flood losses are acts of man. Human encroachment upon the floodplains of rivers accounts for the high annual flood losses" (White, 1945, p. 2). White argued that instead of relying on engineering to prevent floods, people should modify their behavior within their environment to mitigate against loss (Burton and Kates, 2008). His landmark insights and policy recommendations on floodplain management eventually earned him the title "Father of Floodplain Management." White's participation in the drafting of floodplain management policies, and particularly his role in developing and reforming the flood insurance program, marked a significant advancement for geographers' involvement in hazard risk reduction. Furthering his influence, White advised many students at the University of Chicago and later at the University of Colorado, Boulder, where he served as director of the Natural Hazard Center, one of the premier hazards and disaster research centers in the world.

Two of White's early students and frequent collaborators, geographers Robert Kates and Ian Burton, built upon his work pertaining to human actions within hazardous environments. Kates and Burton conducted groundbreaking studies in hazard vulnerability and resilience, examining (1) why people live in hazardous environments, (2) what factors make them vulnerable to disasters within these environments, and (3) how they recover from the disasters affecting these environments. White, Kates, and Burton published numerous studies examining how human-environment interactions will result in disasters if humans do not modify their behavior (Burton et al., 1978; White et al., 2001). The combined works of Barrows, White, Burton, and Kates laid the foundation for the field of modern natural hazards geography.

From this early work by hazard geographers, the subfield has grown; at the root of this diverse body of hazard research is the interaction between people and their environment. Some prominent examples include Susan Cutter's research on social vulnerability, which explores factors that cause some people and places to be more vulnerable to disaster events than others, in addition to the ways in which vulnerability is assessed and measured (e.g., Cutter, 1993, 1996; Cutter et al., 2013). A student of Cutter's, Deborah Thomas's work on hazards and health geography has brought new understanding on health outcomes following disaster events and has pushed forward the role of GIS and other spatial technologies in disaster management (e.g., Thomas et al., 1999, 2015; Thomas, 2018). Thomas Cova's work has also greatly advanced the use of spatial technologies in hazard management, particularly through his groundbreaking research on evacuation modeling, evacuation vulnerability, and wildfire hazards (e.g., Cova and Johnson, 2002; Cova et al., 2009, 2011, 2021). In advancing the field's understanding of hazards and land use management, J. Kenneth Mitchell has published influential research on flooding in megacities and climate change mitigation (e.g., Mitchell, 2005, 2015). Burrell Montz and Graham Tobin, through their independent and collaborative work on flood management, have significantly contributed to such topics as the influence of structural mitigation on the development of high-risk landscapes, the impact of hazards on real estate, and community resilience to environmental hazards (e.g., Tobin, 1999; Tobin and Montz, 2004; Montz and Tobin, 2008; Montz, 2017; Montz et al., 2017). Advancing understanding of land use through a historical geographic lens, Craig Colten's generative research examines community resilience and adaptation to changing environments in coastal areas by understanding past policies and land management practices (e.g., Colten, 2005, 2009). This is just a small sample of U.S.-based hazard geographers and their contributions to the discipline of geography and the disaster management professions in a U.S. context. The next section describes some of the professional roles geographers assume within emergency management and homeland security.

ROLES OF THE GEOGRAPHY PROFESSION IN EMERGENCY MANAGEMENT AND HOMELAND SECURITY

Geographic literacy is an increasingly desired competency within emergency management and disaster science. Though geographic literacy encompasses a diverse range of knowledge and skill sets, the ability to understand the complex interactions between humans, the environment, and hazards, as well as the ability to apply geographic methods and techniques in the analysis of the *where* question, has become essential in practice. In their 2016 report, The Next Generation Emergency Management Core Competencies Working Group identified *geographic literacy* as one of four key knowledge areas desired in future emergency managers. Within their report, the team states:

> Emergency management professionals must possess a foundational understanding of the geographic configurations of hazards, vulnerability, and risk. This comprehensive understanding better enables emergency managers to determine the day-to-day risks they are addressing. Geographic literacy is evident in the ability to conceptualize the interconnections, interactions, and implications of complex environments, as well as the ability to utilize available analysis and technological tools to track environmental changes that result in changing risk profiles.
>
> (FEMA Higher Education, 2016, p. 4)

Geographers perform critical functions within emergency management and homeland security such as identifying and profiling of hazards and threats, conducting risk assessments, and modeling environmental change. The four traditions of geography (Pattison,

1964) described earlier provide an organized means for discussing the roles, functions, and professional job titles of geographers engaged in emergency management (see Table 3.1).

First, geographers with knowledge and skill sets within the *spatial analysis tradition* possess expertise in tools and techniques such as GIS. This spatial technology allows users to visualize and analyze spatial patterns. During the pre-disaster phases, GIS facilitates the hazard mitigation planning process by providing valuable analyses that can be integrated into risk and vulnerability assessments. For example, the HAZ-MAP (2021) spatial databases identify links between chemical and occupational diseases while the HAZUS computer modeling program estimates losses generated from earthquakes, flooding, and high winds (FEMA 2021). GIS is also commonly used in the development of evacuation plans and in determining optimal routes for moving resources to and from affected areas (Cova, 1999). In the post-event context, Cova (1999) notes that GIS is useful in creating and maintaining spatial databases of damage assessment data and tracking the status of household and community recovery. Policy-makers and emergency managers often use GIS during disaster recovery in order to identify and visualize where road networks, schools, businesses, and homes need to be rebuilt (Richardson, 2009). For example, the USGS Earthquake Hazards Program produces ShakeMaps, which provide decision-makers with near-real-time spatial data on ground shaking and the associated intensity produced by an earthquake (USGS, 2021). Additionally, GIS coupled with Global Positioning System (GPS) technologies now assists search-and-rescue teams in navigating disaster-impacted areas that may be unrecognizable post-event (Van Westen, 2000). Within homeland security, agencies such as the Central Intelligence Agency (CIA) hire geographers to serve as cartographers that provide maps to senior policy-makers and members of the Executive Office.

As with GIS, *remote sensing* is a valuable tool for detecting, monitoring, and visualizing hazards and vulnerability. Remote sensing is defined as "a method of collecting information from a distance by instruments carried typically on aircraft or spacecraft" (Fussell et al., 1986, p. 1510). Remote sensors utilize imagery acquired through aerial

TABLE 3.1. Sample of job titles held by individuals trained in Geography.

Area Tradition	Spatial Tradition
Transportation Planner	GIS Analyst / Specialist
Urban Planner / City Planner	Remote Sensing Analyst / Specialist
Location Analysts	GeoSpatial Intelligence Analyst
Area Specialist	Analytical Methodologist
Historic Preservationist	Cartographer
GeoIntelligence Specialty	Surveying and Mapping Technician
Foreign Services Officer	Geodedic Scientist
Market Analyst	Photogrammetrist
Human-Environment Tradition	**Earth Science Tradition**
Floodplain Coordinator	Fluvial Geomorphologist
Park Ranger / Forest Manager	Climatologist
Emergency Management Planner/Coordinator	Physical Geographer
Environmental Planner	Hydrologist
Sustainability Manager	Snow / Avalanche Scientist
Hazards Analyst /Hazard Mitigation Planner	Fire Ecologist
Environmental Affairs Specialist	Water Resources Specialist / Manager

Source: Adapted from AAG (2020)

photographs, radar technologies, satellite, or unmanned aerial vehicles such as drones. This imagery assists users in identifying features on the landscape, carrying out change detection analyses, and acquiring information that may be difficult to obtain, as may be the case in remote locations affected by a disaster.

Remoting sensing technologies are useful for monitoring a wide range of phenomena from river health and flow regimes (Gardner et al., 2020) to urban land surface temperatures and their risk to human health (Mirzaei et al., 2020). This technology is also instrumental in identifying patterns in climate change and predicting sea-level rise (Yang et al., 2013). Analysts use satellite and aerial imagery to: measure and study aridification processes in sub-Saharan Africa; monitor El Niño–Southern Oscillation (ENSO) patterns to predict shifts in atmospheric circulation and sea-surface temperatures in the tropics (De Jong et al., 2004); and detect smoke plumes and monitor wildfire spread rates (San-Miguel-Ayanz and Ravali, 2005). During hazard mitigation, remotely sensed imagery is used to create digital elevation models (DEMs) that assist land use planners in managing zoning and development activities in volcano-, flood-, and landslide-prone areas (Tralli et al., 2005). Recently, there has been a greater reliance on drones for acquiring aerial imagery. For example, after Hurricane Harvey in 2017, remotely sensed imagery gathered by drones helped in finding residents stranded by floodwaters, assessing damage, monitoring levees, and creating maps of flooded areas to aid emergency managers in disaster response and recovery activities (NBC News, 2017). It is important to mention that geographers with expertise in GIS and remote sensing may be hired as part of the staff for larger county and state offices of emergency management to support data acquisition, analysis, and mapping. Likewise, geographers may be housed in other government agencies and serve as technical support for various emergency management activities as needed.

The United States Department of Homeland Security's Geospatial Management Office is responsible for (1) acquiring, maintaining, and providing geospatial data, (2) conducting data analysis and creating visualizations such as maps and aerial images, and (3) ensuring that information and data are accessible to the homeland security and emergency management communities (GeoPlatform.Gov, 2020). Within this office, geographers provide remote sensing support for initiatives such as the National Digital Orthophoto Program (NDOP), the Urban Area Imagery Program (UAIP), and the Homeland Security Infrastructure Protection Program (HSIP). These initiatives support the mission outlined in Presidential Policy Directive 8 (PPD-8), which aims to enhance resilience and national preparedness.

Within international intelligence, remote sensing technologies support geospatial intelligence activities such as monitoring terrorist and violent non-state actors, identifying terrorist safe havens, and monitoring movements of resources and individuals across space during times of war (Medina and Hepner, 2013). Aerial photo interpretation is heavily utilized during conflict and aided in the detection and monitoring of enemy combatant movements during Operation Desert Storm and Operation Iraqi Freedom (De Jong et al., 2004). By combining these technologies with geographic literacy and knowledge of cultures and physical landforms, geographers can provide valuable information for an array of intelligence-related activities (Gillespie et al., 2009).

Spatial statistics includes analytical techniques that use location-based data to address questions either exploratory or confirmatory in nature (Goodchild and Longley, 1999). These analyses incorporate statistical methods that examine geographic patterns and answer spatial- and temporal-related questions. Within the GIS platforms, spatial analyses commonly utilized by geographers include cluster detections analyses like the Getis-Ord Hot Spot Analysis, the Anselin Local Moran's I analysis, and Global Moran's I spatial autocorrelation analysis. GIS also facilitates correlational and regression-based analyses such as Geographically Weighted Regression and Ordinary Least Squares analyses (ESRI 2020). In practice, these analyses identify spatial patterns in human behavior related to violent and non-violent crime (Sherman, 1995), terrorist incidents (Medina et al., 2011), and hate crimes (Medina et al., 2018); examine population distribution throughout the day in order to model impacts of a sudden chemical release event on local populations (Kobayashi et al., 2011); and identify spatial, temporal, and spatio-temporal trends in disease spread (Auchincloss et al., 2012). Similarly, remote sensing software packages also enable users to conduct analyses on aerial imagery. One common analysis includes image classification, which allows users to identify different land cover types such as vegetation, urban areas, and water. This can be particularly helpful if users want to use imagery to calculate the aerial extent of floodwaters, identify the number of roofs damaged by a tornado, or determine the amount of acreage burned by a wildfire.

The *area studies tradition*, or regional tradition, emphasizes developing expertise about a particular country or region through knowledge and understanding of a location's language, history, and culture. As Mardsen (2018) observed, this tradition has expanded over the past several decades to now include international and global studies. Geographers specializing in area studies assume various roles in the fields of emergency management and homeland security. Within emergency management, geographers often work in the non-profit sector to provide relief to disaster-impacted areas. They may also work closely with vulnerable populations to enhance disaster resilience. Because of their expertise in regions, languages, and current events, area study geographers can find employment within the homeland security profession assuming roles in the Foreign Service and the military, and in diplomacy, journalism, and international law.

The *human-environment tradition* centers on the interactions between people and their surrounding environment (Pattison, 1964). Notably, hazards geography and land use management originated within this tradition. As described by Susan Cutter, a distinguished geographer at the University of South Carolina, hazard geographers focus on addressing four key questions: 1) how many people are located in hazardous areas, 2) how do people respond to hazards and what factors contribute to these responses, 3) what can be done to mitigate hazards and risks at a particular location, and 4) are people and places becoming increasingly vulnerable to hazards? (Cutter, 1996, p. 529).

Geography programs at the university level have experienced increased interest in courses related to environmental and human-made hazards, with many courses examining topics such as sources of hazards, hazard adjustments, and the human-ecological dimensions of hazards (Cross, 2000). Within this tradition, geographers utilize the geographic methods discussed earlier to examine the intersection of hazards, people, and the built environment (Montz and Tobin, 2010). Hazards-related curriculum coupled with courses pertaining to geographic methods provide students with the knowledge and skill sets to carry out key functions in emergency management and homeland security. Because of this, the human-environment tradition is closely related to the emergency management and homeland security fields, it is not uncommon to see graduates of geography programs employed in various emergency management and homeland security capacities at the local, state, and federal levels. Specifically, geographers in these fields are often responsible for conducting hazard identification and risk assessments, mitigation planning and strategy implementation, and social demographic studies that inform vulnerability assessments. As shown in Table 3.1, the job titles of hazard geographers include hazard mitigation planner, hazards analyst, emergency coordinator, environmental planner, sustainability manager, forest manager, and park ranger.

The *earth science tradition* provides the knowledge base of the physical phenomena that range across all Earth systems including the atmosphere, biosphere, cryosphere, and lithosphere. Table 3.1 lists common job titles of physical geographers that interact with the emergency management and homeland security communities. Though physical geographers may not work in emergency management offices, they often serve in stakeholder roles as subject matter experts. For example, a snow scientist is a critical member of the State Hazard Mitigation Team in mountainous regions. Likewise, fluvial geomorphologists or hydrologists monitor stream gauges in order to identify current and projected flood risk. Climatologists provide regional climatological outlooks that can guide mitigation and climate adaptation plans as well as data and predictions for expected sea-level rise in coastal communities. Within Homeland Security, physical geographers may provide information about water velocity and discharge downstream should a dam fail as a result of a terrorist attack. Similarly, physical geographers with expertise in climatology can provide forecasts that can assist the intelligence community in understanding climate-forced migrations, potential conflict over water resources, and possible civil unrest.

CURRENT CHALLENGES IN THE PROFESSION

Emergency management and homeland security are exciting professions that are continually evolving to best manage the current risks, hazards, and vulnerabilities in the natural and built environments. Geographers, though diverse in the roles and types of involvement they have in these fields, provide valuable knowledge and skills that enhance community resilience. However, geographers often face challenges within the profession that impact activities within emergency management and homeland security. This section highlights three of these challenges.

1. *What is a geographer?* The discipline of geography is pluralistic and the four traditions within geography highlight the breadth of knowledge and skill sets geographers possess. Although the interdisciplinary nature of geography is a strength, especially in the areas of hazards and disaster studies (Kendra, 2007), it sometimes leads to confusion among the public as to what geographers actually do; given that few individuals hold the official job title of "geographer," it comes as no surprise that this confusion exists (Gould, 2016). Limited knowledge and understanding within the emergency management and homeland security communities of what geographers are capable of doing can lead to several negative consequences. In particular, inadequate familiarity of the skill sets geographers possess may result in them being underutilized. This is particularly true for decision-making related to land use; without a full understanding of where and how hazards occur as well as the risks they pose, communities cannot effectively minimize hazard exposure nor plan for disaster events.

2. *Funding challenges.* The practitioner and academic communities experience similar challenges when integrating geographic technologies into workplace and classroom settings. First, the cost of the equipment and software used to carry out GIS, remote sensing, and statistical analyses is expensive and requires routine maintenance and updated costs (Siebeneck et al., 2019). Second, agencies may not have funding available to hire the personnel needed to utilize these technologies. Finally, budget and time constraints make it difficult to ensure that the personnel utilizing these technologies attend workshops and receive ongoing training to keep up with the latest advancements. These issues may be especially pronounced in organizations located in smaller and in more rural communities.

3. *Data challenges*. The acquisition of data to carry out geographic-based analyses and decision-making is a frequent challenge. The data that geographers need to conduct analyses may not exist or must be purchased. Sometimes the quality of the data may not be adequate and in the case of remotely sensed data, there may be issues related to privacy, thus limiting accessibility to the data set (Fletcher-Lartey and Caprarelli, 2016). Another issue can be found in the interoperability of data, meaning the ability to share and transfer files with other organizations. For example, file formats used in performing GIS or remote sensing analyses may be incompatible between different software platforms. Also, shared files may be missing important attribute information such as details about when the file was created, who created the file, what the variables and column headings mean, and details about the unit of analysis (Abdalla et al. 2007). Emergency management and homeland security are highly collaborative fields and rely on cooperation and coordination between various government, private, and non-profit entities (Olszewski and Siebeneck, 2021). This lack of data coordination and availability of metadata can be especially problematic in disaster scenarios when timely information is critical in strategizing and managing response-related activities across jurisdictional boundaries. Another problem is that data may not be current. For example, decision-making undertaken within floodplain management depends on the accuracy of the data used to create Federal Emergency Management Agency (FEMA) Flood Insurance Rate Maps (FIRMs). The National Flood Insurance Program bases insurance requirements and premiums on the flood zones identified by the FIRMs. Local communities also utilize FIRMs when making decisions about development, land use management, and related planning decisions. Yet FIRMs are often outdated and rely on historical flood data without considering the effects of climate change (Lehmann, 2020). Furthermore, not all of the United States is fully mapped. The Association of State Floodplain Managers (2020) identified that 33% of U.S. riverways and 46% of coastlines are mapped, leaving unmapped areas vulnerable to flooding and without the associated mitigation benefits. Geographers often rely on publicly funded data collected through institutions such as the U.S. Geological Survey (USGS), U.S. Census Bureau, National Oceanographic and Atmospheric Administration (NOAA), and FEMA, among others. A challenge of this reliance is that there must be political will on the part of the public and governmental leaders to recognize the value of these data as lack of support can undermine risk reduction measures. For example, the USGS Streamgauging Network provides scientists and practitioners with data on the volume of water passing through a river channel, which is vital in monitoring and managing flood risks, yet the program is underfunded and several major waterways lack sufficient coverage, leaving communities vulnerable to flood hazards (USGS, 2020). The availability of accurate, updated, and accessible data continues to pose challenges for geographers working in the fields of emergency management and homeland security, and ultimately, this can impact the quality of risk-based decisions that have implications for the protection of life and property.

RECOMMENDATIONS FOR THE FUTURE

To ensure that the discipline of geography continues to advance the fields of emergency management and homeland security, we recognize four key areas of growth to improve operations before, during, and after disasters and terrorist attacks.

1. *Ongoing education and training.* As the emergency management and homeland security professions continue to evolve, it is important that agencies encourage employee development and training. Specific to geography and land use planning, employers should encourage and incentivize employees to engage in continual learning throughout their careers. Keeping current with technical advancements in GIS, remote sensing, and spatial analysis is essential in ensuring that methodologies utilized in hazard identification and risk assessment reflect contemporary best practices. Supporting employee attendance at conferences that engage both the practitioner and academic communities can help individuals keep current on these best practices and changes to the field and discipline, but also allows opportunities to increase professional networks, which may be valuable before and after disasters. Conferences such as the Natural Hazards Workshop, the Environmental Systems Research Institute (ESRI) Users Conference, the American Society for Photogrammetry and Remote Sensing (ASPRS) Conference, the American Association of Geographers (AAG) Annual Meeting, and the United States Geospatial Intelligence Foundation (GeoINT) Conference all provide opportunities for geographers working in the emergency management and homeland security professions to gain exposure to current trends in research, practice, and technology. Additionally, promoting ongoing education through attending webinars or in-person courses enables the employee to continue professional growth in their area of expertise, which in turn has benefits for the organization that employs them.

2. *Funding.* Lack of funding and full-time personnel are two challenges that many local emergency management organizations face (McEntire, 2007; Choi, 2008). The combination of these two limitations means that local emergency managers must assume a variety of roles in order to accomplish missions across hazard mitigation, preparedness, response, and recovery (Samuel and Siebeneck, 2019). Unfortunately, organizations may not have sources to acquire software packages and data needed to perform geographic analyses. In conjunction with encouraging employees to seek out training and networking opportunities, organizations must look for opportunities to support employees in utilizing open-source geographical analyses platforms, such as Q-GIS and the Sentinel Toolbox.

3. *Increase collaboration and data interoperability.* In light of the issues stemming from the availability and interoperability of data, the field would benefit from increased efforts aimed at promoting data-sharing; encouraging consistency in the formatting, storing, and updating (of data); and maintenance of metadata files. For example, the hazards and disasters research community can publish data collection protocols, instruments (e.g., surveys, interview protocols), and collected field data via the DesignSafe Cyberinfrastructure as a means to promote data-sharing (Designsafe-CI, 2021). Given that hazards often fail to conform with jurisdictional boundaries, data that can be utilized across communities, regions, and states can increase the quality and efficiency of pre- and post-disaster planning efforts. Some states have spatial data agencies and websites that house, maintain, and update data, aerial imagery, and GIS shapefiles. For example, Utah's Automated Geographic Reference Center maintains the State Geographic Information Database (SGID), which regularly provides data for state-wide hazard mitigation planning efforts. At local levels, GIS user groups provide valuable resources for geographers working in emergency management–related positions as they can share information about where to find data. The need for collaboration and data interoperability can also be expanded to include

non-GIS data sets such as FEMA and HUD data. Consistency in reporting, creating, and storing data will improve the ease of data acquisition and can lead to more impactful geospatial analyses.

4. *Continue to promote geographic literacy.* The FEMA Higher Education community's emphasis on the need for geographic literacy in emergency management is an important step in helping the academic and practitioner communities understand what geographers actually "do." Emergency management and homeland security higher education programs must promote and encourage geographic literacy and the utility of geographic tools in research and practice. This can be achieved through developing a curriculum that incorporates GIS, remote sensing, map reading, hazards, and consideration of geographic space in the identification and management of hazards and vulnerability (Schumann and Tunks, 2020; Siebeneck et al., 2019; Zavar and Nelan, 2020). For working professionals, taking available GIS courses can help increase knowledge and awareness of the benefits of geography and geospatial technologies. For example, the Emergency Management Institute offers a free independent study course, IS 922: Applications of GIS for Emergency Management that introduces the basics of GIS, provides an overview of how GIS is utilized in the field, and describes what products can be produced using these technologies. The abilities of geographers to carry out risk and vulnerability assessments cannot be overstated, and in order to continue to improve risk-informed decision-making, promoting geographic literacy in the academic and professional settings is essential.

CONCLUSION

Geographers contribute to a wide range of professions within emergency management and homeland security. Though the breadth and depth of geography encompasses various topics and subfields, the unifying theme within the discipline is that geographic inquiry addresses questions related to "space, place, and interactions" (Baerwald, 2010, p. 493). Within emergency management and homeland security, those with geography backgrounds and training greatly contribute to the prevention, mitigation, preparedness, response, and recovery functions of environmental and human-induced disasters.

As emergency management becomes more professionalized, the roles of geographers and land use managers is increasingly critical. The recognition by the FEMA Higher Education community of the value of geographic literacy further validates the essential role that geographers and land use planners have in the profession. Space and place are vital in the management of natural and man-made hazards. As losses from disasters continue to increase, the role of geographers and land use managers will be even more important in advancing the profession and informing more effective hazard management strategies.

CLASS DISCUSSION AND ESSAY QUESTIONS

1. Geographers have long been interested in understanding our physical environment to comprehend the complex systems of our planet, including hazards and disasters. In addition, geographers have utilized their knowledge to assist military leaders. How have geographers facilitated a comprehension of natural hazards and anthropogenic conflicts?

2. What are the four traditions of the "geographic enterprise"? Describe the features of each of these perspectives.
3. Technology such as Geographic Information Systems (GIS) and remote sensing play a vital role in emergency management and homeland security. Explain their importance in various disaster cases, including 9/11, Haiti, and others.
4. The Next Generation Emergency Management Core Competencies Working Group identified *geographic literacy* as a critical knowledge set for emergency managers. Why is geographic literacy vital for improved emergency management? How can geographers help emergency management be more proactive and/or improve post-disaster response and recovery operations?
5. Geographers encounter various problems relating to data. What are these challenges and how can they be overcome for the benefit of the emergency manager and others who are interested in hazards, disasters, and terrorist attacks?

REFERENCES

Abdalla, R., Tao, C. V., & Li, J. (2007). Challenges for the application of GIS interoperability in emergency management. In *Geomatics solutions for disaster management* (pp. 389–405).
American Association of Geographers. (2020). *Careers in Geography*. Accessed November 16, 2020 from http://www.aag.org/cs/careers.
Association of State Floodplain Managers. (2020). Flood mapping for the nation: A cost analysis for completing and maintaining the Nation's NFIP flood map inventory. Madison, WI. https://asfpm-library.s3-us-west-2.amazonaws.com/FSC/MapNation/ASFPM_MaptheNation_Report_2020.pdf.
Auchincloss, A. H., Gebreab, S. Y., Mair, C., & Diez Roux, A. V. (2012). A review of spatial methods in epidemiology, 2000–2010. *Annual Review of Public Health*, *33*, 107–122.
Baerwald, T. J. (2010). Prospects for geography as an interdisciplinary discipline. *Annals of the Association of American Geographers*, *100*(3), 493–501.
Barnes, T. J. (2016). American geographers and World War II: Spies, teachers, and occupiers. *Annals of the American Association of Geographers*, *106*(3), 543–550.
Barrows, H. H. 1923. Geography as Human Ecology. *Annals of the Association of American Geographers*, *13*(1), 1–14. 10.1080/00045602309356882
Blackwell Royal Geographical Society (2021). What is Geography? Accessed March 16, 2023 form: https://www.rgs.org/geography/what-is-geography/.
Burton, I., & Kates, R. W. (2008). Gilbert F. White, 1911–2006. *Annals of the Association of American Geographers*, *98*(2), 479–486.
Burton, I., Kates, R. W., & White, G. F. (1978). *The Environment as Hazard*. New York: Oxford University Press.
Burton, I., Kates, R. W., & White, G. F. (1993). *The environment as hazard* (2nd ed.). New York: Guilford Press.
Chester, C. M. (1904). Some early geographers of the United States. *National Geographic Magazine*, *15*(10), 392–404. National Geographic Archive 1888–1994. Accessed January 2, 2021.
Choi, S. O. (2008). Emergency management: Implications from a strategic management perspective. *Journal of Homeland Security and Emergency Management*, *5*(1). https://doi.org/10.2202/1547-7355.1372.

Colby, C., & White, G. (1961). Harlan H. Barrows, 1877–1960. *Annals of the Association of American Geographers, 51*(4), 395–400.

Cova, T. J. (1999). GIS in emergency management. *Geographical Information Systems, 2*(12), 845–858.

Cova, T. J., & Johnson, J. P. (2002). Microsimulation of neighborhood evacuations in the urban-wildland interface. *Environment and Planning: Part A, 34*(12), 2211–2229.

Cova, T. J., Drews, F. A., Siebeneck, L. K., & Musters, A. (2009). Protective actions in wildfires: Evacuate or shelter-in-place? *Natural Hazards Review, 10*(4), 151–162.

Cova, T. J., Dennison, P. E., & Drews, F. A. (2011). Modeling evacuate versus shelter-in-place decisions in wildfires. *Sustainability, 3*(10), 1662–1687.

Cova, T. J., Li, D., Siebeneck, L. K., & Drews, F. A. (2021). Toward simulating dire wildfire scenarios. *Natural Hazards Review, 22*(3), 06021003.

Cotlen, C. E. (2005). *Unnatural Metropolis: Wresting New Orleans from Nature.* Baton Rouge, LA: LSU Press.

Colten, C. E. (2009). *Perilous Place, Powerful Storms: Hurricane Protection in Coastal Louisiana.* Jackson, MS: University Press of Mississippi.

Cross, J. A. (2000). Hazards courses in North American geography programs. *Global Environmental Change Part B: Environmental Hazards, 2*(2), 77–86.

Cutter, S. L. (1993). *Living with Risk.* London: Edward Arnold, p. 214.

Cutter, S. L. (1996). Vulnerability to environmental hazards. *Progress in Human Geography, 20*(4), 529–539.

Cutter, S. L., Emrich, C., Morath, D., & Dunning, C. M. (2013). Integrating social vulnerability into federal flood risk management planning. *Journal of Flood Risk Management, 6*(4), 332–344.

DesignSafe. (2021). Retrieved January 4, 2021, from https://www.designsafe-ci.org/

DesignSafe C-I. (2021). DesignSafe. https://www.designsafe-ci.org/.

De Jong, S. M., Van der Meer, F. D., & Clevers, J. G. (2004). Basics of remote sensing. In *Remote Sensing Image Analysis: Including the Spatial Domain* (pp. 1–15). De Jong and Ven der Meer (eds.) Dordrecht: Springer.

ESRI. (2020). Retrieved January 4, 2021, from https://www.esri.com/en-us/home

FEMA. (2021). FEMA flood map service center: HAZUS. https://msc.fema.gov/portal/resources/hazus.

FEMA Higher Education. (2016). Next generation emergency managers core competencies. https://training.fema.gov/hiedu/docs/emcompetencies/ngcc%20final%20competencies%204-28-2016.pdf.

Fenneman, N. M. (1919). The circumference of geography. *Annals of the Association of American Geographers, IV*, 3–11.

Fletcher-Lartey, S. M., & Caprarelli, G. (2016). Application of GIS technology in public health: Successes and challenges. *Parasitology, 143*(4), 401–415.

Fussell, J., Rundquist, D., & Harrington, J. A. (1986). On defining remote sensing. *Photogrammetric Engineering and Remote Sensing, 52*(9), 1507–1511.

Freeman, T. W. (1961). *A Hundred Years of Geography.* London: Duckworth.

Gardner, J. R., Yang, X., Topp, S. N., Ross, M. R. V., Altenau, E. H., & Pavelsky, T. M. (2020). The color of rivers. *Geophysical Research Letters, 47*, e02020. https://doi.org/10.1029/2020GL088946.

GeoPlatform.gov. (2020). Retrieved January 4, 2021, from https://www.geoplatform.gov/

Gillespie, T. W. et al. (2009). Finding Osama Bin Laden: An application of biogeographic theories and satellite imagery. *MIT International Review.* http://web.mit.edu/mitir/2009/online/finding-bin-laden.pdf.

Goodchild, M. F., & Longley, P. A. (1999). The future of GIS and spatial analysis. *Geographical Information Systems, 1*, 567–580.

Goodchild, M. F. (2007). Citizens as sensors: The world of volunteered geography. *GeoJournal, 69*(4), 211–221.

Gould, P. (2016). *The Geographer at Work*. London: Routledge.

Hartshorne, R. (1939). The nature of geography: A critical survey of current thought in the light of the past. *Annals of the Association of American Geographers, 29*(3), 173–658.

HAZ-MAP. (2021). Information on hazardous chemicals and occupational diseases. https://haz-map.com/.

Holt-Jensen, A. (2009). *Geography History and Concepts: A Student's Guide 4th Edition*. Los Angeles, CA: Sage.

House Hearing, 111th Congress. (2009). The Mumbai attacks: A wake-up call for America's private sector. Hearing before the Subcommittee on Transportation Security and Infrastructure Protection of the Committee on Homeland Security House of Representatives. March 11, 2009. Serial No. 111–6. Retrieved February 25, 2021, from https://www.govinfo.gov/content/pkg/CHRG-111hhrg49944/html/CHRG-111hhrg49944.htm

Kendra, J. M. (2007). Geography's contributions to understanding hazards and disasters. In McEntire, D.A. (ed.), *Disciplines, Disasters, and Emergency Management: The Convergence and Divergence of Concepts, Issues and Trends from the Research Literature* (pp. 15–30). Springfield, IL: Charles C. Thomas Publisher.

Kobayashi, T., Medina, R. M., & Cova, T. J. (2011). Visualizing diurnal population change in urban areas for emergency management. *The Professional Geographer, 63*(1), 113–130.

Koelsch, W. (1969). The historical geography of Harlan H. Barrows. *Annals of the Association of American Geographers, 59*(4), 632–651. Retrieved January 13, 2021, from http://www.jstor.org/stable/2561831.

Lehman, R. J. (2020). Do no harm: Managing retreat by ending new subsides. R Street Policy Study No. 195 February 2020. https://www.rstreet.org/wp-content/uploads/2020/02/195.pdf.

Liu, Y., Bi, J., Lv, J., Ma, Z., & Wang, C. (2017). Spatial multi-scale relationships of eco-system services: A case study using a geostatistical methodology. *Scientific Reports, 7*(1), 9486.

Livingstone, D. N. (1992). *The Geographical Tradition*. Oxford:Basil Blackwell, pp. 434

Maddrell, A. (2008). The 'map girls'. British women geographers' war work, shifting gender boundaries and reflections on the history of geography. *Transactions of the Institute of British Geographers, 33*(1), 127–148.

Marsden, B. (2018). *Geography 11–16 (1995): Rekindling Good Practice*. London: Routledge. 254pp. https://doi.org/10.4324/9781351032704

McEntire, D. A. (2007). Local emergency management organizations. In *Handbook of Disaster Research*. Rodriguez, H., Quarantelli, E.L., and Dynes, RR. (eds.), (pp. 168–182). New York: Springer.

Medina, R. M., & Hepner, G. F. (2013). *The Geography of International Terrorism: An Introduction to Spaces and Places of Violent Non-state Groups*. Boca Raton, FL: CRC Press.

Medina, R. M., Nicolosi, E., Brewer, S., & Linke, A. M. (2018). Geographies of organized hate in America: A regional analysis. *Annals of the American Association of Geographers, 108*(4), 1006–1021.

Medina, R. M., Siebeneck, L. K., & Hepner, G. F. (2011). A geographic information systems (GIS) analysis of spatiotemporal patterns of terrorist incidents in Iraq 2004–2009. *Studies in Conflict and Terrorism*, 34(11), 862–882.

Mirzaei, M., Verrelst, J., Arbabi, M., Shaklabadi, Z., & Lotfizadeh, M. (2020). Urban heat island monitoring and impacts on citizen's general health status in Isfahan metropolis: A remote sensing and field survey approach. *Remote Sensing*, 12(8), 1350.

Mitchell, J. K. (2005). Urban disasters as indicators of global environmental change: Assessing functional varieties of urban vulnerability. In Ehlers, E, and Krafft, T. (eds.), *Earth System Science in the Anthropocene* (pp. 135–152). Berlin: Springer-Verlag.

Mitchell, J. K. (2015). Governance of megacity disaster risks: Confronting the Contradictions. In Fra, U. (ed.), *Risk Governance: The Articulation of Hazard, Politics and Ecology* (pp. 413–440). Springer.

Monk, J. (2017). Washington women: Practicing geography in the US government, 1915–1970s. *Professional Geographer*, 69(4), 683–693.

Montz, B. E., & Tobin, G. A. (2008). Livin' large with levees: Lessons learned and lost. *Natural Hazards Review*, 9(3), 150–157.

Montz, B. E. (2017). When unprecedented becomes the norm. *Journal of Flood Risk Management*, 10(4), 413–414.

Montz, B. E., Tobin, G. A., & Hagelman, R. (2017). *Natural Hazards: Explanation and Integration*, 2nd ed. New York: Guilford Publishing.

National Geographic Resource Library. (n.d.) *al-Idrisi*. Accessed January 27, 2021. https://www.nationalgeographic.org/encyclopedia/al-idrisi/.

National Geospatial-Intelligence Agency. (n.d.). *Mapping the revolutionary war*. Accessed January 26, 2021. https://www.nga.mil/history/1604328852471_Mapping_the _Revolutionary_War_.html.

NBC News. (2017). Hurricanes show why drones are the future of disaster relief. Accessed September 9, 2017. https://www.nbcnews.com/mach/science/hurricanes-show-why -drones-are-future-disaster-relief-ncna799961.

Nunn, S. (2007). Incidents of terrorism in the United States, 1997–2005. *Geographical Review*, 97(1), 89–111.

Olszewski, C., & Siebeneck, L. (2021). Emergency management collaboration: A review and new collaboration cycle. *Journal of Emergency Management*, 19(1), 57–68.

Parr, D. A. (2015). Crisis mapping and the Nepal earthquake: The impact of new contributors. *Journal of Cartographic and Geographic Information*, 65(3), 151–155.

Pattison, W. D. (1964). The four traditions of geography. *Journal of Geography*, 63(5), 211–216.

Richardson, K. (2009). Aceh Province: Continues GIS Work Five Years after Tsunami. Accessed from https://sensorsandsystems.com/building-back-better-aceh-province -indonesia-continues-gis-work-five-years-after-tsunami/ March 16, 2023.

Rebuilding after a disaster. Esri. https://www.esri.com/news/arcwatch/0310/feature .html.

Samuel, C., & Siebeneck, L. K. (2019). Roles revealed: An examination of the adopted roles of emergency managers in hazard mitigation planning and strategy implementation. *International Journal of Disaster Risk Reduction*, 39, 101145.

San-Miguel-Ayanz, J., & Ravail, N. (2005). Active fire detection for fire emergency management: Potential and limitations for the operational use of remote sensing. *Natural Hazards*, 35(3), 361–376.

Schumann III, R. L., & Tunks, J. L. (2020). Teaching social responsibility and geographic literacy through a course on social vulnerability in disasters. *Journal of Geography in Higher Education*, *44*(1), 142–159.

Sherman, L. W. (1995). Hot spots of crime and criminal careers of places. *Crime and Place*, *4*, 35–52.

Siebeneck, L. K., Medina, R. M., Yamada, I., & Hepner, G. F. (2009). Spatial and temporal analyses of terrorist incidents in Iraq, 2004–2006. *Studies in Conflict and Terrorism*, *32*(7), 591–610.

Siebeneck, L., Schumann III, R. L., & Kuenanz, B. J. (2019). GIS applications in emergency management: Infusing geographic literacy in the classroom. *Journal of Emergency Management*, *17*(2), 119–135.

Thomas, D. S. K., Mitchell, J. T., Scott, M. S., & Cutter, S. L. (1999). Developing a digital atlas of environmental risks and hazards. *Journal of Geography*, *98*(5), 201–207.

Thomas, D. S. K., Anthamatten, P., Dowling Root, E., Lucero, M., Nohynek, H., Tallo, V., Williams, G., Simões, E. A. F., & the ARIVAC Consortium. (2015). Disease mapping for informing targeted health interventions: Childhood pneumonia in Bohol, Philippines. *Tropical Medicine and International Health*, *20*(11), 1525–1533.

Thomas, D. S. K. (2018). The role of geographic information science & technology in disaster management. Chapter 16. In Rodriguez, H., Donner, W., & Trainor, J.E. (eds.), *Handbook of Disaster Research* (2nd ed., pp. 311–330). New York: Springer.

Tobin, G. A. (1999). Sustainability and community resilience: The Holy Grail of hazards planning? Environmental hazards: Human and policy dimensions. *Global Environmental Change Part B*, *1*(1), 13–25.

Tobin, G. A., & Montz, B. E. (2004). Natural hazards and technology: Vulnerability, risk, and community response in hazardous environments. *Geography and Technology*, 547–570.

Tralli, D. M., Blom, R. G., Zlotnicki, V., Donnellan, A., & Evans, D. L. (2005). Satellite remote sensing of earthquake, volcano, flood, landslide and coastal inundation hazards. *ISPRS Journal of Photogrammetry and Remote Sensing*, *59*(4), 185–198.

Tuan, Y.-F. (1991). A view of geography. *Geographical Review*, *81*(1): 99–107.

USGS. (2020). Endangered, discontinued and rescued streamgages mapper. https://water.usgs.gov/networks/fundingstability/.

USGS. (2021). ShakeMap. https://earthquake.usgs.gov/data/shakemap/.

Van Westen, C. J. (2000). Remote sensing for natural disaster management. *International Archives of Photogrammetry and Remote Sensing*, *33*(B7/4; PART 7), 1609–1617.

White, G. F. (1945). Human adjustment to floods a geographical approach to the flood problem in the United States. Thesis (Ph.D.). University of Chicago, 1942, pp. 213–225.

White, G. F., Kates, R. W., & Burton, I. (2001). Knowing better and losing even more: The use of knowledge in hazards management. *Global Environmental Change Part B: Environmental Hazards*, *3*(3), 81–92.

Yang, J., Gong, P., Fu, R., Zhang, M., Chen, J., Liang, S., Xu, B., Shi, J., & Dickinson, R. (2013). The role of satellite remote sensing in climate change studies. *Nature Climate Change*, *3*(10), 875–883.

Zavar, E., & Nelan, M. (2020). Disaster drills as experiential learning opportunities for geographic education. *Journal of Geography in Higher Education*, *44*(4), 624–631. https://doi.org/10.1080/03098265.2020.1771684.

Zook, M., Graham, M., Shelton, T., & Gorman, S. (2010). Volunteered geographic information and crowdsourcing disaster relief: A case study of the Haitian earthquake. *World Medical and Health Policy*, *2*(2), 7–33.

CHAPTER 4

Firefighters Protecting a Nation:
Historical Perspectives and a Modern, All-Hazards Approach

Andrew Byrnes

The hero is commonly the simplest and obscurest of men.

Henry David Thoreau

INTRODUCTION

The public has long viewed the fire and emergency services as a reactionary force, one that deals effectively with current, ongoing threats and hazards to the community. Due to the historical mission-creep that has been a part of the fire service for many years, the modern fire service is much more than a reactionary force. Gone, for the most part, are fire departments that only respond to fires. Fire departments now view firefighting as only a sliver of the pie representing the services they are expected to deliver proficiently. The mission of fire and emergency services has taken on an "all-hazards" type of mission inclusive of natural and man-made disasters.

Since the days of the Roman Empire, firefighters have been called upon to protect, support, serve, and stabilize communities, corporations, states, and nations in more ways than just fighting fires. Some 60 years after a fire in Rome claimed 70% of the city, a force to protect Rome from fire was formed. Cartwright, an ancient Roman historian, explains:

> The vigiles (or *cohortes vigilum*) were formed during the reign of Augustus to act as ancient Rome's permanent firefighting service. Evolving from earlier slave teams, the *vigiles* were organized as an urban military unit and eventually recruits came from the Roman citizenry. The body, with a permanent camp of its own and equipment stations dotted around the city, patrolled the streets of Rome each night and also performed certain nocturnal policing duties to ensure public order.
>
> (2016)

Benjamin Franklin, traditionally considered the father of the municipal fire department, first organized "firewards" in Boston in the early 1700s. These firewards were to "give

DOI: 10.4324/9781003350729-4

such necessary orders as may best serve the said Town in suppressing and extinguishing fires" (Bridenbaugh, 2008). To Franklin, it made sense to have such organizations for both large and small cities. His observations of the firewards formed the basis of his vision for the modern fire service – but his vision went further. Franklin advocated for regulations on fire, writing in his own paper, the *Pennsylvania Gazette*, recommending fire codes and standards he termed "prevention." In the February 4, 1735 edition, he famously penned the first use of this age-old phrase:

> In the first Place, as *an Ounce of Prevention is worth a Pound of Cure*, I would advise 'em to take Care how they suffer living Brands-ends, or Coals in a full Shovel, to be carried out of one Room into another, or up or down Stairs, unless in a Warmingpan shut; for Scraps of Fire may fall into Chinks, and make no Appearance till Midnight; when your Stairs being in Flames, you may be forced, (as I once was) to leap out of your Windows, and hazard your Necks to avoid being over-roasted.

Franklin's commonsense approach spawned the modern fire prevention era and the first serious expansion of the fire service's mission since Rome. The fire service embraced Franklin's commonsense mission of prevention, and Rome's heroic mission of response.

In this chapter we will review the history of firefighting in the United States through the decades, as well as some of the major events that shaped the modern, all-hazards approach to disaster planning and response. We will then discuss the expanding role of firefighters in homeland security. In the conclusion, we'll examine current challenges and opportunities that fire and emergency services organizations face when planning for and responding to natural and man-made disasters.

HISTORICAL PERSPECTIVE

Since the dawn of history, as long as humans have experienced fire, there have been those who extinguish and manage it; one who douses the fire as the caravan moves on or one who stacks the wood far enough from the flames to hinder its ignition. Though ancient Rome and early Boston began organizing this critical service, it wasn't until the 19th century that technological advances made the fire service into an organization we recognize today. Cities were more populated, buildings reached higher, and insurance companies formed the foundation of the modern fire code. Technological advances occurred in manual and steam-driven pumping apparatus, fire helmets, basic protective clothing, fire hoses and nozzles, as well as tactics.

The fledgling fire insurance industry drove advances beyond horse-drawn equipment and citizen bucket-brigades, eventually hiring private firefighters tasked with extinguishing fires only in buildings or properties they insured. Volunteer firefighting teams would compete for the uninsured fires, often holding bare-fisted competitions in the street in front of the burning building to see who "got the job." Tim Winkle, of the Smithsonian's National Museum of American History, noted that, "By 1870, nearly every city had shifted from volunteer companies to paid departments. If it hadn't been for the Civil War, that shift might have happened even earlier" (Donahue, 2016).

The emergence of the National Fire Protection Association (NFPA) in 1896, at the threshold of the 20th century, was an important benchmark in the creation of model fire codes, fire service innovations, and personal firefighter safety. The NFPA creates national consensus standards that drive almost every aspect of fire prevention, fire organization and management, fire-safe buildings, firefighter health and safety, hazardous materials response, technical rescue, and personal protective equipment (PPE). NFPA standards emerge and change based on notable incidents, emerging experiences, and current and evolving fire-related research. These are the gold standards for the fire service profession.

1940–1950s

World War II, and the decade that followed it, brought about a society of enormously increased industrialization. Improved transportation routes, such as by roadway, barge, and rail, transporting new and dangerous hazardous materials, led to catastrophic incidents. The April 16, 1947, explosion on the S.S. Grandcamp, a freighter moored in Galveston Bay laden with over 2,000 tons of ammonium nitrate, used for war-time explosives, killed 27 members of the Texas City Fire Department along with an estimated 600 others in the nearby community. The 1949 Holland Tunnel fire and explosion under the Hudson River in New York involved over 4,000 gallons of the highly volatile carbon disulfide, transported by a driver who was not aware how toxic his cargo was; the tunnel was heavily damaged, there were numerous injuries, and one firefighter lost his life.

Because of the increasingly dangerous situations firefighters were facing, the NFPA in the 1940s created performance testing and standards for firefighter protective clothing. Although the fire helmet had been around for over 200 years in various forms, its performance and value were quantified and improved. Important developments in respiratory protection were also realized. Hasenmeier, in his article on the history of firefighting PPE, explains, "Also after World War II, Scott Aviation made breathing equipment for crews working in airplanes at high altitudes. The engineers noticed that the firefighters were still using filter masks and rebreathers that didn't provide adequate breathing air" (2008). From this realization, engineers developed the Scott Air-Pack for firefighters, introduced in 1945.

In the 1950s, a lack of existing fire codes and the failure to enforce new codes and make their requirements retroactive led to some of the most horrific mass casualties ever caused by fire. On December 1, 1958, 90 young students and three nuns were killed at Our Lady of the Angels Roman Catholic School in Chicago when the second-story attic caught fire and collapsed into the hallway, forcing students to jump from classroom windows or be burned alive. Numerous other fires in mental health wards, hospitals, and convalescent and nursing homes throughout the nation brought attention to the need for improved interior fireproof finish materials, minimum egress widths, fireproofing and construction of smoke-free exit corridors and stairways, and centralized dispatch centers. The 1950s also saw practical innovation by fire service professionals like that of Chicago's iconic fire chief Robert J. Quinn. Quinn served the Chicago Fire Department for 50 years, with 21 years as Fire Commissioner. He instituted an Air-Sea Rescue company, began the use of helicopters for fire observations, and started using centrifugal pumps for high-volume and high-pressure water cannons to reach the upper floors of buildings. Quinn is best known for his innovation of the modern aerial ladder/bucket. While observing a tree-trimming crew one day, he realized similar equipment fitted with water nozzles could elevate firefighters into position and provide another means of moving up a building from the outside. He called this invention the "Snorkle," and many of Quinn's other innovations are still in use today.

1960–1970s

The 1960s brought the unrest of the civil rights struggle to many cities. Fire was used as a weapon against the government and against the community. Its devastation and destruction during riots and unrest brought needed attention to the cause. Unfortunately, some firefighters turned fire hoses on demonstrators and so suffered a tremendous loss of community respect and honor. Firefighters then became a frequent target.

A story in *Time* magazine about the Detroit riots in 1967 was typical: "Two Detroit firefighters lost their lives during the unrest. Carl E. Smith, 30, of Ladder 11, was killed by gunfire at the corner of Mack and St. Jean. John Ashby, 26, of Engine 21, was electrocuted by a high-tension wire while fighting a fire at a supermarket at Lafayette and Canton" (Charles, 2017). The unrest killed 43 people and left 5,000 homeless in Detroit; there were 1,682 fires and 417 buildings destroyed in five days of rioting (Charles, 2017). During the Watts riots in Los Angeles in August of 1965, firefighters were routinely fired at and assaulted. A 1967 International Association of Firefighters (IAFF) report after the Watts riots indicated, "692 incidents of harassment and attacks [on firefighters] since the Watts riot of 1965." When the 1960s ended, firefighters were not the good guys anymore. Fire department public outreach programs like fire safety messages for children and community relations took on a new importance.

This new need for fire service force protection brought about many changes. In May, 1968, *Fire Engineering* wrote:

> Planning firefighting operations in riot areas is becoming an administrative necessity for an increasing number of fire departments ... Fire chiefs had to learn quickly that defenses had to be devised against attacks on their men on the fireground ... So, task force and command post have become part of the language of firefighters. Different types of response to alarms, radical changes in firefighting methods, means of safeguarding apparatus and emergency communications procedures had to be planned for use under riot conditions.

The lessons learned in these critical times led to serious, structured, lasting, and essential reform.

In May 1973, the National Commission on Fire Prevention and Control presented President Nixon with a report on the fire prevention and response efforts in the United States entitled "America Burning." The Commission presented the president with 90 recommendations for ensuring fewer fire deaths, better fire education, proposed restructuring of fire department and community priorities, the need for more funding, stronger enforcement of new fire codes, and the formation of the U.S. Fire Administration (USFA) and the National Fire Academy (NFA) to educate and train fire service leadership. President Nixon said the report was "a good beginning" (National Commission, 1973). Nearly 15 years later, the report was revised and republished as "America Burning Revisited" with updated national fire data and objectives.

Through the 1960s and 1970s, firefighter protective equipment consistently improved. The Federal Occupational Safety and Health Administration (OSHA) was formed in 1970 – 74 years behind the NFPA. OSHA regulations became part of a fire department's ever-increasing compliance responsibility. Cultural changes aimed at being safer did not keep up with the safety now possible. The wearing of a self-contained breathing apparatus (SCBA) was being challenged by hundreds of years of tradition. Links had not yet been made between breathing fire smoke and toxic gasses, and the subsequent increased risk of cancer to firefighters. In the mid-1980s as a new firefighter, I was berated by an old fire officer who wondered why I wasn't right behind him going into a fire. He turned around and I wasn't there – I was putting on my breathing apparatus. That was not acceptable to someone who was trained and served without respiratory protection. At the time, fire service tradition didn't allow for innovation – or a culture of safety.

The 1970s were a time of increasing responsibility for the fire service. Prior to that time, emergency medicine and ambulance transports were typically handled by the local mortuary or hospital. In 1973, "America Burning" recommended that the fire service improve the quality and availability of fire injury medical care to improve the survivability of burn victims. "The Commission recommends that fire departments, lacking emergency ambulance, paramedical and rescue services, consider providing them, especially if they are located in communities where these services are not adequately provided by other agencies" (National Commission, 1973, p. 167). Pre-hospital care became the job of the fire service. Immediately, it was set upon by hundreds of more hours of training, multiple new certifications, and a doubling of the department's call volume. Firefighters had added medicine to their toolbox, and now they had to be proficient Emergency Medical Technicians (EMTs) and Paramedics. Exposure to blood-borne pathogens created a new gap in personal protective equipment. Departments had the added expense of ambulances to include in an ever-growing fleet of vehicles.

1980–1990s

The 1980s brought yet another major task – OSHA, the Department of Transportation (DOT), and the NFPA promulgated standards and regulations related to hazardous materials (hazmat) response. Fire departments had always responded to these types of calls; however, little was known about the material itself. Was it biological, radioactive, corrosive, toxic, flammable, or reactive? What was the main concern – the product, its container, or the environment? Fire departments were dangerously behind the curve when the call involved hazardous materials, and more and more injuries were occurring at these incidents. Additional hours of training and certification were required to adequately prepare firefighters for hazmat response. Fire department hazmat teams were tasked with learning and enforcing hazardous materials–related codes, local ordinances, chemical plan reviews, and hazmat inspections for storage, use, and transportation. On top of that level of highly technical management, hazmat teams also had to respond. Response created the need for expensive and perishable equipment, detection and monitoring technology, new and costly hazmat PPE, specialized apparatus to make the response, and ongoing hazmat training added to the fire service mission.

The 1990s continued the trend of adding further responsibilities to the fire service. Technical rescue specialties such as confined space rescue, high-angle rescue, trench rescue, structural collapse rescue, water and ice rescue, advanced vehicle extrication, and wilderness search and rescue all became a part of "Technical Rescue." Each new rescue discipline required time, money, training, equipment, apparatus, policies and procedures, and a specified need for that particular type of rescue, though not all fire service providers offered all of the disciplines. OSHA mandated that response agencies train and be proficient in confined space rescue, and in 1994, the NFPA added a new technical rescue standard outlining the competencies for multiple levels of technical rescue. Beyond these fundamental rescue requirements, departments typically had small but able rope rescue teams and heavy rescue squads performing vehicle extrication.

Terrorism incidents were on the rise in the 1990s. Defined, terrorism is an intentional act or threat designed to coerce the general public into assuming or changing a position related to a social or political cause. These threats were made manifest through many incidents including the February 26, 1993, World Trade Center bombing in New York City – a failed attempt to bring down the towers in order to kill thousands of people. Another game-changing incident occurred on the morning of April 19, 1995, in Oklahoma City. A small domestic terrorist group detonated a homemade bomb, bringing down most of the Alfred P. Murrah Federal Building. The two individuals killed 168 innocent people – 19 of them were children in a daycare inside the building. The blast was so destructive that over 300 buildings in Oklahoma City were destroyed or damaged. "It was the worst act of homegrown terrorism in the nation's history" (FBI, 2020). The threat was real, and the job of responding to terrorist attacks was now mostly on the broad shoulders of the fire service. The fire service realized that they couldn't do it alone.

2000–2010s

September 11, 2001, began as a beautiful clear day. However, that day ended with the nation on its knees; 343 firefighters and 69 other emergency responders died attempting the largest single rescue of people the world had ever seen. The fire service and the nation would never be the same. After the attack, national attention toward firefighters and all emergency responders were at an all-time high. Presidential directives aimed at bringing emergency responders together in unified communication, command, control, and planning efforts were promulgated to great success. Federal agencies, law enforcement, public health, and the fire service developed cooperative interdiction measures and a national terrorism fusion center network designed to provide resources, expertise, and information in order to protect communities and respond cooperatively.

New weaponization of old agents such as Ricin and Anthrax became a reality in this decade. Thousands of "hoax" calls had to be mitigated by responders, never knowing if the next one would be real. Firefighters and other responders now had to become experts in handling these asymmetrical threats involving weapons of mass destruction (WMD) which involved biological agents, radiological materials, bulk industrial chemicals, and explosives. Reaching out and working together as an emergency response community became a necessity. Command posts had to be unified and based on universal principles of organization and mission execution. No one agency could handle a major incident involving these threats. Cooperation is a continuing struggle.

In 2004, the National Fallen Firefighters Foundation was tasked with and delivered on creating 16 Life Safety Initiatives designed to push for a safety culture and advocate for implementing more stringent safety policies. Gone were the days when wearing an SCBA was frowned upon. Researchers had inextricably linked the causation of certain cancers to elements of the fire service.

National standards, state rules, and local policies required the use of PPE in environments that had always been dangerous but never taken seriously, such as the post-fire overhaul phase when firefighters traditionally removed their PPE to "mop up" the fire scene. Innovations occurred in firefighter and chemical PPE, communications equipment, the integration of new technology to include the use of Global Positioning Systems (GPS) for dispatch, as well as firefighter accountability on scene. Thermal imaging cameras became smaller, less expensive, and more reliable. "Reverse 911" became mandatory in most communities, allowing emergency information to be transmitted directly to a person's home through a hardline telephone. This technology has now integrated with cell phones, informing the public during mass evacuation and disaster scenarios.

2010–2020s

The latest decade is experiencing a long-awaited drop in firefighter fatalities. This can be attributed to the U.S. Fire Administration's safety initiatives, such as the Vehicle Safety Initiative created in 2014, which made wearing a seatbelt in fire vehicles a requirement. The 16 Life Safety Initiatives created in 2004 have increased awareness of the causes of fatalities, and the programs implemented have made a difference. New organizations such as the Firefighter Cancer Support Network, founded in 2005, increased awareness of the cancer problem among firefighters as well as recommended programs and procedures for reducing risk: "The mission of the Firefighter Cancer Support Network is to help fire/EMS members and their families cope with cancer and to provide occupational-cancer awareness and prevention training nationwide" (FCSN, 2020). The Firefighter Behavioral Health Alliance was formed in 2011 to "directly educate firefighters/ Emergency Medical Services (EMS) personnel and their families about behavioral health issues such as depression, Post-Traumatic Stress Disorder (PTSD), anxiety and addictions, as well as firefighter suicides" (FBHA, 2020).

Firefighters and emergency responders were finally taking care of their own, on and off the fire scene, and the increasing embrace of the firefighter safety culture desired by the U.S. Fire Administration was coming to pass, as 2019 saw the fewest number of firefighter fatalities since the NFPA began tracking fatality statistics in 1977. That same year saw 48 fatalities, down from an average of 67 fatalities per year during the previous decade. Philosophical changes have been noted regarding the enforcement of safety policies for fire service leaders, helped by the clear positive influences of the initiatives and a changing culture with each new generation of fire service leadership.

ROLE OF THE FIREFIGHTER IN THE DISASTER MISSION

In 2019, local fire departments responded to 1,291,500 fires that caused 3,704 civilian deaths from fire and roughly 16,600 civilian fire-related injuries. Property damage was estimated at $14.8 billion. On average, a fire department responded to a fire in the United States every 24 seconds. For instance, every 93 seconds a house was on fire and every 3hours and 10 minutes, someone died in a fire (Ahrens and Evarts, 2020). In 2018, local firefighters trained in emergency medicine responded to over 23,551,500 medical calls in addition to fire calls (NFPA, 2019). That averages out to a medical call every 1.4 seconds and a fire call every 24 seconds. Add to that the technical rescue calls, the hazmat calls, the over 2 million false alarms, and the calls for public assistance (to name a few) and you'll begin to appreciate the scope of services provided by the American Fire and EMS services. It's also important to remember that these calls don't go away during a disaster, they increase.

Because disasters occur and require the involvement of the fire department, planning must also take place. Benjamin Franklin has been widely credited with the saying, "Failure to plan is planning to fail." Communities and fire service organizations who don't have a disaster plan, or fail to exercise that plan, will struggle to contend with the multitude of challenges these complex and cascading events pose, devastating resources, equipment, and morale. In the event of an earthquake, what does a department do without the knowledge of procedures that might require apparatus to be pulled out of stations, so as not to trap it under the fire station in an aftershock collapse of the building? They are beaten before they begin.

Besides planning, there is also a need to prepare for disasters in other ways. In June 2015, the U.S. Fire Administration published *Operational Lessons Learned in Disaster Response*. The report states, "The time to develop and test an EOP [Emergency Operations Plan] is before the disaster strikes. After-action reports from our country's worst disasters reveal that many fire departments are not prepared." The author found this to be true of his department, and believes it is still true of many fire departments. We still have much work to do in the areas of emergency and disaster planning and exercising. Finding a person who wants to be involved and is passionate about planning is frequently difficult to find in an organization. Those pressed into service are rarely enthusiastic and therefore rarely effective.

Nevertheless, firefighters can be counted on to accomplish the job. In February 2006, David Paulison, then acting Director of the Federal Emergency Management Agency (FEMA), was interviewed by *Fire Engineering*'s Editor-in-Chief, Bobby Halton. Halton asked about the federal response to Hurricane Katrina the previous year. Paulison concluded the interview with this statement about firefighters and their role during a disaster:

> The people running our joint field offices (JFOs) begged me to send more firefighters. They said these firefighters will and can do anything. They said they go out to do community relations work all day, then they come back to the JFO, crank up the barbecue, and cook dinner for everybody and clean up the dishes. If anything breaks, they can fix it. They said they had never had a group of people like this come into the JFOs and do the things they can do. Yes, I am bragging about the American firefighter again. …Who else to better to deal with people who've gone through a disaster than firefighters, who deal with it every day? They were perfect for the job.

Paulison was right, firefighters do not shirk responsibility and do not turn away from people in need, no matter who they are. Historically, nothing much phases the fire service. Traditionally, firefighters have been the "go-to" responders when the call goes out for help – regardless of the color of your uniform or the shape of your badge; we're coming to help, and very soon the bad day is going to get a lot better.

Firefighters do this despite the difficulties their own families face. Their loved ones are equally affected by disasters and the effects of the disaster. Their families are at home, coping without them while they assist others. The fire service "family" is used to this. Families, spouses, children, and partners must be independent when the dishwasher breaks down and their firefighter won't be home for another 48 hours. This speaks to the resiliency, courage, skills, and resourcefulness of the person at home. For the most part, spouses/partners signed up for that life. Firefighters call home to assure their families that they're okay, and families reassure their firefighter that they are prepared and ready for the challenge without them as everyone then goes about their work. It's the passion and drive to serve that keeps the fire service so strong; no disaster will thwart that mission.

ROLE OF THE FIREFIGHTER IN THE HOMELAND SECURITY MISSION

Disaster response is part of securing the homeland. Asymmetrical threats and responses to WMD incidents are not uncommon to the fire service. A new culture has emerged that some call the "purple responder," a blend of red and blue, firefighters and law enforcement. The National Incident Management System (NIMS), mandated in the aftermath of September 11, 2001, through Homeland Security Presidential Directive/HSPD-5 by then President George W. Bush, was designed to forever link emergency response into a whole responder, whole community, "all-hazards" cooperative approach:

> (3) To prevent, prepare for, respond to, and recover from terrorist attacks, major disasters, and other emergencies, the United States Government shall establish a single, comprehensive approach to domestic incident management.
>
> (15) This system will provide a consistent nationwide approach for Federal, State, and local governments to work effectively and efficiently together to prepare for, respond to, and recover from domestic incidents, regardless of cause, size, or complexity. To provide for interoperability and compatibility among Federal, State, and local capabilities, the NIMS will include a core set of concepts, principles, terminology, and technologies covering the incident command system; multi-agency coordination systems; unified command; training; identification and management of resources (including systems for classifying types of resources); qualifications and certification; and the collection, tracking, and reporting of incident information and incident resources. (White House, 2003)

NIMS (2017) doctrine involves all levels of government (local fire and EMS organizations), nongovernmental organizations, private sector entities, and the community as a whole to "prevent, protect against, mitigate, respond to, and recover from incidents" (p. 1). The introduction to NIMS states:

> Communities across the Nation experience a diverse set of threats, hazards, and events. The size, frequency, complexity, and scope of these incidents vary, but all involve a range of personnel and organizations to coordinate efforts to save lives, stabilize the incident, and protect property and the environment. Every day, jurisdictions and organizations work together to share resources, integrate tactics, and act collaboratively. Whether these organizations are nearby or are supporting each other from across the country, their success depends on a common, interoperable approach to sharing resources, coordinating and managing incidents, and communicating information. The National Incident Management System (NIMS) defines this comprehensive approach.
>
> (2017, p. 1)

Community leadership must support thoughtful emergency plans that call for increased budgets for new equipment, accepting the fact that it may never be used. This can be a difficult sell for short-sighted politicians. In a Senate hearing on the Hurricane Katrina response, Senator Joe Lieberman (I), of Connecticut remarked, "The New Orleans fire department, which was the city's designated lead agency for urban search-and-rescue, owned no boats, none, despite repeated requests to the city over the years to buy some" (U.S. Senate, 2006). It begs the question, "How many lives could have been saved had these requests been funded *before* the storm?" Administrators must support realistic budget requests based on meaningful community risk assessments. Planning and budgetary support are the life-blood elements of a safe and effective response for the fire department's growing mission. All this planning and work has to be done before the first rescue can take place.

While interdiction and prevention of terrorism and terrorist groups is still generally not the mission of the fire service, the emerging cooperative culture is to share information and intelligence if they "see something, report something." Fire departments, by nature, are responders, not preventers. However, cybercrimes and other technology-based criminal and terroristic events can target emergency response agencies prior to a larger attack, thus crippling the department's ability to communicate and coordinate. Protection of critical infrastructure (CI), potential targets for social or political exploitation, and critical community services has been added to the fire service mission. Henderson, in his book *Global Terrorism, The Complete Reference Guide*, emphasizes: "Modern society is vitally dependent on infrastructure: Everything from water supply and power to transportation, communication, and information systems. A properly placed plastic explosive – or computer virus – can cause damage far greater than the effort expended" (2001, p. 19).

Pre-incident protection, which now involves hardening of CI facilities and security systems, is common practice for the fire service. Fire Inspectors no longer look just for fire extinguishers and exit doors – their mission has expanded to ensure these critical nodes are sufficiently hardened. The fire service's role in the overall mission of homeland security has been fully adopted and embraced – we're on the front lines.

CHALLENGES FACING THE FIRE PROFESSION

Every response begins and ends locally. Local fire departments provide the community EMS and technical rescue every day, and during disasters. Major natural disasters such as Hurricane Katrina brought about much-needed changes to stitch together a response to major incidents at all three levels: local, state, and federal. Failures at all three levels created a humanitarian crisis that illuminated fatal flaws in planning, command, and coordination of a national disaster response. The size and scope of the hurricane and all the associated problems that developed quickly, quite simply overwhelmed all three levels of response leading to a paralysis of leadership and services.

The attack on the nation on September 11, 2001, also exposed major vulnerabilities and introduced a level of complexity that could not be imagined and did not fit inside the planning processes used at the time. Terrorism, by law, is investigated and responded to by federal law enforcement (DOJ-FBI) which needs to seamlessly coordinate and rely on local and state law enforcement. Fire departments needed to adjust their operations to include crime scene considerations and processes that would allow for chain of custody, evidence recognition, and preservation. Routine calls now had to be looked at through the prism of a potential terrorist act.

Fire departments needed to become familiar with the progression of how an incident goes from a local response to a federally assisted response; there is a process. When local resources do not have the capacity to deal with the situation, mutual aid with neighboring departments is implemented. Typically, a local community Emergency Operations Center (EOC) which functions as a Multi-agency Coordination Center (MAC) is set up and staffed. When the local EOC and available resources are maximized based on situational awareness and a needs assessment projecting a decline in capabilities, the state is called on for help. Depending on the size of the incident, a state EOC will be activated and the governor informed. At the request of the state EOC, the governor requests disaster assistance from the regional FEMA office. FEMA staff push the governor's needs request to the National Response Coordination Center (NRCC) who request, through the DHS Secretary, a Presidential declaration for a national emergency or major disaster response. If approved, FEMA then creates a Mission Assignment (MA) and associated Mission Assignment Task Order (MATO), which authorize specific federal agencies and resources to respond. Some of these agencies may be the Environmental Protection Agency (EPA),

FEMA, the FBI, the United States Coast Guard, the Department of Defense, the National Oceanic and Atmospheric Administration, etc. The MATO releases federal resources into the area of operations and a JFO is established to coordinate with local incident commanders operating within an Incident Action Plan created through a unified command system that now incorporates federal participating agencies.

MACs are organized under a NIMS-ICS (Incident Command System)–type organization (Operations, Planning, Logistics, Finance, Intelligence/Investigations) or under the National Response Framework construct of Emergency Support Functions (ESFs). Fire departments are routinely involved in three ESFs:

- ESF #4 is Firefighting. This is either wildland firefighting under the direction of local and U.S. Forest Service leadership or structural fires and search-and-rescue operations under the direction of local and FEMA–U.S. Fire Administration leadership.
- ESF #9 is Search and Rescue typically under the direction of local and FEMA–Urban Search & Rescue (USAR) Task Force leadership. USAR Task Forces are capable of all types of technical rescue and extrication.
- And lastly, ESF #10 for Oil and Hazardous Materials/WMD or CBRN (chemical, biological, radiological, nuclear). ESF #10 is initiated if there is a release of oil, chemicals, CBRN, or even the potential for such a release – which is the case in every disaster. ESF #10 is under the direction of the EPA (FEMA 2019).

MACs therefore provide resource management, coordination, communications, planning, and liaison with other MACs, all of which benefit the local response made up of local, state, and federal resources. These critical positions within a MAC must be exercised and evaluated to find the right person to fill these roles. The tense hours before a natural disaster, or the chaos of the terrorist's havoc, is the wrong time to look for the right personnel.

RECOMMENDATIONS FOR THE FUTURE

The challenges and opportunities presented to the modern fire service are the same challenges and opportunities faced by Benjamin Franklin's firewards: new responsibilities, the implementation of new technologies, additional training and educational requirements, new standards and codes along with enforcement responsibilities, and adoption of a progressive culture of safety. For these reasons, fire departments need to become more involved in national-level training through FEMA courses of instruction and nationally sponsored tabletop and full-scale field exercises activating MACs and mutual aid agreements to put into action emergency response plans. It's not a plan until it's been written, trained on, exercised, and evaluated for ease and efficacy. The future is dependent on multi-agency planning, response, and recovery.

There is little doubt that society will require the future emergency responder to be proficient at handling new, emerging hazards and/or threats. The advantage we have is that new technologies are being developed that make the incident safer and more manageable. A culture of safety that didn't exist even 20 years ago, permeates all that responders do. Policies related to an all-hazards approach, requiring cooperation and coordination among federal, state, tribal, and local agencies make the load lighter. These new developments include, but are certainly not limited to, the use of multi-level GPS tracking for firefighter accountability; bio-feedback sensors reporting a firefighter's vital signs in real time to a safety officer; imbedded toxic gas sensors in SCBA packs with toxicity levels wirelessly reported directly to a safety officer; the use of aerial drones for monitoring roof operations or distant hazmat team actions that would otherwise be out of sight for incident safety officers, hazmat officers, and incident commanders.

In the fire service, "where innovation is encouraged, failure is accepted and condoned" (Hewitt, 1995, p. 97). The fire service is ever learning from the failures of the past decades, and yes, centuries. If this wasn't the case, fatalities and injuries would be on the increase instead of the decrease that we are witnessing. Strategic planning, based on new and innovative approaches to prevention and response, continues to be the means of "creating a blueprint of what they [fire service leaders] want their futures to be" (Hewitt, 1995, p. 154). Successful organizations plan to counter future threats and hazards and to respond without repeating the failures of the past. In this way, the fire service maintains its edge against the bad days; society and its interdependencies are protected.

CONCLUSION

The nation has come to respect and rely on the men and women of the fire service to be the "go-to" element when disaster strikes. Whenever an individual, family, community, state, or nation falls into calamity, they know that the men and women of the fire service will be there to assist. For most members of the community, it's their first 911 emergency in 15 years, and it's the responding fire company's fifteenth emergency in the last 24 hours. We're the professionals and we're exceptional at creating calm out of chaos. At the darkest moment, the fire service comes to life and provides needed support and rescue – no matter what the incident may be or how horrible the personal consequences, as evidenced by the events of 9/11.

The fire service has never shirked a responsibility and there have been many heaped upon them since the inception of the service. It's not just about battling fires; it's about protecting the entire community. No incident is too challenging. No rescue too difficult. No disaster too complex. The men and women who serve selflessly for perfect strangers, many times outside of their own communities, always rise to the occasion with their myriad of training, expertise, and experience. The fire service has found a way to accomplish the task of protecting the American public for over three centuries. Franklin would be proud. Doubtless, the fire service will continue to tackle new threats, new hazards, and new challenges, always doing more with less.

CLASS DISCUSSION AND ESSAY QUESTIONS

1. Firefighting traditionally demonstrated a volunteer and reactive approach. How has firefighting changed over the years, and what events have helped it to become more professional and proactive?
2. What is the role of the insurance industry, NFPA, and OSHA in the development of firefighting over the years?
3. Why are firefighters considered the "go-to" responders in time of a disaster or terrorist attack?
4. What Emergency Support Functions (ESFs) are fulfilled by firefighters and why is the fire service equipped and capable of meeting such needs?

5. Firefighters have been given "new responsibilities, the implementation of new technologies, additional training and educational requirements, new standards and codes along with enforcement responsibilities, and adoption of a progressive culture of safety." What successes have been witnessed in this profession, and what challenges remain to be resolved?

REFERENCES

Ahrens, M., & Evarts, B. (September, 2020). *Fire loss in the United States during 2019*. NFPA Research. NFPA No. FLX10. www.nfpa.org/research.

Bridenbaugh, C. (November 4, 2008). [originally published 1938]. *Cities in the wilderness; The first century of urban life in America 1625–1742*. Bridenbaugh Press, pp. 210–212.

Cartwright, M. (December 6, 2016). *Vigiles*. Retrieved September 14, 2020, from https://www.ancient.eu/vigiles/.

Charles, N. (August 24, 2017). What Detroit firefighters saw during the 1967 riot. *Time*. Retrieved September 19, 2020, from https://time.com/4876825/detroit-riots-firefighters/.

Donahue, M. (October 3, 2016). 19th century firefighting artifacts heat-up American history museum. *Smithsonian Insider*. Retrieved September 19, 2020, from https://insider.si.edu/2016/10/19th-century-firefighting-artifacts-heat-american-history-museum/.

FBHA, Firefighter Behavioral Health Alliance. (2020). *Who we are*. Retrieved September 21, 2020, from https://www.ffbha.org/about-us/who-we-are/.

FBI. (2020). Oklahoma City bombing. *FBI, Famous Cases & Criminals*. Retrieved September 21, 2020, from https://www.fbi.gov/history/famous-cases/oklahoma-city-bombing.

FCSN, Firefighter Cancer Support Network. (2020). *Our mission*. Retrieved September 21, 2020, from https://firefightercancersupport.org/who-we-are/our-mission/.

FEMA, Federal Emergency Management Agency. (October 28, 2019). *National response framework*. Retrieved February 27, 2021, from https://www.fema.gov/sites/default/files/2020-04/NRF_FINALApproved_2011028.pdf.

Fire Engineering. (May 1, 1968). Fire department operations under riot conditions. *Fire Engineering* 121(5). Retrieved September 20, 2020, from https://www.fireengineering.com/1968/05/01/300686/fire-department-operations-under-riot-conditions/#gref.

Franklin, B. (February 4, 1735). On protection of towns from fire. *The Pennsylvania Gazette*. Retrieved September 14, 2020, from https://founders.archives.gov/documents/Franklin/01-02-02-0002#BNFN-01-02-02-0002-fn-0002.

Hasenmeier, P. (June 16, 2008). The history of firefighter personal protective equipment. *Fire Engineering*. Retrieved September 20, 2020, from https://www.fireengineering.com/2008/06/16/256552/the-history-of-firefighter-personal-protective-equipment/#gref.

Henderson, H. (2001). *Global terrorism: The complete reference guide*. New York: Checkmark Books.

Hewitt, W. (April, 1995). *Recreating the fire service*. Ottawa, ON: Kendall Publications.

IAFF, International Association of Firefighters. (November 1, 1967). IAFF surveys riots in 11 cities. *Fire Engineering* 120(11). Retrieved September 20, 2020, from https://www.fireengineering.com/1967/11/01/286861/iaff-surveys-riots-in-11-cities/#gref.

National Commission on Fire Prevention and Control. (May 4, 1973). *America burning.* U.S. Fire Administration. Retrieved September 19, 2020, from https://strategicfire .org/wp-content/uploads/2015/04/v2020-america-burning-05.04.73.pdf.

NFPA, National Fire Prevention Association. (November, 2019). Fire department calls. *NFPA News & Research.* Retrieved September 23, 2020, from https://www.nfpa .org/News-and-Research/Data-research-and-tools/Emergency-Responders/Fire -department-calls.

Paulison, D. (May 1, 2006). FEMA's response to Hurricane Katrina. *Fire Engineering.* Retrieved September 23, 2020, from https://www.fireengineering.com/2006/05/01 /192390/femarsquos-response-to-hurricane-katrina/#gref.

U.S. Fire Administration. (June, 2015). *Operational lessons learned in disaster response.* Emmitsburg, MD: Federal Emergency Management Agency – FEMA. www.usfa .fema.gov.

U.S. Senate. (January 30, 2006). *Hurricane Katrina: Urban search and rescue in a catastrophe.* Washington, DC: U.S. Senate Committee on Homeland Security and Governmental Affairs Hearing. Retrieved September 19, 2020, from https://www .govinfo.gov/content/pkg/CHRG-109shrg26751/html/CHRG-109shrg26751.htm.

White House, U.S. (February 28, 2003). *Homeland security presidential directive/HSPD-5.* The White House, U.S. Government. Retrieved September 25, 2020, from https:// georgewbush-whitehouse.archives.gov/news/releases/2003/02/20030228-9.html.

CHAPTER 5

Law Enforcement and Emergency Management:
The Role of Policing during Disasters

Mike Gutierrez and Edward Valla

INTRODUCTION

The profession and discipline of emergency management emerged as the interdisciplinary offspring of sociology, geography, public administration, criminal justice, and psychology. As a field, the practice of emergency management has been informed by police, fire, civil defense, insurance, and many other professions and industries. Often, when an individual hears the words "emergency management," it may evoke the image of a police officer or other uniformed first responders. Even though emergency management has emerged as a stand-alone profession and discipline, complete with industry specific degrees and credentialing, it is still necessary to examine and understand the role of the various professions in disaster management. This chapter will examine the role of law enforcement in disasters. This is necessary because not all jurisdictions have adopted a reformed model of emergency management.

The days of relying on mid-level managers from police and fire departments to fulfill a secondary role as an emergency manager may be numbered. Although many local and state governments have adopted a reformed model of emergency management, there are still many agencies that operate under a classical model. For the purposes of this chapter, a reformed model of emergency management is defined as having a professionally trained emergency manager, which includes having a four-year degree in emergency management from an accredited institution of higher education, and/or possessing professional credentials such as the Certified Emergency Manager from the International Association of Emergency Managers. Additionally, the emergency manager will be housed in a stand-alone Office of Emergency Management and have direct access to the chief executive for their respective level of government. In contrast, the classical or unreformed model is defined as having a law enforcement officer, firefighter, or other public servant serving as the emergency manager. These individuals often lack a formal education in emergency management, will often have dual duties (not solely dedicated to emergency management), and will be housed within the fire or police department. Since there are many agencies that still operate under a classical model and police are usually involved in disasters, it remains necessary to examine the role that law enforcement plays in disasters from both a public safety and an emergency management standpoint.

DOI: 10.4324/9781003350729-5

In order to understand the role that law enforcement plays in emergency management, we have to understand the history, current status, and the future direction of policing. In this chapter, we will examine the history of law enforcement and policing in America, the law enforcement perspective on disasters and terrorism, and the role that police officers fulfill in emergency management. The chapter will conclude with an examination of current challenges and possible solutions facing today's law enforcement and then present some possible solutions.

HISTORY OF LAW ENFORCEMENT AND POLICING IN AMERICA

Policing in the United States and the colonies that preceded the country's founding has evolved over a time period spanning roughly four centuries. The evolution involved moving from informal methods of maintaining social control where church congregations, neighbors, and small communities played important roles in enforcing social mores, community standards, and laws to highly bureaucratized and professional police departments and related law enforcement agencies. We note that the history of policing in America has been well covered by other scholars, and in this chapter, we focus on several broad trends. We provide some commentary on "the origin story" of policing during the colonial period and in the early United States before discussing the establishment of urban police departments in mid-19th-century America. We then highlight some of the major reform efforts to professionalize police departments, concluding with examining some of the current challenges facing law enforcement agencies today.

Policing in the original 13 colonies during the 17th and 18th centuries was largely an endeavor performed by church congregations, neighbors, and small communities, enforcing social mores, community standards, and laws. Crime, to the extent the data are available to show, appears to have been limited. Those crimes to which we have become accustomed by watching the nightly news such as murder, robbery, rape, and burglary were rare events (Walker, 1998, p. 17). Instead, most crimes fell into categories such as cursing, blasphemy, fornication, adultery, and drunkenness (Walker, 1998, p. 17–18). As Samuel Walker notes, the principal agencies of social control were the church, the town meeting, and the family. Church congregations, for example, acted as judge and jury and could impose punishments, the most common of which was a demand that the offender acknowledged wrongdoing in the presence of fellow church members (Walker, 1998, p. 18–19).

The early colonies also established a watch system, which required adult males patrol cities and alert people about criminal activity, fires, and other types of disorder such as prostitution or gambling (Steverson, 2007, p. 11). Boston instituted a watch system by 1636, with other cities following suit. As a crime prevention strategy, the system proved to be inefficient, as watchmen often slept or drank on duty. Pay was minimal, and some of those who had been put on watch were there as a form of punishment (Waxman, 2017, p. 1).

In the Southern colonies, the institution of slavery shaped policing efforts. Slave patrols, the first of which was established in 1704 in the Carolinas, had several interconnected objectives. These included apprehending runaway slaves, deterring slave revolts, and disciplining slaves (Walker and Katz, 2011, p. 26). Notably, the patrollers were not government agents, nor did they perform crime prevention actions. The latter fell mainly to county sheriffs. "Following the Civil War, these vigilante-style organizations evolved in modern Southern police departments primarily as a means of enforcing 'Jim Crow' segregation laws, designed to deny freed slaves equal rights and access to the political system" (Potter, 2013, p. 2).

By the 1830s, the United States had become more industrialized and new waves of European immigrants swelled the populations of its cities. These general trends necessitated changes in policing, and it is during this period that "modern" police departments were established (Walker and Katz, 2011, p. 27). The watch system and other ad hoc or informal mechanisms of social control proved to be ineffective in preventing crime, addressing violent criminal activity, or halting the rioting that plagued some cities (Hofstadter and Wallace, 1973, p. 13–17). Boston established its police department in 1838, with other American cities slowly following their example (Monkkonen, 1981, p. 42). As Gary Potter notes, "By the 1880s, all major U.S. cities had municipal police forces in place, and these organizations shared similar characteristics. Departments were publicly-funded, and accountable to a central governmental authority. Officers served in a full-time capacity. Departments had permanent and fixed rules and procedures, and employment as a police officer was continuous" (Potter, 2013, p. 1).

These early departments would be unrecognizable today. Formal training was negligible. Initially, police did not wear standard uniforms, nor were they armed. It was only in the late 19th century that weapons became standard issue. Police lacked job security and could be fired without cause (Steverson, 2007, p. 15.). Additionally, positions on police forces were a major source of patronage where local politicians rewarded their friends (Walker and Katz 2011, p. 28–29). "Police departments in the political era had no personnel standards as we understand them today. Officers were selected entirely based on their political connections" (Walker and Katz, 2011, p. 28–29).

As it is today, patrolling, or "walking the beat," was the mainstay of police activity during this period. Most patrols were conducted on foot. The work generally involved maintaining order and consisted of arresting vagrants, the intoxicated, or others who disturbed the peace (Steverson, 2007, p. 15). Police also served an important social welfare function with stations serving as de facto homeless shelters. In Philadelphia, for example, police sheltered over 100,000 people a year during the 1880s. Readers may also be surprised to learn that at least in two major cities, police had an active role in the electoral process. This interesting fact is highlighted in the next section with a direct quote, which outlines the roles that police had in the electoral process.

In every city the police duties are numerous and varied, but they are probably more so in Boston than in any other large American city because of the extra functions laid upon the force by state laws. Boston is the only large city in the country (except Baltimore) where the police are required to do work in connection with the listing of voters and the supervision of elections. (McCaffery, 1912, p. 675)

The United States modeled its police forces after those adopted in Great Britain under Sir Robert Peel (Steverson, 2007, p. 8–9; Monkkonen, 1981, p. 41–49). By the late 19th century and continuing in one form or another to the present, federal, state, and local governments, as well as individuals, have led efforts to reform and improve policing. These efforts generally fell into two overlapping areas: (1) addressing police corruption – particularly in urban departments; and (2) improving or professionalizing police departments (Berman, 1981, p. 55–65).

Corruption

It has been well documented that police and politicians maintained a symbiotic relationship. Police officers owed their positions to politicians, who awarded jobs on police departments to those loyal to them. Perhaps one of the best-known examples was the relationship between New York City's Tammany Hall political machine and new police recruits, who were forced to pay a fixed fee for their appointments. "Policemen who secured the confidence of Tammany were promoted, though each advancement required additional fees" (Goodwin, 2013, p. 206–207). In 1894–5, the New York Senate's Lexow Committee's probe into police corruption revealed police involvement in a diverse array of criminal activity including, but not limited to, bribery, extortion, voter intimidation, and various types of fraud (Berman, 1981, p. 55–65).

Improving Efficiency and Professionalism

Police departments across the country took advantage of new technologies and forensic science. Identifying suspects became easier with the development of photography, handwriting analysis, and fingerprinting. August Vollmer, a police chief in Berkeley, California, and considered to be the father of modern policing, adopted a wide range of practices designed to professionalize the field (Douthit, 1975, p. 101–124). He hired college-educated officers and employed bicycles, motorcycles, and radio-equipped cars for patrolling. Vollmer operated one of the first crime labs and used an early variant of the polygraph. He also started a police academy (Steverson, 2007, p. 23).

The primary mechanism through which state and local law enforcement agencies contributed to the counterterrorism mission was by their participation on the FBI's Joint Terrorism Task Forces (JTTFs). As the FBI states on its website, JTTFs are the front line of defense against international and domestic terrorism. The JTTFs investigate allegations of suspected terrorist activity in the United States or against U.S. interests abroad. JTTF membership consists of investigators from federal, state, and local law enforcement agencies and includes other professionals such as intelligence, financial, and language analysts. State and local law enforcement officers who are assigned to JTTFs operate under the same "rules" as an FBI agent. Such individuals have access to FBI computer systems, operate and recruit confidential human sources, conduct investigations, and often become what may be described as a subject matter expert on a particular group. "You wouldn't be able to tell the difference between an FBI agent, a Lowell police detective, a Boston police sergeant, and a Massachusetts state trooper. They're all part of and working together as an integrated team" (Martin, 2016, p. 1).

New York City pioneered the JTTF model in 1980 when it adopted methods that had been used successfully for gang investigations. Prior to the September 11 attacks, 26 JTTFs were established in major U.S. cities. Subsequently, FBI Director Robert S. Mueller III ordered all 56 FBI field offices establish a JTTF. These locally based, multi-agency organizations have expanded to include over 4,400 federal, state, and local investigators and other professionals from 600 agencies (Bjelopera, 2013, p. 13).

Since September 11, 2001, JTTF investigations have disrupted a diverse array of known and suspected terrorist criminal activities ranging from plots aimed at causing mass casualties in the United States to thwarting individuals seeking to join foreign terrorist organizations and providing financial or material support. For example, in 2011, FBI Boston arrested Rezwan Ferdaus for his attempt to provide al-Qa'ida with homemade detonators to be used in improvised explosive devices and for planning to fly a remote-controlled aircraft laden with explosives into the Pentagon. Ferdaus later pled guilty to a series of conspiracy charges including providing material support to al-Qa'ida (Department of Justice, 2012, p. 1). In a similar case, the Denver JTTF arrested Najibullah Zazi for conspiring to attack the New York City subway system on the anniversary of the

9/11 attacks with improvised explosive devices (Department of Justice, 2009, p. 1). What makes the Zazi case significant is that his original intent was to join the Taliban and fight on their behalf. Because of his U.S. citizenship and ability to re-enter the United States, al-Qa'ida recruited and trained him for an operation against a U.S. target.

More recently, some JTTF disruptions have centered upon individuals who attempted to travel to Iraq or Syria in order to join ISIL. In September, 2020, Lirim Sylejmani was charged with conspiring to provide, providing, and attempting to provide material support to ISIL. According to the allegations in the indictment, from November 2015, through February 2019, Sylejmani conspired to provide and provided material support and resources including personnel and services to ISIL in Syria and received military training from the terrorist organization (Department of Justice, 2020, p. 1).

The examples discussed above highlight JTTF investigations and arrests of individuals who sought to act on behalf of foreign terrorist organizations and fall within the broader category of international terrorism. Perhaps more disturbingly, recent JTTF efforts have also disrupted major plots by domestic terrorists. In March 2020, the Detroit JTTF initially arrested six individuals on conspiracy charges to kidnap Michigan Governor Gretchen Whitmer and try her for treason. The FBI became aware of these individuals through their use of social media to broadcast their intention and, most importantly, by a local police department that identified members of a militia group who sought to obtain the home addresses of local law enforcement officers (Department of Justice, 2020, p. 1).

Another important way state and local law enforcement agencies contribute to the homeland security mission is by staffing and operating state fusion centers. As part of an overall effort to improve information sharing after 9/11, fusion centers were established under the auspices of the Department of Homeland Security. Fusion centers:

are state-owned and operated centers that serve as focal points in states and major urban areas for the receipt, analysis, gathering, and sharing of threat-related information between State, Local, Tribal, and Territorial (SLTT) federal and private sector partners.

(Rollins, 2008, p. 1–84)

In Massachusetts, the State Police have general oversight responsibilities for the operation and administration of the Commonwealth Fusion Center (CFC). According to its mission statement, the CFC serves as the primary interface between the Commonwealth and the federal government for information collection, analysis, and dissemination. The CFC frequently publishes intelligence products in collaboration with the FBI and other partners. It will, for example, publish threat assessments regarding major special events such as the Boston Marathon and the Fourth of July celebrations on the Esplanade. "In addition, CFC distributes other intelligence products including periodic bulletins to stakeholders regarding police officer safety, situational awareness, high-profile incident reports, and opioid-related arrests" (Commonwealth of Massachusetts, 2019, p. 1.).

A LAW ENFORCEMENT PERSPECTIVE OF DISASTERS AND TERRORISM

Police, by their very nature and design, tend to always be involved in disaster management. In this section, we will examine how law enforcement officers view their role during disasters or acts of terrorism. This is necessary in order to ensure that those involved in the planning process can understand the culture and mindset of police officers as it relates to their role in emergency management operations.

From the early stages of their career, police officers are instilled with the concept of command presence. During the police academy, which most police officers must attend, they are provided with examples of how officers whose uniforms are clean and pressed, their boots highly polished, and their leather duty belts polished and scuff-free are less likely to be assaulted. The concept of command presence is that you will stand out as authoritative and in command of the scene. During field training, rookie police officers are graded on their appearance, knowledge and application of laws, and their ability to command a scene. In simple terms, when a police officer arrives on scene, they are the ones in charge.

The primary duties of police officers are to prevent crimes, apprehend criminals, and maintain social order. Because of their training and daily operations, police officers tend to view most of their activities through a crime prevention or public safety perspective. A police officer not trained in emergency management may mistakenly fall into believing disaster myths and may view their role in disasters as preventing looting and safeguarding businesses that may be exposed due to the impact of the hazard. It is easy for officers to view their involvement in disasters as falling into one of three activities: 1) Access restriction such as road closures, traffic redirection, and securing facilities used for emergency operations; 2) Crime prevention, which includes responding to looting, assaults, and other property protection calls; and 3) Lifesaving activities, which includes search and rescue, evacuation, and first aid.

After Hurricane Katrina made landfall and the levees failed in New Orleans, there was a widespread call for volunteers to maintain order. The National Guard, contractors such as Blackwater, and law enforcement agencies from around the country were mobilized to assist in response to perceived widespread crime and looting. Many of the officers who responded to New Orleans ended up working in crime prevention operations. This response exacerbated the disaster myths and, subsequently, the perception of law enforcement's view of their role. This led to the widespread idea that looting, crime, and antisocial behavior occurs during and after a disaster. These officers were also tasked with accompanying swiftwater rescue and firefighting crews to prevent assaultive behavior toward rescuers. Law enforcement agencies had to supplement the New Orleans Police Department in these roles, but were also engaged in other activities such as sheltering operations.

Thousands of the people who were evacuated or rescued after Katrina were housed in temporary shelters around the country. Many of the jurisdictions that received evacuees relied upon police personnel to establish and manage sheltering operations. It was apparent there was a need to provide a location where people could temporarily reside and feel secure in their persons and belongings. In coordination with city administration, the Red Cross and other non-profit organizations, as well as many police agencies, were involved in these activities. The challenge for law enforcement personnel was how to maintain control of the centers and make sure that the occupants of the shelter were not placed in dangerous situations. As airplanes and busloads full of people arrived to host cities, it became apparent there may be criminals, sex offenders, and other populations of concern that needed to be considered; this established a sense at many of the shelters that rivaled that of a correctional facility. Police officers were tasked with enforcing curfews at the shelters, searching individuals as they arrived, being aware of drug or alcohol use, and scanning for other threats. Once again, these activities placed police officers in a mindset of viewing their role as enforcers instead of partners in response and recovery.

This section highlighted police officers who often have a self-perception that their role is to prevent crime, arrest bad guys, and enforce rules. This perception manifested again during the COVID-19 response when police officers were used to enforce political preferences or directives that may not have been actual laws. This would indicate that self-perception is also the perception of local, state, and federal administrators. In the following section we will review the actual roles and responsibilities that police officers play in emergency management.

THE ROLE OF LAW ENFORCEMENT OFFICERS IN EMERGENCY MANAGEMENT AND HOMELAND SECURITY

Former Federal Emergency Management Agency (FEMA) Administrator W. Craig Fugate stated that the law enforcement community has two vital roles in responding to disasters: to provide for the safety and security of the community and to be first responders during times of crisis. He reflected in an article titled "From the Administrator: Law Enforcement's Role in Responding to Disasters" in *Police Chief Magazine* (Accessed 2022):

> We ask a tremendous amount of our first responders during disasters and emergencies. They are the first line of defense; they are the first helping hand extended to survivors. Every police officer knows emergencies can happen without notice. Our ability to respond to and recover from disasters is directly influenced by how well-prepared our first responders are and how well we all work together as a team before, during, and after a crisis.
>
> The role of law enforcement in responding to a disaster is very similar to the day-to-day role of public safety and supporting the community. In preparing for a disaster, police officers trust in their training and capitalize on their knowledge of a community. Exercises portraying the situations (large- and small-scale events) help better prepare officers and allow them to fully understand the resources needed for each event and apply that information to each community's needs. Law enforcement officials know their communities best and interact with residents on a daily basis. This knowledge gives them the ability to provide valuable situational awareness to response and recovery groups coming in to help. For example, where will there be language barriers? Does the community have unique challenges? Law enforcement can help communicate this information to the emergency management team and can offer support to other members of the team by simply being a presence in the neighborhoods.
>
> During a disaster, police officers play a key role in many operations including: search and rescue, evacuations, door-to-door checks, and maintaining overall public safety within the community. These are critical actions that support not only their own communities but neighboring towns as well.

The reality is that police officers and law enforcement agencies are involved in all phases of emergency management and play a greater role than just safety and security. In this section we will discuss the roles that law enforcement officers play in emergency management.

Unsurprisingly, state and local law enforcement agencies make significant contributions across the emergency management disciplines from planning and preparedness to response and recovery. For example, police departments assist emergency managers with risk assessment by identifying hazards for a community. Police departments may facilitate planning by designating shelters, evacuation routes, and water distribution points.

These departments frequently participate in tabletop and other exercises to identify and eliminate problems before an actual disaster. Exercises cover natural and man-made disasters, as well as special events. Recently the U.S. Department of Homeland Security Cybersecurity and Infrastructure Security Agency (CISA), NASCAR, the Daytona International Speedway, state and local first responders, law enforcement officials, and local businesses held a tabletop exercise to test response plans around hypothetical public safety incidents on the day of the DAYTONA 500.

Police departments are involved in pre-disaster activities, but not all police officers are involved beyond their day-to-day duties. In other words, the majority of police officers involved in pre-disaster activities usually play their real-life role during exercises. This includes providing an explanation of how they would close roads, handle routine calls for service, secure a perimeter, or respond to an active shooter. Some officers, especially those from jurisdictions that have a classical form of emergency management, do participate in more of the preparedness and mitigation activities. This includes building plans, exercises, and establishing partnerships. In jurisdictions where a police officer serves as the emergency management coordinator, they are responsible for most emergency management–related activities. These officers must complete a set of FEMA courses in order to serve in this role; these provide a baseline to engage in these activities. Oftentimes there will be a member or two from the police department in the Emergency Operations Center (EOC) to coordinate law enforcement efforts. This could be the police chief or his/her designee.

Post-disaster response activities may include search and rescue/recovery, assisting with traffic control, sheltering operations, and quarantine procedures. The Massachusetts Comprehensive Emergency Response Plan template provides a useful snapshot of areas for a local department. Typical activity would include staffing an EOC with primary responsibility for ESF 13 Public Safety and Law Enforcement. The police representative is responsible for coordinating law enforcement resources to support emergency management response operations and providing situational awareness to the EOC manager and police department.

During the Ebola outbreak of 2014, we witnessed the first U.S. biological disaster in modern history. This incident highlighted several shortcomings and identified the need for establishing partnerships with health agencies in terms of emergency management. Police officers were involved in delivering meals to the quarantined individuals and had a difficult time determining how to deliver the food while minimizing their own exposure. This is not a duty that law enforcement typically engages in, but they had to improvise to meet an unmet need. In 2020, as the COVID-19 outbreak unfolded, we witnessed law enforcement officers fulfilling a new role as police officers were tasked with being COVID or mask police. Some jurisdictions relied on police to make sure individuals were wearing a mask and that businesses were complying with the reduced occupancy standards.

In response to the terrorist attacks on September 11, 2001, and the Boston Marathon Bombing on April 15, 2013, police officers responded and fulfilled their public safety roles. On 9/11, many police officers lost their lives while attempting to rescue individuals who were trapped in the burning towers. In both events, law enforcement personnel had to establish a crime scene, preserve evidence, identify/track suspects, and conduct criminal investigations to determine if there were any other threats.

By the very nature of their profession, police officers serve primarily as part of the field operations team when responding to a disaster. However, we have seen the importance of training and including police in other phases of emergency management. Their expertise, insight, and geographical understanding could reduce the likelihood of running into unforeseen roadblocks after a disaster has occurred. In the following sections we will explore some of the current challenges with incorporating or utilizing police to their fullest potential and some possible solutions to these obstacles.

CURRENT CHALLENGES AND POSSIBLE SOLUTIONS

Although there are many challenges that must be overcome in order to utilize law enforcement officers to their fullest capacity, there are a few that are considered critical. The following section will explore how the organizational culture or subculture, public trust issues, limited emergency management training, and a limited understanding of the National Incident Management System impact the use of police officers. These challenges are hurdles that must be overcome in order to fully integrate law enforcement into all phases of emergency management.

Organizational Culture

In society we have cultures, subcultures, and contra-cultures. The law enforcement community has its own unique subculture, complete with signs/symbols, language, codes, and acceptable practices. Earlier in this chapter we mentioned the concept of command presence and the training of police officers. It is necessary to understand how police officers conduct their daily business in order to integrate them into emergency management activities. In this section we will discuss how command presence impacts the perception of police officers and how their training, in its very nature, creates an obstacle.

The concept of command presence is an important part of police officer culture as it allows officers to gain control of the scene and enhance officer safety. However, this is something that police officers need to be cognizant of and be able to switch off when appropriate. Oftentimes when engaging with other members of the emergency management team, police officers still try to command the room; this can be interpreted as arrogance or cockiness. One solution is to increase emergency management training for police officers and educate non-police members about law enforcement culture.

When young police officers enter into the police academy, some may come from the military while others have little to no work experience. During the 13–19 weeks of the academy, police are indoctrinated into a different way of thinking about people. From reading books such as "On Killing: The Psychological Cost of Learning to Kill in War and Society" by Col. Dave Grossman, or listening to speeches from people like Gen. Jim Mattis, police officers develop a cynical view toward non-police individuals. The book by Col. Grossman focuses on the psychological examination of how soldiers' willingness to kill has been encouraged and exploited to the detriment of contemporary civilian society. In other words, it normalizes the concept of righteous violence or killing. Individuals like Col. Grossman and former Secretary of Defense Jim Mattis have contributed to developing the warrior mentality in U.S. special operations soldiers. These ideas have been adopted by many law enforcement agencies to help police understand, cope, and be comfortable with the necessity to use force or deadly force when warranted. Jim Mattis is often cited during police training with the following statement: "Be polite, be professional, but have a plan to kill everybody you meet." (Wilner, 2016), This type of training has led to an "us versus them" mentality among many police officers. Some could argue this also creates an environment where police are hyper-vigilant.

As a former Army Ranger and Police Officer, One of the authors remember sitting through these sessions and being shown videos of police officers who had been assaulted or killed in the line of duty. We are not questioning this approach to police training, but instead highlighting the fact that emergency managers and administrators need to be aware of this culture in order to incorporate police into all phases of emergency management. This is especially critical in today's climate because we have witnessed a decrease in public trust as it relates to police officers.

Public Trust

Many of us recall the feelings or emotions we felt watching the trial of Derek Chauvin for the killing of George Floyd. Whether you were upset about the use of force against George Floyd or the conviction of Derek Chauvin, you were emotionally exposed to criminal justice processes. In recent years, there seems to be a trend to highlight any use of force by police against black Americans because of racial bias. This perception has led to a decrease in trust, an increase in suspicion, and the questioning of policing in America. Whether you support this politically sensitive movement (or not) is irrelevant. What is significant is that there are American citizens who do not trust police and will question the motives of any law enforcement officer, regardless of the circumstance.

Sending police officers to rescue victims or to educate communities during pre-disaster operations may be met with resistance in some communities. It is necessary for emergency managers to be strategic in how police officers will be used when managing emergency situations. One idea would be to have police officers in plain clothes when serving in an emergency management role. Another proposed solution to the public trust issue is to provide communities with open access (transparency) to police department data when appropriate.

As professors of emergency management, our students are sometimes required to engage in research projects in every college-level course that they complete. When the Office of Emergency Management is housed within a police department, citizens often have a difficult time accessing planning or emergency management information. This is a carryover from the dated culture of law enforcement agencies, reinforcing that secrecy is necessary and it should be difficult for everyday citizens to receive information. Some departments' response to inquiries for information is to tell people to file a "Freedom of Information Act" official request, which reinforces the perception of unapproachability. In addition to reimaging how police are viewed through a public trust lens, we also need to consider exposing police officers and the public to more emergency management training.

FEMA Training

Police officers are subjected to an extensive training regimen. This includes a 13–19- week police academy where cadets learn about the penal code, code of criminal procedure, basic defensive tactics, basic firearms, and police driving. After completing the police academy, officers usually attend a 4–6-week in-service or in-house training program. This allows departments to train new police officers on department policies and procedures, advanced use-of- force training, extended firearms training, and developing an understanding about the unique organizational culture. Once the classroom portion of police training has been concluded, police officers are then required to complete a 4-week (minimum) field training program. During this process, a rookie police officer is partnered with a veteran officer who has received special training. An officer in field training will be responsible for controlling the scene, applying the applicable law, determining a course of action, and completing any necessary documentation. Finally, all police officers are required to attend annual refresher training, and this may vary from state to state.

There is no question that police training programs are lengthy, but may not be totally adequate for preparing police officers. What is lacking is emergency management training. Some police officers, especially those assigned in an emergency management role, do complete the minimum courses identified as requirements by FEMA although the average police officer is not required to complete any FEMA training. If the emergency management profession wishes to continue to rely on police officers to staff/manage shelters, participate in exercises, and inform planning/policy direction, then it is necessary to require FEMA training courses to be a part of mandatory police training. By receiving specialized training, police officers will be equipped with the ability to view disasters through an emergency management lens and not just a crime prevention lens. There is an old saying in the military and in law enforcement that police or military operators are hammers, and to a hammer, everything looks like a nail. Emergency managers could collaborate with police administration to require emergency management training that would give officers an additional tool for their tool belt. Much like the police academy training that provides police officers with their guiding doctrine, policies, and legislation as the basis for their authority, FEMA training would provide police officers with an understanding of federal laws and other requirements during disaster operations. This would also allow police officers to develop an understanding of the National Incident Management System (NIMS) and the Incident Command System (ICS).

National Incident Management System and Incident Command System

One of the major problems for police officers who are assigned to an Office of Emergency Management (OEM) is prioritizing the emergency operations organizational chart over their daily operations organizational chart. Law enforcement agencies are designed as paramilitary organizations, complete with a hierarchical chain of command. When a police officer is assigned to an OEM, they have or will acquire a specialized skill set. As such the officer may be placed on the OEM organizational chart at a level higher than command staff members. This can create an issue as higher-ranking officers may be reluctant to adjust their normal chain of command to accommodate the ICS structure.

Police officers may also be reluctant to accept the NIMS response structure as a result of their normal chain of command. Unlike fire departments that are proficient in the NIMS structure and promote scene management to individuals who have specialized credentials or are better suited for the task at hand, police officers are reluctant to place these individuals over their police command ranks. Police officers who lack NIMS training will revert to their training and daily operating system, which may be problematic in some instances.

This also connects back to the police culture, as we can train the police officer who is assigned to the OEM in ICS and NIMS, but unless the rest of the chain of command acknowledges this, it will be a moot point. It remains necessary to instill the emergency management culture at all levels in police departments in order to successfully integrate police departments into all phases of emergency management. Administrators have to guide police departments to develop an understanding that the old adage of "I have a badge and gun, therefore I am in charge" no longer applies.

CONCLUSION

In this chapter we addressed the history of policing and discussed the role that police officers play in emergency management. In some sections of the chapter it may appear as if the roles and responsibilities of police officers were simplified or minimized. The reality is police officers fulfill a critical role in emergency management and will continue to be an integral part of the emergency operations plan. It is necessary to emphasize that policing is not synonymous with emergency management or disaster operations. It is also necessary to clearly outline the roles and expectations of police officers in emergency management, as it is counterproductive to assume that police officers are fully aware of their role.

The purpose of this chapter is to highlight the importance of the role that police officers play in the disaster cycle and identify how emergency managers could improve this partnership. Our police officers deserve to be trained in emergency management so that they are set up for success and enthusiastic about participating in planning, exercises, or in meeting other emergency management needs.

By creating an emergency management training program designed for police officers and establishing a disaster-centric culture within law enforcement agencies, it allows OEMs to be better suited to integrate police personnel in all phases of emergency management. Even if a time comes when all jurisdictions have adopted a reformed model of emergency management, police officers will still be involved in the emergency management cycle. Having police officers available is invaluable, but it is imperative that their involvement be implemented in an appropriate manner that will foster an environment where the objectives of disaster planning and response can be achieved seamlessly.

As a final closing point to this chapter, the authors want to thank our brave police officers for doing a job that is often thankless and for their willingness to serve in a profession where good deeds rarely make the headlines. Stay safe while standing the gap and remember "nemo me impue lacessit."

CLASS DISCUSSION AND ESSAY QUESTIONS

1. According to the authors, what is the difference between the traditional and reformed model of emergency management? Does the model used matter? If so, why?
2. Initially, there were no formal police organizations and matters of law enforcement were handled by churches. What were the possible advantages of this approach? What were the drawbacks?
3. Politicians and policing were closely connected when police departments were created. Why was it important to prohibit political influence over law enforcement?
4. What is a Joint Terrorism Task Force (JTTF)? Who is involved in the JTTF? And, why is the JTTF necessary to better prevent and react to terrorist attacks?
5. What are disaster myths, how do they relate to law enforcement, and what lessons in this regard were learned from the Hurricane Katrina experience?
6. What roles do police officers perform before, during, and after disasters? Why are their services and expertise essential?

7. How was the "public trust" damaged during the arrest of George Floyd? What lessons were learned from this experience and from the response to the riots that followed?

BIBLIOGRAPHY

Berman, Jay S. "The Taming of the Tiger: The Lexow Committee Investigation of Tammany Hall and the Police Department of the City of New York." *Police Studies: The International Review of Police Development* 3, no. 4 (1981): 55–65.

Bjelopera, Jerome P. "The Federal Bureau of Investigation and Terrorism Investigations." FAS. Last modified April 23, 2013. fas.org/sgp/crs/terror/r41780.pdf. (CRS Report No. R41780).

Carte, Gene E., and Elaine H. Carte. *Police Reform in the U.S.: The Era of August Vollmer, 1905–1932.* Berkely: University of California Press, 1976.

Chermak, Steven. "Law Enforcement's Information Sharing Infrastructure: A National Assessment." *Police Quarterly* 16, no. 2 (2013): 211–244.

"CISA, NASCAR, Daytona International Speedway and Local Partners Conduct Joint Exercise to Keep Daytona 500 Fans Safe." *Security Magazine*, January 7, 2021. https://www.securitymagazine.com/articles/94298-cisa-nascar-daytona-international-speedway-and-local-partners-conduct-joint-exercise-to-keep-daytona-500-fans-safe.

Commonwealth of Massachusetts. "Comprehensive Emergency Management Plan." 2019. https://www.mass.gov/lists/comprehensive-emergency-management-plan.

Commonwealth of Massachusetts. "Executive Order No. 476: Designating the Commonwealth Fusion Center as the Commonwealth's Principal Center for Information Collection and Dissemination." January 3, 2007. https://www.mass.gov/executive-orders/no-476-designating-the-commonwealth-fusion-center-as-the-commonwealths-principal.

Commonwealth of Massachusetts. "Overview of the Department of State Police's Commonwealth Fusion Center." January 18, 2019. https://www.mass.gov/info-details/overview-of-the-department-of-state-polices-commonwealth-fusion-center.

Douthit, Nathan. "August Vollmer, Berkeley's First Chief of Police and the Emergence of Police Professionalism." *California History Quarterly* 52, no. 2 (July 1975): 101–124.

Federal Bureau of Investigation. "Joint Terrorism Task Forces." htttps://www.fbi.gov/investigate/terrorism/join-terrorism-task-forces.

"From the Administrator: Law Enforcements Role in Responding to Disasters." Accessed January 11, 2021 Available at https://www.policechiefmagazine.org/from-the-administrator-law-enforcements-role-in-responding-to-disasters

"Fusion Centers." Department of Homeland Security. Last modified September 19, 2019. https://www.dhs.gov/fusion-centers.

"Fusion Center Foundational Guidance." Department of Homeland Security. Last modified March 30, 2021. https://www.dhs.gov/fusion-center-foundational-guidance.

Goodwin, Doris K. *The Bully Pulpit: Theodore Roosevelt, William Howard Taft, and the Golden Age of Journalism.* New York: Simon and Schuster, 2013.

Hadden, Sally E. *Slave Patrols: Law and Violence in Virginia and the Carolinas.* Cambridge: Harvard University Press, 2001.

Hofstadter, Richard, and Michael Wallace. *American Violence: A Documentary History.* New York: A.A. Knopf, 1973.

"How the FBI Stopped the "Violent Overthrow" and Kidnapping of Gov. Whitmer." *News Channel 3*. Last modified October 8, 2020. https://wwmt.com/news/local/how-fbi-stopped-violent-overthrow-kidnapping-michigan-gov-whitmer.

Martin, Phillip. "While You Sleep: Boston's Joint Terrorism Task Force, Part One." *WGBH*. Last modified November 15, 2016. https://www.wgbh.org/news/2016/11/15/local-news/while-you-sleep-bostons-joint-terrorism-task-force-part-one.

McCaffery, George H. "Boston Police Department." *Journal of Criminal Law and Criminology* 2, no. 5 (1912): 672–690.

"Model Partnership New York Joint Terrorism Task Force Celebrates 35 Years." Federal Bureau of Investigation. Last modified December 8, 2015. https://www.fbi.gov/news/stories/new-york-jttf-celebrates-35-years. (for fnote 29).

Monkkonen, Eric H. *Police in Urban America, 1860–1920.* Cambridge: Cambridge University Press, 1981.

Potter, Gary. *The History of Policing in the United States.* Eastern Kentucky University School of Justice Studies, 2013.

Rollins, John. "Fusion Centers: Issues and Options for Congress." FAS. Last modified January 18, 2008. https://fas.org/sgp/crs/intel/RL34070.pdf. (CRS Report No. RL34070).

Steverson, Leonard A. *Policing in America: A Reference Handbook (2007 ABC-CLIO).* https://ebookcentral-proquest-com.maritime.idm.oclc.org/lib/maritime/detail.action? docID=305262.

"United States v. Adam Fox, et al., United States District Court, Western District of Michigan, Case 1:20: MJ 416," Criminal Complaint dated October 6, 2020. Available at https://www.justice.gov/usao-wdmi/press-release/file/1326161/download.

"United States v. Rezwan Ferdaus, United States District Court, Massachusetts, Case 1: 11-CR–10331-RGS," Indictment dated September 29, 2011 and the Criminal Complaint dated September 28, 2011. Available at https://www.investigativeproject.org/documentts/case_docs/1690.pdf and https://www.investigative project.org/documents/case_docs/1702.pdf.

"U.S. Attorney's Office District of Massachusetts," November 1, 2012. Press release, "Man Sentenced in Boston for Plotting Attack on Pentagon and U.S. Capitol and Attempting to Provide Detonation Devices to Terrorists." Available at http://fbi.gov/boston/press-releases/20122/man-sentenced-in-boston-for-plotting-attack-on-pentagon-and-u.s.-capitol-and-attempting-to-provide-detonation-devices-to-terrorists.

U.S. Department of Justice. *The Attorney General's Guidelines for Domestic FBI Operations*, 1–46, 2008. justice.gov/archive/opa/docs/guidelines.pdf.

"U.S. Department of Justice Press Release 'Najibullah Zazi Indicted for Conspiracy to Use Explosives against Persons or Property in the United States'." September 24, 2009. Available at https://www.investigativeproject.org/documents/case_docs/1065.pdf.

"U.S. Department of Justice Press Release 'Najibullah Zazi Pleads Guilty to Conspiracy to Use Explosives Against Persons or Property in U.S., Conspiracy to Murder Abroad and Providing Material Support to al-Qaeda'." February 22, 2012. Available at https://www.investigativeproject.org/documents/case_docs/1186.pdf.

"U.S. Department of Justice Press Release 'United States Citizen Who Joined ISIS Charged with Material Support Violations'." September 16, 2020. Available at https://www.justice.gov/opa/pr/united-states-citizen-who-joined-isis-charged-material-support-violations.

Walker, Samuel. *Popular Justice: A History of American Criminal Justice*. New York: Oxford University Press, 1998.

Walker, Samuel, and Charles M. Katz. *The Police in America: An Introduction*. 7th ed. New York: McGraw Hill, 2011.

Waxman, Olivia B. "How the U.S. Got Its Police Force." *Time*, May 18, 2017. https://time.com/4779112/police-history-origins/.

Wilner, Michael. "Be Polite, Be Professional, but Have a Plan to Kill Everybody You Meet." *The Jerusalem Post*, 2016.

CHAPTER 6

Emergency Medical Services:
A Diverse, Complex and Essential Profession for Disasters and Terrorist Attacks

Peter Burke, Steve Holley, and Margaret Mittelman

INTRODUCTION

Emergency Medical Services (EMS) in North America provide pre-hospital medical care and transport to medical facilities. EMS agencies are typically staffed by Emergency Medical Technicians (EMTs) and/or more advanced Paramedics who may be certified or licensed at various practice levels. In broad terms, agencies in emergency medical services operate at three levels: emergency first responder, basic life support (BLS), (which includes Emergency Medical Responder and/or EMT), and advanced life support (ALS), which can be comprised of Advanced EMTs and/or Paramedics. Agencies may also use a tiered system with a combination of resources at various levels. Unlike other public safety agencies such as police and fire, which are almost always municipal, county, or regional, EMS agencies may be government functions, healthcare system–associated, or private. Government-functioning EMS agencies are most often associated with fire departments, as often EMS personnel act as firefighter/EMTs fulfilling a dual role. When associated with healthcare systems, EMS personnel respond as part of an ambulance crew, providing care and transportation. Private ambulance services hire EMS personnel to provide care and transportation. Ambulances are often staffed with two personnel, one to drive and another to provide patient care. In some instances, ambulances may be staffed with three personnel as alternatively for higher priority calls, a third EMT or Paramedic may be taken from another responding agency or apparatus.

While other government functions have a direct and straightforward mission, EMS has various roles, not always directly related to each other. Comparatively, a community's economic development department has the detailed responsibility of developing a given community's economic vitality and supporting it with an appropriate framework, process, and other needs such as housing. Similarly, a police department has responsibility for law enforcement functions and a fire department, firefighting and rescue operations. However, the roles of EMS span public safety, health care, and public health (Thiel and Jennings, 2012). EMS is unique because it has an apparent initial mission of lifesaving, but it also has roles in healthcare and community paramedicine, public health, and in

DOI: 10.4324/9781003350729-6

some instances, rescue operations, hazardous materials response, and emergency management. Nationally, 60% of emergency medical services are delivered by fire departments, making it one of the many services typically provided by public organizations.

An additional consideration is that EMS is one of a few government-provided services that generate significant revenue for service delivery. As a result, EMS is nearly alone in charging a fee for a public safety service. However, that paradigm shifts as governments attempt to turn to cost recovery for services over taxation. This difference causes some EMS agencies to consider revenue generation in addition to response or other operational concerns. This has also driven some of the expansion of EMS into health care.

These differences can add layers of complexity when responding to disasters or terrorism incidents. These complexities include lines of authority, jurisdiction, and funding. Furthermore, there may be operational concerns related to the scope of practice and training. This chapter covers the history of Emergency Medical Services, a description of EMS services performed routinely and during disasters and terrorist attacks, the role of EMS in emergency management and homeland security and concludes with challenges and recommendations.

HISTORY OF THE EMS PROFESSION

The history of EMS traces back to battlefield medical care, with origins as early as the Napoleonic and U.S. civil wars. The primary functions were immediate battlefield care and the transport of injured soldiers. Despite a lengthy history, civilians were slow to adopt formal systems, relying on physician house calls or funeral home hearses to transport patients to hospitals.

From the late 1800s through the 1960s, despite the formation of rescue squads and ambulance services, there was minimal progress in the formalization of pre-hospital care. Incidentally, it is worth noting that there were two service delivery models used in EMS. The first model is the patient-to-hospital approach where patients are stabilized and provided with life-saving interventions at the scene or en-route to definitive care. The other model, often used in Europe, brings medical care to the patient, sometimes eliminating the need for transport to a hospital. Debate continues as to which model ultimately provides better patient outcomes. Additionally, without focusing on details, there has been an extensive debate on which pre-hospital interventions offer the best patient outcomes. The clearest example is the constant updates to cardiopulmonary resuscitation (CPR), which now focus on perfusion rather than respiration (Lacocque, Freeman, and Kelly, 2019).

Ambulance services started in Cincinnati and New York in the late 1860s (Bucher, Johnson, and Zaidi, 2017). EMS services were expanded during the 1950s but remained unregulated. In the 1950s and 1960s, three events pushed EMS toward modernization. One such event was the development of CPR. Another was the national focus directed toward medical issues and their effect on mortality, primarily heart disease, cancer, and strokes. Lastly, a report titled "Accidental Death and Disability: The Neglected Disease of Modern Society" detailed the occurrence of critical injuries and the lack of an organized system to treat injuries and transport those patients. The report was primarily based on automobile injuries increasing because of the new federal highway system (Division of Medical Sciences, 1966).

That report forced legislation that formed the Federal Department of Transportation (DOT) and the National Highway Traffic Safety Administration. Within the legislation were the first regulations for EMS, oriented at training levels. The DOT regulated EMS based on the principle that EMS was primarily a transport function rather than a medical function (Shah, 2006).

Despite those nascent pushes being nearly 60 years old, EMS providers to this day still view patients as belonging to one of two categories: traumatic injuries or medical illness. This approach is a result of the foundational EMS system and training curriculum.

In 1973, the EMS Systems Act (93rd Congress, 1973) was passed, providing further funding and federal government support for EMS modernization. However, that legislation still had a light touch on standardization, leaving service delivery methods to state and local agencies. That has resulted in a highly decentralized system with few similarities outside of the typical neighboring state and regional idiosyncratic services, and in many cases, the services between adjacent communities. It's important to consider that in many areas, EMS is provided by the fire department. However, the next community over may be served by a private company, and the next, served by a non-profit. Seemingly non-traditional methods may serve even large cities. For instance, Virginia Beach, Virginia, a city of nearly half a million residents, is partially served by a volunteer rescue squad.

Since 1973, technological and pharmaceutical advances have been made, improving the quality of care provided. The metrics used to validate the quality of care on traumatic injuries or acute medical illness patients necessitated rapid response. Entire EMS systems are predicated on the idea of having advanced life support EMTs at bedsides within eight minutes of request. This principle requires an enormous investment to maintain that level of capability and service.

Many of the patients that EMS agencies respond to do not require advanced levels of care. A consideration is that using highly skilled and expensive resources on non-critical incidents is inefficient from a cost perspective and takes resources out of service for other emergencies that may be critical (Blackwell and Kaufman 2002; Shah et al. 2005). Evaluation of best practices for EMS delivery is vexing because of the wide variety of agencies, service delivery areas, and delivery methods. Further, implementing advanced dispatch and resource management systems and methods in a nationally decentralized service is complicated with no clear regulatory path. Cultural impediments on the part of EMS agencies, which place agency in the "emergency" function of the role, are additional barriers.

EMS has a future, particularly highlighted by the COVID-19 pandemic, in expanding its role within public health and providing community paramedic services. These services are not directly aligned with the emergency function but have an overall impact on the community's health and may reduce future service demands.

These expanding and changing roles can make integration into disaster response somewhat more complicated. Departments and agencies with more defined roles or that are more institutionalized may have fewer challenges responding to and scaling up for larger emergencies or disaster responses.

RELATION TO DISASTER AND TERRORISM

It is useful to consider the day-to-day roles and responsibilities of EMS agencies and their training levels before considering their function in disasters and terrorism. EMS is considered the nation's front-line health service provider, focusing on responding to sick or injured patients and transporting them, if necessary, to definitive care (an appropriate hospital for their illness or injury). EMS systems operate at a basic life support (BLS) level, meaning they provide non-invasive interventions such as splinting, bandaging, vital signs, and primary assessment. Other systems operate at the advanced life support (ALS) level allowing providers to perform invasive interventions such as intubation, intravenous access, medication administration, and electrical cardiac therapy. Many systems operate a tiered system using BLS ambulances for lower-acuity patients, reserving ALS ambulances for high-acuity patients. First Responder agencies or units within agencies are non-transport EMS services that provide initial care before turning the patient over to a transport ambulance.

Calls are screened at dispatch centers and acuity is assigned using numerical priorities 1 through 3. The most acute and life-threatening scenarios are considered priority 1, and the least, priority 3. Agencies employ various degrees of call-screening, with some much more rigorous than others. More rigorous call-screening, combined with dispatch triaging, can allow busier systems to be more efficient by assigning only the necessary resources.

Some EMS agencies may also adopt additional roles, most frequently technical rescue, that involve scenarios such as trench collapses, persons in confined spaces, and water rescues. In most municipalities, rescue work is handled by the fire service. However, in some systems, that role has been assimilated by EMS, requiring additional training and expense. In some cases, multiple agencies may have overlapping capabilities that may provide fodder for turf wars.

Another additional role is community paramedicine, sometimes referred to as mobile integrated health care (MIH) or mobile integrated health care–community paramedicine (MIH-CP), which is gaining ground in North America. MIH requires EMS providers to partner with healthcare systems to provide pre-emptive or preventive follow-up with patients. Often that includes primary healthcare measures, such as ensuring medications are being taken as prescribed, taking vital signs, and providing physician's information on the patient's condition. One goal of MIH is to reduce unnecessary hospital readmissions and catch patient issues before they become acute. A benefit is that an MIH interaction takes much less time than a patient transport. MIH provides the additional benefit of financial savings, reducing the risk of penalization for readmissions. By reducing the risk of such penalties, system reimbursement innately increases. However, agencies that have implemented MIH strictly for the financial aspects have not made the programs fully self-sustaining.

When disasters strike, it falls doctrinally on local EMS agencies to respond to their community's lifesaving needs. Depending upon the incident's scope and scale, EMS agencies have various roles that may change as the incident evolves.

A primary concern during emergencies, catastrophes, terrorist attacks, and other disasters is the loss of life; this is also the first metric provided in historical recounts of disasters or evening news stories. Naturally, the role of government is to minimize that loss of life. Even if not provided by a government agency, the role of EMS is to establish a system to limit harm and save lives. During any incident, a primary concern for EMS is the actual or estimated number of patients, as knowing that number will allow the EMS and healthcare system to plan for how and where they will be transported for care.

Disasters may result in a mass casualty incident (MCI), requiring the triage, treatment, and transportation of large numbers of patients. Mass casualty incidents are singular events resulting in multiple patients and may overwhelm the EMS or healthcare systems. Disasters may also destroy, overwhelm, or limit local healthcare systems' capacity requiring a pivot to field care or field hospitals.

During a disaster, EMS responses are predicated on the nature of the disaster itself. Attacks result in penetrating traumatic injuries, flooding may result in drownings, and prolonged power outages may result in hypothermic patients. Each of those will require a different approach while utilizing the same systems. Some disasters may require the search for and rescue of victims. While typically referred to colloquially as Search and Rescue, they are two distinct parts. The search part involves using techniques, some very technical, to locate victims. Often thought of from a wilderness perspective, there are also searches necessary in other instances such as following explosions or building collapses, which use specialized fiber optic cameras, listening devices, and robotics. Rescue removes the victim from harm, which may be as simple as carrying them or as complicated as shoring-up a collapsed building and cutting them out using torches.

MCIs are broken into levels by a local or regional plan according to the number of patients and the severity of their injuries. Establishing the level of MCI allows EMS, the healthcare system, and appropriate hospitals to prepare for an influx of patients. After rescuing victims, if necessary, or establishing safe areas to work, EMS providers or other first responders will start triaging patients.

Depending on the event, first responders may go to the victims where they are, especially if they cannot escape, and triage them in place, moving the most critical first. In other events, victims may come to the rescuers, which may be challenging as the initial rush of victims may not be the most injured but simply the ones able to escape, allowing responders to bypass them and go to the most injured at the incident. After the initial response, or at an incident with a large geographical footprint, casualty collection points (CCPs) may be established to aid in triaging patients. Recent events have proven that at large MCIs, a combination of approaches will be necessary, with some providers immediately going to the scene of the incident when safe, and others forming CCPs and potentially assisting at hospitals.

As an example, during active shooter events, Rescue Task Forces (RTFs) are formed with EMS providers joining with law enforcement to enter an area where the shooting occurred to treat and remove patients. While that is happening, many victims may flee the scene and look for assistance in parking lots or streets, while others will seek care directly at hospitals.

The next priority is to start treating patients; treatment is typically limited to life-saving interventions or pain management. A treatment area is established adjacent to where patients will be arriving. The treatment area will hold patients until they are able to be transported to hospitals or otherwise released from the scene.

The treatment area may be formed from a CCP or may be a separate area more conducive to treating patients. The treatment area needs to be proximate to the scene but also close enough so that victims can be carried, or if they are able, can walk to it. Depending on the situation, the area may need to be covered, temperature controlled, and well lit. Additionally, an area may need to be secured, searched, and screened for secondary devices before being used as a treatment area. Security may also be necessary to protect first responders and victims from further harm.

As victims are triaged and treated, transportation plans must be developed and quickly enacted. There are many factors at play in transporting patients, the first is ensuring the most severely injured get transported to the appropriate hospitals – significant traumatic injuries to trauma centers and burn injuries to burn centers. Care must also be taken not to overwhelm single hospitals, if possible, by sending less acute patients to hospitals further away. Medical coordination systems may also assist by providing hospital bed counts and tracking each patient from triage through to their destination hospital. Another consideration is to ensure that routes to hospitals are kept open for ambulances.

Lastly, the use of helicopters to transport patients will need to be considered. EMS play a vital role in air transport where certified paramedics and nurses sit side by side to care for the injured while in the air.

Ideally, triage, treatment, and transport are happening nearly simultaneously, with the initial arriving units assigned to triage and the next, to treatment. Once triage and treatment are underway, ambulances start transporting based on the priority condition of the patients. All of this occurs within the incident command system, potentially under the operations section or an EMS branch.

A key consideration for the incident commander, operations sections chief, or branch director is to ensure that the number of resources requested will support the number of patients. For MCIs with patients numbering in the double to triple digits, it should be assumed that the initial event will be overwhelming to all but the largest cities. In some instances, it may require ambulances to make multiple trips to hospitals, as happened in West Warwick, RI, following the Station Nightclub fire, when ambulances made the relatively short transport to nearby hospitals and immediately returned to pick up additional patients.

While the initial focus will be on the triage, treatment, and transport of patients, planning for the arrival of people seeking out family members from the disaster may need to be considered. The establishment and staffing of a family reunification center are important to provide parents and other loved ones a place to gather and await information.

Another critical consideration is the safety of responders. While there is something to be said for the bravery of risking one's life to save another, in a disaster context, rescuers and EMS providers need to ensure that they can continue treating patients by not jeopardizing themselves. This requires a risk management approach by first evaluating hazards and establishing appropriate controls to mitigate or lessen that hazard.

Hazard assessment will change based on the nature of the incident and may be dynamic as the incident evolves. With a more polarized and technological society, hazards may not be initially considered, as terrorist attacks may be complex and coordinated using explosives and small arms. Fire may be used as a weapon or as a distraction, and a cyberattack could disrupt dispatch and communications systems. During unintentional or natural incidents, hazards may persist, including areas with contaminated floodwaters or dangerous atmospheres.

Some of the risk management work can be completed before incidents occur. A local or regional Threat and Hazard Identification and Risk Assessment (THIRA) can allow communities to work with stakeholders to identify threats and hazards within their communities and plan responses. While it is clearly impossible to predict or plan for all scenarios, coastal communities can prepare for flooding in the same way that a city can plan for an event in a high-rise building.

As part of addressing threats and risks raised during a THIRA, EMS agencies can prepare for what their role may be during disasters and attacks beyond triage, treatment, and transport. As an example, post-9/11, when the specter of chemical attacks was a grave concern, Atropine and 2- PAM chloride autoinjectors were widely distributed to EMS to treat organophosphate or nerve agent exposure. Building on that, many agencies trained EMS providers to wear chemical protective clothing (CPC) in order to treat, decontaminate, and transport victims from a chemical weapons attack. Many of those programs continue to evolve, addressing new threats and emerging concerns. Another recent example of addressing a new threat would be the treatment and transport of patients infected with the Ebola virus in 2014.

In addition to the catastrophe's nature, there is a distinction between a noticed and non-noticed event or disaster. A noticed event is one in which sufficient notice for planning is provided in advance to the emergency management structure; examples include predicted weather events and large gatherings. No-notice events may or may not be anticipated but will occur with little or no notice, such as a chemical leak or transportation accident.

As outlined in "Why Was Boston Strong?," Boston's initial response to the marathon bombing went exceptionally well because of planning, pre-positioned resources, and a robust urban healthcare system. Despite the bombing itself being a no-notice event, the marathon was a notice event and sufficient resources were on hand to respond (Leonard et al. 2014).

Conversely, an already busy EMS system may not have sufficient resources immediately to respond to a no-notice active shooter attack or a major worldwide disaster, like a pandemic. During the COVID-19 pandemic, EMS personnel made do with fewer resources, including personal protective equipment (PPE) and adapted to changing circumstances. Rather than send a whole team into a home to deal with COVID victims, the family took the patient to the doorstep where one paramedic provided treatment. Often, family members were encouraged to transport victims to the hospital (Lindquist, Mittelman, and Fisher, 2021).

During a disaster, EMS's success is partially dependent on the effort applied to planning and resourcing for both notice and no-notice events. It is also reliant on the structures in place to support the EMS providers in the field. Crisis researcher Patrick Lagadec (1993, p. 54) wrote in *Preventing Chaos in a Crisis*, "the ability to deal with a crisis is largely dependent on the structures that have been developed before chaos arrives. The event can, in some ways, be considered as an abrupt and brutal audit; at a moment's notice, everything that was left unprepared becomes a complex problem, and every weakness comes rushing to the forefront."

Through its core mission, EMS has been involved in disaster response since the beginning of coordinated disaster responses. EMS is integrated into local, regional, and state mutual systems. Staffed ambulances were subject to a 2020 Emergency Management Assistance Compact request for New York to assist with the response to COVID-19. Federally funded civilian (Disaster Medical Assistance Teams) and Department of Defense (Homeland Response Force) systems exist to augment local responders.

ROLE IN EMERGENCY MANAGEMENT AND HOMELAND SECURITY

EMS can be a locally funded and administered system, often fully or partially integrated with the local fire service. It may be supported and operated through local healthcare systems. In other instances, it may be a holdover to pre-regulation times and be a private non-profit service. Most uniquely compared to additional public safety or municipal functions, it may be private and for-profit. These different models alter agencies' roles within their communities and within emergency management functions.

Every community knows who their Fire or Police Chief is, or at least who provides firefighting or law enforcement services, respectively. However, that is often much less clear for EMS services. Many communities may not have that exact authority figure, instead relying on an account executive, for example. Larger communities typically have much more built-out EMS and EM systems where roles are more clearly defined.

However, emergencies and disasters strike rural areas where there may not be clearly defined roles or enough resources to fill defined roles.

For example, an explosion in West Texas that killed 15 people was initially responded to by the local fire department and local non-profit private ambulance service. The blast caused $200 million in damage to the community of only 2,800 residents. This indicates that small agencies may find themselves immediately responsible for disaster response when their typical responses are usually more mundane (Matthews, 2018). That is not to say that size or funding source is the only indicator of performance or preparedness; it may, however, be a complicating factor.

Regardless of funding source or jurisdiction, EMS is a partner with other public safety agencies relative to emergency management in the best cases. It may serve as liaison with emergency operations centers, fusion centers, and healthcare systems in the most mature system.

The Fire Department City of New York (FDNY) Chief of Counterterrorism explained as much in his statement to The House Sub-Committee on Intelligence and Counterterrorism (Currao, 2019). He said, "The FDNY cannot operate at our highest capacity without working hand-in-glove with our partners at the NYPD, New York City Emergency Management (NYCEM), the Port Authority of New York-New Jersey (PANYNJ), the Metropolitan Transit Authority (MTA), the United States Coast Guard (USCG), the New York State Division of Homeland Security and Emergency Services, Federal Bureau of Investigation (FBI), the Joint Terrorism Task Force (JTTF), and many departments and first responder agencies here in New York and across the country."

The FDNY provides EMS service, along with other agencies, to New York City. His statement illustrates a wide variety of agencies and stakeholders and solidifies that EMS has a distinct role within disaster response. Where nearly all emergency incident objectives would include preserving or saving lives as a primary goal, EMS is the resource needed to meet that requirement. He goes on to describe additional improvements, including EMS integration with law enforcement to form Rescue Task Forces.

Depending on the type of disaster, there are more technical responses and operational aspects that may be utilized. In the event of a chemical release, EMTs may be expected to administer medical countermeasures or don PPE and operate in a contaminated environment. For example, they may be expected to participate in search-and-rescue operations and provide care while an injured victim is removed from a collapsed building or trench (Deramus and Ruemke, 2020).

EMS may become a de facto healthcare system managing patients' long-term medical needs in other events while definitive care is unavailable. While this is unique for urban EMS, rural agencies may encounter this as a matter of course with much longer transport times to hospitals. This may become much more important during long-term sheltering operations following storms.

For instance, during COVID-19, EMS agencies took on additional roles providing testing, contact tracing, and ultimately, vaccination. COVID-19 also showed the adaptability and resilience of EMS personnel. Lindquist, Mittelman, and Fisher (2021) stated: "Some important changes were incorporated into the EMS that may remain. Stricter policies were adopted to assure personnel and equipment were safe from contamination. Likewise, improved guidelines assured better patient care, and EMS personnel were able to provide better service with less resources and personnel."

It is useful to consider the strategic, tactical, and task levels of EMS in the instance of a disaster. The strategic level is high-level goal and objective setting. The tactical level is developing the method and resources to meet the strategic goals and objectives. The task level is physically carrying out the assigned tactics. Tasks support tactics; tactics support strategy. The strategy is aligned with the organization's mission in lifesaving.

The strategic level starts with a "size-up" in formalized decision-making processes. This is the intelligence and information gathering phase. Information is critical to making an adequate EMS size-up to include: the location(s) of the incident, the type of incident, the scale and magnitude of the incident, hazards at the incident location(s), access routes to the incident location and from the incident to hospitals, the number of casualties and resource needs.

Those pieces of information allow incident commanders to create objectives. For tactics to be successfully developed from objectives, they should be SMART: specific, measurable, attainable, relevant, and time oriented. For mass casualty incidents, EMS would either be the incident commander (IC), a member of the unified command (UC) team, or a branch director or division supervisor within the incident command system. Post-9/11, all agencies and personnel are trained in and use the National Incident Management System, standardized roles, and specific terminology.

An example of a SMART EMS objective at a multi-vehicle car collision would be that EMS units will triage all patients at the vehicle accident site within 15 minutes of arrival. From the IC, that objective would allow supervisors to assign that task to resources and, if necessary, to request more resources if needed to meet that objective. The exact tactic would be to use Ambulance 1 and Ambulance 2 to triage patients. An additional tactic would be to use Engine 3 and Ambulance 3 to establish a treatment area. The tasks associated with each of the tactics are the physical work, using the triage system, and speaking with individual patients.

Triaging is a method of categorizing patients based on their injuries and likelihood of survival. Differing systems may be used, but they all require the color-coding of patients; red for the most critical, yellow for those who need care but will survive, green for those with minor injuries, and black for those deceased or expected to die.

In the case of a disaster or terrorism incident, EMS leadership would work together with other responding agencies to ensure that their objectives are part of the Incident Action Plan and that they are appropriately resourced to meet them. When used and communicated effectively, the command structure and incident planning process provide an opportunity to remove redundancy and align priorities. Further, it assists in interagency cooperation, mainly when strategies, tactics, or tasks are interlinked. A clear example of that inclusivity is when EMS requires law enforcement for protection as happened during door-to-door searches following Hurricane Katrina. This can also occur during the formation of joint EMS and law enforcement Rescue Task Forces used during an active shooter or other hostile event.

CURRENT CHALLENGES AND RECOMMENDATIONS

Like any public sector service, EMS's most considerable challenge is reacting to a larger, more demanding, and more complex society. EMS must mature along with its public safety counterparts of the fire service and law enforcement agencies while at the same time recognizing that its role in the community is somewhat broader. In addition to response, these agencies play an integral role in the development and social health of communities (Asllani and Fisher, 2019). This maturation is not to say that many agencies are not fulfilling this broader role, but nationally, there is both a lack of federal support and national drive.

An additional challenge is to support emergency management, disaster relief, and community resiliency needs while still meeting communities' daily needs. EMS's role within the more extensive healthcare system must be fully explored. Leveraging relationships with the community and healthcare organizations may allow EMS agencies to better align with stakeholders during disasters. Additional community engagement will also serve to solidify EMS's role as a community lifeline. The newly released Federal Emergency Management Agency community lifelines indicate that EMS spans the gap between "safety and security" and "health and medicine." While not being specifically addressed by either community lifeline, citizens rely on EMS for critical incidents. Additionally, EMS personnel are playing a greater role in pre-hospital care.

Service demand has increased since the inception of EMS, partially driven by an aging population. For instance, the number of calls for elderly falls has increased substantially. There is no reason to expect a decrease in service demand; agencies must keep pace with the communities' needs while remaining financially sustainable. In many instances, this may mean that agencies can only provide baseline services lacking the depth or bandwidth to do in-depth emergency planning.

EMS is fortunate in that it will continue to have customers and demand. It can be best prepared for the future by establishing cooperative relationships with others and ensuring that it is represented when and where appropriate. To accomplish this, EMS agencies must have professional staffing available. To remain sustainable, EMS agencies should ensure that they are using sound management practices including adopting technology, using data-driven approaches to decision-making, and utilizing scalable or regionalized assets.

The service demand increase will be further exacerbated by expansion into health care and public health. The COVID-19 pandemic will have a lasting impact on Emergency Medical Services (Friese 2020). EMS will likely be tasked with additional responsibilities related to pandemic preparedness and infectious disease. Some of these changes are using respiratory and eye protection on every call and transporting patients to urgent care centers. Social distancing has become part of EMS training and some agencies have changed protocols for cardiac arrest care. Major disasters like a pandemic demand more of EMS personnel in terms of adapting to life-threatening conditions, working with fewer resources, and requiring personal sacrifice of time and family relationships.

The COVID-19 pandemic showed a greater need for pre-hospital care provided through EMS personnel. EMS providers have fought to have Medicare pay for treatment in place and for transport to alternative locations like doctor's offices and urgent care centers. The pandemic has made these services an essential part of providing care, and it is anticipated that these modifications in service will likely continue after the crisis is over. Call volumes for EMS and ambulance services have dropped by 30%–40%. People are calling less for non-essential services. This trend is also likely to continue after the pandemic and change the way EMS services are funded. Government and the healthcare industry are relying more on EMS and realize that EMS is not just providing a ride to the hospital.

The EMS system will benefit from better education and training, incorporating clinicals at hospitals and "ride alongs" with EMS agencies for students, and requiring critical care courses and other certifications for EMS professionals. Universities and other training agencies need to adopt new teaching methods like virtual simulations, flipped classrooms, and hybrid courses that combine online and face-to-face instruction (Allred, McCarthy, and Fisher, 2021).

With the above information in mind, the following recommendations are derived from this review:

- EMS, fire, and law enforcement agencies have a broader role, such as mobile integrated health care–community paramedicine (Goodwin and Lane, 2018), disaster response, and emergency medical dispatch in their communities that go beyond response. Greater national recognition and funding needs to be considered with this broader role.
- EMS's role within the more extensive healthcare system should be fully explored by leveraging relationships with the community and healthcare organizations to better align with stakeholders' needs.
- Because EMS service demand has increased since its inception, agencies need to explore additional funding sources to keep pace with the communities' needs while remaining financially viable.
- To remain sustainable, EMS agencies should ensure that they are using sound management practice including the use of the most current technology, using data-driven approaches to decision-making, and utilizing scalable or regionalized assets.
- The EMS system of delivery and services has changed because of recent events. Education and training programs need to prepare students and professionals to meet these changes and adapt to any future challenges.

CONCLUSION

Emergency Medical Services play an integral role in any disaster response that involves casualties. Because EMS is relatively new and has many deployment and operational characteristics, its role is less clear than other public agencies. Furthering EMS agencies' operational and planning capacity will allow them to integrate into incident command structures and systems more readily. EMS's ultimate objective is to save lives via patient care interventions and transport to definitive care hospitals. Ensuring systems are poised to meet that daily demand and scale up into disaster response must be the focus of EMS moving forward.

CLASS DISCUSSION AND ESSAY QUESTIONS

1. Unlike many other first responder organizations, emergency medical technicians may be associated with government, healthcare or private providers. How does this diversity benefit or potentially complicate emergency management?
2. What are the two service delivery models used in EMS, and what are the advantages and drawbacks of each model?
3. What is the difference between basic life support and advanced life support, and how do these two concepts relate to disasters and terrorist attacks?
4. How does triage, treatment, and transport relate to mass casualty incidents? What can EMS providers do to deal with disasters or terrorist attacks that create an excessive number of victims?

5. What other agencies and departments do Emergency Medical Services work with in emergency management and homeland security? Why is communication, collaboration, and coordination necessary among these groups?
6. How did the COVID-19 pandemic change Emergency Medical Services?

REFERENCES

93rd Congress of the United States. 1973. S.2420 - Emergency medical services systems act. https://www.congress.gov/bill/93rd-congress/senate-bill/2410 (accessed June 8, 2021).

Allred, S., K. McCarthy, and J.R. Fisher. 2021. The COVID-19 pandemic's impact on students in a paramedic study program. *Journal of Security, Intelligence, and Resilience Education* 11(1): 1–24. https://jsire.org/the-covid-19-pandemics-impact-on-students-in-a-paramedic-study-program/ (accessed June 13, 2021).

Asllani, H., and J. Fisher. 2019. Effective communication in public services in a diverse language and cultural landscape: A challenge for teaching and training. In Chova, L.G., Martínez, A.L., and Torres, I.C., eds. *EDULEARN19 Proceedings*. Palma: IATED Academy, pp. 9386–9393.

Blackwell, T.H., and J.S. Kaufman. 2002. Response time effectiveness: Comparison of response time and survival in an urban emergency medical services system. *Academic Emergency Medicine* 9(4): 288–295.

Bucher, J., R.W. Johnson, and H.Q. Zaidi. 2017. *A Brief History of Emergency Medical Services in the United States*. Irving, TX: Emergency Medicine Residents' Association (EMRA). https://www.emra.org/about-emra/history/ems-history/ (accessed June 8, 2021).

Currao, T. 2019, May 6. *Local Efforts to Counter the Terror Threat in New York City*. Washington, DC: The House Sub-committee on Intelligence and Counterterrorism. https://homeland.house.gov/imo/media/doc/Testimony-Currao.pdf (accessed June 13, 2021).

Deramus, K., and B. Ruemke. 2020. *Program Guidelines*. Washington County (Texas) EMS Special Operations Divison. https://www.washingtoncountyems.net/wp-content/uploads/2020/01/wordspecops_manual_6_14_2013.pdf (accessed June 13, 2021).

Division of Medical Sciences, Committee on Trauma and Committee on Shock. 1966. *Accidental Death and Disability*. Washington, DC: The Neglected Disease of Modern Society, National Academy of Sciences-National Research Council.

Friese, G. 2020, April 20. What changes in EMS will persist after the national emergency is over? *EMS1*. https://www.ems1.com/future-of-ems/articles/what-changes-in-ems-will-persist-after-the-national-emergency-is-over-IdPry6MCr0phO9Tt/al-emergency-is-over-IdPry6MCr0phO9Tt/ (accessed June 13, 2021).

Goodwin, J., and P. Lane. 2018. *Mobile Integrated Healthcare and Community Paramedicine (MIH-CP)2nd National Survey*. Clinton, MS: National Association of Medical Technicians (NAEMT).

Lacocque, J., C. Freeman, and S. Kelly. 2019, February 5. *From Bedside to Curbside: Prehospital Clinical Research Update*. Irving, TX: Emergency Medicine Residents' Association (EMRA). https://www.emra.org/emresident/article/prehospital-clinical-research/ (accessed June 7, 2021).

Lagadec, P., and J.M. Phelps (translator). 1993. *Preventing Chaos in a Crisis: Strategies for Prevention, Control, and Damage Limitation.* New York: McGraw-Hill.

Leonard, H.B., C.M. Cole, A.M. Howitt, and P.B. Heymann. 2014. *Why was Boston strong? Lessons from the Boston Marathon Bombing.* Cambridge, MA: Harvard Kennedy School. https://www.hks.harvard.edu/sites/default/files/centers/research-initiatives/crisisleadership/files/WhyWasBostonStrong.pdf (accessed June 13, 2021).

Lindquist, C., M. Mittelman, and J.R. Fisher. 2021. Lessons learned from the lived-experience of EMS personnel during the COVID-19 pandemic. Utah Valley University. Unpublished paper.

Matthews, P. 2018, April 9. TX ambulance service rebuilds following blast. *Firehouse.* https://www.firehouse.com/ems/news/21001096/west-tx-ambulance-service-rebuilds-following-blast (accessed June 13, 2021).

Shah, M.N., P. Bishop, E.B. Lerner, R.J. Fairbanks, and E.A. David. 2005. Validation of using EMS dispatch codes to identify low-acuity patients. *Prehospital Emergency Care* 9(1): 24–31.

Shah, M.N. 2006. The formation of the Emergency Medical Services system. *American Journal of Public Health* 96(3): 414–423. https://doi.org/10.2105/AJPH.2004.048793.

Thiel, A.K., and C.R. Jennings. 2012. *Managing Fire and Emergency Services*, 4th ed. Washington, DC: International City/County Management Association (ICMA).

CHAPTER 7

Public Administration and Emergency Management:
The Ties that Bind

Abraham David Benavides

INTRODUCTION

Our world history is filled with natural disasters that have devastated population centers. From early disasters like earthquakes in Antioch, AD 526 and Aleppo, AD 1138, to cyclones, typhoons, tsunamis, volcanoes, and floods (Pappas and Means, 2020) all have caused devastation to population centers. In addition to these natural disasters and many others not mentioned, today we have man-made disasters like hazardous material emergencies, infrastructure failures, nuclear catastrophes, transportation accidents, terrorism, war, cyberattacks, and mob violence to name just a few (Brunsma and Picou, 2008). As we continue our journey in the 21st century, we as a society will be confronted with many additional types and varieties of disasters. The key to our survival and orderly recovery will be how we organize ourselves to confront the challenges placed before us.

As you have read in previous chapters, emergency management or disaster science is the process whereby individuals and organizations come together to prepare, plan, mitigate, respond, and recover from calamities. Although no concrete definition is standard in the field of emergency management, some have said it is an "effort to plan how to deal with disasters in the most effective manner" (McEntire, 2018, p. 6). Others have noted that it is "the management of risk" (Waugh, 2000, p. 3). Still others have said it is "applying science, technology, planning, and management to deal with extreme events" (Drabek and Hoetmer, 1991, p. xvii). This understanding clearly places emergency management as a field in which action and implementation are key in carrying out what is best for individuals and the community or society.

What then is the tie between emergency management and public administration? What is public administration? What relationship do these two fields have in assuring the health and safety of our communities? Finally, how can practitioners manage and respond to the various aspects of these emergencies? These questions will be addressed and responded to in the ensuing sections.

The following chapter begins with a brief history of public administration highlighting the major events that solidified the field as a major area of study in terms of administration and management of government. At this point, the relationship or ties that bind emergency management to public administration are discussed. Although in academia

DOI: 10.4324/9781003350729-7

there is a slight friction or tension between the two fields, in practice they are hand-in-glove in carrying out programs that benefit those affected by disasters. Next, the various roles in public administration and emergency management/homeland security are examined to see how closely these two professional fields work together. The current challenges that confront both fields are considered with an emphasis on collaboration and shared leadership to encounter head-on the threats that face our nation. Finally, recommendations and suggestions for how these two fields can continue to work together are proposed and discussed for the benefit of society.

HISTORY OF THE PROFESSION OF PUBLIC ADMINISTRATION

Public Administration is simply and intricately the art, science, and profession of administration and management (Lynn, 1996) in the public sector. It is not politics although closely associated, nor policy and policy making even though these play a major role in administration and management. Public administration is the process of carrying out the will of the people through their elected representatives by appointed officials selected to implement that will. Therefore, throughout history, public administration has played a significant role in realizing how governments are created, work, and deliver services to the people. In E.N. Gladden's work on the history of public administration, he traces the history to early civilizations noting that even before written records, societies developed practices to manage their affairs. He goes on to mention early societies in the Middle East such as the Persians, Egyptians, Babylonians, Greeks, Romans, and others and shows how they managed their affairs through administration. He also notes the rise of western kingships during the Middle Ages and cites examples of administration in these forms of monarchy (Gladden 2019). The very early history of public administration is rich in text and examples – far too many to mention here – that illustrate administration in action. Nevertheless, that history, in part, has shaped how we view the role of administrators in society today.

Although some textbooks begin the U.S. history of public administration during the Progressive Era (1870–1925), some argue that we should not ignore the first century of our country's administrative history (Luton, 1999). Therefore, the history of public administration in the U.S. should start with the founding of the nation. It is clear that a number of cities existed before the Declaration of Independence or the U.S. Constitution. These cities received the authority to act through administrative charters – the right to administer their cities in shape and form from either England or Spain. A look at the first charter of the City of Philadelphia in 1691, for instance, shows the administration of the city by a mayor, aldermen, councilmen, justice of the peace, a recorder, clerk, coroner, sheriff, and water bailiff (Lloyd, 1894). Many of these positions and titles are still used today, over 300 years later. All these positions were appointed, and the office holders were expected to administer the affairs of the city with equity and honesty. The city of Boston and other New England towns had similar charters. These early documents clearly reveal the importance of public administration in the everyday order of affairs of these early settlers. Karl (1976) notes that the British, French, and German influence was enormously felt in how the government of the United States was founded and eventually administered.

By far the most important founding document that exemplifies public administration is the U.S. Constitution. Signed in 1787 and ratified in 1788, it remains a formidable document for the legitimacy of public administration. Although the word "administration" does not appear in the document, it is implied by what it states – how the government is organized. Administration is also implied by what it asks of its participants to do or administer – how it operates. For instance, in Federalist 51, James Madison clearly articulates the need for administration "by men over men":

> But what is government itself but the greatest of all reflections on human nature? If men were angels, no government would be necessary. If angels were to govern men, neither external nor internal controls on government would be necessary. In framing a government which is to me administered by men over men, the great difficulty lies in this: you must first enable the government to control the governed; and in the next place oblige it to control itself.

(Federalist Papers)

The role of administration was clearly on the minds of the founders as the whole purpose of the constitutional convention was to improve the administration of government as they experienced deficiencies with the Articles of Confederation (the governing document of the time). Charles R. Wise (1993) notes that, "The express need for a strong executive originated in our constitutional historical experience. It should be remembered that what led to the calling of the convention in Philadelphia were real problems of governing under the Articles of Confederation, problems so severe that the attendees quickly abandoned the task of amending the Articles in favor of adopting a whole new Constitution" (p. 258). He concludes his comments by saying that, "The Constitution may not have made public administrator's players in the separation of powers in an explicit sense, but it certainly did so in an operational sense. Does this in itself confer constitutional legitimacy on public administration? I would argue that it does" (p. 260). Our history has shown that Congress does use its constitutional authority to create administration as is plainly seen in the passage of the Homeland Security Act of 2002, which created the Department of Homeland Security shortly after the September 11, 2001, terrorist attacks in New York City, Pennsylvania, and Washington, D.C. (Department of Homeland Security 2020). This Act delegated the appropriate powers to the new agency to coordinate emergency management for the homeland. Finally, it is evident in the writings of Alexander Hamilton in the *Federalist Papers* that a strong executive was necessary. It was clear that the president would have power of appointment and that these appointees, when confirmed, would be subject to his "superintendence" (The Federalist Papers Number 72). In other words, an administrative structure would be in place to run or administer the federal government through the Executive Branch. As the nation grew, various government agencies were created to address specific public policy concerns by regulation and to promote stability usually in consequence of some crisis (Roberts, 2013).

Incremental growth, a civil war, reconstruction, and a spoils or patronage system in the mid-1800s typified the growth of administration during this early period and onward. Politicians appointing friends, political campaign contributors, and campaign workers selected for positions in their administration (Van Riper, 1958) typified the latter. Unfortunately, many of them were not trained for their new positions, which led to inefficiencies and poor public service. There were far more office seekers than there were positions in the federal government, and this eventually led to the death of a president. James A. Garfield was assassinated in 1881 by a would-be office seeker disgruntled because he did not receive the position he desired (Doenecke, 1981). These practices changed with the passage of the Pendleton Act, commonly known as the Civil Service Act of 1883. This Act was key in introducing a merit system or fairness into government employment. In essence, the Act required among other items:

- For open, competitive examinations for testing the fitness of applicants for the public service.
- A period of probation before any absolute appointment or employment aforesaid.
- That no person in the public service is for that reason under any obligations to contribute to any political fund, or to render any political service, and that he will not be removed or otherwise prejudiced for refusing to do so.
- That no person in said service has any right to use his official authority or influence to coerce the political action of any person or body. (Pendleton Act of 1883, p.1)

The reason this Act is significant to public administration is because it is one of the first pieces of legislation that marks the beginning of the current modern public administration. It introduces professionalism, accountability, and several other principles into the field, which are foundational administrative beliefs and values today.

A number of scholars have written about the modern history of public administration (Green et al., 1998; Raadschelders, 1997; Stillman, 1989; Waldo, 1984). Some have used time periods that coincide with our government's history and describe major events in public administration. Others use the discipline's theories and practices as benchmarks to highlight major events in public administration. For instance, Urby and McEntire (2013) write about the importance of applying and integrating public administration into emergency management and disaster education. In their study, they identify seven periods in public administration to demonstrate the theoretical growth of the field over time. They note a classical period, an emergence of human behavior or human relations, a period of orthodoxy, a neoclassical stage, a new public administration awakening, a new public management or reinventing government phase, and finally a new public service movement. Other scholars in public administration have also generated such divisions (Llorens, Klingner, and Nalbandian, 2018; Fry and Raadschelders, 2014; Raadschelders and Stillman, 2017; Starling, 2011. Table 7.1 illustrates some of these periods in greater detail by combining a number of historical eras to show the growth in public administration over the years.

CONNECTIONS BETWEEN PUBLIC ADMINISTRATION AND EMERGENCY MANAGEMENT

As noted above, public administration has a rich history tracing its roots back to the Constitution of the United States. On the other hand, emergency management as a field is relatively new (in its modern formation) and many of its functions and operations are still found within fire and police departments at the local government level. Local government, non-profit management, government finance, public policy, human resources, urban planning, and emergency management, among other disciplines, are all considered categories or disciplines that make up public administration. In other words, public administration is seen as an umbrella-type discipline in which many of these other professions find a home. In essence, the administration of what is public and how services are delivered to that public is what helps determine if a discipline would fall within the realm of public administration. In the case of emergency management or disaster science, it falls neatly within the broad umbrella of public administration.

The tie that binds both disciplines together is the U.S. Constitution. Although this is not a history chapter of emergency management, it should be noted that even as early as 1803, the U.S. Congress passed legislation to provide relief to Portsmouth, New

TABLE 7.1. Periods in the History of Public Administration

Period	Approximate Years	Description or Characterization
Pre-Founding	1601–1776	Monarchy, city charters from England and Spain, Articles of Confederation, independence
Constitutional	1787–1828	The Constitution, end of revolutionary war, Louisiana purchase, Lewis & Clark expeditions
Patronage	1829–1882	Patronage or the spoils system, movement west, trail of tears, the civil war, reconstruction, various states become part of the union including Texas and California
Professionalism	1883–1932	The Progressive Era, the merit system, council manager form of government, women's vote, efficiency, effectiveness, scientific management, the great depression, the classical period in public administration, WWI
Performance	1933–1964	Orthodoxy period, human relations movement, civil service system continues, growth of the administrative state, WWII, Korean War
The People	1965–1979	Neoclassical period, New Public Administration, social equity, affirmative action, civil rights movement, Vietnam War, Watergate – ethics in government
Privatization	1980–Present	New Public Management, Reinventing Government, non-profit management, Challenger explosion, Berlin Wall, Hubble telescope, Gulf War, rise in terrorism and September 11, 2001
Partnerships	2002–Present	Collaborative public management, new public service, public service motivation, Iraq War, Ebola, COVID-19

Source: Adapted and modified from various sources including: Llorens, Klingner, and Nalbandian (2018); Fry and Raadschelders (2014); Raadschelders and Stillman (2017).

Hampshire, because of a damaging fire on their seaport (Schroeder et al., 2001). Similar legislation was passed for a number of disasters during the 1800s and into the 1900s (Drabek and Hoetmer, 1991; FEMA 2021b). In addition, Congress passed the Federal Civil Defense Act of 1950, created the Federal Emergency Management Agency (FEMA) in 1978, and approved the Disaster Relief and Emergency Assistance Amendments of 1988 or the Stafford Act. It authorized the Post-Katrina Emergency Management Reform Act of 2006, adopted the Sandy Recovery Reform Act of 2012, passed the Disaster Recovery Reform Act of 2018, and because of the Stafford Act there have been various presidential disaster declarations in recent years (FEMA 2022). As Patrick Roberts (2013) notes, "The federal government has been involved in disaster relief from the beginning of the republic, which suggests that it is an enduring feature of the social contact" (p. 180). In essence, emergency management is closely tied to our definition of public administration as it is linked to the Constitution by Acts of Congress that allow it to act, perform, and function for the health and welfare of the nation's people. This commonality in disciplines is what provides for cooperation and redundancy, as coordination is necessary to respond to disasters.

The relationship in practice exhibits a harmony and unison that is rarely found between two other disciplines. For instance, is the emergency manager housed within the fire department of a city strictly an emergency manager or also a public administrator? Per our definition above, he or she would be both. Why? Because the primary responsibility is to serve the public. The secondary responsibility is to serve that public via the particular profession of emergency management. The same could be said for the city manager, financial manager, parks and recreation manager, economic development manager, etc. Their primary responsibility is the public service. The only difference is the manner (particular professional expertise) in which that service is carried out. Each has refined skills particular to their specialty areas contributing to the community with that inherent sense of public interest.

Disasters involve most members of the society in which they occur and thus most often require a solution by government. We often see government or public administration as stepping in and helping address serious or wicked problems that individuals or a community cannot solve on their own. This outside assistance is vital in helping a municipality respond to and recover from a disaster. The same could be said for terrorism. Like disasters, terrorism affects whole societies and a government solution or response is warranted. Large-scale events like disasters and terrorism require a response, both in terms of preparing for such events and in responding to them. Therefore, it is essential that government or public administrators establish policies and procedures that cover all aspects of the emergency management cycle.

One area that demonstrates the unity between the disciplines is nicely displayed in the National Incident Management System (NIMS). Over time and with experience, the country realized that many of our emergency response plans, systems, and technology were inoperable. In other words, first responders could not talk with each other because of different radio frequencies, different policies and procedures, different ideas and philosophies about emergency response, and the lack of a common language between branches of the police, fire, military, and local emergency managers. A sad and unfortunate event that perhaps illustrates the flaws in the system was best captured by the terrorist attacks in New York City on September 11, 2001. The system in reality was fractured, splintered, and lacked a joint response plan. Jim Dwyer and Kevin Flynn of the *New York Times* reported the following in July of 2002:

> Those clear warnings, captured on police radio tapes, were transmitted 21 minutes before the building fell, and officials say they were relayed to police officers, most of whom managed to escape. Yet most firefighters never heard those warnings, or earlier orders to get out. Their radio system failed frequently that morning. Even if the radio network had been reliable, it was not linked to the police system. And the police and fire commanders guiding the rescue efforts did not talk to one another during the crisis.
>
> Cut off from critical information, at least 121 firefighters, most in striking distance of safety, died when the north tower fell. Rescuers' ability to save themselves and others was hobbled by technical difficulties, a history of tribal feuding and management lapses that have been part of the emergency response culture in New York City and other regions for years.
>
> When the firefighters needed to communicate, their radio system failed, just as it had in those same buildings eight years earlier, during the response to the 1993 bombing at the trade center. No other agency lost communications on Sept. 11 as broadly, or to such devastating effect, as the Fire Department. Throughout the crisis, the two largest emergency departments, Police and Fire, barely spoke to coordinate strategy or to share intelligence about building conditions.

(Dwyer and Flynn, 2002)

The system that is in place today is in part a response to the lack of cooperation and coordination that resulted from those terrorist attacks. Congress created the Department of Homeland Security (DHS) through the passage of the Homeland Security Act on November 25, 2002. The successful coordination of events following those incidents in the Office of Homeland Security in the White House was its predecessor. In essence, all or part of "22 different federal departments and agencies" were unified to "become a more effective and integrated Department, creating a strengthened homeland security enterprise and a more secure America that is better equipped to confront the range of threats we face" (DHS 2020). Now that the organizational structure was in place (an Act of Congress with authority from the Constitution to create administrative agencies), it was time to concentrate on process and policy. Therefore, DHS concentrated in pulling together from its knowledge base a system or protocols that were originally issued in 2004 by DHS as guidance in responding to all types of emergencies. According to FEMA, NIMS is a system that guides all levels of government as well as private and non-profit sectors. NIMS is an effort:

> to prevent, protect against, mitigate, respond to, and recover from incidents. NIMS pro-vides stakeholders across the whole community with the shared vocabulary, systems, and processes to successfully deliver the capabilities described in the National Preparedness System. NIMS defines operational systems, including the Incident Command System (ICS), Emergency Operations Center (EOC) structures, and Multiagency Coordination Groups (MAC Groups) that guide how personnel work together during incidents. NIMS applies to all incidents, from traffic accidents to major disasters.
>
> (National Incident Management System, 2017, p. 1)

As future local government managers, it will be essential to be familiar with the processes and resources available in responding to emergencies of various types. The National Incident Management System is a "living document" that has and will most likely continue to have newer iterations to maintain pace with new incidents, technology, techniques, and processes that makes the preparation, planning, and response to emergency more efficient.

Another illustration of how public administrators and emergency managers work together to serve the public occurred during the COVID-19 pandemic of 2020. Public administrators and emergency managers in the city of Dallas, Texas, worked tirelessly to ensure that their homeless unsheltered population was cared for and housed, and that those with COVID-19 were isolated before returning to community shelters. Benavides and Nukpeazh (2020) note that the city converted the Kay Bailey Hutchison Convention Center into a temporary shelter for overnight and daytime guests. The city, through their Office of Homeless Solutions, also contracted with local hotels to rent rooms for the homeless and coordinated weekly 8:00 a.m. meetings with community partners including emergency managers to assist this population. The elaborate plan included provisions for isolation and quarantine for all guests and included securing a Housing and Urban Development emergency solutions grant to work with local shelters that had budget short-falls. It should be noted that eventually the city of Dallas bought four hotels with CARES Act funding to serve this population in the future through temporary, transitional, and rapid rehousing (Kalthoff, 2020).

Finally, in terms of professionalism, most disciplines have active professional orga-nizations that provide their members continuing education, regional and national con-ferences, and a number of other supporting activities. In public administration, there are a number of these organizations but the oldest and one of the most respected is the American Society for Public Administration. Since 1939, it has promoted effectiveness in government and has sought to advance excellence in public service (ASPAnet.org). In the fall of 2020, one of its publications highlighted how public servants could assist during the pandemic; it was called *COVID-19 – Public Service during a Pandemic*. The publication illustrates through its many articles the connection between public administration and issues related to emergency management such as a pandemic. The publication covers 15 short and very interesting readings on the COVID-19 pandemic. They come from various points of view and are all very instructive. Another professional organization, the International City/County Management Association (ICMA), was established in 1915 for local government managers. It is an organization intent on furthering ethical principles in local government management (ICMA 2019). ICMA working with Ron Carlee recently prepared a comprehensive overview of various disasters that local governments have experienced in recent years. It provided valuable lessons learned and recommendations for dealing with emergencies. Professional organizations in public administration are continually seeking to provide its members vital information and training opportunities in the discipline of public administration and emergency management.

ROLES OF PUBLIC ADMINISTRATION IN EMERGENCY MANAGEMENT/HOMELAND SECURITY

This section explores the various topics and roles that have a bearing in responding to emergencies and are found in both public administration and emergency management. This review is not extensive but cursory, as each topic in itself is worthy of a full book chapter. Additionally, not every applicable topic or role is addressed, only those that appear to have a standing in both disciplines. First, however, it is essential to understand how, organizationally, various levels of government respond to emergencies and request assistance from other levels of government. In a federalist system of government, the concept of devolution or the subsidiarity principle (Benavides and Nukpezah, 2020; Nukpezah, 2017) dictates that the level of government closest to the people (the local government) should be the one that responds to an emergency before any other level of government is invited to assist. For instance, Homeland Security Presidential Directive-5 given on February 28, 2003, states:

> The Federal Government recognizes the roles and responsibilities of State and local authorities in domestic incident management. Initial responsibility for managing domestic incidents generally falls on State and local authorities. The Federal Government will assist State and local authorities when their resources are overwhelmed, or when Federal interests are involved. The Secretary will coordinate with State and local governments to ensure adequate planning, equipment, training, and exercise activities. The Secretary will also provide assistance to State and local governments to develop all-hazards plans and capabilities, including those of greatest importance to the security of the United States, and will ensure that State, local, and Federal plans are compatible.

> (Homeland Security Presidential Directive-5 2003)

It is clear that the federal government respects and values local control and holds local authorities as key members in determining when and how higher levels of government can assist them. In the words of Kay Goss (2018), "The overall goal of the Federal Emergency

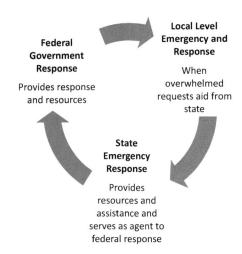

Federal Government Response

Provides response and resources

Local Level Emergency and Response

When overwhelmed requests aid from state

State Emergency Response

Provides resources and assistance and serves as agent to federal response

FIGURE 7.1. Requesting Aid from Higher Levels of Government

Management Agency (FEMA), emergency management programs, and the profession of emergency management is to have the disaster system be federally supported, state managed, and locally executed." Figure 7.1 illustrates how the process can work.

Following this pattern, we can see the logic behind the response structure, as local governments know their areas best. At the same time, we can see the wisdom in having the state and federal governments ready to assist and respond with their vast resources when called upon. The following role areas – mitigation, business continuity, preparedness, mutual aid agreements, responding to emergencies, recovery functions, and after-action reports – highlight areas that are common to the disaster management cycle. These steps in emergency management can vary with prevention sometimes being added as a fifth step. Federal and state governments are also involved in these areas but the focus here is local governments. The final two sub-areas of leadership and vulnerable populations are themes or topics that are more generalizable to all levels of government yet essential to the overall understanding of emergency management.

Mitigation

Mitigation is the process whereby an organization assesses its potential risks and mitigates or reduces those risks by eliminating hazards that can cause injury to human life or physical damage to property. It is an essential step in the phases of emergency management because individuals and organizations can reduce the chance or at minimum lessen the effects of a disaster. Most often mitigation looks at what already exists in the environment and assesses its potential for risk. At the local government level, mitigation has been typified by zoning regulations that prevent building in flood zones and prohibiting other questionable building practices. The construction of levees and the upkeep and maintenance of floodways, creeks, and canals are also mitigation activities. Additionally, building codes that require reinforced buildings in earthquake prone areas and the prohibition of construction in coastal areas prone to flooding are but a few examples of easing potential damage. Local governments need to look to their local land use planning documents and master plans and ensure that new construction projects are located within safe, suitable areas for development. Business continuity planning is an example of a mitigation activity and is described below.

Business Continuity/Continuity of Operations

The concept of business continuity or the continuity of operations has been around for many years. Nevertheless, it was never really implemented in most organizations nor thought about seriously until 2020. The COVID-19 pandemic brought to light the importance of having contingency plans not just for businesses but also for local governments, educational institutions, churches, non-profits, and many other organizations. How do you continue to provide services during an emergency? If you cannot use your current place of business to provide services, how can you provide them in another way? These and many other questions should be addressed by the organization. It is remarkable to see how many organizations in all sectors were able to adapt because of technology. It is also sad to see that many others had to close or failed to provide services because they were not able to adjust or modify their service delivery. Richard Long (2017) defines the concept as "the advance planning and preparation undertaken to ensure that an organization will have the capability to operate its critical business functions during emergency events. Events can include natural disasters, a business crisis, pandemic, workplace violence, or any event that results in a disruption of your business operation" (p. 1). At the federal government level, U.S. Policy Directive 40 (PPD-40) directs the FEMA administrator to ensure that the federal government can continue to operate through a range of emergencies that may befall the country. In essence, it established the process whereby the government can continue to operate "in case of catastrophic events" (p. 1). FEMA has created a toolkit called the Continuity Guidance Circular that provides information on developing the capacity to have a continuity of operations for all levels of government and their private and non-profit partners (FEMA 2022).

Preparedness

Preparedness is the process of conducting various activities that ensure an individual or community is ready for an emergency. It has the potential to increase a community's readiness by ensuring that essential tasks were completed before a potential disaster. For instance, at the local government level, a community can make sure that an emergency operations center (EOC) is operable and ready for use. This would include trainings and exercises to be certain that everyone knows their roles. Other trainings and exercises would also be appropriate including mock disaster drills that involve the community. Ensuring that equipment and other technology is in good order is also essential. Depending on your location in the United States, providing disaster-appropriate information to residents can make a difference between being prepared for a disaster and not being informed. For example, in most communities in north Texas, tornado sirens are tested every first Wednesday of the month. Most buildings have signs or indications for tornado shelters, and many individuals and organizations are signed up to receive alerts from the National Weather Service. In short, preparedness "is a continuous cycle of planning, organizing, training, equipping, evaluation, and improvement activities that ensures effective coordination and the enhancement of capabilities to prevent, protect against, respond to, recover from, and mitigate against disaster events" (Upstate Medical University, 2021, p. 1). Mutual aid agreements and coordination are examples of preparedness and are described below.

Mutual Aid Agreements and Coordination

As noted previously, most likely when a disaster strikes, it is essential to have other governments that are ready and willing to assist in any way possible. For this to happen smoothly, previous arrangements should have been made to make the assistance possible. For instance, if a fire were so large in a community that it requires assistance from the neighboring town, most would be grateful if they came. However, who pays for their gas, water, and wear and tear on their equipment? Who covers insurance? What if a firefighter is injured, and who pays the associated medical costs? There is much more to coordinating a response from another jurisdiction than just making a phone call to the mayor of the city next door and having them come over. Therefore, many cities have entered into what are called mutual aid agreements that are arrangements that spell out the items noted above and many more. In essence, they are agreements that formalize the "sharing of emergency aid and resources among governments and organizations at all levels" (Astho, 2021). Obviously, these agreements need to be done in times of calm, not emergencies. Elements in a mutual aid and assistance agreement may include: procedures for requesting and providing aid, payment, reimbursement and allocation of costs, notification procedures, roles and responsibilities of individual parties, protocols for interoperable communications, workers' compensation, liability, and immunity, among others (Astho, 2021).

Coordination and collaboration within and between cities can be vital in securing the appropriate response to address emergencies. Ana-Marie Jones (2015) suggests that sustainable partnerships need to be ensured before, during, and after disasters. She goes on to say that, "collaboration across sectors has long been assumed, expected, advocated, romanticized, and even scapegoated in the face of failure." Real collaboration, she believes, is essentially misconstrued and unappreciated. Jones emphasizes that, "most of the struggles and failures around collaboration stem from unrealistic expectations and a lack of understanding of the component pieces involved" (p. 1). Table 7.2 shows elements for true collaboration.

Conversations about collaboration in public administration have been around for a number of years (Bryson, Crosby, and Stone, 2015; Agranoff, 2006; McGuire, 2006). It is evident that for emergency management it is essential that mayors and public administrators learn to collaborate effectively. Agendas, "norms, working styles, world views, and opportunistic motives of partners" (Zeger Van der Wal, 2020, p. 764) are all items that must be considered.

Responding to Emergencies

Responding has always been a challenge for local governments over the years. Our federalist system is clear that local governments should respond first, then the state, and finally the federal government. It is essential that local governments understand their capacity to respond to emergencies that are prevalent in their area so that they know when to call on the next level of government for assistance. Our geographic make-up in the United States helps to identify which disasters will most likely hit the area in which a city is located. This is not always the case, but in most circumstances it is true. For instance, in the central United States, tornadoes are expected; in the south and southeast, they expect hurricanes; the west coast is known for earthquakes, fires, and mudslides; the Midwest is known for floods and tornadoes; and in the northeast, they expect snowstorms. Knowing what to expect helps local governments prepare and respond appropriately to the disaster

TABLE 7.2.   Elements for True Collaboration

- **Choose to collaborate:** enter a collaboration with eyes wide open by making the collaboration an intentional act, alert to its pitfalls, costs, and multiple steps in a pathway.
- **Be honest/trust:** be brutally honest because without honesty there is no trust between partners; acknowledge the weaknesses of each collaborating partner.
- **Celebrate/leverage differences:** understand and honor each collaborating organization's diversity as a genuine competitive advantage.
- **Stay focused on common goals, values, and needs:** do not deviate from these shared purposes. Avoid veering off into goals that only the strongest voice wants.
- **Protect your collaborators from idiosyncrasies of one's own bureaucracy:** when entering a collaboration, it is essential to know each collaborating organization's pitfalls, and then actively protect collaborative partners from experiencing them.
- **Create micro-successes:** most organizations cannot sustain a long process to reach a goal; each collaborating organization has to break down the long process into tiny steps along the way for which they can achieve success.
- **Embrace technology:** use technology to create an electronic "place" (e.g., Google Docs, Dropbox, or "the Cloud") that every collaborating partner can access.
- **Seek clarity:** spell out the path for all collaborating partners and agree on the level and depth of each organization's responsibilities, procedures, and communication standards.
- **Commitment and Responsibilities:** understand the time and effort it will take to maintain relationships with other organizations. Stay committed and work reasonably with your partners.

Source: Adapted from: Ana Marie Jones (2015); Bahadori et al. (2015)

or emergency in their area. A number of scholars have written about responding to emergencies from an evolving disaster response system to emergency response essentials (Van Fenema and Romme, 2020; Larson et al., 2006; Comfort, Ko, and Zagorecki, 2004; McEntire, 2002; Auf der Heide, 1989). It is interesting to note that of all the areas in emergency management, this topic of response is the best known to most people because we can immediately see the outcomes. On television or social media, images of a disaster show up instantaneously for all to see the government's response. Public administration and emergency management are closely tied in this phase of the response. Both first responders such as firefighters, police, medical professionals, emergency managers, and local appointed administrators as well as elected officials all carry out their responsibilities to ensure the health and welfare of the members of their community.

Non-profit organizations such as the American Red Cross, Catholic Charities, Latter-day Saints Charities, The Salvation Army, Southern Baptist Disaster Relief, and the United Way Worldwide are among a number of other national, regional, and local non-profits that provide essential services in the response to emergencies. The U.S. Chamber of Commerce Foundation provides a comprehensive list of non-profits working in disasters separated by areas such as preparedness, response, and recovery (U.S. Chamber of Commerce Foundation, 2021). The work of these non-profit or non-governmental organizations is essential in the response to emergencies. Organizations like Team Rubicon, a 501(c)3, can really make an impact in both the response and recovery efforts by using the expertise of military veterans (Team Rubicon Disaster Response 2022). National Voluntary Organizations Active in Disasters (VOAD) also promotes cooperation and collaboration and helps communities affected by disasters (VOAD 2022). Waugh and Streib (2006) noted, "The involvement of nongovernmental actors builds the capacity of communities to deal with future disasters. The disaster experience can speed recovery and make communities more resilient when a disaster strikes again" (p. 133). The private sector also contributes significantly to any emergency response. Cooperation and partnerships can be established with Home Depot, Lowe's, Sam's Club, Costco, Coca-Cola, General Mills, Johnson and Johnson, etc. to provide supplies and cash donations. According to the Public Affairs Council, millions of private organizations have donated to various emergencies in recent years (Public Affairs Council 2022).

Recovery

Many have seen the horrific news clips of various disasters in recent years and the damage they have caused both in terms of human life and property damage. Many have also been aware of the emotional and physical toll experienced by those affected by a disaster. So now what? The hurricane-force winds moved inland, the tornado stopped twirling, the earth ceased trembling, the fire finished burning, and so now, what is to be done? The recovery phase of any disaster or emergency is of vital importance. However, recovery can have different meanings to different people. For instance, rebuilding, reconstruction, restoration, rehabilitation, and restitution (Phillips, 2015; Quarantelli, 1998). Assessments must be made immediately after disasters and leaders must prioritize what should be done first, second, third, etc. After all residents have been cared for and are in a somewhat stable situation, putting things back together must begin. There are stages of recovery, and the actions that should be taken are determined by the stage at which a community happens to be (Phillips, 2015).

Public administrators have a keen focus on recovery for two reasons. First, they need to ensure that they are reimbursed for any expenditures to which they are entitled from the federal government. FEMA as the agent for the federal government follows a strict process for reimbursements, and local governments need to make certain that they follow all rules and procedures to ensure they receive those funds. FEMA's website provides the needed information. It has a program overview section, information on how to apply for public assistance and training, policy guidance, and fact sheets (FEMA 2022). Although this part of emergency management is not "exciting," it is critical in ensuring the city's stability in the long run. Second, the recovery phase is closely tied to economic development. As a community rebuilds its roads, schools, neighborhoods, and businesses, it has the opportunity to reshape its infrastructure and reimagine its future. The Organization for Economic Cooperation and Development (OECD) defines economic development in part as the "capacity of a defined area to improve its economic future and the quality of life for inhabitants. It makes an important contribution to national economic performance and has become more critical with increase global competition, population mobility, technological advances, and consequential spatial differences and imbalances. It can reduce disparities between poor and rich places, and add to the stock of locally generated jobs and firms" (OECD 2022 p.1). As communities recover from disasters it should be essential to keep in mind the importance of how that recovery develops. Finally, the private sector may contribute to disaster recovery through finances and public private partnerships (Chandra et al., 2016). These efforts are central to the whole recovery process.

After-Action Report or Review

Once the recovery is completed, one of the most essential yet sometimes least practiced exercises is that of writing the after-action report or review. Initially, after-action reports were developed and used by the United States Army in the 1970s as a learning methodology or tool to evaluate the performance of various exercises (Gurteen, 2000). It has since become a popular method for analyzing program performance in government and business. Disasters or emergencies will happen but how do we learn from them? What did our community do right and execute correctly? What did not work and where do we need improvement? What do we need to adjust or modify to improve the response the next time? These and many other questions need to be asked and addressed so that cities and organizations can learn from their successes, avoid mistakes, and provide needed information to stakeholders. Todd Henshaw (2012) suggests that it is not only a tool for cultural change but through purposeful action steps, the organization can learn. Table 7.3 shows seven action steps that can be taken.

Leadership

It probably seems obvious that leadership during a disaster is not only important but also essential. Nevertheless, sometimes leaders forget how to lead when leadership is most

TABLE 7.3.   Action Steps for After-Action Reports or Reviews

1. **Schedule After Action Reviews consistently** to learn from both successes and failures. "Postmortems" have a negative connotation that discourages participation and enthusiasm. AARs should be held during or immediately after successful and non-successful events, using the positive positioning of improving your own performance and not that of someone else.
2. **Gather relevant facts and figures** related to the team's performance. If project deadlines have been missed, product standards are being ignored, or client feedback is disregarded in the team's execution, these facts set the foundation for an AAR that is grounded in relevant data.
3. **Make participation mandatory** and involve all team members in the discussion – even customers, partners, and suppliers can be included. Each participant will likely have a different perspective on the event, and this serves as a key input into the AAR. Everyone's voice is important, so you must be able to receive criticism from a few levels down. Open-ended questions that are related to specific standards or expectations will encourage involvement.
4. **Have a three-pronged focus:** performance of team members, the leader, and the team as a whole. Keep the attention on facts and outcomes: what are the strengths and weaknesses of each? This focus keeps the discussion centered on what the team can control (as opposed to what is happening at headquarters or on another team).
5. **Follow the "Rules of Engagement."** To encourage honest participation and mutual trust, AARs must be: confidential (joint learning is shared, but individual comments are not), transparent, focused on individual and team improvement and development, and in preparation for "next time."
6. **Share learning across the organization.** Many organizations, including Huber and Microsoft, use databases or blogs to make the lessons of AARs available via Intranet to all of their teams. It is inefficient to withhold key learnings from other teams and allow them to make the same mistakes or prevent them from replicating best practices.
7. **Consider scheduling a Before Action Review (BAR)** prior to your next significant event. The team would benefit from a review of lessons learned and potential integration of these lessons into the new plan or performance standards.

Source: Todd Henshaw (2012) After Action Review

needed. Take the case of Mayor Ray Nagin from New Orleans during and after Katrina in 2005. He failed to lead when he should have acted on behalf of the public interest and later went to jail for receiving kickbacks on Katrina recovery projects (Brinkley, 2006; Waugh and Streib, 2006; Zucchino, 2014, Murphy and Perlstein 2014). Leadership can be the pivotal link in helping a community recover quickly. On the other hand, the lack of leadership can have the opposite effect by stalling recovery, mismanaging government funds, and causing community residents to suffer needlessly. Peter Drucker (2001) once said that leadership is not just about doing things right; it is about doing the right thing. There are many leaders that are very capable and can achieve much, but the question should always be asked, are they doing the right thing? A study of leadership and emergency management will find that leadership in public administration or, for that matter, many other fields, has some of the same concepts, principles, and guidance for potential leaders. Some of the traits and skills needed to lead are coordination, decisiveness, experience, goal orientation, communication, facilitation, the ability to handle stress, listening skills, open mindedness, responsibility, the capacity to prioritize, and the ability to think critically (Chandler, 2020). Many other scholars have offered similar lists with aptitudes and qualities because leadership is one character trait that can be taught and learned. Denhardt, Denhardt, Aristigueta, and Rawlings (2020) have five simple suggestions for those wanting to develop leadership skills:

- Examine the traits, skills, and commitments associated with leadership, and try to assess your own strengths and weaknesses.
- Learn about leadership by observation; study examples of leadership and excellence.
- Experiment with your own behavior. Practice using leadership skills in your daily life.
- Model important values. They play an important role in leadership in organizations.
- Assume leadership. Engage in leadership experiences. Become involved.

Leadership is sometimes canonized in the form of legal statutes. For instance, in Texas, as in most other states, the mayor of the city (or the mayor's designee) has the responsibility and is the key figure to lead in times of emergencies (Texas Government Code § 418.1015). Nevertheless, because many mayors are part-time and most often have other professions, the importance of staff such as a city manager becomes vital. The city manager has the real power in cities that have a council manager form of government and therefore must take a leadership role "behind the scenes" to provide the essential guidance to the political leaders who are in charge by state statute. In many cases the city manager hires an emergency management coordinator to carry out the day-to-day operations of emergency management (Texas Government Code § 418.1015). Establishing a proactive emergency management structure within a city will go a long way in securing the safety of the community. For instance, designating an emergency management coordinator (most often found in fire departments), establishing an emergency operation center (EOC), and a number of other proactive moves will show leadership in this area. This type of leadership, through state statutes, provides legal authority and in many cases is thrust upon the willing and unwilling. Therefore, it should be understood how it works, the limits of power, the charge, the obligation as an elected or appointed official, and the responsibility to the residents of the community.

Vulnerable Populations

There are various degrees of preparedness among the residents in any given community. Some of this preparation or lack thereof is by personal choice, for instance not to act or take precautionary steps. For example, having a 72-hour emergency kit or a tornado shelter (if in a tornado-prone area), or a designated place to meet family members if an emergency occurs are all optional. On the other hand, there are some segments of the population in our various communities that are vulnerable to disasters, not by any lack of preparedness on their part but because of various social determinants like income, lack of employment, health, education, housing, food insecurity, social exclusion, race, etc. (Mikkonen and Raphael, 2010; Fraser, 2013), which have placed them at a disadvantage from the start. Resourced communities are more resilient and better equipped to respond and recover from emergencies than socially vulnerable communities (Gaynor and Wilson, 2020). Public administration has a history of caring for the vulnerable and unrepresented (Frederickson, 2015). Martin-Howard and Farmbry (2020) note that "following questions about structural and social inequalities in the late 1960s and early 1970s, we have witnessed a half century of administrative considerations of issues of representation, inclusion, and distribution of resources as part of a broader exploration of enhanced quality of life for historically marginalized groups" (p. 839). Having this basic understanding of valuing all people, and having traveled down the road of social improvement, it was once again a shock, yet not unexpected, to see how pronounced the pandemic affected minority communities. COVID-19 has highlighted some of the deficiencies in our systems and the needs in many low-income communities that need to be addressed (Martin-Howard and Farmbry, 2020; Wright and Merritt, 2020). Therefore, it is essential to understand that these populations should not be overlooked, and future public administrators and emergency managers need to take responsibility to care for all residents, especially the socially vulnerable. Regardless of resident preparation and capacity, city leaders are under the obligation to help all residents.

CURRENT CHALLENGES

Among the many challenges facing public administration with respect to responding to disasters, combating terrorism, and the role of homeland security today, is the identity of what we call "emergency management" as a true field or discipline of study. It is not subservient to other fields as has been noted, and it can claim equal rights to a heritage back to the U.S. Constitution. Public administration through emergency management is capable of performing an essential function for the community. Practitioners, scholars, organizations, and community residents all recognize emergency management as a professional area of study. Therefore, it is among the many other professional fields, such as planning, finance, accounting, economic development, law, health, education, and public safety, to name a few, that serve the public and have the public interest at heart. Collectively, these fields are grouped together and intertwined with shared similarities to public administration. Although professionally different – because of their technical expertise – these fields need to learn to work with each other to solve problems that affect the whole community. For instance, during the Ebola outbreak in Dallas, Texas, in 2014, it was a challenge for public safety through their first responders – firefighters and police – to work with the health profession through their medical first responders

– nurses, doctors, and the Dallas county health officials (Soujaa et al., 2021; Benavides et al., 2017). This misunderstanding by professionals on how to address and resolve a pandemic emergency was troubling. Firefighters and police wanted to attack the problem as their professions teach, put the fire out or put them in jail. On the other hand, the medical first responders and county health department officials were busy conducting contact tracing and quarantining those suspected of having contact with the virus. The lack of communication and misunderstanding of the other's profession and expertise, and what skills they could bring to the table to fight the pandemic, was never really explored. Thus, it is evident that different disciplines have different ways, methods, and protocols for addressing disasters, calamities, or emergencies. Therefore, it is essential to reach out and understand the other disciplines in public administration and within the public sector that have the same goal of serving the community.

It is interesting to note that Patrick Roberts argues that "citizens, members of Congress, disaster managers, presidents, and the media inadvertently shape what counts as a disaster and how much responsibility the federal government has in addressing it" (2013, p. 176). Hence what gets categorized as a disaster, emergency, or catastrophe can be as broad or as limited as the public chooses to make it. Nevertheless, there are some fundamental challenges to the field today that should be noted. In 1985 William J. Petak wrote an article entitled "Emergency Management: A Challenge for Public Administration." In it, he listed eight challenges that are still very much relevant today. Although written in the 1980s, the statements provide an outline for considering challenges faced today. They are:

1. Policy Makers view other current problems as more pressing and important. There are insufficient advocates within the internal workings of legislative bodies, which results in a lack of political support and necessary resources.
2. Constituencies and advocacy groups supporting hazard management policy do not represent a powerful political force, except perhaps after a disaster occurs. Thus, legislation tends to be enacted in the immediate wake of a disaster, often under urgent circumstances and on the basis of incomplete information.
3. Political and/or economic costs are seen as disproportionate to the benefits of solving problems, thus deterring legislators from taking action.
4. Hazard problems are rife with complexity and uncertainty and are not necessarily responsive to conventional economic reality.
5. Technical and administrative capacities of local governments are limited in dealing with the complexity of the problems.
6. Intergovernmental and interorganizational complexity often leads to lack of coordinated response, distrust, and conflict.
7. Factual issues are not easily reconciled with social values and there is an inability in the regulatory process to integrate facts, values, and judgement due to the lack of critical information, the bias in factual judgements, and the liability of value judgements.
8. Increasing prospect of public liability resulting from a disaster is of increasing concern. Source William J. Petak (1985).

Another list that could be generated is one looking at challenges as types of disasters or emergencies. For instance, some view climate change as a challenge. Politics aside, the reality is that extreme weather events have been more frequent in recent years. Jane Bullock and George Haddow (2019) suggest that the capability and the capacity of our nation's emergency management system to respond to these more complex events is at a breaking point. The Federal Emergency Management Agency (FEMA), state and local emergency managers, voluntary agencies, and the business sector are doing their best to meet the increased demand required to respond to and recover from these extreme events. There is no such thing as a simple disaster anymore

(FEMA 2020 p. 1).

They go on to list enhancing community mitigation (or risk reduction) efforts as a second challenge and cybersecurity and an all-hazards approach as the third. On the latter, they note that there is nothing inherently wrong with an all-hazards approach except when overemphasis is placed on just one type of emergency such as nuclear attack planning or terrorism at the expense of other natural disasters. They also note the importance of preparing our IT systems against cyberattacks and ransom wear.

Society will continue to face challenges; how it responds to those challenges, how neighbors help neighbors, how governments work with residents, non-profits, the private sector, universities, and other levels of governments will mark the success it will have. The overall challenges are great; however, working together will accomplish the overall goal of being prepared for, responding to, and recovering from disasters.

RECOMMENDATIONS FOR THE FUTURE

In the coming years, how our society responds to emergencies will continue to be a main issue of concern. Emergencies, disasters, calamities, pandemics, and tragedies will continue to be faced by communities. How we prepare, mitigate, respond, and recover from these challenges will be the measure of how well our society prospers. Communicating in all its forms and variants is by far one of the most important undertakings that both public administrators and emergency managers need to consider. FEMA, universities, non-profits, and private organizations have all created, to one degree or another, "communication tips" to help individuals, organizations, and governments reach out to their constituents. Communicating the right information to the right people, at the right time, in the right place, and with the right medium is essential. The following suggestions are recommendations for how to appropriately communicate with others in emergency situations.

Eastern Kentucky University shares five communication tips to help public administrators succeed as emergency managers (Eastern Kentucky University 2020). They compile these steps by referencing various sources including FEMA's Continuity Resource Toolkit (FEMA 2018). They note the importance of making the message clear: keeping it simple, avoiding jargon, and providing background information. Second, they advise keeping the message consistent. The message should be provided by one voice to avoid miscommunication and repeated several times so it will sink in. Third, the message should be timely and recurring providing updates that may arise. This continual communication will help keep people calm. Fourth, they advise tracking social media. Here they suggest the importance of keeping up to date with the mediums available for communication. Various forms of social media can be ideal for communicating with large numbers of people in a timely manner. Checking social media as well can be vital to the emergency manager. Finally, they recommend carefully adopting the most appropriate medium and level of communication to reach the individuals affected, for instance, radio, TV, the Emergency Alert System, social media, text messaging, and AMBER Alerts depending on the emergency.

Another key recommendation is to avoid trying to lead on a solo basis. It is essential that a team is formed that can help respond to emergencies. The team is key in providing advice, expanding the network of contacts, and offering needed support and encouragement during times of crisis. ICMA has noted that the "manager cannot and should not try to lead a crisis alone or in isolation. The pre-crisis work with elected officials, with other city staff, and with the external relationships are all designed to build a team. The team provides mutual support among team members and permits appropriate delegation of tasks and diversity of perspectives" (2019, p. 38). Leadership before, during, and after an emergency is indispensable.

Cooperation and collaboration are other crucial areas that deserve attention. As most disasters are shared responsibilities involving a number of agencies in the response, as well as those individuals affected, learning how to share power and manage an incident with others is necessary. Pearce and Conger (2003) note that shared leadership is "a dynamic interactive influence process among individuals in groups in which the objective is to lead one another to their achievement of group or organizational goals" (p. 1). In other words, shared leadership can be found in various places within and without the organization. It "moves beyond the traditional model in which leadership is conceived around a single individual wielding power and influence in a unilateral and largely downward fashion. Shared leadership involves peer or lateral influence and at other times involves upward or downward influence" (Denhardt et al., 2020, 218–19). Much of the leadership theory and a current trend in public administration is collaboration, shared leadership, network governance, and in working with others to collectively accomplish a given task.

FEMA's strategic plan 2018–2022 outlines three ambitious goals that can also be seen as recommendations. These strategic initiatives are composed of the following elements:

1. To create or build a culture of preparedness in the country.
    1.1 Incentivize Investments that Reduce Risk, Including Pre-disaster Mitigation, and Reduce Disaster Costs at All Levels
    1.2 Close the Insurance Gap
    1.3 Help People Prepare for Disasters
    1.4 Better Learn from Past Disasters, Improve Continuously, and Innovate

2. To prepare or ready the nation for catastrophic disasters
    2.1 Organize the "BEST" (Build, Empower, Sustain, and Train) Scalable and Capable Incident Workforce
    2.2 Enhance Intergovernmental Coordination through FEMA Integration Teams
    2.3 Posture FEMA and the Whole Community to Provide Life-Saving and Life-Sustaining Commodities, Equipment, and Personnel from all Available Sources
    2.4 Improve Continuity and Resilient Communications Capabilities

3. To reduce the complexity of FEMA.
    3.1 Streamline the Disaster Survivor and Grantee Experience
    3.2 Mature the National Disaster Recovery Framework
    3.3 Develop Innovative Systems and Business Processes that Enable FEMA's Employees to Rapidly and Effectively Deliver the Agency's Mission
    3.4 Strengthen Grants Management, Increase Transparency, and Improve Data Analytics (FEMA 2021a)

Building a culture of preparedness, preparing the nation for another catastrophic disaster similar to or worse than the COVID-19 pandemic, and making it easier to work with FEMA are all achievable goals or worthy ambitions. These goals or recommendations for the nation are achievable and as each one is worked on, the nation will be the beneficiary.

Finally, one additional recommendation would be the importance of public administrators, city managers, department directors, line managers, supervisors – all those involved in local government administration – to recognize that disaster preparedness, mitigation, response, and recovery are functions of everyone's role and responsibility at the local level. City leaders need to understand that emergency management is not just a fire and police function. It is more than that. Leaders need to engage all key players in focusing more on proactive approaches (mitigation and preparedness) than simply reactive approaches (response and recovery). As public administrators embrace this broad-minded outlook, a collective cultural shift will occur (from "it is only the emergency manager's role" to "it is everyone's role in government." The country's past experience with the COVID-19 pandemic has made this very clear to everyone.

CONCLUSION

Governments may not be able to protect their residents from all catastrophes, especially those unknown calamities that await us in the future. However, they certainly can make real efforts in preparing the nation for disasters. This chapter looked at the history of public administration highlighting its connection to the U.S. Constitution. The reform movement via the Progressive Era was mentioned and the link that emergency management has to the Constitution. The National Incident Management System was explained and, in this context, how, within our federalist system, emergencies are viewed as local events. When local governments become overwhelmed and cannot respond on their own, they request assistance from the state government. At this point, if state resources are insufficient the federal government is called upon to provide necessary resources and funding. During this process, it was noted that the non-profit and private sectors are also involved in responding to emergencies. This assistance is extremely valuable in both the response and recovery phases.

Responding to and recovering from emergencies was also noted as was the importance of leadership. The various roles in public administration and emergency management/homeland security were examined such as mutual aid agreements, collaboration, vulnerable populations, business continuity, and after-action reports. The current challenges that confront both fields were considered with an emphasis on collaboration and shared leadership. Although it is not known when or where the next disaster will strike or how severe or intense it may be, what can be depended upon is the ability of the various forms of government through their public administrators and emergency managers to prepare their communities and nation.

CLASS DISCUSSION AND ESSAY QUESTIONS

1. What is public administration and why is this profession essential to a well-functioning government?
2. What is the relationship between public administration and emergency management? What unites these two professions in a common purpose?

3. This chapter reveals that governments will typically be required to work with neighboring jurisdictions or state and federal representatives. What are the advantages of these partnerships? What are the pitfalls? How can these challenges be overcome?

4. In 1985 William J. Petak wrote an article entitled "Emergency Management: A Challenge for Public Administration." He identified the challenges facing emergency management and public administration professionals. Are these still valid today? Why or why not? What can be done about them?

5. How can communication, collaboration, and coordination be improved in emergency management and public administration going forward?

REFERENCES

Agranoff, Robert (2006) Inside Collaborative Networks: Ten Lessons for Public Managers Special Issue. *Public Administration Review*, 66, 56–65.

American Society for Public Administration (ASPA) (2020) COVID-19 Public Service During a Pandemic. *PA Times*, 6(2). www.aspanet.org.

Association of State and Territorial Health Officials (Astho) (2021) *Mutual Aid and Assistance Agreements Fact Sheet*. Astho Legal Preparedness Series Emergency Authority & Immunity Toolkit. https://www.astho.org/Programs/Preparedness /Public-Health-Emergency-Law/Emergency-Authority-and-Immunity-Toolkit/ Mutual-Aid-and-Assistance-Agreements-Fact-Sheet/.

Auf der Heide, E. (1989) *Disaster Response: Principles of Preparation and Coordination*. Toronto, ON: C.V. Mosby Company.

Bahadori, Mahammadkarim, Hamid Reza Khaankeh, Rouhollah Zaboli, and Isa Mamir (2015) Coordination in Disaster: A Narrative Review. *International Journal of Medical Reviews*, 2(2), 273–281. https://www.researchgate.net/publication /291355963_coordination_in_disaster_a_narrative_review.

Benavides, Abraham David, Laura Keyes, David A. McEntire, and Erin Carlson (2017) The Logic of Uncertainty and Executive Discretion in Decision Making: The Dallas-Fort Worth Metroplex Ebola Response. *Journal of Public Management and Social Policy*, 24(1), 3–20.

Benavides, Abraham David, and Julius A. Nukpezah (2020) How Local Governments are Caring for the Homeless during the COVID-19 Pandemic. *American Review of Public Administration*, 1–8. https://doi.org/10.1177/0275074020942062.

Brinkkley, Douglas (2006) How New Orleans Drowned. *Vanity Fair June*. https://www .vanityfair.com/news/2006/06/brinkley_excerpt200606.

Brunsma, David, and J. Steven Picou (2008) Disasters in the Twenty-First Century: Modern Destruction and Future Instruction. *Social Forces*, 87(2), 983–991. https:// doi.org/10.1353/sof.0.0149.

Bryson, John M., Barbara C. Crosby, and Melissa Middleton Stone (2015) Designing and Implementing Cross-Sector Collaborations: Needed and Challenging. *Public Administration Review*, 75(5), 647–663.

Bullock, Jane, and George Haddow (2019) Challenges Facing Emergency Mangers Today. *Risk and Resilience HUB*. https://www.riskandresiliencehub.com/challenges-facing -emergency-managers-today/.

Chandler, Robert C. (2020) *The Marks of a Leader*. FEMA Training. www.FEMA.gov.

Chandra, Anita, Shaela Moen, and Clarissa Sellers (2016) What Role Does the Private Sector Have in Supporting Disaster Recovery, and What Challenges Does It Face in Doing So? Rand Corporation Objective Analysis Effective Solutions, Document Number PE-187-CCRMC. https://www.rand.org/pubs/perspectives/PE187.html.

Comfort, Louise K., Kilkon Ko, and Adam Zagorecki (2004) Coordination in Rapidly Evolving Disaster Response Systems: The Role of Information. *American Behavioral Scientist*, 48(3), 295–313.

Department of Homeland Security (2020) *Creation of the Department of Homeland Security.* https://www.dhs.gov/creation-department-homeland-security.

Denhardt, Robert B., Janet V. Denhardt, and Maria P. Aristigueta (2020) *Managing Human Behavior in Public and Nonprofit Organizations*, 5th ed. Los Angeles, CA: SAGE.

Doenecke, Justus D. (1981) *The Presidencies of James A. Garfield & Chester A. Arthur.* Lawrence, KS: University Press of Kansas, 95.

Drabek, Thomas E., and Gerard J. Hoetmer, editors (1991) The Evolution of Emergency Management. By Drabek. In *Emergency Management: Principles and Practice for Local Government.* Washington, DC: International City Management Association, pp. 3–29.

Drucker, Peter (2001) *The Essential Drucker: The Best of Sixty Years of Peter Drucker's Essential Writings on Management.* New York: Harper Collins.

Dwyer, Jim, and Kevin Flynn (2002) Fatal Confusion: A Troubled Emergency Response; 9/11 Exposed Deadly Flaws in Rescue Plan. *New York Times*, July 7, Section 1 Page 1.

Eastern Kentucky University (2020) *5 Communication Tips to Help Emergency Managers Succeed.* https://safetymanagement.eku.edu/blog/5-communication-tips-to-help-emergency-managers-succeed/

FEMA (2018) Continuity Resource Toolkit. https://www.fema.gov/emergency-managers/national-preparedness/continuity/toolkit#cgc.

FEMA (2020) Assistance for Governments and Private Non-Profits after a Disaster. https://www.fema.gov/assistance/public.

FEMA (2021a) FEMA Strategic Plan. https://www.fema.gov/sites/default/files/2020-07/strat_plan_2018-2022.pdf.

FEMA (2021b) History of FEMA. https://www.fema.gov/about/history.

FEMA (2022) https://www.fema.gov/about/history.

Fraser, Michael (2013) Bringing It All Together: Effective Maternal and Child Health Practice as a Means to Improve Public Health. *Maternal and Child Health Journal*, 17(5), 767–775.

Frederickson, George (2015) *Social Equity and Public Administration: Origins, Developments, and Application.* New York: Routledge.

Fry, Brian R., and Jos C. N. Raadschelders (2014) *Mastering Public Administration: From Max Weber to Dwight Waldo*, 3rd ed. Washington D.C.: CQ Press and Sage Publications Ltd.

Gaynor, Tia Sheree, and Meghan E. Wilson (2020) Social Vulnerability and Equity: The Disproportionate Impact of COVID-19. *Public Administration Review*, 80(5), 832–838.

Gladden, E. N. (2019) *A History of Public Administration Volume 1: From the Earliest Times to the Eleventh Century Routledge Revivals.* New York: Routledge Taylor and Francis Group.

Goss, Kay C. (2018) FEMA Challenges Ad Responses, 2017–2018. *Domestic Preparedness.* https://www.domesticpreparedness.com/resilience/fema-challenges-responses-2017-2018/.

Green, R. T., H. L. Schachter, M. W. Spicer, L. G. Nigro, W. D. Richardson, B. J. Cook, R. M. Cawley, R. A. Schuhmann, P. P. Van Riper, and L. Gulick (1998) Symposium: Essays on the History of Public Administration. *Administrative Theory and Praxis*, 20(1), 14–90.

Gurteen, David (2000) Introduction to After Action Reviews. *Gurteen*. Published January 2000. http://www.gurteen.com/gurteen/gurteen.nsf/id/aars-intro.

Henshaw, Todd (2012) After Action Reviews. *Nano Tool Management Wharton Work*, April. https://executiveeducation.wharton.upenn.edu/thought-leadership/wharton-at-work/2012/04/after-action-reviews/.

Homeland Security Presidential Directive-5 (2003) Management of Domestic Incidents. February 28, 2003. https://www.dhs.gov/publication/homeland-security-presidential-directive-5.

International City County Management Association (ICMA) (2019) Leadership and Professional Local Government Managers: Before, during, and after a Crisis, *ICMA Leading Edge Research*, Ron Carlee, Old Dominion University. https://icma.org/sites/default/files/19-117%20Crisis%20Leadership%20Report-FINAL.pdf

Jones, Ana Marie (2015) Promoting Cross-Sector Collaboration. *Regional Disaster Response Coordination to Support Health Outcomes: Summary of a Workshop Series, Institute of Medicine*. https://doi.org/10.17226/21713.

Karl, Barry D. (1976) Public Administration and American History: A Century of Professionalism. *Public Administration Review*, 36(5), 489–503.

Kalthoff, Ken (2020) Dallas Buys Quarantine Hotels. *5 NBCDFW News*, December 9, 2020.

Llorens, Jared J., Donald E. Klingner, and John Nalbandian (2018) *Public Personnel Management: Contexts and Strategies*, 7th ed. New York: Routledge.

Larson, Richard C., Michael D. Metzger, and Michael F. Cahn (2006) Responding to Emergencies: Lessons Learned and the Need for Analysis. *Journal of Applied Analytics*, 36(6), 483–635.

Lloyd, Tho (1894) The First Charter of the City of Philadelphia, 1691. *The Pennsylvania Magazine of History and Biography*, 18(4), 504–509.

Long, Richard (2017) What Is Business Continuity? – Business Continuity 101. *MHA Consulting*. https://www.mha-it.com/2017/08/01/what-is-business-continuity/.

Luton, Larry S. (1999) History and American Public Administration. *Administration and Society*. https://doi.org/10.1177%2F00953999922019094.

Lynn, Laurence E. (1996) *Public Management as Art, Science, and Profession*. Chatham, N.J.: Chatham House Publishers, Inc.

Martin-Howard, Simone, and Kyle Farmbry (2020) Framing a Needed Discourse on Health Disparities and Social Inequities: Drawing Lessons from a Pandemic. *Public Administration Review*, 80(5), 839–844.

McEntire, David A. (2018) Learning More about the Emergency Management Professional. FEMA Higher Education Program. https://training.fema.gov/hiedu/docs/latest/dave_mcentire_learning_about_emergency_m anagement_professional.pdf.

McEntire, David A. (2002) Coordinating Multi-Organizational Responses to Disasters: Lessons from the March 28, 2000 Fort Worth Tornado. *Disaster Prevention and Management*, 11(5), 369–379.

McGuire, Michael (2006) Collaborative Public Management: Assessing What We Know and How We Know It, Special Issues. *Public Administration Review*, 66(s1), 33–43.

Mikkonen, Juha, and Dennis Raphael (2010) *Social Determinants of Health: The Canadian Facts, York University, School of Health Policy and Management*. https://thecanadianfacts.org/.

Murphy, Paul, and Mike Perlstein (2014) *Ex-New Orleans Mayor Ray Nagin Sentenced to 10 Years*. New Orleans, LA: WWL-TV. https://www.usatoday.com/story/news/nation/2014/07/09/ray-nagin-new-orleans-mayor-sentencing/12397415/.

National Incident Management System (2017) Third Edition, October, FEMA. https://www.fema.gov/sites/default/files/2020-07/fema_nims_doctrine-2017.pdf.

Nukpezah, Julius A. (2017) The Financial and Public Health Emergencies in Flint, Michigan: Crisis Management and the American Federalism. *Risks, Hazards & Crisis in Public Policy*, 8(4), 284–311.

Organization for Economic Cooperation and Development Smarter Local Economic Development, OECD Better Policies for Better Lives. https://www.oecd.org/cfe/leed/local-development.htm.

Pappas, Stephanie, and Tiffany Means (2020) Top 10 Deadliest Natural Disasters in History: Reminding Us How Powerful Mother Nature Is. *Live Science*. https://www.livescience.com/33316-top-10-deadliest-natural-disasters.html.

Pearce, C. L., and J. A. Conger (2003) *Shared Leadership*. Thousand Oaks, CA: Sage.

Pendleton Act of 1883, Public Law 47–27. *US Statutes at Large* (1883), 22, 403–407.

Petak, Williams J. (1985) Emergency Management: A Challenge for Public Administration. *Public Administration Review*, 45, 3–7.

Phillips, Brenda D. (2015) *Disaster Recovery*, 2nd ed. Boca Raton, Florida: CRC Press Taylor & Francis Group, LLC.

Public Affairs Council Private Sector Stepping Up During Disasters. *Impact*. https://pac.org/impact/private-sector-steps-disaster-response.

Quarantelli, E. L. (1998) The Disaster Recovery Process: What We Do and Do Not Know from Research. Disaster Research Center. http://udspace.udel.edu/handle/19716/309.

Raadschelders, J. N. (1997) The Progress of Civil Society: A 19th Century American History of Governments. *Administration and Society*, 29(4), 471–489.

Raadschelders Jos, C. N., and Richard Stillman (2017) *Foundations of Public Administration*. Irvine, California: Melvin & Leigh Publishers.

Roberts, Patrick S. (2013) *Disasters in the American State: How Politicians, Bureaucrats, and the Public Prepare for the Unexpected*. New York: Cambridge University Press.

Rossiter, Clinton ed., (1961) *The Federalist Papers, Library of Congress* https://guides.loc.gov/federalist-papers/full-text

Schroeder, Aaron, Gary L. Wamsley, and Robert Ward (2001) The Evolution of Emergency Management in America: From a Painful Past to a Promising but Uncertain Future. Chapter 24. In Ali Farazmand (ed.), *Handbook of Crisis and Emergency Management*, pp. 357–418.

Soujaa, Ismail, Julius Nukpezah, and Abraham David Benavides (2021) Coordination Effectiveness during Public Health Emergencies: An Institutional Collective Action Framework, *Administration & Society*, 1–2. https://doi.org/10.1177/0095399720985440.

Starling, Grover (2011) *Managing the Public Sector*, 9th ed. Belmont, California: Thomson Wadsworth.

Stillman, R. J. (Ed.) (1989) *The American Constitution and the Administrative State: Constitutionalism in the Late 20th Century*. New York: University Press of America.

Team Rubicon Disaster Response. https://teamrubiconusa.org.

Texas Government Code § 418.1015. https://statutes.capitol.texas.gov/Docs/GV/htm/GV.418.htm.

Upstate Medical University (2021) Emergency Management, Four Phases of Emergency Management. https://www.upstate.edu/emergencymgt/about/phases.php.

Urby, Heriberto, and David A. McEntire (2013) Applying Public Administration in Emergency Management: The Importance of Integrating Management into Disaster Education. *Journal of Homeland Security and Emergency Management*, 11(1), 39–60. https://www.researchgate.net/deref/http%3A%2F%2Fdx.doi.org%2F10.1515%2Fjhsem-2013-0060.

U.S. Chamber of Commerce Foundation (2021) Descriptions of Nonprofits Working in Disasters. https://www.uschamberfoundation.org/corporate-citizenship-center/descriptions-nonprofits-working-disasters.

Van Fenema, Paul C., A. Georges, and L. Romme (2020) Latent Organizing for Responding to Emergencies: Foundations for Research. *Journal of Organization Design*, 9 (11). https://doi.org/10.1186/s41469-020-00074-z

Van Riper, Paul P. (1958) *History of the United States Civil Service*. Evanston, IL: Row, Peterson and Company, 60–61

Voluntary Organizations Active in Disasters VOAD. https://www.nvoad.org.

Waldo, D. (1984) *The Administrative State*, 2nd ed. New York: Holmes and Meier.

Waugh, William L. Jr. (2000) *Living with Hazards, Dealing with Disasters: An Introduction to Emergency Management*. Armonk, NY: M.E. Sharpe.

Waugh, William L. Jr., and Gregory Streib (2006) Collaboration and Leadership for Effective Emergency Management. *Public Administration Review*, 66(1), 131–140.

Wise, Charles R. (1993) Public Administration Is Constitutional and Legitimate. *Public Administration Review*, 53(3), 257–261.

Wright, James E., and Cullen C. Merritt (2020) Social Equity and COVID-19: The Case of African Americans. *Public Administration Review*, 80(5), 820–826.

Zeger Van der Wal (2020) Being a Public Manager in Times of Crisis: The Art of Managing Stakeholders, Political Masters, and Collaborative Networks, *Public Administration Review* 80(5). https://doi.org/10.1111/puar.13245

Zucchino, David (2014) C. Ray Nagin, Former New Orleans Mayor, Sentences to 10 Years in Prison. *Los Angeles Times*. https://www.latimes.com/nation/nationnow/la-na-nn-ray-nagin-new-orleans-sentenced-20140709-story.html.

CHAPTER 8

Public Information Officer Functions in Emergency Management:
Operating in Good Times and Bad

John R. Fisher

Effective emergency response depends on communication – the ability to maintain situational awareness through the constant flow of information.

(FEMA IS-700.b, 2020, p. 172)

INTRODUCTION

During Hurricane Katrina, communications systems failed. The breakdown of communications continued after the storm, impeding information flow and response and recovery operations. In New Orleans, where most of the city was flooded, the combined effects of wind, rain, storm surge, breached levees, and flooding knocked out virtually the entire infrastructure – electrical power, roads, water supply, and sewage. Communications systems were also severely impacted.

Thomas Stone, who was the Fire Chief in St. Bernard Parish, stated, "We lost our communications system, and when you are not able to communicate, you can't coordinate your response. You never think that you will lose your entire infrastructure" (FEMA IS-700.b, 2020, p. 172). When those involved in post-disaster operations lose their ability to communicate, at that point the human factor – the public information officer (PIO) – becomes crucial to the success of emergency management. The PIO is the bridge that keeps the public informed and safe.

This review of the role of public information officers in emergency management examines the history of public information and PIOs, their involvement in disasters and terrorism, and their functions and operations in emergency management. The chapter concludes by describing current issues related to PIOs and making recommendations.

DOI: 10.4324/9781003350729-8

HISTORY OF PUBLIC INFORMATION AND
PUBLIC INFORMATION OFFICERS

This section provides a brief history of the use of public information by government. It differentiates public affairs from public relations. It also covers a short history from the Civil War to the present.

To understand public information, it is necessary to comprehend how it relates to public relations and public affairs. While public relations promotes a company to the public, public affairs relates to sharing information that affects the public directly, like legislation, safety messages, or utility services (Hawin, 2016). The distinction is in terms of whether the information is commercial or not.

In other words, public relations is used in the implementation of marketing and product campaigns and is often viewed as an extension of advertising. Although companies can be involved in public affairs, if the information is service-oriented, the term "public affairs" is most often reserved for government agencies and the military.

In the realm of public affairs, public affairs officer is often used interchangeably with public information officer (PIO), although the latter term is used more often in emergency services agencies. The term "spokesperson" is also used, although a spokesperson could also be a company or organization's executive officer or a government agency's elected official. Spokespeople may be elected or appointed by a group of people to represent them on issues of importance.

Spokespeople have existed as long as there have been disasters and a need to share information. The prophets of the Old and New Testaments were considered oracles. There were others who warned the citizens of Greece and Rome of impending doom. Over time, many leaders of government shared information with their respective citizens.

For instance, Mitchell (2020) describes how the Lincoln administration used public information deception to persuade the public to support conscription in the Civil War. In World War I, U.S. President Wilson formed the Committee on Public Information with the goal to influence American opinion toward the war effort in Europe. Edward Bernays joined the Committee on Public Effort and, as a member of the Foreign Press Bureau, helped develop propaganda to destroy the morale of the enemy. While Ivy Lee was the first to open a public relations agency after World War I, Bernays is given credit in the interim period between the wars for developing the principles and concepts that guided public relations. Bernays and Lee took PR from the publicity model of P.T. Barnum to a two-way model of communication where both organizations and the public benefit (Bernays, 1972; Basen, 2014).

Propaganda rose to new heights during World War II. Historian Bruce Catton, who served as a public information officer from 1941 to 1948, coined the phrase "government by public relations" (Lee, 2009, p. 389). Catton condemned Washington's preoccupation with public relations because its goal was to make government look good rather than doing the right thing. Catton told of how government lied about closing down night life, not because the country needed to conserve energy, but because government wanted to "impose 'sacrifices' on the public at home, to arouse public emotion and help shape public psychology" (Lee, 2009, p. 389). Catton denounced public relations in government, indicating that the "PR-ization" of government and politics has led to a lack of citizen confidence in government. Public information officers should not be "press agents" for government but rather channels of information (Lee, 2009, pp. 391, 393).

In 1913, as a result of a controversy over administration of forest rights, the Gillett Amendment was attached to the Deficiency Appropriation Act, stating, "Appropriated funds may not be used to pay a publicity expert unless specifically appropriated for that purpose." The next effort to restrict government use of publicity was in the early 1970s during the Vietnam War and Watergate scandal when legislation further limited the use of government money for publicity, propaganda, or to influence congressional legislation. According to Taylor and Kent (2016), these measures restrict the ability of public information officers at the federal level to do their jobs. The result is information chaos that does little to encourage trust in government or foster public engagement.

In 1950 with the advent of the Federal Civil Defense Administration, the U.S. government began an all-out public information campaign to prepare for the eventuality of atomic warfare. School children drilled on how to "duck-and-cover" to save their lives if a blast occurred. While these measures may have reduced American anxiety about war, in actuality they would have been of little value in an actual conflict where atomic weapons were used (Pruitt, 2019; Jacobs, 2010). Training is given today to prepare students for a possible active school shooting or terrorist attack (Blad, 2018).

In 1979, in response to the growing need to manage disasters, President Carter established the Federal Emergency Management Agency (FEMA), which had a dual mission of emergency management and civil defense. Public information officers were assigned and had an integral role in preparing and keeping communities safe during disasters (FEMA, 2021).

Prior to 2001, emergency management and public information officers focused on preparing the public for natural disasters. After the attacks on September 11, 2001, the focus turned toward terrorist attacks. In 2002, President George W. Bush signed the Homeland Security Act, and FEMA became part of the Department of Homeland Security. Then in 2005, Hurricane Katrina hit New Orleans and surrounding areas, resulting in more than 1,800 deaths. It was ranked as the costliest natural disaster in U.S. history. An all-hazards approach was adopted that considered both natural and human-caused disasters. These changes required adaptation and a greater role for PIOs in preparedness and protection as well as emergency response. With the introduction of the National Incident Management System (NIMS) in 2004, public information became enshrined as one of the principal functions of disaster response (FEMA, n.d.; FEMA, 2016).

PUBLIC INFORMATION OFFICERS IN DISASTERS AND AFTER TERRORIST ATTACKS

Blue skies versus grey skies are figures of speech used by emergency responders to describe conditions for preparation and response to disasters. Under blue skies, response agencies prepare for those days when grey skies bring disasters. In these normal times, PIOs work with the media to provide the public with information that they can use to mitigate against hazards and to prepare for future disasters. FEMA claims that 95% of a PIO's work is conducted in non-emergency times, and 5% of time and effort is directly related to disasters (FEMA IS-0029, 2020, p. 2).

How true is the 95/5 rule for PIOs? Do PIOs actually spend only two weeks per year working in crisis mode? The answer depends on which agency the PIO works for. PIOs for larger police or fire departments may be in front of the cameras multiple times per week. However, many small emergency management departments for counties and cities may have only one person in the emergency management position, who also serves as PIO. In other situations, the PIO role may be carried out by a part-time person who works also as a police or fire officer or by someone else from the county or city administration. In these situations, the 95/5 rule likely applies.

PIOs are busiest during crises. In fact, their work schedule becomes hectic. While it is difficult during planning and preparedness stages to get news media coverage, in a disaster the press demands for information are enormous and continuous. The 95/5 rule is reversed. Most news coverage happens during disasters. In contrast, it may be difficult to get any coverage during the planning and preparedness stage.

During a disaster or terrorist attack, PIOs provide information to keep the public informed so they can protect themselves and take other necessary action. Under the direction of government officials, PIOs provide information about evolving events to the public through the press and social media. They also share information about what the government is doing to respond to the incident.

The following case studies provide a sense from the PIO's point of view of the lessons learned and the pressures faced in disaster situations. In the first case, Francisco Sanchez, Harris County Texas PIO, explains lessons he learned from being a PIO during Hurricanes Katrina and Rita. In the second case, Karen Takai describes the pressures she faces as a Type 1 disaster PIO. The third describes how PIOs handled the 2015 San Bernardino terrorist attack.

Hurricane Katrina

When Hurricane Katrina struck New Orleans on August 29, 2005, government was unprepared from the local level to the federal level. Over 1,200 people died as a result. After being criticized by the public, the media, and legislators, FEMA conducted its own study of mistakes made during the disaster response. The report describes manpower problems, a lack of focus on natural disasters, and confusion by officials in responding to the disaster (Ahlers, 2006).

"Katrina was the first time I managed a joint information center," says Sanchez. "Up to that time, that was probably the largest joint information center we'd ever established along the Gulf Coast. A lot of lessons came out of there, and the biggest is we need to communicate to the public not just what they need to know, but what they want to know."

While Sanchez had an excellent working relationship with the media in Houston and Harris County, for the first time he had to face a hostile media covering Hurricane Katrina. Outside the Astrodome was a satellite city of media trucks and reporters.

It was a unique challenge to face the media that based on what they were experiencing in New Orleans, came in with an adversarial attitude, and really they were advocating for the public because the public was demanding to know who was doing something right.... We had to prove to the media and public that we were doing something at the Astrodome to respond and help our neighbors. So we opened up the doors to the Astrodome and let the media come in and talk to the evacuees. The world got to see that someone was doing it right and evacuees were getting the help they needed.

So the biggest takeaway was it's not enough to say, "Here's what you need to know." Let's understand what the public wants to hear and see – and they want to hear and see that someone is taking it seriously, that we're doing the best we can with the resources we have.

The second takeaway was that we needed an advocate for the joint information center concept. We operated a 24/7 joint operation center that probably never had fewer than 20 people staffing a shift. Since then we have gone from having to do that on the fly to having one of the most robust capabilities of doing regional emergency public information.

(McKay, 2013)

The Yarnell Fire

The Yarnell Fire 30 miles outside Prescott, Arizona, quickly became a Type 1 disaster when the fire overran and killed 19 wildland firefighters. Before the deaths, the fire was like many wildland fires; it didn't merit a news story. Within hours following their deaths, the fire had become an international story. As reporters besieged the small town, the fire continued to rage from 300 to 8,300 acres, causing the evacuation of Yarnell and Peeples Valley. In addition to the lives lost, the fire had destroyed 127 buildings in Yarnell and two in Peeples Valley.

In the midst of an incident, all decisions have to be made quickly. Sometimes it seems like anything that can go wrong will go wrong, says Karen Takai (2014). She describes what it is like to be lead PIO for the Type I Southwest Incident Management Team. By the time Takai gets into the field on a major event, she has 125 messages. She hands her cell phone off to an assistant PIO who screens calls and takes the most pressing requests.

Phones, electricity, and water systems are down and chaos is everywhere. The sheriff is evacuating communities and directing evacuees to shelters that have not yet been set up. Members of the media are showing up everywhere, and rangers are calling me to get someone to corral them. The situation is still in the initial attack phase – and I have only three staff members.

(Takai, 2014, p. 25)

Takai asserts that she was given a call center with 25 phones. "After a day of angry cellphone calls, I check with the center manager and he or she finds out that only six phone lines are working" (Takai, 2014, p.26). People are complaining that they can't get through. She sends emails with releases to update agencies, the media, the local community, and Washington, DC, administrators, but many don't go through because of software limitations.

Calls come in from the Members of Congress, the State's Governor, Washington, DC, administrators, and a multitude of others. Needless to say, not all are happy about response time and the level of information being forwarded. Again, the outside world is plugged into a multitude of different social media formats, their electricity and cell phones are working, and everyone wants information immediately. Unfortunately, Takai comments that they do not have electricity, phones, and social media at their fingertips.

PIOs are continually trying to play catch up. Takai soon found out that to meet social media demands, the social media PIO needs to work outside the event area so access to the Internet is not hampered by failed technology at the event.

San Bernardino Terrorist Attack

On the morning of December 2, 2015, two terrorists – a man and a woman – attacked 80 employees of the San Bernardino County health department, who were attending a training and a Christmas party. The attackers killed 14 people and wounded 22 others before fleeing in their SUV. Four hours later they were stopped and killed in a shoot-out with police. Soon after the initial shooting, the press started arriving on the scene (Braziel et al., 2016).

While the two police officers assigned part-time to public affairs at the San Bernardino Police Department had reported on serious crimes, they had never been spokespeople for a national story of such significance as the terrorism shootings at the Inland Regional Center on December 2, 2015. Back-up PIO Vicki Cervantes was the first to arrive at the scene of the attacks. Before long, she was dealing with 70–80 reporters. The lead PIO was on vacation.

The three members of the county police's public affairs office arrived at the designated media staging area, where they saw Cervantes surrounded by reporters. They set up a Joint Information Center at the county Emergency Operations Center, where office staff started answering calls from all over the world. They used the county's interactive electronic screen so that updated information could be seen from every desk. This assured that only acceptable information was released to the public. Media coverage was monitored on four 55-inch televisions.

Because rumors were rampant, a decision was made to include the PIOs in all command-level briefings and strategy meetings. The PIOs received reliable up-to-the-moment information and were able to provide input. Brittany Rios, who had joined the county PIOs office in 2014, handled social media. She sent her first tweet at 11:18 a.m. about street closures. Eight minutes later she sent out a tweet confirming an active shooter incident. By the end of the day, she had sent out 42 posts, providing the mass media and public with valuable and immediate information. Because of the close cooperation with police officials, she was always informed and able to pre-prepare information. When the information was released, she immediately tweeted the updates.

Local politicians asked what they should say if the media called. They were advised by the county's community liaison to not comment, but to let police officials release any information. Because of good relationships with the police, most did as they were asked. The major problem PIOs faced was the speed at which the incident was moving and the pressing demands of the media. A 1-800 number was only set up later to answer public calls for information because of all that was happening. Although the incident ended after four hours, the JIC was kept in operation for two days.

NIMS, ESFs, and Public Information Goals and Structures

This section describes some of the changes in how PIOs respond during disasters in terms of the introduction of the National Incident Management System (NIMS) and the role of public information officers within it. It also explores the relationship of public information to the Joint Information System (JIS), Incident Command System (ICS), Emergency Operation Centers (EOCs), and the Joint Information Center (JIC).

The National Incident Management System was adopted in March 2004, as a part of Presidential Directive-5 by George W. Bush. The system is administered by the Federal Emergency Management Agency. According to FEMA, "the National Incident Management System (NIMS) provides a systematic, proactive approach to guide departments and agencies at all levels of government, non-governmental organizations, and the private sector to work seamlessly to prevent, protect against, respond to, recover from, and mitigate the effects of incidents, regardless of cause, size, location or complexity, in order to reduce the loss of life and property and harm to the environment" (FEMA IS-0029, 2020, pp. 4–5).

NIMS is a national approach that applies to all jurisdictions at all levels of government. It is comprehensive because it is usable across all functions of government. It is designed to fit a "full spectrum" of hazards and incidents regardless of size, location, or complexity. It is meant to improve coordination and cooperation between the public and private sectors on a variety of emergency management activities. And, it provides a "common standard" for incident management (FEMA, n.d., p. 1).

Public information is a key consideration in NIMS. It is "the processes, procedures, and systems to communicate timely, accurate, and accessible information on the incident's cause, size, and current situation to the public, responders, and additional stakeholders (both directly and indirectly affected)." Public information is coordinated and integrated across all jurisdictions and organizations involved in incidents. These include local, state, and federal governments, private businesses, and non-profits.

Aside from NIMS, FEMA has organized emergency support functions (ESFs) into 15 areas, known as the ESF 15. Function #5 is designated as the Information and Planning Annex. As part of this function, information is gathered, analyzed, processed, and disseminated about potential hazards or actual incidents. Communication plans support the emergency operation plans for all response activities for the whole community. Messages are developed to inform the public of ongoing emergency services, protective measures, and other life-sustaining actions that facilitate recovery (FEMA, 2019).

One of the goals of NIMS and ESF 15 is to ensure that a Joint Information System is promoted. This, in turn, requires a lot of collaboration between Public Information Officers who work in the Incident Command System, Emergency Operations Centers, and the Joint Information Center.

The Joint Information System

The Joint Information System is an extremely important command and coordination objective. It "integrates incident information and public affairs into a unified organization that provides consistent, coordinated, accurate, accessible, timely, and complete information to the public and stakeholders during incident operations" (FEMA IS-700.b, 2020, p. 154).

While communication failure is often a result of the failure or destruction of infrastructure, it can also occur because communication systems among agencies and jurisdictions are incompatible. Such was the case in the World Trade Center on 9/11, when police heard the command to evacuate but firefighters did not because of incompatibility or failure of communication systems. Of the 412 emergency workers who died, 343 were firefighters, 37 were police officers of the port authority, and 23 were New York City police officers.

NIMS recommends that public safety communications and information systems need to be interoperable, reliable, scalable, portable, resilient, redundant, and secure. Interoperable means the system is able to communicate within and across agencies and jurisdictions. Reliable systems function in any kind of emergency. Scalable means the equipment can be used in any size of incident. Portable equipment should be built using standardized technology and frequencies. The equipment is resilient if it is able to perform when damaged or infrastructure fails. It is redundant if alternate communication methods are available when the primary systems go out. It is secure if it protects sensitive or classified information. The equipment is not only important for communicating among first responders, but it is also used for gathering and disseminating incident information. In a crisis situation, life-and-death decisions depend on the information.

While it is important to ensure that communications technology works, it is not the only JIS activity. Other activities include (a) developing and delivering coordinated inter-agency messages; (b) developing, recommending, and executing public information plans and strategies; (c) advising on public affairs issues that could affect the incident manage-ment effort; and (d) addressing and managing rumors and providing accurate informa-tion (FEMA IS-700.b, 2020, p. 155).

PIOs also serve in the Joint Information Center as part of the Joint Information System. The Joint Information Center is attached to the Emergency Operations Center.

Incident Command System

The command component of NIMS provides a flexible, standardized incident manage-ment structure that includes the Incident Command System. Originating in the 1970s during massive wildfire-fighting operations in California, the Incident Command System has a number of benefits that impact incident management. It clarifies chain of command and supervision responsibilities, and improves accountability. It also improves communi-cation by using interoperable communications systems and plain language. ICS provides an orderly, systematic planning process and fosters cooperation between diverse disci-plines and agencies. It not only provides an organizational structure, but also allows for planning, building, and adapting that structure.

ICS has been called a "first-on-scene" structure, because the first responder on the scene takes charge until the situation is resolved, a more experienced responder arrives, or the Incident Commander asks someone else to take over. The Incident Commander has responsibility for the overall management of the incident. A command staff usually supports the management function, although in small incidents, the incident commander may manage the event without other command staff.

Figure 8.1 shows the basic Incident Command structure:

Because the Incident Command System is flexible, it allows for coordinated and collaborative incident management, where additional resources are required and pro-vided from numerous organizations within a single jurisdiction or outside jurisdic-tions. Cross-jurisdictional coordination and common processes and systems such as ICS are important when an incident requires response from many local emergency management and response agencies. It provides for more complex incidents that affect a region or the whole nation, as in the Deepwater Horizon oil spill in 2010. The use of ICS is applicable to all types of incidents, regardless of their size or cause (FEMA IS-0029, 2020). ICS has also been used to manage planned events, like the 2002 Olympics in Salt Lake City.

Depending on the nature of the incident or disaster, the command staff may expand to include safety, information, and liaison personnel. In an incident, the PIO, with his or her special training and skills, could be assigned to work in a number of positions. The PIO could be assigned to work as an interagency liaison or information officer as part of the Incident Command Staff.

Information therefore plays a significant role in the Incident Command System. For instance, the ICS 300 training course lists the following responsibilities for the Information Officer:

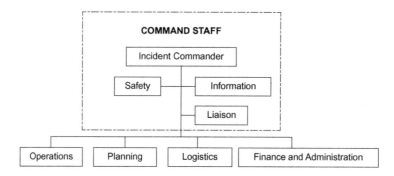

FIGURE 8.1.   Incident Command Structure System

- Determine, according to direction from the Incident Commander (IC), any limits on information release.
- Develop accurate, accessible, and timely information for use in press/media briefings.
- Obtain IC's approval of news releases.
- Conduct periodic media briefings.
- Arrange for tours and other interviews or briefings that may be required.
- Monitor and forward media information that may be useful to incident planning.
- Maintain current information, summaries, and/or displays on the incident.
- Make information about the incident available to incident personnel.
- Participate in planning meetings (FEMA-ICS300, 2018).

Liaison Officer responsibilities also include:

- Act as a point of contact for agency representatives.
- Maintain a list of assisting and cooperating agencies and agency representatives.
- Assist in setting up and coordinating interagency contacts.
- Monitor incident operations to identify current or potential interorganizational problems.
- Participate in planning meetings, providing current resource status, including limitations and capabilities of agency resources.
- Provide agency-specific demobilization information and requirements (FEMA-ICS300, 2018).

Emergency Operations Center

Emergency Operations Centers are off-site locations where staff from multiple agencies coordinate support or resources for incident command. Not all communities will have an operating EOC during normal times, although if there is an emergency manager, he or she will likely work out of the EOC. The emergency manager works with all agencies or organizations, government, non-profit, or private, involved in the planning, preparation, protection, and prevention of hazards.

When partially activated, the EOC may be monitoring a credible threat, risk, or hazard and asked to support the response needs of an incident commander. When fully activated, the EOC, including personnel from a variety of public, private, and non-profit agencies supports the response to a major incident.

While the purpose, authorities, and composition may vary widely, EOCs generally perform the following functions:

- Collecting, analyzing and sharing information;
- Supporting resource needs and requests, including allocation and tracking;
- Coordinating plans and determining current and future needs; and
- In some cases, providing coordination and policy direction (FEMA IS-700.b, 2020).

Elected officials may be present in the EOC. They may serve as the spokespeople or faces of the response. They are assisted by PIOs.

Joint Information Center

During a larger disaster event, a Joint Information Center is set up – often in or around the Emergency Operations Center. It is a physical centralized location that includes representatives of affiliated agencies, local jurisdictions, government partners, private sector parties, and non-government agencies, which work together to coordinate and support communication needs for the media and public. Members of the JIC (including PIOs and volunteers) respond to public inquiries, issue emergency advisories, monitor the media and social media, and control false rumors (Hughes and Palen, 2012).

PUBLIC INFORMATION OFFICER FUNCTIONS

Whether part of NIMS, ESF 15, JIS, ICS, EOC, or the JIC, the Public Information Officer performs vital roles when a disaster occurs. According to FEMA, "PIOs in public safety and emergency management organizations are responsible for ensuring that the affected public receives accurate and timely information during an emergency" (FEMA IS-0029, 2020, p. 1).

Many PIOs worked in the media before coming to an emergency agency. They bring with them the experience and education of journalism and their contacts. When they begin working for government agencies, they change loyalties although they continue to maintain previous working relationships. Much of their knowledge and skill is learned on the job from experience. In smaller jurisdictions, the PIO may also do unrelated work in addition to public relations, such as administrative tasks or part-time policing or fire training.

PIO functions are therefore many and diverse, and may include:

- Providing emergency warnings and public information.
- Advising the Incident Commander or EOC director on public information matters.
- Gathering, verifying, coordinating, and disseminating accurate, accessible, and timely information.
- Handling inquiries from the media, public, and elected officials.
- Conducting rumor monitoring and response.

In addition, PIOs may be involved in intergovernmental (local, state, tribal, and territorial) affairs, congressional affairs, and private sector outreach.

The main duty of a PIO is to convey accurate and timely details about emergency situations to the press, the general public, and any other individuals or groups impacted directly or indirectly. Additionally, they are responsible for keeping an eye on the public information landscape during a crisis, dispelling untrue rumors, and rectifying any misinformation. As a valuable part of a community's emergency management team by providing relevant and timely information, PIOs can greatly influence the media's coverage of an incident. Press stories generated by the PIO may provide critical information that will save and protect lives (Mangeri, 2016). Because of PIOs, "people can make better decisions that contribute to the overall response goal of saving lives and protecting property" (FEMA IS-0029, 2020, p. 1).

Because of these important roles, the PIO should be called up immediately when a disaster happens. The first information (often in a press release) should go out to the media within the first hour of the incident. Through the press and social media, the public is informed of key information like the threat, the size, and the scope of the incident so they can take appropriate actions to keep themselves safe (Mangeri, 2016). In addition, websites and other social media should be updated.

The jurisdiction should also create a communication plan that includes draft news releases, media lists, and contact information for elected officials and community leaders, private sector organizations, and non-profit organizations. Getting information to the public and stakeholders as part of the communications plan means PIOs work an ongoing information cycle. First, they gather and verify information, ensuring it is complete and accurate. They coordinate the gathering and sharing of information with other public information personnel who are part of the local organization or in other agencies or jurisdictions. Finally, as part of the cycle, they disseminate timely, accurate, and complete information to the public and stakeholders. The information PIOs disseminate could include lifesaving measures like evacuation routes (FEMA IS-700.b, 2020, pp. 157–158).

As can be imagined, one person serving as the PIO is not sufficient for managing media and public requests for information, particularly for larger incidents. It's important to have an adequate staffing level to manage requests and to ensure that all personnel have a common operating picture and understand the expectations of them during an incident. All stakeholders – public and private – should have the same information about the incident so they can make informed decisions based on the community's needs and available resources (Mangeri, 2016). This is the overarching objective of the PIO.

Besides having a sufficient number of PIOs, it is also imperative that they are knowledgeable and trained. The Federal Emergency Management Agency provides a number of resources that give general information and guidance for PIOs, including FEMA's Basic Guidance for Public Information Officers (FEMA-517, 2007) and courses offered locally or at the Emergency Management Institute in Emmitsburg, Maryland. State and federal government offer courses for PIOs that include NIMS training, as well as learning about the role, function, and skills required to be a Public Information Officer (Hughes and Palen, 2012). Many steps to improve public information can and must be taken before and after disasters occur.

Before the Incident

Before the incident, according to Mangeri (2016), PIOs assist with outreach activities such as:

- programs designed to educate the public about local threats, hazards, and potential mitigation techniques.

- development of materials that promote family or business preparedness, mitigation strategies that are targeted to the community based on the community makeup, including various cultures and languages, and to assist people with special needs.
- maintaining the capability to communicate valuable information about evacuation, sheltering, and other important disaster response and recovery information to the entire community.
- meeting the requirements of individuals with special needs, including those with cognitive and functional needs as well as language barriers.
- providing information to the community in multiple formats such as braille and large print.
- translating materials into languages commonly found within the community.

When not involved in an incident, PIOs meet these responsibilities by running awareness programs and organizing public safety events. They write stories for local papers, speeches for the leaders, or publish materials such as flyers or brochures for the agencies they support. They may also be charged with maintaining websites and other social media. In doing these tasks, their jobs are more like the work of traditional public relations people.

Planning

One of the main responsibilities of a PIO before a disaster is to facilitate planning that relates to the information sharing function. Communications policies and information management procedures are coordinated across organizations before a disaster occurs. This planning includes collaboration with a host of organizations and agencies. It identifies what information is regarded to be essential and designates how it will be collected and shared. Such planning also designates communications systems and platforms, equipment standards, and system users (FEMA, 2014, pp. 4–13).

Because communication is extremely important in a disaster situation, four types of communication should be considered in the planning process (FEMA, 2014, pp. 4–12). Strategic communications focus on decisions about resource priorities, determination of roles and responsibilities, and courses of action. Tactical communications occur between command and support personnel as well as cooperating agencies and organizations. Support communications assist strategic and tactical communications by providing as an example ordering, dispatching, and tracking information for logistics centers. Public communications provide emergency alerts and warnings, as well as other information to keep the public safe. By considering these four types of communications, a robust public information strategy may be established.

Training and Exercises

Training is another important aspect of PIO activities in non-emergency times (FEMA IS-0029, 2020, p. 3). It is important that the PIO have a good understanding of local government in general, the local emergency management system, and its relation to tribal, state, and federal entities that become involved in disasters. For instance, the PIO must know basic emergency management concepts, the Incident Command System, and the National Incident Management System. FEMA suggests that PIOs complete

Incident Command System training at the 100, 200, and 300 levels. PIOs should learn the national standards set forth in the National Incident Management System (IS-700). These courses and others are found at the website of FEMA's Emergency Management Institute. Many of the courses can be taken as independent study (IS) courses (FEMA, 2007).

In addition, the PIO must have excellent writing and editing skills, since they will help to create the local Emergency Operations Plans (EOP). The public information communications plan, which is part of the EOP, outlines how public information will be acquired and distributed in disaster situations. Because planning is insufficient in and of itself, exercises should be conducted in order to prepare PIOs for actual incidents (FEMA IS-700.b, 2020, p. 158).

Utah Valley University's *Disaster Response and the Public* course (ESMG 4200), suggests other topics PIOs might learn about to improve public communications:

- Media coverage of emergency management and its impact on disaster public policy.
- Issues in communications and mass media.
- Media portrayals of emergency leaders.
- Crisis management and communication plans.
- The role of the PIO in emergency planning, mitigation, response, and recovery.
- Emergency preparedness and the role of media relations.
- Information dissemination before, during, and after a disaster (e.g., press releases, news briefings, and fact sheets).
- Interviews for television or radio.
- Using social media in disasters (e.g., websites, Facebook, Twitter, and other social media platforms).
- Live-streaming and the disaster press conference.
- Risk communications and vulnerable populations.
- Case studies in disaster communications.

During Incidents

During the incident, all PIOs should typically follow the incident action plan, which contains incident objectives established by the Incident Commander or unified command. This addresses tactics and support activities for the planned operational period. PIOs, like other personnel, provide situational reports to the Incident Commander, who records the incident status and specific details for the past operational period. As often as needed, they provide status or spot reports, which include vital and time-sensitive information (FEMA, 2020, pp. 188–189). In addition, other PIOs fulfill a variety of roles in EOCs and the JICs. In these situations, PIOs work with an even larger group of individuals, departments, and organizations.

Regardless of where they are located in an incident, the FEMA-517 (2007) guidance document indicates PIOs have four information functions:

- information gathering,
- information dissemination,
- operations support, and
- liaison activities.

Information gathering. PIOs coordinate with response agencies, their PIOs, and incident command posts to gather information about the incident. They monitor and analyze media coverage for accuracy and content. They respond to media reports to stop rumors, correct inaccuracies, and provide details the public may need to know. They do research and writing to provide media releases, fact sheets, and graphic support, as well as develop video documentation and photographs. In the 2015 Hildale, Utah, flash flood, PIOs used a drone to assist in search efforts and provide video footage of the riverbed to the media.

Information dissemination. PIOs handle events such as news conferences, media briefings, and visits of senior officials of affected areas and other functionaries. PIOs serve as the primary contact for the news media and may also act as spokesperson at news briefings and press conferences. They provide web support and answer public inquiries online, in person, or from call centers.

Operations support. Disasters affect everyone including vulnerable populations. PIOs meet the needs of special needs groups and people requiring language translation. They also work in the Joint Information Center, maintaining and supporting operations, the facilities, and other resources that are required for specific needs.

Liaison. Generally, PIOs serve a liaison function by linking response and recovery operations and key programs with elected officials, community leaders, and other government and non-profit and private support agencies. As liaisons and information officers in the Incident Command Center, PIOs report to the Incident Commander and link key operations areas with the Emergency Operations Center, Joint Information Center, and other entities.

PIO Audiences

When performing their functions, PIOs must keep in mind three different audiences. The first set are the elected officials and decision-makers. These leaders have to have up-to-date information so they can make decisions about how to respond in a disaster. They decide whether the public should evacuate or whether to issue a disaster declaration. Decision-makers should know the worst-case and the best-case scenarios so they can make the best decisions for the public in a crisis situation. In normal times, elected officials and local authorities should be educated so they understand their roles in crisis situations and can plan and make policies to mitigate against potential hazards (McKay, 2013).

Partners are the second audience. These include PIOs from other agencies, other jurisdictions, non-profits, private businesses, and other stakeholder groups. Working through other PIOs, the agency PIO needs to inform partner agencies and stakeholders about what is actually happening and any plans so that they have a common operating picture. This helps them to adjust their plans and make decisions for dealing with the threat (McKay, 2013).

The final audience is the media and the public. These groups need to be kept current about what is happening at the moment, allowing people to make decisions to keep themselves safe (McKay, 2013).

Relations between the PIO and the Media

Because the media is a key partner for PIOs, they must understand media objectives and develop mutually beneficial working relationships before disasters happen. The media want timely, accurate, and complete information both before and during an incident. While journalists can often get the story from social media and government agencies can tell their story through social media, they need each other to ensure the story is both factual and important for the public. PIOs are consequently the bridge between government officials and journalists. Their role is to get accurate information to journalists at the right time to meet deadlines and to provide the news their audience needs. The media and PIOs share a common goal of keeping the public informed. PIOs can make the public aware and prepared for hazards by working with the media (Nelson and Hsiung, 2018).

Just as some people in emergency agencies may view reporters as aggressive and quick to publish any tidbit of information (factual or not), there are some reporters who see PIOs as barriers to getting information and reporting a story. Both views are wrong. Most reporters want to provide the public important information that will keep them safe, and most PIOs see their job as helping journalists tell their stories. PIOs are the means of ensuring reporters get factual information in a timely manner, but they are also in the business of rumor control. This is even more important because media organizations are short-staffed and have high turnover, which could result in inconsistent reporting.

"As a former journalist," Hsiung wrote, "I could not have been as successful without the trust, faith, and respect I had with local Public Information Officers. And that was not something that just came about – I had to make the effort to make that initial connection, and then I had to work at it. As we learned about one another and relationships were forged, it was the PIO who facilitated further successful connections between myself and other members of their organization" (Nelson and Hsiung, 2018).

Because of the high turnover among journalists, it is vitally important that PIOs establish working relationships with journalists. It's a mistake to wait for a crisis for PIOs to get to know the local media. Social media may be a good way to connect, but personal networking is the means of building good working relationships between journalists and government agencies. The PIO links reporters and subject matter experts within government organizations. Journalists have a limited amount of time and space to tell a story and frequently lack the means to get feedback and provide follow-up. PIOs can provide the information reporters need so that follow-up becomes easier. By collaborating with mass media, PIOs can manage media and community information needs before incidents so the public gets guidance on preparedness and risk-reduction strategies. This cooperation will help build the reputation of the emergency management organization in both the eyes of the public and the media.

One way of building a working relationship with local press is for emergency agencies to have a workshop for local mass media to provide general information on emergency management principles and processes. The workshop provides the PIO an opportunity to answer questions about how information is disseminated during an incident or planned event. It provides an understanding of roles and responsibilities of emergency personnel during an incident response. It also helps reporters to get background information for accurate reporting during emergencies. It is the job of the PIO to keep media and the community informed before and during an emergency. PIOs can't wait for a crisis to meet local journalists for the first time (Mangeri, 2016).

Another typical challenge that PIOs face is managing the media during a crisis or incident. Usually, the media are restricted to areas where they will be kept away from harm. Incident Commanders are also concerned about the security of the incident – maintaining privacy of individuals involved and keeping the scene secure so that evidence is not destroyed. The media, on the other hand, want to get as close as they can to the incident to get the best pictures and images, as well as the most salient facts about the situation. They would prefer to talk to the Incident Commander directly as well as witnesses and people involved in the event. PIOs are left serving two masters; they have to meet the demands of the Incident Commander, but also fulfill the needs of the media. Because the press area is outside the perimeter of the event, PIOs have to get permission from the Incident Commander so the media can get close to the incident or bring the Incident Commander out to speak to the media.

In many ways, social media has changed the way journalists and PIOs do business. Often it is witnesses or people involved in the incident who are first to report on the emergency situation. They have information and pictures before PIOs and journalists. Neither the PIO nor the Incident Commander are in control of the information because of citizens who have access to the scene with their cell phones and other digital devices (Hughes and Palen, 2012).

CURRENT CHALLENGES

Public safety PIOs face a number of challenges in fulfilling their role of providing information to the public to prepare, protect, and help them respond in a crisis. They must understand and adapt to social media, which has changed the way the media gather news and the way the public gets news. Social media creates citizen reporters. In a disaster or emergency, everyone can potentially report the news on social media and this can complicate the PIO's job. Furthermore, new technology makes the PIO's job easier in some ways and more difficult in other ways. At one time, PIOs in government agencies had the best technology; now they are challenged to keep up. Each of these issues will be discussed in turn.

Social Media

Traditionally, members of the public got their information about emergency and disaster events from emergency officials and the news media. Because of the advent of social media, public access to information has both increased and become almost instantaneous. The public now get much of their information on the Internet. Bloggers have become an important source of information for the public and the media, and they must be included in an emergency organization's communication plans. Social media has challenged the notion that emergency officials are the only legitimate source of information about disasters or other emergency events.

PIOs were largely seen as the middlemen between information and news reporters before social media made information easier to get and more readily available. In the digital age, it is easier for news agencies to get information from other sources without getting information from PIOs (Davis, 2010). The media now compete with each other to be the first to publish the news; if they can get information more readily from other sources (like social media) than through PIOs, they will certainly do that.

PIOs therefore have to prove their value to the media. It becomes even more important for PIOs to be the first to give the media details they can't get elsewhere. Social media has shortened the news cycle. Therefore, PIOs must collect and disseminate information in a much shorter time frame, as well as in a compressed format for it to be current and relevant (Hughes and Palen, 2012).

In addition, PIOs need to provide accurate news, thus establishing themselves as the legitimate and authorized source for news. This is important because inaccurate and incomplete information creates rumors and misinforms the public. When providing information in a crisis, it is even more important that the information be accurate to ensure public safety. When PIOs are bypassed, the chances for false and inaccurate information are even greater (Davis, 2010).

Citizen Reporters

Citizens have always been first to arrive upon the scene. Now, not only are they witnesses and responders in emergencies, but they have also become citizen reporters. Equipped with digital devices, they can break the news story and provide video footage as well as provide witness information to the media. For instance, when a plane landed on the Hudson River in February 2009, it was a passenger who posted a picture on Twitter using the camera on his cell phone. This phenomenon of a citizen journalist who witnesses an event and is first to report requires heightened skills to keep up with citizen journalists, to ensure accuracy, and provide meaningful updates to the public and the media (Takai, 2014).

With this in mind, the Public Information Officer needs to monitor and control messages being provided to the public if at all possible. False information can compound the problems of the PIO by making it more difficult to respond, but also more difficult for the public to be kept safe. It's important that people monitoring social media report the misinformation to the PIO on the scene so that false information can be corrected on Facebook and other social media outlets (Hughes and Palen, 2012). The advent of social media has expanded the need for help in analyzing and gathering information from the multiple social media channels. Volunteers, who are part of the virtual operations support team, assist by performing online tasks that can be done remotely, which does not require them to be in the JIC or anywhere near the incident.

The PIO and Technology

As noted, the role of PIO has changed in response to new technological tools, particularly the cell phone and social media. The public wants real-time news about large events whether close by or far away. The PIO's goal is to provide the public with relevant and timely information about an event; this requires the use of technology. While one PIO can handle a small event, many PIOs may be required for larger events with multi-media requirements of print, video, or electronics. With changing technology and social media, larger events may require from 10 to 20 PIOs.

It used to be that government agencies had the latest and best tools. Today the public has the best technology and PIOs have to keep up, sometimes by using their own equipment. The minimum equipment needed to work an event is a cell phone, tablet, and a satellite phone, as cell phone coverage is likely to be down in a disaster. Such equipment is often owned by the PIOs because their agencies can't afford it.

RECOMMENDATIONS

To be successful in working with the media, PIOs need to be both responsive and transparent. Since social media has changed how reporters gather news and how the public gets information, PIOs must disseminate information to the news media and reach the public directly. All of this suggests that hiring the right person to be a PIO is essential.

Being Responsive and Transparent

The Society of Professional Journalists claims that a growing trend in government is to prohibit their staff from talking to journalists without first talking to a government authority, like a PIO (Thompkins, 2018). As an example, police officers are most often restricted from talking to journalists. A study indicated that nearly 60% of police journalists report "successfully" interviewing police officers some of the time or rarely, while 26.1% said that they were never able to interview police officers (Thompkins, 2018; Carlson, 2012).

The problem is that government officials do not trust journalists. This complicates the role of PIOs because their success in reaching the public depends on having strong relations with the media. In small rural communities, for example, newspapers are closing down and, where there are papers, the number of journalists is on the decline. PIOs can deal with this problem by being more responsive to the needs of small hometown journals specifically, and large media outlets overall. PIOs can make it easier for journalists to cover emergencies and public safety news by training agency staff and using their skills to share information with the media.

Engaging with Social Media

Because most people and most journalists now get their news from social media, it is imperative that PIOs go there too. They must develop their organizational communication capacity to reach the public on social media (Fletcher and Kascsak, 2018). PIOs must do more to contribute to the flow of information on social media, and correct any erroneous stories that appear when disasters occur. This suggest that PIOs must monitor, make sense of, and then react to social media posts by citizens.

Finding and Training the Right Person to Be a PIO

While most universities have public relations programs, very few have programs to educate Public Information Officers. The difference is distinct because the roles of each are so different. Public relations people are advocates and promoters of their organizations. PIOs, in contrast, disseminate information that is important to protect and keep the public informed and safe. While both are asked at times to protect their organizations and their leaders, the primary responsibility of the PIO is to the public, not the organization.

Because most public safety PIOs are agency staff or former journalists, they come with little training to be Public Information Officers. For this reason, FEMA offers PIO training, including a PIO awareness course (IS-29), public information basics (E/L0105), advanced public information training (E/L0388), and a Master of Public Information Officer program (E0389, E0393, and E0394). Experience, however, may be the best training for PIOs. PIO training should include media skill-building, including writing news stories and press releases, press conferences and TV interviews, and social media usage. Successful PIOs learn to identify key messages, develop talking points, and practice skills in responding to questions and thinking quickly on their feet.

PIOs should also be trained in emergency and disaster response and recovery. While public safety agency personnel may come to the job of PIO with this training and plenty of experience, former journalists should be trained in the all-hazards approach to emergency management. FEMA offers courses online in the Incident Command System (IS 100 and 200) and the National Incident Management System (IS-700). More advanced ICS training (ICS-300 and 400) is offered by state emergency management departments.

CONCLUSION – NEW INFORMATION PATHWAYS

In every after-action report, communications have been high in the list of issues to be corrected in a disaster. The public expectation for good, accurate, and timely information in a disaster has not changed. But, technology has changed, and the broadcast media is no longer the key source of information. This has profound impacts upon the role of the PIO.

Traditionally, the Public Information Officer provided the media with information and the media shared that information with the public. With the advent of social media, the PIO can speak directly to the public through social media. Often the media become dependent upon the public information officers because they lack the resources to cover the story in-depth themselves (Hughes and Palen, 2012).

The role of the Public Information Officer is changing from gatekeeper to translator. A gatekeeper manages and constrains the flow of information. In the past, PIOs engaged primarily in one-way communication. That role is clearly changing as the relationship with the public has become more complex and messages involve multi-channel communication between the public and the PIO. As a translator, the Public Information Officer must put the information into a format that is better understood by others within the organization and in the public. Public information is less constrained by NIMS procedures. PIOs operate more autonomously in order to provide up-to-date and timely information to the public (Hughes and Palen, 2012).

Social media has altered many PIO functions. PIOs are consequently not only monitoring social media to obtain relevant and useful information, but they also must analyze that information. They may also be involved in documenting emergency incidents through the use of video photography and using online resources in identifying rumor and false information. In addition, PIOs coordinate and communicate with digital volunteers to collect, assess, and share information (Hughes and Palen, 2012).

Because the public relies on their phones and social media apps to acquire the information they need, obtaining timely information is expected now more than ever. This is one of the central duties of the Public Information Officer. Keeping it accurate is the other responsibility and it is more challenging (McKay, 2013).

CLASS DISCUSSION AND ESSAY QUESTIONS

1. Why has public information been so important to governments and government leaders over time?
2. What do the cases reveal about the job of a public information officer during disasters? Would it be overwhelming? How could you deal effectively with the demand for information sharing and management under such trying circumstances?

3. What organizational structures have been put in place to deal with disasters and how do they relate to the public information officer?
4. How has social media altered the traditional relationship between the media and the PIO? What should be done about this change?
5. What type of training is required to ensure a PIO is successful?

REFERENCES

Ahlers, M. M. (2006, April 14). Report: Criticism of FEMA's Katrina Response Deserved. *CNN Politics*. http://www.cnn.com/2006/POLITICS/04/14/fema.ig/.

Basen, I. (2014). World War I and the Birth of Public Relations. *Journal of Professional Communication*, 4(1), 15–19. https://doi.org/10.15173/jpc.v4i1.2611.

Bernays, E. L. (1972). The Birth of Public Relations: It Started with Sex. *Management Review*, 61(3), 60.

Blad, E. (2018). Do Schools' "Active-Shooter" Drills Prepare or Frighten? *Education Digest*, 83(6), 4.

Braziel, R., Straub, F., Watson, G. & Hoops, R. (2016). *Bringing Calm to Chaos: A Critical Incident Review of the San Bernardino Public Safety Response to the December 2, 2015, Terrorist Shooting Incident at the Inland Regional Center*. Washington, DC: Office of Community Oriented Policing Services.

Carlson, C. (2012). Censoring through Public Affairs Officers. *Quill*, 100(3), 63.

Davis, P. (2010). The Public Information Officer and Today's Digital News Environment. *FBI Law Enforcement Bulletin*, 79(7), 1–8.

Dickman, K. (2013, September 17). 19: The True Story of the Yarnell Hill Fire. *Outside Magazine*. https://www.outsideonline.com/1926426/19-true-story-yarnell-hill-fire.

Dickman, K. & Damron, W. (2015). On the Burning Edge: A Fateful Fire and the Men Who Fought It. New York: Ballantine Books.

Dickman, K. (2018, October 30). What We Learned from Yarnell Hill Fire Deaths. *Outside Magazine*. https://www.outsideonline.com/2356386/what-we-learned-yarnell-hill-fire#close.

FEMA. (2007). Basic Guidance for Public Information Officers (PIOs). FEMA Publication, 517. https://www.fema.gov/media-library-data/20130726-1824-25045-3342/fema_517_basic_guidance_for_public_information_officers__pios__2007.pdf.

FEMA. (2014, October). Unit 4: NIMS Communications and Information Management Student Manual in IS-0700.A: National Incident Management System, An Introduction. https://www.msema.org/wp-content/uploads/2018/10/is0700a_studentmanual_l4.pdf.

FEMA. (2016, June). Emergency Support Function #5 – Information and Planning. https://www.fema.gov/media-library-data/1470149907591-1ec94844d9f05ba47a448af75c1ffc08/ESF_5_Information_and_Planning_20160705_508.pdf.

FEMA. (2018, March). ICS 300 – ICS Organizational Structure and Elements. https://training.fema.gov/emiweb/is/icsresource/assets/ics%20organizational%20structure%20and%20elements.pdf.

FEMA. (2019, October 29). Emergency Support Function Annexes. https://www.fema.gov/media-library/assets/documents/25512.

FEMA. (2020, June). IS-0700.B: An Introduction to the National Incident Management System – Instructor's Manual. https://training.fema.gov/emiweb/is/is700b/4ig/igis0700b.pdf.

FEMA. (2020, July 1). IS-0029.A: Public Information Officer Awareness. https://emilms.fema.gov/IS0029a/curriculum/1.html.

FEMA. (2021, January 4). History of FEMA. https://www.fema.gov/about/history.

FEMA. (n.d.). NIMS: Frequently Asked Questions. https://www.fema.gov/pdf/emergency/nims/NIMSFAQs.pdf.

Fletcher, S. & Kascsak, M. (2018, October 22). Role of the PIO: Being Responsive and Transparent. Engaging Local Government Leaders (ELGL). https://elgl.org/role-of-the-pio-being-responsive-and-transparent/.

Hawin, P. (2016, December 19). Public Affairs vs. Public Relations: What Is the Difference? *PR Daily*. https://www.prdaily.com/public-affairs-vs-public-relations-what-is-the-difference/.

Hughes, A. L. & Palen, L. (2012). The Evolving Role of the Public Information Officer: An Examination of Social Media in Emergency Management. *Journal of Homeland Security & Emergency Management*, 9(1), 1–20. https://doi-org.ezproxy.uvu.edu/10.1515/1547-7355.1976.

Jacobs, B. (2010). Atomic Kids: Duck and Cover and Atomic Alert Teach American Children How to Survive Atomic Attack. *Film & History*, 40(1), 25.

Lee, M. (2009). Origins of the Epithet 'Government by Public Relations': Revisiting Bruce Catton's War Lords of Washington, 1948. *Public Relations Review*, 35(4), 388–394. https://doi-org.ezproxy.uvu.edu/10.1016/j.pubrev.2009.06.005.

Mangeri, A. (2016, April). Strategies for a PIO to Share Information in Times of Crisis. *American Military University in Public Safety*. https://inpublicsafety.com/2016/04/strategies-for-a-pio-to-share-information-in-times-of-crisis/.

McDonough, B. & Talty, S. (2016). My Lost Brothers: The Untold Story by the Yarnell Hill Fire's Lone Survivor. New York: Machete Books.

McKay, J. (2013, December 2). Lessons Learned for Facing the Public in Disaster. *Emergency Management*. https://www.govtech.com/em/disaster/Facing-the-Public-in-Disaster.html.

Mitchell, E. (2020). *Lincoln's Lie: A True Civil War Caper through Fake News, Wall Street, and the White House*. Berkley: Counterpoint.

Nelson, K. & Hsiung, C. (2018, October 29). The Vital Role of the Public Information Officer. *Engaging Local Government Leaders (ELGL)*. https://elgl.org/the-vital-role-of-the-public-information-officer/.

Pruitt, S. (2019, March 26). How "Duck-and-Cover" Drills Channeled America's Cold War Anxiety. *History.Com*. Retrieved March 13, 2021, from https://www.history.com/news/duck-cover-drills-cold-war-arms-race.

Takai, K. (2014, July 1). Providing Information during Disasters and Incidents. *Fire Management Today*, 24–27. https://www.frames.gov/documents/usfs/fmt/fmt_74-1.pdf.

Taylor, M. & Kent, M. L. (2016). Towards Legitimacy and Professionalism: A Call to …: Full Text Finder Results. *Public Relations Review*, 42(1), 1–8. https://doi.org/10.1016/j.pubrev.2015.09.012.

Thompkins, A. (2018, September 5). SPJ Research Suggests That a Surge in PIOs Negatively Impacts Journalism. *Poynter*. https://www.poynter.org/newsletters/2018/spj-research-suggests-that-a-surge-in-pios-negatively-impacts-journalism/.

Weather Channel. (2014). America Burning: The Yarnell Hill Fire Tragedy and the Nation's Wildfire Crisis. https://www.youtube.com/watch?v=begTiksUwqc.

RESOURCES

FEMA's Independent Study website at www.training.fema.gov/is lists several free, web-based training courses about ICS and NIMS.

Visit FEMA's Emergency Management Institute (EMI) at training.fema.gov. EMI offers several classroom-based, on campus and field deliveries of ICS and NIMS courses for different audiences.

Outside magazine released the documentary film, The Granite Mountain Hotshots and the Yarnell Hill Fire (Dickman, 2013; Dickman, 2018), in which friends, relatives, colleagues, including Brendan McDonough—the lone survivor of the Granite Mountain Hotshots-speak out.[48]

The U.S. Forest Service released a series of videos on November 10, 2014, that were shot by wildland firefighters on the day of the Yarnell Hill tragedy. The Forest Service website notes: "To be transparent with the public, the videos are presented exactly as they have been received. The redactions were done before these videos came into the possession of Arizona State Forestry."[49] In its coverage of these videos, Outside magazine posted and article and video excerpts.[50]

The Weather Channel released a documentary, America Burning: The Yarnell Hill Fire Tragedy and the Nation's Wildfire Crisis (2014).[51][52] Kyle Dickman, a former firefighter and former editor of Outside magazine, published the nonfiction book, On the Burning Edge: A Fateful Fire and the Men Who Fought It (2015; Dickman, 2013; Dickman, 2018).[53] Brendan McDonough published his first-hand account, My Lost Brothers: The Untold Story by the Yarnell Hill Fire's Lone Survivor (May 3, 2016).[54]

Columbia Pictures released a film adaptation of the Yarnell Hill Fire in 2017, titled Only the Brave.

CHAPTER 9

Professionals and Volunteers in Non-Profit Organizations:
Understanding Their Vital Role and Impact in Emergency Management

Tina Bynum, Heriberto Urby, and Arthur J. Simental

INTRODUCTION

The professionals in non-profit organizations play a pivotal role in disaster management and have done so for a long time with even more expectations from them for the foreseeable future. Their contributions must also be understood and not underestimated. In fact, it is our contention that the role and impact of those who work and volunteer for non-profits should be expanded – and not diminished in any way. Non-profit organizations are those that provide social benefits and private goods or services, many of them not covered by the government or other types of organizations. Non-profit organizations, as opposed to for-profit organizations, "are created to fulfill one or more needs of a community" (Allen and Sawhney, 2019, p. 14). Moreover, non-profits function in their unique political and cultural context, ownership structure, financial, and capital structure (Renz, 2016).

A United Nations' definition stipulates that non-profit organizations are:

> organizations that do not exist primarily to generate profits, either directly or indirectly, and that are not primarily guided by commercial goals and considerations. NPIs [non-profit institutions] may accumulate surplus in a given year, but any such surplus must be plowed back into the basic mission of the agency and not distributed to the organizations' owners, members, founders, or governing board.
>
> (Bowman in Renz, 2016, p. 565)

Examples of non-profit organizations include, among others: hospitals, universities, churches, national charities, and foundations. It is organizations such as these that address diverse needs in society, which augment the important work of emergency managers and homeland security personnel, and others, during and after times of crises, disasters, and catastrophes.

As with many other organizations, including those for-profits mentioned earlier, "non-profits succeed because they offer value and make a valuable difference in

DOI: 10.4324/9781003350729-9

the communities and societies they emerge to serve" (Renz, 2016, p. xxxii). Moreover, "those with socially innovative ideas hone and develop them to become functioning organizations that make a difference – that achieves a social impact" (Renz, 2016, p. xxxii).

The non-profit entity, often organized to operate under a 501(c)(3) tax-exempt designation, is designed for associations, corporations, funds, or foundations operating for religious, charitable, literary, or educational purposes. These organizations must be led and managed by professionals effectively, to-wit:

1. *Govern, Lead, and Manage with Strategic Focus.* For example, non-profit organizations are led by leaders, visionaries who look and act forward-thinking (that is, strategically – and with managers who run the day-to-day operations in a similar fashion).
2. *Do not fall prey to the "Run It Like a Business" Cliches.* We have learned much from public organizations – and how related professionals run them. Thus, there is no imminent need to rush to business or other forms of strategic or tactical procedures or processes.
3. *Market and Communicate Effectively.* Professionals must engage in these activities successfully so that the needs of the organization and those whom they serve are met.
4. *Perform Well and Deliver Social Value.* The individuals in these non-profit organizations must formulate and implement the goals they have established in the first place (Renz, 2016).

Most important to the discussion in this chapter, is the role of non-profit professionals and volunteers in disaster management. Here are just some of what these indispensable individuals do:

- Provide medical care, water, food, and other supplies and services to victims and survivors of disasters and catastrophes.
- Manage donations effectively, especially so that they do not become a "disaster within a disaster."
- Provide assistance that government and government organizations do not.
- Help survivors of disasters and man-made disasters recover.

The following chapter will shed light on what non-profit professionals and volunteers do when disasters or terrorist attacks occur. It will pay particular attention to mental health issues in disaster management and the support non-profit organizations provide. For instance, many professionals (e.g., Social Workers and others) involved with non-profit organizations assist during disasters, including for physical, social, and mental health needs. This includes work within all phases of the disaster life cycle, with special emphasis on the response and recovery phases after a disaster or catastrophe has occurred. The professionals who lead and serve are required in non-profit organizations in order to function most effectively during disasters. An example of this is the individuals who work in Voluntary Organizations Active in Disaster (VOAD), a group of volunteer organizations consolidated to align their support and services in a way that minimizes interruption to the primary first response objectives. These organizations serve at the local level as part of the whole-community approach to disaster management as well as across state, tribal, national, and international levels. As stipulated in the disaster management incident command system, the size and scope of VOADs' assistance depends on the nature of the incident and the needs of the community affected. The functions of those who work and serve in non-profits or VOADs are largely similar when engaging their support and services in the United States or even internationally. The professionals and volunteers in non-profit organizations have a history of humanitarian relief that spans generations and they possess valuable skills in dealing with complex humanitarian emergencies. One such case is the ongoing Ukranian conflict with Russia, which will be covered in the chapter as well.

THE HISTORY OF NON-PROFIT ORGANIZATIONS AND RELATED PROFESSIONALS

Though voluntary associations in early America differed from modern-day non-profits (e.g., between public and private realms and the mainly different role of government and the rights and responsibilities of citizenship), Renz (2016) pointed out that they resembled each other in many important ways:

- they were self-governing;
- they were created by members who had been given delegated powers from governing boards;
- they had no owners or stockholders;
- they were exempt from taxation since they were public bodies; and
- they could accept donations and bequests for charitable purposes, such as supporting education and relief for the poor.

Renz also illustrated several eras of historical associations in America and they are summarized briefly below:

1780–1830

The most famous of observations made about voluntary associations in the New Republic was by none other than the French visitor, Alexis de Tocqueville:

Americans of all ages, all conditions, and all dispositions constantly form associations. They have not only commercial and manufacturing companies, in which they all take part, but associations of a thousand other kinds – religious, moral, serious, futile, general or restricted, enormous or diminutive. The Americans make associations to give entertainments, to found seminaries, to build inns, to construct churches, to diffuse books, to send missionaries to the anitipodes. In this manner they found hospitals, prisons, and schools.

1860–1920

This next historical era produced "associations, private charities, and giving and volunteering [that] all played prominent roles in the Civil War, which provided opportunities for further advancing the claims of private eleemosynary enterprise" (Hall in Renz, 2016, 9). As an example, in 1873, the stock market collapse brought hard times and impoverishment for workers everywhere. Andrew Carnegie, a major capitalist in early America, catapulted to prominence during the next decade, amassing huge amounts of wealth. What made this important innovator somewhat unique – at the time and even perhaps in terms of today – was his willingness to usher in motivation for himself and other aspiring millionaires to establish "institutions of various kinds, which will improve the general condition of the people; in this manner returning their surplus wealth to the mass of their fellows in the forms best calculated to do them lasting good" (Hall in Renz, 2016, p. 12).

Thus, the citizenry could become "a nation of joiners" (Hall in Renz, 2016, p. 12). In a subsequent historical era discussed later in this paper, this would later change (see discussion related to Robert Putnam).

1890–1930

During this era, Carnegie and John D. Rockefeller took turns in influencing the development of non-profit organizations. Carnegie was first involved in "establishing the largest foundation of all the Carnegie Corporation of New York, for the general purpose of 'advancement and diffusion of knowledge and understanding'" (Hall in Renz, 2016, p. 14). Shortly thereafter, Rockefeller "applied to Congress for a charter for a $100 million foundation dedicated to 'the betterment of mankind'" (Hall in Renz, 2016, p. 14).

However, even more philanthropists beyond just Carnegie and Rockefeller devoted much precious time of theirs to creation and development of grantmaking foundations and other charitable vehicles – not the least including The Community Chest and the Charities Federation. In the short term at least, these important entities helped "make the establishment and management of charitable endowments more efficient" (Hall in Renz, 2016, p. 15). Add to this associations-based emphasis on the transformation of fundraising, and the strides made by non-profit organizations during this important historical era of advancements are evident.

1930–1980

Incremental growth continued during this New Deal period of government and the transformation of many lives during World War II and afterward. This crucial era saw the professionals in non-profit organizations take on more for-profit ventures and vice versa. Also, for-profits entered into the non-profit realms of volunteerism, and good and services. "According to political scientist Robert Putnam, all forms of civic engagement – voting, attending public meetings, church attendance, and participation in athletic associations such as bowling leagues" (Putnam, 2000; Hall in Renz, 2016, p. 21) waned considerably during the 1960s. Thus, organizations' and individuals' joinders with one another were replaced mainly by religious associations, which continued to expand (i.e., joinders still made possible but more so through religious collaborations). The latter began to take their place "to provide specific kinds of services (child day care, elder care, education, health services) and to engage in advocacy, lobbying, and public education than to promote generalized sociability and civic engagement" (Hall in Renz, 2016, p. 21).

1980–2000

During this more modern era of development, those involved in non-profit management became much more professional in nature and even more competitive with for-profit markets. In order to survive this environment of skilled management and what Osborne and Gaebler called "Reinventing Government" (i.e., doing more with less, contracting out, privatization, etc.), "Non-profits had to become more commercial and more entrepreneurial to survive. Whether non-profits' commitments to missions of public service could survive such relentless attention to the bottom line remained in doubt as the 21st Century dawned" (Hall in Renz, 2016, p. 26).

The New Century and the Transformation of Philanthropy

The very latest era of non-profit institutional development is based on results-oriented philanthropy that concentrates on efficiency and an expansion into globalization (i.e., where international non-profit entities are strongly involved – and not just U.S.-centric based). In sum, many more individuals across the world are now involved – and this expansion includes more than just Americans. Conclusively,

> within a quarter of a century, philanthropy has gone from being centered in North America and Western Europe and focused on aid by advanced industrial nations to developing countries to a genuinely transnational collection of enterprises and initiatives sustaining complex multidirectional flows of aid and influence.
>
> (Hall in Renz, 2016, p. 29)

RELATION TO DISASTERS/TERRORISM

The leaders, managers, and volunteers involved in non-profit organizations are consistently involved when all types of natural disasters occur. Disasters, by their very nature, create a host of problems ranging from death and injury to unemployment, homelessness, and emotional distress. At times, these challenges can be overcome by governments, businesses, and the victims and survivors themselves. But, in many cases, the service of non-profit professionals and volunteers is needed to address immediate and long-term needs.

These professionals and volunteers are not only involved in natural disasters. They are also engaged when there is violent conflict. The professionals and volunteers in non-profit organizations play a unique role in responding to and supporting humanitarian crisis. Geopolitical conflicts are a unique incident in the context of homeland security and emergency management. One notable historic example of a non-profit engaged in humanitarian crisis is the American Red Cross's work spanning numerous historic conflicts such as World War I through the Korean and Vietnam wars. But, perhaps the involvement is best seen in this excerpt from an American Red Cross report on its efforts during World War II:

> The Red Cross mobilized in support of the U.S. military, our Allies and civilian victims of World War II. We enrolled more than 104,000 nurses for military service, prepared 27 million packages for prisoners of war, shipped more than 300,000 tons of supplies, and collected 13.3 million pints of blood for the armed forces. In nearly every American family, someone was a Red Cross volunteer, donor or blood donor, or received Red Cross services.
>
> (ARC, 2022)

Another example from the International Committee of the Red Cross in responding to the atomic bombings of Hiroshima and Nagasaki:

> In August 1945 the Japanese Red Cross Society, later assisted by the International Committee of the Red Cross (ICRC), were among the first organizations to bring assistance to the sick, wounded and dying in Hiroshima and Nagasaki. Although the Japanese Red Cross hospital in Hiroshima was nearly destroyed, its stone walls were still standing and thousands of people flocked to it for help and safety
>
> (ICRC, 2015)

These are but two historic examples of non-profits engaged in emergency management efforts.

Regardless of these notable cases, the impacts of terrorism, intrastate conflict, nation-state aggression, and the ensuing humanitarian implications are not events or issues that the typical American emergency manager has regularly experienced since the end of World War II. In addition, civil defense has largely been dormant since the end of the Cold War where the principal risk to the United States was largely considered to be that of a nuclear attack from the Soviet Union. But there have been very visible cases (the Balkans, Rwanda, and Syria) where the expertise of professionals and volunteers in the non-profit sector have been increasingly essential. And, today, the focus has shifted to homeland security due to the threat of terrorism (e.g., 1993 World Trade Center bombing, Oklahoma City bombing, 9/11, the Boston Marathon bombing, etc.). We have also witnessed the devastating impacts of riots in 2020 and on January 6th. The implications of mounting international or domestic conflict are causing us to again focus more on humanitarian crises. This brings up the contemporary example of humanitarian crisis and non-profits engaged in support being the Russian military invasion of Ukraine.

The case of Ukraine is poignant in what has been referred to as a Humanitarian Crisis. These types of human-created disasters include the evacuation of millions of refugees and internally displaced persons, many of whom were trapped, unable to escape the barrage of explosions and devastation wrought by the invasion of Russian troops into their territory and way of life. In the war-torn country of Ukraine, a true Complex Humanitarian Emergency (CHE) is the term we should be using to describe the situation there instead of a mere Humanitarian Crisis as is mentioned far too often in the news (Coppola, 2011). A Humanitarian Crisis is more representative of situations related to famine and hunger in a population. In contrast, a Complex Humanitarian Emergency is utilized to describe those who experience travails, deaths, injuries, and more as a result of war and military/political conflict.

The Russian military invasion of Ukraine is a unique example of a humanitarian crisis, being the result of armed conflict between the Russian Federation and Ukraine. On February 24, 2022, Russian military forces entered into Ukraine and began to inflict unprecedented damage to infrastructure while also decimating cities through bombings which injured and killed thousands of civilians (ACAPS, 2022). The impact of Russia's invasion of Ukraine has created a large-scale humanitarian crisis. Specifically:

> around 13 million people are estimated to be stranded in affected areas. Some people chose to stay or were unable to flee and are hiding in basements or subway stations. The movement of civilians is limited because of shelling and mines planted along roads, which hinders their access to basic goods and services. Shelling has also led to water and electricity cuts. Safe evacuation of civilians from besieged areas is facilitated through humanitarian corridors, which are often temporary and subject to change. People in need of humanitarian assistance have increased from 2.9 million before the 24 February escalation to 15.7 million after the escalation, with numbers expected to continue increasing because of continuing hostilities. About 24 million people are estimated to be affected by the conflict.
>
> (ACAPS, 2022)

The mass exodus and relocation of millions of Ukrainians is but one of several cascading disasters occurring within this humanitarian crisis requiring nothing less than an international response and support from governments and the private and non-profit sectors working in unison. As the war in Ukraine continues, the situation will continue to become more dire and severe in terms of its impacts. As of May 2022, the latest reports of the toll on the civilian population from Russia's invasion were staggering:

> Over 260 attacks on healthcare in Ukraine were recorded between 24 February and 29 May. This number constitutes over 77% of the total attacks on healthcare worldwide in the same timeframe. Attacks on healthcare have damaged and destroyed health facilities and supplies, and killed and injured patients and personnel. Targeting healthcare affects people's ability to access medical care, including those with injuries, pregnant women including those with obstetric emergencies, and people with non-communicable diseases, such as diabetes and cancer, needing ongoing treatment and care. Evacuation of patients and medical aid delivery to harder to reach areas, such as those with intense fighting, is challenging and people are facing shortages of medicines and medical supplies. About 50% of pharmacies in Ukraine are expected to be closed and many health workers cannot work or are displaced because of the fighting. Over 12 million people are estimated to need health assistance in Ukraine.
>
> (ACAPS, 2022)

The response from the non-profit community to this humanitarian crisis globally has been extraordinary. Hundreds of non-profit organizations worldwide have worked to provide support and respond to the war in Ukraine. The thousands of professionals and volunteers in non-profit organizations engaged in Ukraine have been providing a range of services including:

- Medical assistance
- Medical supplies
- Non-medical supplies (including food)
- Water, sanitation, and hygiene
- Emergency housing
- Long-term assistance
- Financial support (cash/cash vouchers)
- Logistics
- Other supplies
- Animal services (Charity Navigator, 2022).

This aid has been further supplemented with millions of dollars in donations in support (Smith, 2022). These services attempt to more comprehensively address holistic response and recovery from the impact of the humanitarian crisis. Thus, the scale of the response and recovery in Ukraine is massive. As a case in point, here is an example of one non-profit's impact during the war in Ukraine with animal rescue:

> Since Russia launched its invasion of Ukraine 100+ days ago. IFAW's Disaster Response team, together with our partners has directly helped more than 42,000 animals, most of which were cats and dogs but also tigers and bears. We have been working tirelessly to support refugees and their pets, source dog and cat food / supplies for animal shelters, fund zoos, and facilitate animal rescues. We began working with animal shelters in Ukraine following the 2014 Russian invasion and will continue to be there for the pets and wildlife caught in this conflict.
>
> (IFAW, 2021)

Humanitarian crisis, especially that of the war in Ukraine, raises several key issues and areas of inquiry while highlighting the important role non-profits play in emergency management. The list of services discussed, while not comprehensive, paints a clear picture of the extent of support and services non-profits provide well beyond traditional emergency management capabilities geared toward typical disaster life cycles, limited in scope, impact, and geographical area. Ukraine presents a rare unique challenge in that the entire country is under siege, faced with a highly dynamic and shifting landscape that may change within hours due to the ongoing military incursion and shifting war fronts. War affects every aspect of the response to this massive humanitarian crisis. A key point of reflection: men, women, children, people from all walks of life, first responders, volunteers, reporters, soldiers, etc., have all lost their lives in this deadly conflict. War and conflict are not isolated phenomena; domestically how would the United States respond to a similar crisis? One critical report highlights that the United States and the Federal Emergency Management Agency (FEMA) are not prepared to handle the response to a conflict within the U.S. (Quinton, 2019). It is imperative that the lessons learned from the war in Ukraine be studied, applied, and rapidly put into practice to strengthen emergency management systems, including the incorporation and partnership of the private sector and non-profits for a more holistic approach.

ROLES IN EMERGENCY MANAGEMENT/HOMELAND SECURITY

Volunteerism is a long-held American pastime. For instance, Benjamin Franklin is often credited with creating the first organized volunteer programs in the United States, although humans helping their fellow humans is as old as humanity. In the early days of organized volunteerism, groups of people could come together to serve the specific needs of their community. Some would rally around the poor to provide food and shelter, others to provide more cheery holidays, and then there were those who come together to assist in disasters, all of whom are still a part of the American fabric as well as international humanitarianism today. Humans as social beings gather for a variety of reasons, to celebrate, to mourn, to play, and to serve each other. When disasters occur, each of these reasons to organize is evident. Disasters tend to bring out the best in people who want to help, but even the help can be especially taxed during disasters.

Organized disaster management has a long history as well, but nowhere near as long as volunteerism. Interestingly enough, it was the volunteers that came together to form structured emergency services. In 1736, Ben Franklin created the first community-centered volunteer fire department, the Union Fire Company, in Philadelphia, Pennsylvania (Franklin and Bigelow, 1869). In 1863, the International Committee of the Red Cross was formed as an international relief organization to provide humanitarian services to the war-injured (American Red Cross, n.d.a). In 1881, the American Red Cross was formed in Dansville, New York, and provided aid for the first time to those affected by forest fires in Michigan (American Red Cross, n.d.a). Volunteers were there to help explore the new frontier as the United States grew. Ladies Aid Societies organized to render medical aid and provide supplies during the Civil War after which a number of volunteer organizations sprang up such as the Salvation Army, the YMCA, and Volunteers of America, etc. By the end of World War I, community organizations such as the Boy Scouts of America, Rotary Clubs, and Lions Clubs were established. During the Great Depression and into World War II, the immense human need for support and services necessitated the creation of soup kitchens, bread lines, clothing, and other goods for mere survival. Volunteers contributed anything and everything they could to bring some relief to the suffering. Women trained as nurses to join the auxiliaries of the military to serve abroad. Thus began the United States' involvement in international humanitarian services (FEMA, 2015).

Over time, these and other services evolved a set of national standards and efforts to manage emergencies and disasters both at the career level as well as at the volunteer level, both of which practice the same way as collaborating professionals. Today, more than two-thirds of American firefighters are volunteers (Fahy, Evarts, and Stein, 2021) and according to FEMA (2015), volunteer agencies "serve a critical role in the emergency management field from helping communities prepare for and mitigate the effects of disasters to providing immediate response and long-term recovery services. Without the support, dedication, and expertise of voluntary agencies, the government would be unable to address all the needs of disaster-affected communities." Partnerships between disaster response agencies, volunteers, and other community members provide a holistic approach to emergency management that ensures resiliency as disasters become more frequent, more intense, and more widespread.

As community volunteers started to partner and organize their efforts, many have become non-profit organizations over time. But volunteering during disasters is not synonymous with all non-profit volunteering nor are all non-profit organizations active during disasters. It is a very specific group of people who may be a part of a non-profit organization that has disaster support and services as a part of its overall mission. The American Red Cross (ARC) is one such example of an organization with a long history of working closely with the disaster management community. While much of the mission of professionals in the ARC is to serve people during community disasters, these individuals also assist during smaller emergencies such as the loss of a home due to fire or another hazard. Those that work and serve in the Salvation Army (SA) also have a long-time history of assisting during disasters. They, too, provide services to the community outside of disaster assistance. Others who assist include those involved in faith-based organizations, food pantries, soup kitchens, and other local volunteer efforts. Like the ARC and SA, these individuals have identified other community service functions in their organizational missions. What makes them an essential partner in the emergency and disaster management community are their skills with certain functions emergency managers need that are not usually provided by first responders or other government agencies.

The following agencies are an example of the unique contributions these non-profit, non-governmental, voluntary organizations make to the disaster management community.

The American Red Cross. As previously mentioned, the American Red Cross – the oldest and most commonly recognized community service organization – was formed in 1881 with an initial mission to "organize a system of national relief and apply the same in mitigating the sufferings caused by war, pestilence, famine and other calamities." The charter aligned with the United States' ratification of the provisions adopted at the Geneva Convention "for the protection of victims of conflict" and later included "a system of domestic and international disaster relief, including mandated responsibilities under the National Response Framework coordinated by the Federal Emergency Management Agency" (American Red Cross, n.d. b).

The Salvation Army. In an effort to "fight for the lost souls of men and women," William and Catherine Booth worked to evangelize to the poor, hungry, homeless, and destitute of mid-1850s London, England. Deemed the "Christian mission" as a "volunteer army" in an 1878 report, Booth named his organization the Salvation

Army. Although the Salvation Army's main mission is to preach Christian values to those in need, it also provides many services to the community through its religious evangelism, many social service programs, and its disaster response services. Since the Galveston Hurricane in 1900, the Salvation Army started providing emotional and spiritual care, basic comforts and necessities, and long-term recovery needs through these services and with the financial resources they raise every year (The Salvation Army, n.d.).

Faith-Based Organizations. Faith-based organizations (FBOs) are charitable or non-profit organizations that are affiliated with a religious group or are inspired by religious beliefs. Much like the Salvation Army, faith-based organizations' primary mission is to evangelize, support, and serve their faith communities, but they can include many different faith traditions or religions. Faith-based organizations have always been a support and service to their typically local communities by providing aid and spiritual support to the poor, homeless, hungry, sick, disadvantaged, and disenfranchised (Hands of the Carpenter, n.d.). Many food kitchens and pantries are operated by FBOs, for example. FBOs are unique voluntary organizations in disaster management as they are intimately familiar with their local communities. They know their neighborhoods, their people, their culture, and their habits and they are skilled at administering to their communities' specific and unique needs. They are also often in close connection with leaders within the community and can serve as conduits with personnel outside of their community. Thus, FBOs are an extremely important partner to the emergency management community and they are particularly adept at servicing the long-term needs of their communities during recovery.

In addition to the professionals who work and serve in non-profit organizations in the United States, volunteers are an integral part of managing emergencies and disasters across the globe. Many organizations have developed based on the beliefs, ideologies, and interests of the volunteers that congregate and consolidate into structured organizations to both serve their unique missions and objectives and their communities or constituents. Because many are non-profit organizations, they require a number of volunteers in order to operate effectively to provide most of their funding resources to the community to support their services. Likewise, the emergency and disaster management community requires the support and services of volunteers as their resources cannot effectively administer the career personnel necessary to manage the scope and scale of today's emergencies and disasters (FEMA, n.d.a.).

Today's emergencies and disasters require a well-organized approach to all phases of emergency management. The National Preparedness Goal (NPG) outlines the mission areas that integrate the concept of Whole Community in its approach to emergency and disaster management (DHS, 2015). As the professionalism of emergency and disaster management as a discipline evolves, all community partners must be part of the process along each of the mission areas of the NPG. Because of the partnerships between the emergency and disaster management community and voluntary organizations, these organizations now have a seat at the table and are integrated into the overall emergency management process.

The NPG is divided into five mission areas depicted in Figure 9.1: prevention, protection, mitigation, response, and recovery. Each of these mission areas denotes a specific set of strategies and functions to manage disasters. Although most voluntary organizations are involved in the response and recovery missions and as they become more integrated into the emergency management community, their insights and recommendations are emerging in the Prevention, Protection, and Mitigation missions.

FIGURE 9.1 IS-0230.e: Fundamentals of Emergency Management, National Preparedness Goal Mission Areas. FEMA Emergency Management Institute (n.d.b).

Prevention

While virtually all of the mission areas of the NPG have an all-hazards orientation, the prevention mission is focused on "avoiding, preventing, or stopping a threatened or actual act of terrorism" (DHS, 2015). The interesting caveat in this is that many of those that work and serve in these voluntary organizations can provide a remarkable benefit to this mission area. For example, the Department of Homeland Security (DHS) has included faith-based organizations, in particular, through its Center for Faith-Based and Neighborhood Partnerships Resources with its prevention mission focused on human trafficking. This could help prevent terrorists from entering the United States or facilitate reporting of this type of activity. The DHS's *Blue Campaign Faith-Based and Community Toolkit* provides houses of worship with the content and messages that may be used to spread awareness of radicalism within their community and provide a safe place for victims to report their experiences and seek refuge (DHS, n.d.). Those working within organizations like the American Red Cross and the Salvation Army use their national platforms to understand how terrorist ideology and transnational organized crime impact the education and training they generate for their local chapters to employ in their preparedness and response planning and activities.

Protection

Protection "includes the capabilities to safeguard the homeland against acts of terrorism and manmade or natural disasters. It focuses on actions to protect our people, our vital interests, and our way of life" (DHS, 2015). Those leading and serving within non-profit and volunteer organizations have a daily presence in the lives of their communities. Whether it is through the Red Cross, faith-based organizations, or others, these professionals and volunteers have an understanding of their community and their finger on the pulse of potential hazards and threats. Thus, they can provide valuable insights to emergency management personnel.

Mitigation

Mitigation is "focused on the premise that individuals, the private and non-profit sectors, communities, critical infrastructure, and the Nation as a whole are made more resilient when the consequences and impacts, the duration, and the financial and human costs to respond to and recover from adverse incidents are all reduced" (DHS, 2015). As in the protection mission, knowing the threats and hazards of a community aids in developing processes, policies, and procedures to reduce the effects of a disaster/emergency. Again, non-profit and volunteer organizations are strategic partners in this mission due to their unique understanding of their community and its people.

Response

The response mission "includes those capabilities necessary to save lives, protect property and the environment, and meet basic human needs after an incident has occurred... emphasizes saving and sustaining lives, stabilizing the incident, rapidly meeting basic human needs, restoring basic services and technologies, restoring community functionality, providing universal accessibility, establishing a safe and secure environment, and supporting the transition to recovery" (DHS, 2015). The professionals and volunteers in non-profit and volunteer organizations are a part of the community that have local capacities to deal with the public needs. Additionally, when catastrophic incidents occur, a much broader set of partners are able to provide access to goods and services on a large scale. They are a vital link to providing additional support to response personnel and may often be a primary source of logistical needs in the early hours and days after an incident.

Recovery

"Recovery includes those capabilities necessary to assist communities affected by an incident to recover effectively. Support for recovery ensures a continuum of care for individuals to maintain and restore health, safety, independence and livelihoods, especially those who experience financial, emotional, and physical hardships. Successful recovery ensures that we emerge from any threat or hazard stronger and positioned to meet the needs of the future" (DHS, 2015). Given that the leaders and volunteers in non-profit organizations serve an important role in their community's recovery process anyway, it is incumbent upon disaster/emergency management professionals to include them in this phase as they can carry this phase into the longer term efficiently.

As can be seen, efforts to reduce the impact of emergencies and disasters are wholly embedded in the emergency management process. Professionals and volunteers bring a set of skills that can have an invaluable impact on the emergency management workforce (Waters, n.d.). These individuals and non-profit and volunteer organizations are skilled in their own business planning and disaster mitigation needs. For example, their knowledge and experience can augment the emergency management's core capabilities requirements as outlined in Figure 9.2. These human resources help them to be particularly useful in assisting the community with their disaster management efforts.

As has been demonstrated, it is important to know how the National Preparedness Goal relates to non-profit and volunteer organizations assisting in disasters/emergencies. As the nation focuses on its Whole Community, diversity, equity, and inclusion mission, having some understanding of the NPG provides avenues for these organizations to get more involved in all phases of disaster/emergency management as opposed to just providing assistance when incidents occur. The professionals and volunteers in these organizations are stakeholders with a seat at the table to influence policy decisions, planning, and

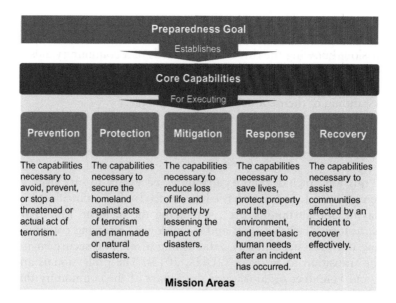

FIGURE 9.2.   FEMA National Preparedness Goal Core Capabilities.

related processes. It is important for non-profit and volunteer organizations to ensure they are part of these discussions by becoming an integrated part of their emergency management communities.

Most of these non-profit and volunteer organizations operate within the Emergency Support Functions of the National Response Framework (NRF). The NRF is "a guide to how the nation responds to all types of disasters and emergencies that is built on scalable, flexible, and adaptable concepts identified in the National Incident Management System" (DHS, 2019). NIMS defines operational systems that guide how personnel works together during incidents to align key roles and responsibilities for emergencies and guides all levels of government, non-governmental organizations, and the private sector to work together to prevent, protect against, mitigate, respond to and recover from incidents. NIMS also provides stakeholders across the whole community with the shared vocabulary, systems, and processes to successfully deliver the capabilities described in the National Preparedness System (NPS). Accordingly, the NPG is one of six elements of the NPS that focuses on the Whole Community approach (DHS, 2019). These doctrines are structured to help jurisdictions, citizens, non-governmental organizations, and businesses:

- Develop whole community plans.
- Integrate continuity plans.
- Build capabilities to respond to cascading failures among businesses, supply chains, and infrastructure sectors.
- Collaborate to stabilize community lifelines and restore services.

The professionals and volunteers involved in non-profit and volunteer organizations are an integral part of the Whole Community within this system. What is important to note is how volunteer organizations factor into this phased process. In fact, they are becoming more and more included in all phases of the cycle rather than just the response and recovery phases as in the past. It is within these phases of the emergency management cycle, along with the NPG, that the professionals and volunteers of the non-profit organizations began partnering as a specific community dedicated to assisting during emergencies and disasters.

Voluntary Organizations Active in Disaster (VOAD)

As illustrated earlier, many volunteer organizations independently served to assist in disasters, but it was often in a disorganized approach that revealed a number of problems resulting from limited training, inadequate information, and limited communication and coordination regarding how to address community needs. When Hurricane Camille occurred in 1969, many expressed dismay that the "help came to the survivors haphazardly"(NVOAD, n.d.). As a result of the Hurricane Camille experience, seven volunteer organizations assembled to discuss ways to coordinate and communicate to better serve their communities during disasters. According to NVOAD (n.d.):

> in 1970, seven national disaster response organizations convened for the first time to find a way to better coordinate responses and more effectively serve disaster survivors and their communities. As an outcome, National VOAD was formed as a forum for sharing knowledge and coordinating resources – money, materials and muscle – throughout the disaster cycle: preparation, response and recovery.

Thus, the National Voluntary Organizations Active in Disaster (or NVOAD) was established in 1970. The VOAD is now one vital organization or a coalition of organizations that provide assistance to emergency management agencies during or after a disaster.

Today, there are currently 56 VOADs and over 70 national organizations (faith-based, community-based, and other non-profits) nationwide connected to VOADs within the United States (NVOAD, n.d.). Today's volunteer organizations are especially adept at coordinating the methods and resources to address disaster/emergency management needs, so they play an integral part in the disaster management ecosystem. In fact, FEMA has within its National Response Framework a core capability dedicated to these organizations, the *Volunteer and Donations Management Support Annex*.

However, non-profit organizations in general have a certain set of legal rules to follow in the course of their business. Likewise, partner organizations in the VOAD have other legal implications based on their specific emergency and disaster management roles. For example, handling donations requires that non-profits be registered with the Internal Revenue Service (IRS) as U.S. 501(c)(3) public charities in order to avoid circumstances of private benefit and private inurement. State and local authorities have their own set of rules and regulations that ensure donations are being used for the specific purpose of assisting the community experiencing a disaster or emergency incident. These funds are generally prescribed for food, clothing, shelter, trauma counseling, and other immediate needs during and following an incident. Finally, non-profits may provide grants for long-term recovery efforts that also carry with them certain rules and regulations (National Council of Non-profits, n.d.). Federal tax law requires that donations be handled solely by a qualified non-profit organization (IRS, 2014).

Volunteer organization liability must also be considered in the event a volunteer gets injured, dies, or performs a function that results in the same for another. Under FEMA funding, the non-profit Public Entity Risk Institute (PERI) developed the Citizen Corps

Volunteer Liability Guide (CCVLG), which provides an overview of liability and suggests ways to address these and other liability concerns (FEMA, 2009). Likewise, states have developed laws for the protection of volunteers that include Good Samaritans and other volunteers, volunteer immunity, liability limitation, shield laws, and charitable immunity. The *State Liability Laws for Charitable Organizations and Volunteers* – 4th Edition, provides an overview of a variety of laws for volunteer protection; however, it is important to note that these protections vary from state to state (NPRMC, 2009).

Non-VOAD Organizations

Other non-VOAD organizations and individual volunteers play an active role in disaster/emergency management. For example, the Department of Homeland Security oversees the Citizens Corps program that partners with the local community to provide training, education, and volunteers "to strengthen the collaboration between government and community leaders from all sectors to encourage citizens' preparedness and to make communities safer, stronger, and better prepared to respond to all hazards and all threats" (DHS, 2013). One element of this program includes the Community Emergency Response Team (CERT) that trains individuals within a community "in basic disaster response skills, such as fire safety, light search and rescue, team organization, and disaster medical operations. CERT offers a consistent, nationwide approach to volunteer training and organization that professional responders can rely on during disaster situations, allowing them to focus on more complex tasks" (FEMA, n.d.c.). Again, these opportunities for volunteers and volunteer organizations adhere to the Whole Community approach in overall disaster/emergency management.

As effective communications issues during emergencies persist, one group of volunteers can be especially helpful with their skills in amateur radio operations. Guglielmo Marconi invented the radio wave–based wireless telegraph system, which led to many amateurs developing radio communications systems in the late 1800s and early 1900s. Over time, these radio operations became useful during World Wars I and II and other wars, as well as for major disasters such as the 9/11 terrorist attacks in the U.S., and Hurricanes Katrina and Maria.

Amateur radio operators have served the emergency management community since 1952 as part of the early days of civil defense. Today, the Radio Amateur Civil Emergency Service (RACES), managed through federal protocols under the civil defense authority, includes volunteers that "serve their respective jurisdictions pursuant to guidelines and mandates established by local emergency management officials" (USRACES.org, n.d.). They are:

- Licensed radio amateurs.
- Certified by a civil defense agency.
- Able to communicate on amateur radio frequencies during drills, exercises, and emergencies.
- Activated by local, county and state jurisdictions and are the only Amateur Radio operators authorized to transmit during declared emergencies when the President of the United States specifically invokes the War Powers Act.

RACES operators are activated by a local civil defense official and function under the protocols of NIMS in order to most effectively collaborate and communicate across jurisdictions during disasters and emergencies. Some amateur radio operators may be affiliated with the Amateur Radio Emergency Service (ARES) and activated before, during, and after a disaster/emergency by a local American Radio Relay League (ARRL) official. Unlike RACES, which is strictly limited to official civil-preparedness activities in the event of an emergency-communications situation, ARES is a non-commercial organization of volunteer radio operators (who may maintain co-membership in RACES) who use their own equipment to provide communication assistance during disasters/emergencies (ARES, n.d.). In addition to some confusion about the differences between RACES and ARES operators, they are usually independently affiliated and not part of the VOAD network.

CURRENT CHALLENGES

The professionals and volunteers engaged with non-profit and volunteer organizations do face challenges as they integrate within the emergency management community. Most of these tend to be administrative and operational in nature such as learning about the National Preparedness System, integrating efforts within the NIMS and incident command structure, managing and vetting unaffiliated volunteers specific to disasters/emergencies, and managing the influx of donations when large disasters/emergencies occur. The ways in which these issues can be addressed were outlined earlier. However, two specific areas that need further development include attention to social and environmental justice and the manner in which mental health care is incorporated into the overall goals of these organizations before, during, and after disasters/emergencies in their communities.

Social and Environmental Justice

Many professions, including the profession of Social Work, concentrate their endeavors on Social Justice to ensure that all people from all social classes are treated equally, with no disproportionate disparity of treatment made between them. The individuals involved in non-profit organizations also work on the noble goal to establish Environmental Justice, which has been defined in many ways.

One definition states that Environmental Justice is "the fair treatment of meaningful involvement of all people regardless of race, color, national origin, or status in life [social or economic] with respect to the development, implementation, and enforcement of environmental laws, regulations, and policies" (U.S. EPA, n.d.).

"Another related definition of Environmental Justice proposes not only the equal involvement and treatment of all people but the right of all people to high levels of environmental protection [water, food, land, etc]" (National Association of Social Workers, n.d.).

> An environmental justice concern arises when some level of government is considering taking an action that might disproportionately impact a vulnerable populations: for example, when polluting sources such as chemical factories, bus depots, urban freeways, or power generating plants cluster in areas where the residents are already burdened with pollution, health and social problems, or economic disadvantage, or when that population has little clout, has been discounted by government for some reason, has not had an opportunity to participate in the decision-making process, or has been discriminated against.
>
> (Hill, 2017, p. 177)

Yet a third definition denotes Environmental Justice as "the study of the relationships between living things and the environment" (Webster's English Dictionary, n.d.). The main focus of all three definitions – whichever one is chosen – is the idea that all people equally experience high levels of environmental protection, and no group is excluded nor disproportionately affected adversely in responsible uses of ecological resources: water, air, food, land, etc. This philosophy of equality for all (sameness) – no matter one's station or status in life – is an integral part of a social worker's and other professionals' institutional training, specifically, as they stand up for everyone, and for one's quality of life. Oftentimes, aspirations toward equality only become a call for equity (i.e., fairness) – but it is equality (i.e., sameness) that all professions should truly seek to obtain. Emergency managers would add to the quality of life: and to their happiness (Phillips, Neal, and Coppola, 2017).

In essence, it is argued that marginalized and underserved communities are not to experience disproportionality of impact by climate, drought, or pollution. "Place" therefore matters, and these marginalized groups should not be singled out to bear the brunt of communities where garbage is burned, poor water quality is maintained, or where factories' smokestacks full of pollution abound.

The Social Workers' Code of Ethics demands that these professionals "should engage in social and political action that seeks to ensure that all people have equal access to the resources, employment, services, and opportunities they require to meet their basic human needs and develop fully" (Code of Ethics). Likewise, emergency managers and homeland security professionals follow similar beliefs in their respective evolving disciplines. For instance, many of these same Social Justice and Environmental Justice tenets are carried forth in these professions by caretaking of marginalized and disadvantaged groups – although emergency management refers to these populations as socially vulnerable populations. These groups include, for example, racial minorities, the poor, infants, women with children, the elderly, those with physical and mental disabilities, etc., that are cared for and taken into account (e.g., during evacuations and other strenuous types of post-disaster response and recovery activities).

Similar to social workers, emergency managers and other professional groups must demonstrate empathy toward these marginalized and disadvantaged groups such as those mentioned earlier. These groups have not had a voice, either politically or socially, and much care must be taken to see that their special and specific needs are met, especially during times of crisis and other calamities. Furthermore, professionals in all settings must continue to hone cooperation, collaboration, communications, coordination, advocacy, and organizational skills to help all socially vulnerable populations, as well as any other persons needing protection in Social Justice and Environmental Justice circumstances.

Conclusively, basic human rights must be protected and the fight against many human violations must continue. Non-profit organizations operated or overseen by social workers, emergency managers, homeland security professionals, and others, can – and do – assist with pressing international wicked problems (i.e., seemingly unresolvable ones) related to: apartheid in Africa; ethnic cleansing; genocide; infertility practices related to a woman's ability to bear children; and much more. These grave injustices must be prevented by these non-profit organizations, or at least mitigated where and when able to do so. Campaigns for Social Justice, Environmental Justice, and protection of socially vulnerable populations must continue, respectively, spearheaded by social workers, emergency managers, homeland security professionals, and other related personnel. The ultimate goal of these indispensable non-profit organizations is that the world – dare we say, each of us – hold steadfast and protect those most marginalized and disadvantaged people on Earth.

Mental Health Care in Disaster/Emergency Management

Another major challenge in disasters and emergency management relates to mental health. Disasters/emergencies can present a number of issues during the incident and in the ability to recover emotionally from the incident. According to the Pan American Health Organization (2012):

> The last decade has been marked by major disasters around the globe. Regardless of their origin, these events have deeply impacted the population living in the affected areas. The loss of life, serious injuries, destroyed homes and other property, displacement, and family separation creates serious disruptions and repercussions in people's lives, and can affect their mental health and psychosocial well being. With time, most of those affected will manage to recover on their own, depending on the circumstances. Some, however, will need more attention, care, and treatment.

Mental health and psychological well-being are thus an integral part of the disaster/emergency management process.

Non-profit organizations and volunteers have always possessed the mission to help others and this assistance consisted of food, shelter, and clothing to serve the basic needs of their communities. However, the professionals and volunteers in these organizations increasingly provide emotional support for the scarring from traumatic events, a common phenomenon as a result of disasters/emergencies. As the emergency management community recognizes the impact of incidents, more attention must be given to mental health support with improved processes, policies, procedures, and partnerships. Using the skills and experiences of the non-profit and volunteer community adds to a holistic approach to the services and care the community needs. Many organizations and programs have developed to address mental health needs for disasters/emergencies.

Therefore, one of the hallmarks of volunteers and non-profit organizations' work is their ability to provide mental health services to affected communities by disasters/emergencies. Many organizations have volunteer mental health professionals or programs to assist those suffering from the effects of major incidents. These affected individuals can include both citizens and first responders; therefore, there are several ways they can obtain comfort, support, and clinical intervention to deal with and recover from their disaster/emergency experiences.

The U.S. Department of Health and Human Services Office of the Assistant Secretary for Preparedness and Response developed a fact sheet of their current assets and capabilities for disaster behavioral health (DHHS, n.d.). This fact sheet identifies various volunteer organizations and programs available for disaster/emergency incident survivors.

- **The Medical Reserve Corps (MRC)** provides volunteer licensed mental health providers that are specifically trained to respond to disasters/emergencies as part of the Emergency Support Function #8, a component of the NRF capabilities discussed earlier in this chapter.
- **The National Disaster System (NDMS) and Federal Occupational Health (FOH)** are federal services that can be deployed as part of the federal response to large incidents and for federal responders.
- **The Employee Assistance Program (EAP)** "is a voluntary, work-based program that offers free and confidential assessments, short-term counseling, referrals, and follow-up services to employees who have personal and/or work-related

problems. EAPs address a broad and complex body of issues affecting mental and emotional well-being, such as alcohol and other substance abuse, stress, grief, family problems, and psychological disorders. EAP counselors also work in a consultative role with managers and supervisors to address employee and organizational challenges and needs. Many EAPs are active in helping organizations prevent and cope with workplace violence, trauma, and other emergency response situations" (OPM.gov, n.d.). EAPs are provided by many employers and can provide support to those suffering the effects of a disaster/emergency, but not all employers provide EAPs, therefore necessitating mental health care through other means.
- **The Department of Health and Human Services** also provides several grants and benefits that support mental healthcare programs during disasters.

Other non-profit and volunteer organizations provide support to their local communities in the form of:

- **The NVOAD Disaster Emotional Care (DEC) Guidelines** that provide a common core for state and local VOADs to address emotional support needs during disasters (NVOAD, 2020). These guidelines help VOAD members use their own standards of education, licensure, and certifications in emotional care to provide assistance specifically for disaster emotional care.
- **Faith-based organizations** that are skilled at providing numerous services to assist during disasters and, in particular, during the recovery process. For instance, the National Disaster Interfaith Network (NDIN, n.d.) provides guidelines on how faith-based organizations can use their services to assist during disasters and for recovery. This includes recommendations on how to address disaster survivors specifically with examples of how to talk with them and how to address their own mental health as these experiences are traumatic to the survivors and can cause vicarious traumatization to the mental healthcare workers as they work with them.
- **Critical Incident Stress Management (CISM)**, which is a concept started in the fire service to address the traumatic experiences first responders are often exposed to. CISM consists of various resources that can include a crisis management briefing to large groups referred to as a "town hall meeting" to provide a basic understanding of stress and trauma along with ways to cope with the disaster/emergency. A Critical Incident Stress Debriefing (CISD) is also a component of CISM that provides a smaller group format to assist those affected with a more structured method of group intervention, education, and resources for further care. These additional resources can include individual, pastoral, peer support, and EAP care, for example, for the community (National Interagency Fire Center, n.d.).
- **Peer Support programs** that provide responders with mental health care as part of the overall disaster/emergency management process. Peer supporters are trained individuals within the first responder, non-profit, and volunteer organizations that support their peers by providing immediate comfort, stress management, and referrals that help avoid the stigma of mental health needs for professionals responding to disaster/emergency incidents. The National Alliance on Mental Illness (NAMI, n.d.) provides information and guidance on what peer support is and how it is utilized in the disaster/emergency management community.

As noted, there are many ways that victims, survivors, and emergency responders can obtain mental healthcare services related in disaster/emergency incidents. Professional mental healthcare providers that specialize in disaster/emergency stress and trauma often volunteer their services to assist in the immediate needs of the incident while offering ongoing services individually in-person and through telehealth methods providing increased convenience and confidentiality to their clients. Today's disaster mental health care serves as a preventative method as "psychological first aid" to those affected by disaster/emergency incidents. These services provide a holistic, Whole Community approach that easily integrates with the NPG's mission areas across the emergency management community.

RECOMMENDATIONS FOR THE FUTURE

The following are ten recommendations that non-profit and volunteer organizations should consider as they continue to provide their services and support to the emergency management community:

1. Reinforce and expand the role and impact of non-profit professionals in disaster/ emergency management.
2. Engage with the emergency management community regularly as part of the whole community approach (e.g., participate in planning, training, and exercises with the local, regional, state, tribal, national, and international governments).
3. Practice harmonious interorganizational relations and avoidance of inter-agency conflicts (e.g., by engaging in cooperation, collaboration, communication, and coordination designed into existing and new burgeoning systems).
4. Manage administrative challenges more effectively in non-profit organizations (e.g., fundraising, human resources, training and professional development).
5. Avoid "disasters within disasters" through the effective management of donations, resources, materials, and volunteers and expand all capabilities in all organizational settings.
6. Provide greater assistance to refugees and internally displaced persons in countries where serious migration issues abound.
7. Hone and develop socially innovative non-profit organizations as "functioning organizations that make a difference – that achieve a social impact" (Renz, 2016, p. xxxii) to address social and environmental justice needs.
8. Keep marginalized and socially vulnerable populations at the forefront of viable actions to achieve positive, viable outcomes.
9. Focus on the diversity, inclusion, and equity issues necessary for today's societal needs.
10. Address and improve upon mental health care particularly as it pertains to all types of disasters, terrorist attacks, and conflict.

CONCLUSION

This chapter focused on the history and nature of non-profit organizations, identified their relation to disasters/terrorist attacks/international conflict, discussed the role of related professionals and volunteers in emergency management/homeland security, mentioned various challenges being confronted today, and suggested recommendations for improvement.

The chapter indicated that non-profit organizations have become more prevalent over time because of the gaps that were evident in government operations and business activities. It highlighted that VOADs as an organized conglomerate of non-profit and volunteer organizations can assist in addressing community needs after disasters and provide a system to the emergency management community with affiliated and unaffiliated volunteers. The chapter also revealed the vital contributions non-profit professionals and volunteers make when complex humanitarian crises (i.e., Ukraine) occur.

While the contributions of non-profit professionals and volunteers are great, major opportunities exist to improve social/environmental justice. These individuals can support FEMA's 2022–2026 Strategic Plan, which outlines key goals of: instilling equity as a foundation of emergency management, protecting the environment and promoting climate change resilience, sustaining a Whole Community approach to prepare the nation, and guaranteeing rights are protected through disaster assistance. There is also a dire need to address mental health needs after disasters and types of incidents.

As has been argued throughout the chapter, the professionals and volunteers involved in non-profit organizations are a key resource that can augment a community's ability to manage disasters/emergencies due to their unique skills and abilities. By being included in all phases of emergency management, these professionals and volunteers can help us to better deal with all types of disasters, terrorist attacks, and humanitarian crises.

CLASS DISCUSSION AND ESSAY QUESTIONS

1. What are the features or key characteristics of non-profit organizations in comparison to businesses and government entities?
2. Why were non-profit organizations established in history and what caused them to expand in number and scope in the United States and elsewhere around the world?
3. What problems do disasters and acts of violence create, and why are non profit organization's services required?
4. Do volunteers need to be coordinated by professionals involved in non-profit management after a disaster or terrorist attack? Why or why not?
5. How do non-profit professionals relate to other phases of emergency management (mitigation, preparedness, response, and recovery)?
6. What is the role of the National Voluntary Organizations Active in Disaster?
7. What can be done to better harness or prepare non-profit professionals for future disasters and conflict situations?

REFERENCES

ACAPS. (2022). Ukraine Conflict Overview. https://www.acaps.org/country/ukraine/crisis/conflict.

Allen, J. M. and R. Sawhney (2019). *Administration and Management in Criminal Justice: A Service Quality Approach*, 3rd ed., Los Angeles, CA: Sage.

Amateur Radio Emergency Service (ARES) (n.d.). What Is ARES/RACES? Amateur Radio Emergency Service (k7yca.org).

American Red Cross (n.d.-a). Red Cross Timeline: Exploring Significant Dates in Red Cross History. https://www.redcross.org/about-us/who-we-are/history/significant -dates.html.

American Red Cross (n.d.-b). Our Federal Charter. https://www.redcross.org/content/ dam/redcross/National/history-federal-charter.pdf.

American Red Cross. (2022). Our History, https://www.redcross.org/about-us/who-we -are/history.html.

Charity Navigator. (2022). Crisis in Ukraine. https://www.charitynavigator.org/index .cfm?bay=content.view&cpid=9366.

Coppolla, D. P. (2011). *Introduction to International Disaster Management*, 2nd ed., New York: Elsevier.

Department of Homeland Security (DHS) (n.d.). DHS Center for Faith-Based and Neighborhood Partnerships. https://www.dhs.gov/faith.

Department of Homeland Security (DHS) (2013). Privacy Impact Assessment for the Citizen Corps Program. Privacy Impact Assessment for the Citizen Corp Program (dhs.gov).

Department of Homeland Security (DHS) (2015). The National Preparedness Goal, 2nd ed., September 2015. https://www.fema.gov/sites/default/files/202006/national_pre- paredness_goal_2nd_edition.pdf.

Department of Homeland Security (DHS) (2019). National Response Framework. 2nd ed. (fema.gov).

Fahy, R., B. Evarts, and G. P. Stein (2021). NFPA: US Fire Department Profile 2019. https://www.nfpa.org/-/media/Files/News-and-Research/Fire-statistics-and-reports /Emergency-responders/osfdprofile.pdf.

FEMA (n.d.a). DHS Center for Faith-Based and Neighborhood Partnerships Resources. https://www.fema.gov/emergency-managers/individuals-communities/faith#human -trafficking.

FEMA (n.d.b). Emergency Management Institute: IS-230.E Fundamentals of Emergency Management. https://training.fema.gov/is/courseoverview.aspx?code=IS-230.e&lang=en.

FEMA (n.d.c). Community Emergency Response Team. https://www.ready.gov/cert.

FEMA (2009). Citizen Corps Volunteer Liability Guide: An Overview of Legal Issues and Approaches to Address Liability for Emergency Volunteers. https://www.hsdl.org/ ?abstract&did=34079.

FEMA (2015). IS-288-A: The Role of Voluntary Organizations in Emergency Management. https://training.fema.gov/is/courseoverview.aspx?code=is-288.a.

Franklin, B. and J. Bigelow (1869). *Autobiography of Benjamin Franklin*. Philadelphia, PA: J.B. Lippincott & Co.

Hands of the Carpenter (n.d.). *What Is a Faith-Based Non-profit Organization?* https:// www.handsofthecarpenter.org/what-is-a-faith-based-non-profit-organization/.

Hill, P. (2017). *Environmental Protection: What Everyone Needs to Know*. New York: Oxford University Press.

Internal Revenue Service (IRS) (2014). Disaster Relief: Providing Assistance throutgh Charitable Organizations. https://www.irs.gov/pub/irs-pdf/p3833.pdf.

International Committere of the Red Cross (ICRC) (2015). 70 Years on Red Cross Hospitals Still Treat Thousands of Atomic omb Survivors. https://www.icrc.org/ en/document/70-years-red-cross-hospitals-still-treat-thousands-atomic-bomb -survivors

International Fund for Animal Welfare. (2021). Help for Ukraine Supporting Refugees & Pets, Animal Shelters & Rescue. https://www.ifaw.org/action/ukraine-emergency-aid-update?utm_source=google&utm_medium=cpc&utm_campaign=BA_DMT_Ukraine_30DG00001&cid=7013k000001a9aw&ms=UONDF220320103&gclid=CjwKCAjw7vuUBhBUEiwAEdu2pDWGo9SwRtNOVqG2fZLZbSty_MhgvoWowsiy3dmOo9bBSDAXVEcYrxoC-kwQAvD_BwE.

Lucie, Q. (2019). How F E M A Could Lose America's Next Great War. *Homeland Security Affairs* 15, Article 1. https://www.hsaj.org/articles/15017.

National Alliance on Mental Illness (NAMI) (n.d.). Public Safety Professionals. https://www.nami.org/Your-Journey/Frontline-Professionals/Public-Safety-Professionals.

National Association of Social Workers (n.d.). Code of Ethics. www.socialworkers.org.

National Council of Non-Profits (n.d.). Disaster Revocery: What Donors and Non-profits Need to Know. https://www.councilofnon-profits.org/tools-resources/disaster-recovery-what-donors-and-non-profits-need-know.

National Disaster Interfaith Network (NDIN) (n.d.). Faith Communities and Disaster Mental Health Factsheet. https://n-din.org/wp-content/uploads/2021/08/11_NDIN_TS_DisasterMentalHealth.pdf.

National Interagency Fire Center (NIFC) (n.d.). Critical Incident Stress Management. https://www.nifc.gov/resources/taking-care-of-our-own/about-critical-incident-stress-management.

National Voluntary Organizations Active in Disaster (NVOAD) (n.d.). About Us. https://www.nvoad.org/about-us/.

National Voluntary Organizations Active in Disaster (NVOAD) (2020). Disaster Emotional Care Guidelines National VOAD Emotional and Spiritual Care Committee. https://www.nvoad.org/wp-content/uploads/Disaster-Emotional-Care-Guidelines.pdf.

Non-Profit Risk Management Center (NPRMC) (2009). State Liability Laws for Charitable Organizations and Volunteers. https://www.probonopartner.org/wp-content/uploads/2016/01/stateliabilitylawsforcharitiesandvolunteers.pdf.

Office of Personnel Management (OPM) (n.d.). What Is an Employee Assistance Program (EAP)? https://www.opm.gov/faqs/QA.aspx?fid=4313c618-a96e-4c8e-b078-1f76912a10d9&pid=2c2b1e5b-6ff1-4940-b478-34039a1e1174.

Pan American Health Organization (2012). Mental Health and Psychosocial Support in Disaster Situations in the Caribbean Core Knowledge for Emergency Preparedness and Response. https://iris.paho.org/bitstream/handle/10665.2/3188/MentalHealthPsychosocialSupport.pdf?sequence=1&isAllowed=y.

Phillips, B. D., D. M. Neal, and G. R. Webb (2017). *Introduction to Emergency Management*, 2nd ed. Boca Raton, FL: CRC Press.

Putnam, R. D. (2000). *Bowling Alone: The Collapse and Revival of American Community*. New York: Simon and Schuster.

Renz, D. O. & Associates (2016). *The Jossey-Bass Handbook of Non-profit Leadership and Management*, 4th ed. Hoboken, NJ: John Wiley & Sons, Inc.

Smith, K. (2022). How Companies Are Responding to the War in Ukraine: A Roundup, Boston College, Center for Corporate Citizenship. https://ccc.bc.edu/content/ccc/blog-home/2022/03/companies-respond-to-war-in-ukraine.html.

The Salvation Army (n.d.). Doing the Most Good: History of the Salvation Army. https://www.salvationarmyusa.org/usn/history-of-the-salvation-army/.

U.S. Environmental Protection Agency-(U.S. EPA) (n.d.). www.epa.gov.

USRACES.org (n.d.). Radio Amateur Civil Emergency Service (RACES). USRACES. ORG.

Waters, A. (n.d.). The Role of Volunteers in All-Hazards Planning and Disaster Management. https://www.galaxydigital.com/blog/the-role-of-volunteers-in-disasters.

Webster's English Dictionary (n.d.). www.webster-dictionary.net.

CHAPTER 10

Professionals in the Department of Homeland Security:
The Swiss Army Knife of America's Defense and Protection

Jackson Roberts and David A. McEntire

INTRODUCTION

In the 9/11 national review, investigators and legislators made it very clear that there was insufficient coordination or communication among the more than 20 organizations and agencies that were tasked with homeland security. For instance, some of the culprits of 9/11 – specifically Khalid al-Mihdhar and Nawaf al-Hazmi had been linked to previous terrorist threats. These individuals had been identified as individuals who were preparing for terrorist attacks in Bangkok, but unfortunately, were not monitored after they left this country and used fraudulent passports to enter the United States (Kean, 2003). Despite various clues and threats, the perpetrators were able to enter America, obtain pilot's licenses, and board those fateful flights that would effectively change the course of domestic and foreign policy, as well as our involvement in the Middle East over the next 20 years. The mistakes made and lack of coordination across intelligence agencies created the need for a reorganization of government to compile and examine information provided from various sources in order to more effectively deter terrorism and protect the American homeland. Thus, the formal profession of Homeland Security was created.

Since its creation of the Department of Homeland Security (DHS) in November of 2002, there has been a constant tension between the DHS professionals and some of the various organizations within it. As with any business or organization, when a new group, individual, or entity is created or placed in a position of authority, there is the potential for conflict. The balance of power is disrupted, and people become resistant to change. The creation of the Department of Homeland Security not only altered the balance of power, it also led to the greatest change in the federal government since the National Security Act of 1947 (Cusick et al., 2021). Thus, the establishment of the Department of Homeland Security was no small or insignificant reorganization. Among other changes, policies and procedures were rewritten, and agencies that previously acted with little oversight now had to report to DHS. In addition, countless positions were created, eliminated, or moved while new legislation and budgets had to be written to accommodate the

DOI: 10.4324/9781003350729-10

new goals and means for accomplishing them. The transition was definitely not without its tensions or conflict.

Despite these challenges, however, the profession of Homeland Security is a necessary one, and the partnerships within it are just as essential. The Department of Homeland Security has the central responsibility for many of the goals relating to security within the American border. For instance, DHS oversees border security, disaster response, pandemic response, and other operations on domestic territory. This vast and critical list of responsibilities places the Secretary of the Department of Homeland Security on the President's cabinet, a testament to the importance of his or her duties. The DHS is therefore in a unique position to coordinate a great deal of information between a large variety of sources and fields, and it shares that information with the President to allow him or her to make critical decisions on policy, military action, disaster response, or any other emergency that may threaten the American people. All of this requires a vast population of DHS professionals trained in a number of different fields.

In the following chapter, we will discuss the history of the Homeland Security from its creation and first iterations, along with the relationship the Homeland Security profession has to disasters and terrorism including its oversight of the Federal Emergency Management Agency (FEMA) and primary mission of antiterrorism. Then, the roles in emergency management and homeland security will be discussed highlighting the DHS professionals' specific tasks and actions within these two fields and some other related functions. Afterwards, the paper will review the current challenges the DHS faces today such as inter-organizational strain, COVID-19, and border issues. Recommendations for the future of the DHS profession will be discussed including better staffing and training of its personnel and how to be more prepared for disasters in the future.

HISTORY OF THE HOMELAND SECURITY PROFESSION

Prior to the creation of the Homeland Security profession, politicians traditionally referred to the United States as "the nation" and policies concerning the territorial United States as "the union." The concept of "the Homeland" was virtually unused prior to the creation of the DHS in 2002. In spite of this fact, the need for the Homeland Security profession was recognized as early as 1980 because of mounting threats – both internal and external. However, the creation of such a department would be difficult as it would require a great deal of time, money, legislation, and effort. For these reasons, no serious action was taken in creating a central homeland security organization until the events of 9/11 emphasized the need for it again and justified the required expenditures.

When the concept of DHS was first introduced, it came in the form of the "Office of Homeland Security," which operated within the White House. This office was established by President George W. Bush through executive order 13228. On September 22, 11 days after 9/11, the first Director of the Office of Homeland Security (OHS) was appointed. The individual chosen for the task was Pennsylvania Governor, Tom Ridge. Tom Ridge would be key in the creation of the subsequent Department of Homeland Security along with the necessary policies, positions, legislation, and allocation of funds for such a change. Around the same time, the Homeland Security Council, similar to the National Security Council, was formed. This was a group of high-level individuals selected to personally advise the President on issues surrounding homeland security from counterterrorism and public health to economic threats. The first "generation" of agents in the OHS, later DHS, had a great many growing pains in front of them.

In "The Department of Homeland Security" publication, released in June 2002, the DHS was tasked with becoming one department with a variety of professionals whose:

> primary mission is to protect the homeland; to secure our borders, transportation sector, ports, and critical infrastructure; to synthesize and analyze homeland security intelligence from multiple sources; to coordinate communications with state and local governments, private industry, and the American people about threats and preparedness; to coordinate our efforts to protect the American people against bioterrorism and other weapons of mass destruction; to help train and equip first responders; to manage federal emergency response activities; [and have] more security officers in the field working to stop terrorists and fewer resources in Washington managing duplicative and redundant activities that drain critical homeland security resources.
>
> (Bush, 2002)

This, of course, was and is no small or simple list of tasks. The responsibilities are much easier said than done and they require a great number of people with specific skill sets to properly accomplish such a diverse mission.

From the very beginning and up to the current day, there were and are tensions regarding a seeming return to civil defense. Much of this contempt came from FEMA personnel who saw its role reduced post-9/11 under DHS. In 2003, FEMA was absorbed wholly into the DHS as a part of the Emergency Preparedness and Response Directorate of the Department of Homeland Security. It lost much of its autonomy, funding, and connection to the President until 2007 when the value of the Federal Emergency Management Agency was reiterated after Hurricane Katrina. Despite the return of their name and a degree of independence, the conflict and tension between FEMA employees and DHS professionals still remain to one degree or another.

Major legislation that has created, changed, or further developed the role of the DHS professional occurred over time. Of course, the first piece of relevant legislation was *The Homeland Security Act of 2002*. The Department of Homeland Security was officially formed via this act one year after the 9/11 attacks. This act resulted in a number of changes – the most substantial, of course, being the creation of the Department of Homeland Security by combining over 20 different agencies and organizations including FEMA, U.S. Customs and Border Protection, the Coast Guard, and numerous others under the "umbrella" of DHS. This act also brought about changes such as a new cabinet-level secretary to represent Homeland Security and oversee the more than 18,000 employees who fall under DHS (Samuels, 2002). The Homeland Security Act of 2002 was followed by the Comprehensive Homeland Security Act of 2003. This act further identified what DHS would do and how its mission would be implemented. It was more focused on accomplishing goals rather than establishing the DHS organization in the first place.

A subsequent piece of legislation which is related to the DHS is the *Intelligence Reform and Terrorism Prevention Act of 2004 (IRTPA)*. This act was an amendment of the National Security Act of 1947 and created the Office of the Director of National Intelligence, effectively reorganizing the entire intelligence community. In some respects, this act brought over a dozen intelligence agencies under one roof, reporting to the Director of National Intelligence who was the newest member of the National Security Council and advises the President directly. This act also created the Information Sharing Council to advise the President about coordination between various federal agencies and departments to make effective policy (BJA, 2004).

An additional and significant piece of legislation which affects the DHS professional is the *Implementing Recommendations of the 9-11 Commission Act of 2007*. This Act altered section 1016 of the Intelligence Reform and Terrorism Prevention Act (IRTPA) and also amended the Homeland Security Act of 2002. It defined key terms such as "homeland security information," "information-sharing environment," "terrorist information," and "weapons of mass destruction." These definitions have been key to determining constitutionality of policy and the creation of further policy surrounding these topics. The act also established guidelines for fusion centers to "develop, publish, and adhere to a privacy and civil liberties policy that is consistent with Federal, State, and local law." Fusion centers are central locations that facilitate the sharing of information between organizations in government such as the FBI, DHS, and Department of Justice, for example (BJA, 2007).

THE RELATION OF HOMELAND SECURITY PROFESSIONALS TO DISASTERS AND TERRORISM

As can be imagined, the professionals in the Department of Homeland Security are heavily involved in both disasters and terrorist attacks since DHS has primary responsibility in overseeing all threats to the homeland. This section of the chapter will discuss in further detail those responsibilities and provide some examples of DHS professionals' actions in relation to terrorism and in disasters. The portion of the chapter will likewise mention some challenges that DHS professionals have had in responding to terrorism or disasters.

Terrorism

For better or for worse, terrorism is the number one priority for professionals in the Department of Homeland Security. According to the DHS website, "Protecting the American people from terrorist threats is the reason DHS was created and remains our highest priority" (DHS, "Preventing Terrorism" 2022). Terrorism is a very general term with a wide variety of threats and possible sources of attack. To combat this, DHS hires diverse professionals, overseeing a plethora of agencies and fields to prevent terrorism. This includes Secret Service Agents, Border Patrol Agents, transportation security personnel, and others that address threats on critical infrastructure such as the chemical sector.

Disasters

FEMA is the primary federal agency when it comes to disasters, and as of 2003, it falls under the organization of the Department of Homeland Security. This federal entity focuses on reducing or reacting to natural disasters or technological events such as earthquakes, hurricanes, tornadoes, floods, industrial fires, and major hazardous materials incidents. It therefore employs individuals who promote all types of mitigation, preparedness, response, and recovery objectives. But, FEMA employees also have a role in dealing with the consequences of terrorist attacks and they are becoming more involved in cybersecurity planning today as well.

Weaknesses Revealed in Hurricane Katrina

The two-fold mission of DHS has not been without controversy. Almost immediately after DHS was created, the professionals in this organization experienced several major challenges. These were due, in large part, to the heavy emphasis being placed on terrorism when DHS was created. Emergency management was being neglected and overshadowed. When Hurricane Katrina made landfall on August 25, 2005, numerous shortcomings and weaknesses in the preparedness and response system were identified. An article written by Chris Edward (2015) identifies five that will be discussed below:

1. Confusion. In a bipartisan report in 2006 on the Hurricane Katrina response, it was stated that "federal agencies…had varying degrees of unfamiliarity with their roles and responsibilities under the National Response Plan and National Incident Management System." It also revealed that government actors perceived "general confusion over mission assignments, deployments, and command structure." One potential reason for this could be due to most of FEMA's executives being political appointees with no experience in disaster response.
2. Failure to Learn. The federal government was quickly overwhelmed in the response to Hurricane Katrina, despite many preparations and warning signs. It was common knowledge that a major hurricane was probable in Louisiana and government agencies, including FEMA, had run the "Hurricane Pam" simulation a year before, where a similarly sized hurricane fictitiously made landfall in New Orleans. When Hurricane Katrina formed, the forecast accurately predicted landfall. Despite the intended preparations and warnings, the response in Hurricane Katrina was poor and showed that critical lessons learned in these simulations and preparations were not being ingrained properly.
3. Communications Breakdown. A House of Representatives report regarding the Katrina response stated that there was "a complete breakdown in communications that paralyzed command and control and made situational awareness murky at best" (Govinto, 2005). Despite a number of grants given to and through FEMA for emergency communications over the past few decades, agencies could not effectively communicate and this revealed a massive waste of resources. Incidentally, this breakdown of information-sharing was also a major issue in the 9/11 response where agencies, such as police officers and firefighters, were unable to properly communicate to share information and coordinate action, contributing to the danger and confusion.
4. Supply Failures. Emergency supplies were acquired prior to the hurricane, but they were quickly depleted. It took days to transport these supplies to critical facilities such as the New Orleans Superdome. FEMA perhaps also wasted millions of dollars' worth of supplies and resources. There have been stories of FEMA spending millions of dollars to ship ice to disaster-affected communities without it ever being utilized. It was also reported that FEMA paid $900 million for mobile homes which FEMA's own regulation kept from being used at all because they were to be located in flood plains, which was known at the time of the purchase.
5. Indecision. While allocating medical supplies, making decisions for placement of personnel and funds, and executing plans, government leaders in the local and federal government were slow and indecisive. The deceased were left out in the elements, rotting for days as officials tried to determine what to do about

recovery of human remains. While FEMA waited on Louisiana for a decision on body recovery, the governor of Louisiana blamed the delay on FEMA for laziness. Law enforcement and evacuation was also delayed greatly by bureaucratic paralysis when decisions had to be made.

THE PROFESSION'S ROLE IN EMERGENCY MANAGEMENT AND HOMELAND SECURITY

As can be seen, the professionals involved in Homeland Security have many responsibilities and have encountered a wide variety of weaknesses. In this section, the chapter will review in detail the specific roles, responsibilities, and tasks that DHS professionals fulfill in Homeland Security, with a focus on their functions in response to terrorism disasters and other events that don't quite qualify as natural or man-made disasters.

Functions in Homeland Security and Terrorism

The Secretary of Homeland Security is responsible for all functions relating to the Department of Homeland Security. "Under the Secretary's leadership, DHS professionals are responsible for counterterrorism, cybersecurity, aviation security, border security, port security, maritime security, administration and enforcement of our immigration laws, protection of our national leaders, protection of critical infrastructure, cybersecurity, detection of and protection against chemical, biological, and nuclear threats to the homeland, and response to disasters" (DHS, "Secretary of Homeland Security" 2022). There are several major priorities the Secretary and others have for homeland security. These are listed below in more detail.

- Counterterrorism. According to DHS's own site (DHS, "Counterterrorism" and "Prevention Terrorism" 2022), the professionals in DHS focus on primary goals to defend against terrorism. First, they collect, analyze, and share actionable intelligence. DHS professionals work with multiple intelligence sources to get accurate, timely, and actionable intelligence. They must then rapidly distribute this information to the correct agencies and individuals necessary to prevent such threats. DHS has the broadest customer base. That is to say, the organization has a large group of individuals and organizations with which to gather and share information. For this reason, the professionals involved in DHS require cutting-edge integrated intelligence systems to coordinate and prevent terrorism.
  A second goal of these professionals is to detect and disrupt threats. Decentralized terrorist groups have shifted largely away from open propaganda and recruitment in favor of cyber recruitment and chat rooms where they are less likely to be detected. It is consequently critical that plans made to harm the American homeland be detected and disrupted before much, if any damage at all, can occur. "DHS is using its full breadth of law enforcement, border security, immigration, travel security, and trade-based authorities to proactively prevent, identify, investigate, disrupt, and dismantle these organizations."
- Cybersecurity. Cybersecurity is one responsibility that largely affects each of the other responsibilities of the professionals in the Department of Homeland

Security. Weak cybersecurity leaves us vulnerable to threats from terrorism, compromised borders, fragile infrastructure, and compromised government operations, to name a few. It is very important then, to have strong cybersecurity measures in place. To do so, DHS tasks the maintenance of its cybersecurity to the professionals in the Science and Technology Directorate. This is an organization within DHS which "conducts and supports research, development, testing, and evaluation" on servers and systems within DHS including the Cybersecurity and Infrastructure Security Agency (CISA), the FBI, Immigration and Customs Enforcement (ICE), FEMA, the United States Coast Guard (USCG), Department of Justice, and others. DHS's Science and Technology Directorate (S&T) partners with the private sector entities such as small businesses, international organizations, and other agencies to develop advanced cyber capabilities and remain ahead of our enemies in cybersecurity. CyLab is one example of that effort to remain ahead. CyLab is "a joint initiative between CISA and S&T to create an advanced analytics, multi-cloud environment that will facilitate secure strategic and critical cybersecurity problem-solving as early as 2024" (DHS, "Cybersecurity/Information Analysis R&D" 2022).

- Aviation Security. As threats to the United States evolve, so does our security and defense against those threats. In the aviation field, professionals within the U.S. Department of Homeland Security are "working to raise the baseline for aviation security across the globe by putting in place strengthened security measures, both seen and unseen, at all last-point-of-departure airports in 105 countries around the world" (DHS, "Aviation Security" 2022). This increased focus on aviation security includes enhancing passenger screening, heightened screening of electronics, increasing security protocols, deploying advanced technology, expanding canine screening, and establishing additional pre-clearance locations. Most, if not all, aviation security is handled by the Transportation Security Administration (TSA) which DHS oversees (DHS, "Fact Sheet: Aviation" 2022).

- Border Security. Professionals within the Department of Homeland Security closely oversee the United States Coast Guard and Immigration and Customs Enforcement, and also work with the Canadian and Mexican governments to promote border security. The primary security line is made up of professionals in the form of border patrol agents, air and marine agents, and even agriculture specialists. Technology and manpower on the border drastically increased following the events of 9/11 from less than 10,000 border patrol agents in 2001 to over 20,000 today; the results of this increase are impossible to dismiss. As of 2018, over 1,000 apprehensions and 75 criminal arrests occur daily on the border of the United States. Border security also seizes almost 5,000 lbs. of narcotics at the border daily. Each one of these arrests and seizures prevents and disrupts another potential threat (DHS, "Border Security" 2022).

- Port Security. Port security professionals work closely with Border Security, though port security is facilitated and controlled mostly by the United States Coast Guard. The Coast Guard monitors ports and the open ocean to identify and intercept unauthorized vessels that may be carrying unauthorized immigrants, illegal drugs, contraband such as guns or chemicals, and counterfeit bills, to name a few. Another major actor in port security is the DHS's Science and Technology Directorate, S&T. In addition to their role in cybersecurity discussed above, this directorate also maintains the Air, Land, and Sea Port of Entry Security Program, which develops and promotes technical capabilities to further secure the border on land, air, or sea to detect and prevent the transportation of illicit personnel and goods. Each month, the Coast Guard seizes over 5,000 lbs. of drugs (DHS, "Air Land and Port of Entry Security" 2022).

- Maritime Security. Professionals within maritime security in DHS work toward "the combination of preventive measures intended to protect persons, cargo, ships' stores, shipping, and port facilities against threats of intentional unlawful acts" (LawInsider, 2022; DHS ---2022). Thus, maritime security is the combination of the above two fields and will not be discussed further.
- Administration and Enforcement of Immigration Laws. Administration and enforcement of the federal statutes regarding immigration rests primarily on the shoulders of professionals within the U.S. Immigration and Customs Enforcement (DHS 2020). ICE is involved at the northern and southern borders of the United States and collaborates with border patrol agents. However, most agents and assets under the jurisdiction of ICE are put to use within the borders of the United States. ICE professionals seek to promote a lawful workforce and enforce immigration laws against employers who exploit unauthorized workers by taking advantage of their situations and providing insufficient working conditions and compensation. ICE professionals also identify and remove illegal aliens who are criminals, fugitives, or others, including those who falsify documents for unlawful activity. Currently, ICE leaders are also concerned with, and seeking to improve, the safe and humane detention and removal of those who are subject to these arrests and removals (ICE, 2022).
- Protection of National Leaders. The Secret Service was formed in 1865 to combat forfeiting money and later was given responsibility for protecting government leaders on a state and federal level (USSS 2022). In 2003, professionals within the Secret Service were placed under the jurisdiction of the Department of Homeland Security. The Secret Service's main responsibility today is to protect government leaders, buildings, and special events. To do this, agents use a multitude of tools including, but not limited to, technology, intelligence, and traditional bodyguards. High-value targets including the President, Vice-President, and foreign leaders when they visit the homeland are protected by special agents selected through a difficult vetting process who must meet the job's high demands. Buildings such as the White House are protected by the uniformed division of the Secret Service, though members of the uniformed division may sometimes travel with high-value targets as well. The uniformed division also trains and maintains five special units: the canine unit, emergency response unit, counter sniper team, motorcade support team, and the crime scene search unit. In many ways, the Secret Service can be loosely compared to the military in their training, demands, and missions (DHS, "U.S. Secret Service" 2022).
- Protection of Critical Infrastructure. Infrastructure is vulnerable in multiple dimensions including physically, financially, and in the cyber realm. Thus, Department of Homeland Security professionals must be vigilant in multiple dimensions to keep it secure. As previously discussed, cybersecurity is a large vulnerability in almost any career field today. Even basic necessities such as water, heat, food, and medicine can be compromised, delayed, shut down, or held hostage due to a cyberattack on the relevant computer system. Using the methods discussed earlier, professionals within DHS defend against, deter, and punish any who attempt to or successfully compromise critical infrastructure such as in the Colonial Pipeline attack where the FBI assisted in recovering ransom money

paid out to hackers. Professionals within DHS also rely heavily on the collection of intelligence to defend against physical threats. As discussed earlier, DHS professionals gather intelligence from a multitude of agencies and sources. They then use this information to protect high-value targets in infrastructure, thwart potential attacks, and when necessary, maintain a physical presence to guard and protect a specific location or building.

- Detection and Protection against Chemical, Biological, and Nuclear Threats. Another significant threat to national security in terms of physical destruction and number of casualties in a minimal amount of time is chemical, biological, radiological, nuclear, and explosive (CBRNE) threats. Any one of these when employed in a densely populated area, could cause billions of dollars in damage and produce millions of casualties in seconds to minutes. Professionals within DHS are very concerned with any potential threat that may involve any CBRNE capability, and the organization will go to great lengths to prevent the above-described outcome from coming to fruition. These professionals employ all tools and capabilities, from cybersecurity and intelligence gathering to border security in countering or dealing with CBRNE-related threats, constantly seeking to mitigate any potential fallout from one of these disasters. One major way they do so is through their "National Strategy for Chemical, Biological, Radiological, Nuclear, and Explosives, or CBRNE, Standards." This strategy explains the need for CBRNE standards and equipment, explains what that equipment is, and provides high-level goals with plans to reach those goals (DHS, "CBRNE" 2022).

- Response to Disasters. The primary individuals utilized in responding to any type of disaster – whether man-made, natural, economic, or any other kind – include those within that are deployed through the Federal Emergency Management Agency. The self-proclaimed mission of FEMA is "to help people before, during, and after disasters. Floods, hurricanes, earthquakes, forest fires, or whatever the disaster, FEMA leads the federal government's response as part of a team of responders" (DHS, "FEMA" 2022). FEMA oversees nearly every aspect of disaster response under supervision and jurisdiction of DHS. Professionals in this organization allocate emergency funds, equipment, personnel, and supplies. They help establish mass casualty hospitals and shelters for those injured or displaced, coordinating with private businesses to get basic operations back up and running, such as cell towers and gas. FEMA officials also coordinate removal and identification of corpses as well as debris removal. In any aspect of a disaster response, FEMA can either respond directly or coordinate a response with another team to re-establish operations and provide life's necessities as rapidly as possible (FEMA, 2022).

CURRENT CHALLENGES CONFRONTING DHS PROFESSIONALS

After reviewing the history of the Department of Homeland Security and the roles professionals fill in this organization, it is clear to see that there are a whole host of problems that could potentially be encountered. These include strains with FEMA, questionable pandemic responses, the border crisis, threats to infrastructure, and the increased possibility of terrorism and various disasters. Below we will discuss some of the primary challenges DHS professionals faced in 2022.

Strain with FEMA

From the beginning of their relationship, professionals within FEMA and DHS have experienced some tensions stemming from jealousy, resentment, and resistance to change. These issues have been acknowledged by employees and spectators of FEMA and DHS alike. While the relationships between these two professional groups have improved over the past decade, precious time has been wasted due to interorganizational bickering. There is still some degree of mistrust between those who focus on terrorism and those who concentrate on disasters. And it is difficult to know for sure how many resources should be spent on terrorism vs. natural and other disasters.

COVID-19

One of the most recent and "vivid" of these challenges is that of the COVID-19 pandemic. Prior to entering America early in 2020, COVID-19 was well preceded by its reputation and had already put many individuals and organizations, including DHS, on alert. Action was taken to curtail the arrival of COVID-19, such as a travel ban into America from China. The emergency restrictions would not stop there. Shortly after discovering the first case of COVID-19 in America, the federal government ordered isolation for all families requiring that they stay confined within their homes for two weeks to reduce the infection rates and keep hospitals from being overrun by the influx of infections. Professionals within DHS, in conjunction with the Department of Defense and the Department of Health and Human Services, established several emergency response measures including identifying major hospital needs and services, supplying thousands of emergency personnel and funds, and even anchoring the "US Comfort" (a navy ship with medical capabilities) in New York to assist in COVID-19 treatment. There was also a great deal of communication with and dependence upon the Centers for Disease Control and Prevention (CDC) and Dr Anthony Fauci, Director of the National Institute of Allergy and Infectious Diseases. However, a whole host of conflicting recommendations from a variety of organizations, as well as the CDC and Dr Fauci himself, made it very difficult to proceed effectively or efficiently through the COVID pandemic.

Border Crisis

Today, America faces the worst border crisis in our history (BBC 2021). Illegal border crossings have skyrocketed since 2018, and in 2021 the Border Patrol reported 1.7 million encounters with aliens at the southern border, the highest recorded in history. Also, according to internal Border Patrol estimates, almost 300,000 immigrants evaded detection and entered the country illegally. Even with the record rates seen in 2021, there are no signs of this crisis calming down any time soon. In the prior six months, there have been over one million encounters with aliens at the southern border, 240 of which were proven to have affiliation with violent gangs. This outpaces the record numbers recorded in 2021, and in April alone, there were 165,000 encounters. There have been over 150,000 encounters each month in the last year, eight of which were record-breaking recordings (USCG, 2021).

Despite these staggering numbers, the worst may yet come. With the expiration of Title 42, a key border policy, the DHS Office of Intelligence anticipates over one million immigrants crossing the southern border in just six weeks, an unprecedented volume of immigrants and nearly 200% more than has ever been processed in a six week period. "Intel stats [show that] there are tens of thousands just waiting in Mexico...[and Border Patrol] capacity will be reached...and we will be forced to release subjects on the street. This will cause even more to flood across the border. We will see something we have never seen before. The border will be open for narcotics to cross since everyone will be processing" (Giaritelli, 2022). This anticipated rush will rapidly overwhelm border patrol agents and their ability to monitor, admit, and apprehend individuals. Those who would typically be identified and apprehended to enter the border of the United States with malicious intent and illegal contraband, could endanger those around them and cause a threat to national security if a large number of them are not stopped and their plans promptly thwarted (Senate Republican Conference, 2022).

A weak border also affords enemies of the United States much more leniency and less oversight, allowing them to potentially cause serious harm to tens of thousands of people. As discussed in the introduction, had there been proper monitoring on the individuals who executed the acts of 9/11, we perhaps could have kept these individuals from entering America or, at least, from obtaining a pilot's license. We face these same weaknesses today, which allow criminals and others to enter the nation. Weak borders allow individuals and contraband (drugs and weapons) to enter without our knowledge. We have been extremely lucky that there has been relatively little impact in America compared to some other countries thus far, but border security is a major concern in countering terrorism and remains to be properly addressed.

Infrastructure Concerns

As discussed earlier in the Protection of Critical Infrastructure section of DHS History, there is a large variety of threats to infrastructure. Infrastructure is defined as "the basic physical and organizational structures and facilities (e.g., buildings, roads, power, supplies) needed for the operation of a society or enterprise" (Oxford, 2023). For the average American, this includes things such as highways and roads, gas stations, grocery stores, and facilities and services related to water treatment and delivery, the provision of electricity, and internet connection. Since there is such a variety of entities and facilities that provide such a variety of goods through different delivery systems, locations, and technological systems, there is a great margin of error where something can go wrong or be attacked. This wide range of attack possibilities makes it extremely difficult for DHS professionals to prepare for and mitigate against every possible outcome.

It is not possible to discuss in this chapter every conceivable type of infrastructure that may be compromised through accidents or malicious intent. But one of the most prevalent issues is cyberattacks. The primary means by which infrastructure is or will be attacked in the 21st century is through cyber capabilities. Earlier in the chapter, the Colonial Pipeline attack was mentioned along with how ransomware was used to take control of the pipeline's servers and hold them for ransom until $4.4 million in bitcoin was paid. This ability to attack a server or site from thousands of miles away is unprecedented and has brought with it exponential growth in risk and threat to the government and private sector as we become more dependent upon the conveniences of connected systems and technology. It must be address intentionally and thoughtfully going forward.

Terrorism and Disasters

Terrorism is the primary reason for the creation of the Department of Homeland Security and it remains a high priority to this day. However, like infrastructure, it is simply impossible to imagine every possible terrorist attack and seek to prevent or mitigate their effects. Professionals in DHS and other government agencies must do all they can to protect Americans and our way of life. This will remain a difficult task since possible targets include political leaders, government buildings, agricultural systems, the economy, etc.

There are also a variety of challenges relating to disasters:

- Insufficient Mitigation Activities. It has been acknowledged numerous times in this chapter that it is unrealistic to expect any person or organization to effectively mitigate every possible emergency scenario at all times. However, many disasters have occurred in America that could have been avoided. One such example is the massive losses that occurred in 2021 during raging wildfires in California. Reports had been shown for years suggesting that the California forests were at high risk for fire and suggested that action be taken, but none was. There is no shortage of these avoidable threats in America. And, unfortunately, most leaders and citizens do not pay attention to disasters until they occur.
- Lack of Training. General Patton was widely quoted as saying "a pint of sweat in training equals a gallon of blood in combat," and the same is true in most any situation. Any amount of time, money, and effort given in training will repay exponentially in actual response, but this is not always happening to the right degree. DHS has been criticized for not properly training their employees or even senior leaders to be able to meet the demands of their respective positions. Untrained individuals are indecisive, make bad decisions when they are made, and tend to blame others when confronted. These are not admirable qualities and actions that only amplify the fallout of a disaster and further delay needed aid to individuals affected.
- Poor Responses. As illustrated during the Katrina response, FEMA and DHS professionals had not fully learned from their simulations and scenarios to properly prepare for actual disasters. This creates sub-optimal reactions like we saw in Katrina, where hundreds of hours, millions of dollars, and immeasurable amounts of effort were wasted. Effective responses save resources exponentially, but also require major improvement in the other three areas discussed here to take effect. One cannot respond better until funding is provided for more frequent training and better mitigation activities.
- Limited Budgets. As with any government agency, funding is a major and recurring issue when it comes to dealing with challenges. In 2021, DHS was allotted $49.7 billion, not including the $2.4 billion allotted for the Secret Service, which according to the budget, falls under that given to the Department of the Treasury (Govinfo, 2021). While this may seem like a great deal of funding, it can be depleted quite rapidly. DHS requires funding for a number of sources including recruiting and retaining personnel; ordering, repairing, and maintaining equipment; updating and upgrading cyber capabilities; and providing salaries for its more than 200,000 employees. This lack of funding negatively affects every other field discussed here.

RECOMMENDATIONS FOR PROFESSIONALS ANTICIPATING THE FUTURE OF DHS

Going forward, there are many different ideas and suggestions concerning the improvement and continued upgrade of DHS and the organizations it oversees. For the sake of this chapter, the focus will be four recommendations relating to the challenges discussed above. The remainder of the chapter will discuss how DHS professionals could become more effective by improving relations with FEMA, ensuring adequate staffing, promoting proper training, and providing necessary equipment to facilitate better responses to disasters and terrorist attacks in the future.

Improve Relations with FEMA

Perhaps the easiest of the four suggested improvements is to strengthen relations between DHS and FEMA. This improvement would, comparatively, require very little funding, equipment, and effort. It may indeed take time, but this is entirely dependent upon the personnel involved. After nearly 20 years of being partners, professionals within DHS and FEMA should ensure they have policies and roles for each other that are clear, well defined, and understood by both parties. Once each party understands their role, it is important that every individual involved seeks progress toward a common goal. If each party feels united with and supported by their peers, then change can occur rapidly. Leaders can established a unified culture, and those below that level will have additional reason to support this integration.

Staffing

Staffing is, arguably, the most difficult improvement to make since it is a demand that relies largely on larger budgets and supply. If funding is limited or if there are no individuals seeking employment or none that are otherwise qualified to be employed, then there is little that can be done by DHS as a whole. That being said, professionals within DHS can currently do quite a bit to improve staffing. First of all, DHS can facilitate recruitment efforts. Typically, one must actively seek out a job with the government in order to obtain one. Private companies advertise job openings in apps, outdoor signage, commercials, and word-of-mouth. The government, with the exception of the Department of Defense, does not advertise job openings using these means. Rather, it is much more typical for one to specifically seek out, contact, and employ using one of these agencies. Another way staffing could be improved is in making careers in the DHS more competitive in the job market. Whether this be done through higher salaries, additional benefits, or any other form of incentive, the more desirable DHS recruiters can make employment for their current and future employees logically attract a wider population pool to employ from. This will allow the DHS to have greater ability to choose more-qualified individuals instead of less-qualified due to lack of supply, and they will more easily retain these qualified individuals long-term, allowing them to continue making positive change as they progress themselves, creating a long-lasting positive momentum within DHS and its accompanying agencies.

Training

Once properly staffed, it is imperative that the staff be trained. Regardless of success in staffing, if positions are filled with underqualified and unprepared individuals, numbers are increased but quality suffers. At the senior management and lower levels, each individual should know their position and role in any given function, as well as how to accomplish critical tasks typically performed by others. Murphy's law states that anything that can go wrong, will go wrong. To that end, it should never be assumed that an individual will always be available; the organization must be able to function without them. Cross training will be imperative not only to fill in that position when needed but also prepare for upward movement within the agency. This level of training and understanding certainly requires time and funding, but the positive results produced from it when correctly executed on a large scale are immeasurable and irreplaceable. Each person should have this level of training before a terrorist attack or disaster strikes, execute their role and overall mission with ease, and then be able to identify what went well and where improvements can be made to further advance the organization.

Equipment

The final suggestion for improvement is in equipment. Even with a harmonious culture as well as a fully staffed and well-trained team, very little can be done without the proper equipment. Like the other suggestions mentioned, this recommendation is also expensive. Top-of-the-line equipment and the newest technologies never come at a cheap price, but they certainly do accomplish the task the best. Old equipment can be found for a bargain, but this equipment performs poorly and requires frequent maintenance and replacement. What is needed is a balance between these two extremes. Especially in a DHS professional's roles of counterterrorism, disaster response and cybersecurity, it is critical that they be provided the necessary funding to provide well-functioning equipment which is reliable and efficiently accomplishes its necessary tasks. Equipment necessary for DHS professionals could include technological equipment such as computers, printers, WIFI routers and servers, and supplies for personnel on the ground such as gloves, helmets, food, and shelter, or any other material necessary to accomplish unique or odd tasks. It is important to reiterate, however, that regardless of how new one's equipment might be, if there are not sufficient personnel trained to use it effectively, then the time and effort to obtain that equipment is wasted. DHS leaders should ensure the professionals in the organization have the latest equipment and know how it is to be utilized.

CONCLUSION

As mentioned, 9/11 illustrated the drastic need for the creation of the profession of Homeland Security. It showed us that it was imperative to have officials and well-trained personnel within a centralized organization with the primary responsibility to protect the homeland. There have certainly been ups and downs throughout the department's history. Hundreds of great successes are rarely discussed because they do not affect us negatively. In contrast, there are great failures such as 9/11 and the Katrina response in addition to the ongoing tensions with FEMA and DHS professionals. As time goes on, professionals involved in DHS will continue to work diligently to keep us, the American people, safe from threats that beset us. In spite of terrorist threats and natural disasters and the vulnerabilities of our technological systems, infrastructure, and our border, we should be grateful there is a vast number of employees working to ensure our safety. Despite the challenges such as COVID-19, the border crisis, and cybersecurity, we remain a relatively safe and protected people thanks to their efforts.

Our current safety, however, is always at risk of being disrupted. New threats are constantly coming into play, jeopardizing our safety and our way of life. It is important that we recognize the weaknesses in our policies and protection systems, and work hard to turn our vulnerabilities into strengths. With proper funding, human resources, training, and relationships between organizations, we can surely take our protection of our peace and rights to the next level. Our enemies want to hurt us now, but DHS professionals and those in other agencies will seek to protect us long into the future.

CLASS DISCUSSION AND ESSAY QUESTIONS

1. Why was the concept of homeland security originally envisioned and why did the Department of Homeland Security finally get established?
2. How did the new Department of Homeland Security impact government and why did FEMA employees feel resentment about the sweeping changes taking place at the federal level?
3. What problems did Hurricane Katrina reveal according to Chris Edward?
4. What roles and responsibilities does DHS have in relation to terrorism?
5. Why is staffing and training vital for the Department of Homeland Security and FEMA?

REFERENCES

BBC. 2021. "What Are President Biden's Challenges at the Border?" *BBC News*. https://www.bbc.com/news/world-us-canada-56255613.

BJA. 2007. "9/11 Commission Act." Bureau of Justice Assistance. https://bja.ojp.gov/program/it/privacy-civil-liberties/authorities/statutes/1283.

BJA. 2004. "The Intelligence Reform and Terrorism Prevention Act of 2004 (IRTPA)." Bureau of Justice Assistance. https://bja.ojp.gov/program/it/privacy-civil-liberties/authorities/statutes/1282.

Bush, George W. 2002. "The Department of Homeland Security – Dhs.gov." The Department of Homeland Security. https://www.dhs.gov/sites/default/files/publications/book_0.pdf.

Cusick, Julia, Sam Hananel, Peter Gordon, Madeline Shepherd, Jerry Parshall, Laura Rodriguez, Mara Rudman, et al. 2021. "Redefining Homeland Security: A New Framework for DHS to Meet Today's Challenges." Center for American Progress. https://www.americanprogress.org/article/redefining-homeland-security-new-framework-dhs-meet-todays-challenges/.

DHS. 2020. "Immigration Enforcement." Homeland Security. https://www.dhs.gov/topic/immigration-enforcement-overview.

DHS. 2022a. "Air, Land, and Port of Entry Security." Homeland Security. https://www
.dhs.gov/science-and-technology/air-land-and-port-entry-security.

DHS. 2022b. "Aviation Security." Homeland Security. https://www.dhs.gov/aviation
-security#:~:text=Enhanced%20screening%20of%20personal%20electronic
,framework%20for%20public%20area%20security.

DHS. 2022c. "Border Security." Homeland Security. https://www.dhs.gov/topics/border
-security.

DHS. 2022d. "Counter Terrorism and Homeland Security Threats." Homeland Security.
https://www.dhs.gov/counter-terrorism-and-homeland-security-threats.

DHS. 2022e. "Cybersecurity/Information Analysis R&D." Homeland Security. https://
www.dhs.gov/science-and-technology/cybersecurity-information-analysis-rd.

DHS. 2022f. "Fact Sheet: Aviation Enhanced Security Measures for All Commercial
Flights to the United States." Homeland Security. https://www.dhs.gov/news/2017
/06/28/fact-sheet-aviation-enhanced-security-measures-all-commercial-flights
-united-states.

DHS. 2022g. "Federal Emergency Management Agency (FEMA)." Homeland
Security.   https://www.dhs.gov/employee-resources/federal-emergency-manage-
ment-agency-fema#:~:text=The%20Federal%20Emergency%20Management
%20Agency's,of%20a%20team%20of%20responders.

DHS. 2022h. "History." Homeland Security. https://www.dhs.gov/history.

DHS. 2022i. "Immigration and Customs Enforcement." Homeland Security. https://
www.dhs.gov/topics/immigration-and-customs-enforcement.

DHS. 2022k. "Maritime Safety and Security." Homeland Security. https://www.dhs.gov
/science-and-technology/maritime-border-security.

DHS. 2022l. "National Strategy for Chemical, Biological, Radiological, Nuclear, and
Explosives (CBRNE) Standards." Homeland Security. https://www.dhs.gov/national
-strategy-chemical-biological-radiological-nuclear-and-explosives-cbrne-standards.

DHS. 2022m. "Preventing Terrorism." Homeland Security. https://www.dhs.gov/publi-
cations-library/preventing-terrorism.

DHS. 2022n. "Preventing Terrorism." Homeland Security. https://www.dhs.gov/topics/
preventing-terrorism.

DHS. 2022o. "Secretary of Homeland Security." Homeland Security. https://www.dhs
.gov/topics/secretary-homeland-security.

DHS. 2022p. "U.S. Secret Service (USSS)." Homeland Security. https://www.dhs.gov/
employee-resources/us-secret-service-usss.

Edwards, Chris. 2015. "Hurricane Katrina: Remembering the Federal Failures." Cato
.org. https://www.cato.org/blog/hurricane-katrina-remembering-federal-failures#:~
:text=Perhaps%20the%20most%20appalling%20aspect,%E2%80%8Bof%E2
%80%90%E2%80%8Bstate%20headquarters.

FEMA. 2022. "About Us." FEMA.gov. https://www.fema.gov/about.

Giaritelli, Anna. 2022. "Border Officials Expect Biden to End Trump Title 42 Border
Policy in April." Washington Examiner. https://www.washingtonexaminer.com/
policy/border-officials-expect-biden-to-end-trump-title-42-border-policy-in-april.

Govinfo. 2005 "H. Rpt. 109-377 – A Failure of Initiative: Final Report." https://govinfo
.library.unt.edu/katrina/conclusion.pdf.

Govinfo. 2021. "Department of Homeland Security – Govinfo.gov." 2021 Budget.
https://www.govinfo.gov/content/pkg/BUDGET-2021-BUD/pdf/BUDGET-2021
-BUD-13.pdf.

ICE. 2022. "Immigrations and Customs Enforcement." ICE. https://www.ice.gov/.

Kean, Thomas, et al. 2003. "The 9/11 Commission Report – Govinfo.gov." https://www.govinfo.gov/content/pkg/GPO-911REPORT/pdf/GPO-911REPORT-24.pdf.

LawInsider. 2022. "Maritime Security Definition." Law Insider. https://www.lawinsider.com/dictionary/maritime-security.

Oxford. (2023). "The Oxford Essential Dictionary of the U.S. Military." https://www.oxfordreference.com/display/10.1093/acref/9780199891580.001.0001/acref-9780199891580-e-4001;jsessionid=92C4EA12C1DA2E9C053647A4BECF89E6.

Samuels, Richard. 2002. "Homeland Security Act." Encyclopædia Britannica, Inc. https://www.britannica.com/topic/Homeland-Security-Act.

Senate Republican Conference. 2022. "Biden's Border Crisis Is the Worst in American History His … - Politico." https://www.politico.com/f/?id=0000017f-d8bd-d522-ab7f-debd59400000.

USCG. 2019. "United States Coast Guard." USCG Annual Performance Report. https://www.uscg.mil/Portals/0/documents/budget/FY19-USCG-APR.pdf.

USSS. 2022. "Resources." Home | United States Secret Service. https://www.secretservice.gov/.

CHAPTER 11

The Role of Public Health in Emergency Management:[1]
Preparedness, Pandemics, Present and Future Challenges post-COVID-19

Arthur J. Simental and Tina Bynum

For he who has health has hope; and he who has hope, has everything.

– Owen Arthur

INTRODUCTION

Public health – a profession that can be traced back to the late 1700s in the United States – plays a vital role in each and every community across the nation. In addition, public health emergency management plays an important role in emergency and disaster response. This was clearly demonstrated during the COVID-19 pandemic, which is the greatest contemporary example of a public health response to a global pandemic and its impact on the U.S. healthcare and quarantine systems. According to the Johns Hopkins University, Center for Systems Science and Engineering's COVID-19 Dashboard, there have been 236,940,594 total COVID-19 cases worldwide; 4,837,772 deaths from COVID-19; and 6,418,953,258 total COVID-19 vaccine doses administered (JHU, 2021). COVID-19 demonstrated strengths and weaknesses across our public health and healthcare systems, and the lessons learned from the pandemic will guide the future of public health, medicine, and health-systems strengthening.

However, disease outbreaks and pandemics are not a new phenomenon. Disease outbreaks of pandemic proportions have occurred throughout the history of humanity and have left their mark on the world. Some pandemics have famously affected the course of history and also played a role contributing to the outcome of various wars. A key example includes the Great Plague of Athens during the Peloponnesian War in 430 BC that killed an estimated 100,000 Athenians over five years, or nearly 25%–30% of the population of Athens and is attributed as helping Sparta win the war (Martin, 2021). The exact source of the disease is still a mystery and suspected causes range from smallpox to measles to typhus (Martin, 2021). Another example is the Medieval "Black Death" bubonic plague in the mid-1300s that killed an estimated 20 million people in Europe (about a third of

DOI: 10.4324/9781003350729-11

Pandemic Outbreak/ Pathogen	Year(s)	Estimated Deaths *
Black/Bubonic Plague	1347–51	200–225 million
Spanish Flu (H1N1)	1918–1919	50 million
HIV	1981–Present	32–43.8 million
Cocoliztli, Mexico	1545–1548	15 million
Smallpox, Mexico	1520	8 million
COVID	2019–Present	6.6 million
Cocoliztli	1578	2 million
Cholera	1899–1923	1.5 million
Asian Flu	1957–1958	1.1 million
Hong Kong flu	1968–1970	1 million
Russian Flu	1889–1890	1 million
Swine flu (H1N1)	2009–2010	150,000–575,000
Russian plague	1770–1772	100,000
Great plague of London	1665–1666	100,000
Great plague of Marseille	1720–1723	40,000
Ebola	2014–2016	11,300
MERS	2012–Present	866
SARS	2002–2003	774

* Data derived from various news, medical agency, and historical sources.

FIGURE 11.1.   Listing of Notable Pandemic Outbreaks since 1300

the population), and also ran rampant in China, India, Persia, Syria, and Egypt several years before reaching Europe (History.com, 2020).

There are many other examples spanning nearly every century of recorded history from the Antonine Plague of AD 165–180 and the Plague of Justinian, AD 541–543, to the Great Plague of London 1665, cholera pandemics 1–6 of 1817–1923, Spanish flu 1918–1919, and many other more contemporary examples in recent history including the H1N1 pandemic of 2009–2010 and Ebola in 2014–2016 (Piret and Boivin, 2021) (see Figure 11.1). As disease outbreaks continue to shape humanity, it is more important than ever to understand their history and impacts, and implement the lessons learned to strengthen the systems and capabilities needed to prevent, mitigate, prepare for, respond to, and recover from them holistically, systematically, and equitably.

With this introduction in mind, the origins and history of public health are explored in this chapter. Furthermore, this chapter examines public health in the context of emergency management with emphasis on the roles, functions, and activities during emergencies and disasters. It also discusses challenges and opportunities for improvement.

PUBLIC HEALTH AND ITS HISTORY

Charles-Edward Armory Winslow defined public health a century ago in 1920. He said this profession is:

> the science and art of preventing disease, prolonging life, and promoting physical health and efficiency through organized community efforts for the sanitation of the environment, the control of community infections, the education of the individual in principles of

personal hygiene, the organization of medical and nursing service for the early diagnosis and preventive treatment of disease, and the development of the social machinery which will ensure to every individual in the community a standard of living adequate for the maintenance of health, so organizing these benefits as to enable every citizen to realize his birthright of health and longevity. — CEA Winslow

(Boston University School of Public Health [BUSPH], 2015)

From this definition, public health is a broad concern with implications across all aspects of life at the societal, public, and private organizational, community, and individual levels (CDC, 2014a). Public health plays a role in safeguarding our health innumerably, from monitoring the air we breathe, to assessing the water we drink and the food we eat, to promoting safety in our places of work and the environment in which we live. According to the World Health Organization, "Public health aims to provide maximum benefit for the largest number of people" (CDC, 2014a). Assuring the public's health is an essential aspect of governance.

Furthermore, because public health touches all aspects of human life, there are complex interrelationships that exist between human activities and factors that influence and determine the health of a population (ODPHP, 2021). This concept is called the *determinants of health*, or "the range of personal, social, economic, and environmental factors that influence health status" (ODPHP, 2021). Determinants of health are categorized broadly and range from: "Policymaking, social factors, health services, individual behavior, biology and genetics" (ODPHP, 2021) and "reach beyond the boundaries of traditional health care and public health sectors; sectors such as education, housing, transportation, agriculture, and environment" (ODPHP, 2021). For example, personal behaviors such as illicit drug use, excess drinking, and poor diet and exercise have an effect on one's health, just as a lack of access to health care, high medical costs, and lack of transportation contribute to adverse patient and community outcomes. Living in an environment with poor public safety, lack of clean drinking water, exposure to environmental toxins, and poor personal hygiene and sanitation will also play a role in one's health. These *determinants of health* capture the complex interrelated factors that impact public health.

KEY TERMS:

EPIDEMIC OR OUTBREAK

Occurrence in a community or region of cases of an illness, specific health-related behavior, or other health-related event clearly in excess of normal expectancy. Both terms are used interchangeably; however, *epidemic* usually refers to a larger geographic distribution of illness or health-related events.

(CDC, 2014a)

PANDEMIC

Event in which a disease spreads across several countries and affects a large number of people.

(CDC, 2020c)

ENDEMIC

Disease or condition present among a population at all times.

(CDC, 2014b)

EPIDEMIOLOGY

Study of the distribution and determinants of health-related states among specified populations and the application of that study to the control of health problems.

(CDC, 2014b)

QUARANTINE

Separates and restricts the movement of people who were exposed to a contagious disease to see if they become sick.

(CDC, 2017m)

ISOLATION

Separates sick people with a contagious disease from people who are not sick.

(CDC, 2017m)

DETERMINANT

Factor that contributes to the generation of a trait.

(CDC, 2020a)

CLINICAL CARE

Prevention, treatment, and management of illness and the preservation of mental and physical well-being through the services offered by medical and allied health professions; also known as *health care*.

(CDC, 2020a)

HEALTH SYSTEMS

Comprising all the organizations, institutions and resources that are devoted to producing health actions.

(Arteaga, 2014)

SANITATION

Basic sanitation is described as having access to facilities for the safe disposal of human waste (feces and urine), as well as having the ability to maintain hygienic conditions, through services such as garbage collection, industrial/hazardous waste management, and wastewater treatment and disposal.

(CDC, 2017d)

MIASMA THEORY OF DISEASE

Many in the early to mid-nineteenth century felt that cholera was caused by bad air, arising from decayed organic matter or miasmata. "Miasma" was believed to pass from cases to susceptibles in diseases considered contagious. Believers in the miasma theory stressed eradication of disease through the preventive approach of cleansing and scouring, rather than through the purer scientific approach of microbiology.

(UCLA, n.d.)

PREVENTION VS. TREATMENT

Treatment: Treatment programs aim to reduce or minimize the adverse effects of an already existing problem or condition. Such practices are vital, but limited because they often do not address the underlying cause of the issue.

Prevention: Preventive interventions aim to reduce the new instances of a problem or undesirable condition. Such efforts may address personal and environmental factors.

(KDHE and KUCCHD, 2015)

CENTERS FOR DISEASE CONTROL AND PREVENTION (CDC)

A U.S. federal government agency whose mission is to protect public health by preventing and controlling disease, injury, and disability. The CDC promotes healthy behaviors and safe, healthy environments. It keeps track of health trends, tries to find the cause of health problems and outbreaks of disease, and responds to new public health threats. The CDC works with state health departments and other organizations throughout the country and the world to help prevent and control disease. The CDC is part of the U.S. Public Health Service of the Department of Health and Human Services (DHHS). Also called Centers for Disease Control and Prevention.

(NIH, n.d.)

WORLD HEALTH ORGANIZATION (WHO)

A part of the United Nations that deals with major health issues around the world. The World Health Organization sets standards for disease control, health care, and medicines; conducts education and research programs; and publishes scientific papers and reports. A major goal is to improve access to health care for people in developing countries and in groups who do not get good health care. The headquarters are located in Geneva, Switzerland. Also called WHO.

(NIH, n.d.)

As noted in the introduction, the history of diseases is lengthy as is the history of public health itself. This section provides a holistic overview of public health practices starting with a discussion on early public health practices by ancient humans. Examples of public health events are explored and an overview of the origins of epidemiology is described in a brief examination of John Snow's investigation of cholera epidemics in

London, England in 1854. Lastly, this section transitions to focus on the public health origins and history in the United States.

Ancient Public Health

Public Health has a vast history with evidence of public health practices dating back to ancient human history. According to Petri S. Juuti, Tapio S. Katko, and Heikki S. Vuorinen, "the first purposeful construction of water supply, bathrooms, toilets, and drainage in Europe dates back to second millennium B.C., which is over 4,000 years ago to provide some perspective" with improvements in sanitation as some of the earliest examples of activities taken to improve public health (BUSPH, 2015). These constructs by ancient Greeks and Romans around 500 BCE included engineering feats such as the famed aqueduct systems that contributed to public health.

The history of public health is seen through various activities and events spanning ancient human history to present day. Table 11.1 depicts examples of different public health events and the activities throughout history. This list of events is not all encompassing but represents the broad range of events and activities that encompass public health. Examples are organized into four areas: sanitation and environmental health; pandemics; disaster preparedness, response, and biological warfare; and prevention and policy.

John Snow – The Father of Epidemiology

Several individuals have had a profound impact on the understanding of public health. Dr John Snow was one of them. He was a practicing obstetrician and anesthesiologist and a founding member of the London Epidemiological Society. He is regarded as "the father of modern epidemiology" thanks to his novel, pioneering, investigative work studying cholera epidemics (Tulchinsky, 2018). Cholera was rampant in the 19th century, causing a number of epidemics globally.

> Cholera is an acute diarrhea caused by infection with the bacterium, Vibrato cholera. It is endemic in over 50 countries and also the cause of large epidemics. Since 1817, cholera spread rapidly throughout the world largely due to inadvertent transport of bilge water in ships mainly from the Bay of Bengal. The Indian subcontinent has been a long-term focus of cholera and the source of six worldwide epidemics between 1817 and 1923. The seventh cholera pandemic, which began in 1961, affects on an average 3–5 million people annually, with 120,000 deaths with large scale epidemics in Haiti, Yemen and in central Africa in the second decade of the 21st century.
>
> (Tulchinsky, 2018)

John Snow conducted novel investigations on cholera epidemics in London, England in 1854, during which time he investigated and traced 600 deaths that occurred over a ten-day period during an outbreak in the Soho district of London (Tulchinsky, 2018). By careful observation and tracing patterns of disease spread, John Snow was able to deduce and theorize that the acute gastrointestinal illness was likely stemming from food or water (Tulchinsky, 2018). Furthermore, he was able to observe and learn from the relatives of the deceased that nearly all who died had consumed water from the Broad Street

TABLE 11.1.   Examples of Various Notable Historical Public Health Events/Activities.

Sanitation and Environmental Health	"Around 500 BCE, the ancient Greeks and Romans actively practiced community sanitation measures" (CDC, 2014a). Examples include the construction of water supply, bathrooms, toilets, and drainage, aqueduct systems.
	"Public Health Act of 1848 in the United Kingdom provided a central board of health and placed responsibilities for sanitation in the hands of boroughs" (CDC, 2014a).
	"In 1970 the Environmental Protection Agency, which protects human health by safeguarding air, water, and land was established" (CDC, 2014a).
	Love Canal New York
	"Love Canal is an abandoned canal project branching off of the Niagara River near Niagara Falls and is also a neighborhood of 800 homes built directly adjacent to the canal. From 1942 to 1953, the Hooker Chemical Company, used the canal as a chemical waste dump, disposing of around 21,000 tons of toxic chemicals, including at least twelve known carcinogens. Hooker capped the 16-acre hazardous waste landfill in clay and sold the land to the Niagara Falls School Board. Public awareness of the disaster unfolded in the late 1970s when investigative newspaper coverage and grassroots door-to-door health surveys began to reveal a series of inexplicable illnesses – epilepsy, asthma, migraines, and nephrosis – and abnormally high rates of birth defects and miscarriages in the Love Canal neighborhood" (Kleiman, 2021). "President Jimmy Carter declared a state of emergency in 1978 and again in 1981 relocating the families living in the affected area" (Kleiman, 2021).
	Per- and Polyfluoroalkyl Substances (PFAS/PFOS)
	PFAS/PFOS water contamination across the nation leads to regulation of a class of chemicals known as "forever chemicals" that do not break down in the environment (H.R.535 – 116th Congress, 2019).
Pandemics	1777 Vaccination Against Smallpox
	"Disease is noted as the primary cause of death for the Continental Army, General George Washington mandates vaccination against smallpox during the Revolutionary War... First large-scale military preventative care measure in history" (Geppert and Paul, 2019).
	1918 Spanish Flu
	"The 1918 influenza pandemic was the most severe pandemic in recent history. It was caused by an H1N1 virus with genes of avian origin...It is estimated that about 500 million people or one-third of the world's population became infected with this virus. The number of deaths was estimated to be at least 50 million worldwide with about 675,000 occurring in the United States. Mortality was high in people younger than 5 years old, 20-40 years old, and 65 years and older. The high mortality in healthy people, including those in the 20-40 year age group, was a unique feature of this pandemic" (CDC, 2018l).

(Continued)

TABLE 11.1.   (Continued)

Disaster Preparedness, Response and Biological Warfare	"Biologic Warfare – Plague used as a weapon of war during the Siege of Kaffa 14th century AD" (CDC, 2014a). 1763 – Smallpox blankets given to Indians during the French and Indian war (Fenn, 2000). 9/11 – "After the September 11, 2001, terrorist attacks on the United States, approximately 400,000 persons were exposed to toxic contaminants and other factors that increased their risk for certain physical and mental health conditions. Shortly thereafter, both federal and nonfederal funds were provided to support various postdisaster activities, including medical monitoring and treatment. In 2011, as authorized by the James Zadroga 9/11 Health and Compensation Act of 2010, the CDC World Trade Center (WTC) Health Program began providing medical screening, monitoring, and treatment of 9/11-related health conditions for WTC responders" (Azofeifa et al., 2021). 2014 Dallas Ebola Incident in the United States – A man travels from Liberia to Dallas, Texas, unknowingly infected with Ebola causing a small travel associated outbreak in the United States for the first time (McEntire & SFHEA, 2019). This incident caused great concern for potential risks of future biothreats and a lapse in biohazard preparedness.
Prevention and Policy	"1500 BCE, Leviticus, the third book of the Hebrew Bible, is believed to be the first written health code in the world. The book deals with personal and community responsibilities and includes guidance regarding bodily cleanliness, sexual health behaviors, protection against contagious diseases, and isolation of lepers" (CDC, 2014a). Tobacco Laws "1964 Surgeon General Dr. Luther Terry releases a landmark report on smoking-related lung cancer and bronchitis, the first report detailing the connection between tobacco and chronic disease" (USPHS, n.d.). Car Safety Laws Speeding, reckless driving, collisions, and pedestrian fatalities in the early 1900s would lead to an overhaul of automobile safety and legislation (Smithsonian, n.d.). "In the early 1960s, many state legislatures passed laws requiring seat belts or seat belt anchors in new cars. This movement grew into a comprehensive government response to auto safety issues. In 1966, Congress authorized the federal government to set safety standards for new cars. By 1968, seat belts, padded dashboards, and other safety features were mandatory equipment" (Smithsonian, n.d.). 1980s – Dioxins in tampons found to cause increased risk of toxic shock syndrome (TSS) in women causing death, leading manufacturers since to remove chemicals linked to TSS in feminine hygiene products (Heid, 2016). COVID-19 mask mandates and social distancing are put in place to prevent community spread of COVID-19. Mandatory vaccination requirements for public and private sector employees, including federal employees, the military, and critical industries such as health care.

water pump, after which he then persuaded local authorities to remove the pump handle. Remarkably, within a few days the epidemic had ended (Tulchinsky, 2018). In his report to the Committee on Scientific Inquiries in Relation to the Cholera Epidemic of 1854, John Snow writes, "I found that nearly all the deaths had taken place within a short distance of the pump...With regard to the deaths...there were sixty-one instances in which I was informed that the deceased persons used to drink the water from Broad Street, either constantly or occasionally" (Tulchinsky, 2018). Snow's work demonstrated that contaminated water caused the cholera outbreak and led to legislative reforms and an overhaul of London's water and sewage systems (Tulchinsky, 2018). Lastly, Snow's work would later help disprove the prevailing theory behind cholera outbreaks of the time: the Miasma Theory of disease causation, which suggested that "cholera was caused by airborne transmission of poisonous vapors from foul smells due to poor sanitation" (Tulchinsky, 2018). Snow's approach and perspectives on disease changed our understanding of the etiology of disease and would lead to changes in the field of epidemiology.

In the years that followed John Snow's innovative approach to epidemiological investigations, public health would continue to evolve and undergo new eras of transformation and evolution of the practice of public health. Public Health in its early years focused on sanitation and clean water. Philosophy and social reform theories and sentiments started to arise during the Enlightenment era of the 18th century linking public health to good governance and economic interests. "In the early 1800s, Jeremy Bentham and his disciples (the theoretical radicals) developed the philosophy of utilitarianism which provided a theoretic underpinning for health policy and wider social policies. One theme was that the reduction of mortality and improvements in health had an economic value to society. Healthy workers were more able to contribute to the economy of the state. Implicit in utilitarianism was the notion that one could measure 'evil' by the degree of misery that was created (or relieved) by a particular action. To Bentham the welfare of both the wealthy and the poor could be achieved most efficiently with good government" (BUSPH, 2015). It was further recognized that poor health was largely impacting poor populations compared to wealthy or affluent populations (BUSPH, 2015). Studies started to emerge exploring the factors contributing to the public's health.

For instance, "in 1842, Sir Edwin Chadwick, a British social reformer, published 'Report on the Sanitary Condition of the Labouring Population of Great Britain,' which showed that life expectancy was far lower in towns than in the countryside" (Harvard Public Health, 2021). Sir Edwin Chadwick believed that government intervention could improve people's lives through reform and provide benefits of a healthier population increasing productivity and reducing support costs (BUSPH, 2015). Chadwick argued that what was really needed to improve the population's health was more civil engineers and not physicians, to undertake improvements for environmental and sanitation such as drainage of streets, delivery of clean water, and removal of sewage and other noxious substances (BUSPH, 2015). "These social, economic, political, and philosophical developments all contributed to the emerging idea that the public's health was a legitimate interest of government" (BUSPH, 2015), leading to continued reform and changing the way public health was viewed.

The culmination of this work would lead to major reforms and passing of the following landmark legislation:

- 1846 The Nuisances Removal Act was passed, giving local justices the power to prosecute and fine landlords for infractions having to do with sanitation (poor housing, garbage, cesspools and faulty drains).

- 1848 The Public Health Act created a General Board of Health in London that could direct localities to create local boards empowered to deal with environmental filth.
- In the 1850s The Epidemiologic Society of London was formed, consisting of local physicians, ex-military commanders, and civil servants who presented papers related to public health issues.
- 1853 John Snow presented "The comparative mortality of large towns and rural districts and the causes by which it is influenced." This intersection of statistics, philosophy, and economy sparked a new agenda for social reform (BUSPH, 2015).

These events and developments served as the underpinning for the foundation of future public health activities and revolutions. Discovery, innovation, theory advancement, studies and the development of public authorities, organizations, and professional societies dedicated to exploring and improving public health contributed greatly to driving changes across the social, environmental, and political spectrum. Growing political and public support for public health actions to improve population health would play an equally important role in advancing impactful change that would greatly reduce further incidence of disease.

Public Health in the United States (1700s – 2000s)

Public Health history in the United States is discussed in this section, including a brief history of key events. Then the origins and creation of the United States Public Health Service and Centers for Disease Control and Prevention is explored. This is followed by a Key U.S. Public Health Developments Timeline and concludes with a contemporary discussion on present-day public health focusing on Public Health in the 21st Century, Public Health Core Sciences, and the Ten Essential Public Health Services.

Public Health in the United States followed similar patterns of growth, advancement, and evolution compared to the United Kingdom.

> The US also underwent a rapid transition from a rural, agricultural society to one that was intensely urban and industrial. Inventions such as the cotton gin that promoted agricultural production, but also decreased the need for farm workers, driving many to the cities for work. Economic growth and inventions spawned factories and textile mills in US cities.
>
> (BUSPH, 2015)

Early Public Health in the United States during the 1700s focused public health activities around key legislation providing relief for Sick and Disabled Seamen through a Congressional Act in 1798 establishing the U.S. Marine Hospital Service and a network of marine hospitals (BUSPH, 2015). During the 1800s health care and public health services continued to expand and key public health activities would take place such as the introduction of smallpox vaccination in the United States; the establishment of public record systems for births, deaths, marriages and other key population metrics; disease reporting; immigration health screenings and inspections; and the foundation of hygienic laboratory services that would later evolve into the National Institutes of Health (BUSPH, 2015). The late 1800s would be known as "the most sweeping revolution medicine has ever seen" (NIH, NIAID, 2012). The 1900s would become an era of continuous transformation for public health. A report from the U.S. Institute of Medicine, *Future of Public Health – 1988*, describes public health in the 20th century as a great paradigm shift of disciplinary practice from disease prevention to the promotion of overall health:

> In the early twentieth century, the role of the state and local public health departments expanded greatly. Although disease control was based on bacteriology, it became increasingly clear that individual persons were more often the source of disease transmission than things. "The work of the laboratory led the Board to define the existence and character of an increasing number of the most dangerous diseases and to provide medical means for their control" (Rosenkrantz, 1972). Identification and treatment of individual cases of disease were the next natural steps. Massachusetts, Michigan, and New York City began producing and dispensing antitoxins in the 1890s. Several states established disease registries. In 1907, Massachusetts passed a law requiring reporting of individual cases of 16 different diseases. Required reporting implied an obligation to treat. For example, reporting of cancer was later added to the list, and a cancer treatment program began in 1927. It also became clear that providing immunizations and treating infectious diseases did not solve all health problems. Despite remarkable success in lowering death rates from typhoid, diphtheria, and other contagious diseases, considerable disability continued to exist in the population. There were still numerous diseases, such as tuberculosis, for which infectious agents were not clearly identified. Draft registration during World War I revealed that a substantial portion of the male population was either physically or mentally unfit for combat (Fee, 1987). It also became clear that diseases, even those for which treatment was available, still predominantly affected the urban poor. Registration and analysis of disease showed that the highest rates of morbidity still occurred among children and the poor. On the premise that a healthier society could be built through health care for individuals, health departments expanded into clinical care and health education. In the early twentieth century, the New York and Baltimore health departments began offering home visits by public health nurses. New York established a campaign for education on tuberculosis (Winslow, 1923). School health clinics were set up in Boston in 1894, New York in 1903, Rhode Island in 1906, and many other cities in subsequent years (Bremner, 1971). Numerous local health agencies set up clinics to deal with tuberculosis and infant mortality...As public agencies moved into clinical care and education, the orientation of public health shifted from disease prevention to promotion of overall health. Epidemiology provided a scientific justification for health programs that had originated with social reforms. Public health once again became a task of promoting a healthy society. In the twentieth century, this goal was to be achieved through scientific analysis of disease, medical treatment of individuals, and education on healthy habits. In 1923, C. E. A. Winslow defined public health as the science of not only preventing contagious disease, but also of "prolonging life, and promoting physical health and efficiency" (Winslow, as quoted in Hanlon and Pickett, 1984)...Federal activities in public health also expanded during the late nineteenth century and the early twentieth century.

(Institute of Medicine, 1988)

Two major driving forces of public health in the United States include the U.S. Public Health Service (USPHS) and the Centers for Disease Control and Prevention (CDC). The following section briefly discusses the origin of these agencies and their respective roles. The roots of these agencies can be traced back to the early years of the United States. Today they continue to serve as a global model for public health and global health security.

Origins of the U.S. Public Health Service

> *The roots of CDC, as well as a number of other federal agencies in the Department of Health and Human Services (HHS), lie in the historic work of PHS.*
>
> (CDC Museum – Roots of the CDC, n.d.)

The U.S. Public Health Service has over 200 years of service and traces its origins back to the Marine Hospital Service established in 1798 when President John Adams signed into law the Act of Sick and Disabled Seamen (USPHS, n.d.). In 1870, the Marine Hospital Service was reorganized, and John Maynard Woodworth was named the first Supervisory Surgeon (later renamed the Surgeon General) (NIH, NIAID, 2012).

> The first Surgeon General was John Maynard Woodworth (1837–1879), the medical hero of Union General William Tecumseh Sherman's (1820–1891) Civil War "March to the Sea." The National Quarantine Act of 1878 gave the MHS substantial quarantine authority and an epidemic disease surveillance system to coordinate with state and local quarantine operations. This was followed by a number of supplementary acts, including an 1890 act authorizing interstate disease control and an 1893 act extending MHS authority over all infectious diseases.
>
> (NIH, NIAID, 2012)

Maynard then "adopted a military model for this medical staff, assigning a cadre of mobile, uniformed physicians to various marine hospitals" (NIH, NIAID, 2012). In 1889, "Congress established the United States Public Health Service Commissioned Corps within the Marine Hospital Service, organizing officers along military lines with titles and pay corresponding to Army and Navy grades" (USPHS, n.d.).

In 1902, Congress renamed the Marine Hospital Service the Public Health and Marine Hospital Service (PHMHS) and expanded its disease prevention responsibilities to include research of human diseases, sanitation, water supplies, and sewage disposal (USPHS, n.d.). Finally, in 1912 the PHMHS was renamed the Public Health Service as Congress continued to expand the service's scope and increase its responsibilities (USPHS, n.d.) (Figure 11.2). The next major expansion of the Public Health Service would occur in 1944 during World War II, with the passage of the U.S. Public Health Service Act, expanding the service to include nurses, scientists, dietitians, physical therapists, and sanitarians (USPHS, n.d.). Since then, the U.S. Public Health Service has continued to play a role as a major driving force in public health. Presently, during the COVID-19 pandemic the U.S. Public Health Service has played a critical lead role in the response. The severity and scale of the COVID-19 pandemic has led to even further expansion of the service that has surged and rapidly expanded to meet this great global health emergency.

Creation of the CDC

According to the CDC, the CDC originally evolved from the U.S. Public Health Service, Office of Malaria Control in War Areas (MCWA), an agency established in 1942 during World War II to control malaria around military bases through Southeastern United

FIGURE 11.2. Historic Photo of U.S. Public Health Service Officers, 1912 (Source: USPHS, n.d.)

States (CDC, 2021f). After World War II the MCWA would continue its work and reformed with a broader disease control mission.

> The Public Health Service established the Communicable Disease Center (CDC) in 1946 to work on malaria, typhus, and other infectious diseases... In the next 60 years, minor changes were made to the name (Center for Disease Control, Centers for Disease Control, Centers for Disease Control and Prevention), but the initials, CDC, have remained the same. Through the years, CDC's work has expanded to include all infectious diseases, as well as occupational health, toxic chemicals, injury, chronic diseases, health statistics, and birth defects. Reporting today to the Department of Health and Human Services and working in collaboration with public health partners, CDC tirelessly leads the fight against known, new, and emerging diseases around the globe. At the same time, CDC leads prevention efforts to reduce the burden of preventable and chronic diseases.
>
> (CDC Museum, Roots of the CDC, n.d.).

Thus, after successfully reducing malaria in the United States, "on July 1, 1946, the U.S. government established the Communicable Disease Center in Atlanta to continue the work of MCWA and to serve as the nation's public health agency" (CDC, 2021f). Today, the now Centers for Disease Control and Prevention has vastly expanded to include multiple Centers, Institutes, and Offices. An organization chart of the present-day CDC can be seen in **Figure 11.3**.

The CDC's mission is "to protect America from health, safety and security threats, both foreign and in the U.S. Whether diseases start at home or abroad, are chronic or acute, curable or preventable, human error or deliberate attack, CDC fights disease and

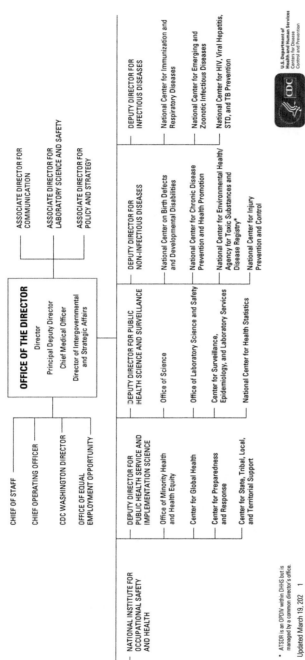

FIGURE 11.3.   CDC Organization Chart (Source: CDC, 2021i).

CDC in the 21st Century

- **On the cutting edge of health security** – confronting global disease threats through advanced computing and lab analysis of huge amounts of data to quickly find solutions.
- **Putting science into action** – tracking disease and finding out what is making people sick and the most effective ways to prevent it.
- **Helping medical care** – bringing new knowledge to individual health care and community health to save more lives and reduce waste.
- **Fighting diseases before they reach our borders** – detecting and confronting new germs and diseases around the globe to increase our national security.
- **Nurturing public health** – building on our significant contribution to have strong, well-resourced public health leaders and capabilities at national, state and local levels to protect Americans from health threats.

CDC's Role

- Detecting and responding to new and emerging health threats
- Tackling the biggest health problems causing death and disability for Americans
- Putting science and advanced technology into action to prevent disease
- Promoting healthy and safe behaviors, communities and environment
- Developing leaders and training the public health workforce, including disease detectives
- Taking the health pulse of our nation

FIGURE 11.4. CDC in the 21st Century and CDC's Role (Source: CDC, 2019g).

supports communities and citizens to do the same" (CDC, 2021g). The CDC's role in the 21st century is depicted in Figure 11.4.

Since the CDC's humble beginnings with the U.S. Public Health Service's MCWA Office, the agency has continued its disease prevention efforts and significantly expanded them to holistically focus on promoting and improving overall health, and has become the premier global public health agency supporting local, state, tribal, territorial, and international public health efforts. "CDC secures global health and America's preparedness by revitalizing our public health infrastructure, stopping the spread of contagions and vector-borne diseases, and addressing bioterrorism threats" (CDC, 2020h). The CDC works to "prevent, detect, and respond to diseases wherever they are to save lives and so that diseases don't come into the United States" (CDC, 2020h). During the COVID-19 pandemic, the CDC has been a leader in the COVID-19 response and worked tirelessly to safeguard the United States.

Key U.S. Public Health Developments Timeline

Public Health has an extensive history in the United States, stemming over four centuries to the present day. Table 11.2 depicts a timeline of key developments from the U.S. National Library of Medicine's *The History of the Public Health Service*, the Boston University School of Public Health's *Public Health in the United States*, and the David J. Sencer CDC Museum's *CDC Timeline 1940s–1970s*.

Public Health in the 21st Century

Present-day public health practice has vastly changed since its inception thanks to significant breakthroughs and advancements in science, technology, engineering, and medicine.

TABLE 11.2.   United States Public Health History Timeline 1700s–2000s

1700s

- 1798 – Congress passes the Act for the Relief of Sick and Disabled Seamen and authorizes formation of the U.S. Marine Hospital Service (MHS), which was the forerunner of the Public Health Service (PHS). Seamen often became ill while at sea and often were unable to find adequate health care in port cities. Their health was viewed as essential to the developing country and a network of marine hospitals, mainly in port cities, was established by Congress in 1798 to care for sick and disabled seamen. Seamen were taxed 20 cents a month in order to raise funds to pay physicians and support the network of hospitals. This tax was abolished in 1884. From 1884 to 1906 funds were raised by a levy on merchant ships and after 1906, funds were allocated by the U.S. Congress.

- 1799 – Castle Island in Boston Harbor was chosen as the temporary site for the first marine hospital. Dr Thomas Welsh, a Harvard College graduate and participant in the Revolutionary War battles at Lexington and Bunker Hill, was appointed as the physician in charge.

- 1799 – Boston establishes the first board of health and the first health department in the United States. Paul Revere is named as the first health officer.

1800s

- 1804 – The Boston Marine Hospital is established in the Charlestown section of Boston. Dr Benjamin Waterhouse was appointed the physician in charge from 1807 to 1809.

- 1800 – Dr Benjamin Waterhouse introduced smallpox vaccination to the United States.

- 1842 – Lemuel Shattuck, a Massachusetts legislator, established the first U.S. system for recording births, deaths, and marriages. Largely through his efforts, Massachusetts legislation became the model for all the other states in the Union. Among Shattuck's many contributions were his proposal for a standard nomenclature for disease; establishment of a system for recording mortality data by age, sex, occupation, socioeconomic level, and location; the application of data to programs in immunization, school health, smoking, and alcohol abuse.

- 1849 – The Massachusetts legislature appointed a Sanitary Commission "to prepare and report to the next General Court a plan for a sanitary survey of the State," with Shattuck as Chief Commissioner and author of its report. The report (1850) was enthusiastically received by the *New England Journal of Medicine*, but the 50 recommendations in the report were otherwise ignored. Twenty years later the Secretary of the Board of Health of Massachusetts based his plans for public health on Shattuck's recommendations.

- The 1870 reorganization [of the Marine Hospital Service] also changed the general character of the Service. It became national in scope and military in outlook and organization. Medical officers, called surgeons, were required to pass entrance examinations and wear uniforms. In 1889, when the Commissioned Corps was formally recognized by legislative action, the medical officers were given titles and pay corresponding to Army and Navy grades. Physicians who passed the examinations were appointed to the general service, rather than to a particular hospital, and were assigned wherever needed. The goal was to create a professional, mobile, health corps, free as possible from political favoritism and patronage, and able to deal with the new health needs of a rapidly growing and industrializing nation.

- Epidemics of contagious diseases, such as smallpox, yellow fever, and cholera, had devastating effects throughout the 19th century. They killed many people, spread panic and fear, disrupted government, and caused Congress to enact laws to stop their importation and spread. As a result of these new laws, the functions of the MHS were expanded greatly beyond the medical relief of the sick seamen to include the supervision of national quarantine (ship inspection and disinfection), the medical inspection of immigrants, the prevention of interstate spread of disease, and general investigations in the field of public health, such as that of yellow fever epidemics.

- 1874 – The Massachusetts State Board of Health instituted a voluntary plan for weekly reporting of disease by physicians.

(Continued)

TABLE 11.2.   (Continued)

- 1884 – Massachusetts passed legislation requiring the reporting of "diseases dangerous to the public health" and imposed fines for not reporting.
- 1887 – A small "Hygienic Laboratory" was established at the marine hospital on Staten Island to aid in the diagnosis of infectious diseases among passengers of incoming ships. The laboratory later moved to Washington, D.C., and eventually evolved into the National Institutes of Health.
- 1891 – The Immigration Act of 1891 required that all immigrants entering the US be given a health examination by PHS physicians. The law stipulated the exclusion of "all idiots, insane persons, paupers or persons likely to become public charges, persons suffering from a loathsome or dangerous contagious disease," and criminals. The largest inspection center was on Ellis Island in New York Harbor.
- 1894 – The first epidemic of polio strikes the United States.

1900s
- 1900 – Some estimates indicate that the human immunodeficiency virus (HIV) was transmitted from monkeys to humans as early as 1884–1924, but was either unrecognized or failed to initiate human to human transmission until later.
- 1902 – The U.S. Congress expanded the scientific research work at the Hygienic Laboratory and gave it a definite budget. The legislation required the Surgeon General to organize conferences of local and national health officials in order to coordinate state and national public health activities. The Marine Hospital Service was renamed the Public Health and Marine Hospital Services (PHMHS) to reflect its broader scope.
- 1906 – Congress passed the Federal Meat Inspection Act requiring the Department of Agriculture to inspect meats entering interstate commerce. They also passed the Food and Drugs Act. The law forbade adulteration and misbranding of foods, drinks, and drugs in interstate commerce, but contained few specific requirements to ensure compliance.
- The working environment and its effect on worker's health became a major area of study for the Public Health Service starting in 1910. Investigations in the garment making industry, as illustrated by these women making flowers, revealed unsanitary conditions and an excessive rate of tuberculosis. Other studies were done of silicosis among miners, sanitation and working conditions in the steel industry, lead poisoning in the pottery industry, and radiation hazards in the radium dial painting industry.
- 1912 – The PHMHS was renamed the United States Public Health Service, and it was authorized to investigate human diseases such as tuberculosis, hookworm, malaria, and leprosy, as well as sanitation, water supplies and sewage disposal.
- 1916 – Johns Hopkins University founded the first school of public health in the United States with a grant of $267,000 from the Rockefeller Foundation. The Rockefeller Foundation later supported schools of public health at Harvard University and the University of Michigan.
- 1918 – The influenza pandemic of 1918 struck. It is believed to have caused at least 25–50 million deaths worldwide.
- 1925 All states begin participating in national reporting of disease.
- 1938 Congress passed the Federal Food, Drug, and Cosmetic Act of 1938, and major amendments to the law were made in 1954, 1958, and 1960. Today the law requires manufacturers to provide scientific proof of a new drug's safety. The law also makes dangerous or falsely labeled cosmetics and therapeutic devices illegal. Enforcement of these laws is the mission of the Food and Drug Administration (FDA), which is tasked with ensuring that foods are safe. It also ensures that drugs and medical devices are safe and effective, and that cosmetics are harmless. Provisions are also made to ensure accurate labeling and that radiofrequency emissions from electronic devices are not hazardous to consumers.

(Continued)

TABLE 11.2. (Continued)

- 1946 July 1, Malaria Control in War Areas, a program within the U.S. Public Health Service, transitions into the Communicable Disease Center (CDC).
- 1946 CDC stations the Laboratory Division at the Lawson Veterans Administration Hospital in Chamblee, Georgia.
- 1947 CDC acquires the U.S. Public Health Service Plague Suppressive Laboratory which includes an epidemiology division.
- 1947 Emory University deeds 15 acres of land to the Federal Government for the development of CDC headquarters on Clifton Road in Atlanta, Georgia.
- 1947 CDC establishes the Veterinary Public Health Division, focusing on protecting and improving both animal and human health.
- 1947 CDC offers disaster aid in response to multiple chemical explosions in Texas City, Texas. Subsequently, CDC is designated as the official response agency for future epidemics and disasters.
- 1947 CDC is transferred from the State Relations Division and established as a field station under the immediate direction of the Chief of the Bureau of State Services of the U.S. Public Health Service.
- 1948 CDC investigations expand to include, typhus, dysentery-diarrheal, fly control-poliomyelitis, viral encephalitis, plague, Q fever, brucellosis, creeping eruption, rabies, histoplasmosis, insecticides, and rodenticides.
- 1948 Richard Doll and Bradford Hill conducted a landmark epidemiologic investigation of the cause of the remarkable increase in lung cancer that had occurred during the 20th century. They identified lung cancer patients in 20 London hospitals and enrolled a comparison group of non-cancer patients and conducted a case-control study. Somewhat to the surprise of Doll and Hill, the study found that the one consistent difference between lung cancer patients and the non-cancer controls was that the cancer patients were more frequently smokers, and they were heavier smokers. In retrospect, the study was quite carefully done and quite convincing. Nevertheless, it initially stirred much controversy, even among the medical community. Smoking was extremely prevalent, even in physicians, and many refused to believe that it could be a cause of cancer. Other studies were conducted which corroborated these findings, and eventually the importance of the study was recognized, not only for establishing the link between smoking and lung cancer, but for establishing the role of case-control studies. At the time, case-control studies were infrequently done, and careful standards for their conduct had not been established.
- 1948 The Framingham Heart Study began with the goal of identifying the factors that contribute to cardiovascular disease by following its development over a long period of time in a large group of disease-free participants. The researchers recruited 5,209 men and women between the ages of 30 and 62 from the town of Framingham, Massachusetts, and began the first round of extensive physical examinations and lifestyle interviews that they would later analyze for common patterns related to cardiovascular disease. Since 1948, the subjects have continued to return to the study every two years for a detailed medical history, physical examination, and laboratory tests. In 1971 the Study enrolled a second generation – 5,124 of the original participants' adult children and their spouses – to participate in similar examinations.
- 1949 CDC becomes a division of the Bureau of State Services of the U.S. Public Health Service, primarily concerned with assisting state health authorities.
- 1949 The United States is declared free of malaria as a significant public health problem.
- 1949 Last case of naturally-occurring smallpox is reported in the United States.

(*Continued*)

TABLE 11.2.   (Continued)

- 1949 Medical discoveries and public health campaigns have almost eliminated deaths from the common diseases of childhood such as measles, diphtheria, scarlet fever, and whooping cough. As a result of these successes nearly 20 years were added to the average life expectancy at birth between 1900 and 1950 – from 47 to 67 years.
- 1949 As epidemic diseases were brought under control the Public Health Service began to shift its attention to other areas such as cancer, heart disease, health in the workplace, and the impact of environmental problems, such as toxic waste disposal, on health. But the Public Health Service is still called upon to investigate outbreak of disease such as Legionnaire's, toxic shock syndrome, and now the deadliest epidemic of our age – AIDS. Much of the work of the early plague fighters and sanitarians is now carried out by the scientists at the Centers for Disease Control and Prevention (CDC) in Atlanta, Georgia.
- 1951 Malaria is considered eliminated from the United States.
- 1951 The Epidemic Intelligence Service (EIS) is established, recognizing the need for an adequate corps of trained epidemiologists who can be deployed immediately for any contingency, including chemical or biological warfare.
- 1951 CDC begins a program to study public health insect problems connected with water resource development.
- 1951 Two field stations are established: one to study the effect of economic poisons (pesticides) on humans, and the other to study tropical diseases.
- 1952 Polio cases surge in the U.S. Early testing of the vaccine developed by Jonas Salk is encouraging.
- Reorganization of the CDC reduces the number of branches into five well-defined spheres of activity: Epidemiology, Training, Technology, Laboratory, and Administrative.
- 1953 Under President Eisenhower, Congress created the Department of Health, Education, and Welfare (HEW).
- 1953 CDC reports first case of rabies in a bat.
- 1953 The Communicable Disease Center National Surveillance Program is developed to maintain constant vigilance over communicable diseases, to respond immediately when an outbreak occurs.
- 1953 The U.S. Public Health Service becomes part of the newly created Cabinet-level Department of Health, Education and Welfare after the Federal Security Agency is dissolved.
- 1953 First EIS investigations on environmental exposure to trichloroethylene and occupational exposure.
- 1954 A large scale clinical trial of the Salk vaccine begins.
- 1954 The EIS is expanded to include other professional disciplines besides medicine.
- 1959 Rene Dubos published a landmark book entitled "The Mirage of Health" in which he convincingly argued that the decline in mortality since 1850 was not primarily due to laboratory medicine; it was due to control of infectious disease as a result of sanitation and improvements in nutrition. He also pointed out that Western health was not optimal and that life expectation at age 45 had improved little. Moreover, one out of four Americans spent at least some time in mental hospitals. Increasing levels of drug dependency (all kinds of drugs) also indicated that health was not optimal. Dubos took the position that medicine's concept of specific etiologies (and therefore magic bullets that could cure disease) was misleading. He said that disease is complex and tends to be rooted in social, physical, and cultural environment in which people lived.
- 1964 The National Aeronautics and Space Administration (NASA) approaches CDC for help in working out methods that would ensure that germs from Earth do not get transported into space and vice versa.

(Continued)

TABLE 11.2.　(Continued)

- 1967 The Quarantine Service, one of the oldest units of the U.S. Public Health Service, is transferred to CDC.
- 1970 The Occupational Safety and Health Act was passed by Congress, and the Occupational Safety and Health Administration was founded in 1971.
- 1970 The Environmental Protection Agency (EPA) was established to consolidate federal research, monitoring, standard-setting and enforcement activities to ensure environmental protection.
- 1979 HEW's educational tasks were transferred to the new Department of Education and responsibility for health was given to the newly organized Department of Health and Human Services (HHS).
- 1979 Smallpox is declared eradicated by the World Health Organization. The eradication of smallpox, one of the deadliest and most dreaded diseases, was the result of a massive global effort utilizing case finding and vaccination. The last known case occurred in 1977 in Somalia.
- 1980 President Jimmy Carter signed into law the Comprehensive Environmental Response, Compensation and Liability Act (CERCLA or Superfund). This historic new statute gave EPA the authority to clean up uncontrolled hazardous waste sites and spills.
- 1981 Dr Michael Gottlieb and his associates report on four previously healthy young men who had developed Pneumocystis carinii pneumonia. They hypothesized that this was a new syndrome of acquired immunodeficiency caused by a sexually transmitted infectious agent.
- 1992 The agency is renamed Centers for Disease Control and Prevention (CDC) to reflect a broader role and vision. The agency is asked by Congress to continue using the initials "CDC."
- 1999 CDC launches National Pharmaceutical Stockpile (now the Strategic National Stockpile), a stockpile of drugs, vaccines, and other medical products and supplies, to provide for the emergency health security of the United States and its territories.

2000s

- 2000 Measles declared eliminated from the United States.
- 2001 CDC learns of the first case of inhalational anthrax in the United States since 1976. The person, a 63-year-old Florida man, is infected by anthrax sent through the mail. He is the first of 22 victims of this domestic terrorism event.
- 2001 CDC responds to the World Trade Center and bioterrorist anthrax attacks.
- 2001 The Children's Health Act establishes the National Center on Birth Defects and Developmental Disabilities (NCBDDD) at CDC. The Act expands research and services for a variety of childhood health problems and authorizes the establishment of Centers of Excellence at both CDC and NIH to promote research and monitoring efforts related to autism.
- 2001 National Institute for Occupational Safety and Health (NIOSH) provides technical assistance for responder safety and health in the World Trade Center rescue and recovery.
- 2001 National Center on Birth Defects and Developmental Disabilities (NCBDDD) established.
- 2002 The Institute of Medicine issued a report entitled "Who Will Keep the Public Healthy?" The report concluded that "public health professionals must have a framework for action and an understanding of the forces that impact on health, a model of health that emphasizes the linkages and relationships among multiple determinants affecting health. Such an ecological model, the committee believes, is key to effectively addressing the challenges of the 21st century."
- 2003 Severe Acute Respiratory Syndrome (SARS) is first discovered in Asia. CDC responds by providing guidance for surveillance, clinical and laboratory evaluation, and reporting

(*Continued*)

TABLE 11.2.   (Continued)

- 2003 Morbidity and Mortality Weekly Report (MMWR) reports the first identification of bovine spongiform encephalopathy (BSE) in the United States.
- 2003 A package containing ricin and a note threatening to poison water supplies is discovered in a South Carolina postal facility, becoming the first potential chemical terrorism event involving ricin in the United States.
- 2003 United States experiences an outbreak of monkeypox, the first time human monkeypox is reported outside of Africa. CDC deploys teams of medical officers, epidemiologists, and other experts to several states to assist with the investigation.
- 2004 Rubella is eliminated in the United States.
- 2005 The Surgeon General releases A Call to Action to Improve the Health and Wellness of Persons with Disabilities and highlights disability as a major public health issue. The call to action appeals to all Americans to help improve the quality of life for people with disabilities through better health care and understanding.
- 2006 CDC responds to a multi-state mumps outbreak involving more than 6,500 reported cases. This resurgence predominantly affects college-aged students living in the Midwest, with outbreaks occurring on many different Midwestern college campuses.
- 2006 CDC's Emergency Operations Center (EOC) activates for Tropical Storm Ernesto.
- 2008 CDC's Emergency Operations Center (EOC) activates for Hurricane Dolly, Tropical Storm Edouard, Hurricanes Gustav, Hanna, and Ike.
- 2009 CDC identifies the novel H1N1 influenza virus. The H1N1 flu pandemic demonstrates CDC's unique ability to assess and explain risk.
- 2010 In the aftermath of the 7.0 magnitude earthquake in Haiti, CDC response effort helps prevent 7,000 deaths from cholera.
- 2010 National Institute for Occupational Safety and Health (NIOSH) provides technical assistance for responder safety and health in the Deepwater Horizon containment and cleanup.
- 2014 The first case of Ebola is reported in Guinea in March; the disease spreads into the neighboring countries of Liberia and Sierra Leone. CDC activates its Emergency Operations Center to respond to the largest Ebola outbreak in history affecting multiple countries in West Africa. CDC helps coordinate the response at the national level, providing health education and assisting with database management. CDC trains teams of people who can do contact tracing, finding everyone who came in direct contact with a sick Ebola patient.
- 2016 CDC responds to lead contamination in the Flint, Michigan water supply.
- 2016 CDC's Emergency Response and Recovery Branch leads efforts to support countries impacted by Hurricane Matthew.
- 2017 Public health officials announce that drug overdoses have become the leading cause of death for Americans under age 50, with more than two-thirds of those deaths coming from opioid painkillers.
- 2017 CDC responds to Hurricanes Harvey, Irma, and Maria.
- 2018 Whole-genome sequencing becomes the new PulseNet gold standard for subtyping pathogens that cause foodborne illness.
- 2019 CDC activates its Emergency Operations Center (EOC) on Monday, September 16, 2019, to enhance the inter-agency response to the current investigation into lung injury cases with e-cigarette product use, or vaping.
- 2019 CDC reports 704 cases of measles in the United States since the beginning of 2019, representing the largest number of cases reported in the country in a single year since 1994.
- 2019 CDC activates the EOC for Ebola outbreak in eastern Democratic Republic of the Congo (DRC). CDC lab research shows two treatments effective against DRC Ebola strain.

(Continued)

TABLE 11.2. (Continued)

- 2020 CDC maps America's high levels of physical inactivity.
- 2020 Public health screenings begin at three U.S. airports for 2019 novel coronavirus (2019-nCoV).
- 2020 CDC activates Emergency Operations Center (EOC) on Monday, January 20, to support public health partners responding to the outbreak caused by a novel (new) coronavirus first identified in Wuhan, Hubei Province, China.
- 2020 CDC confirms person-to-person spread of new coronavirus in the United States.
- 2020 A CDC-developed laboratory test kit to detect 2019 novel coronavirus (2019-nCoV) begins shipping to select qualified U.S. and international laboratories.
- 2020 The World Health Organization (WHO) names the new disease COVID-19.
- 2020 CDC launches the SARS-CoV-2 Sequencing for Public Health Emergency Response, Epidemiology, and Surveillance (SPHERES) consortium, expanding the use of whole-genome sequencing (WGS) of the COVID-19 virus.
- 2020 June 25 marks the end of the 2018 Ebola outbreak in the eastern part of DRC.
- 2020 CDC discovers active ingredient, nootkatone, for development of new mosquito/tick insecticides and repellents.
- 2020 CDC launches a national campaign, Hear Her, which highlights warning signs of pregnancy-related death.
- 2020 Africa is declared free of wild poliovirus, the second virus eradicated from the continent since smallpox 40 years previously.

Source: U.S. NLM, 2012; BUSPH, 2015; David J. Sencer CDC Museum, 2021.

This section provides a discussion of the foundational aspects of present-day public health practice. The Public Health Core Sciences, Core Functions and Essential Services of Public Health, and Ten Essential Public Health Services are briefly explored.

Public Health Core Sciences

Public health practice is based on core sciences and scientific methods used to implement public health approaches by practitioners. These methods come from a series of core sciences that provide the foundation for public health activities shown in Figure 11.5. Working in concert, these five core sciences allow public health practitioners to find the answers they need to protect and promote the public's health; "one science alone cannot answer the questions and provide a solution; it is the application of these core sciences together" (CDC, 2014a).

The Core Sciences of public health include public health surveillance, epidemiology, public health laboratories, public health informatics, and prevention effectiveness.

1. **Public Health Surveillance.** Public health surveillance is "the ongoing, systematic collection, analysis, and interpretation of health-related data essential to planning, implementation, and evaluation of public health practice – *Field Epidemiology*" (CDC, 2018k).
2. **Epidemiology.** "Enables us to determine where diseases originate, how or why they move through populations, and how we can prevent them" (CDC, 2014a). Epidemiology is the "study of distribution and determinants of health-related states among specified populations and the application of that study to the control of health problems. – *A Dictionary of Epidemiology*" (CDC, 2018k).

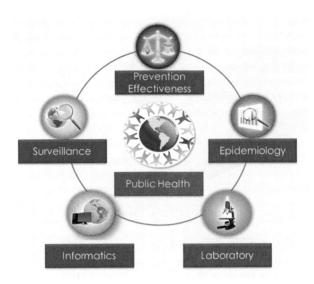

FIGURE 11.5.   Public Health Core Sciences (Source: CDC, 2014a).

3. **Public Health Laboratories**. "Public health laboratories focus on diseases and the health status of population groups. They perform limited diagnostic testing, reference testing, and disease surveillance. They also provide emergency response support, perform applied research, and provide training for laboratory personnel" (CDC, 2018k).

4. **Public Health Informatics**. "Public health informatics is the systematic application of information, computer science, and technology to public health practice, research, and learning. – *Public Health Informatics: Improving and Transforming Public Health in the Information Age*" (CDC, 2018k).

5. **Prevention Effectiveness**. "Prevention effectiveness is the systematic assessment of the impact of public health policies, programs, and practices on health outcomes by determining their effectiveness, safety, and costs. – *Prevention Effectiveness: A Guide to Decision Analysis and Economic Evaluation*" (CDC, 2018k).

Core Functions and Essential Services of Public Health

In addition to the Core Sciences, there are Public Health Core Functions that focus on Assessment, Policy Development and Assurance. "In 1988, the Institute of Medicine defined three core functions of public health agencies that must be carried out at all levels of government for the overall public health system to work effectively" (CDC, 2014a). These functions are further delineated through the Ten Essential Public Health Services. The Three Core Functions of Public Health can be seen in Figure 11.6.

Ten Essential Public Health Services

The core functions of public health can be broken down further through the ten essential public health services (EPHS). "These services are not a prescription for what public health agencies should be doing. Instead, they are intended to serve as a descriptive tool to capture the field of public health and to communicate what public health provides"

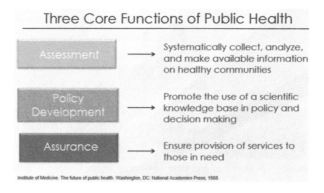

FIGURE 11.6. Three Core Functions of Public Health (Source: CDC, 2014a).

(CDC, 2014a). In 2020, a multi-organizational collaborative effort was undertaken to update the EPHS to bring the framework in line with current and future public health practice (CDC, 2021e). The result of this work modernized the framework that was originally developed in 1994. "The 10 Essential Public Health Services provide a framework for public health to protect and promote the health of *all people in all communities*" (CDC, 2021e). This update places equity in the center, as the new framework seeks to remove structural barriers and obstacles while promoting fair and just health opportunities for all. The updated framework for the Ten Essential Public Health Services can be seen below in Figure 11.7.

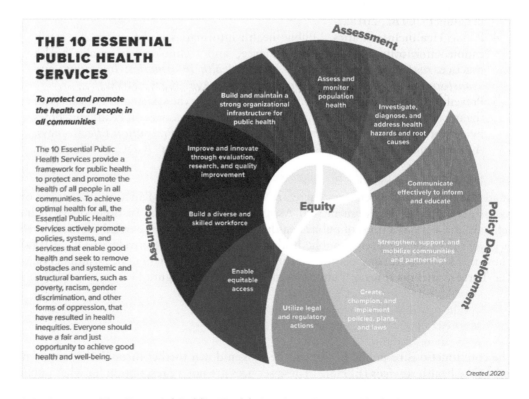

FIGURE 11.7. Ten Essential Public Health Services (Source: CDC, 2021e).

RELATION TO DISASTERS/TERRORISM

The role of public health in relation to homeland security and emergency management is explored in this section. Public Health has always played an essential part in the response and recovery to emergencies, disasters, terrorism, war, and conflict throughout history. These roles continue to evolve and are shaped by events such as 9/11, the 2009 H1N1 pandemic, Hurricane Sandy 2012, the 2014–2016 Ebola outbreak, and others.

PUBLIC HEALTH AND EMERGENCY MANAGEMENT

The Public Health role in Emergency Management is based on the National Response Framework's Emergency Support Function (ESF) #8 – Public Health and Medical Services. While Public Health has a broad range of interests and authority over general public health concerns, public health activities during an emergency or disaster focus on providing ESF-8 support to impacted communities. Public Health support and emergency activities are further explored in this section.

Emergency Support Function 8 – Public Health and Medical Services

The National Response Framework is the current doctrine guiding the principles of emergency response as outlined in the 2002 National Homeland Security Strategy. The framework was developed from an existing 1970s Federal Response Plan in direct response to the terrorist attacks of September 11, 2001. The nation needed to establish a concerted effort to manage incidents of national significance, thereby resulting in a series of doctrines immediately following the tragic events of 9/11. However, over a short period of time and as a result of subsequent incidents, such as Hurricane Katrina in 2005, these doctrines required revisions to make response and recovery capabilities more scalable and applicable across a wider range of emergencies. This resulted in the transition from the original National Response Plan immediately post-9/11, to the National Response Framework (NRF) core guidelines and Emergency Support Functions (ESF) Annexes. The Annexes comprise 15 protocols that provide the structure for coordinating federal interagency support for anything from transportation to utilities and public works, to communications and long-term community recovery, to public health and medical services, or ESF-8.

Emergency Support Function (ESF) #8 – Public Health and Medical Services – "provides the mechanism for coordinated Federal assistance to supplement State, tribal, and local resources in response to a public health and medical disaster, potential or actual incidents requiring a coordinated Federal response, and/or during a developing potential health and medical emergency" (FEMA, 2016). The scope of ESF-8 covers anything related to the health and wellness of the impacted community and its first responders including its mental health. This includes several functional areas outlined by FEMA (2016, p. 2):

- Assessment of public health/medical needs
- Health surveillance
- Medical care personnel
- Health/medical/veterinary equipment and supplies
- Patient evacuation

- Patient care
- Health/medical/veterinary equipment and supplies
- Blood and blood products
- Food safety and security
- Agriculture safety and security
- All-hazard public health and medical consultation, technical assistance, and support
- Behavioral health care
- Public health and medical information
- Vector control
- Potable water/wastewater and solid waste disposal
- Mass fatality management, victim identification, and decontaminating remains
- Veterinary medical support

The medical needs of people "at risk" or with "special needs" as described in the Pandemic and All-Hazards Preparedness Act and in the NRF Glossary are also included in ESF-8 capabilities. ESF-8 serves as an ongoing function for those who may have medical and other functional needs before, during, and after an incident (FEMA, 2016).

During a pandemic, the ESF-8 protocol is initiated and in continuous effect to assess the situation and determine and provide the necessary medical resources to an affected community. Because a pandemic by definition is a global phenomenon, federal resources through its ESF-8 function must also continuously track the vector-borne disease itself, consult on treatments and preventive measures, engage public education campaigns, provide technical assistance and support, and assist with any other impact the pandemic may have both in the United States and, to the extent its humanitarian responsibility allows, to other countries. The ESF-8 process is part of the entire emergency management response system under the National Incident Management System (NIMS) doctrine. NIMS was also developed as part of the national response to the terrorist attacks of 9/11. This doctrine provides a system of response and recovery capabilities to incidents of varying size and significance. NIMS provides a scalable method to conduct operations, incident planning, managing logistics, as well as administering and financing the needs of an incident. More importantly, NIMS is not solely a federal response mechanism. It was designed to manage an incident from the bottom-up, meaning the local personnel maintain priority management over an incident. As an incident grows in size and scale, additional resources from adjoining jurisdictions and levels of government (including the state and ultimately the federal government) unite to manage the response through to recovery. With a pandemic, the incident is clearly of a size and scope to necessitate a full-scale response at all levels of government as well as engaging the participation of the private sector and individual citizens. Everyone must participate in managing the impact of a pandemic because pandemics require much longer responses than some other major disasters like hurricanes and wildfires that may only require weeks and months of support.

U.S. Quarantine System and Pandemics

The USPHS and the CDC operate a network of Quarantine Stations at international Ports of Entry across the nation. U.S. Quarantine Stations serve as part of the federal quarantine system designed to limit the introduction and spread of contagious diseases in the United States (CDC, 2021j). A map of U.S. Quarantine Stations and their Jurisdictions can be seen in **Figure 11.8**. U.S. Quarantine Stations stem back to the founding of the U.S. Public Health Service and are one of its oldest legacy functions. In 1976, federal quarantine functions were transferred to the CDC who continues to operate and manage

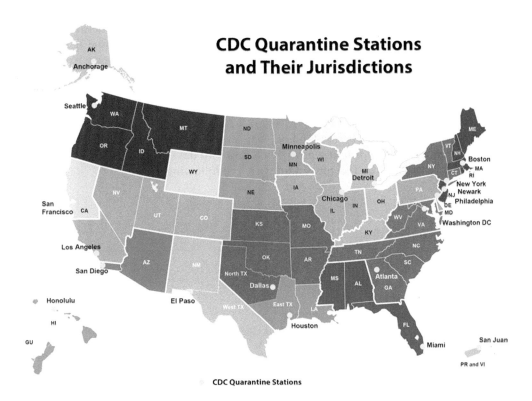

FIGURE 11.8.   Map of U.S. Quarantine Stations (Source: CDC, 2021j).

them in the present day with uniformed Quarantine Public Health Officers and Medical Officers from the CDC's Division of Global Migration and Quarantine and U.S. Public Health Service Officers (CDC, 2021j). A brief snapshot of U.S. Quarantine Station history can be seen in **Figure 11.9**.

U.S. Quarantine Stations have unique federal quarantine authority. "CDC has the legal authority to detain any person who may have an infectious disease that is specified by Executive Order to be quarantinable. If necessary, CDC can deny ill persons with these diseases entry to the United States. CDC also can have them admitted to a hospital or confined to a home for a certain amount of time to prevent the spread of disease" (CDC, 2021j). Activities taken to prevent the spread of communicable disease include

Brief U.S. Quarantine History

- **1799** The first quarantine station and hospital in America was built in 1799 at the port of Philadelphia after a yellow fever outbreak in 1793.
- **1878** The National Quarantine Act was passed in 1878, shifting quarantine powers from state to federal government.
- **1944** The Public Health Service Act formed the federal government's quarantine authority in 1944.
- **1967** CDC (National Communicable Disease Center) took over federal quarantine functions in 1967.
- **1970s** CDC reduced the number of quarantine stations from 55 to 8 because infectious diseases were thought to be a thing of the past.
- **2004-2007** Number of quarantine stations increased to 20 because of concerns about bioterrorism after World Trade Center attack in 2001 and worldwide spread of disease after SARS outbreak in 2003.

FIGURE 11.9.   U.S. Quarantine Station History Snapshot (Source: (CDC, 2021j).

undertaking quarantine and isolation. Quarantine "separates and restricts the movement of people who were exposed to a contagious disease to see if they become sick" (CDC, 2017m), whereas isolation "separates sick people with a contagious disease from people who are not sick" (CDC, 2017m). Quarantine and isolation are two of the oldest public health actions that have been implemented to curb the spread of disease. "The practice of quarantine, as we know it, began during the 14th century in an effort to protect coastal cities from plague epidemics. Ships arriving in Venice from infected ports were required to sit at anchor for 40 days before landing. This practice, called quarantine, was derived from the Italian words *quaranta giorni* which mean 40 days" (CDC, 2020n). The list of Quarantinable Diseases by Executive Order are the following:

1. Cholera
2. Diphtheria
3. Infectious tuberculosis
4. Plague
5. Smallpox
6. Yellow fever
7. Viral hemorrhagic fevers
8. Severe acute respiratory syndromes
9. New types of flu (influenza) that could cause a pandemic (CDC, 2021j).

Quarantine activities are conducted in partnership with an extensive network of domestic and international agencies and organizations across all levels of government and the private sector. Partnerships play a critical role in public health and conducting quarantine activities. An example of these partners include:

- U.S. Customs and Border Protection
- U.S. Fish and Wildlife Service
- U.S. Department of Agriculture: Animal Plant and Health Inspection Services
- U.S. Coast Guard
- U.S. Food and Drug Administration
- U.S. Department of State
- U.S. Department of Homeland Security
- DHS: Countering Weapons of Mass Destruction Office
- U.S. Department of Transportation
- Federal Aviation Administration
- Transportation Security Administration
- Federal Bureau of Investigation
- Travel industry
  - Port officials
  - Airlines and cruise lines
- Medical care
  - Emergency Medical Services
  - Local and state public health departments
  - State public health laboratories
  - State and territorial epidemiologists
  - Hospitals and health care providers
- International partners including:
  - Canadian/Mexican border authorities

- World Health Organization
- Public Health Agency of Canada
- Overseas panel physicians
- International Organization for Migration, and foreign governments (CDC, 2021j).

U.S. Quarantine Stations therefore conduct a variety of activities from illness response to public health surveillance activities, migration, and inspections of items entering the United States. Examples of activities conducted by medical and public health officers at U.S. Quarantine Stations include:

Response
- Respond to reports of illnesses on airplanes, maritime vessels, and at land-border crossings
- Distribute immunobiologics and investigational drugs
- Plan and prepare for emergency response

Migration
- Monitor health and collect any medical information of new immigrants, refugees, asylees, and parolees
- Alert local health departments in the areas where refugees and immigrants resettle about any health issues that need follow up
- Provide travelers with essential health information
- Respond to mass migration emergencies

Inspection
- Inspect animals, animal products, and human remains that pose a potential threat to human health
- Screen cargo and hand-carried items for potential vectors of human infectious diseases

Partnerships
- Build partnerships for disease surveillance and control (CDC, 2021j).

The CDC's Division of Global Migration and Quarantine and the historic efforts of the Quarantine and Border Health Services Branch have played a pivotal role in responding to the COVID-19 pandemic and other public health emergencies by working tirelessly to stop the spread of ill travelers domestically and internationally within the United States. Although COVID-19 has been a primary concern since the start of the novel pandemic, other communicable disease outbreaks have also occurred requiring simultaneous responses. Incidents like the reoccurring Ebola outbreaks in the Democratic Republic of the Congo; disease outbreaks among evacuees during Operation Allies Welcome, which prompted great concern and required close multi-organizational partnership, coordination, public health monitoring and surveillance, and mass vaccination campaigns for "measles, mumps, rubella (MMR), and varicella (chickenpox) to Afghan evacuees who are temporarily staying at eight military installations in the United States"; and even a rare case of Monkeypox in the United States in 2021, have required tremendous effort by the CDC's Division of Global Migration and Quarantine to stave off these concurring public health emergencies (CDC, 2021o, 2021p;DHS, 2021). The Quarantine Stations have historically played a monumental role in the history of public health since the early years of the United States and continue to demonstrate their importance. What remains to be seen is how the federal quarantine system will evolve post-COVID-19. Moving forward, Quarantine Stations will continue to be an integral part of public health efforts to combat future disease outbreaks and pandemics.

Case Study – 2014 Dallas, Texas, USA Ebola Incident

The capabilities of the public health system in the United States are best exemplified by actual events. In October of 2014, a very rare incident – a small Ebola outbreak – occurred in the United States when a man named Thomas Duncan traveled from Liberia to Dallas, Texas, USA. David McEntire captures the many challenges faced during this incident in his report, *The Dallas Ebola Incident as an Indicator of the Bioterrorism Threat: An Assessment of Response with Implications for Security and Preparedness*. The excerpt from the report below describes how the first U.S. Ebola outbreak occurred:

> Concerning outbreaks of Ebola began in the African nation of Guinea on December 28, 2013, when a two-year-old child died from hemorrhagic fever. By March 2014, 59 deaths in Guinea were attributed to Ebola, and cases were subsequently reported in Liberia. Five months later, the World Health Organization put the death toll at 3,091 people and announced that the fatality rate was at an appalling 70%. As this outbreak unfolded, a man named Thomas Duncan cared for his landlord's daughter, who was infected with the disease. A short time later he boarded a plane from Africa and landed in Dallas, Texas, on September 19, 2014. Duncan started to run a fever on September 24 and checked into the Presbyterian hospital the next day. Thinking that Duncan had some strain of routine flu, doctors and nurses sent him home. Duncan's condition continued to deteriorate, and on September 28, Duncan returned to the hospital by ambulance and was isolated. Two days later, tests confirmed he was infected with Ebola. On October 8, 2014, Duncan succumbed to the disease and passed away. During Duncan's treatment in the hospital, two nurses were also infected. Nina Pham became the first person to be infected by Ebola transmission in the United States. She developed a fever on October 10, 2014, and was isolated until she was declared Ebola free on October 24, 2014. Amber Vinson was another nurse who became concerned about possible infection when she felt sick while traveling to Ohio to make wedding plans. She returned to Dallas on October 13 and reported to the hospital on October 14. She tested positive the next day, was treated, and declared Ebola free on October 22. While the loss of Duncan's life from Ebola was undoubtedly tragic and the recovery of infected nurses was fortunate, the large numbers of fatalities in Africa and the spread of the disease in the United States certainly illustrated the serious nature of this outbreak. The Ebola episode severely challenged decision makers in the medical community and in local/state government, and the costs associated with treatment and response were substantial. Although this small occurrence in the US proved to be extremely difficult, a wide-scale outbreak would clearly be even more overwhelming.

> (McEntire, 2019)

This incident is notable for the numerous problems faced during the response and recovery. It became apparent there are unique challenges and issues between the emergency management community and the public health, healthcare, and medical communities. McEntire notes that challenges ranged from lack of scientific and technical expertise, public messaging, assessment, response and treatment protocols, a lack of understanding of public health emergency response and authorities, quarantine and isolation, sanitation, decontamination, and hazardous waste disposal and transportation, and false assumptions about roles and responsibilities during a public health response between organizations and their capabilities to respond to public health incidents (McEntire, 2019). When examining the assumptions and beliefs of agency roles and responsibilities during the

Ebola incident, it can be inferred that this misunderstanding came from a greater lack of understanding of how public health and emergency management communities operate together during incidents, especially public health emergencies of this unique and rare nature involving diseases (known or novel) that are classified as potential weapons of mass destruction and highly hazardous agents. Shaping these perceptions are undoubtedly movies such as the popular 1995 *Outbreak* whose plot revolves around a fictitious Ebola-like virus outbreak in a small California town or *Contagion*, released in 2011, depicting a more truthful version of potential events and response to a novel flu pandemic inspired by previous epidemics such as SARS (IMDB, 1995a, 2011b). These movies depict large-scale quarantines, federal government, military, and CDC involvement to "save the day" or "bring in the cavalry," as one agency expected during the Dallas-Ebola incident. Despite these expectations that are harbored through popular culture surrounding these types of events, this simply is not the case. The unique and rare nature of such public health emergencies and the greater lack of awareness, education, understanding of roles, responsibilities, and capabilities between the communities of homeland security, emergency management, first responders, public health, medicine, and health care, continue to challenge responses to these types of incidents. The greater implications can be seen during the present COVID-19 pandemic, where now the impact is of national and global scale and significance.

Current Challenges

Never before has man had such capacity to control his own environment, to end thirst and hunger, to conquer poverty and disease, to banish illiteracy and massive human misery. We have the power to make this the best generation of mankind in the history of the world – or make it the last.

Address before the 18th General Assembly of the United Nations (366), September 20, 1963, Public Papers of the Presidents: John F. Kennedy, 1963

The global scale of the COVID-19 pandemic has stressed and, in some areas, overloaded public health systems worldwide beyond capacity. This has exacerbated existing problems and challenges. The COVID-19 pandemic has been a proving ground for many great failures and successes. From these great experiences the world has learned much and, in its resolve, worked to overcome what will undoubtedly be known as the greatest disaster of the 21st century. This section reviews two overarching challenges affecting public health – Chronic Public Health Underfunding and Technology and Legacy Systems – followed by a discussion of COVID-19 challenges observed during the COVID-19 response including Challenges with the U.S. Federal Quarantine System and Public Health Workforce, Strategic Public Health Reserves, Public Health Response Challenges, Politics, Misinformation, Public Messaging and Communication, Information Sharing and Intelligence, and Homeland Security Partnerships.

Chronic Public Health Underfunding

One major issue affecting public health and healthcare emergency management has been chronic public health underfunding. A 2020 report on public health funding noted that public health emergency preparedness funding continues to be significantly cut and reduced; "CDC funding for public health preparedness and response programs decreased between FY 2019 and FY 2020, from $858 million to $850 million and has been cut in half over the last decade. The Hospital Preparedness Program – part of the Office of the Assistant Secretary for Preparedness and Response in the U.S. Department of Health and Human Services – is the single source of federal funding to help regional healthcare systems prepare for emergencies. Its budget was $515 million in FY 2004 and $275.5 million in FY 2020" (Farberman et al., 2020). While this report captures shortfalls of the last decade, public health funding has been on a downward trend extending back to the 1960s. "From the late 1960s to the 2010s, the federal share of total health expenditure for public health dropped from 45 percent to 15 percent" (Haseltine, 2020). The implications of the loss of funding are widespread, most notably in the loss of jobs and a capable public health and healthcare workforce. Sustainable funding is paramount to global health security and will be vital beyond the COVID-19 pandemic.

Technology and Legacy Systems

Public Health requires a technological overhaul to the systems it has in place that serve as the foundation for conducting its activities and operations. These legacy systems greatly hinder the ability to conduct timely public health activities and require intensive manual data entry as a direct result of a lack of strategic investment and acquisition of capabilities needed to support largescale pandemics and data collection. Due to the overwhelming volume of COVID-19 cases and contact investigations being undertaken, many organizations have begun investing in upgrading technologies to adapt how they operate, collect, and share information. Lack of funding has historically been an issue complicating acquisitions.

COVID-19 Challenges

The COVID-19 pandemic has proven to be one of the greatest global health disasters in a century. In the United States, the pandemic response will undoubtedly be studied for years to come. Efforts are already underway by multiple organizations and commissions reviewing and examining the public health response. Many challenges have been experienced from the onset of the response to COVID-19 and range from debates about the source of the virus, intelligence and information sharing, legal issues and implications affecting public health program activities, misinformation, public messaging and communication, which has greatly impacted the effectiveness of key public health activities such as mass vaccination and testing, critical personal protective equipment and response supply shortages, manufacturing challenges, and even domestic and international politics. The following section explores some of the key challenge areas observed during the COVID-19 pandemic response.

Challenges with the U.S. Federal Quarantine System and Public Health Workforce

As noted earlier, the Federal Quarantine Station Network plays a vital role in national pandemic preparedness and response. Quarantine Stations are some of the oldest units of the U.S. Public Health Service stemming back to the origins of the agency and now part of the CDC's Division of Global Migration and Quarantine, National Center for Emerging and Zoonotic Infectious Diseases (CDC, 2020n). Due to the vast number of COVID-19 infections since the start of the pandemic, quarantine stations have been inundated with overwhelming numbers of ill travelers greatly taxing the quarantine station system. "As the pandemic response continued, staff experienced unprecedented and increasing numbers of illness responses, contact investigations and implementation of travel restrictions all while continuing to appropriately respond to routine station duties and responsibilities" (FEB Chicago, 2021). In the meantime, responses to simultaneous public health emergencies were still occurring such as Ebola and disease outbreaks among evacuees during Operation Allies Welcome. This is symptomatic of greater issues affecting public health and healthcare workers as a whole while managing the COVID-19 pandemic. Extended emergency responses have negative impacts ranging from fatigue, burnout, turnover and retention issues, as well as impacts to mental health and overall wellness of the public health and healthcare workforce (Stone et al., 2021).

Further, healthcare workers witness high death numbers under their care, experience extreme work hours, are prone to getting sick themselves, and may have to live away from their families. Of great concern are growing trends, nationally dubbed as the "Exodus" of public health workers, while healthcare workers also face threats of violence, being fired, and the stress caused by polarized politics surrounding COVID-19 (Baker and Ivory, 2021). In a survey of public health workers, as of September 2020 "23.6% fewer respondents planned to remain in the U.S. public health workforce for three or more years compared to their retrospectively reported January 2020 plans. A large-scale public health emergency response places unsustainable burdens on an already underfunded and understaffed public health workforce. Pandemic-related burnout threatens the U.S. public health workforce's future when many challenges related to the ongoing COVID-19 response remain unaddressed" (Stone et al., 2021).

As a result of these issues, the U.S. Federal Quarantine System is currently under review by the National Academies of Sciences, Engineering, and Medicine Committee on Analysis to Enhance the Effectiveness of the Federal Quarantine Station Network based on Lessons from the COVID-19 Pandemic (NASEM, 2022). "An ad hoc committee of the National Academies of Sciences, Engineering, and Medicine will assess the Centers for Disease Control and Prevention's (CDC) Division of Global Migration and Quarantine (DGMQ) and the federal quarantine stations strategies, policies, infrastructure, and resources dedicated to mitigating the risk of onward communicable disease transmission in the context of ongoing changes in the global environment, including large increases in international travel, threats posed by emerging infections, and the movement of animals and cargo" (NASEM, 2022). The results of this and other studies will identify recommendations for the current national quarantine system. This is likened to the Commission on 9/11, the recommendations of which were enacted into law. Although the COVID-19 pandemic is uncertain, reviewing, evaluating, and reimaging the future federal quarantine system and its posture to increase health security is a national imperative. Future systems need to be capable of adapting to the vast volume of cases experienced during COVID-19.

Strategic Public Health Reserves
Lastly, as the pandemic rages on, resources are continuously stretched in all sectors as national production globally is slow to recover. Stored reserves like the Strategic National Stockpile became quickly depleted during the first six months of COVID-19. It is noted that stockpiles of critical supplies had been low from previous incidents at the onset of the pandemic. Now, moving into the third year of COVID-19, long-term issues with supply shortages are emerging from subsequent crises with fragile supply chains, shipping, and manufacturing shortfalls brought on by the pandemic. These deficiencies extend

well beyond emergency and key medical supplies. Shortages have emerged with most consumer goods and are anticipated to continue until the pandemic is resolved. Moving forward, rethinking how strategic resources and reserves are developed, maintained, and managed will be critical to future incidents and providing relief at critical times.

Public Health Response Challenges, Politics, Misinformation, Public Messaging and Communication

Overwhelmingly, the greatest overarching challenge during COVID-19 has been the conflicting approaches, political beliefs, public messaging, false narratives, misinformation, and efforts that have gravely undermined the response to COVID-19. From the onset of COVID-19 there were challenges by the Trump Administration to accept and act on the sincerity of the threat of COVID-19. President Trump at one point declared the COVID-19 pandemic to be a hoax devised by Democrats (Egan, 2020). Medical experts and scientists tried further to raise the alarm at the growing threat from COVID-19 but were repeatedly ignored or silenced in some cases (Stanley and Sun, 2021). This came to light when emails from a group of experts from multiple federal agencies and academic institutions surfaced. "The 'Red Dawn String,' Dr Caneva said, was intended 'to provide thoughts, concerns, raise issues, share information across various colleagues responding to Covid-19,' including medical experts and doctors from the Health and Human Services Department, the Centers for Disease Control and Prevention, the Homeland Security Department, the Veterans Affairs Department, the Pentagon and other federal agencies tracking the historic health emergency" (Lipton, 2020). Famously, their email chain known as "Red Dawn" would evolve into "Red Dawn Breaking, Red Dawn Rising, Red Dawn Breaking Bad and, as the situation grew more dire, Red Dawn Raging" (Lipton, 2020). Further, federal pandemic response planning early during COVID-19 forecasted widespread shortages and challenges to come but enacting this plan was hindered by the Administration's slow response and continued downplaying of COVID-19 (Baker and Sullivan, 2020). Ultimately, critical time was lost waiting for the federal government to act that could have been used to ramp up production of critical medical supplies such as masks, personal protective equipment, ventilators, sanitation, and sterilization products that would later face catastrophic shortages and require implementation of the Defense Production Act to overcome and boost vaccine development efforts (Lupkin, 2021).

Continued denials and political efforts later shaped other aspects of the COVID-19 response. Numerous denials came directly from President Trump and his Administration, "the President has declared at least 38 times that Covid-19 is either going to disappear or is currently disappearing" (Wolfe and Dale, 2020). The country became split on how to deal with COVID-19. Republicans and President Trump continued to downplay the pandemic as a harmless flu, whereas Democrats and others sought to take action to prevent the spread of the novel disease (Berman, 2020; Wolfe and Dale, 2020; Rieger, 2020; Beer, 2020; Green and Tyson, 2020). Major contention emerged over the use of shutdowns, testing, quarantine, isolation, and mask mandates to combat COVID-19. This caused healthcare systems in New York, Washington, and California to become overwhelmed with COVID-19 patients, followed by other states and major population centers around the nation (Hersher et al., 2020; Forgey and Choy, 2020).

Another major factor contributing to healthcare systems being overwhelmed was due to a failure to provide federal disaster support, crisis leadership, coordination, resources, and assistance. Arguments and competition ensued over basic and critical medical supplies from ventilators to personal protective equipment such as N-95 masks between the federal government vs. state and local governments, the private sector, and even families.

The Trump Administration had "been reluctant to provide the needed federal support until recently and has told states to get the equipment to fight COVID-19 on their own [vii]. States and healthcare systems are in a free-for-all in competition against other states, FEMA, the Department of Health and Human Services, and the federal government for these critical emergency supplies" (Simental and Bynum, 2020; Fabian, 2020). Extreme shortages of critical medical supplies such as ventilators became normal as resources were exceeded by the vast volume of COVID-19 patients being hospitalized requiring intensive care. Ventilators in particular became a national issue in the fight over resources; at one point hospitals began having to split ventilators and share them among patients, a practice that had only been done twice prior at previous emergencies in the United States, one time being after the 2017 Las Vegas Mass Shooting (Rosenthal et al., 2020). One quote from a hospital captured how dire the situation had become, "The Other Option Is Death" (Rosenthal et al., 2020). This was notably a major deviation from decades-old established national disaster response policy upending long-held practice and expectations set out in the National Response Framework and subsequent plans.

Additionally, another major issue emerged when vaccinations became available. Anti-vaccination movements rose and became a political issue on the premise that vaccinations violated civil rights and liberties (Cole and Mach, 2021). Some states refused to do testing and undertake public health activities to prevent the spread of COVID-19 such as Florida whose Governor infamously opposes all COVID-19 mandates, whereas others took action largely along the established political lines (Luscombe, 2021). Misinformation challenges have been compounded by evolving science and changing public health guidelines causing ire and confusion among the public and private sector organizations, particularly with schools (Brangham and Norris, 2021; Eldred, 2021). Further issues were exacerbated by challenges and attacks on public health officials' credibility, science, and politics (Finn, 2021; Baker and Ivory, 2021). "State and local public health departments across the country have endured not only the public's fury, but widespread staff defections, burnout, firings, unpredictable funding and a significant erosion in their authority to impose the health orders that were critical to America's early response to the pandemic" (Baker and Ivory, 2021). It is of great concern that these attacks have included harassment and death threats toward public health workers (Mello et al., 2020).

Lastly, legal challenges and political efforts took shape to undermine public health authorities and law that continue to the present day. "Legislators have approved more than 100 new laws – with hundreds more under consideration – that limit state and local health powers. That overhaul of public health gives governors, lawmakers and county commissioners more power to undo health decisions and undermines everything from flu vaccination campaigns to quarantine protocols for measles" (Baker and Ivory, 2021). This is complicated by changing narratives, evolving science, and public messaging from public health agencies and political leaders that at times have been conflicting and confusing and further compounded by misinformation spread through social media. Undoubtedly, this will be an area of great interest and research post-COVID-19 in examining lessons learned and developing efforts to combat future pandemics.

Information Sharing and Intelligence
Lack of standardization in communicating and sharing information between local, state, and federal public health agencies is a big issue hindering the COVID-19 response. This dovetails with the issues of technology and legacy system acquisitions. Within public health and health care, there are numerous reporting methods that are highly inconsistent across the country. Some efforts in recent years have been undertaken to standardize

reporting of communicable diseases and develop reporting tools that would boost timely response; improve communication and data collection and sharing; and improve overall public health surveillance activities by organizations like the Council of State and Territorial Epidemiologists (CSTE) and the Association of State and Territorial Health Officials (ASTHO) (CSTE, n.d.).

Homeland Security Partnerships

Even with the concerted national effort to respond to emergencies including public health disasters, which is well documented in the emergency response doctrine of NIMS and the NRF, there is still a lack of comprehensive partnering between the emergency or public safety management community and the public health community. Interestingly enough, strategies for pandemic management have been developed for at least the past 40 years, but putting the strategy into actionable response has been particularly challenging for the emergency management community.

Despite these strategies, federal coordination activities notably struggled to manage and implement key elements of the national disaster response system during the pandemic. Some of these activities centered around national leadership and politics, leading to the hoarding of key resources during the early months of the pandemic. This led to power struggles and competition to acquire key supplies and resources. Federal, state, and local governments, public and private sector organizations, healthcare agencies, and response organizations to include individuals and families, were all competing against one another resulting in bidding wars in the desperate struggle to acquire personal protective equipment, N-95 masks, ventilators, and other key items.

Recommendations for the Future

> *To prevent the hardship of this last year from happening again, pandemic preparedness must be taken as seriously as we take the threat of war. The world needs to double down on investments in R&D and organizations like CEPI that have proven invaluable with COVID-19. We also need to build brand-new capabilities that don't exist yet.*

> **Bill and Melinda Gates, Our Annual Letter 2021**

Public Health as a discipline will undergo a transformation post-COVID-19. The lessons learned from this history-defining global pandemic of the 21st century will set the stage for the future of public health. These changes will serve to support the next era of public health activities and the evolution of future post-pandemic healthcare systems. Recommendations to holistically revolutionize public health to prepare for future pandemics and public health emergencies will be important. These suggestions are numerous:

- Public Health post-COVID-19 will require major systemic changes firmly rooted in law to strengthen public health systems and ensure future public health emergencies, and pandemics will be dealt with swiftly, using the best available science and technology, and are free from political interference.
- Funding and resources must greatly be increased to build sustainable and resilient public health systems capable of withstanding and responding to future pandemics.

- Establishment of standardized public health reporting, communication, information, and intelligence sharing systems are needed to streamline responses and operational processes domestically and internationally.
- Strategic investment and planning into systems, technologies, information sharing, intelligence, surveillance, and monitoring capabilities are needed to modernize public health operations.
- Significant investment into establishing robust global public health quarantine, surveillance, intelligence, and early warning systems are needed to counter future pandemics.
- Continued expansion, maintenance, and development of robust public health partnerships are needed to deliver essential public health services and ensure equitable health outcomes.
- Further development of and investment in Public Health education, communication, training, and workforce development globally are required to create the human capital needed to adequately respond to future pandemics.
- Significant investment into global public health research, research partnerships, and public-private sector and academic institution coalitions including the manufacturing sector is needed to expand on national capabilities to respond to public health emergencies and pandemics.
- Strong, dedicated, and continuous legislative, policy, political, and legal support will be required to enable meaningful and impactful short- and long-term change.
- Engagement of local emergency managers in the state and federal design of healthcare emergency management and response is needed.
- More consistent and equitable engagement of local healthcare coalitions is required, including response guidelines for chain of command and the ability to exercise statutory- defined emergency response powers.

CONCLUSION

Those who fail to learn from history are doomed to repeat it.

Sir Winston Churchill

Public Health plays a vital role in each and every community across the nation. Public health touches all aspects of human life where complex interrelationships between human activities and factors exist that influence and determine the health of a population. Public health plays a role in safeguarding our health innumerably, from monitoring the air we breathe, to assessing the water we drink and the food we eat, to promoting safety in our places of work and the environment in which we live. While the world is presently experiencing a global pandemic, it is important to note that disease outbreaks of pandemic proportions have occurred throughout the history of humanity and have each left their mark on the world. The lessons learned from the global COVID-19 pandemic will set the stage for the future of public health, health care, and medicine.

As the world moves forward from the COVID-19 pandemic of the 21st century, Public Health as a discipline must be thoroughly examined. Changes must be made to systematically strengthen public health and healthcare systems. Strategic investments, partnerships, coalitions, plans, strategies, and development of new technologies, and resources need to be allocated and acquisitioned now to create resilient, sustainable public health and healthcare systems capable of withstanding and responding to future pandemics. As the saying goes, "Those who fail to learn from history are doomed to repeat it" (Sir Winston Churchill). In the context of Public Health and Healthcare, the next great pandemic will represent a continued, existential risk to global health security and may have potential to threaten the very future of humankind. Diseases capable of causing pandemics are natural, biological Weapons of Mass Destruction. If the fight against pandemics and future disease outbreaks is not treated with such seriousness as the risk of war, then we risk the very future of the world and the survival of the human species. We are in a great race against nature itself, and we are losing as dangerous pathogens and bacteria tirelessly seek to evolve and spread into the world.

CLASS DISCUSSION AND ESSAY QUESTIONS

1. What is public health and when and why was this profession created?
2. How did John Snow change our understanding of illness and disease in the world?
3. What are the determinants of health?
4. What roles does public health play in emergency management and homeland security?
5. What are the chronic problems facing public health and healthcare emergency management?
6. What lessons have been learned as a result of the COVID-19 pandemic?
7. What systemic challenges exist and how can they be overcome?

NOTE

1. Special thanks to Anna Shaum, MPH

REFERENCES

Arteaga, O. (2014). Health Systems. In Michalos, A.C. (Ed.), *Encyclopedia of Quality of Life and Well-Being Research* Dordrecht: Springer. https://doi.org/10.1007/978-94-007-0753-5_3390.

Azofeifa, A., Martin, G.R., Santiago-Colón, A., Reissman, D.B. and Howard, J. (2021). World Trade Center Health Program — United States, 2012–2020. MMWR Surveillance Summary;70(No. SS-4):1–21. http://doi.org/10.15585/mmwr.ss7004a1externalicon.

Baker, M. and Ivory, D. (2021). Why Public Health Faces a Crisis Across the U.S. https://www.nytimes.com/2021/10/18/us/coronavirus-public-health.html.

Baker, P. and Sullivan, E. (2020). U.S. Virus Plan Anticipates 18-Month Pandemic and Widespread Shortages. https://www.nytimes.com/2020/03/17/us/politics/trump-coronavirus-plan.html.

Beer, T. (2020). All the Times Trump Compared Covid-19 to the Flu, Even after He Knew Covid-19 Was Far More Deadly. https://www.forbes.com/sites/tommybeer/2020/09/10/all-the-times-trump-compared-covid-19-to-the-flu-even-after-he-knew-covid-19-was-far-more-deadly/?sh=2573fb4ff9d2.

Berman, R. (2020). Remember the Pandemic? https://www.theatlantic.com/politics/archive/2020/08/larry-kudlow-pandemic/615676/.

Boston University School of Public Health. (2015). A Brief History of Public Health. https://sphweb.bumc.bu.edu/otlt/mph-modules/ph/publichealthhistory/index.html.

Brangham, W. and Norris, C. (2021). How the Latest CDC Guidance on COVID-19 Is Creating Unnecessary Confusion. https://www.pbs.org/newshour/show/how-the-latest-cdc-guidance-on-covid-19-is-creating-unnecessary-confusioncovid-confusion.

Centers for Disease Control and Prevention (CDC). (2014a). Introduction to Public Health. In: Public Health, 101 Series. Atlanta, GA: U.S. Department of Health and Human Services, CDC. https://www.cdc.gov/training/publichealth101/public-health.html.

Centers for Disease Control and Prevention (CDC). (2014b). Introduction to Public Health. In: Public Health, 101 Series, Epidemiology. Atlanta, GA: U.S. Department of Health and Human Services, CDC. https://www.cdc.gov/publichealth101/epidemiology.html.

Centers for Disease Control and Prevention (CDC). (2020c). Identifying the Source of the Outbreak. https://www.cdc.gov/coronavirus/2019-ncov/science/about-epidemiology/identifying-source-outbreak.html.

Centers for Disease Control and Prevention (CDC). (2017d). National Center for Emerging and Zoonotic Infectious Diseases (NCEZID), Division of Foodborne, Waterborne, and Environmental Diseases, Global Water, Sanitation, & Hygiene (WASH), Sanitation & Hygiene. https://www.cdc.gov/healthywater/global/sanitation/index.html.

Centers for Disease Control and Prevention (CDC). (2021e). Center for State, Tribal, Local, and Territorial Support, 10 Essential Public Health Services. https://www.cdc.gov/publichealthgateway/publichealthservices/essentialhealthservices.html.

Centers for Disease Control and Prevention (CDC). (2021f). Celebrating 75 Years of CDC and 70 Years of Malaria Elimination from the United States: A Photo Essay. https://www.cdc.gov/malaria/features/CDC_anniversary_photo_essay_Jun2021.html.

Centers for Disease Control and Prevention (CDC). (2019g). Mission, Role and Pledge. https://www.cdc.gov/about/organization/mission.htm.

Centers for Disease Control and Prevention (CDC). (2020h). Securing Global Health and America's Preparedness. https://www.cdc.gov/about/24-7/securing-global-health.html.

Centers for Disease Control and Prevention (CDC). (2021i). CDC Organization Chart. https://www.cdc.gov/about/organization/orgchart.htm.

Centers for Disease Control and Prevention (CDC). (2021j). U.S. Quarantine Stations. https://www.cdc.gov/quarantine/quarantine-stations-us.html.

Centers for Disease Control and Prevention (CDC). (2018k). Public Health 101 Series. https://www.cdc.gov/training/publichealth101/index.html.

Centers for Disease Control and Prevention (CDC). (2018l). History of 1918 Flu Pandemic. https://www.cdc.gov/flu/pandemic-resources/1918-commemoration/1918-pandemic-history.htm.

Centers for Disease Control and Prevention (CDC). (2017m). Quarantine and Isolation. https://www.cdc.gov/quarantine/index.html.

Centers for Disease Control and Prevention (CDC). (2020n). History of Quarantine. https://www.cdc.gov/quarantine/historyquarantine.html.

Centers for Disease Control and Prevention (CDC). (2021o). Monkeypox in the United States. https://www.cdc.gov/poxvirus/monkeypox/outbreak/us-outbreaks.html.

Centers for Disease Control and Prevention (CDC). (2021p). February 2021 Democratic Republic of the Congo: North Kivu Province. https://www.cdc.gov/vhf/ebola/out-breaks/drc/2021-february.html.

CMS.gov. (2021). Emergency Preparedness Rule. https://www.cms.gov/Medicare/Provider-Enrollment-and-Certification/SurveyCertEmergPrep/Emergency-Prep-Rule.

CDC Museum. (n.d.). Roots of the CDC. https://www.cdc.gov/museum/app/roots/roots.html.

Cole, D. and Mach, D. (2021). ACLU: Civil Liberties and Vaccine Mandates: Here's Our Take. https://www.aclu.org/news/civil-liberties/civil-liberties-and-vaccine-mandates-heres-our-take/.

CSTE. (n.d.) Cross Cutting: Border/International Health. https://www.cste.org/members/group.aspx?id=87618.

David, J. and Sencer CDC Museum. (2021). CDC Timeline 1940s–1970s. https://www.cdc.gov/museum/timeline/1940-1970.html#1940.

DHS. (2021). Operation Allies Welcome Completes Vaccination Campaign for Measles and Varicella for Afghan Evacuees. https://www.dhs.gov/news/2021/10/04/operation-allies-welcome-completes-vaccination-campaign-measles-and-varicella-afghan.

Egan, L. (2020). Trump Calls Coronavirus Democrats' 'New Hoax'. https://www.nbc-news.com/politics/donald-trump/trump-calls-coronavirus-democrats-new-hoax-n1145721.

Eldred, S. (2021). Parents, Teachers Baffled by Inconsistencies in US Schools' Quarantining, Tracing Rules. https://www.usatoday.com/story/news/education/2021/11/15/quar-antine-tracing-rules-us-schools-inconsistent-confusing/8590419002/?gnt-cfr=1.

Fabian, J. (2020). Trump Told Governors to Buy Own Virus Supplies, Then Outbid Them. https://www.bloomberg.com/news/articles/2020-03-19/trump-told-gover-nors-to-buy-own-virus-supplies-then-outbid-them.

Farberman, R., McKillop, M., Lieberman, D., Delgado, D., Thomas, C., Cunningham, J. and McIntyre, K. (2020). The Impact of Chronic Underfunding on America's Public Health System: Trends, Risks, and Recommendations. https://www.tfah.org/report-details/publichealthfunding2020/.

FEMA. (2016). Emergency Support Function #8 – Public Health and Medical Services Annex. https://www.fema.gov/sites/default/files/2020-07/fema_ESF_8_Public-Health-Medical.pdf.

Federal Executive Board Chicago. (2021). Champion of COVID Response, CDC – Chicago Quarantine Station Team. CDC Division of Global Migration and Quarantine, Centers for Disease Control. https://chicago.feb.gov/wp-content/uploads/2021/05/CC-Chicago-Quarantine-Team-CDC.pdf.

Fenn, E.A. (2000). Biological Warfare in Eighteenth-Century North America: Beyond Jeffery Amherst. *Journal of American History*, 86(4), 1552–1580. https://doi.org/10.2307/2567577.

Finn, T. (2021). Fauci Says Sen. Paul's Attacks 'Kindle the Crazies' Who Have Threatened His Life. https://www.nbcnews.com/politics/congress/fauci-says-sen-paul-s-attacks-kindle-crazies-who-have-n1287299.

Forgey, Q. and Choy, M. (2020). Trump Downplays Need for Ventilators as New York Begs to Differ. https://www.politico.com/news/2020/03/26/trump-ventilators-coro-navirus-151311.

Geppert, C. and Paul, R.A. (2019). The Shot That Won the Revolutionary War and Is Still Reverberating. *Federal practitioner: For the health care professionals of the VA, DoD, and PHS*, 36(7), 298–299.

Green, T. and Tyson, A. (2020). 5 Facts about Partisan Reactions to COVID-19 in the U.S. https://www.pewresearch.org/fact-tank/2020/04/02/5-facts-about-partisan-reactions-to-covid-19-in-the-u-s/.

Harvard Public Health. (2021). Magazine of the Harvard T.H. Chan School of Public Health, Innovations through Public Health History: A Sample of "Next-Generation" Ideas from the Past. https://www.hsph.harvard.edu/magazine/magazine_article/innovations-through-public-health-history/.

Haseltine, W. (2020). Underfunding Public Health Harms Americans Beyond Covid-19. https://www.forbes.com/sites/williamhaseltine/2020/10/21/underfunding-public-health-harms-americans-beyond-covid-19/?sh=3153a1ae419c.

Heid, M. (2016). The Truth about Your Tampons. https://time.com/4422774/tampons-toxic-cancer/.

Hersher, R., Fadel, L. and Kaste, M. (2020). How New York, California and Washington Are Dealing With COVID-19. https://www.npr.org/2020/03/25/821285193/how-new-york-california-and-washington-are-dealing-with-covid-19.

History.com. (2020). Black Death. https://www.history.com/topics/middle-ages/black-death.

H.R.535 – 116th Congress. (2019). PFAS Action Act of 2019. Retrieved January 13, 2020 from https://www.congress.gov/bill/116th-congress/house-bill/535.

Institute of Medicine (US) Committee for the Study of the Future of Public Health. (1988). The Future of Public Health. In *A History of the Public Health System*. Washington, DC: National Academies Press (US), 3. https://www.ncbi.nlm.nih.gov/books/NBK218224/.

IMDB. (1995). Outbreak. https://www.imdb.com/title/tt0114069/.

IMDB. (2011). Contagion. https://www.imdb.com/title/tt1598778/.

John, F. and Kennedy Presidential Library and Museum. (1963). John F. Kennedy Quotations, *September 20, 1963, Public Papers of the Presidents: John F. Kennedy, 1963*. https://www.jfklibrary.org/learn/about-jfk/life-of-john-f-kennedy/john-f-kennedy-quotations.

John Hopkins University. (2021). COVID-19 Dashboard. https://coronavirus.jhu.edu/map.html.

KDHE & KUCCHD. (2015). Kansas Department of Health and Environment with the KU Center for Community Health and Development, Community Tool Box Module 7: Developing an Intervention. https://ctb.ku.edu/en/developing-intervention.

Kleiman, J. (2021). SUNY Genesco, Love Canal: A Brief History. https://www.geneseo.edu/history/love_canal_history.

Lipton, E. (2020). The 'Red Dawn' Emails: 8 Key Exchanges on the Faltering Response to the Coronavirus. https://www.nytimes.com/2020/04/11/us/politics/coronavirus-red-dawn-emails-trump.html.

Lupkin, S. (2021). Defense Production Act Speeds Up Vaccine Production. https://www.npr.org/sections/health-shots/2021/03/13/976531488/defense-production-act-speeds-up-vaccine-production.

Luscombe, R. (2021). Florida's Governor Celebrated His Anti-mandate Covid Laws. Now Omicron Is Here. https://www.theguardian.com/us-news/2021/dec/04/covid-omicron-florida-republican-ron-desantis.

Martin, C. (2021). The Plague of Athens Killed Tens of Thousands, but Its Cause Remains a Mystery. https://www.nationalgeographic.co.uk/history-and-civilisation/2021/05/the-plague-of-athens-killed-tens-of-thousands-but-its-cause-remains-a-mystery.

McEntire, D. and SFHEA. (2019). The Dallas Ebola Incident as an Indicator of the Bioterrorism Threat: An Assessment of Response with Implications for Security and Preparedness. *UVU Journal of National Security*, 5–17. https://www.google.com/url?sa=t&rct=j&q=&esrc=s&source=web&cd=&cad=rja&uact=8&ved=2ahUKEwjUzsLF6Zb1AhUSB50JHRSdBe0QFnoECAMQAQ&url=https%3A%2F%2Fwww.uvu.edu%2Fnss%2Fdocs%2Fspring2020journal1.pdf&usg=AOvVaw1vFjxeyriK80D_VWNivUdH.

Mello, M.M., Greene, J.A. and Sharfstein, J.M. (2020). Attacks on Public Health Officials During COVID-19. *JAMA*, 324(8), 741–742. https://doi.org/10.1001/jama.2020.14423.

National Academies of Science, Engineering and Medicine. (2022). Analysis to Enhance the Effectiveness of the Federal Quarantine Station Network Based on Lessons from the COVID-19 Pandemic. https://www.nationalacademies.org/our-work/analysis-to-enhance-the-effectiveness-of-the-federal-quarantine-station-network-based-on-lessons-from-the-covid-19-pandemic.

NIH, NIAID. (2012). About NIAID, History, Dr. Joseph Kinyoun the Indispensable Forgotten Man, Background. https://www.niaid.nih.gov/about/joseph-kinyoun-indispensable-man-background.

NIH. (n.d.). NCI Dictionaries. CDC. https://www.cancer.gov/publications/dictionaries/cancer-terms/def/cdc.

NIH. (n.d.). NCI Dictionaries World Health Organization. https://www.cancer.gov/publications/dictionaries/cancer-terms/def/world-health-organization.

ODPHP. (2021). Office of Disease Prevention and Health Promotion, Determinants of Health. https://www.healthypeople.gov/2020/about/foundation-health-measures/Determinants-of-Health.

Piret, J. and Boivin, G. (2021). Pandemics Throughout History. *Frontiers in Microbiology*, 11, 631736. https://doi.org/10.3389/fmicb.2020.631736.

Smithsonian. (n.d.). National Museum of American History, Behring Center, Automobile Safety. https://americanhistory.si.edu/america-on-the-move/essays/automobile-safety.

Rieger, J. (2020). 40 Times Trump Said the Coronavirus Would Go Away. https://www.washingtonpost.com/video/politics/40-times-trump-said-the-coronavirus-would-go-away/2020/04/30/d2593312-9593-4ec2-aff7-72c1438fca0e_video.html.

Rosenthal, B., Pinkowski, J. and Goldstein, J. (2020). The Other Option Is Death. *New York Starts Sharing of Ventilators*. https://www.nytimes.com/2020/03/26/health/coronavirus-ventilator-sharing.html.

Stanley, B. and Sun, L. (2021). Senior CDC Official Who Met Trump's Wrath for Raising Alarm about Coronavirus to Resign. https://www.washingtonpost.com/health/2021/05/07/cdc-official-resigns/.

Simental, A. and Bynum, T. (2020). COVID-19 Federal Pandemic Response: Failing National Emergency Management System. https://simentalindustries.com/2020/04/04/failing-national-emergency-management-system/.

Stone, K.W., Kintziger, K.W., Jagger, M.A. and Horney, J.A. (2021). Public Health Workforce Burnout in the COVID-19 Response in the U.S. *International Journal of Environmental Research and Public Health*, 18(8), 4369. https://doi.org/10.3390/ijerph18084369.

The Joint Commission. (2022). New and Revised Emergency Management Standards. https://www.jointcommission.org/standards/prepublication-standards/new-and-revised-emergency-management-standards/.

Tulchinsky, T.H. (2018). John Snow, Cholera, the Broad Street Pump; Waterborne Diseases Then and Now. *Case Studies in Public Health*, 77–99. https://doi.org/10.1016/B978-0-12-804571-8.00017-2.

UCLA. (n.d.). Competing Theories of Cholera. https://www.ph.ucla.edu/epi/snow/choleratheories.html.

US National Library of Medicine. (2012). History of the Public Health Service. https://www.nlm.nih.gov/exhibition/phs_history/seamen.html.

USPHS. (n.d.). Commissioned Corps of the U.S. Public Health Service, Our History. https://www.usphs.gov/history.

WHO. (2021). Health Systems. https://www.euro.who.int/en/health-topics/Health-systems.

Wolfe, D. and Dale, D. (2020). 'It's Going to Disappear': A Timeline of Trump's Claims that Covid-19 Will Vanish. https://www.cnn.com/interactive/2020/10/politics/covid-disappearing-trump-comment-tracker/.

CHAPTER 12

Disaster and Psychology:
Preparation for, Response to, and Recovery from Terror

Rodger Broomé and Eric Russell

INTRODUCTION

Natural and human-caused disasters are a collective psychological shock that impact communities of all different sizes in society. Psychological traumas are crises of existence that shatter the psychophysical stability of human beings, and the preparation, response, and recovery to disasters require a humanistic-existential approach with built-in flexibility to foster resilience. Mass-scale trauma places society's members in a confrontation with life's contingency and disrupts the normal sense of safety and security society normally offers (Solomon et al., 2015). Disasters come in many forms and overwhelm the victims' ability to cope for a substantial period of time, leaving behind lasting effects. The goal of disaster and crisis psychology is therefore to (a) prepare in such a way that mental health resources can be available; (b) response is orderly, yet nimble to meet the particular needs of the situation; and (c) recovery fosters post-traumatic growth and the ability for society to emerge healing with a *new normal*.

Psychology is both the study of the mind and human behavior and the profession of helping people with psychological problems. As such, scientific psychology seeks to generate theoretical understanding and models of mental functioning to be applied in society, while clinical psychology has clinical mental health goals and procedures as a helping profession. Psychology has adopted *the medical model* in parallel to the way physicians work either as medical researchers or as practitioners in society. Moreover, a lot of medical nomenclature has been adopted by the mental health community via the influences of psychiatry, which is the medical specialty focused on treating mental disorders. However, psychological disruptions and functioning are not solely physical *ailments* or *injuries*, but rather these metaphors are used to talk about disruptive thoughts, feelings, and behaviors (Szasz, 2007). Some might actually consider psychological disorders as an existential impact to the human soul or in another metaphor, a moral injury. While many lasting psychological disorders can emerge in the wake of a disaster trauma, this chapter will focus mostly on post-traumatic stress disorder (PTSD) and post-traumatic growth (PTG) and their respective predictors and interventions. Moreover, the theoretical foundation for this chapter will be Terror Management Theory (TMT), which will help the reader understand how human beings have navigated our existential issues in

DOI: 10.4324/9781003350729-12

society for as far back as we can tell from history (Solomon et al., 2015). With a working understanding of TMT, emergency services providers, emergency managers, and homeland security officials can better formulate plans that will reach the hearts and minds of the citizens they serve.

Disaster planning for mental health services involves support for both emergency and disaster workers and the citizens impacted by the event. Furthermore, the mental health professionals will also likely need support during and after they have done their work in a disaster context. As such, there are different domains of care and levels of services needed. Psychological first-aid is the mental health support of people during and directly after a critical incident or disaster event. Because *duty-related trauma* is different than civilian trauma, specialized care that is *culturally competent* will be needed for emergency and disaster workers. Vulnerable populations will also need to be approached with sensitivity to their special needs (Greenleaf, 1977/2002; Lansing, 2012). Finally, supporting community cohesion will necessitate strategies that support various worldviews while supporting unification of the impacted whole of society. Emergency managers need to be aware and work preemptively toward meeting psychological needs of both the responder and citizen for individual and community healing to take place (Russell, 2019). Disaster and crisis psychology planning will require education, training, and empowerment of the emergency and disaster workers that will be on the front lines of disaster response and recovery.

HISTORY OF PSYCHOLOGY: SCIENCE, PRACTICE, AND PATHOLOGY

Psychology is both a science of the mind and a helping profession focused on mental health. While the topic of psychology existed in philosophy stretching back to ancient Greek philosophy as a medical practice and scientific discipline, it was not developed until the end of the 19th century. Initially, there were two related, yet separate branches of psychology: psychoanalysis and behaviorism. Psychoanalysis was born out of hypnosis, developed by Franz Anton Mesmer and originally called Mesmerism (Ellenberger, 1981). Experimental psychology, on the other hand, was an extension of Russian physiologist Ivan Pavlov's famous experiments with canines and the early work of Wilhelm Wundt (Boring, 2008). The application of the natural sciences approach to studying human beings was initiated and quickly became mainstream (Giorgi, 2019). Meanwhile, Sigmund Freud was developing psychoanalysis (i.e., psychodynamic) theory and talk therapy to assist people with their psychological troubles. The bifurcation of these branches originate in the difference in their vision and goals. Freud was developing a clinical psychology to *ameliorate neurosis and psychosis*, and American psychologist James Watson (1913) had adopted the scientific framework of physics to *predict and control* behavior. Therefore, clinical/professional psychology adopted a medical framework (values and nomenclature) and scientific psychology adopted the natural science framework (values and procedures) as a basis for *engineering* a better humanity.

Both of the branches of psychology were developed upon the foundation of Ontological Naturalism. Freud based his theory and practice on biological evolution, founded by Charles Darwin (Ellenberger, 1981). Scientific psychology adopted naturalism as well, which was used by behaviorism in the development of its stimulus-response linear causality, based also on the principles of biological evolution (Watson, 1913). But there were some psychologists like William James, who was troubled about psychological issues that could not be explained by biological mechanisms or environmental factors.

Some of these issues dealt with things like human agency, volition, experiences, free will, and more that the determinism of psychodynamic and behavioral psychology could not or was not able to address (Kaag, 2020). As a response to the biological determinism and reductionistic tendencies (and other ontological and epistemological issues) of the two mainstream branches, Humanistic Psychology or *The Third Force* in psychology was born in the 1950s (Misiak and Sexton, 1973). In short, the human person had been *"lost"* by psychology in the formulation and abstraction of humanity as merely another *organism*.

Existential psychology is one perspective within The Third Force that sprung from existential philosophy that was born in the Enlightenment. Beginning with theologian and philosopher Soren Kierkegaard, existentialism was a philosophy that questioned the issue of human existence and the meaning of life. Kierkegaard's writings on *anxiety* were ahead of their time because he attributed it to the human being's deeply embedded angst about death (1981). Because human beings can imagine and contemplate our own death, all of that which is associated with death or the frailty of life presents salient reminders of our final destiny. As such, non-being haunts being, meaning, that which is life-promoting, life-sustaining, and life-producing is one side of the same coin as that which makes life contingent (Anton, 2021). Therefore, where Freud truncated his theories to comport with biological determinism, for existentialists the role of personal meaning in the human navigation of social life and relationships in the context of death was left unexplained (Becker, 1997). This is particularly true with emergency work and public protection services.

Emergencies and crises are problems that are particularly defined by their time-pressure and consequences. The consequences are related to the damage or destruction of life, property, and situational stability. The time-pressure comes from the need for intervention in order to re-normalize conditions back to their ordinary safety. An existential crisis is any psychological or moral crisis that causes an individual to ask fundamental questions about human existence (APA, 2020). When a situation in life becomes unmanageable for someone's normal resources to cope with it, the sense of being overwhelmed throws them into facing some of the most fundamental questions in life. Moreover, these problems are fundamental to the human condition and basis for the most impacting psychological disorders.

About the time that humanistic-existential psychology emerged as The Third Force, the cognitive revolution in experimental psychology was born. Similar to the concerns of The Third Force about human *meaning*, cognitive psychologists realized that between stimulus and response was *thinking* (Miller, 2003). Cognitive psychology adopted the information processor metaphor for the mind, and with it, adopted a lot of computer science vernacular that over time became uncritically taken too literally (Giorgi, 2015). Discussing psychology in terms of neural networks, nodes, processing speeds, and memory as information storage imposed a machine context on human beings and was only able to explain the *easy problems* of consciousness (Chalmers, 1997). What this amounts to are issues like cognitive capacity, memory stability, heuristics, context priming, and more. But these issues do not explain how confrontations with tragedy, inhumanity, cruelty, and morality reach to the depths of our psyche. The Third Force psychology aimed at inserting the humanity back into psychology and considered issues of the human condition in its particular human context (Bugental, 1964).

Psychiatry developed within the medical community as a medical specialty. Psychiatry is based upon a biopsychological model of the human being, again, following a naturalistic materialist ontology and biological focus. As such, it is typically and uncritically assumed that the mind is a product of the nervous system and psychopharmacology is its primary intervention (Breggin, 1994). The medical model frames mental health in psychiatry with the structures and vernacular of medicine, even though psychiatric disorders are not the result of a lesion or contagion of the nervous system, for this would be neurology (Szasz, 2007). Nonetheless, psychoactive medications are often prescribed to "correct" a chemical imbalance that is believed to be neurochemical deficits or surplus. Once a person is put on psychopharmacological agents, they can create resistance and dependency so that regular monitoring and adjustments are needed (Breggin, 1994). Consequently, there is a risk of dependence on mental health services when medications are used as long-term "solutions" rather than part of a comprehensive treatment plan.

Psychology still operates in a bifurcated system of clinical and research with some overlap between them. The scholar/practitioner model imitates the idea of evidence-based practice for clinicians, but research also showed it having some kind of practical value in society. One challenge is the stigma born out of the medical model regarding the *mental illness* metaphor (Szasz, 2007) that puts a barrier in front of people's understanding of psychology as a subject matter. The textbook version of psychology's subject matter is along the lines of *the study of behavior and mental processes*. Humanistic psychology added to it the study of human nature, experience, and the human condition (Giorgi, 2015). Without pathologizing human suffering, humanistic psychology is aimed at understanding and empowering people to thrive toward their own actualization as human persons. It is within this objective that psychology can better engage the task of preparing, responding, and recovering from emergencies, crises, and disasters. Human psychology is a thread that runs through our existence and is the generative source of human meaning.

THE PSYCHOLOGY OF DISASTERS AND TERRORISM

While it can be argued that psychology of human survival has been part of the human condition since the dawn of time, early deliberate forms of *mental skills* were developed in the West by the Stoics and the East by Asian philosophers. In the United States, much of the psychology of disasters and terrorism was developed by the military. Particularly, issues emerged after World War I that put the psychology of the soldier on the institutional radars of the U.S. and Allied Forces (Hacker Hughes, McCauley, and Wilson, 2019). The psychology of terrorism is not generally focused on the emergency response and recovery workers; rather, it was aimed at the detection and prevention of attacks (Stedmon, and Lawson, 2013). A single case inquiry was conducted on the lived-experience of a police officer engaging an active shooter (Broomé and Russell, 2018). More studies focused on the experiences of first responders would be useful to inform clinical practice and promote a better understanding in society. This is because it is presupposed that clinicians specializing in trauma are equipped for working with emergency professionals; however, there is too often a lack of cultural competency with these unique people for the responder to readily engage in seeking help.

Natural disasters are devastating, and yet, terrorist attacks involve an inhumane malevolence that adds a sickening psychological dimension to tragedy to create horror. The goal of a terror attack is to overwhelm the community's sense of cosmological safety and security. Our sense that the world, and those in it, basically support human life and our existence itself is *shattered* in terms of its meaningfulness (Greening, 1997). It is nearly impossible to talk about terrorism without having a moral thread run through the discussion. Terrorists violate the sanctity of life, moral virtues, and fundamental humanity of their victims, motivated by political goals that are justified by (often twisted) ideological values. Goldberg (1997) speaks about the malefic personality as one that uses *magical thinking* as part of the process of motivating and justifying the inhumane killing of others. The magical thinking has dimensions of supernatural or metaphysical notions that point toward a twisted sense of a higher ideal or superordinate achievement. This is very different from the abnormally lower levels or absence of empathy that defines a psychopath (Baron-Cohen, 2011). Terrorists do not necessarily *feel evil* due to the moral justifications that make their terror "means" justified by the imagined "ends." The moralizing of terrorists' plans is the way that they *"switch off"* their empathy, often accompanied with some form of dehumanization of their *targets*, enabling them to execute their horrific cruelty (Baron-Cohen, 2012). It is technology that has also enabled terrorists to attack on the massive scales that they do.

Human beings have a natural aversion to homicide. This aversion can be circumvented by technology and the advanced technology of auto-loading firearms, explosives, chemical, biological, and radiological weapons that make homicide efficient and expansive. In fact, it was the development of Newtonian Physics and the continual advances in physics that led to the industrialization of the modern world (Kaku, 2021). Studies on warfare in the 19th and 20th centuries show that the more realistic the training of soldiers is, the more likely the natural aversion to killing is circumvented (Grossman, 2009). This is true in the deployment of weapons of mass destruction (WMDs), yet the procurement or construction of WMDs is a premeditated process that must have sustained motivation and justification from ideologically charged political goals. As such, the psychological impact on victims is embedded with the ill-will of humans' inhumanity to humanity. At this time, there is little discussion about the political institutions' role and responsibility in the psychological recovery from terrorism.

It is the relative infrequency of terrorist attacks but their grave impact that makes psychological services challenging to "put in place." Even with the assistance of supercomputers and other technology, emergencies with their exigent characteristic make it difficult to statistically plan for in terms of human impact. Moreover, technocracies tend to operate on typicalities or normative measures for budgeting. Mutual aid agreements in the fire and emergency services have been the way individual communities have addressed their own stand-alone services being overwhelmed. But on the grand scale, the 911 Commission Report (Kean et al., 2004) taught the United States that interoperability was needed to put mutual aid operations into action. The inclusion and role of mental health services was a challenge that was found to be needed at Ground Zero. However, it was not anticipated that psychosocial dysfunction would plague first responders and disaster workers for decades following the clean-up (Smith and Burkle, 2018). Therefore, the longitudinal trajectory of need for mental health services and their costs is something that needs planning and ideas about funding them.

Medications are often taken for granted, but when a disaster or terrorism attack impacts a community, many people on medications can be left without pharmacological support. This is true for psychopharmacological agents that many people use to assist with managing their psychological disorders. Under normal circumstances, weaning a client off of a psychopharmaceutical is a therapeutic goal that must be handled well (Breggin, 2013). There is some controversy in the mental health professions about the overuse of psychiatric drugs, and has been for over 30 years (Breggin, 1994). Regardless of where a particular clinician lands on the range of professional perspectives on the matter, a disaster that impacts access to dispensing medications can create significant problems for people needing them. In the case of 9/11 disaster workers, the long-term effects of the varieties of medications given and potential drug interactions were not well anticipated (Smith and Burkle, 2018). Therefore, the reality that surfaced for the United States was that there really was no way to plan for the magnitude of sedition and destruction executed on the City of New York's people.

RELATION TO EMERGENCY MANAGEMENT
AND HOMELAND SECURITY

Psychology is a discipline that studies the minds of individuals, or individuals as parts of groups, which often makes it considered the science and practice of an individual's problems. Sociology, however, deals with human factors on a macro-level analysis, which means the structures and functioning of institutions is its area of expertise. Sociologists have had a greater interest and voice in emergency management and homeland security; however, it is individual care for both disaster workers and the civilian population that is needed both immediately and in the long term. After nearly two decades, first responders, disaster workers, and the general population of New York City still require mental health care related to the complex traumas of the terrorist attack (Smith and Burkle, 2018). While one might say this is an event for which everything could not be planned, mental health systems were still operating in peacetime normality. It is also not reasonable to believe that people can suffer an iconic/horrific event and not have lasting signs and symptoms of its impact. Therefore, the goal of emergency planning for psychological impacts is not to believe that such plans will avoid or block the impacts, but that we anticipate this dimension of humanity will need immediate and long-term support.

The Homeland Security piece of psychology is largely aimed at intelligence and profiling potential perpetrators of events. But a politically controversial aspect of Homeland Security that is a challenge is the control of the immigration across the southern border. The goal of controlling the border will have consequences for those people who are detained in detention centers for an indefinite amount of time under very abnormal conditions. Humane treatment of detainees that are entering the continental United States without legally required authorizations is a challenge that has not, up to the time of this writing, been psychologically healthful. It is unknown how such psychological impacts of the "experienced incarceration" will affect the children particularly. While considering the humanity of those migrating to the United States that may or may not have already complex trauma problems, most of the terrorists and organized crime perpetrators crossing the border have their own psychological peculiarities.

Terrorists have often experienced enough hardship through civil wars and other conflicts that their worlds and minds understand that which can be most terrifying. Terrorism works by creating fear among the target population so that the society itself is dysfunctional in various ways (Stedmon and Lawson, 2013). By studying terrorists' motivations and planning processes, the prediction of a deployment of terror and potentially intercepting it is vital to saving lives. Terrorism psychologists are exploring innovative ways to fight terrorism by focusing on situations that are neglected, but relevant for terrorism, such as (a) terrorists lying about intentions, (b) examining people when they are observed secretly, and (c) interviewing terrorism suspects together instead of always using solo interrogation (Stedmon and Lawson, 2013, p. 92). This means looking at how meaning/making is done with terrorists, in addition to their use of deception, misinformation, and malefic creativity are all subjects of study.

The planning phase of emergency managers needs to involve creating mental health worker networks, training, and mobilization to match the needs of the disaster. What we learned in the COVID-19 pandemic was that in normal circumstances, there were not a lot of mental health professionals that could take on many more clients than they had. Under emergency and disaster executive orders, many states authorized teletherapy to be used with fewer, if any, restrictions than before. As with any emergency, all that is typically normal becomes under time-pressure, and dire consequences. Therefore, emergency managers need to encourage policy makers to build in flexible standards to the system.

ROLES OF MENTAL HEALTH WORKERS

While during the emergency response, therapy delivery services might not be practical, other acute psychological interventions can support both emergency and disaster workers and citizens needing support. Further, because emergencies are exigent circumstances that are critical incidents impacting people, the special clinical activities of psychometric testing and therapy with people suffering a diagnosed psychopathology is not the focus. Rather, it is the psycho-social support of people suffering an abnormal situation that might have exceeded their normal coping capacities. People who may be useful providing emergency psychological support services might include, but not be limited to, public health workers, clergy/chaplains, emergency responder peer support members, mental health para-professionals, educators, and of course, licensed mental health professionals. Non-mental health workers should be trained in psychological first-aid (PFA) so that they can be utilized when needed (Everly and Lating, 2017).

There are some foundational *knowledge* and basic *skills* and *abilities* (KSAs) that are needed for one to perform emergency psychological services. We are sensitive to the fact that people might have transferable skills and knowledge from non-psychology origins that do work for PFA (Everly and Lating, 2017). Further, FEMA (2016) provides guidance in ways in which systems for counseling and training supports can be created. Therefore, when an emergency psychological support group, division, or task force is being set up in an emergency, the section chief over this mission should consider those for whom the services are being provided and match the knowledge, skills, and abilities of the PFA providers as best as is practical and feasible. Emergency Managers need to be aware that mental health professionals are experts in psychology but might lack experience and understanding emergency contexts and the structure and functions of the Incident Command System (ICS) (Federal Emergency Management Agency [FEMA], 2011). Emergency Managers need to seek and recruit mental health professionals that can be trained and educated in emergency planning, response, and recovery so that they can navigate these situations appropriately for the various people they will engage. On the other hand, the psychologists and other mental health experts can be leveraged by the Emergency Manager to provide initial and ongoing psycho-education. Psycho-education can include, but is not limited to, stress management, interpersonal communication skills, leadership, mental performance skills, and also PFA. The continuing education (CE) and in-service training of first responders should annually include these areas of psycho-education. The goal of a psychological first-aid program is to prepare people for providing such support and then planning how such support will be deployed.

For emergency responders, the Critical Incident Stress Management (CISM) programs have had mixed reviews on success. Originated by Dr Jeffrey Mitchell, his group process known as a Critical Incident Stress Debriefing (CISD) is a mental health support group process that involves a mental health professional and peer-members that starts factual, moves to a cognitive level, deepens to the emotional level, and returns to the cognitive level with some psycho-educational strategies for the responders to take away (Mitchell, 2003). CISM also involves other non-psychotherapy interventions to help responders during their deployment and demobilization in the aftermath for those not ready for long-term mental health care. Mitchell (2003) points out that there are critics of his model and the practice of CISD, but these are most often misapplications of the intervention or use with inappropriate populations. CISD was intended and designed for the emergency worker (Mitchell, 2003). However, those with experience participating as a peer-member in CISDs can also be important access points and supporters of psycho-education and ongoing stress management and wellness programs in emergency response agencies. It is the mental health promotion before the crisis that lays the foundations for resilience afterwards.

Therefore, the mental health professional should be someone enlisted to work with the responders on a regular basis, and through doing so, becomes a wise and trusted guest among the members of the group. This work can include leadership consulting, psycho-education, crisis interventions, and assistance in emergency planning from a psychologist's perspective (Kirschman et al., 2015). But to do the good that they might, the emergency psychologist has to win the respect and trust of the leaders and the troops. This is not an easy task and waiting until there is a crisis will be too late. Paton (2006) found that social support is essential to fostering PTG in emergency workers who have been exposed to a traumatic event. A comprehensive and holistic wellness program is needed in place prior to the strike of disaster. Emergency Managers need to investigate and take into consideration what their local agencies have in place and how he or she might help improve and integrate it into the overall emergency response plan.

CHALLENGES IN EMERGENCY MENTAL HEALTH – THE MEDICAL MODEL

Emergency Managers need to discard the disease model of mental health from their understanding and discussions about psychological well-being. There is a contradiction here between what we have written in terms of *psychological first-aid* and discarding the disease model. The contradiction comes from the fact that society understands psychology as "mental health" and so it is a necessary place to begin discussions about psycho-physical wellness. Szasz (2007) points out that *mental illness* is a metaphor or analogue because brain injuries and diseases affecting the central nervous system are the work of a neurologist. The concept of mental illness gives people who are struggling the felt-sense that they have "caught it" like the flu. Because of the mental scripts of medicine, it places the person with a psychological problem in the patient role, which implies that the doctor role is both the *authority* and the one with a *cure*. Psychologists are experts in the study of the mind and mental health practices. But the "talking cure" was a term made popular by Freud in the early 20th century, and now psychotherapies are regarded as talk therapies. Even the word "therapy" comes from the Greek term θεραπεύω (therapeuō), which means to serve another by helping them heal or to help cure them. Therapy then implies a medical problem-solving framework, but it is the one that the mainstream mental health industry uses. While we are stuck with it for now, it is important that we do not impose a pathophysiological notion on the people we intend to serve when putting together psychological support programs in emergency management.

An organizational structure and culture of wellness is vital to the other components of a comprehensive emergency psychology program. Too often, the *bureaucrats* in a government organization are sufficed by merely having the ability to claim to have a wellness program. Perhaps this is having an Employee Assistance Program available to employees and some stress management training on a fairly regular basis. But this is insufficient, especially when every other facet of the organization operates like a typical bureaucracy – depersonalized and mechanical (Russell, 2019). The Emergency Manager must persuade leadership to care and be on board with serving an emergency psychology program plan. Paton (2006) says that a vital factor in fostering post-traumatic growth (PTG) in emergency and disaster workers is *social support*. Conversely, organizational hassles are cited as the most common and server stressors for emergency responders (Kirschman, 2018; Violanti and Paton, 2006). The employees of an emergency response agency must have the kind of management that consists of quality leaders that demonstrate overt support for their people on a consistent basis. It cannot wait until tragedy strikes the organization for the leadership to try building a rapport with the troops. Therefore, an Emergency Manager might consider looking at the kind, frequency, and volume of leadership training and education of the administrators and mid-level supervisors as part of an emergency psychology program.

One can understand how the medical model of psychology and the bureaucratic workings of emergency response agencies are cut out of the same mental schema. Wender (2008) points out that the natural sciences framework of the mainstream social sciences is the foundation for the bureaucracy of law enforcement, and we would add, government services altogether. Of course, this same naturalist scientific model is the foundation for medical science from which psychiatry gets its worldview and mainstream clinical psychology interfaces. In fact, the insurance companies motivate the adoption of the medical model (e.g., diagnostics, psychometrics, treatment plans, etc.) by requiring criteria consistent with the medical metaphor. The implication of the medical model on those trained in a scientist, bureaucratic, and rational mentality is that it also imposes a medicalized interpretation on psychological suffering. That means, psychological discomfort or undesired thoughts and so forth are experienced psychophysically as symptoms of a disease rather than normal human responses to human problems. The medical model provides the mental illness metaphor, which also brings with it the metaphors of mental injury, mental scars, and mental cures – all of which do not materially exist. What if we began looking at mental phenomena as adaptive processes acquired through engaged action in the world with the horrific or darker side of existence? After all, humankind is not built with the natural hides, teeth, and claws that other species are and must rely on our creativity, innovation, and technologies to survive. When those things collapse or are destroyed by disaster, then we are, in a sense, out in the wild and must adapt to these raw circumstances (Solomon et al., 2015).

For the population-at-large, many people are already in treatment for a mental disorder and a disaster can disrupt their care, particularly if mental health professionals are needed to respond to provide crisis psychological support. Moreover, an abrupt discontinuation of psychological medications can present some serious withdrawal problems for people accustomed to using them (Breggin, 2013). The availability of prescribers, medication inventory access, and distribution is likely going to put some people's mental health in jeopardy. This, too, is in the context of widespread mass trauma. Emergency Managers should be working with mental health professionals to plan ahead for these contingencies. Moreover, addictions in the population are often functional and therefore not being treated. Something policy-makers realized quickly during the COVID-19 pandemic was that closing down liquor stores, even for a few days, created problems for people that had alcohol dependency. Alcohol withdrawal in some situations can be so acute as to be fatal. Finally, Emergency Managers must consider that there are people with multiple mental disorder diagnoses, and these can be treated with a collection of medications. Withdrawal from multiple medications all at once poses a serious medical and psychological emergency (Breggin, 2013). In any case, emergency planning for mental health issues is a multidisciplinary task among the helping professions.

RECOMMENDATIONS FOR THE FUTURE

Psychological First-Aid Training is a topic not taught in most basic training or academy programs, although there are often some stress management and self-care units that are part of the curriculum. There is not typically any training on how to provide PFA for each other or citizens in crisis. Because the PFA does not take a pathologizing approach or assert the medicalization of trauma in its theory and training, it can be adopted by certification and education programs for first responders, volunteer corps, clergy, educators, etc. (Everly and Lating, 2017). Because Emergency Managers have a lot to plan that is actually about material and physical consequences, it is important for them to keep the psychological issues on their planning and resources lists.

Funding of emergency agencies is always a challenge and mutual aid agreements are often put in place to compensate for the lack of personnel and resources in major emergencies and disasters. Likewise, mental health resources should be set up for mutual aid assistance across jurisdictions. This is where some flexibility in terms of licensure, standardization, and delivery of services must be considered. Each state has its own authority and professional licensing requirements, so that means that mental health workers from one state may not be typically allowed to practice in a neighboring state. The time is now to pre-draft executive orders to make sure that when terror or disaster strikes, mental health workers are granted the authority and ability to help.

University and college psychology and mental health programs should be involved and made ready to mobilize. Again, putting some PFA into the standard curriculum can make ready students and faculty to help where appropriate. Displaced people, particularly children, do not really need much more initially than presence and emotional support. This is exactly what *first- aid* means in the psychological sense (Everly and Lating, 2017). Moreover, universities and college can prepare to collect data on the psychological impacts of terrorism and disaster, which can be used for analysis and understanding the needs better. Too often, the exigent circumstances of an emergency or disaster are a good time to record observations, statements, and narratives from those involved in crisis mitigation, but also those victims of the impact. Journalists typically make it right to the "eye of the storm," but scientists and research assistants do not. Research like this would take planning ahead and Institutional Review Board (IRB) supervision in the planning of such research projects. Such research projects need to be set up longitudinally so that the study can provide trending in the psychological issues of various demographics.

For sure, mental health issues cannot wait until the crisis for emergency managers to begin thinking about interventions. Like other resources it will be too late for some, and less effective overall. This is not a box to be checked, but a serious coalition of mental health leaders must be involved. Perhaps it is time for the United States to have a

Psychologist General in parallel to the Surgeon General that can lead in these matters of mental health crises (Schneider, 2019). It may not be a bad idea for each state to have an executive branch mental health authority with funding to empower states to put systems in place. It is economically needed and morally imperative to start thinking about the overall mental health of society (Schneider, 2019). Emergency Managers should seek a local qualified expert to assist in setting up local systems and pre-arranging resources, including mutual aid response from other areas.

CONCLUSION

Psychology has had a history of theoretical and philosophical disagreements as well as a variety of different goals for itself and society. However, the traumas of war, terrorism, and natural disasters are undisputed in terms of their impacts on populations which are seemingly permanent to some degree. Therefore, when terrorism or disaster strikes, communities and their emergency workers need to be as prepared as possible, including having psychologically supportive interventions and systems in place. The stigma of mental health connected to the medical model of psychiatry has kept psychological problems largely behind closed doors and a personal, private matter. But when the community is decimated with mass death, injury, and destruction, such a perspective about psychological problems undermines getting people the help they need. As noted earlier in the work, Emergency Managers must plan for emergency psychological services and resources beforehand, so that their community can heal and have a better chance at emerging with a new normal in the aftermath (Russell, 2019).

In order to plan, we must learn from the past. But unless researchers are prepared to deploy into the disaster area in a similar fashion as journalists, our disasters become unknown pasts from which we cannot learn. Recording observations, statements, documents, and other social artifacts is important to reconstruction and analysis of every disaster. Of course, law enforcement will collect evidence to indicate fruits of a crime or terror attack, but there is a need for social scientists of all kinds to go out into the affected area and collect data for analysis. It takes pre-planning of such activities and training so that it can be done safely and effectively. Disaster and terror attacks are part of human history and will continue. Perhaps it is time to make mental health a higher priority in emergency planning, response, and recovery efforts.

CLASS DISCUSSION AND ESSAY QUESTIONS

1. What are the academic and professional roots of psychology?
2. Natural disasters produce psychological impacts for victims and survivors alike. Why is this the case, and why would a terrorist attack be even more emotionally and mentally damaging?
3. Why is it important that those involved in psychological interventions be familiar with emergency management terminology and processes?
4. What is a Critical Incident Stress Debriefing and why is it controversial?
5. Why is the medical model of mental health treatment problematic?
6. How can Psychological First-Aid training benefit those involved in emergency management and homeland security?

REFERENCES

American Psychological Association [APA]. (2020). Existential crisis. *APA Dictionary of Psychology* [online]. Retrieved from https://dictionary.apa.org/existential-crisis.

Anton, C. (2021). *How nonbeing haunts being: On possibilities, morality and death acceptance.* Teaneck, NJ: Fairleigh Dickinson University.

Audi, R. (2009). *The Cambridge dictionary of philosophy* (2nd ed.). New York: Cambridge University.

Baron-Cohen, S. (2012). *Zero degrees of empathy: A new theory of human cruelty and kindness.* New York: Penguin Books.

Baron-Cohen, S. (2011). *The science of evil: On empathy and the origins of cruelty.* New York: Basic Books.

Becker, E. (1997). *The denial of death.* New York: Free Press.

Blackburn, S. (2008). *Oxford dictionary of philosophy.* New York: Oxford University Press.

Boring, E. (2008). *A history of experimental psychology.* New Delhi, IMD: Cosmo Publishing.

Breggin, P. R. (2013). *Psychiatric drug withdrawal: A guide for prescribers, therapists, patients, and their families.* New York: Springer.

Breggin, P. R. (1994). *Toxic psychiatry.* New York: St. Martin's Publishing.

Broomé, R. E., & Russell, E. J. (2018). The phenomenological psychology of a police officer stopping an active shooter. *Journal of Theoretical and Philosophical Criminology, 10*(2), 53–70.

Bugental, J. F. T. (1964). The third force in psychology. *Journal of Humanistic Psychology, 4*(1), 19–26. https://doi.org/10.1177/002216786400400102.

Cambridge (2021). Technocracy. In *Cambridge dictionary.* Retrieved from https://dictionary.cambridge.org/us/dictionary/english/technocracy.

Chalmers, D. J. (1997). *The conscious mind: In search for a fundamental theory* (Revised ed.). Oxford: Oxford University Press.

Ellenberger, H. F. (1981). *The discovery of the unconscious: The history and evolution of dynamic psychiatry.* New York: Basic Books.

Everly, G. S., & Lating, J. M. (2017). *The Johns Hopkins guide to psychological first aid.* Baltimore, MD: Johns Hopkins University.

Federal Emergency Management Agency [FEMA]. (2016). Crisis counseling assistance and training program guidance: CCP application toolkit, Version 5.0. *United States Department of Homeland Security* [online]. Retrieved from https://www.samhsa.gov/sites/default/files/images/fema-ccp-guidance.pdf.

FEMA (2011). National incident management system: Guide to credentialing of personnel. *United States Department of Homeland Security* [online]. Retrieved from https://www.fema.gov/pdf/emergency/nims/nims_cred_guidelines_report.pdf.

Giorgi, A. P. (2019). *Psychology as a human science: A phenomenologically based approach* (2nd ed.). Colorado Springs, CO: University Professors Press.

Giorgi, A. P. (2015). In search for the psyche: A human science perspective. In K. J. Schneider, J. F. Pierson, & J. F. T. Bugental (Eds.), *The Handbook of humanistic psychology: Theory, research, and practice* (2nd ed., pp. 61–72). Thousand Oaks, CA: Sage.

Goldberg, C. (1997). *Speaking with the devil: Exploring senseless acts of evil.* New York: Penguin Group.

Greening, T. (1997). Chapter 5. Posttraumatic stress disorder: An existential-humanistic perspective. In S. Krippner & S. M. Powers (Eds.), *Broken images, broken selves: Dissociative narratives in clinical practice.* New York: Brunner/Mazel. 125–135.

Greenleaf, R. (1977 [2002]). *Servant-leadership: A journey into the nature of legitimate power and greatness.* Mahwah, New Jersey: Paulist Press.

Grossman, D. (2009). *On killing: The psychological cost of learning to kill in war and society.* New York: Back Bay Books.

Hacker Hughes, J., McCauley, M., & Wilson, L. (2019). History of military psychology. *Journal of the Royal Army Medical Corps, 165*(2), 68–70. https://doi.org/10.1136/jramc-2018-001048.

Kaag, J. (2020). *Sick souls, healthy minds: How William James can save your life.* Princeton, NJ: Princeton University Press.

Kaku, M. (2021). *The god equation: The quest for a theory of everything.* New York: Doubleday Books.

Kean, T. H. et al. (2004). 9/11 commission report. *National Commission on Terrorist Attacks Upon the United States* [online]. Retrieved from http://govinfo.library.unt.edu/911/report/911Report.pdf.

Kierkegaard, S. (1981). *The concept of anxiety: A simple psychologically orienting deliberation on the dogmatic issue of hereditary sin* (R. Thomte & A. B. Anderson, Eds.). Princeton, NJ: Princeton University.

Kirschman, E. (2018). *I love a cop: What police families need to know* (3rd ed.). New York: Guilford.

Kirschman, E., Kamena, M., & Fay, J. (2015). *Counseling cops: What clinicians need to know.* New York: Guilford.

Lansing, K.M. (2012). *The rite of return: Coming back from duty-induced PTSD.* High Ground Press.

Moran, D., & Cohen, J. (2012). *The Husserl dictionary.* New York: Continuum International Publishing.

Miller, G. A. (2003). The cognitive revolution: A historical perspective. *TRENDS in Cognitive Sciences, 7*(3), 141–144. Retrieved from https://www.cs.princeton.edu/~rit/geo/Miller.pdf.

Misiak, H., & Sexton, V. S. (1973). *Phenomenological, existential, and humanistic psychologies: A historical survey.* New York: Grune & Stratton.

Mitchell, J. (2003). *Crisis intervention & CISM: A research summary.* Ellicott City, MD: International Critical Incident Stress Foundation.

Paton, D. (2006). Posttraumatic growth in protective services professional: Individual, cognitive and organizational influences. *Traumatology, 11*, 335–346.

Russell, E. (2019). *In command of guardians: Executive servant leadership for the community of responders* (2nd ed.). Cham, Switzerland: Springer Nature.

Schneider, K. (2019, July 24). It's time the U.S. had a psychologist general: The country is in a mental health crisis and nobody is in really charge. *Scientific American* [online]. Retrieved from https://blogs.scientificamerican.com/observations/its-time-the-u-s-had-a-psychologist-general/.

Smith, E., & Burkle, F. M. (2018). The forgotten responders: The ongoing impact of 9/11 on the ground zero recovery workers. *Prehospital and Disaster Medicine, 33*(4), 436–440. https://doi.org/10.1017/S1049023X1800064X.

Solomon, S., Greenberg, J., & Pyszczynski, T. (2015). *The worm at the core: On the role of death in life.* New York: Random House.

Stedmon, A. W., & Lawson, G. (2013). Terrorism psychology: Theory & application. *Journal of Police and Criminal Psychology, 28*(2), 91–93. https://doi.org/10.1007/s11896-012-9108-4

Szasz, T. (2007). *The medicalization of everyday life: Selected essays.* Syracuse, NY: Syracuse University of New York.

Violanti, J., & Paton, D. (2006). Who gets PTSD?: Issues of posttraumatic stress vulnerability. Springfield, IL, Charles C. Thomas.

Watson, J. B. (1913). Psychology as the behaviorist views it. *Psychological Review, 20*(2), 158–177. https://doi.org/10.1037/h0074428.

Wender, J. M. (2008). *Policing and the poetics of everyday life.* Chicago, IL: University of Illinois.

Wertz, F. J. (2018). Beyond scientism: Toward a genuine science of psychology. In R. N. Williams & E. E. Gantt (Eds.), *On hijacking science: Exploring the nature and consequences of overreach in psychology.* New York: Routledge/Taylor & Francis Publishing. 107–119.

GLOSSARY OF TERMS

Desire to Serve: The inspiration that brings one into an emergency services career so that they can serve the needs of others (Russell, 2019).

Easy Problems of Consciousness: Explanations of *how* the brain processes environmental stimuli, integrates information, and how people report internal (psychological) states (Chalmers, 1997, pp. xi–xii).

Empathy: The state of being emotionally and cognitively in-tune with another person, particularly by feeling what their situation is like from the inside, or what it is like for them (Blackburn, 2008, p. 113).

Hard Problem of Consciousness: Explanations for *why* information processing by the brain is accompanied by an inner-experienced life (Chalmers, 1997, p. xii). Also see:: Lived experience.

Healing: The act of making a person of a community whole from both physical and psychological trauma (Greenleaf, 1977/2002, p. 50).

Lived Experience: The conscious state as personally lived through and experienced in the first person…or process that can be identified as the stream of consciousness (Moran and Cohen, 2012, p. 195).

Materialism: The view that the world is entirely composed of matter. Also called physicalism since physics has shown that matter itself resolves into forces and energy, and is just one amongst other physically-respectable denizens of the universe (Blackburn, 2008, p. 225).

Metaphor: A figure of speech (or a trope) in which a word or phrase that literally denotes one thing is used to denote another, thereby implicitly comparing the two things (Audi, 2009, p. 562).

Naturalism: The two-fold view that (1) everything is composed of natural entities – those studied in the sciences…whose properties determine all the properties of things, persons included…and (2) acceptable methods of justification and explanation are continuous, in some sense, with those in science. Today most American and other philosophers of mind are naturalists of some stripe, largely because of what they see as the lessons of continuing scientific advances, some of them spectacular, particularly in the brain sciences (Audi, 2009, pp. 596–597).

Psychological First-Aid: A mental health analogue to physical first-aid. A supportive and compassionate presence to stabilize and mitigate acute distress, as well as facilitate access to continued care (Everly and Lating, 2017, pp. 3–4).

Scientism: An influential misconception of science based on dogmatic philosophical assumptions: Ontological materialism, epistemological hypothetico-deductive causal explanation testing, and an arrogant preeminence of science over all other ways of knowing the world (Wertz, 2018, p. 2).

Technocracy: A government or social system that is controlled or influenced by experts in science or technology; the fact of a government or social system being influenced by such experts (*Cambridge Dictionary*, 2021).

Terror Management Theory: A theory proposing that control of death anxiety is the primary function of society and the main motivation in human behavior. Accordingly, awareness of the inevitability of death (mortality salience) motivates people to maintain faith in the absolute validity of the cultural worldviews (i.e., beliefs and values) that give their lives meaning and to believe that they are living up to those standards, thus attaining a sense of personal value or self-esteem that buffers them against the frightening recognition of their own mortality.

CHAPTER 13

Aviation Tools for Emergency Management and Homeland Security:

Types, Functions, and the Future of Aviation for Emergency and Disaster Response

Jack Edwin Troutt III

INTRODUCTION

An old gentleman cannot move, is in distress, and needs to be evacuated from his home, which is damaged with a two-foot-square hole in the roof. He is one of thousands that needs rescuing due to high water that has flooded the city, leaving many roads impassable and complicating rescue efforts. The solution? Up. A helicopter would lower a rescuer to the roof of the house to assist the gentleman. Not a trivial feat considering the small size of the roof of the house, the surrounding trees, and power lines that make maneuvering the helicopter a delicate process, necessitating that the helicopter hover at a slightly higher altitude to avoid these obstacles. A rescue swimmer is then lowered to the roof, first to rescue other family members that are on the roof itself, and then to rescue the gentleman, who has to be carried from the downstairs part of the house to the attic. This individual is then lifted by the hoist on the helicopter through the hole in the roof. The date is September 2, 2005, four days after Hurricane Katrina made its second landfall over the coasts of Louisiana and Mississippi. Lieutenant Commander Steve Kelley and Petty Officers Guy Touchton and Chase Matthews would go on to rescue 97 survivors of Hurricane Katrina in New Orleans over two days and 20 hours of flying ("We Were There," 2005).

While the concept of aviation and flight has been around for hundreds of years, effective flight has only been around for about 120 years. However, during this time there have been amazing developments in aviation technology that have been able to provide emergency responders with invaluable tools. Aircraft have provided professional pilots the ability to travel at high speeds, to go where land and water vehicles cannot, to rescue people when no other option is available, to deliver supplies faster when time

DOI: 10.4324/9781003350729-13

is of the essence, and to provide data and coordination ability when seconds count and information is vital. What follows here will try to discuss some of the important aspects of aviation with regard to emergency response. However, there first needs to be a brief discussion of the history of aviation.

HISTORY OF THE PROFESSION

Aviation and its technology and inspiration have a long and storied past. A logical start to understanding this history would be with some of the earliest figures that dealt with a fantasy of flight, such as Alexander the Great. Alexander the Great, who lived from 356 BCE to 323 BCE, was in some myths thought to have a basket carried by four Griffins that he would use to survey his kingdom (Shaw, 2014). Another story that showed a dream for flight was the Greek myth of Icarus and Daedalus, as told in the tale by the Roman Publius Ovidius Naso (commonly called Ovid) and recalled in Greek myth in his work "Metamorphoses," which was completed around 8 CE (Quezzaire, 2017). The story focused on Icarus and his father, Daedalus, and their attempts to escape King Minos by crafting wings to fly out of feathers and wax. Not heeding the advice of his father, Icarus flew too close to the sun causing the wax to melt, and Icarus fell to his death.

Moving to actual flight, humanity would start small. The first man-made flying objects were likely kites created in China during the Warring States time (475 BCE to 221 BCE) ("The Earliest 'Aircraft'," 2018). In 1505–1506, Leonardo da Vinci would produce his *Codex on the Flight of Birds*, which contained his thoughts and sketches on the nature of flight and his designs for a flying machine called an ornithopter, which is a man-made aircraft that flaps its wings much like a bird does (Jakab, 2013).

Hundreds of years later in 1783, the brothers Joseph-Michel and Jacques-Étienne Montgolfier would launch their first balloon in Annonay, France (Sharp, 2019). The flight, though unmanned, was successful enough to catch the attention of King Louis XVI of France. The King would observe another demonstration on September 13, 1783, and this time the balloon was occupied, with a sheep, a duck, and a rooster. A little more than a month later, the first human flight took place on October 13 with one passenger, Jean-François Pilâtre de Rozier aboard. A few years later, the frameless parachute would be created by André-Jacques Garnerin, proving that you not only need to think about going up, but coming down. Using a balloon, he would make the first parachute jump in 1797, releasing himself from the balloon and using a parachute not dissimilar to a modern umbrella (*Encyclopedia Britannica*, 2019). Later, in 1891, Otto Lilienthal would make some of the first manned flights, utilizing gliders (Berliner, 1997).

While the first human to take flight, and then the first to try to use a parachute, are critical to the important events of history, several years passed before the next milestone in aviation occurred, which was the first powered flight. Brothers Orville and Wilbur Wright would be both newspapermen and operators of a bicycle shop before turning their attention to aviation. On December 17, 1903, Wilbur took the first powered heavier-than-air aircraft on a 59-second flight over the shores of Kitty Hawk, North Carolina (History .com, 2019). Finding a somewhat less than receptive audience in the United States, the brothers took their aircraft to Europe, giving flight to dignitaries and performing shows before returning to America in 1909. After returning, the brothers built a successful company selling their aircraft to both U.S. and European customers. While a significant achievement, the first flights by the Wright Brothers initially required a catapult to get the aircraft into the air. However, just three years later, Alberto Santos-Dumont would be the first to launch an aircraft under its own power. In his original design, his aircraft, the 14-bis would be launched from his No. 14 balloon; he worked to perfect the aircraft, and in 1906 became the winner of the Archdeacon Cup for the first aircraft to take off under its own power (Crouch, 2019).

With the invention of manned, powered flight, further aviation developments would start to happen quickly. In 1909, Louis Bleriot would make the first successful flight across the English Channel, and less than 20 years later, Charles Lindberg would complete the first non-stop solo flight across the Atlantic (The Library of Congress, 2003). Just five years after that, Amelia Earhart would replicate the feat in 1932. Going back slightly, in 1915, the first all- metal aircraft would take off at the Döberitz Airfield outside of Berlin. Previously, aircraft up to that point had been made of wood and fabric, and while the first all-metal airplane would fly in 1915, the common aircraft construction would remain primarily wood and fabric until the 1930s, when stronger engines and lighter metal construction techniques were developed. In 1930, British inventor Frank Little would invent the jet engine as a system of aircraft propulsion that would become commonplace in the years following the Second World War. In 1947, Charles Yeager would be the first man to break the sound barrier in level flight; in 1961, just 57 years after the Wright Brothers' first flight, Yuri Gagarin would be the first man into space.

There are countless other notable moments within the history of aviation, such as the first passenger flight (1908), first cargo flight (1910), first modern airliner flight (1933), first jet- powered flight (1939), and so on. There are far too many firsts and significant events to mention here, but it comes without question that in today's modern society, aviation and all the facets that come with it is integral to our society. It enables goods to be delivered across the world in a matter of hours, while allowing people to travel to places that, before aircraft, would have taken them days or weeks to arrive. It enables new understandings of our world through discoveries that could only happen at altitudes higher than the ground, and has also enabled us to respond to emergencies and disasters faster than ever before.

RELATION TO DISASTERS AND TERRORISM

Of course, the history of aviation in respect to technological development and geographic accomplishments is only part of its history. Within the realm of emergency management and homeland security, aircraft can be the source of a crisis or security situation, and aviation itself can unfortunately be part of the disaster. Either as an aircraft accident or by intentional acts such as the September 11, 2001 attacks, there is the possibility for aviation to be the disaster as much as the prevention of the disaster. Given the number of key features of aviation, aircraft accidents can create unique and large-scale emergencies for responders. Things like highly flammable fuel, high passenger counts, which can mean high injury and fatalities, and the fact that victims can be in the aircraft or on the ground can complicate disaster responses.

Aircraft accidents have unfortunately been common throughout history. Even the Wright Brothers crashed their aircraft a number of times before their first successful flight. The first recorded death as a result of an aircraft accident actually happened in a balloon back in 1785. Pilâtre de Rozier, along with passenger Pierre Ange Romain, died when the balloon they were traveling in caught fire during their attempt to cross the English Channel on June 15, 1785 (Lemaire and Kasserman, 2021). Much later, one of the more widely known aviation disasters occurred when the Hindenburg caught fire and crashed. In this case, the Hindenburg was a rigid- structure dirigible, a lighter-than-air aircraft that contained an internal rigid structure. To stay aloft, the Hindenburg utilized hydrogen, which is lighter than air, but also highly flammable. As the aircraft was landing over Lakehurst, New Jersey, the airship caught fire, crashing into the ground and killing 36 people, including 13 passengers, 22 crewmembers, and 1 ground crew member (Feigenbaum, 2007).

Forty years later, another significant accident would result in the largest single loss of life due to an aircraft accident. On March 27, 1997, two 747's, one owned by Pan Am, the other by KLM, would collide on a runway at the Los Rodeos Airport on the island of Tenerife in the Canary Islands. The causes of this accident would be numerous, including radio communication difficulties and issues with what would eventually be called crew resource management. In the end, 583 people would die due to the KLM aircraft trying to take off while the Pan Am aircraft was taxiing on the runway (Ziomek, 2020). Other aircraft disasters include horrific accidents such as the 2000 crash of the Air France Concorde, in which 109 passengers and crew died along with four people on the ground (Riding, 2000), or the crash of TWA Flight 800 which saw the death of 230 people onboard when the aircraft crashed off the coast of Long Island (Pedzich, 2014). It also means that accidents can happen far from the airport where local emergency response and rescue organizations can be ill-prepared to handle disasters such as the crash of Japan Airlines Flight 123, which killed 520 passengers and crew when their 747 crashed into a mountainside in Gunma, Japan ("Japan Marks," n.d.).

Of course, aviation accidents and disasters are not the only source of emergency and security-related issues. Indeed, aviation can be the tool for intentional crashes and terrorist actions that can cause great devastation and a potential for large loss of life.

One unfortunate method to instill terror in a populace is to bomb or otherwise destroy an aircraft, often with the large loss of innocent lives. Indeed, one such incident was the bombing of Air India Flight 182, which resulted in the loss of 329 people onboard the Montreal to London flight (Dean et al., 2017). The aircraft was found to have broken up over the Atlantic Ocean as a result of a bomb planted by the same organization that was responsible for another bomb that detonated at the Narita International Airport, killing two baggage handlers just an hour before the plane crashed. Another disaster that had security implications was the crash of Pan Am Flight 103 over Lockerbie in Scotland (Warner, 2001). The flight, on its way to New York from London, crashed in Scotland after a bomb that was hidden in a cassette player exploded. The resulting crash killed all 270 people onboard and was eventually blamed on Libyan nationals.

Hijacking, or taking over an aircraft or other vehicle unlawfully, is another unfortunate aspect of aviation. The first recorded hijacking of an aircraft occurred relatively early in aviation's history, in 1931, when Peruvian Revolutionaries hijacked a Pan American aircraft in order to drop leaflets over Lima (Aviation Security, n.d.). The 1970s brought a number of high-profile hijackings, including the hijacking of four aircraft in a coordinated effort by the Popular Front for the Liberation of Palestine (PFLP), which then flew the planes to Dawson's Field near Zarka, Jordan (Homeland Security Digital Library, n.d.). The PFLP demanded that in exchange for the hostages that were aboard the respective flights, they wanted the release of several of their members held in jail in Europe. Eventually all the hostages would be released in exchange for the release of the prisoners. In 1971, the hijacking of Northwest Orient Airlines Flight 305 would end in a far more mysterious manner (Federal Bureau of Investigation, n.d.). In this instance, a man calling himself D.B. Cooper would demand four parachutes and $200,000. After receiving his demand, D.B. Cooper would release 36 hostages, but then order the plane to take off and head to Mexico City. Once airborne, Mr Cooper strapped on a parachute and jumped out of the back of the plane with the money and was never seen again. It goes without saying that probably the most horrific and currently well-known hijacking was the hijacking and subsequent crashing of four aircraft on September 11, 2001 (National Commission on Terrorist Attacks Upon the United States, 2004). On that day, hijackers took over four aircraft and subsequently crashed two into the World Trade Center in New York City, while a third crashed into the Pentagon. Passengers on the final fourth aircraft, on learning of the fate of the other hijackings, attempted to overpower the terrorists; during the ensuing struggle the aircraft crashed into a field outside of Shanksville, Pennsylvania. All told, including those on the ground and inside the buildings struck by the aircraft, over 2,700 people would die as a result of these hijackings.

RELATION TO EMERGENCY MANAGEMENT AND HOMELAND SECURITY

Aviation can be a powerful tool in response to multiple types of disasters including search-and-rescue operations, hurricanes, terrorist incidents, and forest fires. Aircraft have been used to rescue people from all manners of disasters, either from hurricanes, fires, at sea, or even people lost in the woods (CNN, 2019). These relationships will be outlined here, with the subsequent section taking a deeper look at the specific roles and responsibilities that aviation assets managers and organizations have within the security and disaster response field.

Within these roles that aviation can fulfill, there exists a wide array of relationships between aviation and both emergency management and homeland security. If looked at from the U.S. government perspective, the vast number of relationships between aviation and those tasked with managing and overseeing emergency response and security operations typically falls within the Department of Homeland Security and its operational and support components. These components include the United States Coast Guard, United States Customs and Border Protection, Federal Emergency Management Agency, and the Transportation Security Administration, to name a few. Some of the operational components will have their own air and aviation assets, such as the United States Coast Guard and States Customs and Border Protection, while others, such as the Federal Emergency Management Agency, will serve as coordination and support aviation operations while not having any aviation assets of their own, or those that they do have would be limited in nature.

Of course, the Department of Homeland Security is not the only government organization that has aviation assets that can assist in emergency management and homeland security operations. Other federal government organizations such as those under the Department of Defense or Department of Transportation, can also be found to be critical in times of need. There also exists a multitude of state, county, tribal, and local aviation assets that can come to assist in times of need and crisis. These assets represent a vast array of equipment that can perform a wide variety of vital functions in times of disaster or for security considerations.

The greatest advantage of aviation is the speed that it can provide to any disaster. As such, one of the main focuses for any aviation response to a disaster is to enable the rapid movement of materials and disaster responders to where they are needed. One of the most visible responses to natural and man-made disasters is that of aircraft search-and-rescue operations. As well as dropping supplies, aircraft can also be used to drop other things in an effort to mitigate disasters, such as aircraft fighting fires.

Aviation can also provide invaluable tools for assessment of damage, as well as command and control functions during and after a disaster. Aviation assets have the ability for responders to get the "big picture" when it comes to assessing the impact from any disaster, either natural or man-made, while also allowing decision-makers the chance to better direct resources, given a more complete picture of the disaster environment. Depending on the nature and location of any disaster emergency, first responders can be on-site relatively quickly. It goes without saying that aviation assets can provide a multiplier effect for emergency responders when dealing with a disaster, particularly a large-scale one. Depending on the disaster, there could be a variety of emergency response organizations, either from the local, state, tribal, or federal levels (Federal Emergency Management Agency, 2008).

In addition, there exists a need for aircraft to play an active role in weather-related operations. The primary, and possibly most critical and public role that aviation plays in this regard is the gathering of information related to weather and its potential impacts to the United States. The Hurricane Hunters group is probably the most well-known aviation weather support group within the United States. Today, the Hurricane Hunters are made up of the 53rd Weather Reconnaissance Squadron (WRS) based in Biloxi, Mississippi, and the National Oceanic and Atmospheric Administration (NOAA) Aircraft Operations Center (AOC) in Tampa, Florida (Williams, 2015). Aviation assets can accomplish other missions such as cloud seeding to try and mitigate droughts through the inducement of rain in hard-hit areas.

In the realm of security, aviation has taken on new roles and responsibilities in the current day. Security and local police organizations have long utilized fixed-wing and rotary aircraft in order to accomplish their roles. Increasingly, however, more and more organizations have turned to unmanned systems to help in accomplishing their security roles. Local law enforcement organizations, in particular, have started to utilize unmanned systems since the cost of such systems is usually far below that of traditional fixed or rotary systems and they require far less training to operate. Both unmanned and traditional aircraft can carry a wide variety of intelligence, surveillance, and reconnaissance (ISR) sensors such as video, infrared, and even chemical and radioactive detector instruments, depending on the tasking at the time.

Finally, it must be said that in terms of security considerations, federal, state, county, tribal, and local law enforcement agencies provide critical security for aviation resources and aircraft to prevent those that would use aviation assets to do harm. Probably the most well-known organization with regard to this effort is the Transportation Security Administration. The Federal Aviation Administration also plays a critical role in the security of aircraft, ensuring that an airport's aircraft operating areas are also secured. However, once again, it is not only the federal government's responsibility to provide this security, but also the state and local governments and organizations as well.

ROLES IN EMERGENCY MANAGEMENT AND HOMELAND SECURITY

As promised in the previous section, there needs to be a more detailed discussion of the various specific roles and responsibilities that oversee the various aircraft and aviation assets in emergency situations. Professional aviators provide weather reconnisance, fire fighting, engage in search-and-rescue operations, assess damages, and help to distribute relief supplies.

Weather Reconnaissance

As mentioned previously, the organizations that provide aircraft for the Hurricane Hunters are the 53rd Weather Reconnaissance Squadron based in Biloxi, Mississippi, and the NOAA Aircraft Operations Center (AOC) in Tampa, Florida. These groups operate under the National Hurricane Operations Plan when studying hurricanes (Office of the Federal Coordinator for Meteorology, 2019). The Plan seeks to define both roles and responsibilities when it comes to tropical and sub-tropical weather systems in the Atlantic Ocean, Gulf of Mexico, Caribbean Sea, and the Pacific Ocean. As part of the Operations Plan, items such as liaison meetings between the National Oceanic and Atmospheric Administration, U.S. Air Force Reserve Command, the Federal Aviation Administration (FAA), and Department of Defense (DOD), Policy Board on Federal Aviation, and mission coordination between the various federal and local aviation agencies are organized. This coordination will be accomplished by a designated Chief, Aerial Reconnaissance Coordination, All Hurricanes (CARCAH), whose duties include coordinating with impacted Air Traffic Control (ATC) facilities, notifying flight crews when other research missions will be in the area and publishing the Tropical Cyclone Plan of the Day. Under the document, all flight plans into the Weather Reconnaissance Area (WRA) must be filed with the FAA, as well as priority flight handling by local ATC personnel, mission descriptions, and altitude restrictions and communication procedures.

Aside from the established NOAA AOC and 53rd WRS, several other government organizations contribute to weather support during tropical cyclones. The National Aeronautics and Space Administration (NASA) operates weather research aircraft, while the Naval Research Laboratory and the National Science Foundation/National Center for Atmospheric Research maintain their own research aircraft (Office of the Federal Coordinator for Meteorology, 2019). All these aircraft would still operate under the National Hurricane Plan when conducting research and information gathering flights on hurricanes.

Firefighting

All firefighting aircraft operations are coordinated via the National Wildfire Coordinating Group (NWCG) (National Wildfire Coordinating Group, 2017). This group's primary mission enables wildland fire operations among the various federal, state, and tribal groups. These groups include the Bureau of Indian Affairs, Bureau of Land Management, Fish and Wildlife Service, Forest Service, International Association of Fire Chiefs, Intertribal Timber Council, National Association of State Foresters, National Park Service, and the United States Fire Administration.

When responding to a fire under the NWCG guidelines, the Air Tactical Group Supervisor (ATGS) has the primary coordination of the incident airspace and traffic (National Wildfire Coordinating Group, 2017). The ATGS serves as the primary link between ground and air assets and will also prioritize missions and ensure that proper equipment and personnel are assigned to those missions. Assisting the Group Supervisor could potentially be a Helicopter Coordinator (HLCO), who would coordinate and direct helicopter operations during the incident, and an Airtanker Coordinator (ATCO), who would coordinate airtanker operations and assets. Management of the aviation assets directly at the site of the operations would be under the control of the Aerial Supervision Module (ASM). The ASM would function as a two-person crew, consisting of a lead-trained aircraft pilot and an ATGS, trained personnel that would operate from the same aircraft over an incident location. During the operation, the aircraft could operate as both a lead aircraft and as an ATGS as the situation warrants. The variety of aircraft used in fighting fires is limited only by the design specification of the aircraft. Fixed-wing, rotary-winged, single-engine, multi-engine, and Unmanned Aircraft Systems (UAS) have all found roles in firefighting activities.

Another significant use of aircraft in fighting fires is the use of aircraft to deploy ground personnel to critical locations. Both helicopters and fixed-wing aircraft can provide platforms to carry firefighters to locations in wilderness areas. Helicopters can either land or employ rappel operations in heavily forested areas (National Wildfire Coordinating Group, 2017). Fixed-wing aircraft, if lacking a suitable landing area, can be used to deploy firefighting personnel via parachute. These specially trained firefighters, called smokejumpers, will carry all the tools and equipment that they will need for 48 hours with them into remote locations after jumping out of the aircraft.

During low-level aircraft operations (lower that 500 feet above the ground), lead aircraft will perform reconnaissance and identify retardant drop locations for larger air-tanker firefighting aircraft (National Wildfire Coordinating Group, 2017). Airtanker aircraft would follow the lead plane and drop their retardant or water load as given by the flight profile of the lead aircraft and the prevailing conditions. In addition to fixed-wing aircraft, helicopters can actually be a more efficient way to drop water on fires if there are close water sources available. Helicopters can also drop with greater precision, which can be extremely useful when trying to save local assets such as buildings and homes. Of course to be as efficient as possible, helicopters need close, reliable water sources. Sometimes given a lack of options, even swimming pools have been used as sources of water.

Search and Rescue

Organizing search-and-rescue efforts, particularly when coordination needs to be conducted across various federal and local organizations as well among search aircraft, can be tricky. For the 48 contiguous states and including Mexico and Canada, the Air Force Rescue Coordination Center handles this task for inland operations (United States Air Force, 2014). This group coordinates directly with the FAA alerting system and also maintains coordination with Search and Rescue Satellite-Aided Tracking information. The Center has the responsibility to receive distress calls, investigate those calls, and then dispatch search-and-rescue aviation assets that include both state and local fixed- and rotary-winged aircraft. For off-shore search and rescue, at least within the waters of the United States, the U.S. Coast Guard has the responsibility for coordination of maritime rescue activities (United States Coast Guard, n.d.). Both inland and offshore maritime search-and-rescue operations must conform to the National Search and Rescue Plan of The United States (National Search and Rescue Committee, n.d.). This Plan, maintained by the National Search and Rescue Committee, is agreed to by the committee members, which include the U.S. Coast Guard, the Federal Emergency Management Agency, the Federal Aviation Administration, the Maritime Administration, the Department of Defense (U.S. Northern Command), the Department of Commerce, the Department of the Interior, the Department of State, the Federal Communications Commission, and the National Aeronautics and Space Administration.

Damage Assessment and Response Coordination

Depending on the disaster, there could be a variety of emergency response organizations, either from the local, state, tribal, or federal levels (Federal Emergency Management Agency, 2008). Typically, any disaster that necessitates a large aviation response will have a designated Operations Section Chief. This individual will be responsible for all activities at the tactical level while also in charge of implementing the Incident Action Plan (IAP). This IAP will be the means to respond to the disaster by providing clear guidance for both operational and support activities.

At the outset of a disaster, the Operations Section Chief can establish what is called an Air Operations Branch (Federal Emergency Management Agency, 2008). This branch would establish safe and effective use of aircraft and aviation resources including helicopters, fixed-wing aircraft, and unmanned aerial systems. Coordination between the various different assets requires the designation of specific coordinators and base managers. Oftentimes in a large-scale natural disaster, airports that are vital for fixed-wing operations may be off-line, requiring fixed-wing aircraft to be deployed from locations further away from the actual disaster site. Helicopters and unmanned aerial systems typically can operate much closer to the disaster locations, given the much smaller area requirements for landing and takeoff. As such, air support supervisors are critical to coordinate between air assets closer to the disaster with those that are based at locations farther away.

Once the initial disaster scene is secured, local emergency response coordinators and emergency managers will want to get an assessment of the damage, especially if the damage is widespread, such as damage from a hurricane or earthquake (Federal Emergency Management Agency, 2016). Usually such damage assessments are conducted as "fly-overs," which provide opportunities to assess any damage and needs that are obviously visible from the sky. While visual damage assessment is probably the most common, other typical airborne sensors such as thermal imagers and hazardous material detection devices could also be employed, depending on the situation and needs-at-hand. Such assessments would not replace on-the-ground responders, unless the location is inaccessible by ground means. There could also be property damage or disaster victims that would not be visible by air, which would necessitate a close inspection by ground personnel.

Delivery of Aid

Primary to the requirements of delivering supplies and personnel to the disaster is the ability to get the people and supplies close to the area where they are needed. This often necessitates aircraft transporting supplies a great distance to the nearest suitable airport and then other aircraft, such as helicopters or smaller fixed-wing aircraft, or ground transportation methods carrying the supplies to their final destinations. This also requires a relatively intact airport close to the disaster and a logistical plan for the aircraft traffic and supply logistics, something that may be difficult in the wake of a large-scale disaster.

Aircraft can be used to drop relief supplies while in flight as well. Since the early days of aviation, goods and materials have been dropped from aircraft to those waiting below. Food, water, medicines, and other goods that are not easily damaged can be dropped from relatively low altitudes and at slower speeds to deliver directly to those that need such supplies, and can avoid considerations such as ground transportation and other final transportation logistical concerns. However, doing so in a disaster area brings some added issues. Typically dropping goods and materials from aircraft require a clear area for the goods to land safely, something that might not be available given any damage as a result of any disaster. Also, there could be security concerns in dropping the supplies, such as a rush to obtain the dropped goods which could lead to local disturbances. The danger of dropped supplies not landing in the intended landing area and the risk of collateral damage to property and people that are already suffering in the wake of a disaster are also concerns (Dillenburger et al., 2013).

CURRENT CHALLENGES

Although there is a clear linkage between the professionals involved in aviation and emergency management and homeland security, this does not imply that their role is without challenges. Current problems include air traffic management and new regulations emanating from our post-9/11 world. Each will be discussed in turn.

Air Traffic Management

While aviation can help in many different ways to respond and assist in recovery operations, natural and man-made disasters can also bring their own issues for aviation as well. As just discussed, there is a vital need for coordination among aviation assets, particularly in crowded airspaces that can occur in the aftermath of any disaster.

A robust air traffic management system is vital in the before, during, and after phases of a disaster. Before a disaster, aircraft will be needed to assist in evacuations, pre-delivery of emergency supplies, and coordination and movement of response assets. During a disaster, emergency teams will need to be kept advised of data that is acquired through aviation assets, either through such programs as the aforementioned NOAA Hurricane Hunters, or more localized data acquisition assets. The emergency crews can then take this data and respond accordingly. Finally, aircraft resources including recovery, medical, security, media, and data gatherers need to have an effective traffic system to operate in after a disaster. This can be particularly difficult on a local scale as some aviation tools and equipment such as radar, radio, and even landing fields could have been severely damaged or destroyed during the disaster. In all these phases, a diverse mix of fixed-wing, rotary, and unmanned aircraft systems will all need to have space allocated within the area of operations.

The key event for most aviation traffic management in response to disasters came in response to the Hurricane Katrina disaster. Hurricane Katrina made initial landfall in southeast Florida on August 25, 2005 as a Category 1 storm, before heading back out over the Gulf of Mexico, where it strengthened to a Category 5 hurricane. It made its final landfall as a Category 3 hurricane with sustained winds of 120 miles an hour (United States Department of Commerce; National Oceanic and Atmospheric Administration, n.d.).

After the hurricane, it was discovered that aviation assets were more important than ever, and the effective management of that traffic is vital. The images coming out of locations such as New Orleans and the surrounding areas of people being airlifted from their own homes proved this point more than any other disaster in a time of worldwide information sharing and the internet. After Hurricane Katrina devastated the Gulf Coast, the FAA developed its Airspace Management Plan for Disaster to have a more effective and efficient airspace management system (Federal Aviation Administration, 2012).

The plan was developed to have better coordination between the FAA and various federal, state, local, and tribal/territorial entities that may all have aviation resources that could assist in disaster response situations. The plan provides a framework that helps planners and response members better utilize and work within the National Airspace System. More importantly, the plan tries to mitigate the disaster impact on aviation operations while also effectively managing the traffic of flights within the disaster area at the designated airports being used for recovery efforts.

Tools that the plan would utilize to have an impact on the effective flow of airspace aircraft traffic would be warnings such as Advisory Special Notices, Airspace Coordination Areas (ACA), and Temporary Flight Restrictions (TFR). Special Notices would be cautions issued so that pilots would be aware of dangerous conditions around disaster areas and take appropriate actions. Airspace Coordination Areas could also be designated, which is a large volume of airspace area where various airspace designations may have changed, or indicates increased activity by aircraft traffic that would otherwise not be present, such as military operations under the Defense Support to Civil Authorities (DSCA) program.

The strongest tool available to airspace traffic managers during a disaster response would be the temporary flight restrictions. These restrictions can cover a wide variety of aircraft and flying restrictions and would be delivered via the notice to airman information service (NOTAM). Restrictions could include the restriction of all aircraft from a certain area, allowing only certain pre-approved aircraft access, such as rotary rescue aircraft, or requiring that all aircraft must have prior permission systems where aircraft are essentially given "slots" to operate within the airspace traffic system. Other restrictions that might occur would be things such as altitude restriction to certain types of aircraft (i.e., rotary-wing active search-and-rescue operations only allowed up to a certain altitude above ground level), and landing zone ingress and egress procedures and directions.

In order to actively monitor and coordinate these special airspace designations and aircraft traffic, the FAA may use local airport and navigation facilities if available and operational. Additionally, the FAA may also request the services of more military-type assets, such as E-3, E-2, or P-3 aircraft to provide mission coordination and relief mission conflict avoidance within the TFR. These Command, Control, Communications (C^3)-type missions utilizing more military assets will have to have prior FAA approval before they can operate in designated zones, and they are prevented from providing actual Air Traffic Control functions. Those functions normally operated by the FAA including direct monitoring and flow of aircraft would still remain with the FAA at the local and regional level.

New Regulations in a Post-9/11 World

Aviation and its structure was changed significantly in the aftermath of the September 11 attacks. On that day in 2001, 2,600 people would die at the World Trade Center in New York City, while 125 people died at the Pentagon in Washington D.C. Altogether, 256 people died on the four hijacked planes (National Commission on Terrorist Attacks Upon the United States, 2004). In response, a commission was set up to study the failings that could have contributed to the events of that day and advise on security and response changes for the future. In the Commission's report (2004), five areas of improvement were recommended including:

- Unifying strategic intelligence and operational planning against Islamist terrorists across the foreign-domestic divide with a National Counterterrorism Center.
- Unifying the intelligence community with a new National Intelligence Director.
- Unifying the many participants in the counterterrorism effort and their knowledge in a network-based information-sharing system that transcends traditional government boundaries.

- Unifying and strengthening congressional oversight to improve quality and accountability.
- Strengthening the FBI and homeland defenders (p. 399–400).

However, even before the report had been submitted to Congress, several pieces of legislation had been created and approved. The most important for aviation and transportation security at the time would be the Aviation and Transportation Security Act (United States Congress, 2001). This legislation would represent a dramatic shift in the way the nation's aviation security would be treated. Most importantly, this piece of legislation would create the Transportation Security Administration (TSA), an organization that would be charged with security screening at airports for both domestic and international travelers departing within the United States, assessing threats to transportation systems, the determination of watch-lists for passengers traveling on aircraft, airport security, and the inspection of cargo and passenger materials traveling within the nation's transportation networks. The TSA would be created as an agency under the Department of Transportation.

Additionally, the Aviation and Transportation Security Act would preview one of the Commission's recommendations and mandate the sharing of security threat information within government agencies including the Federal Aviation Administration. One of the mechanisms to facilitate this new interagency cooperation was the creation of the Transportation Security Oversight Board. The Board would be made of seven members that would include the Secretary of Transportation, the Attorney General, the Secretary of Defense, the Secretary of the Treasury, the Director of the Central Intelligence Agency, one member to represent the National Security Council, and one member representing the Office of Homeland Security (United States Congress, 2001).

Eventually, the Transportation Security Administration would be moved to the newly-created Department of Homeland Security. This department of the federal government, created via the Homeland Security Act of 2002, would be tasked to further improve inter-agency communication and intelligence-sharing by bringing together several different agencies charged with protecting the United States (United States Congress, 2002). Included in this new department would be the aforementioned TSA, and also the U.S. Customs and Border Protection, U.S. Coast Guard, U.S. Secret Service, and the Federal Emergency Management Agency, among others. While these groups would maintain their same mandates, it was felt that if they belonged within the same federal command structure, the systematic barriers that prevent information-sharing before September 11 would not exist within the same organization.

RECOMMENDATIONS FOR THE FUTURE

There are several opportunities to advance the role of aviation professionals in the future. Some of these include the use of unmanned technology and addressing security needs. Both will be discussed in this section of the chapter.

Unmanned Technology

It goes without saying that unmanned technology is the area poised for the most significant growth in the field of aviation. New technology is being developed on a daily basis that will impact almost every facet of the current aviation environment.

To start with, advances in Unmanned Aircraft Systems (UAS) and Unmanned Aircraft Vehicles (UAV) technology have added new capabilities in advanced weather prediction technologies. A recent experiment undertaken by the National Oceanic Atmospheric Administration's Unmanned Aerial Systems Sensing Hazards with Operational Unmanned Technology (SHOUT) attempted to use a NASA Global Hawk to predict hurricane activity during the 2016 hurricane season (Kren et. al., 2018). This UAS was equipped with 88 dropsondes, which are expendable devices created to study atmospheric conditions, and the UAS could remain on its mission for up to 24 hours, researching supplementary weather observations and prediction capability.

When conducting search-and-rescue operations, unmanned systems can allow for faster searches of missing people and increased coordination among the emergency personnel. For instance, a climber on Broad Peak in the Himalayas was found during a search mission using a common commercial drone (McRae et al., 2019). Unmanned systems can have a number of sensors and detection equipment fitted to assist in a search, such as communication equipment to better aid in coordination between responders when communication can be interrupted (McRae et al., 2021).

Some other lesser known, but still vital, aircraft weather assistance can come during wildfire incidents. A recent experiment with the University of Wyoming Atmospheric Science aircraft to study several parameters during the Rapid Deployments to Wildfires Experiment (RaDFIRE) (Clements et al., 2018). The University of Wyoming Aircraft, a King Air 200T, was deployed to the Pioneer Fire on August 29-30, 2016. During these two observation days, the King Air was equipped with various sensors including a W-band Wyoming Cloud Radar (WCR) and Wyoming Cloud Lidar (WCL), both of which could provide remote sensing information.

In addition to being an information and detection asset for fire responders on the ground, development is also ongoing for using unmanned systems to provide firefighting capability. In 2021, Google's parent company, Alphabet Inc., requested permission from the Federal Aviation Administration to begin testing an unmanned system that would be able to actually drop or spray firefighting materials directly on a fire (Grant, 2021).

There can obviously be a downside as well with any new technology. While unmanned systems can gather a wealth of information that incident commanders can use in their efforts, there is also the concern that ancillary information during emergency operations can also be collected and used in non-emergency capabilities (Hill, 2017). As such, privacy concerns have been raised by groups such as the American Civil Liberties Union on what information is collected during emergency responders' drone use, as well as how any information that is collected is stored.

Such technology is not limited to simply government operators, and that has proven to be an issue in any disaster response. Private and "hobbyist" unmanned system ownership and usage has increased as the cost of ownership of such systems has dropped dramatically. As such, there are increasing issues with civilian operators flying unmanned systems over fires and other emergency response areas without permission in order to "get a better look." These "hobbyist" drone operations put both themselves and emergency responders at risk with these unauthorized flights. Since the flight range is somewhat limited for smaller commercially-available unmanned systems that anybody can buy, civilian operators have to get in relatively close proximity of fires. This can put the operator at risk, particularly with a dynamic wildfire that can grow or shift in direction at a moment's notice. Because of this, people within the emergency disaster area might be impeding response to the area. Probably the most critical however, is that if unauthorized UAS operations are detected within an area of operation that has active aviation operations, air assets that would have otherwise been tasked with disaster response such as fighting a fire, are removed from the area in order to protect the pilots and those onboard the aircraft (Edge, 2018). With the removal of these air assets, fires can grow and become more dangerous to any at-risk people or property and disaster response can become far more complicated. To combat this, some locations in the United States have laws that would see any UAS pilot who flies their craft in any unauthorized area during an emergency facing criminal and civil penalties as well as significant fines.

In the near future, standards for the integration and operation of unmanned systems should be established to enable greater coordination among the various agencies that might respond to a disaster or incident. With the potential for multiple agencies responding to a single disaster such as a hurricane, and each agency potentially bringing their own equipment and technology, there exists the possibility for interference between the various systems. A standard for functionality including radio frequencies used, and reliability would also help develop better usability for unmanned systems. However, given the current rapid development of such technology, it should be noted that any establishment of standards and integration should not come at the cost of development and innovation. Investigation should also be established for air mobility solutions that would enable evacuation without the use of manned piloted vehicles. Such a system could be dispatched to a disaster location, loaded with an injured person, and then be sent automatically back to a safe location without the need for a piloted vehicle.

Finally, law enforcement and security organizations have also begun to utilize unmanned systems. Groups such as the U.S. Customs and Border Protection have been using unmanned systems such as the Predator B aircraft since 2006 (Gambler, 2017), and local law enforcement agencies have begun to utilize small unmanned systems for their own purposes (Police Foundation, 2018). With this increased use of unmanned system by law enforcement and security organizations, there is also the concern about privacy as well as civil rights issues in the utilization of these technologies. While law enforcement agencies have used traditional aircraft in the past, the surge of potential unmanned systems heightens some concerns on how these systems will be used and what policies and procedures will need to be put in place regarding their use.

Post-9/11 Security

After the events of September 11 and subsequent new regulations with regard to security, airports around the country would undergo a transformation. As highlighted in the 9/11 Commission's report, there were identified shortcomings in the screening of the hijackers, and procedures that could have been improved (National Commission on Terrorist Attacks Upon the United States, 2004). But simply increasing security at passenger checkpoints would not be sufficient to avoid new and existing security threats in a post-September 11 world. Almost all aspects of aviation would see some form of increased security, or hardening.

At the time of the attacks on September 11, security technology largely consisted of x-ray screening technology for bags and walk-through metal detectors for passengers and items on their person. While these pieces of technology were deemed adequate at the time, deficiencies were noted and improvements logically deemed necessary. New technology such as full-body "backscatter" devices would begin to be implemented in 2008, and fully deployed to all airports by 2013 at a cost of 2.1 billion dollars (Jansen, 2016).

While a number of police and security agencies already use airborne aviation assets extensively, including fixed-wing, rotary-wing, and unmanned systems, the same advances in sensor and communication technology can also assist these groups as well. However, there is again the same risk within the U.S. legal system about what these aviation tools can do and what data they can collect from the instruments they use, like the tools utilized by emergency managers. Case law is constantly evolving on these subjects, and care must be given to how such things are used and what data is collected during their use, especially with new unmanned systems.

CONCLUSION

Aviation tools can be an invaluable asset for emergency managers. Aircraft and unmanned systems can provide the ability to give responders the resources to see things that they wouldn't be able to see on the ground. They provide the ability to go places that ground or water-based transportation may not be able to go, especially if normal avenues of travel are destroyed by an emergency or disaster. They enable the movement and delivery of vital supplies that may otherwise have been too far away from the disaster to be of use. They provide the data on local conditions necessary to effectively manage the disaster response, including data on weather and local conditions. They provide airborne suppression of difficult-to-access disaster fire locations. In the end, however, they are the tools that the emergency responders can use, but the responders have to know how to use them. As such, these aviation tools need to be effectively managed themselves in order to provide these benefits.

New technology and regulations promise a new set of capabilities that aviation can provide to emergency responders. Unmanned aircraft and systems promise a wide variety of functions that would have been either unthinkable a few years ago or require far more expensive solutions that would have made them too costly. Every year, new technology is developed that increases the potential for these unmanned systems. It will be the role of emergency managers to coordinate and determine how these tools are developed and utilized most effectively and efficiently in the future.

CLASS DISCUSSION AND ESSAY QUESTIONS

1. How did flight move from dreams to actual transportation methods over time?
2. Why is aviation a source of disasters and terrorist attacks? What examples of this can you provide throughout history?
3. Could the functions of fire fighting, weather reconnaissance, search and rescue, damage assessment, and relief distribution occur without professional aviators? Why or why not?
4. Why is air traffic management vital for aviation in and after disaster situations?
5. How is unmanned aircraft technology benefiting and complicating emergency management and homeland security? What can be done to harness this technology while avoiding their negative aspects?

REFERENCES

Aviation Security. (n.d.). Retrieved September 5, 2021, from https://centennialofflight.net /essay/Government_Role/security/POL18.htm

Berliner, D. (1997). Chapter Three: Otto Lilienthal and the Glider. *Aviation: Reaching for the Sky*, 40, 40–51.

Clements Craig, B., Lareau Neil, P., Kingsmill David, E., Bowers Carrie, L., Camacho Chris, P., Bagley, R., & Braniff, D. (2018). The Rapid Deployments to Wildfires Experiment (RaDFIRE): Observations from the Fire Zone. *Bulletin of the American Meteorological Society*, 99(12), 2539–2560.

CNN. (2019, January 9). Helicopter Rescue: Dramatic Footage of Skilful Flying in French Alps. Retrieved August 31, 2019, from https://edition.cnn.com/2019/01/09/sport/skiing-french-alps-rescue-alpine-edge-spt-intl/index.html

Crouch, T. D. (2019). Alberto Santos-Dumont: Brazilian Aviator. *Encyclopedia Britannica*. Retrieved October 23, 2019, from https://www.britannica.com/biography/Alberto-Santos-Dumont

Dean, A. R., Chakraborty, C., & Failler, A. (2017). *Remembering Air India: The Art of Public Mourning*. The University of Alberta Press.

Dillenburger, S. P., Cochran, J. K., & Cammarano, V. R. (2013). Minimizing Supply Airdrop Collateral Damage Risk. *Socio-Economic Planning Sciences*, 47(1), 9–19. https://doi-org.ezproxy.uvu.edu/10.1016/j.seps.2012.09.001

Edge, S. (2018). Drones Clash with Firefighting Efforts. Retrieved from https://ezproxy.uvu.edu/login?url=http://search.ebscohost.com/login.aspx?direct=true&db=pwh&AN=2W61844452415&site=eds-live

Federal Aviation Administration. (2012). Airspace Management Plan for Disasters. Retrieved from https://info.publicintelligence.net/FAA-DisasterAirspaceManagement.pdf

Federal Bureau of Investigation. (n.d.). D. B. Cooper Hijacking. Federal Bureau of Investigation. Retrieved September 5, 2021, from https://www.fbi.gov/history/famous-cases/db-cooper-hijacking

Feigenbaum, A. (2007). The Hindenburg disaster. *Hindenburg Disaster*, 1–29.

Federal Emergency Management Agency. (2008). National Incident Management System. Retrieved from https://www.fema.gov/sites/default/files/2020-07/national_incident_management_system_dec2008.pdf

Federal Emergency Management Agency. (2016, April 5). Damage Assessment Operations Manual. Retrieved from https://www.fema.gov/sites/default/files/2020-07/Damage_Assessment_Manual_April62016.pdf

Gambler, R. (2017). Border Security Additional Actions Needed to Strengthen Collection of Unmanned Aerial Systems and Aerostats Data. *GAO Reports*, 2017: 1–42.

Grant, N. (2021). Google Seeks FAA Authorization to Test Drones for Firefighting. Bloomberg.Com, N.PAG-N.PAG.

Hill, K. (2017). Firefighting Drones to Assist Spokane Police on Investigations of Fatal Car Crashes. The Spokesman-Review. https://ezproxy.uvu.edu/login?url=http://search.ebscohost.com/login.aspx?direct=true&db=pwh&AN=2W63278570284&site=eds-live

History.com Editors. (2019). Wright Brothers. Retrieved October 23, 2019, from https://www.history.com/topics/inventions/wright-brothers

Homeland Security Digital Library. (n.d.). Dawson's Field Hijackings. Homeland Security Digital Library. Retrieved September 5, 2021, from https://www.hsdl.org/c/tl/dawsons-field-hijackings/

Jakab, P. (2013). Leonardo da Vinci and Flight. Retrieved June 8, 2021, from https://airandspace.si.edu/stories/editorial/leonardo-da-vinci-and-flight

Jansen, B. (2016, March 2). TSA Defends Full-Body Scanners at Airport Checkpoints. *USA TODAY*. Retrieved August 30, 2019, from https://www.usatoday.com/story/news/2016/03/02/tsa-defends-full-body-scanners-airport-checkpoints/81203030/

Japan Marks 20th Anniversary of JAL Crash, Worst Single-Plane Air Disaster. (n.d.). The Canadian Press. Retrieved March 15, 2021, from https://ezproxy.uvu.edu /login?url=http://search.ebscohost.com/login.aspx?direct=true&db=pwh&AN =MYO082138065005&site=eds-live

Kren, A. C., Cucurull, L., & Wang, H. (2018). Impact of UAS Global Hawk Dropsonde Data on Tropical and Extratropical Cyclone Forecasts in 2016. *Weather & Forecasting*, 33(5), 1121–1141. https://doi.org/10.1175/WAF-D-18-0029.1

Lemaire, D., & Kasserman, D. (2021). First Manned Balloon Flight. Salem Press Encyclopedia.

McRae, J. N., Gay, C. J., Nielsen, B. M., & Hunt, A. P. (2019). Using an Unmanned Aircraft System (Drone) to Conduct a Complex High Altitude Search and Rescue Operation: A Case Study. *Wilderness & Environmental Medicine*, 30(3), 287–290. https://doi-org.ezproxy.uvu.edu/10.1016/j.wem.2019.03.004

McRae, J. N., Nielsen, B. M., Gay, C. J., Hunt, A. P., & Nigh, A. D. (2021). Utilizing Drones to Restore and Maintain Radio Communication during Search and Rescue Operations. *Wilderness & Environmental Medicine*, 32(1), 41–46. https://doi.org /10.1016/j.wem.2020.11.002

National Commission on Terrorist Attacks Upon the United States. (2004). The 9/11 Commission Report. Retrieved from http://govinfo.library.unt.edu/911/report/ index.htm

National Search and Rescue Committee. (n.d.). National Search and Rescue Plan of the United States. Retrieved August 31, 2019, from https://www.dco.uscg.mil/Portals/9 /CG-5R/manuals/National_SAR_Plan_2016.pdf

National Wildfire Coordinating Group. (2017, April). Interagency Aerial Supervision Guide. Retrieved from https://www.nwcg.gov/sites/default/files/publications/pms505.pdf

Office of the Federal Coordinator for Meteorology. (2019). National Hurricane Operations Plan. Retrieved August 25, 2019, from https://www.ofcm.gov/publica-tions/nhop/nhop2.htm

Pedzich, J. (2014, November 1). TWA Flight 800. *Library Journal*, 139(18), 53.

Police Foundation. (7 C.E. 2018). Police Foundation Launches New Center for Unmanned Aircraft Systems in Public Safety. Business Wire (English).

Quezzaire, P. (2017). Biograohical information. *Ovid*, 1–2.

Riding, A. (2000, July 26). The Concorde Crash: The Overview. *Die in First Crash of a Concorde. The New York Times*. https://www.nytimes.com/2000/07/26/world/the -concorde-crash-the-overview-113-die-in-first-crash-of-a-concorde.html

Shaw, R. J. (Ed.). (2014). History of Flight. Retrieved October 23, 2019, from https:// www.grc.nasa.gov/WWW/K-12/UEET/StudentSite/historyofflight.html

Sharp, T. (2019). The First Hot-Air Balloon. Space.com. Retrieved October 23, 2019, from https://www.space.com/16595-montgolfiers-first-balloon-flight.html

The Earliest "Aircraft". (2018). *China Today*, 67(4), 66–69.

The Editors of Encyclopedia Britannica. (2019). André-Jacques Garnerin. Retrieved October 23, 2019, from. *Encyclopedia Britannica Website*: https://www.britannica .com/biography/Andre-Jacques-Garnerin

The Library of Congress. (2003). Timeline of Flight: The Dream of Flight. Retrieved June 8, 2021 from https://www.loc.gov/exhibits/dreamofflight/dream-timeline.html

United States Coast Guard. (n.d.). U.S. Coast Guard Office of Search and Rescue (CG-SAR). Retrieved August 31, 2019, from https://www.dco.uscg.mil/Our -Organization/Assistant-Commandant-for-Response-Policy-CG-5R/Office-of -Incident-Management-Preparedness-CG-5RI/US-Coast-Guard-Office-of-Search -and-Rescue-CG-SAR/

United States Congress. (2001). S.1447 - Aviation and Transportation Security Act. Retrieved from https://www.congress.gov/bill/107th-congress/senate-bill/1447

United States Congress. (2002). H.R.5005 - Homeland Security Act of 2002. Retrieved from https://www.congress.gov/bill/107th-congress/house-bill/5005?q=%7B%22search%22%3A%5B%22department+of+homeland+security%22%5D%7D&s=3&r=1

United States Air Force. (2014, April 4). Air Force Rescue Coordination Center: CONR-1A. Retrieved August 31, 2019, from https://www.1af.acc.af.mil/Library/Fact-Sheets/Display/Article/289622/air-force-rescue-coordination-center/

United States Department of Commerce; National Oceanic and Atmospheric Administration. (n.d.). Hurricane Katrina - August 2005. Retrieved August 19, 2019, from https://www.weather.gov/mob/katrina

Warner, M. B. (2001). Lessons of Lockerbie. *National Journal*, 33(46–47), 3586.

We Were There; In their own words, eight people who dealt head-on with one of the greatest disasters in U.S. history share their stories of heroism and survival. Difficulty grew as rescue efforts moved to smaller rooftops. (2005, September 18). Florida Times Union, D. https://link.gale.com/apps/doc/A136931748/STND?u=utahvalley&sid=bookmark-STND&xid=05f3a1b5

Williams, J. (2015). Into the Eye: Tracing the History of the Hurricane Hunters. *Weatherwise*, 68(5), 37. https://doi.org/10.1080/00431672.2015.1067110

Ziomek, J. (2020). Disaster on Tenerife. *Aviation History*, 31(1), 42–49.

CHAPTER 14

Military Support for Civil Authorities Responding to Domestic Disasters and Emergencies

Limitations, Authorities and Capabilities

Michael L. Smidt

INTRODUCTION

The armed forces of the United States are superbly "manned, trained, and equipped" to fight and win our nation's wars (Armed Forces, 10 U.S.C. § 101(a)(4) and Coast Guard, 14 U.S.C. §§ 101, 102; National Security Strategy, 2017). The United States military stands at the ready, heavily resourced and endowed with awesome warfighting capabilities to defend the United States and its interests.

Not surprisingly, however, that same overwhelming combat power that enables the armed forces to be successful on the battlefield could also translate to incredible resources and capabilities available to respond to domestic man-made and natural disasters and emergencies. Certainly most Americans have seen images on the nightly news of military helicopters and crews (originally designed to perform in combat) rescuing hurricane or flood survivors from the rooftops of homes or businesses. And of late, most have seen the *Mercy* and *Comfort*, two military hospital ships, cruise into New York and Los Angeles harbors in response to the COVID-19 pandemic.

Although the armed forces are perfectly well suited to perform prevention and response missions related to large-scale catastrophes, there are many legal and policy limitations on the participation of the armed forces in domestic matters. During most domestic emergencies, the military primarily provides support to civilian organizations such as the Federal Emergency Management Agency under the direction of the Department of Homeland Security, the Federal Bureau of Investigation (FBI), or the Department of Justice. In fact, the U.S. Constitution, as well as federal law and policy, restrains the use of the armed forces domestically.

Nevertheless, there are various laws and policies, when triggered, that provide the needed emergency authorities for the military to play a limited but significant support role to other federal, state, tribal, and local agencies involved in these domestic catastrophes.

DOI: 10.4324/9781003350729-14

This chapter will explore the use of the armed forces during domestic emergencies. First, the chapter will review the history of the armed forces, primarily in the context of supporting civil authorities during domestic challenges. Next, this chapter will discuss the mission of the armed forces in response to terrorism on the mainland including homeland defense, homeland security, and support to civil authorities. Third, this chapter will explore operations focused on man-made and natural disasters. This chapter will also discuss authorities and policies related to natural and man-made disasters such as a Commander's inherent immediate response authority, the use of the military during domestic civil disobediences, special events, chemical, biological, radiological and nuclear disasters, public health emergencies, mass migration emergencies and counter-drug applications. Finally, the chapter will consider some of the current challenges in using the military domestically with a few recommendations for change.

HISTORY OF THE PROFESSION

In 1675, in what might be considered the first significant counter-terror or counter-insurgency operation in the Americas, the Native-American Pokunoket Chief, Metacom, also known as King Philip, led members of the Wampanoag, Nipmuck, Mohegan, Mohawk, Pocumtuck, and Narragansett tribes in an uprising against the New England colonists. The colonists banded together and formed a militia of over 1,000 men and 150 Native-American sympathizers. The fighting lasted 14 months and left 12 frontier towns destroyed. Metacom was eventually captured and beheaded, and some of his supporters escaped to Canada; others surrendered and were sold into slavery. Some have opined that this was one of the first steps taken in carving out a unique American identity. It arguably demonstrated the preference of the early colonists to rely on militias in domestic matters as opposed to maintaining a standing army to provide for the common defense (Brooks, 2017; Warren, 2023; History.com, 2019a; Wikipedia, 2020).

Later on, the colonists believed that King George and the British Parliament had routinely violated their rights. The Framers of the U.S. Constitution sought to avoid recreating an all-powerful executive, an imperial Congress, or a secret or political court. They sought to defuse the power between these branches of government horizontally by separating, describing, and limiting their respective powers and by providing certain checks and balances so no branch could have unlimited power in their own sphere.

The Framers also sought to defuse government power vertically through the concept of federalism where there would essentially be two governments, state and federal, running parallel with one another with most of the power, including the police power, residing with the states. After all, it was the states that created the federal government and not the other way around. The concept of federalism is important to understanding why the active duty and National Guard troops have different authorities even though their uniforms and equipment are virtually identical.

The Framers also had a justifiable and healthy fear of maintaining a large standing army. Early Americans viewed themselves as the victims of an abusive British government, concluding the British Army was responsible for enforcing the abusive practices of King George and the British Parliament. Of all the abuses, the one that seems to have troubled them the most was taxation without any sort of representation in the government. Adding insult to injury, the taxes the colonists were paying were being used to finance the very army that was seen by the colonists as the tool of their repression by the British (Declaration and Resolves, 1774).

Once the colonists gained their independence, they no longer enjoyed the protection of the British armed forces. The newly established republic was on its own and would need to provide for its own defense (U.S. Constitution Preamble). This, along with the experience of an ineffective central government during the War of Independence, taught them they needed an executive branch capable of command and control over the military. From the time of their independence until the ratification of the Constitution, there was no head of state, no king, no prime minister, and no president over the nascent republic. The Framers empowered Congress with the power to tax to support its military efforts.

The oldest branch of the organized armed forces of the United States, the U.S. Army, actually predates the colonies' independence from England, and was established in 1775 by the Second Continental Congress. It was made clear to the Framers during the War of Independence that while they preferred state militias, these alone were insufficient to deal with external foreign threats.

Now that it was on its own, the nascent United States would need to be able to participate in international trade to survive economically. The Framers realized early on that the British Navy would no longer protect American interests at home or abroad; this would require the establishment of a navy. The United States was in need of a federal Navy, and to a lesser degree, a standing conventional federal Army to protect U.S. interests at home and abroad. The benefits of a navy were on full display when President Thomas Jefferson dispatched the Navy and Marine Corps to the Mediterranean Sea to protect U.S. commercial shipping against the so-called Barbary Pirates (Corn et al., 2019).

The Framers built a constitutional framework that sought to reduce the potential domestic coercive power of the military, and particularly the Army. For example, the President is the Commander and Chief of the armed forces (U.S. Const. art II, §2, cl. 1), but it is Congress that authorizes and creates the Army and the Navy that the President commands. Congress is authorized "To raise and support Armies, but no Appropriation of Money to that Use shall be for a longer Term than two Years." In addition to an army, the Framers realized that a navy would be crucial. The Constitution empowers Congress "To provide and maintain a navy." Notice there is a two-year limit on appropriations for the Army in the Constitution, but no such limit on the Navy (U.S. Const. art I, §8, cl. 12 and 13).

The Constitution gives Congress the power to "raise and support" an army and the authority to "provide and maintain" a navy. This difference in language seems to suggest that the Framers were more inclined to support a standing navy as opposed to a standing army. "Raise and support" an army seems to suggest a short-term reaction to a specific problem. Conversely, "provide and maintain" a navy suggests a standing force, a constant force, anxiously engaged in the defense of the nation and its interests abroad.

Finally, the Constitution protects Americans from having to house American forces in their homes, even during a time of war, without their consent or a Congressional mandate (U.S. Const. amend. III). Having to "quarter" troops in their homes would be a form of taxation that would directly benefit the Army. At worst, quartering soldiers in the homes of citizens essentially constitutes a bloodless but effective invasion and occupation by military forces whose dislodgment would be next to impossible; the Army could enforce federal policy against the will of the people. At best, quartering soldiers would create a perception of coercion that would likely chill political activities, especially those critical of the government.

The Constitution allows for the creation of state militias under the command of the Governor (U.S. Const. art. I, § 8, cl. 15, 16; U.S. Const. art. I, § 10, cl. 3; U.S. Const. amend. II and X). The State carries with it "police power," the inherent authority to draft and enforce laws to protect persons and property within its territory (National Guard Bureau, 2019; CLAMO, 2018). The Governor can use the state militia to enforce state and local laws. The Constitution allows Congress to call up the militia into federal service and makes clear that the President is the Commander and Chief of the militia when called into the service of the United States (U.S. Const. art. I, § 8, cl. 15, 16; U.S. Const. art. I, § 10, cl. 3; U.S. Const. art. II, § 2, cl. 1). The National Guard and Air National Guard (both referred to as the National Guard) have come to mean organized state militias, created and trained at federal expense to conduct both federal as well as state missions. The National Guard is essentially two "overlapping organizations": the National Guard of the various states and the National Guard of the United States (CLAMO, 2018; National Guard Act, 73 Pub. L. § 18).

Even though the Constitution protects the state militia system (known in modern times as the National Guard), federal troops have been used domestically at times in U.S. history when the state militia is overwhelmed or where the state itself is seen as condoning activities that the federal government believes trample on the rights of U.S. citizens. Consider, for example, the Whiskey Rebellion in 1794, when President Washington, in his role of Commander and Chief, led the federal forces. Moreover, armed forces participation in responses to natural disasters and emergencies has been significant since the Truman era (Library of Congress, 2017), and will undoubtedly continue into the future.

Modern concepts of homeland defense and homeland security arguably find their genesis in cold war. Following the Second World War and the rapid development and proliferation of nuclear weapons and delivery platforms such as long-range bombers, nuclear submarines, and intercontinental ballistic missiles, many in the United States were concerned about the potential of an adversarial nuclear weapons attack on the United States homeland. Some citizens began building shelters on their private property in an attempt to protect their own families against such an attack. In schools across the nation, children were taught to "duck and cover" should a warning in advance of such an attack go out. The federal government also led efforts to establish community shelters. Equipment such as radiation monitoring kits were distributed as well (Bradbury Science Museum, "Civil Defense and the Cold War"). While there was disagreement over the need for and the efficacy of such shelters, the Federal Defense Shelter Act of 1950 provided significant funding for the shelter initiative. Moreover, the media contributed to the perceived need for shelters and organized civil defense through its doomsday-like predictions of the aftermath of a thermonuclear exchange. Nonetheless, this media-fueled debate energized policy-makers to plan for and resource civil defense requirements and the protection of U.S. citizens in a thoughtful and purposeful manner.

As is the case with most other significant policy matters, the Homeland Defense and Homeland Security experience in the United Sates has been one marked with constant change, both in terms of policy and within the agencies that carry out those critical functions. These changes reflect the evolution of the threats to the United States, the nature, size, and scope of natural disasters, the changes in policy taken by the various Presidential administrations, and the creation and modification of agencies, funding, and laws generated by Congress. For example, one of the most important recent drivers of change was the terrorist attacks of 9/11. These attacks on the United States homeland generated increased funding, a focus on homeland security, the creation of the Department of Homeland Security, and new policies and missions for the Department of Defense, the Department of Justice, and other intelligence agencies. Additionally, new laws were designed to assist in the prevention, detection, and response to potential terror threats.

But it has not just been man-made disasters that have acted as agents of change. The devastation caused by earthquakes and significant storms such as Hurricane Katrina showed that the country remains vulnerable to natural disasters (DHS Civil Defense, 2006). In addition and more recently, the COVID-19 pandemic, mass migration, the civil unrest of 2021, and cyberattacks have demonstrated that the United States is likely to continue to face an evolving set of hazards, threats, and emergencies. For these reasons:

> [C]ivil defense began with the desire to involve Americans in the protection of their fellow citizens and critical infrastructure from destruction at the hands of our enemies. It has evolved over time to encompass coordinated, professional efforts, involving all levels of government, the private sector, and citizens to address wide ranges of disaster and attack scenarios.
>
> (DHS Civil Defense, 2006)

RELATION OF THE MILITARY TO WAR AND TERRORISM

The relationship of the military to war is fairly straightforward. If the United States or its interests are threatened by an enemy aggressor, the President may deploy military assets around the globe in offensive or defensive postures. Throughout history, the U.S. armed services have been sent to many traditional battlefields including those in Europe, Japan, Korea, Vietnam, and Iraq to name a few. When the threat of nuclear war has been heightened as it was during the Cuban Missile Crisis, the military has put out nuclear weapons systems on the highest levels of alert.

More recently, terrorist attacks have also involved the military in active operations. While described in many different ways, terrorism is usually defined by the armed forces of the United States as "the unlawful use of violence or threat of violence, often motivated by religious, political, or other ideological beliefs, to instill fear and coerce governments or societies in pursuit of goals that are usually political" (CJCS Joint Pub. 3-26, 2014). Terrorists often seek to magnify the psychological impact of an attack by targeting locations frequented by civilians, or by using means designed to strike terror in the hearts of potential victims. Their targets do not necessarily or always have significant military value, such as a mosque or shopping mall, but the terrorists believe that attacking the target may have a significant psychological impact, which may in turn contribute to the influence they ultimately seek.

In response to war or terrorism, the government relies on the military to detect, deter, prevent, or defeat threats. But, the threats – whether occurring against our allies or against our national territory – may alter when, where, and to what extent the military becomes involved. And, as will be illustrated, the military is not the only actor involved in war. It is not solely responsible for dealing with terrorism either.

Several measures may be taken by the government to protect Americans, our way of life, and our interests internationally or at home. These measures are commonly known as counterterrorism operations, homeland defense (HD), homeland security (HS), and Defense Support of Civil Authorities (DSCA). While they are separate and distinct operations, they can be overlapping. They can also occur simultaneously, and it is entirely possible to transition from one operation to another during the same incident (CJCS Joint Pub. 3-27, 2018; CJCS Joint Pub. 3-28, 2018; HSC National Strategy for Homeland Security, 2017; DOD Strategy for Homeland Defense and Defense Support of Civil Authorities, 2013; DHS Strategic Plan, 2019).

As will be illustrated, the distinction between them can be somewhat complicated. For instance, what if a terror threat is particularly catastrophic – tantamount to a military attack in terms of potential damage and sophistication? What if the act is planned and set in motion outside of the United States, initiated from overseas, and potentially involves foreign powers? What if the planned act of terror involves a weapon of mass destruction? Such an act of terror could be viewed as a criminal act writ large, and a military lead may be the best option for prevention and/or as a response. Regardless, each of these measures will be discussed below.

COUNTERTERRORISM

Counterterror activities and operations are taken to neutralize terrorists, their organizations, and networks in order to render them incapable of using violence to instill fear and coerce governments or societies to achieve their goals. These types of measures require the participation of many departments and individuals. For instance, the Department of State is the lead federal foreign affairs agency and therefore plays a central role in recommendations of counterterrorism policies. However, the CIA also shares information with the President, who may then decide if a counterterrorism action is warranted and justified.

Nevertheless, it is often the military that launches airborne attacks or sends troops into harm's way to neutralize threats. Visible examples of this include the lengthy military operations in Afghanistan or other quicker strikes in Pakistan, Syria, Iran, or various nations in Africa and Asia. In many cases, the goal of counterterrorism is to attack and kill potential or actual perpetrators so future attacks can be thwarted.

HOMELAND DEFENSE

While the military is most often involved in operations outside of the United States, the Department of Defense is also the lead on large-scale threats against the continental United States. For example, if a foreign power were to attempt to invade or attack the United States, the Department of Defense would take the lead as part of its Homeland Defense mission.

Homeland defense is defense operations against traditional external threats or aggression (e.g., nation-state conventional forces or weapons of mass destruction [WMD] attack), and against external asymmetrical threats that are outside of the scope of HS operations. Homeland Defense is therefore the "protection of US sovereignty, territory, domestic population, and critical infrastructure against external threats and aggression, as directed by the President." It is specifically designed to repel attacks against the U.S. homeland (in contrast to military operations oversees).

HOMELAND SECURITY

If an attack is not of substantial size, scope, and duration to warrant the involvement of the military in homeland defense, the President may decide to activate the homeland security mission. Homeland Security (HS) consists of those national efforts taken to prevent and protect the United States against terror attacks, secure and manage the borders, and enforce immigration. Homeland Security is primarily a law enforcement mission.

Acts and potential acts of terror in the United States are a unique challenge. Acts of terror, if large enough in scope, have aspects of a military attack while also constituting a significant criminal act. An act of terrorism is virtually always a violation of state or federal law. But these events may also threaten security, damage infrastructure, kill or injure people, and cause widespread disruption.

The Department of Justice, acting through the FBI, has the lead for investigating acts of terror and the lead for intelligence collection efforts within the United States against potential terror activities (CJCS Joint Pub. 3-26, 2014; CJCS Joint Pub. 3-27, 2018; CJCS Joint Pub. 3-28, 2018; White House, PDD/NSC, 1995; HSC National Strategy for Homeland Security, 2007). The Attorney General (normally working through the FBI) is responsible for the law enforcement response and criminal investigations (CJCS Joint Pub. 3-26, 2014).

The Department of Homeland Security is the lead federal agency for other aspects of Homeland Security (e.g., investigation, security of borders and critical infrastructure, and consequence management). It addresses and coordinates federal operations in the homeland to anticipate, prepare for, respond to, and recover from terrorist attacks.

In the vast majority of cases, the role of the Department of Defense against acts of terror in the United States is one of providing support to the Department of Justice, the Department of Homeland Security, and to other federal and state agencies (like emergency management) involved in incident management. This brings us to the concept of support to civil authorities.

SUPPORT TO CIVIL AUTHORITIES

In terms of the homeland, the primary focus of the armed forces is Defense Support to Civil Authorities (DSCA). Defense Support to Civil Authorities is support provided by federal military forces, including the National Guard when in a federal status, in response to a request for assistance by civil authorities for domestic emergencies, disasters, special events, and support to civil law enforcement. DSCA is only provided in the homeland, as it is a domestic category of military operations (CJCS Joint Pub. 3-28, 2018). Examples of DSCA may include detection of weapons of mass destruction, flood mitigations (e.g., sandbags), perimeter control, debris removal, etc.

MILITARY ROLES IN DISASTERS/EMERGENCY MANAGEMENT/HOMELAND SECURITY

The military possesses significant potential to respond to and support other agencies involved in emergency management and homeland security. The primary mission of the military is to deter adversaries, and if that fails, to be successful against threats to national security. The military's function, authorities, equipment, and personnel are all focused on its primary mission of defense. However, the military has a history of providing support during disasters, both natural and man-made. Under the direction and lead of the Department of Homeland Security and the Federal Emergency Management Agency (FEMA), the military stands by to provide needed support when directed to do so.

The role of the military in response to disasters and emergencies is generally one of support to other federal, state, and local agencies. Typically, upon request from a state Governor, or at the direction of the President or Secretary of Defense, the military provides support to the local, tribal, state, and federal agencies involved in emergency management (DOD Dir. 3025.18, 2018). Department of Defense support provided to the civil authorities during emergencies and disasters is referred to as Defense Support to Civil Authorities (DSCA). In most cases, the military will seek reimbursement for the support provided to these civil authorities.

The military ordinarily requires two things in order for it to respond to a disaster or emergency. First, the authority, usually in the form of a statute, must exist. While the President is the Commander and Chief of the military, his or her authority to deploy the force during a domestic emergency is limited to whatever inherent authority Article II of the Constitution provides to the President as the Chief Executive and Commander and Chief, and whatever authority Congress has granted to the President by statute or by a funding mechanism such as an appropriation. Statutory authority is important; if it applies, Congress delegates whatever Article I Constitutional authority Congress has to authorize the use of the military to the President, which is then coupled with his inherent Constitutional Article II power. If there is an appropriation of funds by Congress for a given operation, it may be viewed as Congressional approval by implication. Therefore, the military must first identify proper authority, which is usually in the form of a statute, before the military can provide support to domestic civil authorities.

Second, there must be an appropriate approving official. For example, the Insurrection Act provides the authority to use the military during incidents of civil disobedience, but the President must approve such a use of the armed forces (Insurrection Act, 10 U.S.C. §§ 251–255). As will be discussed, in certain emergency situations, even a local military installation commander has the authority to approve the use of his/her troops in response to disasters or emergencies in his/her area. Typically, whether it is the President or a local commander, the approving official issues "orders" to provide the requested support. Some orders are simple verbal directives, while others are formal and detailed, and may include specific guidance such as what Rules for the Use of Force will apply (CJCS Inst. 3121.01B, 2008; CJCS Execute Order, 2009).

As is pointed out by Corn et al., the title "first responder" carries with it a legal connotation as well as the commonly understood use of the term, meaning the first to respond to a serious incident (Corn et al., 2019). First responders should be the first to respond from a legal authority standpoint as well as a pragmatic one. Local and Tribal first responders have the initial jurisdiction, authority, and responsibility to respond first to a disaster or emergency. If they are incapable of handling the incident or are over-whelmed, they can turn to the state government for assistance. The Governor's police power is quite extensive, and he or she can exercise that power by way of the National Guard. Should the state's resources, including the National Guard, prove to be inad-equate, the Governor can ask for assistance from neighboring states or from the federal government and its armed forces. By calling on first responders first, not only are they ordinarily the first to be capable of responding because of location and understanding of the people and area involved, they are also the legal and Constitutional preference based on the notions of federalism, authorities, and funding.

The Robert T. Stafford Relief and Emergency Assistance Act (Stafford Act) was promulgated in 1974 and is the primary federal statutory authority enabling the mili-tary to participate by providing support during disaster relief activities (Stafford Act, 42 U.S.C. §§ 5122 et seq.). The Department of Homeland Security is the lead federal agency in disaster relief operations and the focal point for "natural and man-made crises and emergency planning" (Homeland Security Act, 6 U.S.C. §§ 101 et seq.). As a result of the Homeland Security Act of 2002, the Federal Emergency Management Agency and 22 other agencies became part of the Department of Homeland Security on March 1, 2003. Typically, FEMA is the lead for DHS. Most support to local, Tribal, and state governments by the military falls under one of three categories: 1) Disaster Relief and Emergency Response, 2) Support to Law Enforcement, and 3) Special Events and other Domestic Activities (CJCS Joint Pub. 3-28, 2018).

Disaster Relief

The Stafford Act delegates to the President the power to declare a major disaster or emergency and to provide federal support. This ordinarily follows a request to do so by a Governor where he/she certifies that the state has activated its resources and capabilities, but lacks the ability to effectively respond to the crisis without federal assistance. The Governor must also generally certify they can meet the reimbursement requirements (Stafford Act, 42 U.S.C. § 5170). The statutory definition of a "major disaster" includes such things as hurricanes, tornados, earthquakes, tsunamis, and other similar catastrophic events. The definition covers not only natural disasters, but man-made disasters such as the use of a weapon of mass destruction (WMD) where a fire or explosion is involved (Stafford Act, 42 U.S.C. § 5122(2)). When a major disaster is declared, the Stafford Act gives the President authority to direct a very broad assortment of support activities (Stafford Act, 42 U.S.C. §§ 5170a–5198h).

In addition to a "major disaster," the President can also, under certain circumstances, declare an "emergency" (Stafford Act, 42 U.S.C. § 5122(1)). Unlike a major disaster, the President can declare an emergency *sua sponte*, on his or her own, without a request from a Governor, where the emergency "involves a subject area for which, under the Constitution or laws of the United States, the United States exercises exclusive or preeminent responsibility and authority" (Stafford Act, 42 U.S.C. § 5191(b)). Such an emergency is even more broadly defined than is a major disaster; virtually any use of a WMD would meet the definition of emergency, with or without fire or an explosion which would be necessary for a "major disaster." And unlike a major disaster, in an emergency the President can order support with or without reimbursement.

However, the assistance that can be provided in response to an emergency is more limited than the potential support in a disaster. Each emergency has a $5 million cap unless the President determines there is an immediate and ongoing risk to lives, property, public health, or safety, and also that the proposed aid must be provided in a timely fashion (Stafford Act, 42 U.S.C. § 5193). The President may authorize emergency relief in the form of technical and advisory assistance, issue hazard and risk warnings, broadcast public health and safety information, debris removal, temporary housing, assist local and state governments in the distribution of food, medicine, expedited federal assistance, and other consumable supplies (Stafford Act, 42 U.S.C. § 5192(a)). Therefore, it is important for a participant in a DSCA operation to know whether they are operating under a Presidential declaration of an emergency or a major disaster, what the Governor is requesting, and what the President has approved.

The Department of Defense implementation of the Stafford Act can be found in Department of Defense Directive 3025.18, Defense Support of Civil Authorities (DSCA). The Directive and an associated manual provide guidance for support requests to the Department of Defense (DOD Manual 3025.01, 2017). The Directive applies to the "military departments" and to the National Guard "when under federal command and control." Federal military forces employed for DSCA activities are to remain under federal military command and control at all times, even though FEMA might be in charge over-all of the federal response to the disaster (DOD Dir. 3025.18, 2018).

DSCA is initiated by a request for the Department of Defense assistance from civil authorities or when directed without a request by the President or Secretary of Defense. Requests for military support are to be in writing and will include a commitment to reim-burse the Department of Defense in accordance with "The Economy Act" (Economy Act, 31 U.S.C. § 1535). The Department of Defense must then apply the so-called "CARRLL" factors to evaluate whether the Department should honor the request. The CARRLL fac-tors include:

1) Cost (including the source of the funding and the effect on the Department of Defense budget);
2) Appropriateness (whether providing the requested support is in the interest of the Department of Defense);
3) Readiness (impact on the Department of Defense's ability to perform its other pri-mary missions);
4) Risk (safety of the Department of Defense personnel);
5) Legality (compliance with the laws); and
6) Lethality (potential use of lethal force by or against the Department of Defense)
(DOD Dir. 3025.18, 2018).

Immediate Response Authority

Local military commanders have been given a powerful tool via the Department of Defense policy to assist civil authorities responding to "imminently serious conditions" where the commander believes he or she can provide support that may "save lives, pre-vent human suffering, or mitigate great property damage" (DOD Dir. 3025.18, 2018).

Referred to as "Immediate Response Authority," after receiving a request for sup-port from a civil authority "where time does not permit approval from higher authority," a federal military commander, Head of Department of Defense Components, and/or a responsible Department of Defense civilian official may provide an immediate response by "temporarily employing the resources under their control, subject to any supplemen-tal direction provided by higher headquarters" (DOD Dir. 3025.18, 2018). Certainly this reduction in bureaucracy could potentially result in large gains in responsiveness. Immediate Response Authority serves to reduce approval times because the decision to provide support can be made at the local or regional level. Moreover, because of prox-imity, a local commander is in a much better position to quicky assess the problem and prepare a response. And finally, a local commander is likely to be familiar with area, the civilian first responders and the infrastructure.

The Directive does not place an absolute mileage limit from the relevant installation to the crisis. Instead, the Directive requires that in providing a response, commanders and Department of Defense officials need to "exercise judgement" in determining the maxi-mum allowable response distance. Although the relevant commander or Department of Defense official can provide an immediate response without seeking higher approval, the Directive does contain various notice requirements. The support "shall end when the necessity giving rise to the response is no longer present," such as when other agen-cies can provide sufficient resources. The immediate response must also end not later than 72 hours after the request for assistance is received. Where "appropriate or legally required," support should be provided on a cost-reimbursable basis. However, the support should not be delayed or denied if the recipient is unable or unwilling to reimburse the Department of Defense (DOD Dir. 3025.18, 2018).

The Directive explains that, "Immediate response authority does not permit actions that would subject civilians to the use of military power that is regulatory, prescriptive, proscriptive, or compulsory." This means that even when a commander invokes his or her immediate response authority, the Posse Comitatus Act still applies (DOD Dir. 3025.18, 2018; CLAMO, 2018; CJCS Joint Pub. 3-28, 2018). The Posse Comitatus Act will be discussed below.

Civil Disturbance Operations

This is an area that may see significant changes in the near future. When this chapter was written, violent protests or riots were playing out in many cities across the country in response to the death of George Floyd while in Minneapolis Police Department custody (Hernandez et al., 2020). Immediately after turning the calendar page on 2020, on January 6, 2021, a large group of disgruntled (President) Trump supporters overwhelmed the Capitol Police and stormed the U.S. Capitol Building (Myers and Winkie, 2021). Because many of those involved in the violence questioned the integrity of the election results, there was great concern that violence would once again erupt during the inauguration of President Biden. In response, thousands of National Guard soldiers and airmen were activated and deployed to Washington (Booker, 2021). Thankfully, it appears, the inauguration went off without a hitch.

A little less than a week after the inauguration, some of those National Guard troops headed home. However, thousands remained in Capitol region and for weeks or even months (Dickstein, 2021). Ironically, in certain northwestern cities such as Portland, Oregon, and Seattle, Washington, mob violence appears to have raised its head once more. Unlike those who participated in the January 6, 2021, storming of the Capitol Building, these groups appear to be left-leaning or anarchists (Ailworth, 2021).

The question here is what role the military – both National Guard and active forces – should play in civil disturbances. The general laws, policies, and authorities discussed below have not really changed in years. However, that may not be the case following the tumult of 2020.

As a general rule, local first responders are the first to respond factually and legally to civil unrest. If they are incapable of handling the issue, a Governor may choose to call out the National Guard. If the state is overwhelmed, the Governor may request that the President deploy active duty troops. In certain cases, the President can deploy troops without such a request from a Governor.

Both the Constitution and statutory law give the President the authority to call out the armed forces in response to certain domestic security threats. In addition to being the Commander and Chief, he/she is Chief Executive for the nation and has the Constitutional responsibility to "take care that the laws be faithfully executed" (U.S. Const. art. II, § 1, cl. 1; art. II, § 2, cl. 1; and art. II, § 3). It is his or her duty to ensure that the government is functioning so that the Constitution and federal law, as established by Congress, can be executed and citizens can receive the protections and services the government is supposed to provide. Congress passed the Insurrection Act, which gives the President the authority to use the armed forces during large-scale acts of civil disobedience (Insurrection Act, 10 U.S.C. §§ 251–255).

Pursuant to the Insurrection Act, the President can send federal armed forces to a state dealing with an insurrection where either the state legislature or Governor asks for federal assistance. The President can call into federal service other state militias and "use such of the armed forces as he considers necessary to suppress the insurrection" (Insurrection Act, 10 U.S.C. § 2251). The focus of this particular statute is to assist the state, upon request, in restoring order.

What about when that violence occurs in the District of Columbia where there is no Governor? The President is the Commander and Chief of the Washington, D.C., National Guard. However, he/she has delegated the authority to call out the Washington, D.C., National Guard to the Secretary of Defense, and that has further been delegated to the Secretary of the Army ("About Us," 2021).

Under certain conditions, the Insurrection Act gives authority to the President to act even without a request from the state (Insurrection Act, 10 U.S.C. § 252). Under this provision, the President could authorize the use of federal troops to put down an insurrection led by the state itself, for example, a state's refusal to desegregate public schools where a federal court has ordered such compliance. There is, however, a requirement for the President to determine whether enforcement of the laws by the courts is practical.

In a similar provision, the President can also act without a request under various situations, such as where the state is not enforcing state law, or where the state is refusing to provide certain citizens equal protection. There is also other authority a President could use to enforce federal law should the state refuse to do so, such as the Civil Rights Act (Insurrection Act, 10 U.S.C. § 254). Of course, this is not just limited to potential recalcitrant state actors. This authority could be used against non-state actors as well, such as when activities constitute a rebellion. Whenever the President relies on the Insurrection Act, he/she must order the insurgents to disperse.

The Insurrection Act is a statutory exception to the Posse Comitatus Act (DOD Dir. 3025.18, 2018). Therefore, federal troops involved in combatting an insurrection could be directed to support law enforcement by actively enforcing the law. The Department of Defense tends to refer to these potential operations pursuant to the Insurrection Act as Civil Disobedience Operations (DOD Dir. 3025.18, 2018). A detailed discussion of these operations is beyond the limited scope of this chapter. For those interested in a deeper dive into this topic, consider reviewing the U.S. Army Judge Advocate General's Domestic Operational Law Handbook (CLAMO, 2018). Only the President can authorize the military to participate in Civil Disobedience Operations, and military units involved must remain in the military chain of command (DOD Dir. 3025.18, 2018).

Commander's Emergency Authority

Similar to the President's national authority to respond to an insurrection in accordance with his/her inherent Constitutional powers, or with the statutory authority provided in the Insurrection Act, a local military commander has local-level "Emergency Authority" (DOD Dir. 3025.18, 2018). It may appear to be the same authority as a commander's inherent response authority, but it is not. For starters, unlike the inherent response authority, a commander's emergency authority is an exception to the Posse Comitatus Act, which will be discussed below. There is no civil authority request requirement, and the commander should only respond under the extraordinary emergency authority where authorization by the President is impossible (CJCS Joint Pub. 3-28, 2018).

This authority would only apply where there is a complete breakdown in law and order in the vicinity near the installation. Commanders must use all "available means to seek presidential authorization through the chain-of-command" (CJCS Joint Pub. 3-28, 2018). The disturbance has to be large-scale and should involve only the activities that are necessary to prevent significant loss of life or wanton destruction of property. Additionally, authorized activities must be necessary to restore government functions. A disturbance of a very short duration, but one that potentially causes massive damage or casualties, such as the use of a WMD, would also trigger this authority. It is unclear where the authority for this policy lies, but it appears to be derivative of the President's Article II, Commander and Chief, Chief Executive, and the "take care" clause authority (U.S. Const. art II, § 1, cl. 1; art II, § 2, cl. 1; and art. II, § 3).

Special Events

The Department of Defense supports a wide variety of "special events" every year. These include certain special events designated by the Secretary of Homeland Security as a "National Special Security Event (NSSE)." When so designated, the United States Secret Service, as part of the Department of Homeland Security, becomes the lead federal agency responsible for planning and executing security measures. The Department of Defense may be asked to support security and non-security aspects of these events. Events may be so designated because of their size, importance, dignitaries in attendance, and the like. Planning typically includes an unlikely but possible transition to disaster support and relevant Combatant Commander level commands are often involved in the planning (DOD Dir. 3025.20, 2012 and CJCS Joint Pub. 3-28, 2018). Sensitive Support to special activities is beyond the scope of this chapter, but can be found in the Department of Defense Directive S-5210.36 (U) Provision of DOD Sensitive Support to DOD Components and Other Departments and Agencies of the U.S. Government.

Chemical, Biological, Radiological, and Nuclear Incidents

A Chemical, Biological, Radiological, and Nuclear Incident (CBRN) is essentially an attack, or even an accidental spill, of a hazardous chemical, biological, or radiological substance (CJCS Joint Pub. 4-41, 2016). There are essentially three jurisdictional and lead options for a response to a CBRN incident. The first involves a domestic event. In such a case, the Department of Homeland Security is normally the lead agency. The second involves an incident overseas, where the Department of State is typically the lead agency. However, the Department of Defense can be tasked to perform the duties of the lead agency in either of these two scenarios depending on the facts involved. When the Department of Homeland Security is the lead of a domestic incident and the Department of Defense is in support, it is a DSCA mission for the military. When the Department of Defense is in the lead in a domestic mission, it is a Homeland Defense mission (CJCS Joint Pub. 3-41, 2016).

For the military, support will typically be provided to civil authorities following a request for assistance from the Governor or other state or local officials. DOD CBRN response forces have the requisite equipment, training, and experience. Except where a local commander provides support pursuant to the commander's immediate response or emergency authority, only the Secretary of Defense can approve DOD CBRN support (DOD Dir. 3025.18, 2018).

The planning process for response to a CBRN incident includes considering a wide variety of operational and technical factors. The event may be an accident at a chemical plant, nuclear power plant, or other facility. The event may involve chemical agents (weaponized chemicals or delivery systems designed to incapacitate) or toxic industrial chemicals (TICs). Hazards related to a chemical incident include such things as inhalation, absorption, or ingestion of a lethal or incapacitating gas. Responders must also be concerned with secondary complications such as asphyxiation, smoke inhalation, and fire (CJCS Joint Pub. 3-41, 2016).

"Biological agents are microorganisms and/or biologically-derived compounds or molecules that cause disease in personnel, plants or animals, and/or cause the deterioration of material. Biological agents are divided into two broad categories: pathogens and toxins" (CJCS Joint Pub. 3-41, 2016). Infectious diseases can be quite dangerous because of their ability to reproduce. A biological event can take place anywhere in the world and may take days or even weeks to discover due to the incubation period. A contagious person may move to many locations around the world without showing symptoms. At the outset, a person with a very debilitating disease may exhibit symptoms consistent with a very minor illness. First responder and medical personnel may be the first casualties. Adversaries or terrorists may attack indirectly by going after the food supply or the economy or international trade by attacking animals or crops. Bacteria could be genetically engineered to attack oil or industrial supplies (CJCS Joint Pub. 3-41, 2016).

As to nuclear events, they may include a nuclear detonation, a radiological dispersal device (RDD), a radiological exposure device (RED), or an Electromagnetic Pulse (EMP) attack, which is essentially a high-altitude nuclear detonation where damage is caused by radiation rather than a kinetic blast. RDDs and REDs are far less complicated than an actual nuclear bomb. An RDD, often referred to as a "dirty bomb," uses a non-nuclear explosive device to disseminate radioactive material. A small non-nuclear blast disperses radiological particles into the air, which can then be inhaled into the lungs or embedded in open cuts, sores, or food products. REDs are radioactive sources that are placed to cause injury or death. A RED can be hidden from sight, exposing those who pass by. A RED does not disseminate radiological material, rather, it exposes people to it (CJCS Joint Pub. 3-41, 2016). The Department of Defense must be prepared to mitigate the consequences of a nuclear weapon or radiological device wherever it may be in the world. (DOD Dir. 3150.08, 2018).

Another very important function of the National Guard is the Weapons of Mass Destruction (WMD) Civil Support Teams (CSTs). There are 57 National Guard WMD-CSTs, with at least one in each state. They are on standby 24 hours a day, every day of the year. They are trained to assist civil authorities at a domestic chemical, biological, radiological, and nuclear high-yield explosives (CBRNE) incident site by "identifying CBRNE agents/substances, assessing current or projected consequences, advising on response measures, and assisting with appropriate requests for additional state and federal military forces." They can also provide assistance at hazardous material (HAZMAT) releases (National Guard Public Affairs, 2017).

Under the direction of the Governor, the state National Guard Adjutant General can deploy a CST (consisting of 22 personnel) in response to an incident. They are generally operating in a "Title 32" status, meaning they are funded by the federal government but remain under the command and control of the Governor and state Adjutant General. These units can also be pre-positioned to support special events such as the Boston Marathon, World Series, Super Bowls, papal visits, State-of-the-Union Addresses,

Presidential Inaugurations, activities at the United Nations, and special state events, to name just a few. A CST's vehicles and equipment, including such assets as command suites, communications nodes, analytical laboratories, and analysis equipment can be moved by ground or airlifted into place (National Guard Public Affairs, 2017).

Public Health Emergency and the Coronavirus Response

With the deployment of military personnel all over the world, many of whom live on a military installation, and because many are married to spouses from foreign countries and may visit those foreign countries often, it is not unforeseeable that a public health emergency may develop on a military installation. Should that occur, the Department of Defense has guidance on what to do when there is a public health emergency within the Department of Defense (DOD Dir. 6200.03, 2019). But more likely, the armed forces may be called upon to provide support to civil authorities during a public health emergency (DOD Dir. 6010.22, 2016). Generally, this is likely to involve providing support to the Department of Health and Human Services (DHHS). Support from the Department of Defense may be protecting food and water, medical evacuation, transportation, assisting with quarantine and isolation, providing medical supplies and emergency medical treatment, patient processing, and the management of human remains (CLAMO, 2018).

The Department of Defense's authority to provide medical care to the general public, other than in an emergency situation involving life and limb, is limited because it must first provide care to its own members responding to the emergency; there are also fiscal law limitations on spending funds appropriated for the care of military personnel on others. Other considerations include licensing, credentialing, and malpractice insurance coverage issues.

As this chapter was being written, the United States and the entire world was struggling mightily against the Coronavirus, also known as COVID-19. As has been stated throughout this chapter, even though the Department of Defense has significant assets in terms of personnel, facilities, and equipment, the military is performing a support role to the civilian-lead agencies involved in the fight against this invisible enemy. The Department of Defense set up a web page for the Coronavirus and as stated on the first page, "The Defense Department is working closely with the Department of Health and Human Services and the State Department to provide support in dealing with the Coronavirus outbreak" (DOD, 2020).

As of June 2020, according to the Department of Defense Coronavirus web page, over 55,600 Department of Defense personnel have participated in support of COVID-19 operations. Of that number, 540 are medical personnel, including doctors, nurses, respiratory therapists, and medical support personnel. In addition to medical personnel, 1,080 from the U.S. Army Corps of Engineers have been involved. More than 45,700 National Guardsmen from all 50 states, the District of Columbia, and three territories, as well as more than 5,900 Army, Navy, and Air Force reservists have participated in these operations. The Department of Defense has performed 64 key FEMA mission assignments at a cost of $1.8 billion.

In terms of equipment, the Department of Defense has provided 2,000 ventilators, 20 million N95 masks to FEMA and HHS, 8 million test swabs, $1.1 million in laboratory and diagnostic supplies, 121,309 certified clinical COVID-19 tests, and more than $8.4 million in COVID-19 bio-surveillance activities in more than 30 countries (DOD, 2020). Perhaps some of the most visible Department of Defense support came in the form of the USNS *Comfort* and USNS *Mercy* hospital ships which deployed in March of 2020 (DOD, 2020).

Since June 2020, some of DOD's support has included the use of the Defense Production Act to procure goods and services related to fighting the pandemic. As just one of many examples, in support of the Department of Health and Human Services Strategic National Stockpile, DOD awarded $104 million for the procurement of syringes in advance support of the U.S. COVID-19 vaccination campaign. Other Defense Production Act use included such things as surgical masks, ventilator components, sample collection and processing consumables, flock tip testing swabs, SARS-CoV-2 assays for BD Veritor devices, oral fluid swab tests, molecular diagnostic testing, convalescent plasma products, and reusable isolation gowns to replenish the Strategic National Stockpile (DOD, 2021).

The Defense Production Act also has a role in what is referred to as Operation Warp Speed (OWS), a joint effort with the U.S. Department of Health and Human Services to distribute COVID-19 vaccinations to the American public as vaccine distribution is being executed in phases by the federal government. Currently on the federal government side, there are 64 Centers for Disease Control and Prevention jurisdictions, with industry partners. The military has distributed vaccines to its own population of air personnel, soldiers, and marines. And, in some cases, the National Guard has been deployed in states like New York to support others working in public health.

Of course, military personnel must be ready to respond to a national security emergency at any time and place on the planet. To do so, it must also maintain the health of the force itself. There is always a possibility that a national security emergency could take place while trying to battle the Coronavirus pandemic; military planners must always plan and be prepared to provide military medical personnel and assets to the military in the event of such an emergency.

There was concern in some circles that the federal government would use the Department of Defense to declare martial law in response to the Coronavirus pandemic (DOD, 2020). This of course did not happen. Members of the Trump administration, Congress, and some Governors all sought to assure citizens that there was no plan to declare martial law and under the facts present at the time, the military could not be used to enforce martial law. The first hurdle to using the military to enforce martial law is the Posse Comitatus Act (PCA) which will be discussed below. Unless an exception to the PCA exists, the military cannot be used in a law enforcement role, which is what "martial law" would be. If, however, large-scale riots and civil disobedience were to break out, the Insurrection Act might be triggered. If so, the President could employ the military to quell a rebellion or insurrection.

However, that authority has existed before the Coronavirus – in fact, since George Washington's administration – and it will exist after the Coronavirus is history. Presidents can and have used the Insurrection Act in the past, and will likely do so in very limited situations in the future. It is important to remember that the violence has to be at a level that can trigger application of the authority, which has not happened with the Coronavirus. Additionally, this authority is available to the President, not just for public health emergencies that potentially turn into extremely violent rebellions, but in response to events such as terror or cyberattacks. It is also important to note that Congress gives to the President this authority to respond to civil disobedience and insurrections through legislation; Congress can easily take that statutory authority away should it be abused.

Mass Migration Emergency

Another DSCA mission of the recent past has been mass migration emergencies, or crisis at the border, where the Department of Defense is requested to provide support to the Department of Homeland Security and the other civil authorities involved in the enforcement of federal immigration laws and border security. The Posse Comitatus Act bans military personnel from direct participation in law enforcement activities, including enforcement of federal immigration laws. As will be explained below, National Guard troops in a state active duty status or a Title 32 status could enforce their own state laws dealing with misconduct such as drug smuggling, sexual assault, or kidnapping. All of these might accompany violations of federal immigration law, but probably not the federal immigration laws themselves.

In a Homeland Defense posture, the Department of Defense could be directed to physically seal the border as an act of defense rather than as a law enforcement activity. In a DSCA operation, the armed forces could also provide indirect support to law enforcement agencies such as providing shelter, food, water, communications, transportation, and the like if such a request was made and approved by the appropriate authority (Posse Comitatus Act, 18 U.S.C. § 1385; The National Guard, Title 32 U.S.Code; DOD Dir. 3025.18, 2018).

Counter-Drug

A great deal of military support has been provided to federal, state, and local law enforcement involved in counter-drug operations. While having to steer clear of various limitations such as the Posse Comitatus Act, which prevents the armed forces from direct participation in law enforcement, and the ban on using the military to collect intelligence on U.S. persons, it is a legal and policy-intense area in terms of providing indirect support to law enforcement agencies involved in counter-drug activities. This is because the long-term and steady support the military has provided to the "war on drugs" is not indicative of a disaster or an emergency in the traditional meaning of the words. Counter-drug operations are beyond the scope of this chapter.

Mutual Agreements

Military commanders and the Department of Defense Component heads may enter into mutual aid agreements with any governmental entity, public or private corporation, or association that maintains facilities for fire protection (DOD Manual 3025.01, 2018). A wide array of support can be committed as part of a mutual aid agreement. Moreover, states may enter into interstate agreements with other states, promising support to one another. These state and federal agreements, which are allowable by law, may be referred to as an Emergency Management Assistance Compact (EMAC) (EMAC, Pubic Law Number 104-321).

CURRENT CHALLENGES

There are many challenges with using the armed forces as a tool to resolve domestic issues. There are legal and policy limitations such as the Posse Comitatus Act, among others. There are differences in authorities, command structure, and funding between the National Guard and active duty forces. There are significant limitations when using intelligence assets domestically. Finally, there is the issue of readiness. Does the use of the military to support civil authorities domestically detract from their mission in that equipment and personnel are used in ways not intended? Do these other obligations detract from training time and cause unprogrammed wear and tear on equipment and perhaps personnel?

The Posse Comitatus Act (PCA)

The PCA finds its roots in the 1876 Presidential election following the Civil War. The Republican candidate, Rutherford B. Hayes, defeated the Democratic candidate, Samuel J. Tilden by one electoral vote. During the election, President Grant had sent federal troops to South Carolina, Louisiana, and Florida for use by the U.S. Marshals in maintaining order in polling places. Some believe that Hayes was able to win those hotly contested states because of the actions of President Grant. The result was the PCA in 1878, which precludes members of the Army and Air Force from enforcing law (CLAMO, 2018; PCA, 18 U.S.C. § 1385).

As a general rule, the military must leave enforcement of the law to the civilian professionals. Should a member of the armed forces run afoul of the PCA and "execute" the law in a domestic setting where there is no exception or exemption, the soldier, sailor, airman, or marine could be charged with a crime (PCA, 18 U.S.C. § 1385).

By its express terms, the PCA appears to only apply to the Army and Air Force, but not to the Navy and Marine Corps. Federal courts have tended to interpret the plain language of the statute as only applying to the Army and the Air Force (CLAMO, 2018; U.S. v. Yunis, 1991; U.S. v. Roberts, 1986). However, Congress effectively expanded the reach of the PCA to cover the Navy and Marine Corps when, in separate legislation, it directed members of the Army, Navy, Air Force, or Marine Corps to avoid "direct participation" in law enforcement activities (10 U.S.C. § 275).

Neither the PCA nor this provision of law bans all support to law enforcement; as long as members of the military do not "execute the laws" or become involved in the "direct participation" of law enforcement activities, they are not in violation of the law. Moreover, both statutes recognize that there may be exemptions or exceptions to the two statutes in the Constitution itself or through specific legislation such as the Insurrection Act.

The Department of Defense Instruction 3025.21 and Defense Support of Civilian Law Enforcement Agencies implement both the Posse Comitatus Act and 10 U.S.C. § 275. As a matter of this Department of Defense policy, the PCA limitations placed on the Army and Air Force as a matter of law also apply to the Navy and Marine Corps. These restrictions do not, however, apply to the Coast Guard, despite being a branch of the armed forces. Unless in the service of the U.S. Navy, the Coast Guard belongs to the Department of Homeland Security and is a law enforcement agency performing law enforcement functions (Armed Forces, 10 U.S.C. § 101(a)(4) (2020) and Coast Guard, 14 U.S.C. §§ 101 and 102).

Additionally, the PCA and 10 U.S.C. § 275 do not apply to the National Guard except when federalized and operating in an active duty federal "Title 10" status (NORTHCOM, 2019). Finally, the PCA does not, as a matter of law, apply overseas. (Chandler v. U.S., 1948; D'Aquino v. U.S., 1951; Scowcroft Memo, 1989). However, the Department of Defense has expanded the coverage of the PCA as a matter of policy to "all actions of DOD personnel worldwide." The Secretary of Defense may, however, grant exceptions to this Instruction overseas "based on compelling and extraordinary circumstances" (DOD Inst. 3025.21, 2019).

The law prohibits federal troops from "direct participation" in law enforcement activities. The Department of Defense Instruction gives examples of direct participation such as the interdiction of vehicles, vessels and aircraft, searches and seizures, arrests, apprehensions, stops and frisks, the use of force, evidence collection, surveillance or pursuit, forensic investigations, and other similar examples (DOD Instr. 3025.21, 2019).

There are, however, a number of exceptions where the armed forces are authorized to enforce the law. The Instruction permits some activities that would otherwise appear to be direct participation as legal exceptions to both law and policy. Some of these include:

- The Military Purpose Doctrine. This exception "covers actions the primary purpose of which is to further a military interest." For example, when "Military Police provide general traffic control on civilian streets and highways where large convoys of military vehicles were using a civilian highway or road to get to a U.S. port in order to deploy overseas, investigations of members of the military by military personnel or military law enforcement entities, such as investigations under the Uniform Code of Military Justice; the protection of military personnel, equipment, guests, and classified information."
- Providing information to law enforcement that was incidentally collected during lawful military operations.
- Permitting law enforcement to use military equipment and facilities as well as Department of Defense maintenance and operation of the equipment. This is a complicated exception with significant approvals required.
- When the Insurrection Act is triggered.
- Crimes involving nuclear materials.
- Emergencies involving weapons of mass destruction (WMD).

(DOD Instr. 3025.21, 2019; 10 U.S.C. §§ 271–284; 10 U.S.C. §§ 251–255; 18 U.S.C. § 831)

The Instruction also provides examples of support to law enforcement that does not rise to the level of direct participation, such as providing expert advice on operating and maintaining Department of Defense equipment. These activities are not exceptions to the law, but are not considered to be "direct participation." Examples include:

- Expert advice.
- Training of law enforcement personnel.
- Transfer to federal, state, or local law enforcement officials information acquired in the normal course of Department of Defense operations.

National Guard

In evaluating permissible support to law enforcement, the first question that should be asked is whether the military personnel or organization providing the support belongs to the active duty military, the Army, Navy, Air Force, or Marine Corps Reserves, or the National Guard. If the unit or personnel are members of the National Guard, the second question should be, "under what 'status' are they operating?"

Imagine an active duty soldier standing right next to a member of the National Guard activated in a state status, where both are involved in the same disaster or emergency, both are the same rank, both are equipped and armed in the exact same fashion, both are wearing identical uniforms, and both wear "U.S. Army" name tapes on their uniforms. Under these facts, the active duty soldier cannot enforce the law but the National Guard soldier can. This is true even though the two would be indistinguishable by anyone seeing them in the area of the disaster.

The Constitution allows for the creation of state militias under the command of the Governor (U.S. Const. art. I, § 8, cl. 15, 16; U.S. Const. art. I, § 10, cl. 3; U.S. Const. amend. 2 and 10). The state carries with it "police power," the inherent authority to draft and enforce laws to protect persons and property within its territory (NGB DOMOPS, 2019). The Governor can use the state militia to enforce state and local law. There is no federal PCA equivalent for State forces that prevent a Governor from using the state militia (the National Guard) to enforce the law.

Often referred to as "status" when activated, there are essentially three separate and distinct authorities under which National Guard troops are called to active duty:

1) State Active Duty (SAD). When on SAD, they are under the sole control of the Governor and state government. The requirements to provide support to civil authorities would be limited to state authorities. Guardsmen on SAD are paid by the state, controlled by the state, and disciplined by the state.

2) Title 32 status. This means they are operating under Title 32, National Guard, of the U.S. Code. In this status, they are largely paid for and by the federal government but under the command and control of the Governor and state government. This is the status they are typically under when training for a federal mission. With some limitations, the National Guard can also perform DSCA while in a Title 32 status.

3) Title 10 status. If they are activated under Title 10 of the U.S. Code, they become federal troops, funded by the federal government, removed from the command and control of the state, and under the command of the federal military command structure with the President as Commander and Chief. When in a Title 10 status, their authorities are those of active duty troops; limitations such as the PCA apply to them (NGB DOMOPS, 2019).

National Guard units are normally the preferred military response to domestic disasters and emergencies. They are trained, organized, exercised, and experienced at responding to the sorts of disasters and emergencies they are likely to see in their own States. As a general rule, active federal forces are used only when National Guard units for the state or states affected are overwhelmed or are not capable of responding, or where primarily federal functions or assets are at stake. Another reason for a National Guard preference is that the PCA does not apply to, and does not therefore limit, the National Guard when serving in a state active duty status or in a Title 32 status under state command and control.

When both National Guard and active duty members of the military are involved in a disaster, both are very valuable. While from a jurisdictional standpoint the National Guard may have authorities that the federal military forces do not have, the federal forces may have capabilities the National Guard does not have, such as water purification units. Leaders may be able to use the active forces to participate in non–law enforcement activities freeing up the National Guard to conduct law enforcement activities. During a disaster or emergency response, it would be helpful to place all the units, both National Guard and federal, under one commander that would provide unity of command and utilize all assets to the greatest effect possible.

Not long ago, Congress provided legislation for this very purpose by permitting the creation of a Dual Status Commander (DSC) in a given emergency. Ordinarily, a

National Guard chain of command runs through the National Guard to the Governor as Commander and Chief. The federal troops run through the federal chain of command to the President as Commander and Chief. Where the President and Governor can agree is when an active duty officer with a regular commission can also accept a National Guard commission, or when an officer of the National Guard can also accept a commission in the federal military (32 U.S.C. §§ 315 and 325). These officers can then serve as commanders of both the federal and National Guard forces working a given emergency or disaster. They are in command of both units and the chains of command remain separate and distinct; the commander will typically have a separate staff for both the National Guard and federal commissions (NGB DOMOPS Law and Policy, 2019).

Intelligence Collection on U.S. Persons

Intelligence collection on U.S. persons by the military is extremely limited, restricted, and exceptionally complicated with numerous authorities, oversight, and approvals involved. As a general rule without a special very limited exemption or exception, the military is prohibited from collecting intelligence on U.S. persons. This subject, while exceedingly important, is beyond the scope of a general information chapter such as this. The collection of intelligence on U.S. persons in the United States is primarily the job of civilian law enforcement. On the federal side, this ordinarily means the Department of Justice using the FBI, Drug Enforcement Administration, or some other federal law enforcement agency (TJAGLCS, 2017).

Readiness

Another pragmatic policy reason for limiting military support to civilian authorities is readiness, including the readiness of the personnel and equipment assigned to a military organization (DOD Dir. 3025.18, 2018; TJAGLCS, 2017). As stated above, the bottom-line priority mission for the armed forces is to fight and win our nation's wars. If military resources are deployed to a natural disaster, they may not be available for a national security emergency. Moreover, the wear and tear from disaster relief on resources, from computers to transport ships and aircraft, impacts readiness. If a soldier breaks a leg during a disaster mission, they will not be ready for combat during the time it takes to heal. There is also a training cost to readiness. If an infantry soldier is out fighting fires for the summer, the soldier is taken out of the training pipeline for battle. On the other hand, as with most significant life experience, soldiers typically grow from these experiences. Their units arguably benefit from the opportunity to work together to help solve a critical problem.

Purpose Statute

Finally, another restriction on defense support to civil authorities is fiscal law. First, Congress has the authority to "lay and collect taxes" (U.S. Const. art. I, § 8, cl. 1). Second, no funds can be withdrawn from the Treasury without an appropriation from Congress (U.S. Const. art. I, § 9, cl. 7). When Congress appropriates funds to a government agency, it includes specific instructions as to what the money can be used for. It is often said Congress controls the "purse strings" or the "checkbook."

Typically in an annual appropriation, Congress provides money to the armed forces for, among other things, "operations and maintenance" (O&M). These O&M funds pay for things such as the day-to-day costs of running an armed force, training, exercises, operations, maintenance of equipment and facilities, and some construction and procurement. When, as in most cases, a natural disaster strikes, it is not something that is budgeted for and represents an unfunded contingency operation. The funds spent on the contingency reduce the fiscal resources unless Congress comes up with the O&M funds to cover the unforeseen disaster.

This creates two concerns. First, expenditure of the limited funds that the armed forces has for operations and maintenance on unplanned disasters or emergency responses may adversely impact such things as training and maintenance of equipment and facilities. Compounding this dilemma is the fact that equipment used during the disaster may wear out or reduce the life expectancy of the equipment, which in turn requires more maintenance funding.

The second concern is a Constitutional issue. It is not just about limited numbers of dollars and running out of O&M funding. When Congress appropriates funds for the military to use to train for battle, that is what it must be spent on. If the military instead spends the funds on something else, such as building shelters and feeding the victims of a hurricane, the military is not using the funds for what Congress provided them for in the first place. Using the funds for some other purpose may be a violation of the Purpose Statute. The "Purpose Statute" makes it a criminal offense to spend money for a purpose other than what Congress appropriated the funds for (The Purpose Statute, 31 U.S.C. § 1301). Therefore, when the armed forces participate in emergencies, the military will look to see if they can be reimbursed for some of their expenditures.

RECOMMENDATIONS FOR THE FUTURE

The difficulties in this area spring primarily from limited resources and a generally held conviction that the military should not be involved in intelligence operations or law enforcement activities against U.S. civilians who are not employees of the Department of Defense. The resource issue is an interesting one because in this case, the military has resources and personnel that would be highly useful in responding to emergencies. In fact, they are the only government agency with many of these resources and in the numbers required. In most cases, however, these resources, including personnel, are necessary to be ready for combat. Using them for another purpose, no matter how noble, represents a risk that is tied to readiness and has to be evaluated when deciding to rely on military resources.

The other issue is the proper role of the military. Even if the resources are available, having large numbers of military aircraft and vehicles manned by soldiers in combat gear in a concentrated area following a disaster, will likely cause discomfort for some. They might prefer that their streets were cleared by other than military forces. Additionally, some post-emergency activities certainly appear to be law enforcement or Intel related. This will likely be problematic as Americans have always resisted martial law or anything that resembles it.

What then are the options for improving the situation in the future?

1. Status quo. Do not change anything, keep the status quo: While disasters may be on the rise, the military is not being stressed at the current time with military operations as it has in the very recent past. Readiness is currently being held at

risk because of support to civil authorities, though only those in the armed forces can verify that. It is not likely that the budget exists to "man, train, and equip" FEMA or some other organization to the levels required, so the status quo may be the best alternative.

2. Status quo plus: In this option, resources are essentially maintained at the status quo but exercises, especially those dealing with command and control, are increased so that compatibility and cooperation improve. Plans should be written for foreseeable contingencies, realizing they are likely to change.

3. Expand the authorities of the active duty forces: Repeal or rewrite Posse Comitatus so that during man-made or natural disasters the active forces have more law enforcement authority. Bring them on par with the National Guard in terms of domestic authorities. Continue to increase counterinsurgency and defensive cyber authorities and assets.

4. Provide increases in active and/or National Guard budgets specifically for disaster relief: Approve the increased acquisition of equipment for disaster relief purposes and funds for training and operations.

5. Further limit active duty military involvement but empower the National Guard: Get the active duty military out of the disaster relief business by increasing funding, equipment, and authorities for the National Guard. Create regional National Guard commands where neighboring states are required to respond to disasters as if they were taking place in their own states, but under the control of the Governor where the event takes place.

6. More resources to FEMA: Buy FEMA helicopters, airplanes, trucks, tractors, and the like to relieve the military of this mission. Provide them with more personnel.

The opinion of the author, based on the current severity and frequency of emergencies and disasters, is that Option 1, Status quo, or Option 2, Status quo plus, are the only realistic courses of action because of fiscal and policy limitations. Certainly there are indications that cyberattacks, natural disasters, terror, WMD incidents, and mass migration events may be on the rise, which might mean some of these other options may become more important.

CONCLUSION

The armed forces of the United States have tremendous resources and capabilities that could be and are used in response to man-made and natural disasters and emergencies to relieve human suffering, prevent death, and protect property. The Department of Defense and its military departments are part of the executive branch of government with the President as the Commander and Chief. Congress also plays a vital role in creating and maintaining the military and in drafting legislation regarding its authorized use.

Despite its significant resources and capabilities, the American public prefers that its military refrain from domestic law enforcement and focus on traditional external matters of national defense. Additionally, the military does not have unlimited funding and legally can only spend its money on the purposes for which Congress appropriated its funds. And finally, people and equipment break down. It would be taking a huge risk to degrade readiness by running the military's war-time equipment into the ground while providing support during natural disasters.

DSCA during disasters and emergencies means saving lives and relieving suffering. My experience has always been that soldiers really want to help their fellow Americans who are really suffering. For many, wearing the uniform, whether in combat or responding to a natural disaster, is all about rescuing people. They are generally excited about the opportunities to serve their fellow Americans in a direct and meaningful way. Lives are saved, suffering is relieved, and property is protected.

CLASS DISCUSSION AND ESSAY QUESTIONS

1. What factors led to the creation of the military in the United States, and how has the mission of the military changed over time?
2. Discuss what the terms "homeland security" versus "homeland defense" mean to you. Are they synonymous or do you distinguish between them from a legal, policy, or implementation standpoint?
3. What is the role of the military in Defense Support of Civilian Authorities and the capabilities the military brings when terrorist attacks occur or to disaster response and recovery operations?
4. Summarize the Posse Comitatus Act and discuss its prudence relative to separation of power and limitations on government overreach.
5. Some argue that the military, given their remit as "warfighters," shouldn't be utilized for domestic emergency response agents. Use content from the chapter, or real-world case examples, to argue for or against utilizing the military in certain response scenarios.
6. What challenges exist for the military in emergency management and homeland defense/security contexts, and how can these be overcome in the future?

REFERENCES

Ailworth, Erin, "Inauguration Day Protests in Portland, Seattle Turned Violent," *The Wall Street Journal*, January 21, 2021.

"About Us," District of Columbia National Guard, Accessed January 24, 2021. https://dc.ng.mil/About-Us/.

Armed Forces, 10 U.S.C. § 101(a)(4) (2020) and Coast Guard, 14 U.S.C. §§ 101 and 102. The armed forces of the United States consists of the Army, Navy, Air Force, Marine Corps, Space Force and Coast Guard. However, unless in the service of the U.S. Navy, the Coast Guard belongs to the Department of Homeland Security and is a law enforcement agency primarily performing law enforcement functions.Booker, Brakkton, "About 20000 National Guard Members to Deploy For Inauguration, Officials Say," *National Public Radio*, January 13, 2021.

Brooks, Rebecca Beatrice, "History of King Philip's War," *History of Massachusetts (blog)*, May 31, 2017. https://historyofmassachusettes.org/what-was-king-philips-war/.

Bradbury Science Museum. "Civil Defense and the Cold War," Accessed February 2, 2021. https://www.lanl.gov/museum/news/newsletter/2018/05/civil-defense.php.

Chairman of the Joint Chiefs of Staff (CJCS), Execute Order, "141745Z Aug 9 CJCS Defense Support of Civil Authorities (DSCA)," (August 14, 2009).

Chairman of the Joint Chiefs of Staff (CJCS), Instruction 3121.01B, "Standing Rules of Engagement/Standing Rules for the Use of Force for U.S. Forces," (June 18, 2008).

Chairman of the Joint Chiefs of Staff (CJCS), Joint Publication 3-26, "Counterterrorism," (October 24, 2014).

Chairman of the Joint Chiefs of Staff (CJCS), Joint Publication 3-27, "Homeland Defense," (April 10, 2018).

Chairman of the Joint Chiefs of Staff (CJCS), Joint Publication 3-28, "Defense Support of Civil Authorities," (October 29, 2018).

Chairman of the Joint Chiefs of Staff (CJCS), Joint Publication 3-41, "Chemical, Biological, Radiological, and Nuclear Response (CBRN)," (September 9, 2016).

"A CBRN incident is any occurrence, resulting from the use of CBRN weapons and devices; the emergence of secondary hazards arising from counterforce targeting; or the release of toxic industrial materials (TIMs) into the environment, involving the emergence of CBRN hazards. A USG response would normally be required when local, territorial, tribal, or state authorities are overwhelmed by the incident; if there are some shortfalls in local territorial, tribal, state, or federal response capabilities; or other USG departments and agencies may require a defense support of civil authorities (DSCA) request for Department of Defense (DOD) assistance."

"Radioactive materials cause damage by ionizing effects of neutron, gamma, x-ray, beta, and/or alpha radiation. A population may be exposed to radiation intentionally through two primary methods (other than a nuclear detonation): radiological dispersal devices (RDDs) and radiological exposure devices (REDs)."

"An EMP is unlikely to have a direct health threat on individuals. However, personnel with pacemakers or other implanted devices may be negatively affected. An EMP can also damage electronic equipment, rendering it inoperable, if it is strong enough."

Chandler v. United States, 171 F.2d 921, 936 (1st Cir. 1948), *cert denied*, 336 U.S. 918 (1949).Corn, Geoffrey, Jimmy Gurulé, Eric Talbot Jensen and Peter Margulies, *National Security Law: Principles and Policy*, 2nd ed. (New York: Wolters Kluwer, 2019), 1–7.

D'Aquino v. United States, 192 F.2d 338, 351 (9th Cir. 1951), *cert. denied*, 343 U.S. 935 (1952).Department of Defense (DOD), "Coronavirus: DOD Response," May 28, 2020, https://www.defense.gov/Explore/Spotlight/Coronavirus/.

Department of Defense (DOD), Department of Defense Directive 3025.18, "Defense Support of Civil Authorities (DSCA)," (March 19, 2018).

Department of Defense (DOD), Department of Defense Directive 3025.20, "Defense Support of Special Events," (April 6, 2012). Typical special events include, but are not limited to:
The President's State of the Union Address or other address to a joint session of Congress
Annual meetings of the United Nations General Assembly
National Presidential nominating conventions
Presidential inaugural activities
International summits or meetings
State funerals
The National Boy Scout Jamboree
Certain international or domestic sporting competitions
They may also include things such as:
World's Fair
Super Bowl

Olympics

Special Olympics and Paralympics

World Series

NASCAR [National Association for Stock Car Auto Racing] events

Department of Defense (DOD), Department of Defense Directive 3150.08, "DOD Response to Nuclear and Radiological Incidents," (March 19, 2018).

Department of Defense (DOD), Department of Defense Directive 6010.22, "National Disaster Medical System (NDSM)," (April 14, 2016).

Department of Defense (DOD), Department of Defense Directive 6200.03, "Public Health Emergency Management (PHEM) Within DOD," (March 28, 2019).

Department of Defense (DOD), Department of Defense Instruction 3025.21, "Defense Support to Civilian Law Enforcement Agencies," (February 8, 2019).

Department of Defense (DOD), Department of Defense Manual 3025.01, "Defense Support to Civil Authorities (DSCA)," Vols 1–3 (March 19, 2018).

Department of Defense (DOD), "Strategy for Homeland Defense and Defense Support of Civil Authorities," (2013).

Department of Homeland Security (DHS), "Civil Defense and Homeland Security: A Short History of National Preparedness Efforts," (2006).

Department of Homeland Security (DHS), "The DHS Strategic Plan, Fiscal Years 2020–2024," (2019).

Dickstein, Corey, "Thousands of National Guard Troops Could Remain in DC into March." *Stars and Stripes*, January 22, 2021.

Dual Status Commander, Pub. L. 109-163, 32 U.S.C. §315 and §325 (2020).

Economy Act of 1932, 31 U.S.C. §1535 (2020). The Economy Act is a provision on federal law that allows for the transfer of funds to a federal agency to cover the expenses of the federal agency when the organization transferring the funds was the real recipient of the benefits from the expenditure. For example, if an Army Engineer unit removes debris and clears streets following a major disaster, the entity that benefited from the debris removal may have to reimburse the Engineer unit fits its costs.

Emergency Management Assistance Compact (EMAC) Pubic Law Number 104-321, Stat. 3877 (1996).

First Continental Congress, Declaration and Resolves, N.C.D. 9 (October 14, 1774).

Hernandez, Arelis R., Chelsea Janes, Isaac Stanley-Becker, Brent D. Griffiths, Amanda Erickson and Rachel Van Dongen, "Demonstrators, Police Clash Across Nation in Another Night of Protest." *The Washington Post*, May 31, 2020.

History.com editors, "King Philip's War," History.com, November 13, 2019. https://www.history.com/topics/native-american-history/king-philips-war.

History.com editors, "Whiskey Rebellion," History.com, September 13, 2019. https://www.history.com/topics/early-us/whiskey-rebellion.

Homeland Security Act of 2002, Pub. L. 107-296, 6 U.S.C. §§ 101 et seq. (2020). Homeland Security Council (HSC), "National Strategy for Homeland Security," (2007).

Insurrection Act of 1807, Pub. L. 144-328, 10 U.S.C. §§ 251-255 (2020). The President can respond to an Insurrection with or even without a request from the state under certain conditions. For example, whenever the President considers that unlawful obstructions, combinations, or assemblages, or rebellion against the authority of the United States, make it impracticable to enforce the laws of the United States in any state by the ordinary course of judicial proceedings, he may call into federal service such of the militia of any state and use such of the armed forces, as he considers necessary to enforce those laws or to suppress the rebellion.

The Insurrection Act also directs:

The President, by using the militia or the armed forces, or both, or by any other means, shall take such measures as he considers necessary to suppress, in a state, any insurrection, domestic violence, unlawful combination, or conspiracy, if it-

(1) so hinders the execution of the laws of that state, and of the United States within the state, that any part or class of its people is deprived of a right, privilege, immunity, or protection named in the Constitution and secured by law, and the constituted authorities of that state are unable, fail, or refuse to protect that right, privilege, or immunity, or to give that protection; or

(2) opposes or obstructs the execution of the laws of the United States or impedes the course of justice under those laws.

In any situation covered by clause (1), the state shall be considered to have denied the equal protection of the laws secured by the Constitution.

Library of Congress, Federal Research Division, "Military Support to Civil Authorities: The Role of the Department of Defense in Support of Homeland Defense," (2017).

Memorandum from Office of the Assistant Attorney General to Brent Scowcroft, "Extraterritorial Effect of the Posse Comitatus Act," (November 3, 1989).

Military Support to Law Enforcement, 10 U.S.C. §§271-284.

Myers, Meghann and Davis Winkie, "Entire DC Guard, Plus 500 from MD and Others from VA, Activated after pro-Trump Protesters Storm Capitol." *Military Times*, January 6, 2020.

National Guard Act of 1933, 73 Pub. L. 64, §18, Title 32 U.S.C.

National Guard Bureau Office of the Chief Counsel (NGB), *Domestic Operations Law and Policy*, 2nd ed. Washington DC: National Guard Bureau, (2019).

National Guard Public Affairs, "Weapons of Mass Destruction Civil Support Team Fact Sheet," December 2017. https://www.nationalguard.mil/Portals/31/Resources/Fact%20Sheets/Weapons%20of%20Mass%20Destruction%20Civil%20Support%20Team%20Fact%20Sheet%20(Dec.%202017).pdf.

Posse Comitatus Act (PCA), 18 U.S.C. § 1385. The Statute says, "Whoever, except in cases and under circumstances expressly authorized by the Constitution or Act of Congress, willfully uses any part of the Army or Air Force as a posse comitatus or otherwise to execute the laws shall be fined under this title or imprisoned not more than two years, or both."

Purpose Statute, Pub. L. 97-258, 96 Stat. 917, 31 U.S.C. §1301 (2020).

Robert T. Stafford Disaster Relief and Emergency Assistance Act of 1974, Pub. L. 93-288, as amended, 42 U.S.C. §§ 5122 et seq. (2018).

A major disaster under the Stafford Act includes any natural catastrophe (including any hurricane, tornado, storm, high water, wind driven water, tidal wave, tsunami, earthquake, volcanic eruption, landslide, mudslide, snowstorm, or drought), or, regardless of cause, any fire, flood, or explosion, in any part of the United States, which in the determination of the President causes damage of sufficient severity and magnitude to warrant major disaster assistance under this chapter to supplement the efforts and available resources of states, local governments, and disaster relief organizations in alleviating the damage, loss, hardship, or suffering caused thereby.

In response to a major disaster, the President can provide support such as:

[P]ersonnel, equipment, supplies, facilities, managerial, technical and advisory services, medicine, medical equipment, food, emergency mass feeding, water, other consumables, debris removal, clearance of roads, temporary facilities for schools, dissemination of public information, search and rescue, emergency medical care, emergency mass care, emergency shelter, demolition, warnings, rescue, care and shelter of animals, hazard mitigation, repair, reconstruction, restoration or replacement of local, state or federal government facilities, unemployment assistance, assistance for low-income and seasonal farmworkers, relocation assistance, legal services, crisis counseling, community disaster loans, emergency communications, emergency transportation, fire management assistance, and timber sell contracts.

An emergency in accordance with the Stafford Act is defined as:

[A]ny occasion or instance for which, in the determination of the President, federal assistance is needed to supplement state and local efforts and capabilities to save lives and to protect property and public health and safety, or to lessen or avert the threat of a catastrophe in any part of the United States.

United States v. Roberts, 779 F. 2d 565 (9th Cir. 1986), *cert. denied*, 479 U.S. 839 (1986).

United States v. Yunis, 924 F.2d 1086, 1093 (D.C. Cir. 1991).

U.S. Army Center for Law and Military Operations (CLAMO), "Domestic Operational Law (DOMOPS) Handbook," (2018).

U.S. Army Judge Advocate General's Legal Center and School (TJAGLCS), "Operational Law (OPSLAW) Handbook," (2017).

United States Constitution.U.S. Northern Command (NORTHCOM), "The Posse Comitatus Act," September 23, 2019. https://www.northcom.mil/Newsroom/Fact-Sheets/Article-View/Article/563993/the-posse-comitatus-act/.

As explained by NORTHCOM:

The Posse Comitatus Act (PCA) does not apply to the U.S. Coast Guard, or to the National Guard in Title 32 or State Active Duty status. Although the PCA prohibits only the Army and Air Force as from performing domestic law enforcement activities, another statute, 10 USC Section 275, requires the Secretary of Defense to prescribe regulations to prohibit members of the Army, Navy, Air Force, or Marine Corps from direct participation in a search, seizure, arrest, or other similar activity unless participation in such activity by such member is otherwise authorized by law. Department of Defense Instruction 3025.21 implements the prohibitions required under the PCA and 10 USC Section 275.

These laws and regulations generally prohibit U.S. military personnel from direct participation in law enforcement activities. Some of those law enforcement activities would include interdicting vehicles, vessels, and aircraft; conducting surveillance, searches, pursuit and seizures; or making arrests on behalf of civilian law enforcement authorities. Prohibiting direct military involvement in law enforcement is in keeping with long-standing U.S. law and policy limiting the military's role in domestic affairs.

White House, Presidential Decision Directive/NSC-39, "U.S. Policy on Counterterrorism," (1995).

Warren, Jason W., "King Philip's War," *Encyclopedia Britannica*, March 9, 2023, https://www.britannica.com/event/King-Philips-War.

White House, "National Security Strategy of the United States of America," (2017). See also, Department of Defense (DOD), "National Defense Strategy of the United States of America," (2018); Chairman of the Joints Chiefs of Staff (SJCS), "National Military Strategy of the United States of America," (2018).

Wikipedia, "King Philip's War," May 19, 2020, https://en.wikipedia.org/wiki/King_Philip%27s_War.

CHAPTER 15

The Role of Law in Emergency Management and Homeland Security:
Legal Foundations to Follow and Liabilities to Avoid

Heriberto Urby, Jr.

INTRODUCTION

Law as a profession and practice has existed since antiquity (i.e., ancient times) and perhaps as far back as the Code of Hummarabi used during the 1st dynasty of Babylonian times (i.e., 1755–1750 BC). In the United States, law has existed since the settlement of the American colonies in the 17th century, with the sources of law consisting of: Constitutional Law, Statutory Law, Case Law (e.g., the common law derived from English common law), Treaties, and Administrative Regulations. American lawyers' involvement in emergency management prevention, mitigation, preparedness, and the response and recovery phases of the disaster life cycle is a more recent occurrence. Historically, lawyers were not prepared, adaptable, or even keen on the idea of providing service to emergency managers and their respective personnel.

Only in recent years have U.S. State Bar Associations (on a state-by-state basis) lent their numbers to people afflicted by disastrous events, as the special expertise necessary to help draft legal documents, provide knowledgeable advice, and work through other related tasks require the skills these legal professionals possess. An apparent inability on the part of many lawyers and bar associations to assist citizens and neighbors before, during, and after disaster events has been hampered by noticeable observance that even the best of them have not been formally or practically trained in major aspects of emergency management or homeland security law, related statutes, and pertinent case law, not to mention how to apply and enforce them. These lawyers and representative entities have lacked the true expertise and know-how as to how best help those in these fields do their jobs well. This situation has been especially obvious when it comes to assisting emergency managers, homeland security stakeholders, and related personnel to prevent liability issues before any exposure to lawsuits and their quite often drastic consequences.

DOI: 10.4324/9781003350729-15

As late as the start of the 21st century, the vast majority of U.S. law schools did not provide specialized, unique courses or an ever-larger emergency management law curriculum to effectively train lawyers to help homeland security stakeholders and emergency managers in specific matters of practice related to disaster science. It is not enough anymore, as might have been true in the past, for lawyers to just provide their clients basic general contracts law, torts law, or other areas of more general emphases. The complexity of emergency management and homeland security and science and practice no longer allows for such a luxury. The crux of lawyers' assistance must come from their role in all pre- and post-disaster phases of the disaster life cycle – respectively, prevention, mitigation, preparedness, response, and recovery. Therefore, more discussion in this chapter focuses on lawyers' roles (as voluntary or hired agents) to assist their clients (principals) to follow the law respective to emergency management and homeland security, allowing the important decision-makers in these fields to prevent legal liability in advance if at all possible.

With this in mind, my purpose is to focus on what we know and do not know about the legal profession and its inextricable relationship especially with emergency management practice (Nicholson, 2003d). To help us find better solutions to homeland security and emergency management problems, and for lawyers to assist with the pre- and post-disaster activities brought on by disasters, this chapter is divided into the following several parts for discussion: 1) brief general U.S. history of the legal profession; 2) the law's relation to disasters and terrorism; 3) lawyers' roles undertaken in emergency management and homeland security; 4) current challenges; 5) recommendations for the future; and 6) conclusion, which ties this chapter together.

U.S. HISTORY OF THE LEGAL PROFESSION

Laws and lawyers have existed in the United States since before the 1700s, and a huge precedence of laws has accumulated throughout the short time this great nation has existed. Along with congressional statutes, the United States has the longest-lasting, most enduring constitution of any other nation to date. As mentioned earlier, the majority of the law that is relied upon by courts in the United States comes from the English common law and is followed in many cases still today. Case precedents or "stare decisis" (i.e., let the decision stand) is alive and well. Thus, courts follow case precedence (e.g., the judge will most likely follow the law that was used in prior or precedent cases unless court precedent is changed by the judge's "new ruling" in the matter at hand).

Law schools train lawyers in the law (much of it general law) today, but there was a time in the 19th and early 20th centuries when a person could study the law and pass the bar exam of a particular state without attending law school. However, that is not the case today. Lawyers must study law in a law school, and only become lawyers when licensed to practice by passing the respective bar exam in that state or states. Merely completing law school without passage of the bar exam does not entitle one to status as an attorney or attorney and counselor at law. Put simply, a state of the United States must license one to practice in that particular state, and one becomes known as a lawyer only by satisfactorily attaining qualifications of a lawyer (i.e., satisfy the law curricular requirements of law school *and* passage of a state bar exam).

But graduating from law school and passage of the bar exam does not guarantee that emergency managers or homeland security stakeholders will be advised correctly or even adequately, as most lawyers are not well trained in either emergency management or homeland security law. This must change, and hopefully, sooner rather than later. The areas of the law regarding protection in all phases of the disaster life cycle must be developed to help those who need to act favorably in advance of liability, or even during the time they are in hearings or trials before court tribunals or other hearings' officers. Time is of the essence, thus competent, well-trained lawyers in these important areas must be available to help those avoid liability or know what to do when the time may come that they are sued. Next, a discussion of the law's relation to disasters and terrorism.

THE LAW'S RELATION TO DISASTERS AND TERRORISM

At the outset of this section, it should be noted that disasters and terrorist attacks create liabilities. This occurs no more commonly than in the response phase of the disaster life cycle. Examples include situations where warnings are not issued when they should have been, or when warnings are issued but they are late and do not afford evacuees the opportunity to evacuate carefully and timely, assuming they could in the first place. For instance, during Hurricane Katrina in 2005, many thought that warnings were not issued; in fact, they were issued so late that many did not or could not evacuate even if they wanted to do so. Finally, another case is where warnings that are given in a timely fashion do not always take into account where evacuees will end up sheltering, temporarily or permanently. The latter should always be contemplated and planned for more aggressively, as this is a crucial aspect for emergency managers to most certainly consider.

However, there are other areas of legal import where lawyers' advice is crucial. For example: 1) relative to disputes about employment (e.g., allegations of discrimination); 2) involvement in negotiations regarding payments when cities share dispatch, Emergency Operations Centers, fire equipment, etc.; and 3) allowance of prudent advice given on issues related to Due Process and Equal Protection under the 5th and 14th Amendments of the United States Constitution – these are areas that only the most competent and expert lawyers do best.

Moreover, in order to reduce legal liabilities that can and do occur for emergency managers, homeland security stakeholders, and their personnel, lawyers and emergency managers must work together. William Nicholson, a well-known attorney and author of books on legal issues in emergency management, claimed that "law and emergency management are inherently intertwined, and legal norms in the disaster field are changing and having a significant impact on the profession" (Nicholson, 2003d, Abstract). Most notably, this statement recognized the impact lawyers and their legal work have accomplished for society after experiencing disasters "first-hand" through the last many years. It is as if lawyers and individual state bar associations have come to the realization that "time is of the essence" to put FEMA's admonition into practice that emphasizes protection of civilian populations and property from natural/man-made disasters through the disaster life cycle – prevention, mitigation, preparedness, response, and recovery.

Thus, the paramount recognition now is that the advice and legal work that lawyers conduct through the law on behalf of emergency managers and homeland security stakeholders and their organizations may be almost limitless. That is to say, there are many types of active opportunities – before, during, and after disasters – within which competent counsel can advise specific experts in the professions of emergency management and homeland security. Importantly, these legal experts must provide consistent advice on the prevention of potential liability for legal threats expected, and even those not expected but still a hazard. Put differently, at all times these persons in service to others must be ready to do what is right, as well as do the right thing on behalf of their important clients.

This is key for homeland security stakeholders and emergency managers to accomplish other phases of the disaster life cycle efficiently and effectively, for instance, to conduct mitigation properly (i.e., reduction of the risk through long-term planning), to advance preparedness (i.e., readiness to meet the urgent and immediate needs of victims and their families during disasters), and to effectuate tremendous outcomes as relates to the post-disaster phases of response and recovery as well (i.e., reaching goals for bouncing back or building back better). But what more of the lawyers' roles that are undertaken in emergency management and homeland security? These follow below.

LAWYERS' ROLES UNDERTAKEN IN EMERGENCY MANAGEMENT AND HOMELAND SECURITY

Emergency management and homeland security organizations look to lawyers to obtain valuable legal advice. More specific examples of lawyers' value to emergency managers in helping them avoid liability (in advance) include:

> circumstances of wrongful death, negligent planning, or actions during the disaster, civil right violations resulting from improper use of authority, exceeding the scope of proper practice for emergency management, failure to properly distribute aid, monetary damages resulting from loss of business during an evacuation, and many more.

> (Nicholson, 2003d, p. 14)

Other more specific (and essential) examples indicate that a lawyer:

1) May have to discuss issues related to complex mitigation issues (land use disputes, new building codes or retrofitting requirements, etc.);
2) May provide advice on mutual aid agreements or memoranda of understanding;
3) May provide advice on the creation of city ordinances;
   a. May need to provide advice on contracts with vendors who deal with disasters;
   b. May have to interpret federal laws and regulations or disaster assistance policies,
   c. especially as relates to the Robert T. Stafford Act (perhaps the most important federal legislation to emergency management yet passed);
   d. May have to provide advice on LGBTQ or sex offenders' issues in shelters;
   e. May need to provide specific legal advice re: American with Disabilities Act (ADA) and on matters related to socially vulnerable populations, especially concerning evacuation and other delicate "management circumstances" that may bring about serious liability issues;
   f. May get involved in disputes about payments after disasters and other recovery phase
   g. issues; and

4) Is needed for all pre-trial, trial, and post-trial proceedings, should it come to litigation.

As Nicholson so aptly made clear, "properly trained legal counsel may offer beneficial input [sic] prior to the emergent event that gives rise to possible liability" (Nicholson, 2003d, p. 14). Thus, legal assistance by noble, knowledgeable counsel is indispensable, and attorneys and counselors versed in emergency management and homeland security law is *sine qua non* to homeland security stakeholders' and emergency managers' ability to protect themselves in situations that involve serious emergency management and homeland security liability concerns that cannot – and should not – be taken lightly or overlooked for obvious reasons.

Moreover, lawyers must be competent to decipher the various related homeland security and emergency laws and regulations that pertain to the Stafford Act of 1988 (and its amendments in specific years subsequent), the Homeland Security Act of 2002, the Post Katrina Emergency Management Reform Act of 2006, and the National Response Framework of 2008 (Moss et al., 2009). These multiple layers of law and regulations (i.e., the quagmired complexity of bureaucracy) are difficult to apply when there is a specific need for the federal government to act under diverse provisions of these "simultaneous acts" (referring to the various Acts and policies discussed earlier). These areas of law and regulations must be decided more in terms of "settled law," which, of course, is done best by lawyers and judges well versed in emergency management and homeland security law. This is why lawyers' role in emergency management and homeland security law is salient.

Finally, torts of commission or omission, as well as contracts law and other types of representation, must be regulated by lawyers' good advice, especially as pertains specifically to emergency management and homeland security law. We now undertake the current challenges in doing what has been proposed so far.

CURRENT CHALLENGES

One of the biggest general challenges is that definitive roles have not been expanded for lawyers in the areas of emergency management and homeland security. If lawyers are still not well versed in these areas because law schools and other venues have not equipped them fully, these roles must be identified, classified, and presented as a coherent body of principles or ideas for systematic implementation (i.e., needed so that lawyers may be effective advocates and litigators for these respective clients). Moreover, this is not to mention lawyers getting well educated and trained in emergency management and homeland security law to specifically benefit homeland security stakeholders, emergency managers, and related personnel sooner rather than later.

Another general challenge is that emergency managers must have confidence that their lawyer/advisors know what they are facing in emergency management scenarios with the different activities and prospective liabilities faced by these leaders during each phase of the disaster life cycle, and especially during evolving times of crises and catastrophic disasters in the response phase.

More specific challenges follow. For instance, lawyers in the United States, as in many places worldwide, have suffered from a lack of public trust that they actually do what is in the best interests of their respective clients. The belief is one of rational choice theory, where one will do what is best for himself rather than for someone else, even if the other person is "the client." A more complete understanding of this idea comes from a study of the concept of moral hazard, which supports the idea that lawyers (the agents for clients) possess specialized knowledge of the law their clients (the principals) do not possess. This section refers to Agency Theory (i.e., the principal-agent relationship, where the client is the principal and the lawyer is the agent dutifully representing his/her client).

To expand on this thinking, the major challenge is that mistrust is sown from the client's seemingly disadvantaged position of not possessing the specialized knowledge in this principal-agent relationship with one's lawyer. After all, it is the lawyer who went to law school and is learned in the law. Relationships between lawyer and client are fiduciary in nature (they all should be), and the trusting client believes and holds firm to that belief that his/her lawyer is doing everything to protect the former's best interests – every time. When trust is lacking (as is the case sometimes), the relationship between the lawyer and his client usually suffers irreparable damage. Unfortunately, the consequences are more adversely impacted upon the client-emergency manager or other defendant who has been, or will be, sued.

Even more, the situation of mistrust of lawyers is further complicated because if something does not go as planned (as case results cannot be guaranteed) – for example, a defendant is convicted after going to trial on the lawyer's advice that "I'll win your case and you can go free" – the lawyer may take warranted criticism for leading the client "down the wrong path." Distrust is further cultivated by the client's perhaps mistaken belief that the "noble professional" (the lawyer) did not act in a trustworthy and loyal manner, and somehow, he is dishonest and not worthy of respect. Some other professions like medicine, it seems, receive more latitude for their doctors' life/death decision-making. Patients wait in waiting rooms for hours to see their doctors, and when someone dies, whether a relative or friend, their survivor (may also be a patient of the particular doctor) understands that not everyone can be saved. This seems true even when a person is not a patient of the doctor, and doctors of medicine are still afforded great latitude for decisions made in these life/death circumstances; in essence, the reaction realized by the spectator that death is a reality and was probably imminent for this very sick person. This is not the case for lawyers when dealing with life/death situations, especially on the criminal law side. Mistrust by clients toward some lawyers seems ubiquitous, and this apparent typical culture must be quelled, limited, or at least reckoned with to resolve.

Yet, the foregoing comments seem in drastic contradiction to the statement, "The underlying ethos of the legal profession is service to society, akin to that of a doctor. The aim is to protect citizens from social diseases" ("Legal Profession: A Noble Profession"). However, clients do not always see it this way. When cases are lost (because of the real or perceived notion that it is the lawyer's foremost fault), the lack of trust that developed throughout the attorney-client relationship (especially on the part of the client) is difficult to undo. It seems in these situations that the designation of lawyering as a noble profession is not merited – and certainly not true in the eyes of the client. How do lawyers, then, continue to deserve such a designation, "practice in the noble profession of law"? How do they continue to practice, especially when trust has waned between lawyer-agent/client-principal in recent years? No doubt, lawyers and their bar associations must continue to pursue and form extraordinary and trustworthy relationships in all they do, and in the transactions they undertake to exponentially increase society's trust of lawyers. In fact, they must convince their clients that lawyers are engaged in a noble profession, and are actually representing their clients with the zeal and expertise they deserve and expect.

Miranda provided a good reason that law may remain a noble profession, in spite of a client's lack of trust when he stated, "the law is a profession, one that has standards for entry and rules of ethics that are in place to protect the clients we serve" (Law Remains a Noble Profession). There are other reasons, none better propounded than in 1953 by the eminent and learned U.S. Supreme Court Justice Roscoe Pound when he said, "The practice of law is no less a public service because it may incidentally be a means of liveli-hood." By writing these wise words, Justice Pound emphasized the law as the substantial ideal of service rather than only the maximization of profits (i.e., fees billed in hours, etc.).

Despite earlier comments about a lawyer's apparent diminished vantage point vis-à-vis medical doctors, a lawyer may have a "one up" on "lesser professions" that do not approxi-mate a high status such as medical doctors, engineers, and especially the clergy, because the profession of law has been recognized as "a calling" in unison with "a calling" for physicians, engineers, and the clergy. In essence, this statement may bring into fruition the realization that many also believe that candidates for the bar (i.e., lawyers) are "called to the Bar," not merely admitted to the bar (Pound, 1953). Thus, no one should wonder why all the aforementioned professions, including Law, have confidentiality rules of ethics that are firmly held and cannot be violated without expected dire consequences meted against practitioner-violators. To reemphasize, this fact is no less true with lawyers and their req-uisite adherence to Ethical Codes of Professional Responsibility and Conduct, or risk the consequences of private reprimand, public reprimand, suspension, and/or disbarment.

But what about a lawyer's dual roles, for instance, that of Advocate and as "Officer of the Court"? Do these apparent contradictions, lawyer as advocate while also serving as officer of the court, exacerbate the challenge of the lack of trust? These two dual roles conflict at times, causing even further distrust of lawyers. At the very minimum, the belief that the lawyer is not interested in performing duties in the best interest of the client is magnified because as an advocate, a lawyer has a duty to represent his/her client zeal-ously and protect every legal right they have; as an officer of the court, the same lawyer serves (simultaneously) the judicial system such that the decorum (rules and procedures) of the court is followed, and where the lawyer must advise the court if his client is com-mitting perjury (at the expense of the client who believes the lawyer, as his advocate, will defend him/her at all costs). As one can notice, the designation of the lawyer as advo-cate and officer of the court (at the same time) is problematic. Emergency management and homeland security clients must be taught about how counsel may serve as an able advocate, while also serving competently as an officer of the court. This may help clients improve trust and confidence levels in their counsel.

Even more, expanded examples of challenges of some of the legal problems emer-gency managers and lawyers may face as they try to deal with liabilities (civil cases) and even clients' culpabilities (criminal cases) exist. For instance, politicians and emergency managers were arrested in Italy for neglect. Especially significant to mention is when wicked problems (i.e., those that create uncertainty, such as the COVID-19 pandemic) create inconsistencies among policy-makers, decision-makers, lawyers, and emergency managers, these professionals can all come together and collaborate to resolve problems created by multilevel, intergovernmental governance systems made up of local authori-ties, administrative bodies, and even citizens (and their inconsistent decision-making that creates the uncertainty in the first place). Put differently, conflict in decision-making and variation in public administrative outcomes in Italy during the COVID-19 crisis could be resolved and, especially, understood (Malandrino and Demichelis, 2020).

A second international example presents itself in the case of Paraguay and its advances in the emergency management and legal realms. In Paraguay and other countries where corruption exists and violators of the law may not be brought to justice, lawyers and emergency managers face situations such as these:

the huge fire of August 1, 2004. It occurred at a "shopping center" called Yeua Bolanos. On this particular day, over 2,000 people were inside when a fire began in the bakery. This horrendous incident caused over 400 deaths, burned or injured over 1,000 persons, and wrought a vast amount of property loss and damage. Rich and poor alike perished in this horrendous fire. Nevertheless, the gruesome nature of the incident affected many others in Asuncion [the capitol] and in the surrounding areas. The survivors were affected since they had relatives or friends of victims who were lost in the blaze.

(Urby and McEntire, 2015)

This watershed event in Paraguayan emergency management history, despite the aforementioned rampant corruption (delays in judicial process of wrongdoing were encountered at first) rendered a just sentence of 12 years' confinement against the owner of the commercial shopping center and 10 years' against his son, identified as the culprits who ordered the doors chained when the fire broke out (Urby and McEntire, 2015). It is noteworthy that Paraguay's legal system and emergency management processes, in effect, have begun to create a culture of prevention (in Latin American countries, more like our Mitigation phase) as a national priority. The country even created for its lawyers and emergency managers (everyone in general) new laws and organizations to better deal with disasters in the future.

These two examples provide a general overview of how lawyers and emergency managers may collaborate, synchronize, and advocate for their respective countries and put into practice the laws and emergency management innovations so necessary for homeland security stakeholders and emergency managers to continue to avoid liability. This will allow lawyers to advise them most effectively so that prudent outcomes result for all concerned, and justice is done and not delayed. Coverage of recommendations for the future follows.

RECOMMENDATIONS FOR THE FUTURE

By recognizing and understanding the challenges just presented, we can make various recommendations to address them. One outstanding suggestion that Nicholson presented at length is the indispensable "litigation mitigation" strategy. His beliefs included that for lawyers to succeed with professional zeal and the quest to protect, defend, and promote their emergency management clients, litigation mitigation's three-prong complementary objectives (i.e., in essence, defines this important term) should be employed: 1) reduced exposure to legal claims [the lawyer is able to effectively advise his client in anticipation of liability that may, or does, accrue], 2) improved life safety (the lawyer helps his emergency management client follow Occupational Safety and Health Administration (OSHA) safety and other laws that keep the client and his workers safe), and, 3) enhanced property protection through insurance and other mitigation-type structural and non-structural approaches (Nicholson, 2003d).

Nicholson's admonition that most stands out in this regard "is for legal counsel and emergency managers to rely on and comprehend each other as equal partners for litigation mitigation to be successful" (Nicholson, 2003d, p. 16). He emphasized that, "The attorney must understand the client's business in order to provide the best legal advice" (p. 20). What Nicholson proposed should equally apply to homeland security stakeholders and practitioners. His important admonishment is summarized as follows:

The best attorneys know both the law and their clients' business. Lawyers should spend time in the field with emergency responders and emergency managers to learn about their concerns and perspectives. Only by sharing information on legal concerns and listening respectfully to one another's views can emergency responders, emergency managers, and their attorney advisors enter into a comprehensive alliance. Only through a truly equal partnership can appropriate steps be taken to mitigate and prevent legal liability.

(Nicholson, 2003d, p. 327)

Finally, for these recommendations to work or at least have a chance at some success, homeland security stakeholders and emergency managers should have a much closer connection to lawyers than people think. Understanding each other as equal partners when it comes to life/death situations (e.g., before, during, and after disasters) and building communities' and individuals' resilience involved in prevention, mitigation, preparedness, response, and recovery issues related to homeland security and emergency management is essential and of primary concern. In summary, to help mend serious "dysfunctional fences" (so to speak) between lawyer and client, the following advice is noteworthy: "The nobility of the legal profession lies in the selfless efforts of the legal community to uphold the ideals of the society and the relentless exertions to serve the society" ("Legal Profession: A Noble Profession").

CONCLUSION

The Law has been around for a long time, as evidenced by the "legal footprint" of statutes, laws, case precedent, civil law, etc., in many nations throughout the world. Lawyers in the United States have not had a long history of preparation, adaptability, or service in the emergency management and homeland security disciplines or respective practice. This is due mainly to emergency management as a discipline being around for only some 60 years. Homeland security, at least as a cabinet-level federal department, has existed only since 2002 (i.e., Homeland Security Act). Moreover, most U.S. State Bar Associations have only existed for a few more decades than emergency management as a discipline. Even so, the frequent occurrence of diverse terrorist acts and/or disasters in recent memory should continue to provide opportunities for lawyers to exercise legal expertise, practice in the pre- and post-disaster phases of the life cycle, and help their homeland security and emergency management partners succeed and prevent liability in advance. More opportunities must be opened for lawyers to write and enforce contracts in court judicial "in-law" proceedings from an emergency management and homeland security perspective. This will also allow lawyers to defend homeland security stakeholders and emergency managers sued in tort from civil liability damages and know how injunctions help their clients (or not) when it comes to administrative "in equity" (equitable) lawsuits and much more.

Lawyers' limitations to represent their homeland security and emergency manager clients specifically and reasonably in emergency management and homeland security law must be addressed by law schools and emergency management and homeland security professional organizations alike. This must be accomplished to assist one another with each other's practical challenges, and to ensure that everyone can assist where needed; lawyers to prosecute civil claims for their clients and defend them in criminal court (if necessary). Homeland security stakeholders and emergency managers can also assist their lawyers in understanding their duties and how they practice their craft efficiently, effectively, legally, and ethically (or not).

For instance, homeland security stakeholders and emergency managers should also learn some basic law (as is now the case in many university emergency management and related programs) to help their lawyers with accurate facts, issues, and information. The main point here is that it is integral that lawyers possess precise legal education and/or practical training to facilitate competent performance of their essential jobs in furtherance of their clients' best interests for and in all matters related specifically to emergency management and homeland security.

If all we have suggested takes hold, the voluntary and hired opportunities for lawyers to provide legal assistance to homeland security stakeholders and emergency management personnel and their organizations will, at a minimum, enhance trust of lawyers in furtherance of their practice of a noble profession, not to mention what it does to protect clients legally and ethically and within the highest standards of the effective practice of law. The more that is known about the important profession of law and the role of lawyers in all phases of the disaster life cycle, the more their enormous professional contributions will be appreciated. With learned, competent, and skilled lawyer representation in emergency management and homeland security law, homeland security stakeholders, emergency managers, and other personnel may be provided the highest quality legal advice and services related to terrorism and disasters. This will hopefully allow implementation of the legal preventative remedies provided by qualified, competent counsel in advance of certain liability threats that will benefit all except those who would attempt to file the lawsuit in the first place.

CLASS DISCUSSION AND ESSAY QUESTIONS

1. According to Bill Nicholson, "law and emergency management are inherently intertwined, and legal norms in the disaster field are changing and having a significant impact on the profession" (2003d, Abstract). Explain this statement.
2. Are lawyers typically trained in the areas of emergency management and homeland security law? What are the implications of your answer?
3. Mistrust of lawyers is common in our society. Why is this attitude dangerous for the professionals involved in emergency management and homeland security?
4. What is "litigation mitigation" and why should it be pursued?
5. What other aspects of law relate to disasters, terrorism, emergency management, and homeland security? Why is it important for emergency managers and homeland security professionals to consider these issues?

REFERENCES

Malandrino, A. and E. Demichelis (2020). "Conflict in Decision Making and Variation in Public Administration Outcomes in Italy during the Covid-19 Crisis". *European Policy Analysis*. DOI: 10.1002/epa2.1093.

Miranda, D. P. (2015) "Law Remains a Noble Profession (e-report)". https://www.americanbar.org>gpsolo>, November 2015.

Moss, M. L., C. Shellhamer and D. A. Berman (2009). "The Stafford Act and Priorities for Reform". *Journal of Homeland Security and Emergency Management* 6(1). DOI: 10.2202/1547-7355.1538.

Nicholson, W. C. (2003d). *Emergency Response and Emergency Management Law: Cases and Materials*. Springfield, IL: Charles C. Thomas Publisher, Ltd.

Pound, R. (1953). *The Lawyer from Antiquity to Modern Times*. St. Paul, MN: West Publishing Co. https://www.jstor.org>stable.

Urby, H. and D. A. McEntire (2015). "Emergency Management in Paraguay: A Landlocked Country Not Without Disasters and Accidents". In McEntire, David A. (Ed.), *Comparative Emergency Management: Understanding Disaster Policies, Organizations, and Initiatives from Around the World*. Emmitsburg, MD: Federal Management Agency. http://training.fema.gov/EMIWeb/edu/CompEMMngtBookProject.asp.

CHAPTER 16

Healthcare Emergency Management:

The Role of Relevant Professionals in Healthcare Systems, Facilities, and ESF8

Arthur J. Simental and Lorin Schroeder

> *Make preparations in advance...you never have trouble if you are prepared for it.*
>
> – Theodore Roosevelt

INTRODUCTION

This chapter explores the role of healthcare systems and facilities with emphasis on the associated professional roles, functions, and activities during emergencies and disasters. Healthcare systems are composed of a complex network of primary care and secondary care facilities ranging from frontline urgent care clinics to hospitals, specialized treatment centers such as burn and trauma centers, pediatric facilities, radiology, dialysis, nursing homes, and hospice care.

These healthcare systems have long been the bedrock and leading pillars of medical care in communities across the nation, playing a central role in community health, safety, and development. From an emergency management lens, healthcare systems and facilities such as hospitals and specialized treatment centers have become vital components of the disaster life cycle. Healthcare facilities serve as the primary receiver system where patients can obtain care and exit the response and recovery phases of a disaster upon successfully going through a course or series of stabilizing treatments.

After reviewing the history of healthcare systems and their relation to disasters and terrorist attacks, the following chapter identifies current challenges and provides recommendations for the future. It reflects and discusses issues observed during the COVID-19 response, including triage and ethics, surge capacity and healthcare worker burnout and mortality. As will be demonstrated, it reveals that healthcare emergency managers play a pivotal role in the development of disaster-related programs that have far reaching impacts across multiple jurisdictions spanning large geographic areas. In partnership with local healthcare coalitions, healthcare emergency managers have significant

DOI: 10.4324/9781003350729-16

influence on a wide range of program activities and matters from the establishment of community preparedness stockpiles of critical medical supplies to the development of mass patient decontamination, triage and surge plans needed to manage major influxes of patients after mass casualty events and WMDs. Most notably, healthcare emergency managers have a direct role in all aspects of pandemic preparedness, response and recovery as seen during the COVID-19 pandemic.

HEALTHCARE SYSTEMS AND HEALTHCARE EMERGENCY MANAGEMENT

Healthcare systems are an essential part of every community. Healthcare systems and healthcare emergency management have an important history in the United States. Healthcare emergency management is a newer focus in healthcare with growing importance following the 9/11 terrorist attacks in the U.S. This section explores a brief history of healthcare emergency management in the United States, mentions its relationship to disasters and terrorist attacks, and identifies regulatory requirements that have been developed over time.

According to the World Health Organization (WHO), Healthcare Systems are defined as organizations that are:

> responsible for delivering services that improve, maintain or restore the health of individuals and their communities. This includes the care provided by hospitals and family doctors, but also less visible tasks such as the prevention and control of communicable disease, health promotion, health workforce planning and improving the social, economic or environmental conditions in which people live.

> (WHO, 2021)

This definition from WHO demonstrates the critical role they play in providing healthcare services that range from preventative medicine, treatment, health promotion, advancing the general welfare of the community's workforce, supporting public health maintenance, and recovery. Given the critical roles healthcare systems play in communities as a community lifeline and key critical infrastructure, the need to safeguard healthcare systems from the range of ever-increasing threats, hazards and vulnerabilities post-9/11 is apparent. Healthcare systems and the span of facilities that comprise them in communities have only just begun engaging in emergency management efforts and preparedness activities over the last two decades despite the historic role they have played throughout the history of disasters and even during times of war and conflict.

Healthcare emergency management is thus a newer focus in healthcare with growing importance following the 9/11 terrorist attacks in the U.S. The following section explores a brief history of healthcare emergency management in the United States, the role healthcare plays in emergency management, and the Crisis Standards of Care. Healthcare emergency management in the context of war, terrorism and conflict is also examined through select key events pre- and post-9/11 and the War in Ukraine.

Brief History of Healthcare Emergency Management in the United States

The role of healthcare systems in relation to homeland security and emergency management is explored in this section. Healthcare systems have always played an essential part in the response and recovery to emergencies, disasters, terrorism, war, and conflict throughout history. These roles continue to evolve and are shaped by notable events such as World War II and Pearl Harbor, 9/11, the Boston Marathon Bombing 2013, the 2009 H1N1 pandemic, Hurricane Sandy 2012, COVID-19, the War in Ukraine and many others.

Historically, healthcare systems have served as places of care and healing be it from any type of emergency, disaster, crime, conflict or war. There are innumerable examples going back to the founding of the nation and throughout history, both pre- and post-9/11 demonstrating the role healthcare systems have played in emergency management. These examples also show the need for robust healthcare emergency management programs. To highlight a few for example, pre-9/11 the Tokyo Subway Sarin Attack showed weaknesses in hospital emergency preparedness and demonstrated the need for hospital decontamination systems, expanded surge capacity, patient care triage, protocols to prevent secondary exposure to first receivers and care providers, and many other lessons learned (Okumura et al., 1998). The 2014 Ebola Outbreak in the United States showed weaknesses in healthcare emergency management and as a precursor to COVID-19 general weaknesses in managing public heath communicable disease response, quarantine and isolation policies, and major misunderstandings about organizational roles and responsibilities (McEntire, 2019). This occurred despite years of hospital preparedness funding compounded by minimal regulatory requirements for healthcare preparedness programs, lax healthcare emergency preparedness efforts and organizational cultures often reported among hospital emergency managers, especially in the private sector. These were the pre-regulatory years to note where emergency management programs and the present-day standards governing them were not required by healthcare facility regulatory and accrediting bodies.

Another example the 2017 Las Vegas Country Music Festival shooting where "Sunrise Hospital, a level II trauma Center, treated 214 patients of the hundreds injured at the Route 91 Harvest country music festival in Las Vegas … including 124 with gunshot wounds … Sunrise surgeons performed 58 surgeries in the first 24 hours, 83 altogether." (LUS Health New Orleans, 2019). A key takeaway from the lessons learned of the 2017 Las Vegas Country Music Festival Shooting being "we always need to plan for the unexpected" (LUS Health New Orleans, 2019). This is a lesson that ties back to the conclusion of the 9/11 Commission Report – a failure of imagination. History shows us that events once unimaginable are becoming reality at a more frequent pace then we are able to prepare for them. The response to COVID-19 and the war in Ukraine are the most recent examples and they will be examined in later sections of this chapter. Healthcare emergency management is therefore critical to homeland security, and as these events have shown us a vital part of our communities.

RELATION TO DISASTERS/TERRORISM

Healthcare systems are the final leg of patient care in the complex web and systems of disaster medicine. Because of the relation to disasters and terrorism, and the fact that healthcare systems themselves are not immune to the impacts of incidents of all types be it natural disasters such as flooding, hurricanes and wildfires to cyberattacks, and even direct attacks by enemy forces as seen in the Ukraine War, there is a great need for healthcare emergency management programs. Arguably there has always been a significant need, however this was optional and not a regulatory requirement in the United States until many years after 9/11.

Emergency management in healthcare is a relatively new focus. The incident command system (ICS) has been operational mostly in the fire service since the 1970's with roots traced back to the California fire service (EMSI, n.d.). By the 1980's FEMA (Federal Emergency Management Agency) started to incorporate ICS in the curriculum at the National Fire Academy (EMSI, n.d.). Homeland Security Presidential Directive 5 in 2005 was the beginning of a national focus on ICS for first responders (EMSI, n.d.). During this time, Orange County Emergency Medical Services began adapting ICS for healthcare (CEMSA, n.d.). It wasn't until 2006 that the Hospital Incident Command System (HICS) began to get national attention and help form an organized response to emergency management in healthcare. The California Emergency Medical Services Authority released the most current model in 2014. This most recent model has incorporated lessons learned from national impacts on the healthcare system from numerous real-world events (CEMSA, n.d.).

In 2002 The Joint Commission (TJC) published elements of performance in emergency management for hospitals and a few other healthcare providers. The TJC continues to update these healthcare emergency management standards and surveys participating hospitals for compliance (TJC, 2022). These standards only affected healthcare organizations who sought TJC accreditation but served as guidance for emergency preparedness in others. In 2016 the Centers for Medicare and Medicaid Services (CMS) published new rules and requirements for Medicare and Medicaid providers (CMS, 2021). These new rules identified 17 provider groups, including hospitals, that would now be required to meet emergency management regulations if they were to bill Medicare or Medicaid for services. This cemented need for healthcare emergency management programs as a regulatory requirement for healthcare facilities and nodded to integral role they play as a part of each community's lifeline infrastructure.

Healthcare Emergency Management Regulatory Requirements

In 2001 the Joint Commission on Accreditation of Healthcare Organizations (JCAHO), later known as The Joint Commission (TJC), included emergency management standards in the Environment of Care chapter. These standards were mostly focused on disruptions in the delivery of care from damage to buildings, grounds, loss of utilities, or surge events (CABQ OEM, n.d.). There were only 33 elements of performance (EP's) identified for emergency management. For the most part, the safety officer was responsible for documenting compliance for these EP's as they were a part of the Environment of Care chapter.

During the release of the 2009 TJC standards, emergency management became its own chapter. With this release, TJC identified 111 elements of performance and guidance of how healthcare organizations would be measured for compliance. This new chapter and a 70% increase in EP's encouraged many healthcare organizations to identify an emergency manager to ensure compliance. In 2022, TJC has 207 EP's just for emergency management almost doubling from 2009.

Along with regulations, in 2006 Health and Human Services (HHS) made Federal funding available through Hospital Preparedness Program (HPP) grants. This funding was sent from HHS to state health departments to be distributed to local healthcare organizations (i.e., hospitals) to assist in emergency management preparedness (CHA, n.d.). This funding had state and federal deliverables attached to them. Organizations requesting these funds were required to submit documentation of completion of deliverables to be eligible for funding. This program exists today, but has seen a decrease of over 50% in the past few years. Recent years have seen a focus change from regulators (TJC, CMS, and HHS) demanding that healthcare organizations provide more emergency preparedness activities as a part of doing business and relying less on state and federal grant funding.

THE ROLE OF HEALTHCARE EMERGENCY MANAGEMENT

Healthcare emergency management plays a unique role in the emergency management community. Healthcare facilities serve as an import component of the healthcare and public health critical infrastructure sector with various risks and numerous interdependencies. Healthcare emergency management encompasses aspects of crises standards of care and Emergency Support Function #8 Public Health and Medical Services. These are two core elements of healthcare emergency management are further explored in this section. Additionally, an overview of the National Disaster Medical System and Hospital Preparedness Program is also provided in the ASPR's Healthcare Readiness and Hospital Preparedness Programs section.

Crisis Standards of Care: A Systems Framework for Catastrophic Disaster Response

Crisis Standards of Care (CSC) is the proverbial third rail topic in healthcare. "Crisis Standards of Care provides a framework for a systems approach to the development and implementation of CSC plans, and addresses the legal issues and the ethical, palliative care, and mental health issues that agencies and organizations at each level of a disaster response should address" (CSC, 2012). This subject has enormous ethical and moral dilemmas and conflicting interests, not to mention the legal pitfalls from adjudicated case law to current local and federal statutes covering the ethical and equitable delivery of healthcare in our country. A national committee assembled a seven-volume report to assist in guiding the discussion to establish CSC. This work is crucial for the future of healthcare disaster management and mass casualty response whether it be mitigating a natural disaster or the next pandemic.

EMERGENCY SUPPORT FUNCTION #8 – PUBLIC HEALTH AND MEDICAL SERVICES

The Healthcare role in Emergency Management is based on the National Response Framework's Emergency Support Function #8 (ESF8) – Public Health and Medical Services. Healthcare activities during an emergency or disaster focus on providing ESF8 support to impacted communities. ESF8 support and emergency activities are an expansive conglomeration of many fields from medicine to public health, veterinary care and occupational health and safety. "HHS is the primary agency responsible for ESF8 – Public Health and Medical Services. ESF8 is coordinated by the Secretary of HHS principally through the Assistant Secretary for Preparedness and Response (ASPR). ESF8 resources

Health and Medical Response Lead Partners

HHS leads and coordinates the overall health and medical response to national-level incidents through coordination, along with the following.

- ▶ Department of Agriculture
- ▶ Department of Transportation
- ▶ Department of Defense
- ▶ Department of Veterans Affairs
- ▶ Department of State
- ▶ Agency for International Development
- ▶ Department of Energy
- ▶ Environmental Protection Agency
- ▶ Department of Homeland Security
- ▶ General Services Administration
- ▶ Department of Interior
- ▶ U.S. Postal Service
- ▶ Department of Justice
- ▶ American Red Cross
- ▶ Department of Labor

FIGURE 16.1.   List of Agency ESF8 Partners (OASPRa, 2019).

can be activated through the Stafford Act or the Public Health Service Act. ESF8 – Public Health and Medical Services provides the mechanism for coordinated Federal assistance to supplement State, Tribal, and local resources in response to an emergency" (OASPR, 2019a). Medical Assistance is the primary type of support available through ESF8 led by the U.S. Department of Health and Human Services in coordination with multiple federal agency and other organizational partners including the American Red Cross as seen in Figure 16.1.

Primary ESF8 support provided from the federal government includes a range of capabilities including specialized medical teams, equipment, personnel, and technical support. ESF8 medical support is expansive and adaptable to all-hazards including specialized incidents and operations across the CBRNE spectrum. "Federal public health medical assistance consists of medical materiel, personnel, and technical assistance. These resources may provide response capability for the triage, treatment, and transportation of victims or persons with special medical needs; evacuation of patients; infection control; mental health screening and counseling; environmental health services; and other emergency response needs" (OASPR, 2019a). Brief descriptions of ESF#8 Medical Assistance can be seen in **Table 16.1.** For a full description of these capabilities from the Office of the Assistant Secretary for Response see Appendix A: ESF#8 Medical Assistance Capabilities. USPHS Commissioned Corps, NDMS, and MRC teams are further supported by resources from the Strategic National Stockpile and HHS deployable healthcare facilities such as Federal Medical Stations.

Another type of support provided through ESF8 includes medical surge capacity capability to support healthcare facilities. Medical surge capacity support is contingent upon Presidential major disaster declarations and Stafford Act Disaster declarations and upon request of a state Governor. "When the NRF is triggered by a Presidential declaration of a major disaster or emergency under the Stafford Act, Federal assistance generally

TABLE 16.1. ESF #8 List of Medical Assistance Capabilities (OASPRb, 2019).

ESF #8 List of Medical Assistance Capabilities:

USPHS Commissioned Corps teams

- *Rapid Deployment Force (RDF):* The RDF consists of five pre-identified teams, each with 105 multidisciplinary staff.
- *Applied Public Health Team (APHT):* The APHT is composed of experts in applied public health and can function as a "public health department in a box."
- *Mental Health Team (MHT):* The MHT consists of mental and behavioral health experts who assess stress and suicide risks within the affected population, manage responder stress, and provide therapy, counseling, and crisis intervention.

NDMS teams

The NDMS is a nationwide partnership designed to deliver quality medical care to the victims of, and responders to, a domestic disaster. NDMS provides state-of-the-art medical care under any conditions at a disaster site, in transit from the impacted area, and in participating definitive care facilities. The main NDMS teams consist of the following:

- *Disaster Medical Assistance Team (DMAT):* DMATs provide primary and acute care, triage of mass casualties, initial resuscitation and stabilization, advanced life support and preparation of sick or injured for evacuation.
- *Disaster Mortuary Operational Response Team (DMORT):* DMORTs work under the guidance of local authorities by providing technical assistance and personnel to recover, identify, and process deceased victims.
- *National Veterinary Response Team (NVRT):* NVRT provides assistance in identifying the need for veterinary services following major disasters, emergencies, public health or other events requiring Federal support and in assessing the extent of disruption to animal and public health infrastructures.
- *National Medical Response Team (NMRT):* NMRTs provide medical care following a nuclear, biological, and/or chemical incident.

Medical Reserve Corps

- The MRC is comprised of organized medical and public health professionals who serve as volunteers to respond to natural disasters and emergencies. The MRC program provides the structure necessary to deploy medical and public health personnel in response to an emergency, as it identifies specific, trained, credentialed personnel available and ready to respond to emergencies.

is provided at the request of the Governor (or his/her designee) of an affected State" (OASPR, 2019b). These assets, capabilities and resources available under ESF8 support represent the primary means of which federal support is provided and supports healthcare facilities during disasters. However, response resources are not the only means available to healthcare facilities. The former HSS, Office of the Assistant Secretary of Preparedness and Response now Administration for Strategic Preparedness and Response (ASPR) maintains robust preparedness programs and partnerships supporting healthcare readiness with healthcare facilities nation-wide. Healthcare facility preparedness support is provided through programs such as the Hospital Preparedness Program, Regional Disaster Health Response System, National Special Pathogen System, Workforce Capacity support and other programs including technical assistance. Descriptions of these core programs can be seen in Figure 16.2. Healthcare disaster preparedness and readiness activities are briefly discussed in the next section.

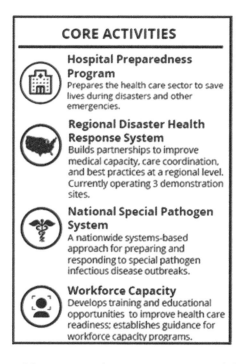

CORE ACTIVITIES

Hospital Preparedness Program
Prepares the health care sector to save lives during disasters and other emergencies.

Regional Disaster Health Response System
Builds partnerships to improve medical capacity, care coordination, and best practices at a regional level. Currently operating 3 demonstration sites.

National Special Pathogen System
A nationwide systems-based approach for preparing and responding to special pathogen infectious disease outbreaks.

Workforce Capacity
Develops training and educational opportunities to improve health care readiness; establishes guidance for workforce capacity programs.

FIGURE 16.2.   ASPR Health Care Readiness Programs Portfolio Fact Sheet (ASPR(a), 2022).

ASPR's Healthcare Readiness and Hospital Preparedness Programs

The Assistant Secretary of Administration for Strategic Preparedness and Response (formerly known simply as Preparedness and Response), now plays a critical role in supporting healthcare emergency preparedness programs. ASPR serves as the administrator of strategic and national ESF8 capabilities and initiatives.

> ASPR's Health Care Readiness Programs help hospitals, health care facilities, and health care systems across the country overcome the complex challenges associated with disaster health care by providing coordinated, life-saving care and broadening the resources available during a disaster or public health emergency. ASPR's Health Care Readiness Programs support the development of new partnerships and provide leadership, funding, training, and technical assistance that enhance the nation's health care preparedness and response capacity. This portfolio of programs and activities engages health care stakeholders from all 50 states, U.S. territories, and freely associated states and from across the health care industry – empowering private health care to share ownership in addressing the risks and vulnerabilities across the spectrum of disaster care delivery. ASPR's Health Care Readiness Programs create connections among health care providers, specialty care providers, response organizations, regional partners, and public health professionals. These programs also enhance education and technical assistance to help health care providers save lives in the face of complex health challenges, including COVID-19.
>
> (ASPR(a), 2022)

ASPR funds a variety of healthcare preparedness programs and readiness activities to engage healthcare systems, healthcare coalitions, networks, providers and facilities before a disaster strikes. These activities include expanding capabilities through equipment, planning, training and exercises in partnership with community response organizations and partners such as emergency medical service, acute care hospitals, emergency management organizations, and other healthcare entities (ASPR (b), 2022). Select healthcare facilities part of Regional Disaster Health Response Systems even have the unique opportunity to exercise with federal and defense agency partners for incidents supporting military healthcare emergencies. Chiefly, Hospital Preparedness Program funding has supported a robust range of emergency preparedness activities and capability development since 9/11 including planning, training, exercises, expanding healthcare facility surge capacity, disaster preparedness, communication and many other key areas with local healthcare systems and facilities nation-wide. Other programs like the National Special Pathogens Program provides expansive support to a network of designated healthcare facilities and treatment centers nationwide to support the response and recovery from unique and special pathogens like Ebola (ASPR (b), 2022). This program is a direct result of lessons learned and failures in the response to the 2014 U.S. Ebola outbreak where multiple persons providing treatment to a traveler carrying Ebola were infected in Dallas, Texas. Demonstrating clear gaps and weaknesses in healthcare systems, medical operations, emergency management and public health and communicable disease prevention and control. The wide range of readiness and preparedness programs works to build and support capacity and capabilities nationwide. These preparedness and readiness investments since 9/11 serve as a robust foundation preparing healthcare systems and facilities for emergency and disaster response, especially when working in concert with federal ESF8 support.

CURRENT CHALLENGES

While there are many lessons learned from the healthcare emergency management response to COVID-19 and volumes yet to be written on the subject over the next decade, this section highlights a handful of contemporary healthcare emergency management issues. The following challenges affecting healthcare emergency management are examined: COVID-19 challenges and healthcare emergency management, COVID-19 healthcare surge capacity, COVID-19 ethics of patient triage during a pandemic, NIMS/ICS implementation and training, and lastly concerns about learned from the War in Ukraine's impact on healthcare systems.

COVID-19 Challenges and Healthcare Emergency Management

COVID-19 has demonstrated the inadequacies healthcare emergency mangers identified and attempted to address during the H1N1 outbreak and the Ebola preparation experienced in the U.S. Moving forward into the future, emergency managers have to keep sight not only on the next pandemic but all the other risks for the organization. The all-hazards approach of emergency management is sometimes lost during the overarching COVID-19 pandemic in relation to the subsequent concurring disasters.

Hospitals especially were hit hard, not just from COVID-19 patients but the everyday patient population as well. Long term care facilities that run at near capacity at any given day were also pushed to extreme limits they were never designed to operate under. These systems have proven more fragile than we had feared and the solution for supporting them is more complex than we allowed ourselves to believe. Moving forward, emergency managers need to not only be a part of the mitigation, preparedness, response, and recovery planning for their community, but also the discussion and reevaluation of local, state, and federal laws and regulations as it pertains to public health emergencies.

COVID-19 Healthcare Surge Capacity

Early on during the initial COVID-19 outbreak when vaccination, therapeutics and effective courses of treatment were unknown, not yet available scores of people in several states such as New York were infected and subsequently hospitalized from the early and very severe strains of COVID-19. The numbers of infected quickly maxed hospital and healthcare systems bed capacities throughout states. Conflicting Trump Administration perceptions on roles, responsibilities and strategic resources compounded this issue which became a slow-moving train wreck as the foundation of pandemic preparedness planning that had taken place over the past decades unraveled. Healthcare surge capacity is a critical issue of national importance. Its effective and efficient management and administration is vital to strategic national security and homeland security interests whether it's for pandemic response, treatment of military casualties or a mass casualty event in general. Moving forward we must deeply examine and explore the underlying science, planning foundations and assumptions that have long driven how we approach this critical topic. If the pandemic has taught the world anything is that many assumptions once thought valid are not. They were deeply flawed or based only on a snapshot of the reality facing the nation when they were created and therefore new methodologies, plans and assumptions must be created and regularly assessed, evaluated and revised to capture the present-day environment in which we find ourselves.

COVID-19 – the Ethics of Patient Triage during a Pandemic

As vital resources dwindled during the COVID-19 response an issue surrounding how to best prioritize resources became a focal point of contention over whether to triage and first prioritize critical COVID-19 treatment and care availability to vaccinated patients vs. unvaccinated patients. There are many ethical dilemmas and conflicts to be navigated as it pertains to triage and prioritization of resources in a resource restricted operating environment where limited resources must be used for the greater good. Pandemic response represents a unique area where potentially thousands upon thousands of patients must be carefully managed and triaged. There are a number of challenges over mis- and dis-information about vaccines and interplay between real and perceived rights over whether to vaccinate or not that trace back to the founding and early years of the nation. Given the unique circumstances of the COVID-19 pandemic it is clear that revised ethical guidelines and new standards of care governing pandemic triage, care and treatment prioritization need to be developed.

NIMS/ICS Implementation and Training in Healthcare Emergency Management

As is the case for nearly everything in healthcare, the biggest challenges are time and money to properly and adequately train healthcare workers in the ICS style of response. CMS and TJC have requirements that local healthcare workers are trained in ICS used within their local jurisdictions. There is also a requirement that leadership is trained in NIMS. During the COVID-19 pandemic the issue of NIMS and ICS integration in healthcare settings become more central as challenges and unfamiliarity with NIMS and ICS created coordination challenges during the public health response.

1. EM.15.01.01 The hospital has an emergency management education and training program. (1-4)
2. The hospital provides initial education and training in emergency management to all new and existing staff, individuals providing services under arrangement, volunteers, physicians, and other licensed practitioners that is consistent with their roles and responsibilities in an emergency.
3. The hospital provides ongoing education and training to all staff, volunteers, physicians, and other licensed practitioners that is consistent with their roles and responsibilities in an emergency:
   • At least every two years
   • When roles or responsibilities change
   • When there are significant revisions to the emergency operations plan, policies, and/or procedures
   • When procedural changes are made during an emergency or disaster incident requiring just-intime education and training
4. The hospital requires that incident command staff participate in education and training specific to their duties and responsibilities in the incident command structure.

(TJC, 2022)

For the most part, healthcare organizations follow the letter of the requirements. The challenge is when these practices must be applied to real world events. Leadership in hospitals, for example in some cases, do not follow NIMS in their day-to-day activities. The result is either freelancing of leadership or having a crash course refresher during the onset of the disaster.

One of the hallmarks of effective emergency management is the attention to training using the NIMS doctrine. NIMS was designed to bring a more structured approach to responding to incidents, but more importantly it brings a holistic approach to incidents that requires collaboration and cooperation across multiple agencies and jurisdictions if the incident is so significant. The integration of leaders, along with first responders, is a necessity in the NIMS process. Leadership trained in NIMS would then understand how early planning and recovery response will enable the organization to not only respond to the emergency but to return to the "normal" level of service delivery. Thus, leadership can more effectively integrate the business needs such as risk management and continuity of operations into the overall process of mitigation, preparedness, response, and recovery. While NIMS and the ICS are fundamental elements of the National Response Framework and the national approach to emergency and disaster response, the implementation of NIMS and ICS in existing complex organizational structures such as healthcare facilities can be challenging.

Leadership is looking for the quickest solution to return operations to the "normal" state as quickly and efficiently as possible. Emergency managers who develop an in-depth Continuity of Operations Plan (COOP) can equip leadership with the tools they need to make the business decisions to relocate services as needed within the organization or the list of needs to expand other service lines to meet the needs of the surge. A comprehensive COOP enables leadership to dive deeper into the inner workings of the organization to better understand the inefficiencies and effective systems before a disaster affects the organization. This cooperation integrates emergency management more into the day-to-day operation of the organization instead of a plan on a shelf in case it is needed.

War in Ukraine's impact on Healthcare Systems

Lastly, the War in Ukraine provides great insights into wartime civil defense response and operations. Healthcare facilities specifically have been used to support a variety of activities during the Ukraine War. In doing so they have also become a target for hostile forces who have deliberately targeted, bombed and destroyed many healthcare facilities across Ukraine. One notable example being "a maternity hospital that was damaged by shelling in Mariupol, Ukraine, on March 9" where pregnant mothers were wounded and had to be evacuated (Cole, 2022). This is but one of many horrific incidents witnessed during the Ukraine War. It is noted that this is not an isolated event either. According to wartime reporting, "Russia's 226 attacks on health-care targets in Ukraine are part of a larger pattern" (Cole, 2022).

As the United States has not suffered from or been exposed to conflict on the Homefront since World War II, it is imperative that the lessons learned from the Ukraine war as they pertain to civil defense and wartime healthcare system operations be closely examined, researched, reviewed and practices, standards and wartime operating guidelines be developed to prepare healthcare systems for potential future conflicts from adversarial nations. While the majority would be perceived to view the threat of war in the United States as a low probability, increased saber rattling and destabilizing actions globally by competing superpowers and rogue nations such as North Korea make this a topic not to be gambled with. Civil defense is a re-emerging topic in defense, homeland security and emergency management. We can either prepare now or wait for disaster to happen. Healthcare systems and critical facilities like hospitals and specialized treatment centers are critical to all efforts be it responding to or recovering from terrorism, disasters and even war be it foreign, domestic or civil as history shows.

RECOMMENDATIONS FOR THE FUTURE

COVID-19 variants are likely, but Americans' "focus should be on preparation, not on panic,"
-U.S. Surgeon General Vivek Murthy

The next era of healthcare emergency management will be unique in that there will likely be a robust evolution in the field driven by the many lessons learned from World War I, the great 1918 Influenza Pandemic, World War II, and 9/11, to the present COVID-19 pandemic and other historic events that served as catalysts for evolutionary changes in healthcare. Building on the lessons learned and challenges from the healthcare emergency management response to COVID-19 and the highlights on the War in Ukraine, a series of recommendations are listed below in reflection:

- Engagement of local emergency managers in the state and federal design of healthcare emergency management and response.
- More consistent and equitable engagement of local healthcare coalitions. Including response guidelines for chain of command and the ability to exercise statutory defined emergency response powers.
- Revising pandemic preparedness planning across all levels of government including the development of new updated methodologies, plans and assumptions that are regularly assessed, evaluated and updated.
- Establishment of new and revised national disaster medicine ethics standards of care guidelines for pandemic operations including the governance of triage and treatment prioritization.
- Establishing a commission to examine and develop standards and practices for Healthcare Civil Defense guidelines and protocols governing healthcare system operations during wartime.

CONCLUSION

In conclusion, change in the field of Healthcare Emergency Management is inevitable. What remains to be seen is how the many, many, many lessons learned are implemented in the years moving forward. How will COVID-19's lasting impact be internalized among the many professions and disciplines in healthcare, medicine, allied fields and subdisciplines including emergency medical services, homeland security, and emergency management? How will the pandemic shape the nature of healthcare systems and concepts such as *One Health* and the changing role of public health redefine communities?

The following quote captures the essence of how healthcare systems and emergency management programs need to posture themselves for the future, "we cannot treat our way out of these problems. We are never going to build enough medical services. Preventing suffering before it happens is the long-term answer for our country. Our goal is to create a community where everybody has opportunity to thrive." — Kelly Kelleher, M.D., M.P.H., director of the Center for Innovation in Pediatric Practice at Nationwide Children's Hospital in Columbus, Ohio, accepting the Hearst Health Prize for population health. If the post-WWI and 1918 pandemic's evolutionary changes to the fields of medicine, healthcare, public health, emergency management and the many innovations and marvels that spawned from those crises are any indication of what's next for global health security; than the future looks bright for the generations who will face the great pandemics in the centuries to come.

CLASS DISCUSSION AND ESSAY QUESTIONS

1. What roles do healthcare systems fulfill in a disaster?
2. What major historical incidents have shaped healthcare emergency management?
3. What are the Crisis Standards of Care?
4. How does ESF8 support healthcare facilities during disasters and crisis?
5. What lessons have been learned during COVID-19 and the Ukraine war in improving healthcare systems?

APPENDIX A: ESF#8 MEDICAL ASSISTANCE CAPABILITIES

From the Office of the Assistant Secretary for Preparedness and Response Webpage: Medical Assistance (OASPR, 2021c). Per the Department of Health and Human Services, Office of Assistant Secretary for Preparedness and Response the following Medical Assistance Capabilities can be provided through Emergency Support Function #8:

USPHS COMMISSIONED CORPS

Rapid Deployment Force (RDF): The RDF consists of five pre-identified teams, each with 105 multidisciplinary staff. The teams serve on a rotating call basis, with the on-call team capable of deploying within 12 hours of notification. RDF teams have a built-in command structure and can provide mass care at shelters (including FMSs), and staff Points of Distribution and Casualty Collection Points. The RDF can also conduct community outreach and assessments, among other functions.

- *Applied Public Health Team (APHT):* The APHT is composed of experts in applied public health and can function as a "public health department in a box." An APHT can deploy within 36 hours of notification and provide assistance in public health assessments, environmental health, infrastructure integrity, food safety, vector control, epidemiology, and surveillance.
- *Mental Health Team (MHT):* The MHT consists of mental and behavioral health experts who assess stress and suicide risks within the affected population, manage responder stress, and provide therapy, counseling, and crisis intervention. The MHT can deploy within 36 hours of notification.

NDMS TEAMS

The NDMS is a nationwide partnership designed to deliver quality medical care to the victims of, and responders to, a domestic disaster. NDMS provides state-of-the-art medical care under any conditions at a disaster site, in transit from the impacted area, and in participating definitive care facilities. The main NDMS teams consist of the following:

- *Disaster Medical Assistance Team (DMAT):* DMATs provide primary and acute care, triage of mass casualties, initial resuscitation and stabilization, advanced life support and preparation of sick or injured for evacuation. The basic deployment configuration of a DMAT consists of 35 persons; it includes physicians, nurses, medical technicians, and ancillary support personnel. They can be mobile within 6 hours of notification and are capable of arriving at a disaster site within 48 hours. They can sustain operations for 72 hours without external support. DMATs are responsible for establishing an initial (electronic) medical record for each patient, including assigning patient unique identifiers in order to facilitate tracking throughout the NDMS.
- *Disaster Mortuary Operational Response Team (DMORT):* DMORTs work under the guidance of local authorities by providing technical assistance and personnel to recover, identify, and process deceased victims. Teams are composed of funeral directors, medical examiners, coroners, pathologists, forensic

anthropologists, medical records technicians and transcribers, fingerprint specialists, forensic odonatologists, dental assistants, x-ray technicians, and other personnel. HHS also maintains several Disaster Portable Morgue Units (DPMU) that can be used by DMORTs to establish a stand-alone morgue operation.

- *National Veterinary Response Team (NVRT):* NVRT provides assistance in identifying the need for veterinary services following major disasters, emergencies, public health or other events requiring Federal support and in assessing the extent of disruption to animal and public health infrastructures.
- *National Medical Response Team (NMRT):* NMRTs provide medical care following a nuclear, biological, and/or chemical incident. This team is capable of providing mass casualty decontamination, medical triage, and primary and secondary medical care to stabilize victims for transportation to tertiary care facilities in a hazardous material environment. The basic deployment configuration of an NMRT consists of 50 personnel.

STRATEGIC NATIONAL STOCKPILE (SNS)

The SNS is a national repository of antibiotics, chemical antidotes, antitoxins, life-support medications, IV administration and airway maintenance supplies, and medical/surgical items. The SNS is designed to supplement and re-supply State and local public health agencies in the event of a national emergency anywhere and at anytime within the U.S. or its territories.

FEDERAL MEDICAL STATION (FMS)

The FMS is an HHS deployable healthcare facility that can provide surge beds to support healthcare systems anywhere in the U.S. that are impacted by disasters or public health emergencies. FMS are not mobile and cannot be relocated once established.

Each FMS comes with a three-day supply of medical and pharmaceutical resources to sustain from 50 to 250 stable primary or chronic care patients who require medical and nursing services. Staffing for an FMS can be provided using displaced local, regional or EMAC providers, or can be provided by the federal government (primary federal staff are Officers of the U.S. Public Health Service Commissioned Corps). Potential roles for an FMS include the following:

- Provide temporary holding and care for patients to decompress a local hospital (increase beds available for patients with disaster-related trauma or illness
- Receive patients from nursing homes and skilled nursing facilities forced to evacuate due to the disaster
- Provide low acuity care for patients with chronic illnesses whose access to care is impeded due to the disaster

Because the equipment and supply cache does not include tents, each FMS requires an appropriate building of opportunity in which to operate. Significant preparation is needed to employ FMSs in support of local, State, Tribal, and Territorial emergency plans. An FMS must be established in a structurally intact, accessible building with adequate hygiene facilities and functioning utilities (hot and cold potable water, electricity, heating, ventilation, and air conditioning, and internet accessibility or capability).

A 250-bed FMS requires roughly 40,000 square feet of open space, while a 50-bed FMS requires about 15,000 square feet. In addition, wrap around logistical services must be coordinated and in place before an FMS can be operational. Some of these include a 10-12 person set up team, contracted support for patient feeding, laundry, ice, medical oxygen, and biomedical waste disposal. Fewer beds can be set up in smaller facilities, but building attributes and wrap around services remain the same.

Once a request for FMS has been approved, the cache of equipment and supplies will be delivered in 24-48 hours, after which 12 hours is planned for set-up. ASPR Regional Emergency Coordinators are the primary points of contact for FMS preparedness by State, local, Tribal and Territorial authorities. CDC Division of Strategic National Stockpile (DSNS) can assist with site surveys and training for receipt and set-up of FMSs.

MEDICAL RESERVE CORPS

The MRC is comprised of organized medical and public health professionals who serve as volunteers to respond to natural disasters and emergencies. The MRC program provides the structure necessary to deploy medical and public health personnel in response to an emergency, as it identifies specific, trained, credentialed personnel available and ready to respond to emergencies.

REFERENCES

ASPR. (2022). Administration for Strategic Preparedness and Response, Healthcare Readiness. https://aspr.hhs.gov/HealthCareReadiness/Pages/default.aspx.

ASPR. (2022). Administration for Strategic Preparedness and Response, Hospital Preparedness Program. https://aspr.hhs.gov/HealthCareReadiness/Pages/default .aspx.

California Hospital Association (CHA). (n.d.). What Is the Federal Hospital Preparedness Program? https://www.calhospitalprepare.org/post/what-federal-hospital-preparedness-program-2.

CEMSA. (n.d.). HICS History and Background. https://emsa.ca.gov/hics-history-and -background/.

City of Albuquerque OEM. (n.d.). https://www.cabq.gov/office-of-emergency-management/documents/JCAHOsPerspective.pd.

CMS.gov. (2021). Emergency Preparedness Rule. https://www.cms.gov/Medicare/ Provider-Enrollment-and-Certification/SurveyCertEmergPrep/Emergency-Prep -Rule.

Committee on Guidance for Establishing Crisis Standards of Care for Use in Disaster Situations; Institute of Medicine. Crisis Standards of Care: A Systems Framework for Catastrophic Disaster Response. Washington, DC: National Academies Press (US); 2012. Mar 21. PMID: 24830057.

Cole, Diane. (2022). Ukraine Invasion, Russia's 226 attacks on health-care targets in Ukraine are part of a larger pattern, NPR. https://www.npr.org/sections/goatsand-soda/2022/03/16/1086982186/russias-strike-on-ukraine-maternity-hospital-is-part -of-a-terrible-wartime-tradi

EMSI. (n.d.). History of ICS. https://www.emsics.com/history-of-ics/#:~:text=ICS %20was%20developed%20in%20the,systems%20for%20managing%20wildland %20fire.

LUS Health New Orleans. (2019). Sharing Lessons Learned. https://www.lsuhsc.edu/ newsroom/Sharing%20Lessons%20Learned.html.

McEntire, D. and SFHEA. (2019). The Dallas Ebola Incident as an Indicator of the Bioterrorism Threat: An Assessment of Response with Implications for Security and Preparedness. *UVU Journal of National Security*, 5–17. https://www.google .com/url?sa=t&rct=j&q=&esrc=s&source=web&cd=&cad=rja&uact=8&ved =2ahUKEwjUzsLF6Zb1AhUSB50JHRSdBe0QFnoECAMQAQ&url=https%3A %2F%2Fwww.uvu.edu%2Fnss%2Fdocs%2Fspring2020journal1.pdf&usg =AOvVaw1vFjxeyriK80D_VWNivUdH.

OASPR. (2019a). HHS, Office of Assistant Secretary for Preparedness and Response, Emergency Support Functions. https://www.phe.gov/Preparedness/support/esf8/ Pages/default.aspx.

OASPR. (2019b). HHS, Office of Assistant Secretary for Preparedness and Response, Medical Surge Capacity Capability. https://www.phe.gov/Preparedness/support/ mscc/Pages/default.aspx.

OASPR. (2019c). HHS, Office of Assistant Secretary for Preparedness and Response, Medical Assistance. https://www.phe.gov/Preparedness/support/medicalassistance/ Pages/default.aspx.

Okumura, T., Suzuki, K., Fukuda, A., Kohama, A., Takasu, N., Ishimatsu, S. and Hinohara, S. (1998). The Tokyo Subway Sarin Attack: Disaster Management, Part 2: Hospital Response. *Academic Emergency Medicine*, 5(6), 618–624. https://doi .org/10.1111/j.1553-2712.1998.tb02471.x. . PMID: 9660290.

The Joint Commission. (2022). New and Revised Emergency Management Standards. https://www.jointcommission.org/standards/prepublication-standards/new-and -revised-emergency-management-standards/.

WHO. (2021). Health Systems. https://www.euro.who.int/en/health-topics/Health -systems.

CHAPTER 17

Nursing and Disasters:
Responding to Victim Needs and Performing Other Essential Functions

Dale Maughan, Allison Swenson, and Joy Cole

INTRODUCTION

Nurses have a long history of responding to disasters. In each unique disaster throughout history, nurses were there, responding and adapting to the circumstances in order to care for and serve those who needed it most. The education and experience of nurses are vital and pertinent to disaster response because of nurses' adaptability, holistic approach to caring, and their experience serving a wide variety of populations. In the following chapter we will discuss the history of nursing as well as the history of nursing related specifically to disasters. We will then explore the roles nurses play in emergency management of disasters and the current challenges nurses face when responding in these situations. Finally, we will identify some recommendations related to needed operational changes to improve the effectiveness of nursing services during a crisis.

HISTORY OF NURSING

Understanding the history of nursing allows us to recognize the impact of nursing on the healthcare system, better understand the effect of societal issues on the profession, and appreciate the rich traditions of nursing. "History shows that societal beliefs about health and illness, Christianity, and the military had strong influences on the evolution and images of professional nursing" (Wilkinson et al., 2020, p. 4). In the following paragraphs we will examine how important events throughout history have shaped and influenced modern nursing.

Nursing in Antiquity

Very little information exists regarding ancient history of nursing. Often, caregivers were assigned the role before they even had a choice. It was their "destiny" or role in society. For example, in the Zuni tribe, if a child was born with the placenta covering the face, that was a sign that they were to be a caregiver; it was their "destiny" (Henly and Moss,

DOI: 10.4324/9781003350729-17

2007). In Greek medicine, healing was centered around shrines or sanctuaries where sick people congregated. Responding to those needing care, "basket bearers" provided comfort and healing to the sick much like a modern-day nurse would. In ancient Rome, the care of the injured and sick was seen as more of a household duty taken on by women who traditionally nurtured their own children and were seen as natural caregivers. No formal education for nurses existed at this time, so much of what was learned occurred through trial and error or was passed on from generation to generation by observation. "Those who acquired a reputation for expert care of the sick...were often sought after to provide care to friends and relatives" (Egenes, 2018, p. 4).

The earliest indication of organized nursing can be seen during the early Christian period when the deaconess would visit and care for those who were sick, poor, orphaned, or far from home. The most well known and often cited as the earliest deaconess is Phoebe, a Greek remembered for the expert nursing care she provided, traveling to the homes of those in need (Griffin and Griffin, 1969). Because most care was given at home, hospitals were only for the destitute or those that had been ostracized. The earliest hospitals were started by nuns and monks who devoted their lives to care for the sick, who were usually placed in beds that lined the walls of the church.

Crimean War and Florence Nightingale

Florence Nightingale hailed from an upper-class family and was well educated in Greek, Latin, mathematics, natural science, literature, German, French, and Italian. "It was assumed that Florence would follow the traditional path dictated for women of the upper class during the Victorian era, which included marriage and the rearing of a family" (Egenes, 2018, p. 4). However, Florence believed she had been called to care for the sick and injured, and despite her family's initial disapproval, she entered the convent of Irish Catholic nursing sisters to learn basic patient care.

In 1854, the Crimean War started. The British, French, and Turks were battling Russia and the British Army was having difficulty handling the wounded and sick soldiers. The French had nursing nuns to care for their sick and wounded; the British had nothing. The British soldiers were dying from diseases rather than their battle wounds. This situation was unacceptable to Florence Nightingale. After obtaining special permission, Nightingale and her band of ladies traveled to Crimea to care for the sick, wounded, and injured. Florence used her knowledge and beliefs about dirt and pathogens to change the care injured soldiers were receiving, and within months was able to decrease the mortality rate dramatically (Wyatt, 2019). Documenting the results of her care, she then used her knowledge of mathematics and statistics to further improve care to the sick.

Once Florence returned to England, she established a nursing school to educate future nurses. Florence made it clear that, "She wanted to establish a secular career for women, similar to law and medicine for men. And she succeeded" (Griffin and Griffin, 1969, p. 77). Florence Nightingale elevated nursing from a lowly craft to a respected profession. We must recognize the beginning of formal nursing education as the founding of the Nightingale School at St Thomas Hospital where emphasis was placed on the proper education of the nurse.

The Civil War

Shortly after the Crimean War, the Civil War ensued in the United States. At the time of this war, there were no "trained" nurses in the United States. Much like in ancient times, more than 3,000 women left their homes to care for the wounded with only the basic knowledge of nursing care they had obtained from caring for their own families (Egenes, 2018). The demands placed on caregivers served as a pivotal event for nursing in the United States. Formal education for nurses became a priority with the goal to better care for the growing population. The establishment of the first school of nursing in the United States began in Philadelphia in 1872 (Egenes, 2018).

The 20th Century

With the 19th century came drastic changes and growth in medicine. Science was now seen as a profession, germ theory was widely accepted, the first vaccine was made, and many diseases became identifiable. Furthermore, late in the 19th century, the number of nurses increased and by the 1890s, two professional organizations for nurses emerged. Hospitals developed their own schools for training nurses and only employed a few graduates, utilizing student nurses for the majority of bedside care. This limitation forced most graduate nurses at this time to serve as private duty nurses working in the homes of their patients.

Beginning in 1914, the casualties incurred during World War I magnified the need for nurses, and approximately 23,000 nurses served in the military (Whelan and Buhler-Wilkerson, 2019). "The success of military nurses in providing essential care during the war insured their participation in succeeding conflicts" (Whelan and Buhler-Wilkerson, 2019, p. 1). Meanwhile, nurses on their home soil addressed the needs of the civilians. This development further propelled nursing into recognition as a profession. Specialized skills obtained during these times allowed nurses to diversify their practice into other areas of health care and by the late 1930s, nurses were the most essential component in competent patient care. This change resulted in a shift of primary care of patients being provided by educated nurses rather than nursing students.

With the advent of World War II, nurses "duplicated the excellent work they had performed in World War I" (Whelan and Buhler-Wilkerson, 2019, p. 1). Unfortunately, post-war circumstances posed new challenges to the profession of nursing. Nurses were seen as heroes during the war but demanding work, poor working conditions, and low pay drew fewer young women to choose nursing as a profession. Despite this setback, the nursing profession provided new educational opportunities and abandoned its racial and gender segregation system, allowing more nurses to graduate.

"From the beginning of humanity, persons have been designated, called, or educated to perform the functions we now refer to as nursing care" (Egenes, 2018, p. 26). Furthermore, nurses consistently show their ability to adapt to the needs of their patients. Nursing is an important profession, honored and respected by those we serve.

RELATION TO DISASTERS AND TERRORISM

Just as a long history of disasters shaped the development of the nursing profession, current challenges continue to highlight the contributions of nurses during extreme situations. According to the American Nurses Association (ANA), "Registered nurses have consistently shown to be reliable responders, and their compassionate nature typically compels them to respond to those in need, even when it puts their own safety or well-being at risk. There is a strong relationship between the nurse and the public who expects that nurses…will respond to their needs in an infectious disease emergency or in other types of disaster resulting in mass injury or illness" (ANA, 2017, para. 1). The ANA recognizes that caring – the hallmark of nursing – propels nurses to respond to a variety of catastrophes. "They are called upon to respond in times of mass casualty – such as a catastrophic weather event (hurricanes/floods) – or when the nature of their work puts them at risk for exposure – such as influenza or other infectious disease pandemics. It is reassuring to know that because of their compassionate nature and the nature of their role as caregiver, registered nurses are typically willing to respond" (ANA, 2017, para. 3).

Professional and personal preparation stand as necessary competencies for nurses responding to disasters. Nurses must engage in advance planning related to care of their own families during an absence, making ethical decisions in extraordinary circumstances, and ensuring self-protection in novel or dangerous situations. Additionally, nurses may be called upon to practice under altered standards of care, and they deserve protection from litigation and punitive actions related to this alteration in expectations.

ROLES IN EMERGENCY MANAGEMENT/HOMELAND SECURITY

According to the American Nurses Association (ANA, 2023) "Nursing is the protection, promotion, and optimization of health and abilities; prevention of illness and injury; facilitation of healing; alleviation of suffering through the diagnosis and treatment of human response; and advocacy in the care of individuals, families, groups, communities, and populations. (ANA, 2023, para.2)." Nursing practice occurs "wherever there is a patient in need of care, whenever there is a need for nursing knowledge, compassion, and expertise…to achieve the most positive patient outcomes in keeping with nursing's social contract and obligation to society" (ANA, 2023 para. 2).

Generally speaking, undergraduate nursing curricula are very similar across programs, built on principles of behavioral, life, and nursing science (ICN, 2019), and driven by standards established by professional nursing organizations and accreditation bodies. The aim of nurse education programs is to prepare nurse "generalists" who can provide care in a safe and competent manner regardless of the setting. The International Council of Nurses' definition of nurses explains that "the nurse is prepared and authorized: 1) to engage in the general scope of nursing practice, including the promotion of health, prevention of illness, and care of physically ill, mentally ill, and disabled people of all ages and in all healthcare and other community settings; 2) to carry out healthcare teaching; 3) to participate fully as a member of the healthcare team; 4) to supervise and train nursing and healthcare auxiliaries; and 5) to be involved in research" (ICN, 2019). In some ways, the profession or discipline of nursing can appear to be somewhat eclectic as nurses can and are expected to fill multiple roles.

According to Veenema (2012, p. 17), "Caring for patients and the opportunity to save lives are what professional nursing is all about, and disaster events provide nurses with an opportunity to do both." This idea is congruent with the "Tenets of Nursing Practice" as outlined by the American Nurses Association (2010) providing a foundation for the knowledge and skills that are valued in all phases of disaster response. The first tenet is that the practice of nursing is individualized. Nurses are trained to see the uniqueness, individuality, and diverse needs of their clients, whether they be a single person or a group of people, like communities. The second tenet is nurses' ability to coordinate care. They value the importance of establishing partnerships and collaborating with others to meet the needs of the whole person or community. The third tenet forms the core of nursing, which is caring. Caring is a common thread through all nursing actions. The fourth tenet is the use of what is called the "nursing process." Although the name is specific to nursing, the process or variation of it is common in many other disciplines. All nursing actions are based on this process of assessing, making a diagnosis, planning, implementing, and lastly, evaluating – only to make the necessary adjustments and cycle through the process again until the desired outcome is realized. Using this process, nurses are constantly monitoring and addressing the human response and utilizing evidence-based knowledge and practice in their interventions. The fifth and last tenet is the nurse's commitment to providing safe and effective care with an ultimate goal to improve outcomes.

The roles filled by nurses in disaster situations flow naturally from their formal education as well as their practice in a variety of clinical settings. Nurse graduates and better yet, nurses who have years of experience, come with the skill set essential for the varied roles they play in disaster settings (Keeling et al., 2015; Ranse and Lenson, 2012; Stanhope and Lancaster, 2014). Nursing skills are valued and essential to the roles that nurses are expected to fill in all aspects of disasters (Stanhope and Lancaster, 2014). Basic nursing skills attained through general nursing education fall within the domains of assessment, health education, advocacy, a holistic approach to patient care, direct care provision, leadership and management, and communication.

Given that the practice of nursing has no boundaries, its presence will be apparent to some degree in disasters of any etiology. Nursing makes up the largest segment of the healthcare workforce today and can play a key role in all aspects or phases of disaster management: preparation, prevention, response, and recovery (Savage et al., 2016; Stanhope and Lancaster, 2014). The role of nurses will vary across all aspects of disaster management, with the ultimate goal to preserve the health of individuals, families, and communities. With the frequency with which disasters occur and the involvement of nurses in those disasters, Veenema (2012) proposes the following: "It is imperative that all nurses acquire a knowledge base and minimum set of skills to enable them to plan for and respond to a disaster in a timely and appropriate manner" (p. 17).

Wilkinson et al. (2020) have identified the following roles in nursing that can apply to all settings and specialties of nursing practice, including disasters: direct care provider, communicator, educator, advocate, counselor, change agent, leader, manager, case manager, and research consumer. In the following paragraphs, some of the key roles filled by nurses during a disaster will be explored.

Advocate – Nurses are educated to be advocates for their patients. This role recognizes the vulnerability of patients whether it be one person or a population and calls for action, which might range from protecting someone from harm or infringement on legal rights to ensuring the pediatric dose of an emergency medication is available in a disaster supply cache. Disasters increase the vulnerability of their victims and nurses are trained to recognize their needs and intervene.

Triage Officer – Nurses are educated to conduct rapid assessments to establish priorities in care. A partially obstructed airway or severe bleeding is addressed before a deformed distal extremity from a fall. With large numbers of victims and limited resources available in disaster settings, the ability to establish care priorities is essential. Effective triage means doing the best for the most. It is interesting to note that the care and compassion aspect of nursing has the potential to interfere with triage assignments as nurses want to fix the problems they identify in the triage process.

Assessor – Nurses are skilled at performing assessments from which valuable data is obtained, documented, interpreted, and used to inform appropriate interventions. Nurses are adept at interviewing to obtain health histories and other essential information, observing for and measuring physiological, mental, emotional, and other indicators of

TABLE 17.1   Disaster nursing roles

	Assessment	Prevention	Response	Recovery
Collaboration	x	x	x	x
Communication	x	x	x	x
Health Screening		x	x	x
Advocacy		x	x	x
Assessment		x	x	x
Triage			x	
Interviewing Skills			x	
Priority Setting		x	x	
Care Provision		x	x	x
Recordkeeping	x		x	
Clinic Management			x	
Leadership		x	x	x
Management	x	x	x	x
Case Management			x	x
Counseling			x	x
Disease Screening		x		x
Education	x	x		x
Change Agent		x		x

health concerns. They are able to provide physical examinations and perform screenings. These same skills can be applied to groups of people or communities in disaster settings.

Care Provider – Care is provided with compassion using a holistic lens, addressing all apparent and potential needs – not just the physical, but the emotional, psychosocial, environmental, spiritual, etc. Having been educated to address health issues across the life span and transculturally, nurses are very flexible in providing care.

Health Educator – Respected and trusted by the public, nurses are expected to know something about everything related to health. Nurses are always teaching in clinical settings and a disaster is no different. During a disaster when handwashing facilities are unavailable nurses can answer questions such as, "What are the hygienic practices that will limit the potential for illness and disease?" and, "What are the consequences of stress on disaster victims and what are effective measures to manage that stress?"

Collaborator – In typical patient care settings, nurses are very comfortable collaborating effectively with members of interdisciplinary teams to accomplish all that is required to provide quality care for patients. In disaster settings, collaboration is essential and may involve working closely with other care providers as well as Emergency Medical Services, law enforcement, sanitation and utility workers, government officials, news media representatives, etc. Table 17.1 provides a comprehensive overview of the many roles that nurses can fill during the disaster cycle.

LIMITATIONS OF NURSING DURING EMERGENCY MANAGEMENT

Nurses repeatedly receive recognition as representing the most trusted profession (Brusie, 2020). This distinction rests on the history of nurses as competent and compassionate care providers, public educators, and patient advocates. Nurses focus on patients' needs first before promoting the interests of medical groups or insurance companies. These qualities position nurses at the forefront in responding to challenges related to public health including relief efforts during disasters and mitigation of bioterrorism and pandemics. As early as 2008, the American Nurses Association recognized the role of nurses in emergency management as they face shortages of resources – both human and material – and addressed the reasonable standard of care that can be expected during emergencies (ANA, 2008). While nurses regularly participate in individual emergency response, the challenges of large-scale emergencies expose some limitations to the profession related to shortages of physical resources, human resources, and intellectual resources.

Despite the knowledge base and skill set typically coming from a general nursing education, formal training in disaster response has not traditionally been a part of nursing curriculum (Ivanov and Blue, 2008; Ranse and Lenson, 2012). The truth is that most nurses who respond to disasters have not received formal education or training in their undergraduate experience or professional development even after licensure. Disaster-related education is not a required topic in most undergraduate programs across the country. Studies have shown that the majority of nurses who do respond to disasters to provide assistance have not received formal disaster training, and they are also not likely to have had previous disaster response experience. These factors result in nurses who are not trained adequately to respond within the expected performance standards during disasters.

Emergency situations present in many ways, including natural disasters, human-caused emergencies, and epidemics of infectious diseases. Recent natural disasters include extreme weather, wildfires, and earthquakes. Human-caused emergencies come in the forms of terrorism, riots, industrial accidents, and transportation catastrophes. Most recently, the COVID-19 pandemic highlighted the emergent nature of infectious diseases and the challenges related to their mitigation. All of these situations share a common theme related to a shortage of resources including physical resources, human resources, and intellectual resources.

Physical Resources

Physical resources include all of the materials needed to provide care including supportive infrastructure, equipment for care providers and patients, and the physical space needed to promote maximum care opportunities while maintaining infection control practices. Recent responses to emergencies revealed the difficulties presented by inadequate or undeveloped resources. In 1995, during the aftermath of the bombing of the Alfred P. Murrah Federal Building in Oklahoma City, communication system destruction resulted in delay of care to people injured during the blast, and nurses faced the task of caring for the onslaught of patients while unable to convey information to doctors, other hospitals, and family members (OK.gov, 2005). During the response to COVID-19, ventilator shortages directly affected patient care as nurses reported harrowing scenes of watching people struggling to breathe because no ventilators were available (Bell, 2020). Following Hurricane Katrina, nurses cared for patients in hospital hallways, waiting rooms, within the flooded community, and even in a football stadium (Nicole, 2007).

Inadequate physical resources during an emergency response situation limit the ability of nurses to maintain the expected standards of care associated with nursing responsibilities. Infrastructure failures may result in poor communication, the inability to transport critically ill patients in a timely manner, and unsafe environments for nurses providing care. A lack of physical space in medical facilities may dictate the discharge of patients who are not "as sick" and leave nurses in a position of perceived helplessness or inadequacy (Bell, 2020). Shortages of medical supplies and equipment may force nurses to abandon some quality and safety measures that would, in other situations, constitute a breach of duty (ANA, 2008).

Human Resources

The nursing shortage in the United States is well documented and despite efforts to address the shortage, the problem continues to expand. During an emergency crisis, the increased number of patients, along with the increased acuity of illness among those patients, magnifies the dearth of nurses available to fulfill their roles. This deficiency results in nurses working in unfamiliar surroundings, accepting responsibility for an increased patient load, and facing increased physical and emotional demands (Nicole, 2007).

While all nurses receive educational offerings that address patient care during emergencies, most nurses work in specialized areas of care. The nurses become very familiar with meeting the needs of the subset of patients in their specialty area, but eventually become less competent in other areas. During times of crisis, nurses may be expected to perform highly demanding tasks and skills that have become less familiar during their day-to-day practice (ANA, 2008).

During the 2018 Camp Fire in California, the California Medical Services Authority responded to the influx of patients but only after the need for medical personnel was termed "desperate" by the CEO of Scripps Health (Hoffman, 2018). During emergencies, nurses may be called upon to take responsibility for more patients, work longer hours, and accept extra shifts. This increase in demand results in nurses who face both physical and emotional exhaustion – factors repeatedly shown to negatively affect patient outcomes. During the COVID-19 pandemic, nurses documented the ill effects of wearing N-95 masks for 12 hours, working consecutive shifts with short recovery periods, and being responsible for more patients than usual (Allabaugh, 2020).

The mental health of nurses also suffers during large-scale emergencies. The sheer emotional toll of a disaster, coupled with the expectation to maintain professionalism, may lead to both short-term and long-term feelings of anxiety, fear, and depression. Nurses who covered a patient with their own bodies during the destruction of Moore Medical Center by a tornado in 2013 (Todd and McConnell, 2013) reported "believing [they] were going to die" during the storm, along with recurring nightmares and panic attacks during subsequent storm seasons (C. Popejoy, personal communication, 2014). Nina Pham, a nurse who contracted the Ebola virus from a patient in 2014, remembers having "end-of-life discussions" with her caregivers, and reports suffering from insomnia and nightmares since her recovery (Herskovitz, 2016).

Intellectual Resources

Nurses frequently rely on high-quality research to keep pace with the emerging needs of patient populations. In some situations, however, research-based practice guidelines may be undeveloped due to the novel nature of a situation. Additionally, experts may disagree about the content of the guidelines and offer nurses conflicting information regarding patient care and personal protection. During the recent COVID-19 pandemic, the World Health Organization (WHO) reported that asymptomatic carriers of the virus possessed very little risk of contaminating others (Howard, 2020). Within 48 hours of this announcement, the WHO retracted the announcement and reported, "There's much unknown" (Howard, 2020, para. 10). Moreover, effective treatment for the virus was unknown and included the use of several medications whose outcome rested on the best-educated guesses offered by epidemiologists (Szabo, 2020).

During disasters, the shortage of adequate physical, human, and intellectual resources presents challenges to nurses. The most important role of the nurse – holistic care for humans – may be diminished by the expectation for nurses to become more adaptable, more resilient, and more competent in generalized skills. As a profession, nursing continues to evolve, and disaster response often acts as a catalyst for changes that further define and expand nurses' capacity to maintain the level of trust expected by response teams and victims.

RECOMMENDATIONS FOR ADDRESSING LIMITATIONS IN NURSING

Many factors hinder the abilities of nurses to adequately respond to disasters and perform at the highest levels of their education and experience. Expectations for nurses during disasters appear in a publication from the International Council of Nurses, "Core Competencies in Disaster Nursing" (ICN, 2019). The general principles of the competencies outlined in the document such as communication, infection control, patient and nurse safety, and ethical behavior stand as foundational concepts to the education of nurses. Nevertheless, implementation of the principles during a disaster calls upon the nurse to perform at higher-than-normal levels of expertise, thus presenting a chasm between educational preparation and readiness to respond. Recommendations to address this deficit include inclusion of disaster-specific educational offerings as a part of licensure preparation, the establishment of protections for nurses working during disasters, and ongoing certification programs that promote the ability of the practicing nurse to respond to the extraordinary demands of disaster response.

Pre-licensure Education

Content overload stands as the major hurdle to introducing novel curricular components in pre-licensure nursing education. For this reason, the inclusion of disaster nursing as an additional requirement presents a challenge. Some nursing programs include a lecture on the triage aspect of disasters, but nursing students receive few opportunities to translate theory to practice in a disaster setting. Simulation has been shown to be an effective method to provide experience in adapting the role of the nurse in novel situations. The inclusion of simulated disasters during each semester of students' nursing education experience would foster a growing sense of responsibility and competence during disasters. Additionally, collaboration among other departments who would be expected to respond to emergencies would allow students to gain a clearer vision of the nurse's role as a manager, delegator, and advocate.

Current governmental standards already require emergency drills at higher education institutions. These drills aim to ensure the safety of the students during disasters. To accommodate the need for nurses to appropriately respond to disasters, these drills could be enhanced for nursing students to include a mock disaster complete with injured people, supply limitations, and ethical dilemmas. As students gain experience with this unusual set of circumstances, they will be better prepared to respond to an actual disaster.

Disaster Protection for Nurses

The ANA Code of Ethics for Nurses with Interpretative Statements contains elements that speak to the nurse's primary responsibility to the patient as well as the nurse's responsibility to recognize the duty to both themselves and others. In disaster nursing, these two statements may leave the nurse in an uncomfortable position related to choosing to provide care to others or maintaining personal safety. In recognition of this issue, the ANA articulated the need for actions from several entities to create an environment of physical, emotional, and legal safety for nurses practicing during disasters (ANA, 2017). To answer the question "Who will be there?," the ANA calls upon the federal government to set a vision for safe response efforts and for states to create "non-punitive environments that enhance the registered nurse's efficiency and capacity" during disaster response (ANA, 2017, p. 4). On a local level, recommendations include corporate provision of operational protocols, supplies of personal protective equipment, and measures to promote physical safety (ANA, 2017).

Nurses must feel safe from recriminations when exercising their duty to protect themselves. During the COVID-19 response, a nurse in Texas was assigned to care for a patient who had not been pre-screened for the virus. The nurse accepted the assignment and later learned that the patient was a carrier of the virus. Later, when the nurse developed a fever and cough, the employer refused to release the nurse from duty. The nurse, at the time of this writing, is on a ventilator in an intensive care unit and has a poor prognosis. While the employing institution failed to maintain policies to protect the nurse, the nurse also failed to recognize the duty of self-protection. Delaying accepting the assignment until testing was completed and leaving the facility during an illness constitute protective actions that the nurse did not utilize – or believed could not be utilized.

Disaster Nursing Certification

The American Nurses Credentialing Center (ANCC) offered a National Healthcare Disaster Certification (NHDC) until 2023 when it was retired. The exam fee was $395 and presented a significant financial barrier to many nurses. The stated purpose of this certification was to provide a valid, reliable assessment of the knowledge, skills, and competencies related to all phases of the disaster response cycle. When the credential was retired, the competencies were absorbed into other credentialing assessments. The certification's retirement leaves a gap in the available resources for both nurses and disaster preparedness officials who can no longer rely on a database of credentialed professionals as a resource when marshalling responders.

CONCLUSION

The relevance of nursing in relation to disaster preparation, assessment, prevention, response, and recovery efforts stands on centuries of precedent that highlight the preparation, adaptability, and commitment to serve in difficult circumstances. Nurses emerge from their basic educational experiences ready to practice in a wide variety of settings, and they develop specialized skills – both hard and soft – that make their contributions during disaster situations invaluable. At this time, some limitations exist that can affect the immediate responsiveness of nurses when asked to perform in unfamiliar environments, but these deficits can be overcome through focused educational efforts and mock disaster response experiences. Historical evidence and current standards of practice demonstrate the ongoing commitment of nurses to serve whenever and wherever they are needed. Natural disasters, wars, terrorism, and pandemics all serve as opportunities for nursing to contribute to response efforts and to further the reputation of being the most trusted profession.

CLASS DISCUSSION AND ESSAY QUESTIONS

1. How did organizations such as the church and individuals such as Florence Nightingale influence the establishment of nursing as a profession?
2. Why did war facilitate the expansion of nursing in the United States and around the world?
3. According to the International Council of Nurses, what are the responsibilities of nurses? How do these duties relate to disasters and terrorist attacks?
4. What resources are required for nurses to better fulfill their roles in emergency management and homeland security?
5. Should education on disasters and terrorism become a standard aspect of education and training in nursing? If so, why?

REFERENCES

American Nurses Association (ANA). (2008) *Adapting standards of care under extreme conditions: Guidance for professionals during disasters, pandemics, and other extreme emergencies* [PDF]. Retrieved June 11, 2020, from https://www.nursingworld.org/~4ade15/globalassets/docs/ana/ascec_whitepaper031008final.pdf

American Nurses Association (ANA). (2017)_Who *will be there? Ethics, the law, and a nurse's duty to respond in a disaster* [PDF]. Retrieved June 11, 2020, from https://www.nursingworld.org/~4af058/globalassets/docs/ana/ethics/who-will-be-there_disaster-preparedness_2017.pdf

American Nurses Association (ANA). (2023) *Scope of practice* [PDF]. Retrieved March 14, 2023 from https://www.nursingworld.org/practice-policy/scope-of-practice/

Allabaugh, D. (2020, May 10). '*It's heartbreaking:' W-B general nurse describes work with covid-19 patients*. The Citizens' Voice. Retrieved June 8, 2020, from https://www.citizensvoice.com/news/it-s-heartbreaking-w-b-general-nurse-describes-work-with-covid-19-patients-1.2626510

Bell, J. (2020, April 15). *The impact of covid-19 ventilator shortage on medical device regulation*. NS Medical Devices. Retrieved May 20, 2020, from https://www.nsmedicaldevices.com/analysis/ventilator-regulation-covid-19/

Brusie, C. (2020, January 7). *Nurses ranked most honest profession 18 years in a row.* Nurse.org. Retrieved May 11, 2020, from https://nurse.org/articles/nursing-ranked -most-honest-profession/

International Council on Nurses (ICN). (2019) *Core competencies in disaster nursing, 2.* Retrieved June 12, 2020, from https://doi.org/https://www.icn.ch/sites/default/files/ inline-files/ICN_Disaster-Comp-Report_WEB.pdf

International Council on Nurses (ICN). (2019) *Disaster training preparedness for health-care personnel.* Retrieved June 12, 2020, from https://www.icn.ch/sites/default/files/ inline-files/ICN_Disaster-Comp-Report_WEB.pdf

Egenes, K. (2018). The nursing profession. In *Issues and trends in nursing: Practice, policy, and leadership* (2nd ed., pp. 3–30). Jones and Bartlett.

Griffin, J. G., & Griffin, J. K. (1969). *Jensen's history and trends in professional nursing* (6th ed.). The C. V. Mosby Company.

Henly, S., & Moss, M. (2007). *Encyclopedia of epidemiology: Vol. 1. American Indian health issues.* Sage.

Herskovitz, J. (2016, October 24). *Texas hospital reaches settlement with nurse infected with Ebola.* Reuters.com. Retrieved May 25, 2020, from https://www.reuters.com/ article/us-health-ebola-texas-nurse-idUSKCN12O2AF

Hoffman, M. (2018, November 5). *Local hospital sending medical response team to the Camp fire.* KPBS News. Retrieved May 10, 2020, from https://www.kpbs.org/news /2018/nov/15/local-hospital-sending-medical-response-team-aid-v/

Howard, J. (2020, June 8). *Coronavirus spread by asymptomatic people "appears to be rare"; WHO official says.* CNN.com. Retrieved June 10, 2020, from https://www .cnn.com/2020/06/08/health/coronavirus-asymptomatic-spread-who-bn/index.html

Howard, J. (2020, June 9). *Who clarifies comments on asymptomatic spread of corona-virus: There's much unknown".* CNN. Retrieved June 10, 2020, from https://www .cnn.com/2020/06/09/health/who-coronavirus-asymptomatic-spread-bn/index .html

Ivanov, L., & Blue, C. (2008). *Public health nursing: Leadership, policy, and practice.* Delmar.

Keeling, A., MacAllister, E., & Wall, B. (2015). *Nurses and disasters: Global, historical case studies* [ebook]. Springer Publishing. https://doi.org/http://www.bls.gov/news .release/osh.t05.htm

Nicole, K. (2007, November 1). *Katrina nurses.* The Chronicle of Nursing. Retrieved April 19, 2020, from https://www.asrn.org/journal-chronicle-nursing/204-katrina -nurses.html

OK.gov. (2005). *After action report Alfred P. Murrah building bombing* [PDF]. Retrieved June 10, 2020, from https://www.ok.gov/OEM/documents/Bombing. After Action Report.pdf

Ranse, J., & Lesson, S. (2012). Beyond a clinical role: Nurses were psychological support-ers, coordinators, and problem solvers in the Black Saturday and Victorian bushfires in 2009. *Australian Emergency Nursing Journal, 15,* 156–163.

Savage, C., Kub, J., & Groves, S. (2016). *Public health science and nursing practice: Caring for populations.* F.A. Davis.

Stanhope, M., & Lancaster, J. (2014). *Foundations of nursing in the community: Community oriented practice* (4th ed.). Elsevier.

Szabo, L. (2020, May 17). *'A lot of strikeouts' in search for COVID-19 cure.* Detroit News. Retrieved May 6, 2020, from https://www.detroitnews.com/story/news/ nation/coronavirus/2020/05/17/covid-cure-search/111791744/

Todd, B., & McConnell, D. (2013, May 24). *A tornado bearing down, a mom in labor: Four nurses face a crisis*. CNN.com. Retrieved May 30, 2020, from https://www.cnn.com/2013/05/23/us/oklahoma-tornado-birth/index.html

Veneema, T. (2012). *Disaster nursing and emergency preparedness: For chemical, biological, and radiological terrorism and other hazards* (3rd ed.). Springer Publishing.

Whelan, J. C., & Buhler-Wilkerson, K. (2019, March 5). *American nursing: An introduction to the past*. Nursing, History and Health Care. https://www.nursing.upenn.edu/nhhc/american-nursing-an-introduction-to-the-past

Wilkinson, J. M., Treas, L. S., Barnett, K., & Smith, M. H. (2020). *Fundamentals of nursing: Theory, concepts & applications* (4th ed.,Vol. 1). F. A. Davis Company.

Wyatt, L. (2019). *A history of nursing*. Amberley Publishing.

CHAPTER 18

Forensic Technicians:
Locating and Analyzing Physical Evidence in Terrorist Attacks

Amie B. Houghton

INTRODUCTION

In October 2000, *CSI: Crime Scene Investigation* debuted on CBS, marking the beginning of countless television shows, podcasts, and documentaries popularizing the various disciplines within forensic science. Although forensic science applications can be traced back several centuries, shows like *CSI* have catapulted the public awareness of forensics to the forefront within the last few decades. Forensic practitioners will argue (and rightfully so) that many of these shows have created an inaccurate depiction of what forensic science truly entails. Though much of the public may have a dramatized understanding of forensics, it does not negate the "real-life" forensic contributions and capabilities used in criminal investigations.

Crime scene investigators hold the primary role of documenting and processing crime scenes. As part of this process, they will identify and collect any item of evidentiary value that could be related to the event. This evidence passes to a crime laboratory where it will undergo scientific analysis and comparison to determine whether the evidence can be associated with a particular person or source. This association, in many cases, provides the foundation for a successful prosecution. Just as in common criminal investigations, forensic practitioners play a vital role in terrorist events as physical evidence recovered can be critical in identifying who was responsible.

Terrorist attacks usually result in chaos that can overwhelm personnel at the scene. If an agency is unprepared, undermanned, or does not have a plan in place on how to properly manage and process the scene, it can destroy an investigation. Proper preparation and planning helps mitigate issues during scene processing and subsequent evidence collection and analysis.

This chapter will describe the historical origins and advancements in forensic science. It will then provide a comprehensive discussion of the roles and duties of various forensic technicians and scientists as they pertain to criminal investigations and terrorist events. Current challenges for processing events associated with terrorist activity will be discussed as well as possible resolutions to pave the way toward the future.

DOI: 10.4324/9781003350729-18

THE ORIGINS AND ADVANCEMENTS OF FORENSIC SCIENCE

Forensic science in its basic essence is the application of science to criminal and civil law. It is common knowledge that the ability to apply aspects of forensic science is a valuable piece of everyday criminal investigations. However, early origins of forensic science can actually be traced back several centuries to investigators and early scientists who founded the rudimentary groundwork of scientific principles as they apply to the law. Ancient history records instances in which various methods were used to identify and compare physical evidence within criminal investigations. Though these examples do not quite mirror exactly what forensic science is today, the techniques involved foreshadow what we now know and have established as forensic science.

Historians attribute the earliest applications of forensic science to China. Evidence in the form of a manuscript stemming from the 3rd century provides one of the earliest examples of the use of forensics. *Yi Yu Ji* ("A Collection of Criminal Cases") describes how a coroner determined a woman, who claimed her husband died in an accidental fire, had in fact murdered him and burned the body postmortem (Saferstein, 2019). A text from 1248, translated as "Washing Away of Wrongs," describes, among many accounts, a murder investigation in a small Chinese village. After a local farmer was found murdered, the investigator determined who the perpetrator was based on insect activity occurring on a tool owned by that individual. Additional books from the 6th and 10th century, *Ming Yuan Shih Lu* ("True Records of the Clarification of Wrongs") and *I Yu Chi* ("Records of Doubtful Criminal Cases") discussed early concepts related to forensic science (Bucholtz & Davis, 2015).

Examples such as these provided a final resolution to cases; however, it was not common practice to utilize a scientific approach to criminal investigations. Not until the late 17th and early 18th centuries did forensic science really begin to establish its roots. In 1686, Marcello Malpighi, an anatomy professor at the University of Bologna, first began documenting fingerprint characteristics. More than a century later, the first scientific paper was published describing the nature of fingerprints. However, neither of these writings indicated the value of utilizing fingerprints as a form of identification. The connection of science to law at this time did not occur due to insufficient knowledge of human anatomy and physiology (Saferstein, 2019).

As prominent physicians and scientists began to gain a better understanding of the human body, some of the first scientific treatises were published on forensic science. In 1775, Carl Wilhelm Scheele, a Swedish chemist, developed a test in which arsenic could be detected in corpses. Valentin Ross, a German chemist, later developed a more precise method for arsenic detection. Mathieu Orfila, considered the "Father of Forensic Toxicology," contributed most significantly in this area of chemistry. Orfila published the first scientific treatise on the detection of poisons and their effects on animals in 1814, ultimately establishing toxicology as an official science (Saferstein, 2019).

Throughout the mid-1800s, several advances furthered the development of various forensic science disciplines. William Nichol invented the polarizing microscope in 1828. In 1839, toxicological evidence was first used in a criminal trial when James Marsh, a Scottish chemist, testified arsenic was the cause of death after he determined its presence in a deceased victim. The first microscopic procedure for detecting sperm was formulated in 1839 by Louis Bayard. During the 1850s and 1860s, the first microcrystalline test for hemoglobin was created and the first presumptive test for blood was developed. The mid-1800s also saw the first applications of photography being utilized to record images of crime scenes (Saferstein, 2019).

In 1879, Alphonse Bertillon, a French identification bureau chief, developed an identification technique known as anthropometry. For almost two decades, this method was believed to be the most reliable way to establish personal identification of an individual based on multiple measurements of bony parts of the human body. Eventually, it was determined that this was not a reliable technique and anthropometry was replaced by fingerprinting. However, Bertillon is still remembered as a pioneer in criminalistics and a major contributor to the development of forensic science (Michelson, 2015).

After anthropometry was discredited, personal identification shifted to fingerprints. Francis Galton conducted the first definitive study of fingerprints. In 1892, Galton published *Finger Prints*, which provided the first statistic proof indicating the unique method of using fingerprints as a means of personal identification. The present system of fingerprint classification is based on the work and principles Galton established (Saferstein, 2015).

Throughout the early 1900s, multiple individuals contributed to a great surge in forensic science advancements. After Dr Karl Landsteiner discovered blood could be identified and categorized into the various blood groups (A, B, AB, O), Dr Leon Lattes devised a technique in 1915 where the specific blood group could be ascertained from a dried bloodstain. In the mid-1920s, a U.S. Army colonel, Calvin Goddard, devised the comparison microscope, the same tool used in modern-day bullet comparisons. Albert Osborne developed the fundamental principles of document examination and published the first significant reference, *Questioned Documents*, still used to this day. Walter McCrone is known as the world's preeminent microscopist through his advancements in analytical chemistry. Hans Gross wrote the first treatise on how multiple scientific disciplines could be applied to criminal investigations.

Another prominent leader in forensics was Edmond Locard. Locard's research and accomplishment garnered the attention of forensic scientists and criminal investigators across the world. Locard is most renowned for what is known as "Locard's Exchange Principle." This principle explains that whenever two objects come in contact with one another, there is an exchange of material between them. This cross-transfer is what provides the basis of being able to identify a suspect who had contact with a victim or was present at a particular crime scene. The research and accomplishments of all of these men helped lay the solid foundations of forensic science (Saferstein, 2015).

Moving into the modern day, the most significant advancement in forensics has been through the discovery of DNA and the ability for DNA typing. In 1984, Sir Alec Jeffreys, a British geneticist, determined a DNA-based method for biological identification. Through his work, Jeffreys developed the first DNA profiling test utilizing Restriction Fragment Length Polymorphisms (RFLP). RFLP analysis focused on highly variable regions (polymorphisms) within the DNA, which allowed for discrimination between individuals. In 1986, this technique was used for the first time in a criminal case in England. A man by the name of Colin Pitchfork was identified as the murderer of two young girls after his DNA was compared to biological evidence recovered from the scene (Zagorski, 2006). The following year, RFLP DNA profiling was first used in the United States in the case of Florida vs. Tommy Lee Andrews. Andrews was tried and convicted for rape and was sentenced to 22 years (Longmire, 2004). In 1988, Timothy Wilson Spencer, also dubbed "The South Side Strangler," received the death penalty after his DNA was discovered at multiple rape and murder scenes in Richmond, Virginia (James, 2009).

In the 1990s, a new technique was developed which replaced RFLP analysis in DNA testing. Polymerase Chain Reaction (PCR) would greatly advance DNA profiling techniques in that a much smaller sample could yield a DNA profile as compared with RFLP technology.

PCR works like a copy machine, where it amplifies certain sections of DNA known as Short Tandem Repeats (STR), copying it millions of times. STRs are short, repeating units of base pairs along the DNA. These sequences repeat multiple times, forming a series with lengths up to 100 bases long (Fan & Chu, 2007). The benefit of using STRs is that these sections of DNA are highly variable between individuals. Twenty specific STR locations (loci) on the human genome have been identified for use in present-day DNA analysis (Federal Bureau of Investigation, (n.d.) Frequently Asked Questions on CODIS and NDIS).

DNA alone does not solve all criminal cases; however, it has become the gold standard in forensic science. DNA evidence is what juries and judges have come to expect to support a solid conviction. Technology has advanced dramatically since the first DNA case 30 years ago. Improved sensitivity and analysis allows for quicker results, identification with smaller samples, and even the ability to distinguish multiple individuals from a mixed DNA sample (Arnaud, 2017).

As history has shown, there have been countless scientific breakthroughs advancing the field of forensics. Although STR typing provides discrimination of an individual, there may be times when the forensic biological sample has too little DNA or the sample is degraded or decomposed, greatly decreasing a promising result through PCR. Additionally, investigations have yielded a complete DNA profile from physical evidence, but there was no individual or reference sample to match to the profile. Within recent years, another type of genetic marker, single nucleotide polymorphisms (SNPs), is being used in cases like this through what is known as DNA Phenotyping. SNPs are base substitutions, insertions, or deletions that can occur at a single position in the genome. They are highly abundant, have a very low mutation rate, and allow for analyzing much smaller fragments of DNA than STRs (Sobrino & Carracedo, 2005). Approximately 85% of human variation is derived from SNPs. These areas contain much of the genetic blueprint that differentiates what people look like; a huge amount of genetic information can be gleaned through using these areas of DNA.

Traditional DNA analysis will match the 20 STR loci from an item of evidence to a known reference sample or database. DNA phenotyping, however, will read parts of the millions of sections within the genome that code for the physical differences between individuals. Information gleaned from these areas can predict ancestry, skin color, hair color, eye color, freckling, and even the physical morphology of the face – all from an unidentified DNA sample. This type of technology allows new leads to identify whose DNA was left at a crime scene or even assist in identifying a victim (Parabon Nanolabs, n.d.). Although SNPs and DNA phenotyping have not replaced STRs in forensic DNA analysis, they are being utilized more often in certain cases like inheritance, missing persons, and situations where no reference sample exists (Budowle & Van Daal, 2018).

An emerging approach to forensic DNA analysis, Genetic Genealogy, has made headlines within the past few years. This technology utilizes autosomal DNA (aDNA) SNPs to determine how closely related individuals might be. aDNA is inherited through ancestral lines, both on the paternal and maternal lines. Therefore, this DNA can be utilized to compare any two individuals, regardless of how they are related. This type of technology has traditionally been used to build family trees and find possible new family members. Recently however, this analytical approach is being employed to solve cases where no reference DNA sample existed. Through this technique, the identity of an unknown individual can be determined by using DNA to identify relatives and then use genealogical research to build a family tree. Then through investigative research, it can be deduced as to who the unknown person may be. Genetic genealogy has been used to identify victims' remains and even suspects in various cases (Parabon Nanolabs, n.d.). In 2018, Joseph James DeAngelo, a 72-year-old former police officer, was identified as "The Golden State Killer" through this exact technology. Police investigators utilized GEDmatch, a free open-source website, which allows users to conduct research or fill in family trees. Through this database, DNA evidence was matched to a pool of potential suspects under the same family tree as DeAngelo (Robbins, 2018).

Approaches and forensic technological advances have continued to improve the analysis of evidence. The future may hold even better methods of how science can be used to solve crime.

FOLLOWING THE EVIDENCE: FROM THE CRIME SCENE TO THE CRIME LABORATORY

The glorification of crime scene investigators and forensic science on television has given rise to the current popularity of this field. However, it has also created a false perception of how real-life forensic practitioners do their job. These television shows promote a cool, sleek vision of crime laboratories and crime scene investigators who within minutes of arrival on scene, find the single important piece of evidence that solves the crime. They utilize immediate laboratory results through automation, along with the ability to enhance faces and reflections on grainy, otherwise impossible to decipher, video recordings. Suspects are identified and arrested within minutes of the crime. Ultimately, the case is solved within 45 minutes or less. Imagery such as this has created an inaccurate, dramatized depiction and expectation of what forensic science is really about. Although their jobs may not be as sensational as primetime television shows depict, crime scene investigators and forensic scientists play an extremely vital role in solving crime.

The overall goal of forensic science is to utilize physical evidence to provide a scientific link between a suspect, a victim, and a crime scene. Per Locard's Exchange Principle, it is known that wherever anyone goes, whatever he or she comes into contact with, they will leave some sort of evidence behind. Paul L. Kirk, a criminalistics professor at UC Berkeley, discussed the importance of this principle:

> Wherever he steps, wherever he touches, whatever he leaves, even without consciousness, will serve as a silent witness against him. Not only his fingerprints or his footprints, but his hair, the fibers from his clothes, the glass he breaks, the tool mark he leaves, the paint he scratches, the blood or semen he deposits or collects. All of these and more bear mute witness against him.

(Kirk, 1953)

The ability to locate and find whatever evidence exists begins at the scene of the crime. A Crime Scene Investigator (CSI) normally conducts this extremely important responsibility. A CSI could be a sworn member of law enforcement who conducts crime scene investigations as a collateral duty. A non-sworn civilian could also serve in this role, where their primary job duty is to process scenes on a daily basis. There are also select individuals, who primarily work in the forensic laboratory, that may respond to a scene for specialized scene processing or recovery of a specific type of evidence such as DNA or latent fingerprints. In short, the goal of the CSI in whatever capacity they may work, is to find the evidence.

The overall duties and scope of the crime scene investigator can be vast. The priority of any CSI, however, is to maintain the integrity of the scene and any evidence contained in it. As a CSI responds to a scene, they will coordinate with the first responders to make sure the scene has been properly cleared of individuals, cordoned off, and secured. From this point, the CSI will assess the scene and begin the steps to document and process the area. Documenting the scene involves several steps. To start, the entirety of the scene and any evidence is photographed, then, depending on the resources of the agency, the scene may also be scanned using 3D laser technology. This type of scanning allows the CSI to capture the entire geometry of the scene, including evidence and/or relevant aspects of the scene in digital format. Additional types of documentation consist of physical measurements and two-dimensional sketches of the scene. Throughout this process, in-depth notes are taken to record any observations or information obtained at the scene. These notes are ultimately used to write the formal crime scene examination report.

Throughout the processing and search of the scene, the CSI will identify, collect, preserve, and package any physical evidence that is discovered. There may be times the CSI must employ the use of chemicals, powders, or light technology to look for and identify other types of evidence that may not be readily visible. Fingerprint powders and chemicals can be used to develop latent fingerprints at a scene. For bloodstain evidence, Bluestar® Forensic, a latent bloodstain reagent that reacts with iron, has replaced what is commonly known as luminol. This reagent allows for searching a scene where a suspected clean-up of blood may have occurred. A positive reaction results in a blue luminescent glow. An alternate light source (ALS) can be used at a scene, utilizing various combinations of light wavelengths and barrier filters to look for biological fluids that may fluoresce under the emitted light source. Countless processing techniques exist and are used at a scene to find multiple types of physical evidence otherwise invisible to the naked eye.

Subsequent to a scene being documented, processed, and the physical evidence identified, it is the CSI's responsibility to make sure the evidence is properly packaged. The evidence must be protected to prevent any damage or contamination. Packaging consists of anything from a simple paper bag to a metal container, depending on the type of evidence it is and what type of laboratory process it will be subjected to; all items of evidence are individually packaged, sealed, and labeled appropriately for further transport and storage.

Once physical evidence has been properly secured from the scene, it will eventually transition over to the forensic laboratory. The laboratory employs a variety of individuals who are trained and educated in various forensic disciplines. The laboratory setting is where forensic scientists will examine the physical evidence. The purpose of examining the physical evidence is to conduct identification and comparison analysis. Identification involves the determination of the physical or chemical identity of an item with as near absolute certainty as existing analytical techniques permit. An example of identification would be identifying a red-brown stain collected at a crime scene as human blood. A comparison analysis subjects a suspect item and a standard or reference sample to the same tests and examinations, keeping in mind that the sole purpose of this analysis is to determine whether the two have a common origin. A comparison example of two items would be matching a shoe impression discovered at a crime scene to a specific shoe obtained from an individual (Saferstein, 2019).

Laboratories have separate and distinct sections, each with its own specific function, space, and equipment. The makeup of each laboratory can vary, although common divisions exist across many of them. The following is a comprehensive list of the various sections commonly found in a crime laboratory:

- **Biology Section:** examines biological/serological evidence and develops DNA profiles from physical evidence.
- **Chemistry Section:** examines narcotics and drug paraphernalia, among other evidence, utilizing instrumentation such as gas chromatography and mass spectrometry.
- **Toxicology Section:** analyzes biological specimens for the presence of drugs, alcohol, poisons, or other foreign substances.
- **Latent Fingerprints:** examines evidence for the presence of fingerprints utilizing various techniques; also conducts comparisons with fingerprints collected from a crime scene to known prints obtained from an individual.
- **Firearms Division:** examines any evidence pertaining to ballistics, including weapons, projectiles, and casings; also conducts range determinations through chemical processing of gunshot residues.
- **Trace Evidence:** identifies any substances that cannot be identified in the chemistry division; substances include items such as paints, glass, fibers, food products, or even building materials (Denmark & Mount, 2010).

Additional sections could include questioned documents, footwear and tire mark impression evidence, and digital evidence to name a few. Although there are many divisions within the laboratory, all forensic scientists work toward the same goal: connecting the suspect, the victim, and the crime scene through scientific analysis of the physical evidence.

A final category of practitioners that deserves mention is crime scene reconstruction analysts. These individuals are tasked with using scientific methods to recreate the events of a crime. Although many different types of reconstruction exist, commonly known disciplines in this area are bloodstain pattern analysis (BPA) and shooting incident scene analysis. Bloodstain analysts identify discrete patterns at a scene to determine what events may have occurred in order to create that specific pattern. BPA can assist in determining the position of the individual when the blood was deposited, the possible type of weapon used, and the possible mechanisms that could have produced the blood pattern on a particular surface (Minnesota Bureau of Criminal Apprehension, n.d.). A shooting incident scene reconstruction involves identifying and reconstructing the trajectory of a projectile path. Observations at the scene can provide information about the projectile, the type of firearm used, intermediate objects in the path of the projectile, direction of travel, and the order of shots (Minnesota Bureau of Criminal Apprenhension, n.d.). Shooting reconstructions will confirm the location of the firearm when the projectile was fired, what surfaces the projectile impacted, and even the position of a victim impacted by the bullet. Analyses such as these can greatly assist the overall investigation in confirming or refuting witnesses' or suspects' explanation of events.

Forensic practitioners serve an important role in helping solve crimes. Although there are many other aspects to a criminal investigation, the identification and collection of physical evidence and the subsequent analysis can lay the foundation for a solid conviction. Forensics provides the link between the suspect, victim, and crime scene through science.

CRIME SCENE INVESTIGATION PROCEDURES
FOLLOWING A TERRORIST EVENT

Forensic science and the various types of expertise within it can be applied to the overall investigations of terrorist attacks. Acts of terror have occurred in multiple cities and countries across the entire globe and affected countless individuals. When these events occur, one of the primary goals is to determine who is ultimately responsible. Examination of the scene and the identification and analysis of the physical evidence is crucial in bringing resolution to the investigation. The evidence recovered can be critical in identifying, charging, and ultimately convicting the responsible individual(s). Although the forensic laboratory analysis of physical evidence from terrorist attacks does not differ from the common criminal investigation, the approach to the crime scene can be drastically different. Because these events create a scene unlike any other, the methods of processing and documenting these scenes and subsequent evidence collection can be unique and need to be conducted appropriately for the specific situation.

A unique aspect of dealing with the aftermath of a terrorist event is determining which agency will take primary jurisdiction of the scene itself. Although the event may occur in a particular city which may fall under a specific law enforcement jurisdiction, the circumstances of the event may dictate who actually will maintain control of the scene. In the United States, the Federal Bureau of Investigation (FBI) is the nation's lead federal law enforcement agency responsible for investigating acts of domestic and international terrorism (Federal Bureau of Investigation, n.d. What Is the FBI's Role in Combating Terrorism?). Therefore, the FBI could be the primary agency in control of the investigation even though a local or state agency has normal jurisdiction of the location. Although a specific agency may take the lead, these events usually involve a multi-agency response. No matter who is in primary control, the roles and responsibilities need to be understood by all involved agencies. Thus, the responsibility of who will handle the documentation and processing of the scene needs to be established.

Just like any other type of scene, it is vital that the forensic investigation begins at the terrorist scene as soon as possible. The earlier this occurs, the better the chances of protecting physical evidence from being contaminated, destroyed, or even lost. However, because scenes that are a result of terrorist actions are by nature very complex, the forensic technicians may not be able to immediately secure the scene and begin their work.

The first and foremost issue of working complicated scenes such as that of a terrorist attack is dealing with the safety of any personnel. Because terrorist events typically involve explosive, chemical, biological, or nuclear weapons, the scene itself may not be safe to enter. A preliminary evaluation should be conducted to assess the scene and determine the course of any action to be taken. The assessment should include any safety concerns and evidentiary considerations. Any hazards need to be identified that could further threaten any public safety personnel. Specialized resources can be called in such as bomb disposal technicians, building inspectors, utility company representatives, or anyone else that can assist in mitigating any hazards. Once safety concerns are handled, the rescue of any living victims can proceed. During this process, personnel should be attempting to preserve evidence and avoid disturbing areas not directly related to any rescue activities (U.S. Department of Justice, 2004).

Security and control of the scene is the next step of the process. A security perimeter should be put in place and access in and out of the scene restricted to only essential personnel. Because events such as these involve multiple agencies, a command post should be established somewhere outside of the perimeter. This will allow for easier communication, points of contact, and authority for other public safety personnel. Once the scene is secured, documentation procedures need to be implemented to protect the integrity of the scene such as personnel entering/exiting the scene, evidence collection, and chain of custody (U.S. Department of Justice, 2004).

Proper resources, equipment, and additional personnel may be needed when dealing with scenes of this magnitude. Although common crime scene processing tools and equipment will be needed, they may not be sufficient in terrorism cases. Light and heavy equipment, hand tools, specialty equipment, and heavy-duty personal protection equipment may also need to be secured (U.S. Department of Justice, 2004).

Many of the common CSI processing and documentation procedures will be employed during the processing of these scenes. A thorough search of the scene needs to be done in a methodical manner. Investigators need to complete written scene documentation through notes indicating all observations and activities completed throughout the process. Photography of the scene and possible 3D laser-scanning will be conducted, all of which will support the written documentation. The identification of physical evidence at the scene will be of extreme importance. All items of evidentiary value will need to be noted, measured, and sketched. The makeup of the evidence processing team for these events may differ from the standard team due to specialized knowledge required for determining what items are most probative. Individuals such as a bomb disposal technician, logistics specialist, safety specialist, medical examiner, and others may need to be involved in identifying possible evidence unique to the event. Once the evidence is identified, it should be documented fully, collected, and preserved to minimize contamination; chain of custody should be maintained to ensure the integrity of the evidence (U.S. Department of Justice, 2004).

At the completion of the scene processing and once all items of evidence have been properly collected, the evidence should be transported and secured with the appropriate agency. The agency who maintained primary jurisdiction of the scene should take custody of all of the evidence or designate who will take control of the items. The evidence will then be distributed to the crime laboratory for further analysis. Ultimately, the forensic scientists will be attempting to identify who and what caused the event based on the physical evidence recovered. Physical evidence has been the essential link to identifying the individuals responsible for acts of terror countless times.

CSI: THE REAL-LIFE STORIES

Some vivid, real-world examples can shed important insight on what occurs during crime scene investigations. Three cases will be mentioned: the Oklahoma City Bombing, the Boston Marathon Bombing, and Pan Am Flight 103.

The Oklahoma City Bombing

At 9:02 a.m. on the morning of April 19, 1995, an explosion occurred in front of the Alfred P. Murrah Federal Building in downtown Oklahoma City. As a result of the blast, 168 people were killed, 19 of them children; hundreds more were injured. A third of the building was completely demolished, dozens of cars were incinerated, and more than 300 buildings were damaged or destroyed. This incident sent shock waves across America and became the most devastating incident of domestic terrorism in U.S. history (Federal Bureau of Investigation (n.d.). Oklahoma City Bombing).

The aftermath of the bombing created a crime scene that stretched throughout a four-block radius from the blast site. The FBI took primary investigative lead on this case, which included the documentation and processing of the scene as well as identifying and collecting any possible physical evidence. The scene processing was a monumental task of digging through rubble, twisted metal, concrete, and debris in the attempt to determine what or who caused the explosion.

Out of all of the evidence, a few items proved to be of vital importance early in the investigation. These pieces of physical evidence played an important role in identifying the main suspect and ultimately connected him to the scene of the bombing. The day after the attack during a search of the rubble, the rear axle of a Ryder truck was located. This piece of evidence yielded a vehicle identification number, which was used to trace the truck to a body shop in Junction City, Kansas. It was through this connection and subsequent interviews of the employees of the body shop that the initial composite sketch was created of the man who rented the van. The man was very quickly identified as Timothy McVeigh, an ex-Army soldier and security guard (Federal Bureau of Investigation (n.d.). Oklahoma City bombing).

Additional examination of evidence determined that the bomb consisted of a combination of agricultural fertilizer, diesel fuel, and other chemicals. Clothing and personal items eventually seized from McVeigh indicated traces of the same explosive chemicals that had been used in the bombing. Through investigative efforts, McVeigh's extremist ideologies were uncovered as well as his anger over the events that had occurred in Waco, Texas, two years prior. Terry Nichols, a friend of McVeigh's, was identified as having helped build the bomb. A third man, Michael Fortier, was also identified; he had been aware of the bomb plot (Federal Bureau of Investigation (n.d.). Oklahoma City Bombing).

It did not take long to identify the individuals responsible for the Oklahoma City Bombing. However, the investigation turned out to be one of the most exhaustive in FBI history. By the end of the investigation, the Bureau conducted more than 28,000 interviews, followed up on around 43,000 investigative leads, collected three-and-a-half tons of evidence, and reviewed nearly a billion pieces of information (Federal Bureau of Investigation (n.d.). Oklahoma City Bombing).

Boston Marathon Bombing

The 117th Boston Marathon was held on the morning of April 15, 2013. This event brought almost 27,000 official entrants and more than 500,000 spectators gathered along the marathon route to the city of Boston that day. Although the first place winners were already past the finish line by 12:36 p.m., a majority of the runners had yet to cross. Several hours later, more and more runners would be approaching the end of their race. At 2:49 p.m., an improvised explosive device (IED) detonated near the finish line on Boylston Street. Ten seconds later, a second IED exploded just 180 yards up the course from the first detonation (Gates et al., 2014). The result of these two explosions took the lives of three individuals: eight-year-old Marton Richard, 29-year-old Krystle Campbell, and 23-year-old Lu Lingzi. In all, 261 people were injured, 16 of whom suffered traumatic amputations (After Action Report, 2014).

Within minutes of the explosions, multiple law enforcement personnel and emergency management officials came together to coordinate priorities. A Unified Command Center (UCC) was established that included the Governor, Mayor of Boston, Secretary of the Executive Office of Public Safety and Security (EOPSS), Massachusetts Emergency Management Agency (MEMA) Director, Massachusetts State Police (MSP) Superintendent, Boston Police Department (BPD) Commissioner, Boston Fire Department (BFD) Commissioner, Boston Emergency Medical Services (Boston EMS) Chief, Director of the Mayor's Office of Emergency Management (OEM), Massachusetts National Guard (MANG) Adjutant General, Massachusetts Bay Transportation Authority (MBTA) Transit Police Department (Transit PD) Chief, and FBI Boston Special Agent-in-Charge (SAC). The UCC was ultimately responsible for making decisions on initial law enforcement response and investigation issues, including that of securing the crime scene. Ultimately, the perimeter of the scene encompassed a 12-block area surrounding the detonations (After Action Report, 2014).

It was not long before multiple items of evidence were recovered from the scene that helped identify the makeup of the IEDs. A joint bulletin was released within days of the event with several photographs of a damaged pressure-cooker container found at the scene. Parts of the pressure cookers, metal and ball bearings, and fabric fragments consistent with backpacks were also recovered and identified. With this information, the FBI was able to ascertain that the bombs were contained in a pressure cooker with nails and ball bearings and hidden in backpacks.

On April 16, surveillance footage was released to the public showing two males, one with a black ball cap and a second with a white cap. Both were carrying heavy backpacks and were walking in the direction of the finish line shortly before the detonations. One of the suspects had also been witnessed placing a backpack on the ground at the second detonation site just moments prior to the explosion. These two individuals were eventually identified as Tamerlan and Dzhokhar Tsarnaev. The days following the bombing led to the death of Massachusetts Institute of Technology (MIT) police officer Sean Collier, who was fatally shot in his patrol car. Shortly after, a Mercedes sports utility vehicle was carjacked; however, the vehicle's owner was able to escape after being held captive for almost an hour. Officers were able to ascertain the location of the carjacked SUV. Upon arrival at the car's location, the two suspects began shooting at the officers and launching homemade IEDs; Tamerlan Tsarnaev was killed during this interaction and Dzhokhar fled the scene. Later that day Dzhokhar was discovered hiding in a boat in the backyard of a Boston resident and was taken into custody (After Action Report, 2014).

During the trial of Dzhokhar, an FBI explosives analyst testified about some of the evidence that was recovered during the course of this investigation. Explosive residue consistent with the bombs was also found at the Tsarnaev residence in Cambridge, as well as in a Honda CRV driven by Tamerlan Tsarnaev. Trace evidence samples seized from the Tsarnaev apartment contained grains of black powder and residue of pyrotechnics. Agents recovered nails, BBs, wire, a battery charger, a fuse, and parts of a pressure cooker from the apartment, all consistent with a homemade bomb like the ones used at the Marathon. Christmas tree lightbulbs were found at the residence, which have the power to set off a low explosive charge. An FBI agent testified in Dzhokhar's trial that the initiator that was used in the bombs at the finish line was a green Christmas tree light bulb strand. Overall, the FBI analyzed approximately 300 pieces of evidence that had been recovered throughout the investigation (NBC, 2015). The physical evidence recovered and the countless hours of investigative efforts by multiple law enforcement agencies provided resolution to this crime. In May 2015, Dzhokhar Tsarnaev was sentenced to death for his participation in the bombing.

Pan Am Flight 103

On December 21, 1988, Pan American Flight 103 took off from London Heathrow Airport bound for New York City. Less than 40 minutes into the flight, the plane exploded over the town of Lockerbie in the Dumfries and Galloway region of southwest Scotland. A total of 259 passengers and crew members were killed, along with 11 residents of Lockerbie when the plane's burning parts plunged into the town.

The plane's wings and tanks carrying 100 tons of jet fuel plummeted into Lockerbie's Sherwood Crescent neighborhood. Other parts of the jetliner came to rest in and around Lockerbie. The rear fuselage and landing gear crashed into Rosebank Crescent. A few miles away, the nose cone landed in a field opposite a church. The victims, along with 300 tons of wreckage, were scattered along an 81-mile-long corridor, measuring 845 square miles, creating a crime scene of massive proportions. Harry Bell, a detective stationed near Glasgow stated, "A crime scene for me was normally a house or a room or a field with a person lying in it. This was just a catastrophe. It was like a battlefield. Nothing could have prepared you" (FBI, 2018).

Scottish police treated the disaster as a massive crime scene. From the very beginning, they preserved anything that might be evidence of what may have caused the crash. The large scene was split into geographical boundaries and drawn into sectors, with a dedicated search and processing team assigned to each. Stuart Cossar, a Scottish detective inspector stated, "When you consider that some of the most critical exhibits or productions of the case were found 80 miles from Lockerbie, it shows you the scale of the search" (FBI, 2018).

During the course of the investigation there were vital pieces of evidence recovered that helped identify what caused the explosion and who was responsible. A fragment no bigger than a thumbnail was found on the ground. It was determined the item came from the circuit board of a radio/cassette player. This crucial piece of evidence, in addition to fragments of a suitcase, helped establish that the bomb had been inside a radio and tape deck in a piece of luggage (FBI, 2018). Also during the recovery effort, a piece of scorched shirt was found containing a fragment that identified the type of timer (FBI, 2003). When the CIA was provided a photograph of this fragment, a Directorate of Science & Technology (DS&T) electronics expert identified it as a timer similar to one used in a previous Libyan terrorist attack. Further analysis confirmed that this particular fragment matched part of a timer circuit manufactured specifically for the Libyans (CIA, 2012).

This evidence provided the link to identifying two Libyan intelligence operatives. In 1991, the United States and Scotland indicted the two operatives for planting the bomb. On January 31, 2001, Abdel Basset Ali Al-Megrahi was found guilty of the bombing; however, the co-defendant, Lamen Khalifa Fhimah, was found not guilty and released.

This particular case required unprecedented international cooperation. Investigators from various agencies combed over 845 square miles of debris; thousands of pieces of evidence were recovered. Retired Special Agent Dick Marquise, assigned to lead the FBI's investigation, credits the Scots' thoroughness in finding critical evidence. Pieces of the suitcase containing the bomb, fragments of a circuit board, and clothing traced to a Malta business all led to identifying the Libyan intelligence officers (FBI, 2018).

THE CHALLENGES OF PROCESSING COMPLEX
TERROR SCENES AND FORENSIC ANALYSIS

In everyday crime scenes, CSIs are faced with multiple challenges. Many issues can arise during a scene examination that can have profound effects on the overall investigation. Was the scene secured properly? Was any item of evidence moved prior to the CSI arrival? Did any fragile items of evidence get destroyed? These, plus countless others, are all concerns of the CSI when they are dealing with any sort of crime scene. However, when applied to a complex terror scene, the resulting answers are compounded and can create an even worse adverse effect on the case.

In traditional crime scenes, the first responding officer immediately secures the scene in an attempt to maintain the overall integrity of the scene and any evidence present. However, this approach may not be initially feasible in terrorist scenes due to the disorder, panic, lack of personnel experience in CSI, and most importantly, the need to attend to any victims. The search for and recovery of victims in these events is the priority. Personnel scouring the scene most likely do not have crime scene and evidence protection first and foremost on their minds. As a result, the mere act of rescuing victims can have a damaging outcome on the scene. Rescue teams, paramedics, police officers, and other first responders may be infiltrating the scene, causing contamination and other degradation of evidence.

Another challenge facing crime scene investigators pertains to determining and managing the actual scene(s) of the crime and personnel who are assisting. First, a terrorist event can create an extensive scene in and of itself. As mentioned earlier, attacks such as the Pan Am Bombing can result in a massive crime scene. How does one decide how big the scene perimeter needs to be? How is it ensured that the entire area that could contain physical evidence is secured, controlled, searched, and processed? When dealing with scenes of this nature, the ability to manage the scene can be overwhelming, as an area stretching for miles creates obstacles for being able to maintain scene integrity and preventing contamination, damage, or loss of evidence. Additionally, due to the high profile nature of the case, there will be a multi-jurisdictional response, resulting in a large turnout of personnel, all from different agencies. The stress of managing a complex scene is compounded with the responsibility of managing all of those who have arrived to assist; maintaining control of these scenes and all of the personnel becomes a huge challenge to make sure everyone is operating under the same procedures and physical evidence is protected.

Events such as this may also create multiple scenes that need to be processed, which require personnel, proper equipment, and sufficient laboratory resources. Depending on the aftermath, there could be numerous scenes or areas that need to be searched and examined for physical evidence. The Boston Marathon Bombing resulted in two separate explosions in two locations. Throughout the days following, there were additional scenes that required thorough processing such as the death scene of the MIT officer, the shootout location between the Tsarnaev brothers, the boat where Dzhokhar was apprehended, and even the apartment where the brothers lived. The amount of manpower needed to process all of these scenes within a short amount of time was substantial, and having the proper equipment was vital. Oftentimes, the responding agencies may not be prepared with the necessary equipment and scene processing tools for dealing with a large-scale incident; the time of the event is not the time to begin putting a disaster crime scene kit together. These events can result in an enormous amount of physical evidence that is collected, all of which will require some sort of examination, analysis, and comparison. Examples such as the Oklahoma City Bombing and many others resulted in the collection of literally tons of evidence, and due to the high profile nature of the case, demands pour in from investigators wanting results as soon as possible. This extensive amount of evidence may overwhelm the laboratory responsible for analyzing the items, causing delays and a longer turnaround time for results.

Another challenge exists because terrorist events commonly involve a multi-jurisdictional response. For example, in the Boston Marathon Bombing there were over a dozen agencies working together immediately following the explosions. Although one specific agency may take the primary jurisdictional role, many individuals from the various agencies will be assisting in the overall investigation; this also holds true to the scene examination. Though one agency will be governing the scene processing, there may be individuals working the scene who may be employed by a different agency. As a result, there could be confusion on procedural processes, such as who will maintain custody of the evidence, which laboratories are going to be utilized to process the evidence, and even something as simple as what type of reporting forms are going to be used. Different agencies use different methods, and if there is confusion on basic procedures, it could be a detriment to the final outcome.

PREPARING FOR THE CRISIS

The overwhelming types of challenges faced by scene investigators and the forensic laboratories during a terrorist event mostly focus on preparation and planning. Although one hopes to never deal with these types of cases, it is inevitable they will happen. When they do, there needs to be plans already in place so that the responding agencies have the proper ability to adequately manage the scene and the physical evidence recovered.

Crime scene management plays a vital role in being able to make sure the scene as well as any evidence located within it maintains its integrity. Because these types of scenes are not encountered every day, there may not be a lot of preparation on how to establish, manage, and control a scene of this magnitude. Planning for the worst is something agencies need to be doing. There should be a process in place for how to approach these complex scenes, how to secure them, what specific roles and duties will need to be filled, how personnel will be managed, and what the procedures should be for evidence collection, processing, packaging, and storing. During the course of the D.C. Sniper investigation, there were several lessons learned based on the issues that arose regarding scene management. Chief Charlie Dean from Prince William County Police Department stated, "Whatever the size of the crime scene, double it." Although this police department had the foresight for pre-planning large scenes like this, during the investigation they were forced to increase the size of the scene once a shooting started in a specific location (Murphy et al., 2004). Additionally, a major issue that arose during this case was the massive law enforcement response to the scenes. At one of the scenes located in Fairfax County, the police officials never expected several hundred local and federal law enforcement officers to show up at their crime scene. Many of these individuals acted independently of one another, expecting they would be the one to break the case. Chief Thomas Manger from the Fairfax County Police Department said, "When I arrived at the Home Depot crime scene, I looked at the parking lot and saw in excess of 200 law enforcement personnel and thought, this is going to be a challenge." Though

Fairfax County had planned for a large turnout, they did not anticipate these types of numbers, nor did they anticipate the need to assign extra patrol officers to manage all those who showed up at the scene (Murphy et al., 2004). A plan needs to be established where the roles and responsibilities of investigative personnel are thoroughly defined. A general list of roles with associated responsibilities should be established so when these events occur individuals can be specifically assigned to those duties. Roles such as scene manager, scene security, search teams, documentation, photographer, sketcher, evidence collection, packaging and many others should have clearly defined tasks. Procedures such as this will assist in being able to effectively manage these complex scenes.

Another important aspect of preparing for complex terror scenes is making sure all of the proper resources are available for processing these scenes. There may be times when specialized equipment will be necessary for proper documentation. Equipment such as 3D Measurement, Imaging, and Realization Technology will be of utmost importance for documenting the scene. 3D laser-scanning allows the crime scene investigator to capture the entire geometry of the scene, including evidence and/or relevant aspects of the scene that may not be observed by the naked eye during the original response. The ability to view and capture the scene through 3D laser-scanning technology ensures the longevity and preservation of the scene and provides crime scene units with unprecedented abilities to evaluate the scene and evidence in a holistic manner. Due to the high cost of this type of technology, not all agencies have a 3D laser within their inventory; as such, departments should have an agreement in place with a partner agency to utilize their resources during large-scale terrorist events.

Mass disaster crime scene kits are another type of specialized set-up. A crime scene response kit is standard throughout agencies. These kits contain any type of equipment needed to document and process a scene. Items like scales, measuring tape, evidence markers, fingerprint powders, evidence packaging, and much more are common to have on hand in a processing kit. However, when it comes to complex scenes there may be additional items needed. Equipment that is more robust may be necessary to sift through rubble, debris, metal, and concrete. Having a prepared mass disaster–type kit already stocked and ready would allow for a more organized response, as a scramble to find and locate equipment once a disaster happens is not the time to put a response kit together.

A fundamental piece of preparation for complex scenes is having a plan for dealing with the analysis of the physical evidence that will be recovered. Knowing there will most likely be a substantial amount of physical evidence that will require analysis, laboratories need to have a plan already in place. As agencies need to prepare for large-scale events, so does the laboratory. Forensic laboratories should evaluate what their capabilities are to manage large amounts of physical evidence in cases like this. They need to develop a contingency plan where they have agreements and coordination in place with cooperating laboratories that can assist in any analysis. These agreements will minimize overload of the laboratory and provide quicker response time for analysis results.

CONCLUSION

The discovery and subsequent forensic analysis of physical evidence is key in the ability to solve crimes, identify perpetrators, and bring justice to victims. The application of forensic analysis has been utilized for centuries. Through technological advances, more and more information can be gleaned from evidence recovered from crime scenes.

Forensic technicians play an important role in crime scene investigations and forensic analysis for all crime scenes, especially those of a complex nature like terrorist events. The ability to locate evidence of the crime is crucial in identifying who is ultimately responsible. Although many techniques of the approach to standard crime scenes will apply, dealing with a large-scale event requires adjustment and a more robust approach in order to properly manage the scene. Planning and preparation for these events is extremely crucial to ensure an organized and effective scene process and evidence analysis. Time will tell when another event may hit; how that scene is secured, managed, and processed could set the stage for how the investigation will play out. Finding that piece of evidence, however small it may be, could be the key to ultimate justice. In the words of Paul Kirk:

> Physical evidence…does not forget. It is not confused by the excitement of the moment. It is not absent because human witnesses are…Only human failure to find it, study and understand it can diminish its value.

(Kirk, 1953)

CLASS DISCUSSION AND ESSAY QUESTIONS

1. How accurate are the portrayals of investigation processes in shows like *CSI*?
2. What were some of the key turning points in the development of forensic science?
3. How has DNA advanced and become a significant factor in the conviction rate of criminals?
4. What lessons about forensic science can be gleaned from the Oklahoma City Bombing, the Boston Marathon Bombing, and Pan Am Flight 103?
5. Although the makeup of each forensic science laboratory can vary, what divisions exist across many of them and what does each section do?
6. What processes are undertaken by forensic technicians to collect and process evidence from the crime scene and how can a CSI more fully ensure that the materials will be admissible and not dismissed in a trial?

REFERENCES

After Action Report for the Response to the 2013 Boston Marathon Bombing. (2014). Retrieved from https://www.policefoundation.org/wp-content/uploads/2015/05/after-action-report-for-the-response-to-the-2013-boston-marathon-bombings_0.pdf

Arnaud, C. (2017). Thirty Years of DNA Forensics: How DNA Has Revolutionized Criminal Investigations. *Chemical & Engineering News* 95(37): 16–20.

Bucholtz, A., & Davis, A. (2015). *Forensic Studies: CSI for the Nonscientist: From Crime Scene to Crime Lab*. San Clemente, CA: San Clemente: Ebooks2go Incorporated.

Budowle, B., & Van Daal, A. (2018). Forensically Relevant SNP Classes. *BioTechniques* 44(5): 603–610.

Central Intelligence Agency (2012). *Terrorist Bombing of Pan Am Flight 103*. Retrieved from https://www.cia.gov/about-cia/cia-museum/experience-the-collection/text-version/stories/terrorist-bombing-of-pan-am-flight-103.html

Denmark, A., & Mount, M. (2010). *Crime Lab Design.* Retrieved from https://www.labmanager.com/lab-design-and-furnishings/crime-lab-design-19493

Fan, H., & Chu, J. (2007). A Brief Review of Short Tandem Repeat Mutation. *Genomics Proteomics Bioinformatics* 5(17): 7–14.

Federal Bureau of Investigation. (n.d.). Frequently Asked Questions on CODIS and NDIS. Retrieved from https://www.fbi.gov/services/laboratory/biometric-analysis/codis/codis-and-ndis-fact-sheet

Federal Bureau of Investigation. (n.d.). *Oklahoma City Bombing.* Retrieved from https://www.fbi.gov/history/famous-cases/oklahoma-city-bombing

Federal Bureau of Investigation. (n.d.). What Is the FBI's Role in Combating Terrorism? Retrieved from https://www.fbi.gov/about/faqs/what-is-the-fbis-role-in-combating-terrorism

Federal Bureau of Investigation. (2003). *A Byte Out of History.* Retrieved from https://archives.fbi.gov/archives/news/stories/2003/december/panam121903

Federal Bureau of Investigation. (2018). *The Bombing of Pan Am Flight 103.* Retrieved from https://www.fbi.gov/news/stories/remembering-pan-am-flight-103-30-years-later-121418

Gates, J., Arabian, S., Biddinger, P., Blansfield, J., Burke, P., Chung, S., Fischer, J., Friedman, F., Gervasini, A., Goralnick, E., Gupta, A., Larentzakis, A., McMahon, M., Mulla, J., Michaud, Y., Mooney, D., Rabinovici, R., Sweet, D., Ulrich, A., Velmahos, G., Weber, C., & Yaffe, M. (2014). The Initial Response to the Boston Marathon Bombing: Lessons Learned to Prepare for the Next Disaster. *Annals of Surgery* 260(6): 960–966.

James, R. (2009). A Brief History of DNA Testing. *Time.* Retrieved from http://content.time.com/time/nation/article/0,8599,1905706,00.html

Kirk, P. (1953). *Crime Investigation: physical evidence and the police laboratory.* New York: Interscience Publishers, Inc.

Longmire, A. (2004). Landmark DNA Court Cases. Retrieved from http://www.ric.edu/faculty/lmsm/Landmark%20%20DNA%20Court%20Cases.pdf

Michelson, R. (2015). *Crime Scene Investigation: An Introduction to CSI.* San Clemente, CA: LawTech Publishing Group.

Minnesota Bureau of Criminal Apprehension. (n.d.). Bloodstain Pattern Analysis. Retrieved from https://dps.mn.gov/divisions/bca/bca-divisions/forensic-science/Pages/forensic-programs-crime-scene-bpa.aspx

Minnesota Bureau of Criminal Apprehension. (n.d.). Shooting Scene Reconstruction. Retrieved from https://dps.mn.gov/divisions/bca/bca-divisions/forensic-science/Pages/forensic-programs-crime-scene-ssrecon.aspx

Murphy, G., Wexler, C., Davies, H., & Plotkin, M. (2004). *Managing a Multijurisdictional Case: Identifying the Lessons Learned from the Sniper Investigation.* Washington, DC: Police Executive Research Forum. Retrieved from https://bja.ojp.gov/sites/g/files/xyckuh186/files/Publications/SniperRpt.pdf

NBC News. (2015). Boston Marathon Bombing Trial: Feds Not Sure Where Bombs Made. Retrieved from https://www.nbcnews.com/storyline/boston-bombing-trial/prosecution-home-stretch-boston-marathon-death-penalty-trial-can-t-n330731

Parabon Nanolabs. (n.d.). The Snapshot DNA Phenotyping Service. Retrieved from https://snapshot.parabon-nanolabs.com/phenotyping

Parabon Nanolabs. (n.d.). Snapshot Genetic Genealogy. Retrieved from https://snapshot.parabon-nanolabs.com/genealogy

Robbins, R. (2018). The Golden State Killer Case Was Cracked with a Genealogy Web Site. *Scientific American.* Retrieved from https://www.scientificamerican.com/article/the-golden-state-killer-case-was-cracked-with-a-genealogy-web-site1/

Saferstein, R. (2015). *Criminalistics: An Introduction to Forensic Science* (11th ed.). Hoboken: Prentice Hall, Inc.

Saferstein, R. (2019). *Forensic Science: From the Crime Scene to the Crime Lab* (4th ed.). Pearson.

Sobrino, B., & Carracedo, A. (2005). SNP Typing in Forensic Genetics: A Review. *Methods in Molecular Biology* 297: 107–126.

U.S. Department of Justice. (2004). *A Guide for Explosion and Bombing Scene Investigation.* Washington D.C.: Washington D.C.: Createspace Independent Pub.

Zagorski, N. (2006). Profile of Alec J. Jeffreys. *Proceedings of the National Academy of Sciences of the United States of America* 103(24): 8919–8920. Retrieved from https://www.ncbi.nlm.nih.gov/pmc/articles/PMC1482540/

CHAPTER 19

Forensic Pathology:
Medicolegal Death Investigation and Management of Fatalities in Mass Disasters and Terrorist Events

Amie B. Houghton

INTRODUCTION

People succumb to death in a variety of ways. Sometimes it is a result of disease, maybe it is from an accidental fall, or there are times it is through the actions of others. No matter the reason, many times a forensic pathologist will determine the cause of death and why the individual died.

The pathologist is responsible for many roles within the overall death investigation. Pathologists work death investigations with causes that vary from natural to violent, pandemics, homicide, and even work-related. Their ultimate goal, however, is always the same: identify the victim and determine what the circumstances were surrounding their death. This overall process falls under the modern-day system known as medicolegal death investigation (MDI). These same goals will hold true when considering fatalities in mass disasters and terrorist events.

Mass disasters can create extremely challenging conditions. A coordinated, effective response is essential when attempting to locate and identify human remains. Victim identification, recovery, and examination are top priority when disasters, whether natural or man-made, occur. If there has not been a disaster plan in place, proper training, and equipment and personnel available, many victims may never be recovered.

Throughout this chapter, the history of pathology and death investigations will be explored. The roles of forensic pathologists will be delineated for standard investigations as well as their management for dealing with fatalities in a mass disaster or terrorist attack. Current challenges for approaching mass casualties will be discussed as well as ways to mitigate those problems for future events.

ORIGINS AND DEVELOPMENT OF FORENSIC PATHOLOGY
AND THE DEATH INVESTIGATION SYSTEM

Forensic pathology is the application of the medicinal science of pathology to the investigation of death. The forensic pathologist serves a vital role within a death investigation, as it is the forensic pathologist who determines *what* caused someone's death and then correlates it to the circumstances of *why* the individual died. Although the term "forensic pathologist" was not coined until the early 1900s, and the official death investigation system took even longer to establish, the roots of this overall process originated long before the 20th century.

The association of law and medicine can be traced as far back as 3000 BCE, to Ancient Egypt. During ancient times, most cultures had religious and social objections to dissection of the dead. However, the Egyptians and Babylonians strayed from these belief systems, and as a result they gained a considerable amount of knowledge of human anatomy over other civilizations (Spitz & Spitz, 2006). Imhotep, the personal physician of King Zozer, has been described as the first figure to stand out clearly from ancient medical practices. The Edwin Smith papyrus, believed to be written by Imhotep, describes various surgery procedures and treatment of trauma. Imhotep has been recognized for diagnosing over 200 diseases in his lifetime, as well as founding the first ever school of medicine. After his death, Imhotep was elevated to a demigod and eventually, his status was exalted to that of a god of medicine and healing (Barton, 2016).

Rudimentary investigations of death can be found in various cultures throughout history. The first recorded murder trial, inscribed on clay tablets, took place in Sumeria around 1850 BCE; three men were sentenced for killing a temple servant, Lu-Innanna (Wilson, 1984). The Code of Hammurabi, which dates back to 1700 BCE from Ancient Mesopotamia, is one of the earliest written legal codes. This code of laws, which consists of 282 rules, established fines and punishments to meet the requirements of justice or laws of retribution. This code is also one of the earliest examples of the concept of "innocent until proven guilty" and established the belief of "an eye for an eye" (History, 2009). The first recorded autopsy conducted to determine cause of death occurred in 44 BCE on the body of Gaius Julius Caesar. Although ancient Greeks were known to have performed dissections of bodies, Caesar was the first recorded murder victim to undergo an autopsy. A doctor by the name of Antistius examined Caesar's remains after his assassination. Antistius recorded 23 stab wounds during his examination of the body. Although Caesar's face and groin sustained a majority of his injuries, one particular stab wound was noted and determined to be the only one that was fatal. This wound, located just under the left shoulder blade, indicated Caesar was most likely struck in the heart or a major artery, causing massive internal bleeding, ultimately leading to the Emperor's death (Sheldon, n.d).

The Middle Ages brought about new developments involving medicolegal investigations. There was greater reliance on medical testimony in cases of physical injury, infanticide, rape, and bestiality. Medicolegal autopsies were performed in Bologna beginning in 1302 on victims of homicide, suicide, and executed criminals. One of the first documents pertaining to postmortem examinations, *His Yuan Lu*, was published in 1250. This Chinese handbook described general postmortem guidelines in addition to physical descriptions of blunt force and sharp force injuries. One particular case in this handbook explained the determination of whether a person had drowned or was deceased prior to being submerged in water (Spitz & Spitz, 2006).

The 12th century marked the true beginning of a medicolegal system where the first coroners were formalized into law in England by King Richard I under the Articles of Eyre. Coroners, initially known as "crowners," were to represent and protect the interests of the Crown in criminal proceedings (Spitz & Spitz, 2006). The crowner was ultimately required to identify the deceased, determine cause and manner of death, and collect any monies or confiscate property (NAS, 2009). The role of the coroner was described as follows:

> The office and power of the coroner are similar to those of a sheriff and consists, first, in inquiring, when a person is slain or dies suddenly, or in prison, concerning the manner of his death. And this must be upon sight of the body; for if the body be not found, the coroner cannot sit. He must also sit at the very place where death happened, and the inquiry must be made by a jury from 4, 5, or 6 of the neighboring towns over which he is to preside. If any be found guilty by this inquest of murder or other homicide, the coroner is to commit them to prison for further trial and must certify the whole of his inquisition, together with the evidence thereon, to the Court of King's Bench.
>
> (Spitz & Spitz, 2006)

In the 16th century, rudimentary death investigators, known as *Searchers of the Dead*, were established in London. These "searchers," made up of a network of women, were initially developed as part of a system to determine the numbers of individuals who succumbed to the plague. London parishes set up this system where these women searchers were to view all corpses, determine what the circumstances were surrounding the death, and then report their results to the parish clerk (Henry, 2016). If the searchers determined infectious disease was the cause of death, authorities were notified and steps would be taken to avoid an epidemic. If, however, the death was suspicious, and murder was suspected, the Constable would be requested and a more thorough investigation, a "Coroner's Inquest," would occur. These searchers were active from at least 1574 until 1836 (Munkhoff, 1999).

American history documents the use of the coroner system as the early colonists implemented British Common Law in the New World. A record of a coroner's inquest was documented in 1635, New Plymouth, where cause of death of a man, John Deacon, was determined to be hypothermia with starvation as a contributing factor. The inquiry into the death stated:

> Having searched the dead body, we finde not any blows or wounds, or any other bodily hurt. We finde that bodily weakness caused by long fasting and weariness, by going to and fro, with the extreme cold of the season were the causes of his death.
>
> (Spitz & Spitz, 2006)

In 1647, the General Court of Massachusetts Bay began teaching medical students the importance of autopsies. It was during this time that they authorized and conducted autopsies on criminals once every four years. March 21, 1665, marked the first recorded application of an autopsy to ascertain medicolegal information in the murder of a man named Sammuel Yeoungman. The coroner's report read:

> Wee the Jury haueing viewed the Corpse of Samuell Yeoungman and finding A Depression in the Cranenum in flesh was Corrupted, and withal finding Corrupt blood betweene the Dura and Piamater, and the braine and several other bruises in the head and body therefore our verdict in that for want of looking after the abousesaid wounds, were Cause of his death.
>
> (Spitz& Spitz, 2006)

Essentially, the report indicated that Mr. Yeoungman had died of blunt force trauma to the head rather than failure of being treated by a doctor, as initially believed (Spitz & Spitz, 2006).

Developments within law and medicine continued to occur in the United States throughout the 1800s. In 1811, Dr Benjamin Rush published "On the Study of Medical Jurisprudence." This particular publication was a first of its kind and served as a guideline for many medicolegal issues. In 1860, the Code of Public General Laws authorized the attendance of a physician in cases of violent death in the state of Maryland, acknowledging the need for coroners to have medical training. One of the first steps in beginning a new medicolegal investigative system in the United States was made in 1883 when the Medicolegal Society of New York was founded. In 1887, the Commonwealth of Massachusetts required a physician, known as the medical examiner, replace the coroner (Spitz & Spitz, 2006).

In the early 1900s, the title "Forensic Pathologist" was coined and was used in death investigations. A shift was being seen from "coroner" to "forensic pathologist." By 1915, Massachusetts and New York City had completely abolished the coroner system and had a fully functional medical examiner department. Dr Charles Norris was appointed the first chief medical examiner of New York on February 18, 1918. Thomas Gonzales eventually succeeded Dr Norris after his death. Under the tenure of both Drs Norris and Gonzales, the New York office became the training ground for pathologists who wished to focus in forensic pathology. Throughout the mid-1900s, forensic pathology continued to advance and progress throughout the United States under prominent pathologists such as Dr Alexander Gettler, Dr Milton Helpern, Dr Alan Moritz, Dr Russell Fisher, Dr Richard Lindenberg, Dr Joseph Davis, Dr Charles Hirsch, Dr Charles Petty, and Dr Werner Spitz (Spitz & Spitz, 2006).

With the advancements in forensic pathology came the growth in the medical examiner system. The first statewide medical examiner system was developed in Maryland in 1939 (Spitz & Spitz, 2006). Subsequently, other states began to shift from a coroner system to a medical examiner system as well. In recent years, there remained a mixture within the states of utilizing either the coroner or the medical examiner system. This became an issue of huge debate, as some states required a coroner to be a physician; other states required only that you must be of voting age and have no felony convictions. However, medical examiners are required to be a physician, but some medical doctors may not have a background in forensics. This caused a major discrepancy on how a death investigation and/or autopsy was conducted from state to state. In 2009, the National Academy of Sciences recommended the coroner system be abolished and all death investigations must be conducted by the medical examiner. Many states have since transitioned to the medical examiner system, with others beginning to follow suit (Quinn, 2018).

The discipline of forensic pathology and death investigations has come a long way from the "an eye for an eye" approach. The pioneers of the field, all the way back in Ancient Egypt and Mesopotamia, provided the framework for our modern-day systems.

THE ROLES AND FUNCTIONS OF THE FORENSIC PATHOLOGIST AND MEDICOLEGAL DEATH INVESTIGATIONS

Forensic pathology is a subspecialty of pathology, which deals primarily with examinations of deceased individuals. A forensic pathologist is a Doctor of Medicine (MD) or a Doctor of Osteopathic Medicine (DO) that is skilled in the investigation of deaths that are sudden, unexpected, and/or violent. Forensic pathologists should be board-certified by the American Board of Pathology. A forensic pathologist can be appointed as a Medical Examiner (ME) through city, county, or state jurisdiction. The designated role of the medical examiner is to conduct the death investigation in order to provide an opinion certifying the specific cause of death. They should not only discover *what* happened but also attempt to answer *why* the death happened. Forensic pathology can be broken into two components: documentation and interpretation. The documentation piece is conducted through the autopsy phase. Interpretation is based on training and experience of the pathologist. However, accurate interpretation can only be accomplished when it is evaluated with the overall circumstances surrounding the death. There must be coordination and correlation between the pathologist's findings at autopsy and the investigation conducted; otherwise, there are higher chances for erroneous opinions on the part of the pathologist (Spitz & Spitz, 2006).

The forensic pathologist has a wide array of responsibilities. These duties include:

- **Positively identifying the deceased**: Identification can be considered presumptive or definitive depending on the method used for comparison. Presumptive identification could be matching personal effects that were recovered with the body or documentation such as a driver's license. Definitive methods, however, are primarily what should be utilized when positively identifying remains. These methods include matching antemortem and postmortem fingerprints, dental records, and DNA.
- **Determining cause of death and finalizing manner of death**: A cause of death is the disease or injury that initiated the lethal chain of events that brought about a person's death. Examples of this would be coronary artery disease, exsanguination (blood loss), blunt force trauma, drug toxicity, etc. The pathologist determines the cause through the autopsy of the individual. The manner of death, however, is determined through the overall death investigation. There are only five different types of manners of death: Natural, Accidental, Homicide, Suicide, or Undetermined. The manner hinges on the circumstances that led to the fatal event. For example, a cause of death could be determined as blunt force trauma to the head. Depending on the investigation, someone may have received these wounds by falling down and hitting their head on a concrete surface. This would be considered an "accidental" death. However, if someone hit the deceased multiple times in the head with a blunt object, this would be considered "homicide." The cause of death is the same in both circumstances, but the manner in which the injuries were sustained is completely different.
- **Documenting any external and internal injuries**: The pathologist will document any injuries through written and photographic documentation, which were discovered on the body during the autopsy. They will determine whether those injuries occurred around the time of death, prior to death, or after death. The pathologist will classify those injuries (blunt force, sharp force, etc.) and provide their opinion on how those injuries may have occurred.
- **Determining postmortem interval**: Postmortem interval (PMI) describes the timeframe of how long has it been since a person died. There is no true accurate methodology to determine time since death; however, there are several factors that can assist the pathologist in making this approximation. These factors include rigor mortis (stiffening of the body), livor mortis (blood settling in the body due to gravity), algor mortis (cooling of the body temperature), stage of

decomposition, insect invasion, death scene indicators, and reliable witness statements. Using a combination of these factors, along with environmental variables the body may have been exposed to, can provide an estimated timeframe of when the individual died.

- **Documenting any natural disease**: During the autopsy, the pathologist will remove and examine all organs from the body. Any natural disease will be documented and a determination will be made whether natural disease was the actual cause of death, whether it contributed to the death, or was unrelated to the death.
- **Requesting additional laboratory testing**: During the course of the autopsy, body fluids and tissue samples are collected as standard operating procedure. The pathologist will request further testing of those samples through toxicology, histology, and microscopy to determine if there might be anything present that caused or contributed to the death of the individual.
- **Collecting any physical evidence from the body**: If there is any physical evidence discovered on the deceased, the pathologist will be tasked to collect and preserve that evidence. Evidence could be an item found in the pocket of the deceased's clothing, or physical evidence of a suspected sexual assault. All physical evidence collected would be turned over to the investigating law enforcement agency for further laboratory testing if needed.
- **Providing expert witness testimony**: Because the pathologist conducts all of the aforementioned tasks and provides an official opinion associated with the death investigation, they may be required to testify on their findings in a criminal or civil court case.

The pathologist serves as an integral component of the medicolegal death investigation process. Individual states dictate through legislature the authority, roles, responsibilities, and types of death investigations the medical examiner will preside over. Although each state may differ slightly, these state laws are based upon the 1954 Post Mortem Examinations Act in addition to guidelines set forth in 1993 by the National Association of Medical Examiners (NAME). State code will dictate when the medical examiner will assume custody of a dead body. These circumstances usually include situations where it appears the death was:

- By violence, gunshot, suicide, or accident;
- Sudden death while in apparent good health;
- Unattended (no one else is or was present);
- Under suspicious or unusual circumstances;
- Resulting from poisoning or overdose of drugs;
- Resulting from diseases that may constitute a threat to the public health;
- Resulting from disease, injury, toxic effect, or unusual exertion incurred within the scope of the decedent's employment;
- Due to sudden infant death syndrome;
- Resulting while the decedent was in prison, jail, police custody, the state hospital, or in a detention or medical facility operated for the treatment of persons with a mental illness;
- Associated with diagnostic or therapeutic procedures;
- Of such a nature that a request is made to assume custody by a county or district attorney or law enforcement agency in connection with a potential homicide investigation or prosecution (Utah Medical Examiner Act, 1981).

When the ME assumes control of the deceased individual in any of the aforementioned types of cases, an investigation into the circumstances surrounding the death will occur simultaneously. The ME's office will employ medicolegal death investigators (MDIs) who investigate any death that falls within the ME's jurisdiction. These investigators will respond to the death scene and work with the primary law enforcement agency who has jurisdiction over the location of where the death occurred.

Three general steps need to be completed when dealing with a medicolegal death investigation. First, there must be a full investigation of the circumstances where information leading up to and surrounding the death of the individual is gathered. This information includes a full investigation of the death scene, witness statements, and obtaining any pertinent victim records (e.g., mental health, medical, social, etc.). This part of the investigation is usually completed by the primary law enforcement agency who holds jurisdiction of the scene location. The second step is the examination of the body. This involves a full documentation of the deceased at the scene, and then the external and internal examination during autopsy. This documentation may consist of photographs, injury documentation, physical evidence collection, and any bodily fluids or tissues obtained from autopsy. This second step is accomplished by the ME's office. The final step in the overall investigation is that all laboratory tests must be concluded. These tests include the toxicology/histology from body fluids and then any physical evidence that may have been sent to the crime laboratory. Forensic scientists within the forensic laboratory will conduct these examinations. Once these steps are finalized, the investigation can possibly close (if no criminal activity was discovered) or it can move forward to criminal prosecution in cases where another individual caused the death.

The death investigation is a collaborative effort between the ME's office, law enforcement, and specialized forensic scientists. Each individual entity holds an important responsibility as it pertains to the investigation. Resolution for a death cannot happen without support from each of these vital disciplines.

MEDICOLEGAL DEATH INVESTIGATION PROCEDURES

There is no justification from the medicolegal standpoint not to follow all scientific procedures for the recovery, transfer, identification, and final disposal of the remains of disaster fatalities.

Jorge Gonzalez Perez

Mass disasters, no matter what the cause, can produce a significant number of victims. Whether the disaster was of natural origin, such as the tsunami that occurred in Thailand in 2004, claiming almost a quarter of a million lives, or a result of terrorist attacks, as was seen on 9/11, the number of victims can be substantial. Because of the nature of these events, the victims are often disarticulated, decomposed, burned, or traumatized in a way that the remains must be identified and subjected to a medicolegal response and investigation.

Identification can be the most common challenge in a mass disaster. In a standard death investigation, the medical examiner is primarily trying to determine how and why an individual died; though they are tasked with identifying who the individual is, in most cases identification may already be known or at least somewhat easily attainable. When dealing with mass disasters, however, the priority is shifted because the causes of the individuals' deaths are directly associated with the disaster. So the main concern becomes the recovery of the remains and the identification of the victims. Rarely is it possible to identify a victim of a major disaster by visual recognition – fingerprints, dental records, or DNA samples are often required for a conclusive identification. Depending on the circumstances, remains could be fragmented due to an explosion or there could be injury due to fire or decomposition, all of which obscures readily identifiable characteristics of that individual. Additionally, when the body is subjected to various forces or events, even the process of discerning what might be human remains or not can be extremely challenging.

When a mass disaster occurs, the medicolegal investigation responsibility consists of several objectives.

- Locate, document, and recover any human remains.
- Positively identify the victims.
- Determine/confirm cause of death.
- Oversee morgue operations.
- Explain the circumstances of death.
- Prepare remains for final disposal.
- Study the event to assist in prevention for the future.

Although these responsibilities seem simple, the process of completing them requires an organized procedure in order to make sure they are effectively accomplished. Over the years, several working groups have come together and established resources in an attempt to provide guidance for managing mass fatalities. Some of these groups include: Interpol – *Disaster Victim Identification* (DVI); National Institute of Justice – *Mass Fatality Incidents: A Guide for Human Forensic Identification*; the National Association of Medical Examiners – *The Medical Examiner/Coroner's Guide for Contaminated Deceased Body Management*; The Pan American Health Organization – *Management of Dead Bodies after Disasters: A Field Manual for First Responders*; and many others. Each of these guides provides various steps on how to approach the disaster and the victims. Consistently, each has similar procedures of how the MDI process should occur, which are described below.

1. **Examination of the scene:** This process involves the identification and location of human remains. Locating and identifying human remains in a mass disaster can be overwhelming. Depending on the nature of the disaster, the environment is extremely challenging, as there could be massive amounts of rubble, water, or burnt debris, all obstacles for locating human remains. However, timely management of the scene is important to prevent further destruction or decomposition of the remains. It is vital to have the correct forensic scientists from various disciplines on scene as soon as possible to work together and begin the process of identifying anything that could be human; examples of these experts would be a pathologist searching to determine whether something is human tissue or not; an odontologist identifying small fragments as teeth; and an anthropologist determining what may be a bone fragment versus a piece of debris. All of these disciplines should be employed at the site during the process of locating and identifying remains. If conditions allow, the location and condition of the victims should be recorded and photographed, just as in standard crime scene examination.

After the remains are recorded, they should be transported to the morgue for further examination. Depending on the disaster, the morgue could be a local medical examiner's office or even a temporary morgue established near the site. Either way, all of the victims and any personal property are eventually removed from the site for further examination.

2. **Collection of postmortem data through forensic examination of the remains:** Once at the morgue site, the medical examiner should employ any available methods in order to positively confirm the identity of the victims. Therefore, all human remains are examined by experts. A multidisciplinary approach to the identification process is extremely important to a successful response and outcome of a mass disaster event. These methods could include:

   • Fingerprints – If the body is in good enough condition, identification of the victim can be expedited through the use of fingerprints. One thing to consider is that there may be many individuals who do not have their prints on record or maintained in a database, making this mode of identification difficult.

   • Odontology – Dental comparison provides a definitive identification and is one of the most reliable forms of identification. However, in order to identify the victim, antemortem records must be obtained through the victim's family or other means.

   • DNA – For some incidents, the remains may be highly fragmented so DNA will be an essential component of the identification process. DNA analysis can identify a victim and associated fragmented remains. There are various ways DNA analysis can provide identification. Direct DNA comparisons can be made from reference samples that belonged to a victim or to a personal item provided by family members. Familial DNA comparison can be conducted against a family member utilizing mitochondrial DNA for maternally related family or Y-chromosomal markers for paternally related family members.

   • Radiology – X-rays taken of the victim can assist the pathologist, anthropologist, and odontologist in the overall identification process. There may also be serialized surgical implants that can be traced through antemortem medical records that will assist in identifying the victim.

   • Anthropological Information – A forensic anthropologist can assist in the recovery, sorting, and analysis of the remains. Additional information can be obtained such as a biological profile of the victim (sex, age, stature, ancestry). There may be times when remains need to be confirmed as human vs. non-human. Remains may be co-mingled and require re-association of disparate body parts and separating recognizable fragments that would require DNA analysis (de Boer et al., 2018).

   Because identification can be determined through fingerprints, dental records, DNA, X-rays, and/or anthropology, all of these experts must come together and focus on the identification of the victims of a particular disaster. This procedure will have each of these entities examine the body or remains recovered. Even if there are not any identifiable features, such as fingerprints or teeth, all experts will conduct an examination, regardless of the condition of the body. Visual identification of the deceased is not considered accurate.

3. **Collection of antemortem data:** Dental and medical records, fingerprints, photographs, and biological samples are obtained from a victim's home or from family.

There should be a location set up for family members to gather. A place should be established to interview relatives of victims. Families should be provided a list of antemortem items that would be useful in identifying any remains. Having a single location will allow for a better line of communication with the families and provide direct access to required information. In every mass disaster, there are scores of families looking for answers. They are anxiously waiting for the confirmation of whether their loved one has been identified in the aftermath. Therefore, having a place where families can directly provide vital information can assist in the overall identification process.

4. **Reconciliation:** Once the postmortem and antemortem data is collected, experts will compare information in order to identify the victims. It is during this phase that positive identification will occur. The goal at this stage is to be able to account for and identify as many victims as possible.

5. **Certifying death and disposition of remains:** Once identification, cause, and manner of death are fully documented, the medical examiner is expected to certify the death through proper documentation. Once this is completed, disposition of the remains will occur. Every family is expected to have the opportunity to obtain the remains of their loved ones. However, depending on the circumstances, public health issues associated with the disaster may dictate the manner in which the remains are handled.

Although there are many resources for mass disaster response, the responsibility of fatality management falls to the medical examiner's office. They are the ones in charge of the documentation, examination, identification, recovery, disposition, and certification of all the remains, as well as all morgue operations. The medical examiner ultimately becomes the face of forensic science to the public. There are governments, agencies, and hundreds or thousands of families looking for answers. The experts from this office are the ones who carry the burden of providing vital information such as victim identification, the number of victims, and the overall magnitude of the disaster that has just occurred.

No day shall erase you from the memory of time.

~Virgil

Forensic anthropologist, Dr. Murry Marks once stated, "We are born with an identity; we need to all die with one as well." This statement holds true, especially when the medicolegal death investigation process involves mass casualties. Whether due to natural disasters or human caused, priority is set on determining the identity of each and every victim. The following three case studies provide details on how this process was implemented.

Camp Fire – Paradise, California

During the early morning hours of November 8, 2018, the deadliest wildfire in California history, known as the "Camp Fire," ignited. The Camp Fire burned for over two weeks, devastating the town of Paradise before it could be extinguished. The fire blazed through Paradise within four hours, eventually burning over 150,000 acres and destroying almost 19,000 buildings. A total of 86 people lost their lives in the fire, some in their cars as they attempted to escape the inferno. Eventually, the cause of the fire was determined to be from an old electrical transmission line owned by Pacific Gas & Electric. However, even understanding what caused it could not provide solace to the many families of the victims who died as a result of the massive blaze (Boghani, 2019).

In the hours after the fire, the uncertainty and pain of families waiting to hear about loved ones was overwhelming. The fact that the scene of the disaster was a massive wildfire made it impossible for medical examiners or personnel to conduct immediate victim recovery, delaying any sort of victim identification. Additionally, the effects of the fire made the mere fact of identifying human remains difficult. On top of this, even if it was possible to recover any remains, the condition of the bodies ruled out some of the standard identification processes such as fingerprints and dental records. Therefore, DNA analysis, using Rapid DNA technology, became the first resort to obtain quick results in the case of the Camp Fire.

The FBI defines Rapid DNA as the "fully automated hands-free process of developing a COIDS Core Loci STR profile from a reference sample buccal swab. The 'Swab in–profile out' process consists of automated extraction, amplification, separation, detection, and allele calling without human intervention." (FBI, n.d.) Rapid DNA is an automated system that can be utilized in the field, allowing for the identification of an individual from a DNA sample within two hours, instead of sending samples to a laboratory where results could take months to obtain. ANDE® was the first company to receive FBI approval to allow accredited National DNA Index System (NDIS) laboratories to process DNA samples from the ANDE® system. These labs could search the resulting ANDE DNA IDs™ against the FBI's Combined DNA Index System (CODIS) without manual interpretation or technical review (ANDE, n.d.).

The Sheriff's Office of Butte County invited the ANDE Corporation to assist at the disaster site in order to analyze DNA samples. With the use of Rapid DNA technology, medical examiners could obtain identification of the victims within hours, providing families with information, and even closure, much quicker than standard DNA analysis. Rapid DNA allows for the analysis of five DNA samples to be processed simultaneously within 90 minutes. This process identified victims in two stages. The first stage, with the assistance of the medical examiner's office, tested multiple samples of human remains in an attempt to determine which DNA samples were viable for identification. Second, the viable DNA samples were then matched to possible next of kin. Three hundred family members volunteered their DNA to be processed for possible matches. Chris Miles, Department of Homeland Security Science and Technology Directorate (S&T) Rapid DNA Project Manager, stated, "Despite the extreme damage to the remains, the Rapid DNA machines were able to quickly make accurate matches and confirm victims' identities. Rapid DNA became a priority tool for the Sacramento County Coroner's Office during this event. I was glad to see we could help bring closure to many families" (DHS, 2019).

Christchurch Terror Attack

During Friday morning prayer on the morning of March 15, 2019, two consecutive mass shootings occurred at the Al-Noor and Linwood mosques in Christchurch, New Zealand. By the end of the massacres, the number of injured totaled 49 and the death toll was at 51. These shootings set in place a series of events that would require a massive response of police, pathologists, and experts to respond. As with most terrorist instances, the total number of victims was initially unknown; however, authorities knew in this case that it was a lot. Experts from around the country responded immediately. Over the next week, they would work around the clock in an attempt to return the victims to their families (Livingston, 2019).

New Zealand police described their efforts to identify the victims as "detailed and complex work, which must be completed thoroughly." Chief Coroner Deborah Marshall explained the importance of identifying the victims as "there could be nothing worse than giving the wrong body to the wrong family." Although correctly identifying victims is always vital in events such as this, the fact that the victims of the terror attack involved Muslim victims created another major hurdle. Not only were authorities tasked with identifying the victims of the attacks, but also pressure to do so quickly was mounting because, according to Islamic tradition, a person must be buried as soon as possible after death, ideally within 24 hours (Guy and Holcombe, 2019). Although the victims' remains could not be processed that quickly, the bodies were returned to their families within a week. A large part of why this process occurred so quickly was New Zealand's use of the Disaster Victim Identification (DVI) process.

The DVI process for this event began less than 24 hours after the first shot was fired. All 51 victims were removed from the mosques and transported via refrigerated storage to the mortuary. The mortuary was set up to process the victims one step at a time. The first station was established as a collection point for any personal property from the victims. The items were photographed, cataloged, and assigned the same DVI number as the body from which it was removed. The items were packaged and maintained with the individual remains. The next station was established for taking fingerprints and footprints. The victims were then moved to the third station where an external examination took place by the pathologists. Any scars or tattoos were documented for possible identification. Victims were then autopsied and documented for injuries, cause of death, and any other possible identifying characteristics. Dental examinations took place at the subsequent station. There were 18 dental experts who worked to assist in this process following the shootings. The fourth step in the process was for paperwork completion and quality control. During this phase of DVI, authorities were working on collecting any form of antemortem evidence or records from the families. This included obtaining information about identifying features and retrieving DNA evidence or fingerprints from their homes. By March 21, almost all of the victims' identities had been confirmed (Livingston, 2019).

Khobar Towers

On the night of June 25, 1996, bombers drove a sewage tanker truck packed with more than 20,000 pounds of TNT into the United States Air Force housing complex located in Khobar, Saudi Arabia. Two thousand U.S. Military members assigned to the King Abdulaziz Air Base were housed in this complex, known as Khobar Towers (Pearson, 2020). That evening, SSgt Alfredo R. Guerrero, a security forces personnel, and two other sentries observed the truck, along with a white car, drive into the complex parking lot. The tanker drove through the lot and stopped directly in front of the north façade of Building 131. The driver and a passenger jumped out of the truck and fled to the white car, which immediately sped off. The security forces immediately started evacuating the building; however, they only made it through the top three floors before an enormous blast occurred as the tanker exploded. The blast propelled pieces of the Jersey barriers and outer walls into the bottom floors. The façades of the top three floors sheared off.

The east and west ends were blasted from their original positions, which caused several floors to collapse (Grant, 1998). Ultimately, the explosion left a crater 50-feet wide and 16-feet deep and destroyed much of the eight-story building, in which Airmen from the 4404th Air Wing were assigned. In the end, the blast claimed the lives of 19 U.S. Airmen and wounded nearly 500 others (History, 2019).

Due to the fact that the victims in this case were members of the Department of Defense (DoD), their remains would fall under the jurisdiction of the Armed Forces Medical Examiner System (AFMES). Under regulations prescribed by the Secretary of Defense, the Armed Forces Medical Examiner can conduct a forensic pathology investigation to determine cause or manner of death of a deceased person if the decedent died at an installation garrisoned by units of the armed forces and the member was on active duty (10 U.S. Code 1471, 1999). Therefore, all of the victims would be autopsied by the AFMES. Additionally, because of the overseas location of the deaths, all of the victims' remains would be flown to Dover Air Force Base located in Delaware, where they would be positively identified and autopsied.

Throughout the night following the explosion, airmen assisted in recovering the remains of the victims from the debris. The bodies were transported from King Abdulaziz to the Air Mobility Command (AMC) Terminal, where they would ultimately be flown back to Dover. Initially, several military officers from the 58th Fighter Squadron were assigned to identify the bodies through visual confirmation. Although this is not protocol, the officers were attempting to gain accountability of their service men. The personnel from Dover Port Mortuary ultimately held the responsibility for making the final positive identification. They informed Lieutenant Colonel (LtCol) Thomas A. McCarthy, operations officer of the 58th, "If you are not absolutely sure, don't say anything...We're not going to use anything you say as positive ID. We're going to use fingerprints, DNA and dental, once they get back to Dover." In 11 of the cases, officers were able to visually identify the remains; however, the remaining 8 could not be identified on site. Ultimately, a list of missing personnel was provided to AFMES for assisting in final identification of the victims (Jamieson, 2008).

Once the remains were transported and autopsied, personnel at Dover were able to positively identify 18 of the 19 remains. One name, however, Senior Airman (SrA) Paul A. Blais, remained on the list of the unidentified. The pathologists studied the forensics of the last set of remains and determined they did not match those of Airman Blais. It was ultimately determined that while medical and military personnel were attempting to positively identify injured airmen who were treated at King Fahd University Hospital, one particular individual was misidentified. Fellow airmen initially identified one of the patients who had suffered severe injuries as Airman First Class (A1C) Christopher B. Lester. Once Dover informed Air Force personnel in Dhahran of the inability to identify the last remaining fatality, they realized the patient at the hospital was most likely SrA Blais and the remains in Dover belonged to A1C Lester. It turned out that both airmen had extremely similar features. Veterans of the bombing explained that both men had similar face shapes and features, hair color, and small mustaches, trimmed exactly the same. Brigadier General Daniel M. Dick studied the ID cards of the two airmen and photographs taken in the ICU and concluded there was "no way in the world" he could tell either of the men from each other. He stated, "These guys could have been twin brothers!" In the end, medical personnel completed fingerprinting, footprinting, and dental mapping of the patient in the ICU. Through comparisons of these records, the patient was positively identified as SrA Blais. Dover personnel matched the medical records of A1C Lester with the last remaining set of remains at the mortuary (Jamieson, 2008).

CHALLENGES OF DEALING WITH THE DISASTER

The Department of Homeland Security's Target Capabilities List (2007) defines fatalities management as:

> the capacity to effectively perform scene documentation, the complete collection and recovery of the dead, victim's personal effects and items of evidence; decontamination of remains and personal effects (if required); transportation, storage, documentation, and recovery of forensic and physical evidence; determination of the nature and extent of injury; identification of the fatalities using scientific means; certification of the cause and manner of death; processing and returning of human remains and personal effects of the victims to the legally-authorized person(s) (if possible); and interaction with and provision of legal, customary, compassionate, and culturally-competent required services to the families of the deceased within the context of the family assistance center.
>
> (Institute of Medicine, 2010)

This complex list of fatality management provides an insight into the depth of the many responsibilities that need to be addressed when dealing with mass disaster fatalities. As a result, there can be many challenges to overcome when these situations arise. The most common challenges consist of preparedness, planning, training, and the availability of expert personnel.

First and foremost, a common challenge is proper planning. Although the United States continues to improve preparedness efforts for mass disaster, there are still short-comings that can occur. When a disaster strikes, the medicolegal response must be organized and planned. Sorting through the aftermath is a daunting task. This response should never be something that is organized at the time of the event. The medical examiner's office should have a disaster plan in place where responsibilities and duties are delineated, equipment can be obtained, additional services are identified, and resources are allocated for such an event. A disaster plan should address several aspects. First, there should be the ability to organize and mobilize a team of necessary and qualified personnel. There will also be material needs and equipment required to properly respond. However, required resources should be in direct relation to the type and magnitude of the event. Planning must be in place to recover remains whether it be a fire, an earthquake, a plane crash, or any other sort of disaster. Personal protective equipment (PPE) must be available to suit the needs of the particular disaster. Heavy duty coverings may be needed instead of the standard gloves and booties normally worn in a death scene. The issue of body preservation and transport will need to be addressed. How will the remains be temporarily stored or transported to the morgue facility? Are there refrigerated holding areas or portable refrigeration units available? Additionally, there is a possibility that temporary work sites must be established for victim processing. The shear number of victims may be too great to be handled at a single facility, or morgue facilities may be too far away to be able to transport victims in a timely and proper manner. All of these aspects should be part of the overall disaster plan so that when the time comes, the medicolegal response can be efficient, coordinated, and timely.

The disaster plan is only the first step in facing the challenges of the impending disaster. Since the question is never "*if* a disaster happens," but "*when* a disaster happens," the plan should be put into practice in order to see any gaps or failures not accounted for. One of the ways this can occur is to integrate the response for mass fatality incidents into planning exercises. Several of these exercises already occur throughout the United States.

"Vibrant Response" is the annual U.S. Northern Command (NORTHCOM) Chemical Biological Radiological Nuclear (CBRN) Response Command Post Exercise, which takes place at Camp Atterbury, Indiana. This exercise brings together military personnel and civilians from various U.S. agencies for three weeks of training on the response to a catastrophic event (US Army North, 2017). Exercises such as this help create a multi-agency, realistic, and challenging training experience where disaster plans can be evaluated for completeness and gaps can be identified that need to be addressed for the future.

During a forum on preparedness for catastrophic events, participants identified the lack of a national comprehensive fatality management strategy and limited resource availability. One of the federal resources allocated for mass disaster is the Disaster Mortuary Operational Response Team (DMORT). DMORT is the Federal National Mortuary Affairs Support system and is made up of ten teams within the various FEMA regions. The members of these teams consist of individuals working within various disciplines centered on aspects of mass disasters. One shortcoming that was noted by this forum is that individuals assigned to DMORT may already be involved in relief efforts within their community before DMORT is even activated, causing a personnel gap in the federal response. Therefore, it is vital that there must be planning within communities for an effective and efficient response (Institute of Medicine, 2010).

Mass disaster situations are naturally challenging to begin with; the addition of potentially hundreds of thousands of fatalities only compounds the issues. Although there is not one specific methodology for response, planning and preparedness can be employed to assist experts when disaster strikes.

CONCLUSION

The field of forensic pathology and the death investigation process play an important function in today's society in understanding how and why someone died. The answers provided by the medical examiner are sought after by law enforcement, government officials, media, medical personnel, and most importantly, the families of the victims. Whether it was an accidental death or something of greater magnitude like an earthquake or bombing, the death investigation delivers answers to those desperately demanding them. Without personnel like the medical examiner, the identities of those victims may never be known. Although these events are challenging and require a lot of planning and preparation, it is important to be ready for not *if*, but *when* disaster happens.

CLASS DISCUSSION AND ESSAY QUESTIONS

1. What is the difference between a forensic technician and a forensic pathologist?
2. What key developments helped to advance the profession of the forensic pathologist?
3. The forensic pathologist has a wide array of responsibilities. List and discuss five of them.
4. When a mass disaster occurs, the medicolegal investigation responsibility consists of several objectives. What are they and why are they essential in assignment of death?
5. What lessons were learned from the mass casualty incident associated with Khobar Towers and why are they important to keep in mind?

6. What measures can be taken before a mass casualty event to improve the forensic
   pathology profession?

REFERENCES

10 U.S. Code §1471. (1999). *Forensic Pathology Investigations*. Retrieved from https://
www.law.cornell.edu/uscode/text/10/1471

ANDE®. (n.d.). *What Is Rapid DNA?* Retrieved from https://www.ande.com/what-is
-rapid-dna/

Barton, M. (2016). *Imhotep – The First Physician*. Retrieved from https://www.past-
medicalhistory.co.uk/imhotep-the-first-physician/

Boghani, P. (2019). *Camp Fire: By the Numbers*. Retrieved from https://www.pbs.org/
wgbh/frontline/article/camp-fire-by-the-numbers/

De Boer, H., Blau, S., Delabarde, T. & Hackman, L. (2018). The Role of Forensic
Anthropology in Disaster Victim Identification (DVI): Recent Developments and
Future Prospects. *Forensic Sciences Research* 4(4): 303–315.

Department of Homeland Security. (2019). *Snapshot: S&T's Rapid DNA Technology
Identified Victims of California Wildfire*. Retrieved from https://www.dhs.gov/sci-
ence-and-technology/news/2019/04/23/snapshot-st-rapid-dna-technology-identified
-victims

Federal Bureau of Investigation. (n.d.). *Rapid DNA*. Retrieved from https://www.fbi.gov
/services/laboratory/biometric-analysis/codis/rapid-dna

Grant, R. (1998). Khobar Towers. *Air Force Magazine*. Retrieved from https://www.air-
forcemag.com/article/0698khobar/

Guy, J. & Holcombe, M. (2019). *CNN New Zealand Rushes to Identify Christchurch
Terror Attack Victims*. Retrieved from https://www.cnn.com/2019/03/17/asia/new
-zealand-mosque-shooting-victims-identification-intl/index.html

Henry, W. (2016). Women Searchers of the Dead in Eighteenth and Nineteenth Century
London. *Social History of Medicine* 29(3): 445–466.

History. (2009). *Code of Hammurabi*. Retrieved from https://www.history.com/topics/
ancient-history/hammurabi

History. (2019). *Khobar Towers Bombing in Saudi Arabia Kills 19 U.S. Airman*.
Retrieved from https://www.history.com/this-day-in-history/saudi-arabia-khobar
-towers-bombing-kills-19

Institute of Medicine. (2010). *Medical Surge Capacity: Workshop Summary*. Forum on
Medical and Public Health Preparedness for Catastrophic Events. Washington, DC:
National Academies Press.

Jamieson, P. (2008). *Khobar Towers Tragedy and Response*. Washington, DC: Air Force
History and Museums Program.

Livingston, T. (2019). An inside Look into How the Victims of the Christchurch Terror
Attack Were Returned to Their Families. *Stuff*. Retrieved from https://www.stuff.co
.nz/national/117406088/an-inside-look-into-how-the-victims-of-the-christchurch
-terror-attack-were-returned-to-their-families

Munkhoff, R. (1999). Searchers of the Dead: Authority, Marginality, and the Interpretation
of Plague in England 1574–1665. *Gender & History* 11(1): 1–29.

NAS Report. (2009) *Strengthening Forensic Science in the United States: A Path Forward*.
Washington, DC: National Academies Press.

Pearson, E. (2020). Khobar Towers Bombing of 1996. *Encyclopedia Britannica*. Retrieved from https://www.britannica.com/event/Khobar-Towers-bombing-of-1996

Quinn, M. (2018). *America's Coroners Face Unprecedented Challenges*. Retrieved from https://www.governing.com/topics/health-human-services/gov-coroner-medical-examiner-drugs-opiods.html

Sheldon, N. (n.d.). *The Earliest Recorded Autopsy in History Was Performed on This Roman Emperor*. Retrieved from https://historycollection.co/julius-caesar-complicit-death-re-examining-earliest-autopsy-history/

Spitz, W. & Spitz, D. (2006). *Medicolegal Investigation of Death: Guidelines for the Application of Pathology to Crime Investigation* (4th ed.). Springfield, IL: Charles C. Thomas Publisher, Ltd.

US Army North. (2017). *Vibrant Response*. Retrieved from https://www.army.mil/standto/archive_2017-04-13/

Utah Medical Examiner Act. (1981). *Utah Code Title 26*, Chapter 4. Retrieved from https://le.utah.gov/xcode/Title26/Chapter4/26-4.html

Wilson, C. (1984). *A Criminal History of Mankind*. New York: Diversion Books.

CHAPTER 20

The Role of Dentistry:
Victim Identification in Mass Casualty Disasters

Kathleen Young

INTRODUCTION

Natural disasters and acts of violence have occurred as long as people have had teeth, and those knowledgeable of teeth are often needed to identify the victims of these different types of events. For their part, the severity of natural disasters – whether they are fires, floods, earthquakes, tsunamis, hurricanes, tornadoes, landslides, or volcanic eruptions – has become more problematic over time. In 2017 alone, 335 natural disasters affected 95.6 million people. These disasters killed 9,697 people and cost a total of $335 billion in damages (Below and Wallemacq, 2018). Over the preceding decade, there were approximately the same number of natural disasters, but the number of people killed was less (Below and Wallemacq, 2018). Deaths from natural disasters are significant and most of the casualties occur in third-world countries with the most recent activity in India, Nepal, and Bangladesh (Below and Wallemacq, 2018).

In addition to natural disasters, there are man-made disasters, which are a more recent phenomenon. These disasters have increased exponentially and Coleman (2006) states that these types of disasters produce a high toll financially – $8 billion per year. Such events are common in industrialized countries, and most often include fires and explosions. Records from the 30 countries that are part of the Organization for Economic Co-operation and Development (OECD) show that since 1974, the number of man-made disasters has risen quite dramatically, although deaths have declined. Nevertheless, according to Coleman (2006), deaths due to industrial accidents are about 1,000 people per decade. This is far fewer than natural disasters. In fact, natural disasters produce ten times more deaths than man-made disasters.

Although the number of natural and man-made disasters is alarming, the greater issue at hand is dealing with the deaths that these types of events cause. Oftentimes, dental records may be the only way to identify a deceased person. There are problems in trying to identify remains when there are no dental records to use as a comparison if one is trying to determine identity by means of forensic odontology. Because the remains are often difficult to identify, trained individuals are necessary to help in the process. This chapter will give a brief history of dentistry and the evolution of the specialty of forensic dentistry, also known as forensic odontology. It will discuss the roles of members of

DOI: 10.4324/9781003350729-20

the dental team and address the need for further training, both by dentists and dental hygienists.

HISTORY OF DENTISTRY

Evidence of dental work has been found in some of the earliest archeological discoveries. A study at Mehrgarh (current-day Pakistan) shows that as early as 4800 BC, people were experimenting with different dental techniques. Researchers found drill holes on at least 11 molars and surmised that since they were in the back of the mouth, they were probably not for decorative purposes. Flint drill bits were found at the same excavation, which produced similar holes in human enamel (Hirst, 2017). In the year 1000, Abulqasis, an Arabic surgeon in Cordoba, wrote many pages on the topic of dentistry in his medical encyclopedia entitled *Al tasrif* (Baron, 2000). In 1530, a book devoted entirely to dentistry was published: *The Little Medicinal Book for All Kinds of Diseases and Infirmities of the Teeth* (History of Dentistry, n.d.). The earliest surviving pair of dentures dates from the 1580s, and we know that most American schoolchildren know about George Washington's false teeth made of cow teeth and hippopotamus ivory (Worsley, 2011).

In the seven centuries between 1000 and 1700 AD, there was not much progress in the dental field. But in the 18th century, dentistry became its own specialty in the medical field (Baron, 2000). France stood out in dentistry, with about 70 books published on the topic in the 18th century including *Treatise on Teeth* by Pierre Fauchard, the Father of Modern Dentistry (History of Dentistry, n.d.). Fauchard was also the first to formally introduce the idea of dental prostheses and dental fillings. Nicolas Dubois de Chemant was one of the first to use porcelain for dentures (Baron, 2000).

America's first known dentist was John Baker, who trained Paul Revere in the fine art of dentistry. He also built a few of George Washington's dentures (Mancini, 2014). The first school of dentistry was established in the United States in 1839, in Baltimore, Maryland. By 1877, fillings with amalgams, bridges, crowns, and root-canal therapy were becoming more commonplace. The first X-ray machine appeared at the beginning of the new century (Baron, 2000). These same dental procedures are currently widely used to compare and identify remains of individuals when no other means of identification are available.

HISTORY OF FORENSIC DENTISTRY

Forensic dentistry (as a subset of dentistry) has been well documented as early as 66 AD. Agrippa, the wife of Claudius, emperor of Rome, was concerned that Lollia Pauline, a rich divorcee, might be a rival for her husband. She gave instructions to her soldiers to kill Lollia and bring back her head. She identified Lollia by a discolored front tooth, thus confirming through "forensic dentistry" that her soldiers had killed the right person (Balachander et al., 2015).

India saw its first forensic dental identification in 1193 when Jai Chand, Raja of Kanauji, was murdered by Muhammad's army and identified by his false teeth (Balachander et al., 2015).

Peter Halket, killed in the French and Indian War of 1758, was identified by his son because of an artificial tooth he had (Balachander et al., 2015).

The first well-known forensic dentist in the United States was Paul Revere. During the Revolutionary War, Dr Joseph Warren, a war hero and second-in-command at the battles of Concord and Lexington, died during the 1775 Battle of Bunker Hill with a bullet to his face. This made it impossible to identify him immediately and he was buried on the battlefield. His brothers later exhumed his body and asked Paul Revere to identify him. Mr Revere was able to do so because he recognized the wiring he had used to fasten Warren's false teeth. Because of this identification, Warren was able to receive a proper military burial with honors (Saunders, 2016; Nola, 2016).

There are numerous individuals that have been identified after death by their teeth; however, these were individual cases and the dentists involved had no formal training in forensic dentistry. Dr Oscar Amoedo, born in Matanzas, Cuba, in 1863, is considered by many to be the father of forensic odontology. He studied at the University of Cuba and the New York Dental College, and attended the International Dental Congress in Paris as a delegate in 1889. Amoedo enjoyed Paris very much and decided to stay, becoming a dental professor at the Ecole Odontotechnique de Paris in 1890. It was during this time that a deadly event initiated his interest in dental and forensic identification (Senn and Stimson, 2010).

This tragic event was a fire at the Bazar de la Charité, and although Dr Amoedo was not directly involved in the identification of individuals, he interviewed those that were; this became the basis of his doctoral thesis. This thesis served as the foundation of a book titled *L'Art Dentaire en Medicine Legale*, which was the first complete text on the subject of Forensic Dentistry (Senn and Stimson, 2010).

Perhaps the most famous modern forensic odontologist is Dr Norman "Skip" Sperber, who has been at the forefront of dental forensic identification after mass disasters for more than five decades. His involvement includes the mid-air collision of Pacific Southwest Airlines Flight 182 in 1978, the 1995 Oklahoma City Bombing, the 2001 World Trade Center attack, and Hurricane Katrina in New Orleans in 2005 (Saunders, 2016).

IMPORTANCE OF FORENSIC IDENTIFICATION

Often in mass disasters (MDs), identification of individuals by dental records may be one of the most reliable ways of ascertaining identity since the most indestructible part of the body is the teeth; they survive unchanged for thousands of years (Balachander et al., 2015). Severe burns due to fires or explosions may make identification by visual means impossible; this is also the case for bodies that have seriously decomposed or that were found in water (Kolude et al., 2010).

Forensic odontology (FO) is considered one of the most reliable methods for identification of victims. A meta-analysis done by Prajapati et al. (2018) compared 20 disasters: accidental, natural, and criminal. Seventeen of the 20 mass disasters included FO in the identification of victims. These disasters included multiple plane crashes, an Australian bushfire, and an Estonian ferry disaster. Of the 23,654 total victims, 3,025 (14.7%) were identified using FO, and another 1,094 (5.31%) were identified using FO plus other methods. Although in this study FO did not account for the majority of identifications, it was an important part of the overall identification strategy.

Teeth have an exceptional ability to survive; unprotected teeth will turn to ash at 540–650 degrees C (1,004–1,202 degrees F). Porcelain crowns can withstand temperatures greater than 1,100 degrees C (2,012 degrees F). Other dental materials such as amalgams and composites (tooth-colored material) may resist temperatures of 101 degrees C (214 degrees F) for 2.5 hours (Furnari, 2018). Because of this incredible survivability, teeth are often a major contributor to the identification of a deceased person. Forensic odontology is one of the most reliable methods to identify victims of disasters. Besides dental work, identification can include pathological conditions such as changes due to age, disturbance of tooth eruption, malocclusion, or other dental disturbances (Kolude et al., 2010).

Although teeth can survive extreme conditions, they can become very fragile during the disaster and so need very careful handling. In one study, Berketa and Higgins (2017) discuss the need for stabilization of the dental structures in fire situations. In 2009, the Victorian (Australia) bushfires were still burning after 4–5 hours; temperatures recorded on some bodies 24 hours later were 600–700 degrees C (1,112–1,292 degrees F). The fragility of tooth structures after a fire requires careful stabilization of the head. Various methods of stabilization to protect the teeth had been used including glue guns, water-based PVA glue, adhesive clear enamel spray, and Clag® paste (wheat paste which can be diluted and used as a spray). No matter what stabilization method or materials were used, it was found that any remains from this fire that were treated preserved better than those left untreated (Berketa and Higgins, 2017).

Once a stabilizing spray is used, care must be taken when transporting the body. Bubble Wrap™ can stabilize the head, and a paper bag or cardboard box can add further protection. Any loose structures must be carefully placed in specimen containers for transportation with the body. Good photographic evidence is also very important (Berketa and Higgins, 2017).

In any disaster, whether man-made or natural, the American Board of Forensic Odontologist has four recommendations when reporting dental identification:

A. Positive Identification

The antemortem and postmortem data match in sufficient detail to establish they are from the same individual. Additionally, there are no irreconcilable discrepancies.

B. Possible Identification

The antemortem and postmortem data have consistent features, but due to the quality of either the postmortem remains or the antemortem evidence, it is not possible to positively establish dental identification.

C. Insufficient Evidence

The available information is insufficient to form the basis for a conclusion.

D. Exclusion

The antemortem and postmortem data are clearly inconsistent. However, it should be understood that identification by exclusion is a valid technique in certain circumstances (American Board of Forensic Odontology, 2018).

TYPICAL FORENSIC ODONTOLOGY TEAMS AND WHAT THEY DO

Rarely does a dentist work alone in the identification of victims; there is usually a team of people supporting the effort. In a large-scale operation, the team consists of several professionals including a forensic dentistry chief who oversees the operation and a dental registrar who helps keep track of all the records.

The Postmortem (PM) team can be subdivided into individuals who deal with surgical exposure, radiography, and clinical examination of the teeth and oral cavity. Dental hygienists can do all of these but the surgical exposure of teeth.

Surgical duties include gaining access to the teeth. Radiology involves exposing, developing, and duplicating postmortem dental X-rays (Brannon and Connick, 2000). With today's digital technology, this has become much easier. The next step in the PM examination is cleaning the teeth with a solution of hydrogen peroxide or diluted bleach. Throughout this process, Brannon and Connick (2000) point out that there needs to be redundancy, meaning more than one dental personnel verifies the findings. A common problem in this phase of identification is psychological burnout and emotional stress. It helps to have a team member watching out for this.

The Antemortem (AM) team must generate and construct accurate dental records that can be compared to the PM dental record. A dental hygienist can facilitate collection of these records and additional dental evidence such as prosthetic appliances, study models, and laboratory prescriptions. Assembling this information may require requesting information from dental offices, labs, and family members. As the dental hygienist does this, the forensic dentist can continue with victim identification (Brannon and Connick, 2000).

A common problem facing the AM team is inadequate or poor-quality AM records. Methods of charting, legibility, and dental forms can vary greatly, making teamwork all the more important (Brannon and Connick, 2000).

Finally, an important part of this process is the records-comparison team. This group begins its work relatively late in the game after the AM and PM teams have collected their information. If the disaster involves 25 or fewer victims, manual comparison is sufficient. If more than 25 individuals are involved, computer technology is employed, greatly enhancing the speed at which the team can work. Even with computers, dental personnel often directly review the charts to verify the computer-suggested matches (Brannon and Connick, 2000).

All of these components require training. Experts in the field of forensic dentistry stress that "disaster preparedness is the key to successful disaster management" (Brannon and Connick, 2000, p. 382).

STORIES TO TELL

There are some vivid examples of the role of dentistry in identifying victims associated with terrorist attacks and disasters. 9/11, Hurricane Maria, and the tsunami in Thailand will be mentioned in this section.

September 11, 2001

Often referred to as "9/11," this terrorist attack, the single deadliest in United States history, killed 2,996 people. Among these were 343 firefighters and 72 law enforcement officers (Congressional Record, 2002). Dr Jeffrey Burkes was the chief forensic dental consultant to the medical examiner's office in New York City, and he oversaw the forensic dentists that came to help in this great crisis. In the early days after the attack, about 40 dentists worked eight-hour shifts. Forensic dentists with impressive experience in the field were "tour commanders." They worked 12-hour shifts and reported directly to Dr Burkes (Dental Practice Management, 2001). There were also many others who volunteered to be on the Disaster Mortuary Operational Response Teams (DMORTs); the number swelled to approximately 350 dentists and dental auxiliaries (Zohn et al., 2010).

This large number of individuals was necessary to avoid delays in the identification of the dead. DMORT team members were paid for their time but had to leave their personal practices for weeks at a time. Those who volunteered were not able to put as much of a time commitment into the work (Zohn et al., 2010).

One of the main issues in dealing with the number of volunteers was the variation in training. After September 11, 2001, dentists were surveyed regarding their forensic odontology training. A total of 62% recorded they had never had forensic odontology training, while 75% expressed an interest in this type of training (Zohn et al., 2010). While there is training available, very few dental or dental hygiene schools offer this training as part of the curriculum.

Hurricane Maria

Eight dentists that were part of the Disaster Mortuary Operational Response Team traveled to Puerto Rico in September 2017, to assist the medical examiners in the identification of bodies. Among these were Drs Lawrence Dobrin and Harry Zohn; both have been involved in many disaster relief operations. Dr Dobrin, the chief forensic odontologist for the City of New York stated, "We need to have compassion for the living and reverence for the victims" (Burger, 2018).

Both Dr Dobrin and Dr Zohn worked 12-hour days in difficult conditions. Among the challenges they faced were inconsistent phone and internet service as well as electricity that went on and off throughout the day. Another issue was many of the people they were working with only spoke Spanish, and neither of these dentists did. However, Dr Dobrin made the point that having the American team there was a great psychological boost to the medical examiner's office, and they really appreciated the support (Burger, 2018).

Tsunami, Phuket, Thailand

A seaquake and tsunami in December 2004, which killed over 230,000 people worldwide, led to a tremendous international effort to identify bodies of the victims. In Thailand, teams working to identify the victims consisted of forensic odontologists, medicolegal experts, police officers, and DNA and fingerprint specialists. In Thailand after the disaster, about 4,280 bodies were placed in refrigerated containers in preparation for identification. The PM (postmortem) forensic team collected detailed dental information including bitewings and/or periapical radiographs (Schuller-Gotzburg and Suchanek, 2007).

Typically, victims of severe destruction can only be identified by three main components: dental status, DNA, and fingerprints. By March 23, 2006, AM (antemortem) cases, which included X-rays and treatment charts from the patient's native country, were numbered at 3,647 and had been entered into the computer. Slightly more PM cases (3,680) had been entered into the computer system. The PM information consisted of bitewing and periapical X-rays and five Polaroid or digital photographs (one frontal, two lateral, and one occlusal view) of both the upper and lower jaw. Using the entered data, the computer was able to compare and classify the information as "probable" or "established," "possible," insufficient evidence," or "excluded" (Schuller-Gotzburg and Suchanek, 2007).

Three months after the disaster, 971 victims had been identified. 837 (88%) of these had been identified by dental status alone. By July 29, 2005, 2,020 victims had been identified: 1,097 (54%) by dental status alone and 331 (16.6%) by a combination of dental and other modes.

Eleven months after the disaster (November 13, 2005), 1,105 victims were identified by dental status alone, which accounted for 54.16% of the total number identified to that point (Schuller-Gotzburg and Suchanek, 2007). Dentistry also played a part in DNA samples used for identification because DNA extracted from the pulp of the canines provided further help with identification (Schuller-Gotzburg and Suchanek, 2007).

These statistics show the importance of dental forensics in the identification of the tsunami victims in Thailand. Several issues emerged, however, including the lack of dental records in poorer countries due to lack of dental care. Because of this, the majority (80%) of dental identifications were made on foreign victims. Fingerprints identified most of the Thai victims, since this data is a part of their identification cards. Another issue was identifying children and adolescents that had very little dental treatment (Schuller-Gotzburg and Suchanek, 2007).

These are just a few of the many stories that could be shared about the role of forensic odontology in mass casualty disasters. There are many others from the past and those yet to be told in the future.

CURRENT CHALLENGES AND POSSIBLE SOLUTIONS

One of the main problems in forensic odontology is the lack of trained personnel. A survey by the *Journal of the American Dental Association* showed that 62% of the respondents had never received any forensic training, although 75% were interested in such training (Zohn et al., 2010). Ideally this type of training should be taking place in dental and dental hygiene schools, but most students graduate without any skills or knowledge in this area. Fortunately, several organizations now have forensic odontology certification programs, and these include the American Board of Forensic Odontology (ABFO, www.abfo.org), the American Academy of Forensic Sciences (AAFS, www.aafs.org), the American Society of Forensic Odontology (ASFO, www.asfo.org), and the International Organization for Forensic Odonto-Stomatology (www.iofos.eu).

Dental hygienists could play a significant role on the forensic teams, but currently there are only a few individuals out of the over 150,000 dental hygienists nationwide that are involved in disaster response. Bradshaw et al. (2016) suggest that hygienists could perform many roles including:

> managing dental personnel, obtaining and standardizing AM dental records, assisting authorities, transcribing data into databases, assisting surgical procedures, exposing radiographs, aiding multiple verifications during PM exams, monitoring team members for fatigue, assisting with PM dental charting and evidence collection, triaging dental records, assisting the search for matches, and sorting charts.

(p. 314)

Brannon and Connick (2000) state that "the disaster team that is not utilizing the DH (dental hygienist) is ignoring an invaluable resource" (p. 383).

Current forensic curriculum is therefore lacking in both dental and dental hygiene schools. Bradshaw et al. (2016) suggest that possible reasons for this might include lack of interest by the faculty, shortage of qualified instructors, and scarcity of time in an often-overcrowded schedule. A possible solution might be to involve local medical examiners in the development of curriculum and teaching the courses. Giving students the opportunity to participate in community disaster drills could also spark an interest.

The ABFO, ASFO, Armed Forces Institute of Pathology, and the University of Texas Health Science Center at San Antonio Dental School all offer courses in forensic odontology (American Academy of Forensic Sciences, n.d.). These are possible resources for instructors at dental or dental hygiene schools to receive additional training. The ABFO also offers a rigorous certification program that requires multiple case study submissions, court depositions, formal training, authoring works on forensic dentistry, formal affiliation with a recognized medical/legal agency, participation in a Mass Fatality Incident (MFI), and service on an odontology committee. All these activities are awarded points; the applicant must reach a certain number of points as well as completing a written test to be qualified for board status (American Academy of Forensic Sciences, n.d.).

Since there is no national standard for training, when volunteers "report for duty" at a mass casualty event there has been no way to assess the skills of the volunteers. It has been suggested that a skill assessment system be developed that could quickly and effectively assess a volunteer's abilities (Zonh et al., 2010). Zohn et al. (2010) advocate for internet-based courses, which would qualify a dentist or dental auxiliary for one of five teams:

- Antemortem Team Qualification
- Postmortem Team Qualification
- Comparison Team Qualification
- Field Team Qualification
- Initial Response Team and Shift Leader Qualification (Zohn et al., 2010, p. 789).

Team leaders would quickly recognize volunteers having training in one or more of the above areas. Personnel could be placed on the team best-suited to their qualifications.

One solution to this lack of qualified forensic odontology specialists is to provide basic forensic training in all dental and dental hygiene schools, then progress on to further mentoring and training. Not all dentists or hygienists are interested in the topic, but a basic introduction could be of great benefit in increasing the number of trained volunteers.

Another issue is the lack of good dental records, especially in third-world countries. A train accident in Zagreb, Croatia, had only 5% of the victims identified, while a plane crash of Slovenian and British nationals yielded a 33% identification of the Slovenians and 100% of the British passengers by dental means only (Obafunwa et al., 2015). As mentioned earlier, this was a problem in the tsunami in Phuket, Thailand. Foreigners visiting from other countries were more easily identified by dental records because there were good records kept in their home countries (Schuller-Gotzburg and Suchanek, 2007).

We may not be able to do anything to improve dental records in third-world countries, but we can certainly make sure that in individual dental offices in more advanced countries, records are complete and accurate. Warnick (1987) stressed both the ethical and moral obligation to keep accurate and adequate dental records. The advent of the digital age has certainly made sharing of these records much easier, but if records are poorly kept or not kept at all, it is extremely difficult to piece together the AM and PM records of disaster victims.

In 1999, Brannon and Connick found that one of the most frequent problems found in records was that dentists failed to chart *existing* restorations or abnormalities. There was definitely a need for a standardized system of recording both existing conditions and treatment received. Thirty years later, this has still not happened as dentists use a variety of record-keeping systems and there is no standardization of dental records.

Failure to put a patient's name on prosthetics has also been a consistent problem. Just a moment of time on the part of the dentist could save the PM teams hours or days of needless work if the patient's name was on a removable appliance (Brannon et al., 1999).

Another issue is that of fragmented dental remains or the inability to adequately recover enough dental structure to do a comparison (Brannon and Kessler, 1999). Brannon et al. (1999) studied ten disasters and found that "lack of remains recovery" (p. 123) occurred in half of them. However, using computers in forensic dentistry has greatly expedited the identification of fragments.

The above problems have all been *external* issues, but there are *internal* problems to be addressed as well. These include stress, lack of experience, and difficulty in identifying esthetic restorative materials.

Seldom mentioned is the stress of the forensic dental teams. A study done by McCarrol et al. (1996) did a comparison of the 31 dentists who had identified the dead from the fire at the Branch Davidian compound with 47 dentists who lived nearby but did not participate in identifying remains. Those who had handled remains had significant stress, related to how many hours they had worked, how much prior experience they had handling remains, their age, and support received from spouses and co-workers during the event.

Brannon and Connick (2000) recommend pairing an older, more experienced member of the forensics team with a younger member to reduce stress. Rotating jobs, group discussions with mental health professionals, keeping the teams small, and humor all play a part in reducing stress.

An unexpected problem of increasingly improved dental materials is that the composite (tooth-colored) restorations are often hard to identify. Brannon et al. (1999) share that in two disasters, the 1989 KC-135 accident at Dyess Air Force Base, Texas, and the 1992 V-22 Osprey experimental aircraft crash in Quantico, Virginia, composite restorations were not found. PM exams had to be redone even though there were multiple substantiations of the initial findings. Patients appreciate the beauty of esthetic restorations, but this presents a challenge for the forensic team.

RECOMMENDATIONS FOR THE FUTURE

As previously stated, education is paramount to increasing the effectiveness of forensic odontology teams. This education should start in the schools and interested students should be directed and mentored with further education. Pairing of experienced and older team members with those less experienced helps with training and reducing stress.

Standardized dental records or at least strong recommendations to keep exemplary dental records is a necessity. Without good AM records, the identification process is greatly hampered. Again, this is accomplished by education that should begin in the schools.

Continuing education units are a requirement for all dentists and dental hygienists to maintain their licenses. There should be more continuing education (CE) offerings related to forensic dentistry and the role of the dental hygienist on the forensics team. In the author's 40 years of CE courses, she has never seen any offerings on forensic dentistry. It is time for this to change, especially as we continue to see mass casualty disasters.

Mental health professionals should monitor all members of the dental forensic team to identify and help individuals deal with stress-related problems. The service the forensic dental team provides to family members of victims is immeasurable, yet it can take its toll on the individuals performing that service. Support from team members, family, friends, and mental health professionals is critical to this work.

CONCLUSION

Forensic dentistry is a very old science; it has been around for centuries. Through the ages, it has improved and modernized, yet the basics still hold. Teeth are the longest-lasting part of the body in a disaster situation whether it be fire, plane crash, tsunami, or an act of war or terror. They can withstand extreme heat and are the hardest substance in the human body (Chun et al., 2014). Teeth hold the DNA signature for the body within the pulp. Teeth show wear, they show dental work, and they tell a lot about the life of the person. Because of all these things, they are a valuable resource in identifying deceased persons.

The field of forensic dentistry needs more training opportunities. Beginning courses could, and should, be taught in dental and dental hygiene schools. Access to online training is now readily available. But more than education, there need to be mentors that help guide new forensic dental teams. International standardization in training and procedure would make it possible for anyone to come from anywhere to help in a mass casualty situation; everyone would be on the same page. There are efforts being made along these lines, and with improved education, training, and support, dental forensic odontology will become even more effective in providing comfort and closure to the families of disaster victims.

CLASS DISCUSSION AND ESSAY QUESTIONS

1. What are some of the first examples of forensic dentistry in history?
2. Why is forensic odontology (FO) considered one of the most reliable methods for the identification of victims?
3. What are the four options of reporting dental identification according to the American Board of Forensic Odontologists?
4. Who participates in Forensic Odontology Teams and what are their respective roles?
5. What lessons about forensic odontology are gleaned from cases such as 9/11, Hurricane Maria, and the tsunami in Thailand?
6. This chapter reveals a shortage of trained personnel that could and should be involved in forensic odontology. What measures can be taken to overcome this challenge?

REFERENCES

American Academy of Forensic Sciences. (n.d.) Retrieved from https://www.aafs.org/home-page/students/undergraduate-and-graduate-degrees-in-dentistry/.
American Board of Forensic Odontology. (2018). Retrieved from http://abfo.org/wp-content/uploads/2012/08/ABFO-DRM-Section-4-Standards-Guidelines-Feb-2018-3.pdf.

Balachander, N., Babu, N., Jimson, S., Privadharsini, C., & Masthan, K. (2015). Evolution of forensic odontology: An overview. *Journal of Pharmacy and Bioallied Sciences*, 7(Suppl 1), 176–180. https://doi.org/10.4103/0975-7406.155894.

Baron, P. (2000). The development of dentistry 1000–2000. *The Lancet, 354*.

Below, R., & Wallemacq, P. (2018). Annual disaster statistical review 2017. Retrieved from www.cred.be/publications.

Berketa, J., & Higgins, D. (2017). Stabilization of dental structures of severely incinerated victims at disaster scenes to facilitate human identification. *Journal of Forensic and Legal Medicine, 51*, 45–49.

Bradshaw, B., Bruhn, A., Newcomb, T., Giles, B., & Simms, K. (2016). Disaster preparedness and response: A survey of U.S. Dental Hygienists. *Journal of Dental Hygiene, 90*(5), 313–322.

Brannon, R., & Connick, C. (2000). The role of the dental hygienist in mass disasters. *Journal of Forensic Sciences, 45*(2), 381–383.

Brannon, R., & Kessler, H. (1999). Problems in mass-disaster dental identification: A retrospective study. *Journal of Forensic Sciences, 44*(1), 123–127.

Burger, D. (March 19, 2018). Compassion for the living and reverence for the victims. *ADA News*,14–15.

Chun, K., Choi, H., & Lee, J. (2014). Comparison of mechanical property and role between enamel and dentin in the human teeth. Retrieved from https://www.ncbi.nlm.nih.gov/pmc/articles/PMC3924884.

Coleman, L. (2006). Frequency of man-made disasters in the 20th century. *Journal of Contingencies and Crisis Management, 14*(1), 3–11.

Congressional record. (October 10, 2002). *Vol. 148*, H7831

Forensic dentistry: Identifying the Victims of 9/11. (2001). *Dental Practice Management*. Retrieved from https://www.oralhealthgroup.com/features/forensic-dentistry-identifying-the-victims-of-9-11/.

Furnari, W. (2018). A cursory review of forensic dentistry. *RDH Magazine*,38(4), 57–63.

Hirst, K. (2017). Mcgrgarh, Pakistan life in the Indus valley before Harappa. Retrieved from https://www.thoughtco.com/hehrgarh-pakistan-life-indus-valley-171796.

History of Dentistry. (n.d.). Retrieved from https://www.adea.org/GoDental/Health_Professions_Advisors/History_of_Dentistry.aspx.

Kolude, B., Adeyemi, B., Taiwo, J., Sigbeku, O., & Eze, U. (2010). The role of forensic dentist following mass disaster. *Annals of Ibadan Postgraduate Medicine*,8(2), 111–117.

Mancini, M. (2014). The time Paul Revere worked as a dentist. Retrieved from http://mentalfloss.com/article/54816/time-paul-revere-worked-dentist.

McCarroll, J. E., Fullerton, C. S., Ursano, R. J., & Hermsen, J. M. (1996). Posttraumatic stress symptoms following forensic dental identification: Mt. Carmel, Waco, Texas. *The American Journal of Psychiatry, 153*(6), 778–782.

Nola, M. (2016). Paul Revere and forensic dentistry. *Military Medicine, 181*(7), 714–715.

Obafunwa, J., Ogunbanjo, V., Ogunbanjo, O., Soyemi, S., & Faduyile, F. (2015). Forensic Odontological observations in the victims of DANA air crash. *Pan African Medical Journal*. https://doi.org/10.11604/pamj.2015.20.96.5360.

Prajapati, G., Sarode, S., Sarode, G., Shelke, P., Awan, K., & Patil, S. (2018). Role of forensic odontology in the identification of victims of major mass disasters across the world: A systematic review. *PLOS ONE*. https://doi.org/10.1371/journal.pone.0199791.

Saunders, M. (2016). Forensic dentistry: A public and social service. *Journal of the American Society on Aging, 40*(3), 49–51.

Schuller-Gotzburg, P., & Suchanek, J. (2007). Forensic odontologists successfully identify tsunami victimsin Phuket, Thailand. *Forensic Science International, 171*(2–3), 204–207.

Senn, D., & Stimson, P. (2010). *Forensic Dentistry* (2nd ed.). Boca Raton, FL: CRC Press.

Warnick, A. (1987). Dentists aid in identification of crash victims. *Journal of the Michigan Dental Association, 69*(10), 553–556.

Worsley, L. (2011). Dental hygiene: Oral history. *History Today, 11*(5). Retrieved from https://www.historytoday.com/lucy-worsley/dental-hygiene-oral-history.

Zohn, H., Dashkow, S., Aschheim, K., Dobrin, L., Glazer, H., Kirschbaum, M., Levitt, D., & Feldman, C. (2010). The odontology victim identification skill assessment system. *American Academy of Forensic Sciences, 55*(3), 788–791.

CHAPTER 21

The Critical Role of Public Works in Emergency Management and Homeland Security:
Promoting and Defending a Seat at the Table

Dave Bergner

INTRODUCTION

No area of the United States is immune from disasters. In recent decades, this nation has endured a number of natural, accidental/technological, and intentional catastrophes – some on a scale, intensity, duration, or type rarely or never before experienced. As all incidents and events begin at the local level, thus prevention, mitigation, planning, preparedness, response, and recovery are primarily the responsibility of local jurisdictions. However, when major disasters strike, the capabilities of even large municipalities and counties can be quickly overwhelmed and assistance from other agencies, jurisdictions, states, and the federal government will be needed. As much of this support may not be immediately available, local jurisdictions must be prepared to handle the first 12–72 hours of an incident themselves. Though police, fire, and emergency medical services have well-defined and highly visible roles, the responsibilities and capabilities of public works agencies are not as well known or understood by the other professions, governing officials, and the general public.

The public works profession includes municipal, county, and tribal public works departments (DPW) and State and territorial departments of transportation (DOT) that are responsible for roadways, traffic control systems, stormwater control, and other functions. Because of the wide range of functions and capabilities, the public works discipline is an important component of overall emergency management as evident by its inclusion in the Federal Emergency Management Agency's (FEMA) Emergency Services Sector. Its involvement often spans a much longer duration and a wider scope of activities than the other professions – police, fire, emergency medical – in the public sector.

Whenever possible, public works initiates preventive measures prior to an anticipated event such as constructing temporary levees to mitigate flooding, staging equipment prior to a hurricane, and activating shifts in advance of a major snowstorm. Even routine

DOI: 10.4324/9781003350729-21

maintenance work, such as cleaning, repairing, and hardening stormwater drainage systems, and keeping roadways in good condition are considered mitigation efforts. When disasters strike, public works maintenance operations clears debris from roadways to provide access for responders and for citizens to evacuate, and repairs roads, bridges, stormwater structures, and traffic control devices. Typically, when other responders have resumed routine operations, public works will still be removing debris, assessing damage, repairing infrastructure, and restoring public services to normal levels.

Defining Public Works

The term "public works" encompasses such a broad range of "infrastructure" services and activities. The perception most people have is that "public works" is street maintenance, trash collection, water and sewer pipelines, and snow removal. To some, "public works" connotes big projects like dams, bridges, airports, and major highways built by the federal Public Works Administration in the 1930s. According to the American Public Works Association (APWA), even its members have difficulty arriving at a common definition because of the "multi-faceted, ever-evolving nature" of this discipline. APWA (2022) defines it as follows:

> Public Works is the combination of physical assets, management practices, policies, and personnel necessary for government to provide and sustain structures and services essential to the welfare and acceptable quality of life for its citizens...The traditional concept of public works is that governmental units provide the services, own the facilities, and are usually funded through taxation. However, the situation often is not that clear-cut today, and other models also exist, which include publicly owned corporations and partial outsourcing. It is not uncommon for the private sector to be involved in delivering public works services as well.
>
> (https://www.apwa.net/MYAPWA/About/What_is_Public_Works/MyApwa/Apwa
> _Public/About/What_Is_Public_Works.aspx)

APWA (2003) identified 145 different public works functions and classified them into eight categories:

1. Transportation – includes streets, bridges, sidewalks, bike paths, airports, seaports, traffic control and storm water management. Public works is responsible for the design, construction, and maintenance of these facilities.
2. Sanitation – covers solid waste, collected by their government forces or by contractors. Some cities also operate their own landfills and recycling operations instead of using county facilities.
3. Utilities – incorporates water, wastewater, gas, and electric functions of a public works department or handled by other departments, governmental entities, or private enterprises. Storm water drainage and flood control may be within a public works department or district authority
4. Buildings and Grounds – comprises the design, construction, maintenance, and management of public buildings and facilities.
5. Municipal Engineering – includes civil and environmental engineering functions such as infrastructure design, technical studies, construction inspection and surveying. The size of a public works department, along with the expertise

of personnel, will determine how many of these functions it performs. Larger departments perform some of their own engineering services; small departments will contract them. Major, complex projects are usually contracted.

6. Fleet management – involves the procurement and maintenance of city-owned equipment and vehicles. Some public works departments manage their own equipment or provide this as a central service for all departments. Many contracts cover part or all of fleet maintenance services.
7. Management and Administration – includes operations management and supervision, financial management and reporting, public relations, procurement of professional services, requesting and evaluating proposals, awarding bids, and contract management
8. Other – suggests various other functions such as parks maintenance, urban forestry, public cemetery operation, airport services, dead animal pickup, etc.

There is no standard organizational structure for local public works agencies. The arrangement depends on statutes and ordinances, population, area size, complexity of operations, and other local factors. Some municipalities place water and wastewater under public works while others use a different department or board. Likewise, planning and development, code enforcement, parks and recreation, facilities, and trash collection services may be within public works or in other departments and agencies. For example, in an urban area comprised of a number of small jurisdictions, water/wastewater service and mass transit are provided by regional authorities. A few municipalities also operate their own electric and gas systems.

In 1987, the U.S. National Research Council adopted the term "public works infrastructure" to include:

highways, streets, roads, and bridges; mass transit; airports and airways; water supply and water resources; wastewater management; solid-waste treatment and disposal; electric power generation and transmission; telecommunications; and hazardous waste management. A comprehension of infrastructure spans not only these public works facilities, but also the operating procedures, management practices, and development policies that interact together with societal demand and the physical world to facilitate the transport of people and goods, provision of water for drinking and a variety of other uses, safe disposal of society's waste products, provision of energy where it is needed, and transmission of information within and between communities.

National Research Council; Committee on Infrastructure Innovation (1987)

However, the focus of this chapter is on the vital surface transportation network of highways, roads, and streets. All other functions depend upon the ability for people, goods, and services to freely move about and are critical for nearly all aspects of emergency management. To illustrate, consider the disruptions to our everyday lives when roadways are obstructed by flooding, snow and ice, storm debris, landslides, earthquakes, wildfires, accidents, and civil disturbances. When these unexpected events occur only public works/transportation agencies can restore access, safety, and mobility to roadways.

Note that the terms "public works," "public works/transportation," "transportation agencies," "department of public works (DPW)," and "state department of transportation (DOT)" are used interchangeably in this chapter due to similarity of functions regarding routine roadway operations and emergency management activities. Furthermore, though federal emergency management and transportation agencies tend to focus on state DOTs, local DPWs are also included or implied.

HISTORICAL PERSPECTIVE

Arguably civilization, as we know it, would not exist if not for "public works." As humankind evolved from inhabiting transitory hamlets to established towns, the need for facilities and systems for the common good became necessary. Early civilizations like Egypt, Babylon, Greece, China, India, and even the Mayan and Aztec civilizations in Mesoamerica had some form of "public works" such as constructing fortifications, roads and bridges, water supply systems (dams, reservoirs, canals, aqueducts), rudimentary sewers, and other community improvements. The Romans are famous for their engineering feats such as roads, canals, and aqueducts, some that are still in use today.

But as these ancient empires declined, so did the maintenance and construction of the infrastructure. For centuries afterward, the roads, bridges, dams, aqueducts, etc. fell into disrepair, destruction, and abandonment. Remarkably, however, some remnants still survive. Throughout Europe in the Dark Ages, roads were rough and dangerous; most travel was on rivers, lakes, and along seacoasts thus spurring the development of ports with wharves, docks, levees, seawalls, and jetties.

Meanwhile, in towns and cities "public works" included erecting defensive high walls, paving streets and market squares with stone, and providing water at public fountains. The density and lack of sewers and other sanitation (human and animal waste, offal, garbage, and trash were dumped in the streets and alleys) contributed to frequent infestations and pestilence.

By the 1600s, towns and cities in Europe were growing as trade expanded and populations rebounded following centuries of devastating plagues. More people were moving to urban areas from the farms and villages as the need for labor in specialized trades and services increased. The need for clean water, better sanitation, and improved land transport (particularly farm-to-market to feed the burgeoning populations) spurred renewed construction of public facilities. After massive fires and natural disasters severely damaged or destroyed large areas of cities, planned rebuilding focused on creating more public spaces, widening streets, improving water supply, and constructing sewers. This was primarily to mitigate the spread of fires but it also improved overall sanitation and relieved congestion.

The Beginning of Public Works in America

Across the Atlantic in the American colonies of the 1600s and 1700s, settlers built most villages and towns on a grid-pattern of streets. In the colonial period and early decades of the United States, travel between settlements by land was difficult as there were few roads. Transportation between the coastal towns and cities was mostly by sea. Likewise, travel to the interior was slow and difficult; rivers provided access from the seacoast up to the fall line where the Appalachian Mountains were a great obstacle. Passengers and freight bound for the western parts of the country had to travel overland, made more difficult by the rough condition of the roads. After the American War of Independence, the new government grappled with the need to improve and extend the nascent transportation network:

> The central issue [was] "internal improvements," a term used loosely in the 1780s to refer to all kinds of programs to encourage security, prosperity and enlightenment. Gradually the first generation identified roads, canals...as the instruments of improvement that urgently needed attention. Eventually the concept narrowed...and became synonymous with public works for improved transportation.
>
> (Lawson, 2001)

At that time, most settlements were still concentrated along seacoasts and navigable rivers. Though segments of roads and "tow paths" ran alongside connecting villages and towns, they were not as convenient nor capable of transporting substantial numbers of people and cargo as boats and rafts were. Roads were few, fairly short, primitive, and as narrow as two feet. The terrain and dense old-growth forests made construction of new roads difficult. Most early roads followed Native American and animal trails. As an example, several trails merged to form the Boston Post Road. The Upper Post Road, originally called the Pequot Path, was used by Native Americans for centuries. The post riders used this trail to deliver mail beginning in 1673. During the 19th century, turnpike companies improved parts of the road, much of which is now U.S. Route 1 (Wikipedia, 2021a). Until the early 1800s, few other long-distance roads existed; most were private toll roads or "turnpikes." As more lands between the Appalachian Mountains and the Mississippi river were settled, George Washington and Thomas Jefferson believed that a trans-Appalachian road was necessary. In 1806 President Jefferson established the first federally funded road to connect Cumberland, Maryland to western settlements on the Ohio River. Construction of the National Road began in 1811 and was completed to Wheeling in 1818. By the 1830s the federal government conveyed part of the road's responsibility to the states through which it runs. Tollgates and tollhouses were then built by the states, with the federal government taking responsibility for road repairs. The National Road is now U.S. Route 40 earning the nickname "The Main Street of America" (Longfellow, 2021).

Yet, as financially and commercially successful as the National Road was, it did not spark other such endeavors. Waterways were still the prime mode of transportation over long distances. The Erie Canal, linking the Hudson River with the Great Lakes, built in the early 1800s with considerable federal funding and from New York state, is one of the more notable "public works" projects of the young nation. Prior to the opening of the canal, local transportation of bulk goods was limited to the use of pack animals. Transport by water was the most cost-effective way to ship bulk goods (Wikipedia, 2021). Because of the enormous success of the Erie Canal other states followed in constructing canals. The Ohio & Erie Canal completed in 1833 linked Cleveland, Columbus, and the Ohio River, and the Wabash & Erie Canal completed in 1853 linked Toledo to Evansville. Pennsylvania then constructed a canal system to Pittsburgh. At its peak, Pennsylvania had almost a thousand miles of canals in operation. By 1840 the country had over 3,000 miles of canals, a complete water route from New York City to New Orleans. Yet, within 20 years the railroad would render most of them unprofitable (US History, 2021).

The first regular carrier of passengers and freight was the Baltimore and Ohio railroad, completed in 1827. By 1850 over 9,000 miles of track were in service. Though private enterprises built and operated the railroads, bonds issued by state governments and other incentives could be considered as a quasi-form of public works. The need for a more diverse extension of railways was extremely apparent after the Civil War. The first transcontinental railroad was completed in 1869 funded by both private-issued and federal government bonds. During the next several decades, construction of other transcontinental railroads across the sparsely inhabited Great Plains and Mountain West was spurred by millions of square miles of land grants from the federal government. The railroads needed towns along their routes to supply water and fuel, supplies and lodging. To encourage settlement, the railroads offered the lands granted to them by the federal government at cheap prices. By the late 1880s immigrants from Central Europe were arriving in large numbers to settle along the routes (Stanford, 2021).

Meanwhile, in the latter decades of the 19th century, cities in the Northeast and Upper Midwest were rapidly growing due to industrialization and the influx of migrants from rural America and immigrants from Europe to work in the mines, mills, factories, foundries, shipyards, docks, slaughterhouses, and railroads. As housing was in short supply, people were crammed into tenements and shanties. The crowded living conditions created public health and social problems. "Transportation systems and the general infrastructure improved, better meeting the increased needs of the middle- and upper-class city dwellers. But, with few city services to rely upon, the working class lived daily with overcrowding, inadequate water facilities, unpaved streets, and disease" (Library of Congress, 2021a).

Though the first public water main in the United States was installed under New York streets in 1830, and the first sewer systems were built in Chicago and Brooklyn in the 1850s, it was several more decades before they were installed in other cities and towns. In the 1890s, the "City Beautiful" movement began in the United States in response to the squalid conditions in large parts of cities. It flourished and greatly influenced urban planning throughout the 20th century (Wikipedia, 2021). The movement cleared slums; widened, graded, and paved streets and sidewalks; constructed broad boulevards and parks; planted trees; installed water and sewer lines; expanded streetcar service; installed streetlights; provided regular street cleaning; and erected monuments and public buildings and venues. It would be reasonable to conclude, therefore, that this was the definitive beginning of modern municipal public works in the United States.

While the urban population in America was growing rapidly, a majority of the population in 1900 (60%) lived on farms or in small towns and villages. Most people, whether living in rural or urban areas, did not travel far; if they did, it usually was by rail or waterways. Outside the cities, roads were dirt or gravel; mud in the winter and dust in the summer. Travel was slow and expensive (Library of Congress, 2021b). In the 1890s, bicycles were very popular, especially for touring in the nearby countryside. Annoyed by the deplorable condition of the roads, a coalition of farmers' organizations and bicyclists' organizations, like the League of American Wheelmen, formed the Good Roads Association. The goal was state and federal spending to improve rural roads. By 1910, the American Automobile Association and other organizations joined the campaign coordinated by the National Good Roads Association. Early organizers cited road construction and maintenance in Europe that was supported by national and local governments. In 1893, the U.S. Department of Agriculture's new Office of Road Inquiry initiated a systematic evaluation of existing highway systems (it became the Office of Public Road Inquiries in 1899; then the Office of Public Roads in 1905; then Office of Public Roads and Rural Engineering in 1915; and Bureau of Public Roads in 1918). In 1939, it was put under the Federal Works Agency and renamed the Public Roads Administration. In 1970, the Public Roads Administration was absorbed into the newly created Federal Highway Administration.

Also in 1893, Charles Duryea produced the first American gasoline-powered vehicle; others, like Henry Ford, soon began manufacturing automobiles, though only the wealthy could afford them. In 1903, Horatio Nelson Jackson and Sewall K. Crocker were the first to drive an automobile across the United States from San Francisco to New

York City in 63 days, 12 hours, and 30 minutes. Most of the journey was on unpaved, unmarked, and often unmapped roads, railroad tracks, and old wagon trails. In 1915, Roland R. Conklin drove the first motor home (a customized Packard pick-up truck) from Long Island to San Francisco. The trip took two months, due to the poor quality of roads at the time. As automobiles became more affordable and use grew, organizations developed cross-country road projects such as the coast-to-coast east–west Lincoln Highway in 1913, and the north–south Dixie Highway in 1915 from Canada to Miami, Florida. Despite those efforts, the lack of well-signed, paved roads outside of urban areas was still a problem. The 1916 Federal Aid Road Act created a national highway construction campaign that continued into the 1920s. During World War I, the difficulties of transportation in France demonstrated that wide, paved roads were critical for mass movement of military personnel, equipment, and supplies. Recognizing the strategic importance in America, Lieutenant Colonel Dwight D. Eisenhower in 1919 led a convoy of 81 motorized Army vehicles from Washington, DC, to San Francisco, a distance of 3,251 miles in 62 days. Unfortunately, little improvement to roads had occurred since Horatio's Drive. As Eisenhower wrote in his November 1919 report to the chief of the Motor Transport Corps, the Lincoln Highway in Utah proved "one succession of dust, ruts, pits and holes."

(https://www.freightwaves.com/news/freightwaves-classics-hell-in-nevada-for
-transcontinental-convoy)

Evolution of Municipal Engineering and Public Works as a Profession

Modern municipal engineering originated in the 19th century in the United Kingdom with the growth of industrial cities. The threat from epidemics of waterborne diseases led to the development of a profession devoted to "sanitary science" that later became "municipal engineering." British legislation granted municipalities powers of paving, lighting, cleansing, supplying with water, and improving their communities, what we now consider as public works:

> By the early 20th century, Municipal Engineering had become a broad discipline embracing many of the responsibilities undertaken by local authorities, including roads, drainage, flood control, coastal engineering, public health, waste management, street cleaning, water supply, sewers, wastewater treatment, crematoria, public baths, slum clearance, town planning, public housing, energy supply, parks, leisure facilities, libraries, town halls and other municipal buildings.

(Wikipedia, 2021)

Recognizing the importance of this emerging discipline and profession, the Association of Municipal Engineers was established in Britain in 1874; it was later renamed the Institution of Municipal Engineers and merged with the Institution of Civil Engineers (ICE) in 1984. ICE was chartered in 1828 "For promoting…the profession of a civil engineer…as applied in the construction of roads, bridges, aqueducts, canals, river navigation, docks…ports, harbors…and in the drainage of cities and towns."

(https://en.wikipedia.org/wiki/Institution_of_Civil_Engineers#cite_ref-6)

As American cities rapidly grew in the late 1800s and early 1900s, so did a myriad of problems. Municipal governments became more professional and progressive with the adoption of the council–city manager structure and the development of public works departments. College-educated civil engineers and trained technicians – rather than inexperienced, uneducated, and often corrupt elected officials and patronage political appointees – were put in charge. They became responsible for street construction and maintenance, water supply, storm-water drainage, sanitary sewers, garbage collection, and sundry other services depending upon locale. Systematic traffic control to deal with the explosive increase in automobiles that were clogging city streets also became a responsibility.

The new generation of professional consultants, design engineers, construction supervisors, and water works directors formed the American Society of Municipal Engineers in 1894. Around the same time the International Association of Public Works Officials (formerly known as the International Association of Street Sanitation Officials) was organized; it was primarily comprised of non-engineers engaged in public works management and service delivery. In 1934 the two organizations merged to form the American Public Works Association (APWA). Its current membership of 30,000 includes elected officials, department directors, division chiefs, superintendents, managers, supervisors, senior operators and technicians, and administrative staff. APWA has through its publications and conferences promoted significant contributions to the various aspects of public works, including emergency management.

The American Association of State Highway Officials (AASHO) was founded in 1914. It strongly advocated for federal-aid funding for the development of highway systems nationwide and to allow major routes to span state lines. Most of what AASHO supported ended up in the Federal Aid Road Act of 1916. This was followed by the Federal Aid Highway Act of 1921 which mandated that 7% of a state's total mileage must be expended only on a primary system of connector interstate roads, the foundation of national numbered routes. In the 1950s, President Eisenhower authorized funding for the planning and construction of what became the Interstate Highway system, now regarded as one of the world's most significant public works projects. In 1973 AASHO's name was changed to American Association of State Highway and Transportation Officials (AASHTO) to reflect a broadened scope that covers all modes of transportation, although mostly for highways.

The foremost distinction between APWA and AASHTO is that APWA membership is open to public works and transportation agencies at all levels of government, related quasi-public authorities, private sector organizations, and individuals. AASHTO membership, on the other hand, is composed only of departments or agencies of the States, Puerto Rico, and the District of Columbia that have official highway responsibility, and the United States Department of Transportation (USDOT). Associate Membership is available to sub-state and federal transportation agencies; port, toll, and highway commissions or authorities; international transportation agencies; city DOTS; and transportation agencies in other counties. Individuals or private sector entities like engineering firms, consultants, and vendors are not eligible.

Though modern public works departments have various configurations and names, all share the basic functions of planning, designing, constructing, and maintaining infrastructure. The more common designation for municipal agencies is "Public Works Department" though some are titled "Street Department" or "Transportation Department." Likewise, county agencies typically are Public Works or Road or Highway departments. Most states use "Department of Transportation" or older terms such as

"Highway Department" or "Bureau of Roads." Regardless of nomenclature, the primary responsibility of these agencies is to design, build, and maintain roadways, bridges, viaducts and tunnels, and stormwater systems, and the installation, maintenance, and operation of traffic control systems. (Note that tolled turnpikes, bridges, and tunnels are often under separate public or private "authorities"). The interconnected systems of highways, roads, and streets is essential to everyday life and critical for emergency management.

Emergency Management Becomes a Distinct Function

Comprehensive emergency management originated during World War II as the Civil Defense (CD) program. Though the obvious mission was readiness for hostile attacks, it set the foundation for peace-time disaster response. The Cold War fears of the 1950s and 1960s kept Civil Defense organizations active and often employed for natural disasters. An example is that sirens installed for air raids were also used for warnings during extreme weather incidents like tornadoes. After the end of the Cold War in the 1980s, the focus on nuclear war evolved to an "all-hazards" approach of Comprehensive Emergency Management. In 1992, the Federal Emergency Management Agency (FEMA) renamed the Office of Civil Defense to the Office of Emergency Management. Most local emergency management functions were typically placed with fire or police departments due to their existing command, control, and communication structures. Public works, however, was commonly considered as support and often not included in the planning phase, a trend still prevalent today.

In the 1980s and 1990s, a number of significant catastrophes occurred that heightened the visibility of public works; major hurricanes in Florida and the Carolinas, several intense earthquakes in the Los Angeles and San Francisco areas, massive floods in the Missouri and Mississippi valleys, tornado outbreaks, extreme winter storms, and even a volcanic eruption (Mt St Helens). The specter of foreign and domestic terrorism in the United States arose with the bombing of the World Trade Center in 1993 and the 1995 bombing of the federal office building in Oklahoma City. Also, large protest demonstrations, marches, and riots in a number of major cities caused much damage. Public works departments were tasked with erecting barricades, traffic detours, and cleaning up after these events. Public works dump trucks have also been parked nose-to-tail as barriers around venues where major events were held, to prevent rioting and acts of terrorism.

However, for years, FEMA lacked a legislative mandate to take action; instead, it was limited to "coordinating" responses, making it difficult to make organizations share resources. This was evident as FEMA attempted to obtain an inventory of generators from various federal departments and agencies in preparation of expected Y2K (January 1, 2000) blackouts. Yet there was still lack of coordination and cooperation among the various disciplines and agencies at all levels of government and general ambivalence about planning and preparation.

That changed with the horrific events of September 11, 2001. The terrorist attacks on the World Trade Center and the Pentagon, and the thwarted attack of a fourth hijacked airliner, were unprecedented. The response of many agencies and jurisdictions was exemplary considering the sheer enormity, both physical and psychological. But the underlying issues that hindered communication, cooperation, and collaboration became more evident later with reviews of what had transpired. Clearly, this was a wake-up call to the nation and dramatically illustrated the need for all levels of government to actively plan and prepare for, protect against, respond to, and recover from a wide spectrum of events, especially those that would exceed the capabilities of any single entity.

Then, in 2005, the weaknesses in the nation's emergency preparedness and response capabilities were again revealed with the devastating impact of Hurricane Katrina. The response of governments was a massive failure. The nation lacked a framework to show how all levels of government fit together in a common system for organizing and managing incidents. Some improvement was demonstrated with Hurricane Rita that soon followed but much more still needed to be done.

> The magnitude, variety and geographic range of these and other crises reinforced the need for comprehensive, inclusive emergency management. The public demanded that governments at all levels must do more and do it more efficiently and effectively. Certainly, the Federal government must be more involved than providing checks for individual and public assistance. During this period, FEMA transformed from being known as a "turkey farm."
>
> (Wildfire Today, 2012)

FEMA, between its founding in 1979 and 1993, had gone through periods of obsession with nuclear war planning, thereby making it unprepared for the 1989 San Francisco earthquake and Hurricanes Hugo and Andrew in 1989 and 1992. The agency became known as the "Turkey Farm" because of its management by third-rate political appointees. FEMA director James Witt then transformed it to one of the most respected agencies in the government during the Clinton administration. Its responses to major disasters such as the 1993 Midwest floods and the 1994 Northridge earthquake showed great improvement, as did increased hazard mitigation efforts. However, after Witt left, the Bush administration completely undid FEMA's progress by appointing incompetent administrators and burying the agency inside the Department of Homeland Security (DHS). The Post-Katrina Reform Act restored some independence to FEMA and requires that a professional disaster manager be Director (Birkland, 2017).

PUBLIC WORKS TRANSITIONS TO COMPREHENSIVE EMERGENCY MANAGEMENT

Because of their unique capabilities, statutory duties, and responsibilities, public works/transportation agencies have over many decades responded to floods, blizzards, ice storms, tornadoes, hurricanes, earthquakes, and other natural disasters. But as these occurrences tend to be infrequent, unanticipated, and vary widely as to scope, size intensity, and duration, local public works departments did little, if any, significant planning and preparation. It was just assumed that cleaning up after a disaster was a task for the maintenance forces while engineers directed major repairs or replacements of damaged infrastructure. Otherwise, the focus was on returning to routine activities and programs as quickly as possible. From that perspective, public works agencies viewed emergencies with a *reactive* rather than *proactive* mindset. The general assumption was that as disasters were unpredictable, variable, and uncommon; therefore little planning and preparation was necessary – or worthwhile – until something actually occurred or was imminent.

Furthermore, as operational command was (and still is) typically the responsibility of fire and/or police, public works would provide whatever support it could, if called upon. It was assumed by most public works officials that their departments were on an "as needed" basis and not as first responders. Even today, the role of public works officials in emergency management is given little regard as reflected in a review of job descriptions for division and department managers. Few recruitment postings mention this as a responsibility nor explicitly require knowledge or experience of the subject. (As an example, a June 2022 recruitment for public works director of Joplin, Missouri, which was devastated by a F-5 tornado in 2011, makes no mention of emergency management responsibilities or qualifications.)

It should be noted that though police, fire, emergency medical services (EMS), and many federal agencies were prominently involved with the aftermath of the 9/11 attacks and the 1995 Oklahoma City federal office building bombing, Public Works (PW) was extensively involved in rescue, recovery, debris removal, engineering assessments of damaged structures, and area traffic control. PW personnel were exposed to the same dangers and hazards as the others.

National All-Hazards Incident Management and Public Works

The 1988 Robert T. Stafford Disaster Relief and Emergency Assistance establishes an *orderly, systematic means of federal natural disaster assistance for state and local governments* in carrying out their responsibilities to aid citizens. Congress's intention was to encourage states and localities to develop comprehensive disaster preparedness plans, prepare for better intergovernmental coordination in the face of a disaster, and provide federal assistance programs for losses due to a disaster (Federal Emergency Management Agency, 2021e).

President George W. Bush issued Homeland Security Presidential Directive 5 (HSPD-5) (Department of Homeland Security, 2021a) in 2003 that created the National Incident Management System (NIMS). This provides a unified and coordinated national approach to domestic incident management so that all levels of government, nongovernmental organizations (NGOs), and the private sector work together regardless of cause, size, location, or complexity of all incidents ranging from local, daily occurrences to those requiring federal assistance. NIMS consists of a core set of doctrines, concepts, principles, terminology, and organizational processes of existing emergency management and incident response systems used by jurisdictions, organizations, and functional disciplines at all levels. It is based on the Incident Command System (ICS) that FEMA adopted as the basis for its response team organization. The Department of Homeland Security, formed after 9/11, expanded and revised what is now known as the National Incident Management System for all agencies and jurisdictions across the nation. Lines of authority and responsibility are clearly defined, and specific positions have roles understood and accepted by all.

The National Response Framework (NRF) identifies 15 Emergency Support Functions (ESF) used to provide federal support to States for presidential declared disasters and emergencies. ESF #3 Public Works is the one most relevant:

- Local, state, tribal, territorial (LSTT) governments are responsible for their own public works and infrastructures and have the primary responsibility for mitigation, preparedness, response, and recovery.
- LSTT governments are fully and consistently integrated into ESF #3 activities.
- When activated to respond, the primary agency for ESF #3 [Army Corps of Engineers] develops work priorities in cooperation with LSTT governments and in coordination with FEMA.
- Local authorities are responsible for obtaining required waivers and clearances for ESF #3.
- LSTT mutual aid and assistance networks facilitate sharing resources to support response.

(https://www.fema.gov/emergency-managers/national-
preparedness/frameworks/response)

ESF #1 Transportation, in contrast, is more about the role of the USDOT though reference is made to state and local public works/transportation agencies:

DOT provides transportation assistance in incident management, including the following:

- Monitor and report status of and damage to the transportation system and infrastructure.
- Identify temporary alternative transportation solutions that can be implemented by others when systems or infrastructure are damaged, unavailable, or overwhelmed.
- Coordinate the restoration and recovery of the transportation systems and infrastructure.
- Coordinate and support prevention, preparedness, response, recovery, and mitigation activities among within the authorities and resource limitations of ESF #1 agencies.

The ESFs are also replicated in state Emergency Operations Plans (EOP):

> The state DOT usually has the leadership role within the state for all matters relating to ESF 1, Transportation: infrastructure, including roads, tunnels, and bridges…as well as for all preparedness activities, response operations, and recovery and mitigation activities related to transportation resources.

(Federal Highway Administration, 2017)

Likewise, many counties and municipalities follow Federal ESFs in developing their own EOPs.

Homeland Security Presidential Directive-8 of 2003 (Department of Homeland Security, 2021b) specifically included public works as "emergency responders" though it was later removed in a revised HSPD-8. (Police and fire were adamantly opposed to public works referring to itself as a "first responder." This author routinely uses the encompassing term of "emergency responder" instead.) Achieving acceptance and recognition by police, fire, and even emergency management professionals was, and still is, problematic, yet public works has clear responsibilities that the other disciplines cannot perform. A common misperception is that the National Guard (NG) handles clearing debris and performing other tasks in the aftermath of disasters.

The involvement of the NG, Army Corps of Engineers (ACE), and the Coast Guard (CG) is a tremendous contribution to response and recovery for catastrophic events such as the 9/11 terrorist attack, Hurricane Katrina in 2005, the Joplin, Missouri, tornado in 2011, Super Storm Sandy in 2012, Hurricane Harvey that flooded Houston in 2017, the devastating 2020 California wildfire season (followed later by huge mudslides), and the 2021 snow and ice storm that crippled most of Texas for a week or more. Though local public works departments and state DOTs were also extensively involved, the news media rarely showed their efforts.

But most disasters and other emergencies are local, not regional, and of lesser scope, size, intensity, and duration. Therefore, municipal and county public works departments will be initially and directly involved though they may need to call for assistance from the state DOT and from neighboring jurisdictions. Depending on the magnitude, a municipality or county may request that the governor activate the National Guard to assist as well.

Local public works departments and state DOTs need to commit more time and resources toward planning and preparing for natural disasters that are likely to occur in their area, such as tornadoes, hurricanes, earthquakes, wildfires, flooding, and landslides. There also is growing concern about "slow-moving" disasters caused by climate change: prolonged heat waves, severe drought, intense storms, extreme flooding (for example, the 1,000-year flood in Yellowstone in 2022) and sea-level rise that is already impacting Miami, Florida, and other East Coast cities.

Most of the significant emergencies and disasters that local public works and state DOTs deal with are natural-caused. Though nothing can be done to prevent a flood, ice storm, tornado, hurricane, or earthquake, there are measures that agencies can implement over time to lessen the impacts. Thus, there is a shift toward enhancing resilience of the infrastructure rather than just preparedness for response. As noted in the AASHTO 2015 report, "Fundamental Capabilities of Effective All-Hazards Infrastructure, Protection, Resilience and Emergency Management for State Departments of Transportation":

> Resilience is "the ability to prepare and plan for, absorb, recover from and more successfully adapt to adverse events" (*Disaster Resilience: A National Imperative*, National Research Council, 2012). DOTs are currently in the process of understanding the impact of the shift in focus from protection of assets to resilience of systems.

Achieving a degree of resilience depends upon the following principles according to AASHTO:

- Redesign infrastructure to reduce or eliminate vulnerability.
- Improve ability to improvise during an event.
- Add redundancies to system to improve ability to reroute traffic through parallel components.
- Have backup components available to quickly replace disrupted functions.
- Allow rerouting of facilities, equipment, personnel, procedures, and communications.

(American Association of State Highway Transportation Officials, 2015)

These principles are applicable for local public works agencies as well. Furthermore, DPWs and DOTs emergency management capabilities should align with the National Preparedness Goal of:

- Prevention: To avoid, prevent, or stop a threatened or actual act of terrorism.
- Protection: To secure against acts of terrorism and man-made or natural disasters.
- Mitigation: To reduce loss of life and property by lessening the impact of disasters.
- Response: To save lives, protect property and environment, and meet basic needs.
- Recovery: To assist communities affected by an incident to rebound effectively.

(FEMA, 2021b Mission Areas and Core Capabilities. https://www.fema.gov/
emergency-managers/national-preparedness/mission-core-capabilities)

The capabilities reflect an all-hazards approach of a broad range of incidents and events that have potential to impact transportation systems operations including "technical incidents" such as major traffic accidents, hazmat spills, train derailments, and massive infrastructure failures (I-35 bridge in Minneapolis in 2007; 2010 San Bruno, California gas pipeline explosion; and 2020 Edenville Dam collapse in Midland, Michigan).

For many public works/transportation agencies, strategic planning for emergencies tends to have lower priority than planning, designing, constructing, operating, and maintaining core infrastructure and services. Without sufficient planning for critical incidents, and ensuring the needed training and resources, DPW/DOT agencies will be ill-prepared to deal with major events. But even the best plans need regular review and updating; moreover, the staff at all levels needs to be kept aware of them. Considerable turnover in personnel at these agencies due to the COVID-19 pandemic has resulted in a significant loss of institutional knowledge and staff experienced in emergency management.

Due to ever-tightening budgets, it is increasingly difficult for communities to obtain the funding for resources needed to respond to major emergencies beyond typical minor-scale events. By working more closely on Mutual Aid Agreements (MAA) with their counterparts in other communities – much like the fire and police departments already do – DPWs and DOTs not only can be better prepared to serve the community but also will save money that would otherwise be invested on additional resources. It is common among local public works agencies to informally coordinate and cooperate with each other in the same general vicinity. Though these should be officially established by Mutual Aid Agreements, it is often the case that "exigency equates to expediency." Or, stated colloquially, "Get it Done." Emergencies frequently happen nights, weekends, and holidays; response cannot wait for a formal resolution or directive to activate a MAA. On a broader scale:

> Several states already have formalized PW mutual-aid networks to develop and maintain a statewide network of PW-related agencies. The principal purpose of these networks is to provide mutual-aid response and recovery assistance to one another when confronted with a natural or manmade emergency or disaster. Participating agencies receive important and significant benefits, such as the protection of both the requesting and the responding agencies from liabilities that may be encountered in a disaster setting.

> (Geary and Fessler, 2011)

As an example, from this author's experience, an F-5 tornado obliterated Greensburg, Kansas, late Friday night May 4, 2007. Greensburg's population was a little over 1,000 and the town was only one square mile in the southwestern part of the state. The tornado was nearly a mile in width and directly hit the town. Public works agencies from the county, the local KDOT depot, adjacent counties, and nearby towns responded. That Saturday morning the State Emergency Management office put out a call to all other entities in Kansas for assistance. This author, as Superintendent for Overland Park, KS Public Works on the eastern side of the state, was notified of the request for aid. Over the weekend, a team was assembled and equipment and supplies prepared and loaded for deployment that following Monday. The team had to travel several hundred miles in a caravan, leading units from several smaller municipalities and the county. Over the next six weeks, we rotated two other teams. They worked with many other entities including the National Guard to clear most of the debris and transfer it to burn pits and landfills further away. As for Overland Park, we were able to rapidly prepare and deploy because we used the same highly detailed plan that we developed two years earlier in response to an Emergency Mutual Aid Compact (EMAC) request for Hurricane Katrina. Though we were "stood down" just hours before departure, the lessons learned from having to build a response team from scratch paid off.

EMAC, ratified by the U.S. Congress in 1996, is the first national disaster–relief compact since the Civil Defense and Disaster Compact of 1950. All 50 states, the District of Columbia, Puerto Rico, Guam, U.S. Virgin Islands, and the Northern Mariana Islands are members. EMAC offers assistance during governor-declared states of emergency or disaster through a responsive, straightforward system that allows states to send personnel, equipment, and commodities to assist with response and recovery efforts in other states. EMAC has been activated nationwide through state emergency management offices numerous times in the past several decades, most notably for 9/11 and for Hurricanes Katrina and Rita in 2005 (EMAC, 2021). Local public works agencies as well as state DOTs have contributed personnel and equipment in most of these catastrophes. Again, from this author's experiences with local, regional, state, and national disasters, the sudden onset of such demands that all agencies have a minimal "standby" capability at all times. Even small agencies should establish "mission ready packages" that are available if only for localized events.

Training

The police and fire disciplines have well-defined qualifications, standards, and credentialing set by national professional organizations and formally adopted by state and local governments. In contrast, little is available, or required, for public works/transportation employees. This lack of professional training and certification keeps public works in low regard by the other disciplines. Though public works/transportation employees are typically required to have nominal NIMS training (typically one or two basic courses) there is not much motivation to pursue additional NIMS or other training. Furthermore, many public works/transportation agencies have not incorporated NIMS concepts, principles, and practices into routine non-emergency work as recommended by FEMA.

Working with the other departments and agencies within their jurisdictions on planning, preparing, and exercises creates opportunities for public works officials to improve communication and collaboration while impressing upon them that they are full and equal partners with a "seat at the table." More to the point, to gain recognition and acceptance, public works officials must be able to "talk the talk" with their counterparts in the emergency management arena and, very importantly, actively participate in meetings, drills, and exercises. From this author's experience, police, fire, and emergency management professionals are unaware of what resources and capabilities public works has and also that our routine operational posture is not 24/7/365 like theirs. Police and fire are required to take more of FEMA's on-line Independent Study (IS) and Incident Command System (ICS) in-person classes depending upon their respective ranks. To get on an equal footing, suggested courses for public works include:

Group A (IS-100 is for all employees; IS-200 for crew leaders and supervisors):

IS-100	Introduction to Incident Command System
IS-200	Incident Command System for Single Resources and Initial Action Incidents
IS-700	Introduction to National Incident Management System
ICS300	Intermediate Incident Command System**
ICS400	Advanced Incident Command System**
	(**300 and 400 courses in-classroom only for supervisors, superintendents, managers, directors)

Group B (for superintendents, managers, directors):

IS-552	Public Works Role in Emergency Management
IS-553	Coordination between Water Utilities and Emergency Management Agencies

IS-554	Emergency Planning for Public Works
IS-556	Damage Assessment for Public Works
IS-558	Public Works and Disaster Recovery
IS-559	Local Damage Assessment
IS-632	Introduction to Debris Operations
IS-633	Debris Management Plan Development
IS-15	Special Events Contingency Planning for Public Safety Agencies
IS 775	Emergency Operations Center Management and Operations
IS 271	Anticipating Hazardous Weather and Community Risk
IS 393	Introduction to Hazard Mitigation
IS-1010	Emergency Protective Measures
IS-1011	Roads and Culverts

Group C (recommended for those with extensive role in planning and collaboration):

IS-703	National Incident Management System Resource Management
IS-706	NIMS Intrastate Mutual Aid
IS 800	Introduction to National Response Framework
IS-860	The National Infrastructure Protection Plan
IS-2000	National Preparedness Goal and System Overview
IS-2200	Basic Emergency Operations Center Functions
IS-2500	National Prevention Framework
IS-2600	National Protection Framework
IS-2700	National Mitigation Framework
IS-2900	National Disaster Recovery Framework
G205	Recovery from Disaster, the Local Government Role

Courses for specific leadership positions in an Emergency Operations Center (EOC) are offered through state emergency management departments or at FEMA's Emergency Management Institute (EMI). Additionally, for roadway maintenance and operations personnel, FHWA's Transportation Security and Emergency Preparedness Professional Capacity Building produced the "National Incident Management System Workbook for State Department of Transportation Frontline Workers" in 2009, a concise overview of NIMS and ICS.

(Federal Highway Administration, 2021b)

Resource Typing of Personnel and Equipment

The Stafford Act Section 219 requires a FEMA report that, "identifies public works repair teams…and assesses the feasibility of developing a national network of teams that can be deployed through EMAC to conduct emergency repairs necessary to restore critical services in an area affected by a disaster." This emphatically recognizes public works/transportation as an essential emergency responder. FEMA Resource Typing of Personnel lists hundreds of positions among the various disciplines but just a few (Director, Supervisor, Safety Specialist, Equipment Operator, etc.) are specific to public works. As an example, this is part of the description for a Public Works Support Team:

1. Supports local public works departments during incident response operations and recovery.
2. Provides backup relief for local public works department staff during extended operations.

3. Supports normal public works operations in addition to emergency response needs.
4. Reviews damage assessments and cost estimates for repair and replacement recorded by the Damage Assessment Team – as Public Works (Authority Having Jurisdiction) determines.
5. Is multidisciplinary and may provide support in the following areas, based on incident need:
   a. Solid waste management
   b. Roadway and bridge maintenance and construction
   c. Traffic management
   d. Fleet management
   e. Building management
   f. Water, wastewater, stormwater, and reuse water management
   g. Public and private utilities
   h. Parks and urban forestry
   i. Other public works functions, as necessary

(https://www.fema.gov/sites/default/files/2020-10/fema_public-works-
support-team_draft-resource-typing-definition.pdf)

The Team Leader must have completed: "IS-100; IS-200; ICS-300; IS-554; IS-556; IS-558; IS- 559; IS-632; and Occupational Safety and Health Administration Hazard Material Awareness."

(https://rtlt.preptoolkit.fema.gov/Public/Position/View/7-509-1377?p=18)

In addition, FEMA's Equipment Resource Typing lists for public works has the most categories due to the wide range of functional responsibilities. Not every jurisdiction has or needs all categories but much of what is listed can be critically needed in a disaster. Keeping vehicles and machines operable and available is just as important. A wheeled loader serves no purpose if it has not been properly maintained and routinely inspected. The majority of FEMA grant funding has gone to other disciplines, notably police, fire, and EMS. Public works needs to be more aggressive in competing for grants that could purchase or upgrade equipment. The following is from FEMA State Homeland Security Grants 2011; though the emphasis is on preparedness for terrorism, it acknowledges an all-hazards approach:

> Activities implemented under SHSP must support terrorism preparedness by building or enhancing capabilities that relate to the prevention of, protection from, response to, and recovery from terrorism in order to be considered eligible. However, many capabilities which support terrorism preparedness simultaneously support preparedness for other hazards. Grantees must demonstrate this dual-use quality for any activities implemented under this program that are not explicitly focused on terrorism preparedness.
>
> (Federal Emergency Management Agency, 2021a)

In other words, equipment, supplies, facilities, etc. procured to counteract terrorism must also be available and used for other emergencies such as natural disasters. For instance, dump trucks, loaders, backhoes, skid-steers, jet-vac trucks, and crane trucks would be available for routine work as well.

The National Response Framework and Public Works

The National Response Framework (NRF) is a guide for all response organizations to prepare for and provide a unified national response to all disasters and emergencies from the smallest incident to the largest catastrophe. It defines the key principles, roles, and structures. Incidents include potential as well as actual emergencies; even planned special events (PSE) should be managed using the NRF and NIMS. The NRF emphasizes that incidents must be managed at the lowest possible jurisdictional level and support obtained from others only when its own capabilities are insufficient. As incidents change in size, scope, and span, the response must also change to meet the demands. Local agencies must be prepared to handle emergencies without state or federal assistance for up to the first 72 hours. Even when the higher levels of government step in, the local jurisdictions will often still be responsible for overall management. The standard organizational structure is based on ICS and requires an Incident Commander (IC). Depending on the situation, the IC may add a Command staff consisting of Officers for Safety, Public Information and Liaison, and General staff comprised of Chiefs for Operations, Planning, Logistics, and Finance sections. If the situation expands and involves multiple agencies and jurisdictions, a Unified Command is established. In this context, public works managers must be prepared that, in some situations, they will either be the Incident Commander or assigned to a position on the Command or General staff. Certain types of emergencies are more likely to have public works assume the lead role, either initially or transferred to them later. For instance, floods or hurricanes can be anticipated and proactive measures taken. Neither police nor fire can prevent or mitigate the impact of these natural events but public works can. And, in the aftermath, public works will be doing the most work and for the longest time in regard to response and recovery.

Another example of where public works/transportation should, quite obviously, assume incident command is snow and ice control. Winter maintenance operations are an opportunity for public works agencies to demonstrate their ability to plan, organize, and implement effective and efficient emergency operations. Snow removal may seem routine in many parts of the country but requires thorough preparation, judgment, decisiveness, and adaptability, the same skills needed for any emergency. Storms will vary considerably and the effort expended by public works/transportation over a period of time may equal or surpass that for other emergencies. In fact, a number of public works/transportation agencies have incorporated NIMS/ICS protocols into their winter operations plans.

Preparedness

Unlike police and fire, who continually train and drill for many specific contingencies, public works/transportation agencies, with a few exceptions, spend little time on planning and preparation for emergencies. Obviously, it is not necessary or advisable to plan for *every* conceivable event. Instead, each agency should perform a threat and vulnerability analysis by reviewing historical incidents, evaluating the likelihood of such to occur again, and estimating the probability of other events. This is known as risk assessment that considers factors such as resources needed, including workforce, to manage multiple incidents simultaneously. FEMA defines preparedness as "a continuous cycle of planning, organizing, training, equipping, exercising, evaluating, and taking corrective action in an effort to ensure effective coordination during incident response." Likely tasks of public works agencies during response operations that should be addressed in planning include:

- Traffic control
- Detours
- Evacuation routes
- Assisting with evacuation rescue
- Site security/perimeter control
- Hazardous material containment
- Debris clearance/removal
- Fatality recovery
- Constructing staging area

(Department of Homeland Security Plan and Prepare for Disasters. https://www.dhs.gov/plan-and-prepare-disasters)

APWA offers the following books and pamphlets useful for developing or revising an Emergency Operations Plan (EOP):

- Emergency Management: Field Manual for Public Works (2003)
- Recovery Operations Field Manual (2010)
- Incident Command System Pocket Guide (2006)
- Writing Your Emergency/Disaster Plan (2005)

Likewise, FHWA also produces guidance to aid state and local jurisdictions in planning for traffic incident operations, incident management for transportation professionals, evacuation planning and operations, traffic management center as information sources for Emergency Operations Centers and Fusion Centers, and traffic planning for special events. The Traffic Incident and Events Management Team focuses its efforts on supporting the needs of local, regional, tribal, and state transportation organizations. The "Simplified Guide to the Incident Command System for Transportation Professionals" and other useful publications are available at https://ops.fhwa.dot.gov/publications/ics_guide/.

The Transportation Research Board (TRB), a division of the National Academy of Sciences, also produces quality reference materials that may be used by public works and transportation in planning for emergency management. The National Cooperative Highway Research Program (NCHRP) produced "A Guide to Emergency Response Planning at State Transportation Agencies" as part of its 525 Transportation Security series. Other projects that may be useful to public works/transportation include:

- 20-6/20-59 (41)   Legal Definition of First Responder
- 20-7/239   Incident Management and Multi-Agency Emergency Response Functions
- 20-59 (11)   Emergency Traffic Operations Management
- 20-59 (19   Transportation Response Options; Role in Public Health Emergencies

- 20-59 (23)   Guide to Emergency Response Planning at State Transportation Agencies
- 20-59 (30)   Role of Transportation in ICS and NIMS
- 20-59 (37)   Debris Management Handbook for Local and State DOTs

Debris management is the most common, most costly, and most contentious emergency function of public works. For those agencies to be reimbursed by FEMA in a presidential-declared disaster, thorough, rigorous documentation of every truckload of debris is compulsory. Stiff procedures and policies must be followed in letting contracts for debris removal and disposal.

The Role of Public Works in Traffic Incident Management

Traffic incidents are unplanned roadway events that affect or impede the normal flow of traffic, increase the likelihood of secondary crashes, and pose a threat to the safety of incident responders as well as the traveling public. Traffic Incident Management (TIM) consists of a planned and coordinated multi-disciplinary process to detect, respond to, and clear traffic incidents to restore traffic flow as safely and quickly as possible. Public works/transportation agencies have a significant role in TIM. Generally speaking, the policies, practices, protocols, and procedures for TIM are very similar to those for all-hazards emergencies. Most traffic incidents are minor and do not involve public works/transportation agencies; however, when they do, then public works/transportation can gain experience working with the other disciplines that also helps to better plan and prepare for other situations.

According to the AASHTO 2015 report, "Fundamental Capabilities of Effective All-Hazards Infrastructure, Protection, Resilience and Emergency Management for State Departments of Transportation":

> DOT efforts have improved emergency response planning and training since 2007. When an emergency occurs, routine day-to-day operations give way to a focused, practiced, and resilient crisis management approach that requires professional skills throughout the breadth and depth of the organization. Traffic Incident Management (TIM) provides processes and procedures for responders (firefighters, emergency medical services, law enforcement, towing and recovery, safety patrols, transportation and maintenance crews, and 911 professionals) to work together as a team to clear incidents safely and quickly. The National Incident Management System (NIMS) and Incident Command System (ICS) integrates best practices into a comprehensive framework for use by emergency management personnel at the local, state, and federal levels.

Chapter 6-I of the FHWA "Manual of Uniform Traffic Control Devices" (MUTCD, 2009) defines a traffic incident as, "an emergency road user occurrence, a natural disaster, or other unplanned event that affects or impedes the normal flow of traffic." It classifies traffic incidents as:

- Minor – expected duration under 30 minutes
- Intermediate – expected duration of 30 minutes to 2 hours
- Major – expected duration of more than 2 hours.

(Federal Highway Administration, 2021a)

Typical causes of traffic incidents include vehicle collisions and breakdowns; debris, large objects, or spills on the roadway; flooding, ice, mudslides, landslides, or avalanches; heavy smoke, dust, or fog interfering with visibility; pavement, bridge, overpass, or tunnel failures; pedestrians obstructing traffic such as during demonstrations; non-accident-related medical emergencies; loose animals on the roadway; police and fire activity on or near roadway. Public works/transportation will definitely be needed in some of these situations. If the duration of the incident exceeds 24 hours, then public works/transportation will usually have command. TIM is based on the principles of NIMS but is more specific and involves "Core Competencies" such as scene management, chain of command, and use of temporary traffic control (TTC). To provide for responder safety, prevention of secondary crashes, and excessive traffic delays, specific TTC measures are required and will vary according to the type, scope, and duration of a traffic incident. Public works/transportation employees have extensive training and experience with TTC practices routinely used while working on roadways. Police, fire, and other responders, however, lack that training and even sufficient basic TTC devices. The FHWA's Office of Emergency Transportation Operations (ETO) states on its Traffic Incident Management website (2009) that:

> Transportation agencies are typically responsible for the overall planning and implementation of traffic incident management programs. These agencies are also involved in the development, implementation, and operation of traffic operations centers (TOC), as well as the management of service patrols. Operational responsibilities by public works/transportation agencies include:

- assist in incident detection and verification
- initiate traffic management strategies on incident impacted facilities
- protect the incident scene
- initiate emergency medical assistance until help arrives
- provide traffic control
- assist motorist with disabled vehicles
- provide motorist information
- provide sand for absorbing small fuel and anti-freeze spills
- provide special equipment clearing incident scenes
- determine incident clearance and roadway repair needs
- establish and operate alternate routes
- coordinate clearance and repair resources
- serve as incident commander for clearance and repair functions
- repair transportation infrastructure.

(Federal Highway Administration, 2021c)

Public works/transportation tasks for TIM are quite similar to those for all-hazards emergencies. As noted in FHWA's "Best Practices in Traffic Incident Management," (2010) "Within transportation agencies, personnel assigned to TIM duties have other full-time responsibilities in maintenance, traffic engineering, intelligent transportation systems (ITS), or emergency management. Unlike public safety agencies, whose personnel devote much of their time to training for emergency or life-threatening situations, transportation personnel are typically not trained in such areas." This is an important point similar, if not identical, to all-hazards emergency response.

(https://ops.fhwa.dot.gov/publications/fhwahop10050x/index.htm)

Since the FHWA launched the TIM for Responders course in 2013, thousands of public works/transportation personnel have taken the four-hour course but thousands more need the training. It is available at online or in-person classes provided by state DOTs and Emergency Management departments, and organizations such as the National Highway Institute (NHI), American Traffic Safety Services Association (ATSSA), International Municipal Signal Association (IMSA), the Responder Safety Learning Network, and APWA. FHWA also offers an eight-hour TIM Train-the-Trainer course.

Public Works Role in Planned Special Events

Lastly, the same principles, concepts, and techniques used for handling emergencies can be applied to planned special events (PSE) such as political conventions, major sports and entertainment events, demonstrations, and parades. Even small jurisdictions will eventually have an event that will draw large crowds. Security, safety, and access in and around the event must be ensured and public works is often involved in some capacity. NIMS and ICS should be used to facilitate the planning, preparation, and implementation of event management. According to the FHWA:

> Unlike traffic incidents, natural disasters, and adverse weather, public agencies typically have access to information on the location, time, duration, and demand expected for a planned special event. Planning for these events also provides an opportunity for agencies to plan, coordinate, share resources, deploy Intelligent Transportation Systems (ITS) technologies, and apply proven traffic management techniques to mitigate any possible adverse impacts. This advanced planning, management, and control of traffic in support of planned special events are not yet commonly accepted or consistently applied practices.

https://ops.fhwa.dot.gov/aboutus/one_pagers/planned_events.htm

More jurisdictions are realizing that PSEs offer valuable opportunities to use multi-agency planning and coordination in a less stressful environment than an unexpected disaster. In essence, the PSEs are a real-life functional exercise allowing the agencies to practice and refine their emergency management skills and develop working relationships among agencies so important in times of crisis.

CHALLENGES AND ISSUES

Public works/transportation agencies face many challenges in planning and preparing for and responding to emergencies and disasters. Budgets have always been an issue; the United States has experienced several severe economic downturns in recent years including the Great Recession of 2008–2010 and the extraordinary COVID-19 pandemic recession of 2020–2021. As of mid-2022 the nation is once again facing a recession while contending with 40-year high inflation. Supply chain problems have plagued every sector of the economy creating shortages of critically needed materials and driving up costs. Governments though have not been immune to shortages and the rise in prices for goods and services which offset tax revenue growth. Add to that the increases in wages and benefits to recruit and retain qualified and skilled employees. Historically, when local and state governments have to trim budgets, roadway maintenance operations take a big hit and that usually means some Reduction in Force through layoffs, furloughs, and freezing vacant positions.

Prior to the pandemic, the public and private sectors were already anticipating and encountering the retirement of millions of the post-World War II or "Baby Boomer" generation. The pandemic induced many of that generation to take retirement earlier than planned, in part due to incentives offered by employers who needed to quickly and sharply reduce their workforces. The pandemic also influenced younger employees to quit because of workplace protocols and mandates, reduction in work hours or wages, and family needs at home (particularly those with young children). By early 2022, as the pandemic eased and demand for workers was high, some employees left in the Great Resignation to pursue other opportunities. Filling the vacancies, especially among the front-line public works/transportation employees considered as "emergency responders" has been difficult due to competition from the private sector and an overall negative image of the jobs. Roadway and traffic maintenance operations workers are the core of public works/transportation emergency response and recovery. Nearly all are required to have Commercial Drivers Licenses (CDL) and many also need USDOT cards. The strict background checks, medical and physical requirements, substance abuse testing, and general working conditions deter many potential applicants and also cause veteran employees to leave. Furthermore, state and county public works/transportation agencies' maintenance workers have traditionally come from rural areas and small towns but that pool of candidates has been shrinking for years. Local and state agencies need to do more to recruit women, minorities, veterans, second-career seekers, and even retirees.

Looking ahead over the next three to five years, turnover in the workforces will accelerate as more older employees reach retirement eligibility and others leave for other reasons. What that means for dealing with incidents, emergencies, and disasters is a front-line workforce that is quite inexperienced and insufficiently trained in NIMS and ICS. Also, increased turnover in police and fire departments and emergency management staffs means that their knowledge of public works/transportation capabilities, policies and procedures, and the important informal working relationships that facilitate communication and cooperation will dissipate over time.

Furthermore, the Federal government tends to continually revise, either by legislation or administrative regulations, the concepts, policies, procedures, mandates, etc. regarding overall emergency management. It is difficult for even large public works/transportation agencies to keep up with changing federal requirements, especially regarding grants for planning and preparation and for reimbursement of expenses for response and recovery.

Again, when local and state government budgets are constrained, funding for major maintenance and construction equipment purchases and upgrades takes a big cut. In emergencies, not having the proper necessary equipment is akin to trying to pound a 20-penny nail with a tack hammer. It might eventually get done but it will take a lot more time and effort. And not be as effective. Relying on contractors for assistance is often problematic as they may not be immediately available or have the needed resources. Contractors are fine when it comes to the recovery phase but availability during the response phase, in those initial hours, can be difficult even with on-call contracts or purchase orders. Another problem with reliance on contractors is that they are not trained in ICS nor have the accessibility to public safety communications systems.

Lastly, the nation's infrastructure is aging, deteriorating, and is generally approaching the end-of-life span. That means that roads, bridges, and tunnels are losing functional and resilience capacity and are more vulnerable to damage and destruction from natural events. The reliability of the surface transportation network is of vital importance not only for normal activities but also for ensuring that responders can access stricken areas and for affected populations to safely evacuate when disasters occur and for follow-on relief organizations to bring in needed supplies and services.

Federal, SLTT, and private sector assets, networks, and systems (including physical, cyber, and human components) contribute to public safety and quality of life through services such as assessing and repairing damage to buildings, roads, and bridges; clearing, removing, and disposing of debris from public spaces; restoring utility services; and managing emergency traffic. With responsibility for hardening security enhancements to critical facilities and monitoring the safety of public water supplies, public works is an integral component of a jurisdiction's emergency planning efforts. In addition, public works departments supply heavy machinery, raw materials, and emergency operators and may also manage contracts for additional labor, equipment, or services that may be needed before, during, and after an incident.

Recommendations for the Future

As mentioned, the roadway/traffic maintenance and operations workforces are the frontline of public works/transportation agencies; among the first to respond in emergencies and usually the last to leave as the recovery winds down. Yet, this workforce is often not recognized by the other responder disciplines, the community, and even governing officials for its contributions. APWA adopted a Public Works First Responder logo several years ago to promote better awareness and understanding (Figure 21.1).

Through its Emergency Management committee, APWA has developed a number of publications including checklists to prepare for, respond to, and recover from earthquakes, floods, hurricanes, ice storms, tornadoes, and wildfires; Public Works Incident Management Manual; Principles of Emergency Management; and Writing Your Emergency/Disaster Plan. Aside from these, there is very little literature specifically addressing the role of public works/transportation in emergency management.

To raise awareness among the other responder disciplines, FEMA, the public, and elected officials at all government levels, public works/transportation has to promote its role in emergency management.

It begins with formally incorporating emergency management into an agency's mission statement and organizational structure. Policies and plans are developed, disseminated, and periodically, at least once a year, discussed in briefings with all employees.

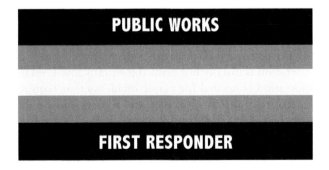

FIGURE 21.1   American Public Works Association First Responder Logo (Source: APWA)

They should also be reviewed every several years, or after a major event, and revised as needed.

Next is to ensure that all employees, depending upon their positions, have the relevant training. For example, a field supervisor may need ICS-200 but an administrative clerk assigned to work in the Emergency Operations Center would benefit from training on the various forms and reports used there. Higher-level employees would need the more advanced ICS courses, perhaps even attending FEMA's Emergency Management Institute.

Participation with police, fire, and emergency management officials (each county and state is required to have an emergency management department or office) in meetings, table-top exercises, and drills is highly important. Having a "seat at the table" is essential to build trust and understanding. If necessary, the public works agency should initiate these discussions if they have been infrequent or if they have not been invited before.

Planning and preparation within public works/transportation agencies for likely hazards and threats should be ongoing. In fact, most already do such for winter road maintenance, hurricane season, and recurring major special events (like college football games, and county and state fairs). Envisioning likely scenarios for a range of incidents helps to be better prepared for the more unlikely. Assessing what the impacts would be and the resources – personnel, equipment, supplies, money and time – needed, comparing with what is currently available, and then determining how to best fill the gaps is essential.

Most important is having well-trained, informed, and skilled personnel. As mentioned earlier, agencies are dealing with high turnover and difficulty filling vacancies. They need to work with the Human Resources departments to revise job descriptions and classification schedules based on the expanded duties, responsibilities, skills, and knowledge required for a workforce capable and ready for all-hazards events from traffic incidents to regional or national catastrophes.

CONCLUSION

Public works/transportation has unique responsibilities, capabilities, and resources vital for situations from traffic incidents and minor emergencies to natural, technical, and terrorism catastrophes. Most emergencies are handled at the local level; but even when state and federal assistance is needed the local agency will still be very much involved. Every public works supervisor or manager must be ready to take charge as the initial Incident Commander or serve in a key position on the Command or General staffs in an Emergency Operations Center. All local public works and state DOT personnel must be trained to properly fulfill their missions. Public works leadership must affirm emergency management as a core function along with design, construction, and maintenance of infrastructure and provision of services.

Public works/transportation also has a distinct role in Traffic Incident Management though it is still not fully recognized by the other disciplines. That is due to the fact that public works/transportation is usually not needed for many low-level incidents. However, public works/transportation is needed for major incidents that require extensive temporary traffic control, detours, and road clearance and repairs. How public works responds to these situations is similar to all-hazards emergencies. The policies, protocols, and partnerships established for Traffic Incident Management are based on the Incident Command System and Unified Command structures employed for other events and disasters. Instituting these practices into routine operations prepares public works/transportation agencies to effectively respond to any emergency.

The national preparedness missions of response and recovery are still the primary emergency management functions of public works/transportation but more attention is being directed toward Mitigation as well. While some may still debate the existence of and causes of global climate change, what is undeniable is that this nation, and other countries, are experiencing increasingly severe and frequent natural disasters. Compounding the impacts of those events is the increase in population density in areas more vulnerable to floods, wildfires, extreme heat, exceptional drought, hurricanes, tornadoes, and sea-level rise. Additionally, the potential for devastating earthquakes in California and elsewhere, volcanic eruptions in Hawaii, and tsunamis along the Pacific Coast are threats that agencies should also prepare for. Public works/transportation agencies, and the Federal government, look for innovative and feasible ways to mitigate the disruptive effects of these events.

Though prevention and protection missions are the domain of national intelligence services and law enforcement, public works/transportation personnel, particularly those that work on the roadways and other public infrastructure, are in a position to observe, detect, and report suspicious activity and conditions that may be related to terrorism. In sum, the public works/transportation discipline, recognized by FEMA as a key element in its Emergency Service Sector, is critical to the security and safety of every community and of the United States as a whole (Cybersecurity and Infrastructure Security Agency, 2021).

CLASS DISCUSSION AND ESSAY QUESTIONS

1. Most people do not really understand what public works is or does. How would you explain the general responsibilities of this organization in government to someone who is unfamiliar with the concept and public department?
2. What changes in societies led to the creation of public works, and how did this profession evolve internationally and in the United States?
3. What functions does public works perform as part of comprehensive emergency management?
4. This chapter recommended training for those working in and with public works. What type of training would be important and why is it necessary?
5. How will retirements and turnover impact public works as it relates to emergency management and homeland security? What can be done about these challenges?
6. Public works wants a "seat at the table." What does this imply as it relates to disaster mitigation and emergency management planning?

REFERENCES

American Association of State Highway Transportation Officials. (2015). Fundamental Capabilities of Effective All-Hazards Infrastructure, Protection, Resilience and Emergency Management for State Departments of Transportation. https://ctssr.transportation.org/wp-content/uploads/sites/54/2017/10/Fundamental-Capabilities-of-Effective.pdf

American Public Works Association. (2003). Essential Role of Public Works in Emergency Management. https://www.apwa.net/MyApwa/Apwa_Public/Focus_on_Public_Works/emergency_management.aspx

American Public Works Association. What Is Public Works? https://www.apwa.net/MYAPWA/About/What_is_Public_Works/MyApwa/Apwa_Public/About/What_Is_Public_Works.aspx Accessed August 22, 2022

Birkland, T. A. (2017, May 3). Close the Turkey Farm. *Pacific Standard*. https://psmag.com/news/close-the-turkey-farm-4039

Cybersecurity and Infrastructure Security Agency. (2021). Emergency Services Sector. https://www.cisa.gov/emergency-services-sector

Department of Homeland Security. (2021a). Homeland Security Presidential Directive 5. https://www.dhs.gov/publication/homeland-security-presidential-directive-5

Department of Homeland Security. (2021b). Presidential Policy Directive / PPD-8: National Preparedness. https://www.dhs.gov/presidential-policy-directive-8-national-preparedness

Department of Homeland Security Plan and Prepare for Disasters. https://www.dhs.gov/plan-and-prepare-disasters.

EMAC. (2021). Emergency Management Assistance Compact. https://www.emacweb.org/index.php/learn-about-emac/emac-history

Federal Emergency Management Agency. (2021a). Homeland Security Grant Program. https://www.fema.gov/grants/preparedness/homeland-security

Federal Emergency Management Agency. (2021b). National Preparedness Goal. https://www.fema.gov/emergency-managers/national-preparedness/mission-core-capabilities

Federal Emergency Management Agency. (2021c). National Preparedness Framework. https://www.fema.gov/emergency-managers/national-preparedness/frameworks/response

Federal Emergency Management Agency. (2021d). Resource Typing Library Tool. https://rtlt.preptoolkit.fema.gov/Public/Combined?p=18

Federal Emergency Management Agency. Public Works Support Team. https://www.fema.gov/sites/default/files/2020-10/fema_public-works-support-team_draft-resource typing definition.pdf).

Federal Emergency Management Agency. (2021e). The Stafford Act. https://www.fema.gov/disaster/stafford-act

Federal Highway Administration, Security and Emergency Management – Briefing for Executives and Senior Leaders in State Departments of Transportation.2017. https://www.fhwa.dot.gov/security/emergencymgmt/profcapacitybldg/docs/hsemexecsr-rleaders/hsem_srexecs.cfm)

Federal Highway Administration. (2021a). Manual of Uniform Traffic Control Devices (MUTCD), Chapter 6-I. 2009 edition. https://mutcd.fhwa.dot.gov/htm/2009/part6/part6i.htm

Federal Highway Administration. (2021b). The National Incident Management System – A Workbook for State Department of Transportation Frontline Workers, 2009. https://www.fhwa.dot.gov/security/emergencymgmt/profcapacitybldg/docs/nims/nims_wkbk.cfm

Federal Highway Administration. (2021c). Office of Emergency Transportation Operations Traffic Incident Management Website. https://ops.fhwa.dot.gov/tim/

Geary, D. and Fessler, T. (2011). Public Works Emergency Management - From Training to Reality. March 23, 2011. https://www.domesticpreparedness.com/preparedness/public-works-emergency-management-from-training-to-reality/

Lawson, J. L. (2001). *Internal Improvements: National Public Works and the Promise of Popular Government in the Early*. Chapel Hill, NC: University of North Carolina Press.

Library of Congress. (2021a). Cities During the Progressive Era. https://www.loc.gov/classroom-materials/united-states-history-primary-source-timeline/progressive-era-to-new-era-1900-1929/cities-during-progressive-era/#

Library of Congress. (2021b). Rural Life in the Late 19th Century. https://www.loc.gov/classroom-materials/united-states-history-primary-source-timeline/rise-of-industrial-america-1876-1900/rural-life-in-late-19th-century/

Longfellow, R. (2021). Back in Time: The National Road. Federal Highway Administration. https://www.fhwa.dot.gov/infrastructure/

National Research Council; Committee on Infrastructure Innovation (1987). *Infrastructure for the 21st Century: Framework for a Research Agenda.* Washington, D.C. doi:10.17226/798. ISBN 978-0-309-07814-6.

National Research Council. (2012). Disaster Resilience: A National Imperative. Washington, DC: The National Academies Press. https://doi.org/10.17226/13457.

National Response Framework https://www.fema.gov/emergency-managers/national-preparedness/frameworks/response.

Stanford. (2021). History of American Railroads. https://cs.stanford.edu/people/eroberts/cs181/projects/corporate-monopolies/development_rr.html

US History. (2021). Rise of American Industry: 25.a. The Canal Era. https://www.ushistory.org/us/25a.asp

Wikipedia. (2021a). Boston Post Road. https://en.wikipedia.org/wiki/Boston_Post_RoadWikipedia

Wikipedia. (2021b). City Beautiful Movement. https://en.wikipedia.org/wiki/City_Beautiful_movement

Wikipedia. (2021c). Erie Canal. https://en.wikipedia.org/wiki/erie.canal

Wikipedia. (2021d). Municipal or Urban Engineering. Wikipedia. https://en.wikipedia.org/wiki/Municipal_or_urban_engineering

Wildfire Today. (2012). Is FEMA a Turkey Farm? December 12, 2012. https://wildfiretoday.com/2008/12/12/is-fema-a-turkey-farm/

CHAPTER 22

The Information Technology Specialist:
From Zero to Hero in Emergency Management and Homeland Security

Jackson Roberts and David A. McEntire

INTRODUCTION

For generations, any threat or task associated with emergency management and homeland security was accurately considered to be handled within blue- and white-collar careers. These careers included men and women in designated uniforms to prevent attacks or respond to disasters, managers on the ground to facilitate the movement of supplies, and other actors who share information and coordinate across organizations. However, in this generation, another player has entered the game: the information technology specialist. Stereotypically imagined as an overweight, poorly dressed, anti-social male with glasses, these information technology (IT) specialists have rapidly found themselves on the front lines of both homeland security and emergency management.

This transition is increasingly important. As the world's information and technology advances, so do the threats and vulnerabilities that this nation faces. For most of this nation's history, threats or hazards could be typically summarized as physical. These threats consisted mainly of warfare or natural disasters. However, the world today is much more connected and complicated and, thus, more vulnerable. For the first time ever, someone can sit down in a basement thousands of miles away and create devastating effects on a mass number of people using technology. One example of this is the recent Colonial Pipeline attack. In one hack, millions of Americans were affected and could have been left without critical needs to fulfill the necessities of their everyday lives if this was not immediately corrected. Of course, this was not the first cyberattack, nor will it be the last. Most experts agree that the threat and consequences of cyberattacks are likely to become worse before getting better.

With this introduction in mind, the following chapter will provide accurate and educational information on five perspectives regarding information technology specialists. It will first provide a detailed history on the creation, development, and major milestones of information technology specialists. Next, the chapter will discuss the relation of IT specialists to terrorism and disasters and identify how these individuals went from support positions to the front line in these disruptive and even dangerous events. The chapter will

DOI: 10.4324/9781003350729-22

then discuss the role of the information technology specialist in homeland security and emergency management, followed by information on the current challenges and threats they face, as well as how we could make these tasks easier legislatively, politically, and organizationally.

HISTORY OF THE IT SPECIALIST

An information technology specialist, more commonly known as an IT specialist, is defined differently within government and private organizations. This section will focus on how information technology specialists are defined and how they operate from a governmental perspective.

Field Engineer (2023) describes an information technology specialist as individuals who:

> can work in various areas of information technology. They work in the help desk to redress the problems that end users face. Specialists can also don roles of software engineers, software developers, database administrators, system analysts, computer security technicians, and network analysts, among others. Regardless of the area they work in, IT support specialist job descriptions will require strong analytical skills, along with familiarity with different operating systems, such as Windows, macOS or Linux, and proficiency in one or more programming languages.

This job description, which requires a diverse and dynamic skill set, illustrates the difficulty in becoming, or even finding, a qualified information technology specialist. One must also consider that an information specialist working in a government capacity not only needs the above qualifications, but they must also be thoroughly screened to receive the proper security clearances, certifications, and access privileges so often needed for information technology specialists working in the emergency management or national security fields.

Regardless of how this profession is defined or described, an information technology specialist is a relatively new concept and position. One would not find the position on any company's payroll, nor would they have interacted with any of these employees throughout most of history. In fact, the first concept of an IT specialist was developed in the 1960s with individuals tasked specifically with the construction and maintenance of computers, though these individuals were typically engineers and the equipment was maintained by other scientists. This is a dramatic difference from today where IT specialists no longer construct computers, as most of their work is in maintaining and repairing software (Wikipedia, 2022).

The need for information technology specialists was fostered almost uniquely by the creation and development of computers. The invention of the "first computer" is a debated topic to say the least, with claims of the earliest machine being invented in 1822 by Charles Babbage (Freiberger, 2020). However, regardless of when the "first" legitimate computer appeared, between the early 1800s and the mid-1950s progress was slow but major milestones were made as computers became more versatile, programmable, and eventually, portable. It was in the 1970s when computers first began to be a common item at home and at work, and thus the first need for information technology specialists was born. Early on, these computers certainly did not show many of the technical vulnerabilities that we see today. As a double-edged sword, these computers were quite simple, meaning there was little margin for error or mistake because the coding itself was not overly complicated. This also meant that very little could be done with them in terms of nefarious actions.

As can be seen in Figure 22.1, the job market for IT specialists has changed dramatically over the last ten years. It illustrates that demand in the job market for qualified personnel in computer and mathematical jobs has outpaced every other major field's growth. It continues to outpace them at an exponential rate and is likely to grow even further as cyber threats appear over time.

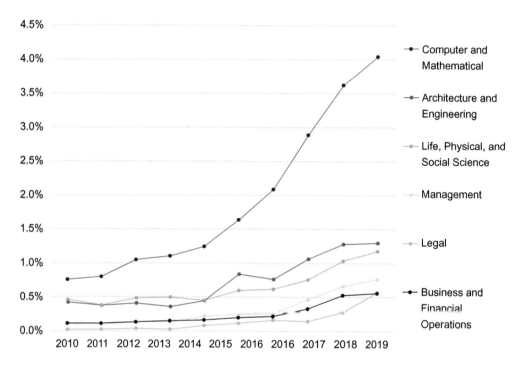

FIGURE 22.1   Growth in Demand in Job Market (Alekseeva et al., 2020)

Current Challenges for the IT Specialist

The Cybersecurity and Infrastructure Security Agency (an organization of the Department of Homeland Security established in 2018) defines and describes five threats to cybersecurity in America. The section below will discuss and provide examples of each of the five individually.

National Governments

Currently, nation-states certainly seem to pose the greatest cyber threat to the United States. According to the CISA report, government are developing capabilities with the intent to cause widespread impacts on U.S. critical infrastructures." Nation-states uniquely possess the institutional stability, funding, and training necessary to build and maintain offensive and defensive cybersecurity divisions. As we grow increasingly dependent upon technology, our enemies are becoming increasingly clever in their attacks on critical government servers and private institutions like banks and retail stores. Imagine if Wal-Mart were to suddenly lose access to their central servers and communication between stores. Billions of dollars would be lost, millions of Americans' identities would be compromised, and concern over identity theft would be nationwide. For these reasons, nation- states pose the greatest threat to the United States.

Some examples of nation-states that pose a threat to national security in America include China, Iran, North Korea, and Russia, who, in particular, have been getting more involved and bolder in cyberattacks against the United States government and the private sector in the West. China primarily practices espionage and intellectual property theft, defined as the stealing of one's ideas, creative products, or other inventions. This can include ideas, logos, and sensitive national security information. In fact, between May 2021 and February 2022, China-based hackers compromised six U.S. state government networks (Kharpal, 2022), giving them access to confidential information and records. Alternatively, Iran routinely seeks retaliation against the United States and primarily uses ransomware against our private sector, compromising and holding for ransom servers, information, and passwords (Das, 2021). North Korea, while not as technologically advanced as many of our other adversaries, seeks to harm the United States through criminal activities on the web such as the robbery of nearly $400 million worth of crypto currency in 2021 (BBC, 2022). Nonetheless, the biggest cybersecurity threat today comes from Russia. In fact, from 2007 to 2016 alone, Russia was responsible for over a dozen significant cyberattacks on foreign nations, starting with satellites of former Soviet countries, first in 2007, then quickly moving on to western nations such as the United States (Windrem, 2016). While there is a plethora of options when executing a cyberattack, Russia has historically leaned slightly toward attacks on government and military networks. It has also focused heavily on political stages and platforms such as flooding social media sites with misinformation to interfere with and influence elections. In some cases, Russia has shut elections down completely as they did with Ukraine in 2014; three days before the election, the election commission as well as its backup servers were disabled overnight by Russian hackers (Windrem, 2016).

Terrorists

Terrorists, like nation-states, recognize America's dependence upon technology and actively seek to disrupt or destroy those services to inhibit our security and way of life. Terrorists, however, do not always have the infrastructure, funding, and time like nation-states to execute effective and wide-range attacks. For these and other reasons, terrorists tend to focus on physical attacks as opposed to those in the cyber realm.

With varying degrees of success, some terrorist organizations who have sought, or do seek, to harm American citizens or government servers in the cyber field include ISIS, al Qaeda, and numerous non-government-sanctioned groups located in China and Russia.

Industrial Spies and Organized Crime Groups

Spies and organized crime groups also pose varying degrees of threat to the United States. These groups primarily focus on espionage and monetary theft. Sometimes it is difficult to distinguish between nation-state espionage and criminal groups because they could be intermingled. In fact, many states sponsor and promote spies and organized crime but deny any involvement whatsoever.

There is very little information about or acknowledged events of cyberattacks by spies typically because governments do not want to show that they have been breached; most of these attacks by spies are done, in fact, for a government. For this reason, America has dealt with cyberattacks from spies with ties to China, Russia, North Korea, Iran, and other countries.

Since the goals of criminal groups are profit-based, these actors are unlikely to make attacks which negatively affect a large portion of the population. In most cases, criminal groups lack a motive to seek to harm nation-states. Money seems to be their major priority.

Hacktivists

A "hacktivist" is defined as "a person who gains unauthorized access to computer files or networks in order to further social or political ends" (Dialogic 2023). Hacktivists pose a relatively small threat to the United States because of their small numbers and their priority focusing on propaganda over damage to infrastructure. In other words, hacktivists seek to support a political agenda and spread propaganda.

The most popular example of a "hacktivist" organization would be Anonymous. Anonymous is an independent group who enacts cyberattacks to promote its value of equality and protect citizens from governments. Anonymous acts with no higher loyalty such as to government or religion; it seeks instead to promote and enforce an ideology or belief. Anonymous has accordingly been involved in numerous government leaks and breaches, though none of these have sought specifically to harm citizens or disrupt everyday life like a cyberattack does.

Hackers

Aside from nation-states, hackers pose the greatest threat to national security. It is true that most hackers lack motive and ability to attack critical networks and infrastructure in the United States. However, the notable and growing number of these hackers present a large threat of isolated and brief disruptions which could, in turn, cause serious damage or impacts. This population of hackers is also growing in skill, making them a unique threat that must be taken into account in the future.

With threats coming from any of these five groups, there are numerous concerns surrounding the vulnerability and security of American servers and systems in both the government and the private sector. As was mentioned earlier under "History of the IT Specialist," it is extremely difficult to even fill the slots required within these organizations. As far as supply and demand are concerned, there is no shortage of demand for IT specialists in any capacity and almost any field within the government or private sector. But the supply is not nearly capable enough of meeting these demands, let alone providing enough supply that one could be picky in choosing the best of the best. Almost universally, incentives like higher salaries, sign-on bonuses, and on-the-job training are being offered for anyone capable or willing to become capable of filling these positions and executing the many tasks required. Even with those who are getting degrees in this field and becoming trained on a basic level, continual training, time, and practice is critical for American companies and government entities to stay up to date with current threats and development in the cyber community.

The above factors alone of an ever-changing and challenging industry should illustrate the difficulty in maintaining a fully staffed and capable information technology team. But it becomes even harder in the government where legislation and limited funding could hinder the ability to recruit, train, and retain qualified individuals.

RELATION OF THE IT SPECIALIST TO TERRORISM AND DISASTERS

As stated in "History of the Information Technology Specialist," those in the information technology field have typically not been associated with disaster response and especially not terrorism. Even up through the 1990s, there was little involvement of information technology specialists in anything other than minor technical problems in the office or at a help desk/call center. However, in the last 20 years, information technology specialists have been exposed to, closely associated with, and heavily involved in terrorism and emergency response. Information technology specialists are now thrust into terrorism and disaster response primarily out of response to our dependency on technological systems. This mainly has occurred post-2000.

For instance, the government has a long history of computer problems both within their systems and on sites or programs utilized for interaction between citizens and government agencies. Some of the most obvious examples are events that occur in every citizen's life, often numerous times. The long delays, hiccups, setbacks, and lost or incorrect information that we all face when filing taxes, renewing a driver's license or passport, or paying tickets, for example, are all typically caused by computer problems in some way, shape, or form. Whether this takes the form of information being lost when it was supposed to be transferred to another system, or just long wait times due to old and outdated computers and servers running slowly with many glitches or errors, an immeasurable amount of time and money is wasted due to computer problems and delays.

The private sector faces much less legislative restriction and delay on time and funding than the government does. The ability of businesses to act quickly and allocate funds more easily makes them much less susceptible to poor systems, overwhelmed servers, and untrained information technology specialists. They are not, however, completely exempt. Any time a business, however large or small, loses the ability to use their computers or those computers are not communicating properly, thousands to millions of dollars are lost. These losses can be due to power outages, glitches or bugs, failed servers, or cyberattacks. Cyberattacks cost all businesses in America $200K annually, with 43% of all cyberattacks worldwide focusing on small businesses; only 14% of owners claim that they are prepared to handle such attacks (Steinberg, 2020).

As our nation and the world began to integrate technology more and more into our lives, we opened up a vulnerability for any hacker around the world for cyberattack. Prior to the 2000s, much of our world still functioned on paper or closed-circuit computers, not connected to the internet, other devices, or other systems. For anyone to steal information or attack these systems, they needed to be within close proximity of the hardware; this could be thwarted by physical limitations such as a guard or even a lock. Today, however, everything from our light bulbs and our doorbells to our banking and even vehicles and air transportation, is connected on the worldwide web. As much as we try to protect these systems, we cannot deny that we enable attacks from a much larger population and the world by being connected worldwide. Nation- states, spies, and terrorists recognized this fact, making government and private sector servers a high-value target for our enemies. A well-placed and timed attack can cost millions, disrupt the lives of millions, and/or take weeks to months for recovery. Thus out of necessity, information technology specialists were given primary responsibility for protecting these essential systems and servers for the American government and its people; they continue to bear this duty.

One of the most recent examples of these attacks occurred in 2021 against the Colonial Pipeline. In the summer of 2021, the Colonial Pipeline (which provides oil from the Gulf Coast to the northeast) was attacked with a "DarkSide" ransomware. After gaining access to and locking down computers and servers controlling the pipeline, the hackers demanded a ransom of $5 million in bitcoin. The pipeline promptly paid the ransom and after regaining control, shut down their servers and some pipelines for the safety of the company and their customers. After publicly announcing the attack and the plans for restarting the system, the Federal Bureau of Investigation (FBI) launched an investigation and was able to recover about $2.3 million worth of the bitcoin ransom, though the full amount ($3.7 million worth of bitcoin) was never recovered (Partida, 2021).

ROLES OF THE IT SPECIALIST IN HOMELAND SECURITY AND EMERGENCY MANAGEMENT

In this section, five roles and their responsibilities will be outlined and discussed, including why an information technology specialist might have information regarding general operations, disaster recovery, business continuity, continuity of government, and their universal role in cybersecurity.

General Operations

The first role to be discussed in this section is in general operations. Prior to any emergency or event in homeland security, there is a substantial amount of time, money, and personnel required to make a team in homeland security and emergency management capable and effective in accomplishing their mission. Once the information technology specialists are hired and trained, they can immediately begin advising the manager of technical and procedural upgrades or changes necessary to ensure security or better accomplish the mission. The information technology specialist(s) can advise on the best equipment to be used for current systems, or to support different systems if needed. While limited by a strict budget, there is a constant demand for newer and better equipment, especially within the government.

When properly equipped (or equipped as best as possible), the information technology specialist needs to ensure that all equipment is programmed and protected. Depending on the agency, there are specific programs that must be downloaded for firewall and password protection, monitoring, tracking, or any other task required by that agency. All of this is done by the information technology specialist prior to issuing or using any of the equipment. In addition to this preparation, every government employee working with technology needs to have extensive training to use that equipment. Each year they must be recertified on technology safety, which entails training on keeping passwords strong and protected, avoiding viruses or phishing, and maintaining the security of all computer and network equipment. Information technology specialists don't necessarily oversee this training, but they must ensure that it is done prior to the use of the equipment and that the training is enforced.

The real work begins here. Once the above criteria are all sufficiently met, a high degree of funding and effort is required to maintain the equipment and training. Parts like batteries go bad, glitches and bugs are found in programs, and mistakes are made in setup, etc. Any one of these issues requires an information technology specialist who will address the problem at hand. Typically, the technology specialist can determine when a part has gone bad and then order and replace the part themselves. They also are typically skilled in troubleshooting. Whenever an error is found or a notification is given that indicates something is not working properly, an information technology specialist must be contacted to report the problem, shut it down, and take the necessary steps to correct it.

Disaster Recovery

Information technology specialists likewise play an important role in every phase of disaster, from preparation to response, and then recovering from disasters. A major way that information technology specialists assist and facilitate disaster recovery is through mitigation measures. Immediately before, during, or after a disaster – whether that be a cyberattack or a natural disaster like a hurricane or a man-made disaster – there is little that can be done by an information technology specialist. It is consequently critical for an information technology specialist to prepare for a variety of diverse and creative potential disasters and problems that could arise in order to mitigate these issues.

One way that information technology specialists can mitigate problems is in the proper securing and saving of data and programs in a way that they can be easily protected or recovered if the traditional storage methods fail. For example, having an off-site backup server allows a quick and near seamless recovery if a fire burns down the primary servers. Backup servers allow those programs to be quickly and easily re-established with the necessary connections and communications.

Another major aspect of recovery is the recovery of data, when necessary. Data recovery is defined as salvaging data that has been lost, corrupted, or damaged from secondary storage, removable media, or files when the data stored in them cannot be accessed in the usual way. This can include restoring uncorrupted files from a secure server in the case of a hack or virus that has corrupted your current software. It could also include the use of software built to combat viruses or other malware by "cleaning" files, then deleting the virus and de-corrupting the software it affected.

Business Continuity

Business continuity refers to the re-establishment and return of normal, day-to-day operations within a private sector business. Despite their best efforts to prepare for and mitigate fallout of attacks and disasters, it is simply impossible to be perfectly prepared for any situation. Thus, there will always be varying degrees of disruption to business operations. If the power goes out, then an information technology specialist may be involved in coordinating the return of power, the restarting of servers and systems used, and repairing any damaged equipment due to the disaster, among other tasks.

Continuity of Government

Similar to business continuity, there are a great deal of operations that must be evaluated, repaired, and re-established following a disaster. However, this also brings many unique challenges. The first of these is the line of succession. Especially in government, it is paramount that there is a clear line of authority and succession when that line is interrupted. Should any individual be unable or otherwise compromised, the line of succession ensures that there is always the necessary authority to authorize possible actions. One way that IT specialists help in this instance is in keeping that line of succession up to date in their systems to avoid "hiccups" as the situation develops. Continuity of government also requires, at times, the relocation of a facility when damaged, destroyed, or compromised. IT specialists also need to designate who in their unit will be responsible for any event in case others are on vacation or otherwise occupied or unavailable.

Cybersecurity

As noted earlier, cybersecurity is a major priority and concern, especially on the domestic and international levels. Cybersecurity is incredibly diverse in scope. It can address phishing methods such as whale phishing (which is using falsified information and emails to target high-level individuals such as CEOs within companies), or spear phishing (which is using falsified information and emails to target specific personnel and their equipment with less regard to their seniority in a company). Cybersecurity also focuses on the use of ransomware, viruses, malware, and others. With the variety of threats and consistency of risk, cybersecurity tends to be the primary responsibility and concern of information technology specialists. Cybersecurity defense and response can be considered in three phases: identifying threats, stopping attacks, and prosecuting those who were involved.

Intelligence in any type of operation for the government, military, or private sector is key. Intelligence facilitates faster, more accurate, and more sure decision-making. When properly informed, one is much more likely to make decisions that benefit their organization and avoid pitfalls that might not have been seen without that intelligence. To this end, it is very important that information technology specialists identify and understand our threats in the cyber realm. When we are able to identify a threat prior to that threat becoming an attack or disaster, we are enabled to predict possible actions and prepare for worst-case scenarios. This identification and preparation for threats does more to minimize the fallout of a disaster than any response, no matter how efficient, could ever hope to do otherwise. This identification of threats also enables law enforcement, domestically and internationally, to pursue and stop these threats long before disaster occurs. This is of course, preferable to preparation for attacks and disasters. However, if law enforcement is unable to stop the attack, information technology specialists can be critical in the prosecution of the identified perpetrators. They can provide evidence and testimony regarding how, when, why, and by whom an attack occurred, enabling law enforcement to prosecute and punish those involved in an attack and prevent future ones. These phases remain true on a private, domestic, and international level of cybersecurity.

RECOMMENDATIONS FOR THE FUTURE

Cybersecurity, and how to mitigate the risks associated with various threats, has been a highly debated topic for as long as a worldwide web has existed. Rights and privileges as old as this nation come under examination when determining policy and law surrounding cybersecurity, making it very difficult to pass effective legislation and allow agencies to form policy in compliance with that legislation. There are also, as discussed, a great variety of threats coming from numerous sources that pose risks to our safety every day, such as from nation-states, terrorists, and hackers. This requires thorough planning and efficient execution to defend the United States and its assets. The information below will discuss possible solutions from legislative, policy, organizational, and practical viewpoints and review pros and cons for each.

Legislative

Any legislation can be a major pro or con, depending on how it is viewed. Legislation can be extremely beneficial in the sense that it can give specific and long-term standards to be set across a wide variety of fields and organizations, and requires compliance under the law, significantly increasing incentives to abide by the legislation. However, legislation can be easily added to or subtracted from, as a negotiation tactic among politicians, which can devalue the original intent of the legislation. Legislation is also highly debated at times and takes a significant amount of negotiation to pass, causing major delays.

Legislation also could inadvertently contribute to problems instead of solving them; that legislation is much harder to fix than the problem itself. For these reasons, the "pro" of this legislation is that it provides a universal and publicly acknowledged law: an iron standard. Nevertheless, some would prefer to see benefits of this legislation and the execution of it come from within organizations and policy rather than government oversight and legislative authority. One recommendation to improve Department of Homeland Security (DHS) professionals would include legislation providing training and requiring employees to report threats that they identify, including a mandatory review and response on these threats within a certain time frame. Legislation could also be passed that outlines the necessary training that would ensure each employee can meet a certain level of competence in their field. These two recommendations would make each DHS professional more prepared to meet threats and more adept at having the resources to stop them before consequences can be realized.

Policy

Policy has undergone major developments to further cybersecurity at the national level. In the 21st century, every president has made cybersecurity a major priority and concern for their administration, providing specific plans and initiatives to protect the cyber realm. Under the Bush administration, we saw the *National Strategy to Secure Cyberspace* (Lemos, 2003). During the Obama administration, this became the *Comprehensive National Cybersecurity Initiative*, calling cybersecurity "one of the most serious economic and national security challenges we face as a nation" (Whitehouse Archives, 2009). Later under the Trump administration, great effort was made, led by CISA, to improve cybersecurity and confront our adversaries (Fidler, 2020). Most recently,

> President Biden has made cybersecurity, a critical element of the Department of Homeland Security's DHS mission, a top priority for the Biden-Harris Administration at all levels of government. To advance the President's commitment and to reflect that enhancing the nation's cybersecurity resilience is a top priority for DHS, Secretary Mayorkas issued a call to action dedicated to cybersecurity in his first month in office. This call to action focused on tackling the immediate threat of ransomware and on building a more robust and diverse workforce.
>
> (DHS, 2022)

Part of this push for action involves 60-day "sprints" announced by Secretary Mayorkas. The first sprint is titled "International Cybersecurity" and is dedicated to international activity from those outlined in the first international "CISA Global" strategy. The second 60-day sprint is titled "Election Security" and focuses on the resilience of the United States' infrastructures and elections and will make election security a top priority for the DHS. "Cybersecurity and Transportation" is the title of the next sprint and will prioritize cyber resilience for transportation systems such as rails and aviation. The next sprint, "Industrial Control Systems" will improve the resilience of industrial control systems such as water treatment plants. "Cybersecurity Workforce" is the subsequent sprint and it seeks to design a more robust and diverse cybersecurity workforce. The final sprint is titled "Ransomware" and uses the Office of the Secretary to reinforce defenses for ransomware across all sectors.

One "pro" in this plan and execution includes the involvement of different sectors. It is easy to look at cybersecurity and get overwhelmed if the government had to do it by itself. Another "pro" to this is having a fixed timeline in the form of 60-day periods in which progress can be measured and people held accountable. One "con" is that the information given publicly was very general. Most citizens would hope that the direction given during these sprints was more specific and measurable.

Organizational

Organizationally, the government has seen a massive uptick in the need for cyber-security-related employees. The Department of Defense built a team of 6,200 cyber-professionals in 2015 to adapt to modern cyber threats. The Central Intelligence Agency (CIA) has likewise stated in multiple reports that they are most interested in applicants who have a master's degree in a cyber-oriented field. The Department of Homeland Security has centralized its focus on cybersecurity and is actively updating policy and priorities to reflect the need for protection and provide it. The U.S. Government Accountability Office (GAO) has made a large effort to hire cybersecurity professionals and has a career segment on its website advertising its constant and open invitation for cyber-oriented individuals to seek employment there. The National Security Agency (NSA) is the United States' leading employer of cybersecurity personnel and actively hunts professionals to recruit. The FBI has initiated "cybersquads" in each of their 56 offices nationwide and hired 6,000 "cyberwarriors" in 2015.

Clearly, the government is recognizing the organizational needs for cyber-personnel, and there are virtually no "cons" in this approach. Organizationally, this is exactly what the nation needs. We need to create a large incentive for people to become proficient in cyber-skills and use those skills to benefit national security in the cyber-realm. It is a huge "pro" to see that on most major actors within the national government, incentives are being provided to draw cyber- professionals to the government's aid; this influx and diversification will only exponentially improve the ability of the United States to defend itself and her allies while effectively counter- attacking our enemies.

CONCLUSION

IT specialists are relatively new to the workforce and the homeland security and emergency management arenas. While our nation still faces many physical threats, there are many threats and vulnerabilities in the cyber-realm. The primary actors of concern are China, Russia, Iran, and North Korea, who each persistently seek unique ways to weaken America on any front through the cyber-realm. Most recently, we have seen Russia meddle in our elections and attack us in other ways.

To face and defeat these threats, we must stay ahead of the curve. Each of these is augmented and defended in the cyber-realm, making the information technology specialist a key actor in the national security and homeland response fields. They are also critical in disaster recovery in the private sector.

Going forward, legislation and policy needs to be carefully crafted to ensure that our own bureaucracy does not strangle our ability to act and react to our enemies in the cyber-realm. Training needs to become more applicable, frequent, and effective. Simply going through motions will do little to help us. Lastly, funding is necessary for any and all improvements recommended here. Funding will enable us to have a fully staffed, well-trained, and well-equipped front line of IT specialists who are ready to protect, defend, and counterattack on a moment's notice which will pay immeasurable dividends to American society.

CLASS DISCUSSION AND ESSAY QUESTIONS

1. What led to the introduction of the IT specialist, and why have these individuals become more important over time?
2. What are the five sources of cyber threats? Which one(s) are more concerning to you?
3. In what ways are governments and businesses vulnerable to cyberattacks? Are the situations similar or different? Explain.
4. This chapter mentioned several terms: business continuity, disaster recovery, continuity of operations, and cybersecurity. What are these terms and how are they related to one another?
5. What legislative, policy, and organizational changes need to be made to prevent or minimize cyberattacks?
6. This chapter focused extensively on the threats associated with information technology and what the IT specialist should do as a result. Can information technology benefit emergency management and homeland security? How can the IT specialist promote the use of technology so as to improve what we do about disasters and terrorist attacks?

REFERENCES

Alekseeva, Liudmila, Jose Azar, Mireai Gine, Bledi Taska, and Sampsa Samila. "The Demand for AI Skills in the Labour Market." VOX, CEPR Policy Portal, May 2020. https://voxeu.org/article/demand-ai-skills-labour-market.

Archives, Whitehouse. "The Comprehensive National Cybersecurity Initiative." National Archives and Records Administration, 2009. https://obamawhitehouse.archives.gov /issues/foreign-policy/cybersecurity/national-initiative.

BBC. "North Korea Hackers Stole $400m of Cryptocurrency in 2021, Report Says." BBC News. January 14, 2022. https://www.bbc.com/news/business-59990477.

CISA. "Cyber Threat Source Descriptions." CISA, 2022. https://www.cisa.gov/uscert/ics /content/cyber-threat-source-descriptions.

Das, Shouvik. "Iranian Hackers behind Biggest Ransomware Attacks of 2021: Report." Mint. February 18, 2022. https://www.livemint.com/technology/tech-news/iranian -hackers-behind-biggest-ransomware-attacks-of-2021-report-11645183640733 .html.

Dialogic. (2023). "Hacktivists." https://www.dialogic.com/glossary/hacktivism.

DHS. "Cybersecurity." Homeland Security, 2022. https://www.dhs.gov/topics/ cybersecurity.

Fidler, David. "President Trump's Legacy on Cyberspace Policy." Council on Foreign Relations, 2020. https://www.cfr.org/blog/president-trumps-legacy-cyberspace -policy.

Freiberger, Paul. "Analytical Engine." Encyclopædia Britannica, Inc., 2020. https://www
    .britannica.com/technology/Analytical-Engine.
Kharpal, Arjun. "China State-Backed Hackers Compromised Networks of at Least 6
    U.S. State Governments, Research Finds." CNBC. March 10, 2022. https://www
    .cnbc.com/2022/03/09/china-state-backed-hackers-compromised-6-us-state-gov-
    ernments-report.html.
Lemos, Robert. "Bush Unveils Final Cybersecurity Plan." CNET. November 13, 2003.
    https://www.cnet.com/tech/tech-industry/bush-unveils-final-cybersecurity-plan/#:~
    :text=The%20Bush%20administration%20signed%20off,that%20companies
    %20adopt%20certain%20measures.
Partida, Devin. "The Colonial Pipeline Ransomware Attack: The Fallout and Its
    Implications." secude.com. June 28, 2021. https://secude.com/the-colonial-pipeline
    -ransomware-attack-the-fallout-and-its-implications/.
Steinberg, Scott. "Cyberattacks Now Cost Companies $200,000 on Average, Putting
    Many out of Business." CNBC. March 9, 2020. https://www.cnbc.com/2019/10/13/
    cyberattacks-cost-small-companies-200k-putting-many-out-of-business.html.
Wikipedia. "Information Technology." Wikimedia Foundation. May 30, 2022. https://en
    .wikipedia.org/wiki/Information_technology.
Windrem, Robert. "Timeline: Ten Years of Russian Cyber Attacks on Other Countries."
    NBC Universal News Group, 2016. https://www.nbcnews.com/storyline/hacking-in
    -america/timeline-ten-years-russian-cyber-attacks-other-nations-n697111.

CHAPTER 23

Lessons about the Distributed Functions of Emergency Management:
Individual Contributions, Interdependencies and Collective Recommendations

David A. McEntire

INTRODUCTION

The chapter summarizes some of the main findings of the book and explores overall lessons generated from the authors' perspectives. It reviews some of the main arguments in each chapter – where the profession is clearly related to emergency management, partially related to emergency management, or insufficiently recognized in emergency management. The chapter also illustrates how each profession correlates to the others. And suggestions for improvement – such as education and training or increased budgetary needs – are identified.

CHAPTER SUMMARIES

As noted in the chapters of this book, there are a variety of professions that are related closely to disasters and terrorist attacks, and none more so than emergency management itself. However, others including geographers, firefighters, and law enforcement officers have close ties to emergency managers. Public administrators as well as public health and public information officers also engage frequently in emergency management functions. But, as this book illustrates, there are a myriad of additional professions that are vital (although sometimes less visible) for our effectiveness in dealing with all types of disasters – whether they be natural, technological, or anthropogenic.

DOI: 10.4324/9781003350729-23

Emergency Management

To start off, Brian Williams's impressive chapter on emergency management provided a great introduction to the book. He notes that emergency managers lie at the core of the emergency management system, and they are therefore able to harness networks to employ requisite knowledge and skills before, during, and after disasters. He reiterates that emergency management has always existed, but it has typically been a reactive profession. Williams provides a good discussion of the Incident Command System (ICS) and underscores the "tension between centralized/decentralized and standardized/flexible approaches to disasters and terrorist attacks" (p. 14). Hurricane Katrina was utilized, along with the discussion of ICS to illustrate the challenges of implementing bottom-up vs. top-down approaches. Fortunately, Williams points out that the responsibilities and focus of emergency managers has expanded, now to include greater emphasis on mitigation. Nevertheless, the emergency management system is facing an intergovernmental paradox where local government has the responsibility to implement in all phases of disasters, but also faces limited capacity.

Perhaps this problem can be overcome if the emergency manager adeptly employs the contributions of all relevant actors. In this sense, Williams notes that, "emergency managers are like symphony conductors. They do not need to know how to play every instrument, but they must know how the symphony functions as parts of a whole and be able to facilitate that functioning for the most beautiful aesthetic" (p. 17). Of course, this will require the "buy-in" from others, but this is difficult since people may not wish to give "funding and support for an event that has not happened and may never happen" (p. 18). Perhaps for this reason, Williams wonders if emergency managers may need to concentrate on the hazards and disaster functions that matter most.

Geographers and Land-Use Planners

Laura Siebeneck, Elyse Zavar, and Rachel Wolfe – the group of respected scholars and students from the University of North Texas's well-known emergency management program – cover geographers and land use managers in the second chapter of this book. Their contribution starts off with a solid discussion of academic perspectives of these professions. They state that, "geography is a pluralistic field that draws on many other areas of study to examine spatial relationships" (p. 27). The work of geographers has heavily influenced mapping and spatial descriptions such as latitude and longitude.

These authors reveal that one of the very important roles of geographers and land use managers is to identify hazards and facilitate mitigation and response. For instance, geographers may provide visualizations for wildfire incident command teams that may enhance the safety of firefighters and minimize the conflagration. Therefore, people in the public, private, and non-profit sectors may rely on geographers.

Another significant finding of the chapter is that Geographic Information Systems is an essential tool for physical human and environmental geographers. Siebeneck, Zavar, and Wolfe reveal that "geospatial data and geographical information systems are essential in the analysis of spatial patterns and oftentimes generate new knowledge and insights in the form of maps" (p. 30). They reiterate that geographic literacy is important in the "Next Generation of Emergency Management Core Competencies," which is a document produced by scholars affiliated with FEMA's Higher Education Program. The chapter on geographers and land use planners also explores the value of remote sensing via drones. Challenges related to funding, data interoperability, education, and collaboration are problematic and must be addressed going forward.

Firefighters

The chapter on firefighters by Andrew Byrnes reveals some very interesting trends about this profession. Firefighting may have initially been reactive in nature when it was first created; however, firefighters have increasingly taken on many new responsibilities. Byrnes, a respected fire instructor in Utah and around the nation, traces the history of the profession from the Roman Empire to the fire wards in Boston, and then to the present day. He explains the shift from volunteer to paid firefighters in many jurisdictions, and shares details about advances in protective gear and other safety equipment. Citing the "America Burning" report, Byrnes reviews some of the many recommendations to implement new fire codes, restructuring of fire departments, and educating communities to reduce deaths. He also points out increased attention and emphasis being given to technical rescues, hazardous materials, and terrorism.

Byrnes discusses the creation of the National Incident Management System (NIMS) and identifies how events like 9/11 and Hurricane Katrina have impacted the profession (e.g., revealing weaknesses such as the lack of funding and providing opportunities for improvement such as the adoption of new technologies). He asserts that, "there is little doubt that society will require the future emergency responder to be proficient at handling new, emergency hazards and/or threats" (p.55). He advocates for increased planning along with followup on after-action reports, education, and strategic planning. In his progressive view, "successful organizations plan to counter future threats and hazards and to respond without repeating the failures of the past" (p. 56).

Law Enforcement

Mike Gutierrez and Edward Valla use their extensive experience and academic knowledge to explore law enforcement as it relates to emergency management. These authors point out that policing didn't initially exist as a profession, but instead was performed by churches and neighbors. In time, modern departments were established as cities expanded and were publicly funded. While police forces have had to address corruption and become more professional over time, the officers in law enforcement increasingly play important roles in disasters and terrorist attacks. Police help with evacuation, sheltering, search and rescue, and quarantines. They fulfill roles in Emergency Operations Centers and assist with planning, training, and exercises. The police are also important players in all things related to terrorism (e.g., counterterrorism, Joint Terrorism Task Forces, fusion centers, etc.).

Gutierrez and Valla reiterate that there are many dangers facing police officers as witnessed on 9/11. They call attention to the culture of policing and underscore the importance of enhancing public trust in this institution. These authors recommend further collaboration with emergency managers. They state, "the reality is that police officers fulfill a critical role in emergency management and will continue to be an integral part of the emergency operations plan" (p. 65).

Emergency Medical Services

The chapter on Emergency Medical Services by Peter Burke, Steve Holley, and Margaret Mittelman is another exploration of the importance of first responder organizations in emergency management. These knowledgeable practitioner scholars indicate that emergency medical technicians and paramedics are engaged in pre-hospital medical care, and in that sense, are the "frontline health service provider".

Burke, Holley, and Mittelman share details about the profession from the battlefields in Europe and in the United States during the Civil War, along with the later appearance of ambulance services in Cincinnati and New York City. They show advances associated with the development of CPR and repeat the findings of reports that call for improvements in emergency care.

Emergency medical technicians (EMTs) and paramedics perform many similar roles as firefighters, particularly when it comes to rescue operations. They also coordinate with hospitals, participate in mass casualty operations, and have now taken on new roles relating to the COVID-19 pandemic. The authors are concerned about the safety of responders, regardless of whether it is in relation to natural disasters, terrorist attacks, or global pandemics. They request additional funding for this profession and recognize the need to prepare for the future. In their view, "EMS's most considerable challenge is reacting to a larger, more demanding, and more complex society" (p. 82).

Public Administration

Abraham Benavides' chapter demonstrates the critical role of public administration in emergency management. For those that are not as familiar with public administration as they want to be, Benavides defines it as "the art, science, and profession of administration and management" in government organizations (p. 88 citing Lynn, 1996). Benavides then provides a great review of the historical development of this profession, including the major factors that shaped how it has unfolded over time.

The respected professor reveals that government steps help address "wicked problems that individuals or a community cannot solve on their own" (p.92). He suggests that emergency management falls "neatly within the broad umbrella of public administration" (p. 90). His chapter argues that public administration principles and practices can help the emergency manager be more effective in cases such as 9/11 or COVID-19. He indicates the value of public administration in several functions and issues such as mitigation, continuity of operations, preparedness, mutual aid, communication and coordination, response, recovery, after-action reports, and vulnerable populations.

Benavides stresses two important priorities for public administrators and emergency managers: leadership and collaboration. He points out that emergency management will benefit from a variety of leadership traits and skills such as "coordination, decisiveness, experience, goal-oriented, communication skills, facilitator, ability to handle stress, listening skills, open-mindedness, responsible, capacity to prioritize, and the ability to think critically" (Chandler, 2020 on p. 101). He recommends to "engage all key players in focusing more on proactive approaches (mitigation and preparedness) than simply reactive approaches (response and recovery")" (p. 106). He notes "it will be essential to be familiar with the processes and resources available in responding to emergencies of various types" (p. 93). In particular, he cites Jones, who underscores the need to have realistic expectations, promote a culture of collaboration, seek common goals, promote trust, harness differences and expertise, celebrate successes, and follow up on commitment. If this type of collaboration can be promoted, it may allow us to move from "it is only the emergency manager's role" to "it is everyone's role in government" (P. 33).

Public Information Officers

Starting off his chapter with the case of Hurricane Katrina, John Fisher reveals that the loss of good communication or ineffective communication will likely have a negative impact upon response operations. For this reason, public information officers are extremely important in emergency management and homeland security. John Fisher, who has an impressive academic background in public information, states that the profession was introduced and became important in the United States during the Civil War. Public information officers also grew in importance during the civil defense era; events like 9/11 "required adaptation and a greater role for PIOs in preparedness and protection as well as in emergency response" (p. 114).

Most of the work of PIOs is completed in normal times. However, when disasters occur, PIOs will be extremely busy. After the San Bernardino terrorist attack, for instance, the PIO had to participate in command-level briefings, work with over 70 reporters, and share details about the event via social media. Fisher declares that "one person serving as the PIO is not sufficient for managing media and public requests for information" (p. 122). In addition to having sufficient personnel, "NIMS recommends that public safety communications and information systems need to be interoperable, reliable, scalable, portable, resilient, redundant, and secure" (p. 118).

Fisher discusses the importance of preparedness (creating plans with sample news releases, media lists, and contact information of government officials). PIOs need to consider the types of information that are needed (e.g., strategic, tactical, support, and public communications). He reveals that PIOs should gather and disseminate information so as to be responsive and transparent. PIOs are the bridge between government and media and their importance cannot be overstated. "In every after-action report, communications have been high in the list of issues. The public expectation for good, accurate, and timely information has not changed" (p. 130).

Non-Profit Management

The chapter by Tina Bynum, Heriberto Urby, and Arthur Simental is an outstanding exploration of the value non-profit managers provide to the emergency management profession. These scholars reveal that those involved in non-profit management have important motives that separate them from their peers in businesses and corporations. In the context of disasters, this means that they help to oversee the provision of medical care, food, water, and other in-kind or financial donations and services to help survivors recover from disasters.

The involvement of non-profit managers in emergency management is extensive and Bynum, Urby, and Simental reveal that it has only grown over time and even expanded internationally. In addition, the "impacts of terrorism, intrastate conflict, nation state aggression and ensuing humanitarian implications" requires the "expertise of professionals and volunteers in the non-profit sector" (p. 139). Complex emergencies, such as the one occurring due to the Russian military invasion of Ukraine, require non-profit managers who are able to address sheltering, medical, financial, and other needs of the victims of this gruesome conflict.

While non-profit managers may operate independently when needs appear, they are likely to communicate, collaborate, and coordinate with others through the Voluntary Organizations Active in Disasters. Bynum, Urby, and Simental indicate that these non-profit managers are increasingly focusing their attention on environmental justice concerns. There is an urgent requirement to address the basic needs of individuals who lack resources and rights. Furthermore, the mental health concerns of disaster victims must be addressed, which echoes the comments provided by Broome and Russell in Chapter 12. Bynum, Urby, and Simental conclude that there must be further engagement between non-profit managers and emergency managers. There are opportunities to improve fundraising, human resource management, and professional development. In spite of these opportunities for improvement, "the professionals and volunteers involved in non-profit organizations are a key resource that can augment a community's ability to manage disasters/emergencies due to their unique skills and abilities".

Homeland Security

As seen, Chapter 10 provides a discussion of the professionals involved in homeland security. Jackson Roberts and David McEntire begin their chapter with the 9/11 terrorist attacks and the sweeping reforms that occurred in government due to the creation of the Department of Homeland Security (DHS). Their work provides a glimpse of the very dynamic evolution of DHS due to its expansion from a White House Office, the inclusion of numerous federal agencies, tensions with emergency management, and further transitions that occurred after the disappointing response to Hurricane Katrina (confusion, failure to learn, communication breakdowns, supply failures and indecision).

Regardless of the organizational challenges and criticisms, the professionals involved in homeland security have a clear relation to terrorist attacks and even disasters. The Department of Homeland Security's mission is to protect "the American people from terrorist threats . . . and remains our highest priority". And, because the Federal Emergency Management Agency (FEMA) falls under DHS, there is a logical relation to natural disasters and technological events as well as the consequence of terrorist attacks.

Jackson and McEntire remind us that "DHS professionals are responsible for counterterrorism, cyberterrorism, aviation security, border security, port security, maritime security, administration and enforcement of our immigration laws, protection of our national leaders, protection of critical infrastructure, detection and protection against chemical, biological and nuclear threats to the homeland, and response to disaster". Sufficient staffing, training, budgetary support, as well as improved relations with FEMA will be needed to tackle the host of problems related to border control, an aging infrastructure, and cyber threats.

Public Health

The next chapter on Public Health was written by Arthur Simental, Tina Bynum, Lorin Schroeder, with special contributions by Anna Shaum. These authors do a fantastic job of revealing the history of public health in Europe and the United States, and how it has been shaped by disease outbreaks and war. They point out advances in public health relating to sanitation and the protection of food, water, and our environment, and underscore how advances in engineering, science, technology, and medicine have helped to protect well-being and save lives.

Simental, Bynum, Schroder, and Shaum mention the core functions of public health (i.e., assessment, policy development, and the provision of services), and then break these down into ten essential functions. They comment that, "public health has always played an essential part in the response and recovery to emergencies, disasters, terrorism, war, and conflict throughout history" (p. 145). As a result of the systemic COVID-19 public health challenges, the U.S. Federal Quarantine System is went under review by the National Academies of Sciences, Engineering, and Medicine Committee on Analysis to Enhance the Effectiveness of the Federal Quarantine Station Network based on Lessons from the COVID-19 Pandemic (NASEM, 2022). Likened to a 9/11 commission, the results of which are likely to shape the future of public health and the U.S. federal quarantine system for decades to come.

One of the great things about the chapter on public health is that it is a timely contribution considering the ongoing COVID-19 pandemic. There is a need to rethink admission into the country as well as quarantines and isolation. There is also a need to increase the professional ties between public health and emergency management and overcome the overloaded capacity with the healthcare and medical communities. The COVID-19 pandemic was "clearly of a size and scope to necessitate a full-scale response at all levels of government as well as engaging the participation of the private sector and individual citizens" (200).

Psychologists

Rodger Broomé and Eric Russell's chapter on psychology is important because this profession is in higher demand in general and vital in terms of all types of disasters. Broomé and Russell reveal that psychology appeared at the end of the 19th century and diverged into the scientific study of psychology and clinical psychology (or the treatment of those impacted by mental disorders). Their informative chapter explores the different branches of psychology including psychoanalysis, behaviorism, humanistic psychology, experimental psychology, and psychiatry. They illustrate that the military helped to develop the psychology of disasters, terrorism, and war, arguing that, "by studying terrorists' motivations and planning processes, the prediction of a deployment of terror and potentially intercepting it is vital to saving lives" (223).

Broomé and Russell go on to state that disasters – whether natural or human-induced – produce individual and collective psychological shock. Victims and survivors can be overwhelmed with grief about the loss of life, injuries, damage to home and property, lost jobs, etc. However, "terrorist attacks involve an inhumane malevolence that adds a sickening psychological dimension to tragedy to create horror" (221). They note how 9/11 impacted first responders, disaster workers, and the general population for decades.

The chapter on psychology then explores various ways to address Post-Traumatic Stress Disorder through psychological first aid, which may include counseling and pharmacological approaches. Critical Incident Stress Management programs have had mixed reviews in terms of success, and there has probably been an overuse of psychiatric drugs over the past three decades. We must eliminate the stigma about mental health and society's use of illness metaphor and question the disease model of mental health critically. For these reasons, emergency managers need to be more aware of psychological issues surrounding disasters and terrorist attacks. They need to seek support services from, "public health workers, clergy/chaplains, emergency responder peer support members, mental health para-professionals, educators, and of course, licensed mental health professionals" (p. 224).

Overall, Broomé and Russell indicate that, "communities and their emergency workers need to be as prepared as possible, including having psychologically supportive interventions and systems in place" (p. 228). They argue that "mental health issues cannot wait until the crisis for emergency managers to begin thinking about interventions" (p. 227). They conclude that, "disaster and terror attacks are part of human history and will continue. Perhaps it is time to make mental health a higher priority in emergency planning, response, and recovery efforts" (p. 227).

Pilots/Aviation

The laudable chapter written by Jack Troutt is probably one of a very few academic examinations of pilots as they relate to emergency management. This faculty member at Utah Valley University explores the development of the aviation profession and indicates the unique relation it has to disasters and terrorist attacks.

Troutt notes that people have dreamed about flight throughout history. This fascination led to the first balloons being used in France in 1783 and caused Orville and Wilbur Wright to work tirelessly to launch the first flight over Kitty Hawk, North Carolina, in 1903. In time, increased experience and changes in technology resulted in the first flights across the English Channel, over the Atlantic, and around the world.

This novel chapter reveals that aviation can be the source of a disaster or attack. There are countless examples including a balloon that caught fire in 1785 over the English Channel, the Hindenburg incident, the Canary Islands crash, the loss of Flight 800, and Concorde in 2000. Aircraft may also be the target or tool of terrorism as has been seen in numerous hijackings and 9/11. In addition to this, pilots and their aircraft can play vital roles in disaster response; they drop retardant on fires in rural settings and gather information about hurricanes through the NOAA Aircraft Operations Center. Pilots assist with evacuation and rescue people who are stranded on rooftops due to major flooding as was seen in the case of New Orleans after Hurricane Katrina. Aviation also helps to perform aerial damage assessment and can deliver people and supplies to the scene of a disaster. Troutt notes that, "one of the main focuses for any aviation response to a disaster is to enable the rapid movement of materials and disaster responders to where they are needed" (p. 237). In terms of terrorism, law enforcement uses fixed-wing aircraft and drones for their roles related to intelligence, surveillance, and reconnaissance. They can also be used to provide video, infrared cameras, and chemical and radioactive detectors.

Despite numerous advantages for emergency management and homeland security, there are notable challenges and opportunities that face the aviation profession. Managing air traffic and airspace is a problem. There needs to be better coordination between the Federal Aviation Administration and the federal, state, local, and tribal territorial groups that rely on aviation. Emergency management needs to take advantage of unmanned aircraft systems and unmanned aircraft vehicles, although there are concerns about drones (hobbyists interfering with official response operation and privacy).

Military

Michael Smidt's chapter on the military is an important contribution for this book, and he is the correct person to provide perspective on this subject since he worked in the Army for several decades. Smidt follows the creation of the military in the United States owing to conflicts with England and Native Americans. While the country could establish a Navy and an Army, it would only be allowed under the restrictions of the Constitution. In time, the military would become an important branch of government; it was influenced heavily by the world wars, the Cold War, and 9/11 (moving from national security and civil defense perspectives to now include the war on terrorism).

The chapter notes that the military has dual roles in the United States – to engage in international combat and to assist in various types of emergencies. In this sense, it has some overlap with the Department of Homeland Security, the Department of Justice, the Federal Bureau of Investigation (FBI), and the Federal Emergency Management Agency. However, the involvement of the Department of Defense inside the United States depends on the legal justification for deploying the military.

The military can become involved in all types of attacks and disasters through the National Guard as well as through Defense Support to Civil Authorities. It has often provided security, participated in search and rescue (with or without aircraft), cleaned up debris, and shared technical expertise if weapons of mass destruction have been utilized. It has provided medical support during the COVID-19 pandemic and assisted with immigrants at the border. In the future, Smidt believes the military could possibly be called on to assist with civil disturbances. However, the military can only be called up for legitimate purposes when the President and states request such outside assistance. The military must be careful not to overstep bounds and jeopardize its readiness for fighting wars.

Lawyers

The chapter on law by Heriberto Urby is a necessary component of this book on how various professions relate to emergency management. Law has existed around the world for several centuries, and lawyers were found immediately after the colonists arrived in what would become the United States of America. However, there was not always a relationship between law and emergency management. Urby states that throughout history, "lawyers were not prepared, adaptable or even keen on the idea of providing service to emergency managers and their respective personnel" (p. 279). Much of this is since, "even the best of them have not been formally or practically trained in major aspects of emergency management or homeland security law" (p. 279).

According to Urby, this is highly problematic. "One of the biggest general challenges is that definitive roles have not been expanded for lawyers in the areas of emergency management and homeland security" (p. 283). It is amply clear that disasters and terrorist attacks can create serious liabilities for everyone involved. For instance, law is necessary to create city ordinances, settle questions about appropriate land use, ensure there is not discrimination within the emergency management organization, identify appropriate mutual aid arrangements, ensure contracts will protect signatories, and verify that federal regulations are interpreted and implemented accurately. In addition, there have been many legal proceedings relating to a variety of disaster operations. The lawsuits against politicians in Italy is a case in point where the community was upset about the lack of warnings about earthquakes in one area of the country. But there have been other legal actions related to the failure to evacuate or shelter certain groups (e.g., the disabled). In addition, Urby points out that there are many new laws pertaining to emergency management and homeland security, so these groups should have close ties to legal counsel. There is a notable need to implement what Bill Nicholson calls litigation mitigation, which suggest that liabilities should be at the forefront of much of what is done to deal with disasters and terrorist attacks (p. 286).

Healthcare Emergency Management

Arthur Simental, Tina Binum and Lorin Schroeder's chapter on the professionals involved in healthcare emergency management defines healthcare systems as organizations and services "that improve, maintain or restore the health of individuals and their communities" (p. 291). As such, they have a close relationship to all types of disasters and terrorist attacks.

Starting at the World War II era, this unique chapter reveals that historical events like the Tokyo Sarin gas attack, 9/11, the Ebola outbreak in 2012, and the Las Vegas Country Music Festival Shooting have shaped the profession in profound ways. Because of ongoing challenges associated with such problematic events, the President, Department of Homeland Security, and The Joint Commission have all required and advocated for a number of changes to improve capacity and operations under emergency conditions.

One of the important changes relates to the Crisis Standards of Care (CSC), which establishes a systemic approach to dealing with disasters and other community emergencies. This is particularly important when mass casualty events take place. Another transformative change is in relation to ESF #8: Public Health and Medical Services. This part of the federal government's plan to deal with disasters and terrorist attacks relies heavily on healthcare emergency management, and requires the collaboration of many private sector partners with the American Red Cross and the U.S. Department of Health and Human Services.

Simental and Schroeder's work on healthcare emergency management exposes many of the weaknesses that have been revealed during the COVID-19 pandemic. There was simply not enough surge capacity. Difficult decisions had to be made about crisis communications and triage, often with mistakes and conflicting priorities. NIMS and ICS training has taken place, but events like COVID-19 reveal that it is more difficult to implement in practice.

Going forward, healthcare emergency management needs to address these persistent problems, gear up for possible war-time disasters, and find ways to prevent healthcare emergencies before they happen.

Nursing

The chapter on nursing by Dale Maughan, Allison Swenson, and Joy Cole provides a very nice exploration into this profession and how it relates to disasters and other extreme events. These authors examine the history of nursing from early times through our modern era. Nurses originally had no formal training, and this service was often performed by family or others who developed a reputation for healing the sick and afflicted.

War was a major reason later why nursing developed as a profession. Florence Nightingale saw the injured and dying during the Crimean War. She had a calling to care for the many soldiers in need and her efforts decreased the mortality rate dramatically. In time, she wanted to educate future nurses and succeeded in making nursing a respected profession. New information about germs and vaccines along with World War I and World War II helped to advance nursing for civilians and in the military.

As the profession has advanced over time, nurses have – according to the American Nursing Association – "consistently shown to be reliable responders" to disasters and other extreme events (p. 310). The International Council of Nurses states nurses are prepared and authorized to, "engage in the general scope of nursing practice, including the promotion of health, prevention of illness, and care of physically ill, mentally ill, and disabled people of all ages in all healthcare and other community settings" (p. 311). Veenema (2012, p. 17) also declares, "caring for patients and the opportunity to save lives are what professional nursing is all about, and disaster events provide nurses with an opportunity to do both" (p. 311 in chapter).

Maughan, Swenson, and Cole cover the many roles nurses perform when dealing with disasters: assessment, health education, and treatment. They also do a great job talking about other functions such as advocacy, health education, and collaboration. They note the challenges of triage and the need for ethical decision-making and altered standards of care. Unfortunately, this can be very challenging.

> The truth is that most nurses who respond to disasters have not received formal education or training in their undergraduate experience or professional development even after licensure. Disaster-related education is not a required topic in most undergraduate programs across the country. Studies have shown that most nurses who do respond to disasters to provide assistance have not received formal disaster training and they are also not likely to have had previous disaster experience.
>
> (p. 314)

The authors conclude that we need more resources (physical and human) in nursing and assert that there must be legal protections in place along with mental health support for those who work in this valiant profession.

Forensic Technicians

Amie Houghton, a former forensic expert with the Naval Criminal Investigative Service (NCIS), provided very intriguing chapters about forensic technologists and forensic pathologists. In her chapter on forensic technologists, Houghton notes that forensic science has a long history but has become increasingly visible due to TV programs such as *CSI* (despite many inaccuracies). As portrayed in the show, crime scene investigators document the scene and collect evidence. This evidence goes to where the use of science is relied upon to settle cases of law and assist in the prosecution or criminals.

This chapter notes that one of the first situations that relied upon forensic technologists was a case in China where a woman killed her husband and later burned his body to cover up the crime. In Bologna, Marcello Malpighi later documented fingerprints that could be used to connect perpetrators to the scene of the crime. Wilhelm Scheele, a Swedish chemist, developed a test to identify arsenic poisoning in corpses. Later on, advances were made to detect sperm in cases of rape, and hemoglobin and different types of blood in cases of murder. Techniques with anthropometry helped people link bones to victims. A major advance occurred when Sir Alex Jeffreys discovered DNA. According to Houghton, DNA, "has become the gold standard in forensic science," and people expect this evidence now (p. 324). Technology has improved in this area with new approaches such as genetic genealogy.

Houghton explains that "the ultimate goal of forensic science is to utilize physical evidence to provide a scientific link between a suspect, a victim, and a crime scene" (p. 325). At first, attention must be given to victims even if, "the mere act of rescuing victims can have a damaging outcome on the scene" (p. 333). As this is occurring, the next priority is to protect the safety of all personnel. Bomb technicians might be required, and the perimeter may need to be secured. At this point, investigations need to occur as soon as possible to gather and protect evidence. Many cases have been solved with this evidence (e.g., pieces of a radio in Pan Am 103, the axle of a truck in the Oklahoma City Bombing, remnants of a pressure cooker at the Boston Marathon Bombing). Very specialized equipment might be needed in this process; Houghton notes that crime scenes (and the scenes of terrorist attacks) are photographed and scanned using 3D-laser technology. As this evidence is collected, it must be carefully preserved with a clear chain of custody. Labs will then process evidence with specialization in biology, chemistry, toxicology, and fingerprint analysis. Others in the lab will examine firearms and trace evidence (such as paints, glass, fibers, etc.).

Houghton also observes that the size of crime scenes can sometimes be complicated. Multi-jurisdictional responses may be necessary but can be problematic. "Because these types of scenes are not encountered every day, there may not be a lot of preparation on how to establish, manage, and control a scene of this magnitude. Planning for the worst is something agencies need to be doing" (p. 334). There is consequently a need to determine roles and responsibilities.

Forensic Pathologists

Houghton's second chapter concentrates attention on forensic pathologists, who determine the cause of death. Forensic pathologists play a vital role in investigating crime scenes and terrorist attacks. They help to identify human remains.

Some of the first information about forensic pathology came from the Egyptians and Babylonians who dissected the dead and provided knowledge about human remains. However, it is the investigation on the body of Gaius Julius Caesar in 44 BCE that would first identify a cause of death. Antistius recorded 23 stab wounds in this well-known murder but identified only two of the wounds as fatal. There were other advances in the Middle Ages regarding injury, infanticide, and rape. In London in the 16th century, women "searchers" would look at the dead to determine if their death was due to the plague. Similar activities occurred among the colonists in 1635 in New Plymouth where hypothermia and starvation were commonplace. A notable advance resulted when Dr Benjamin Rush wrote *On the Study of Medical Jurisprudence* in 1811. This was a guideline for medicolegal issues, and such information helped cities like New York develop expertise in forensic pathology.

Whether called a coroner or a forensic pathologist, these individuals must be board-certified by the city, county, or state. They attempt to determine what happened in the incident and why death occurred. Their role is to identify the deceased, which can be particularly problematic in disasters because these events produce many victims who may be disarticulated, decomposed, burned, etc. In addition, forensic pathologists must document injuries or natural disease, determine when it happened, request testing, collect evidence from the body, provide expert testimony, oversee morgue operations, prepare remains for disposal, and certify deaths on reports.

Houghton lists many resources that will help forensic pathologists including various reports and field manuals. She discusses the importance of fingerprints, dental records, and X-rays, and illustrates the importance of DNA in identifying victims in cases such as the Camp Fire in California. Houghton reiterates the importance of the Target Capabilities List, which focuses on fatality management. Qualified teams, personal protective equipment, refrigerated trucks, and other resources are also helpful as are trained Disaster Mortuary Teams and exercises such as NORTHCOM in Indiana.

Dentists

Kathleen Young, a dental hygiene expert at Utah Valley University, begins her chapter by discussing the various types of disasters that may occur, including terrorist attacks. She reiterates that these events produce death and that, "dental records may be the only way to identify a deceased person" (p. 356).

Young explores some of the first dental techniques that took place in Pakistan as well as the creation of some important manuals in the year 1000 in Cordoba. She discusses some of the first dentures that were used, such as those worn by George Washington. In the 18th century, dentistry became its own medical field. John Baker became the first dentist in the USA, and Baltimore, Maryland, opened the first school to offer education and training on this subject, as fillings, bridges, crowns, and root canals were becoming more commonplace.

However, forensic dentistry began in 66 AD when a discolored tooth verified that Lollia Pauline was indeed the person who was killed. In the United States, Paul Revere was the first person to do similar identifications through dental evidence. He helped identify Dr Joseph Warren's body after he took a bullet to the face in the Battle of Bunker Hill. Nevertheless, it was Dr Oscar Amoedo who is considered to be the father of forensic dentistry. Others, including Dr Norman "Skip" Sperber, became famous for their expertise in forensic dentistry, as Sperber helped to identify many remains after the Oklahoma City Bombing, 9/11, and Hurricane Katrina, among other mass disasters.

Like Houghton, Young reveals that bodies may be obliterated in disasters so forensic dentistry may be required for identification. Teeth can survive in extreme environments, but this may require that the skull and teeth are initially protected with stabilizing glues. The subsequent postmortem analysis may require expertise in surgical exposure, radiography, and clinical examination. Forensic dentistry creates postmortem dental evidence with existing dental records. This allows dentists to determine either positive identification, possible identification, or inconclusive identification due to insufficient evidence.

There are a variety of challenges that forensic dentistry faces. There are many individuals that respond to disasters and terrorist attacks, but they may not have the requisite training in this area. For instance, after 9/11, over 350 dentists and others helped to identify remains. "One of the main issues in dealing with the number of volunteers was the variation in training" (p. 361). A total of 62% of these individuals had never had training in this specialized area, and it is difficult to assess the skills of volunteers who show up to help. In other cases, there may be problems with electricity, phones, the internet, or different languages, as was the case in Puerto Rico due to Hurricane Maria. Finally, there may be a lack of dental records, as was the case after the tsunami affected Thailand in 2004. Charting is often incomplete, and the legibility of dental forms makes records hard to understand at times. Overcoming these types of challenges will vastly improve forensic dentistry in the future.

Public Works

The chapter by Dave Bergner on the role of public works is one of the most unique contributions in the book since very little is written about this profession in emergency management. Bergner helps us comprehend the range of responsibilities and services of public works professionals and how they relate to disasters. He refers to the American Public Works Association in noting that public works is in charge of functions ranging from sanitation and utilities to facilities and fleet maintenance. However, the foremost responsibility is in term of transportation. Regardless, any of the aforementioned areas may be impacted by disasters.

Bergner's chapter does a wonderful job exploring the history of public works in the United States, and explaining why increased attention has been given to disasters over time. Bergner underscores ESF #3, which pays special attention to damage to transportation systems and how local, state, and federal governments may work together to address pressing issues in this area. Bergner also reiterates the importance of promoting resilience because "for many public works/transportation agencies, strategic planning for emergencies tends to have lower priority than planning, designing, constructing, operating, and maintaining core infrastructure and services" (p. 380).

In order to strengthen the role of public works in emergency management, Bergner recommends increased training since "little is available, or required, for public works/transportation employees" (p. 382). He is critical of small budgets for professionals in this area, and he is concerned about the number of individuals that may be retiring in the near future. He also points out "the nation's infrastructure is aging, deteriorating, and is generally approaching the end-of-life span. That means that roads, bridges, and tunnels are losing functional and resilience capacity and are more vulnerable to damage and destruction from natural events" (p. 390). Therefore, the public works/transportation professionals are "critical to the security and safety of every community and of the United States as a whole" (p. 393).

Information Technology Specialists

The chapter by Jackson and McEntire on information technology specialists is another relevant contribution since computers and related technologies are now impacting emergency management in a myriad of ways. Because computers are needed to run government and because cyberattacks are increasing in frequency and severity, "IT specialists have rapidly found themselves on the front lines of both homeland security and emergency management" (p. 396).

Jackson and McEntire provide a discussion of the unique knowledge and skill set that IT specialists need, and then reiterate that having security clearances may be even more important in the future. This is vital since cyberattacks are emanating from nation-states, terrorist organizations, industrial spy and organized criminal groups, hacktivists, and hackers. The chapter also suggests that government needs to increase its ability to react swiftly to threats as they arise.

The Colonial Pipeline attack was used as an illustrative case study in the chapter. It showed the potential costs and disruptions that occur when computers and infrastructure are impacted by cyberattacks. Therefore, more attention needs to be paid to general operations, business continuity, disaster recovery, continuity of government, and cybersecurity. New legislation must be passed to address the threats and issues, and further steps must be taken from a policy and organizational perspective. The chapter concludes with the assertion that we must have a "fully staffed, well-trained, and well-equipped front line of IT specialists who are ready to protect [and] defend . . . [the] American society" (p. 407).

The Interdependence of Each Profession

One of the key findings of this book is that each profession clearly relies to one extent or another on other professions to fulfill their functions relating to disasters and terrorist attacks. That is to say, the responsibilities performed by one agency or organization often require the assistance of other departments and units. The examples are countless, but several will be listed here:

- Williams says, "the emergency manager must effectively navigate the...legislative environment that guides the complex intergovernmental structures that must work in partnership during disaster" (p. 21). He also mentions the importance of dealing with the media in disaster situations.
- In terms of geographers and land use planners, Siebeneck, Zavar, and Wolfe mention that visualization and mapping is essential for wildfire teams. What is more, GIS can help determine where and how to rebuild homes after disasters, and this type of technology may promote better health outcomes after emergency situations. Remote sensing will also prove useful for homeland security infrastructure protection.
- The chapter on firefighting by Andrew Byrnes illustrates that professionals in this area rely heavily on emergency medical care providers to assist burn victims. He notes that "federal agencies, law enforcement, public health, and the fire service developed cooperative interdiction measures and a national terrorism fusion center network designed to provide resources, expertise, and information in order to protect communities and respond cooperatively" (p. 50). He likewise points out that firefighters may help identify what critical infrastructure needs to be hardened to fulfill the homeland security mission. Byrnes further suggests that "fire departments [need] to adjust their operations to include crime scene considerations and processes that would allow for chain of custody, evidence recognition, and preservation" (p. 54).
- Gutierrez and Valla make similar connections between law enforcement and firefighting. They reveal that, "the early colonies...established a watch system, which required adult males patrol cities to alert people about criminal activity [and] fires" (p. 60). These authors reiterate that police departments must take advantage of new technologies related to forensic science (p. 64).
- The chapter on EMS by Burke, Holley, and Mittleman underscores close relations of EMTs with other professionals. They note that EMS personnel often "act as firefighter/EMTs fulfilling a dual role" (p. 74). They also stress that, "the roles of EMS span public safety...public health, and in some instances, rescue operations, hazardous materials response, and emergency management" (p. 74). These authors reveal that "during active shooter events, Rescue Task Forces (RTFs) are formed with EMS providers joining with law enforcement to enter an area where the shooting occurred to treat and remove patients" (p. 78). In addition, EMS partners closely with emergency managers in terms of emergency operations centers, fusion centers, and healthcare systems.

- In his chapter on public administration, Benavides agrees about the importance of geography in identifying risk. His chapter also illustrates that emergency management can and will benefit from the practices of public administrators.
- Simental, Bynum, Schroeder, and Shaum indicate that public health relies on engineering to improve sewage and drainage, as well as effective leadership and management of government.
- Fisher's chapter on public information notes that police and fire may have their own PIOs. These individuals also liaise with emergency managers, elected officials, the media, and non-profit and private organizations.
- Troutt's chapter on aviation indicates that pilots are essential in wildland firefighting. He also reveals that aircraft were utilized to distribute vaccines during the COVID-19 pandemic.
- Smidt's chapter on the role of the military examines several roles for the armed forces, including support for "protecting food and water, medical evacuation, transportation, assisting with quarantine and isolation, providing medical supplies and emergency medical treatment, patient processing, and the management of human remains" (p. 265).
- The chapter on law by Urby indicates that legal issues permeate all aspects of government, including emergency management and homeland security. He agrees with Nicholson (2003d, p. 2) that, "the attorney must understand the client's business in order to provide the best legal advice."
- Broomé and Russell's contribution on psychology indicates that the emergency manager must seek and recruit mental health professionals who understand "stress management, interpersonal communication skills, leadership, mental performance skills, and also PFA" (p. 224).
- Simental and Schroeder's work reveals that the professionals involved in healthcare emergency management may need to coordinate with virtually every major federal government agency and department while fulfilling the responsibilities associated with ESF 8.
- Nurses, as illustrated by Maughan, Swenson, and Cole, follow up on the medical needs of victims who are transported to hospitals by emergency medical technicians. It is especially imperative that nurses must have legal protections while they perform their jobs in normal times and when emergency situations result in triage and the crisis standard of care.
- The chapter on forensic technologists by Houghton reiterates that it is important to know who will take the lead at the crime scene – whether it be the FBI, police, fire, or EMS. She also indicates that forensic technologists may need bomb technicians from the military and other law enforcement personnel to secure the crime scene.
- Young's chapter agrees that there is also a very close relationship between forensic scientists and dentistry. Dentists perform functions that are strikingly similar to the work of forensic scientists (although admittedly much narrower in scope). Forensic scientists may need dentists or dental hygienists to assist in the identification of human remains.
- Bergner's chapter on public works indicates that this government department frequently provides support to fire and police personnel and is often involved in disasters on an "as needed" basis. Public works will be increasingly important to emergency managers in the future as our infrastructure ages and becomes more vulnerable to disasters.

- The chapter on information technologists illustrates that these professionals are very concerned about cyberattacks and therefore perform a central role in the homeland security enterprise.

All these examples indicate that emergency management is indeed a distributed function as noted in the introductory chapter. The success of one professional organization is highly coupled with the activities of the others. Therefore, the system is extremely dependent on the contributions of each individual agency, department, or unit.

INDIVIDUAL CHALLENGES AND COLLECTIVE RECOMMENDATIONS

The chapters in this book identified several problems and potential solutions for the challenges we currently face. For instance, the work of this book teaches the need for improvements in the:

- understanding and practice of intergovernmental relations
- use of technology and equipment to perform a myriad of functions in firefighting and emergency management
- management and sharing of data and information
- utilization of drones for firefighters
- public trust citizens have toward police officers
- staffing for pre-hospital EMS personnel
- engagement with social media
- harnessing of non-profit organizations
- collaboration among FEMA and DHS employees
- overall capabilities and functioning of public health and healthcare emergency management pandemic response
- approaches taken to address disaster mental health
- application of drones in aviation
- the activation of the military in disaster situations
- integration of law into all aspects of emergency management
- protection of nurses against legal liability
- collection and processing of evidence to prosecute perpetrators of violence and identify the remains of disaster victims
- security of computer systems
- ensuring public works has a seat at the table and addressing deficiencies in critical infrastructure.

However, several similar lessons could also be drawn from the important contributions in this book. For instance, each chapter discussed the priority of planning and preparing for a variety of hazards and there was a common theme in much of the book in regard to addressing the needs of vulnerable populations. What is more, virtually all of the chapters discussed the need for additional resources, and the importance of further research, education, and training. There was also a notable assertion that all aspects of emergency management must evolve and improve in dramatic ways to meet the demands of the future. These latter themes will be covered below.

Resource Needs

One of the key takeaways of this book is that each of the professions indicated a lack of resources available for their vital emergency management and homeland security functions. The chapters on emergency management, geography, and EMS suggest that budgets are insufficient for the tasks they are expected to fulfil. The COVID-19 pandemic likewise uncovered the lack of funding to address the many and varied public health challenges that we are facing today. While the military often has more funding than other government organizations, Smidt does state that there are concerns about budgetary issues when the military fulfills roles outside its normal national security mission.

Others seem to suggest similar financial problems. Maughan, Swenson, and Cole illustrate that there is a need for more resources in nursing – physical resources, human resources, and intellectual resources. Broome also indicates that, "funding of emergency agencies is always a challenge" in the context of psychology (p. 227). Houghton's chapter also shows that many resources are required to process crime scenes and evaluate evidence. Those involved in forensic investigations and forensic science will need mass disaster crime kits, scales, measuring tables, evidence markers, fingerprint powder, and evidence packaging, among other things. Others have made similar claims about the lack of resources for homeland security and public works.

With these concerns in mind, it appears the entire system is stretched significantly. As Williams observes, "economic factors pose a challenge...and this often results is a loss of funding for emergency management even when there are foreseeable disasters". This situation is problematic because more resources are required to perform each professional obligation before or after disasters and terrorist attacks.

Research, Education, and Training

Another major finding of this book is that there is a need for additional knowledge and its application in all professions. For instance, Williams says that "the concept of managing networks is a vital aspect that must be a part of the education of future emergency managers" (p.19). He asserts that public and elected officials must be educated on disasters to understand where their communities' vulnerability lies. The chapter on geographers stressed the importance of education on GIS while the contributions on firefighting, law enforcement, and EMS advocated for more training on general emergency management concepts and the use of advanced rescue technology, how to deal with social disturbances, and appropriate responses to pandemics like COVID-19.

Other chapters made similar arguments about the importance of studies and integrating cutting edge techniques in practice. For instance, Benavides says we must focus more on developing skills related to leadership, management, and communication. Fisher notes that, training is an important aspect of PIO activities in the non-emergency times (p. 114). Urby also reiterates that we need better-educated lawyers who know how to handle disaster and homeland security issues. Jackson and McEntire underscore the need for training the diverse types of professionals working in homeland security.

The findings of this book also stress the need for the emergency manager "to seek and recruit mental health professionals that can be trained and educated in emergency planning, response, and recovery so they can navigate these situations appropriately for the various people they will engage" (p. 224). Simental and his colleagues indicate that more efforts should be devoted to the proper training of healthcare workers. Maughan, Swenson, and Cole agree and cite Veenema, who believes, "it is imperative that all nurses acquire a knowledge base and minimum set of skills to enable them to plan for and respond to a disaster in a timely and appropriate manner" (2012, p. 17, p. 312 in book). Houghton states that training is vital for those involved in crime scene operations and evidence processing. Young likewise asserts that one of the major problems in forensic odontology is, "the lack of trained personnel." She believes that education is of paramount importance, that new course offerings should be included in curriculum, and that older and more experienced forensic odontologists should mentor those who are newer to the profession.

Thus, there is almost universal agreement that more needs to be learned about disasters and terrorist attacks, and individuals must continue to advance their education and training in and across their respective professions.

A More Proactive Approach

Finally, each of the chapters in this book suggest the need for an improved vision and more concerted implementation of the various goals in the professions that relate to emergency management and homeland security. For instance, Williams recommends that emergency managers need to understand and correct the "social, political, and economic policy issues that can actually create vulnerability" (p. 20). Byrnes notes the urgency of adopting "a progressive culture of safety" (p. 57). The chapter on law enforcement advocates for a reformed approach of emergency management and Benavides suggests the need for more advocates who will promote disaster policies (p. 103). Simental, Bynum, and Schroeder point out that "Public health will undergo a transformation post-COVID-19" which will require "strong, dedicated and continuous legislative, policy, political, and legal support…to enable meaningful and impactful short- and long-term change" (p. 211). Similar arguments are made in the chapter on healthcare emergency management (i.e., the need for increased cross-sector collaboration, revised planning assumptions, and commissions to provide standards for civil defense type of emergencies).

Others make similar claims about the need for a dramatic improvement of emergency management and homeland security professionals. For instance, Jackson and McEntire state that "new threats…are constantly coming into play, jeopardizing our safety and our way of life. It is important that we recognize our weaknesses in our policies and protection systems, and work hard to turn our vulnerabilities into strengths" (p. 172). These authors therefore emphasize that in order "to face and defeat these threats, we need to stay ahead of the curve" (Jackson and McEntire p. 427). Other chapters in this book promote increased mitigation as well as "building a culture of preparedness".

CONCLUDING THOUGHTS

This exploration into the diverse professions involved in emergency management and homeland security underscores just how valuable each one is for individual communities and society in general. Benavides (p. 104) provides an important quote from Jane Bullock and George Haddow (2019), who state that, "there is no such thing as a simple disaster anymore." As a result, "the capability and capacity of our nation's emergency management system to respond to these more complex events is at a breaking point" (Jane Bullock and George Haddow as cited by Benavides p. 104).

Benavides is also correct to observe that, "in the coming years, how our society responds to emergencies will continue to be a main issue of concern. How we prepare, mitigate, respond, and recover from these challenges will be the measure of how well our society prospers" (Benavides p. 104). Each profession will play a vital role in how the future plays out in terms of disasters and terrorist attacks.

CLASS DISCUSSION AND ESSAY QUESTIONS

1. What professional roles in disasters were you most aware of? What professions did you not fully understand in the context of disasters and terrorism?
2. This book suggests that the various professions involved in emergency management and homeland security are highly interdependent. What examples of this can be given? Are there others in the book that could be mentioned?
3. What recommendations could improve individual professions?
4. What are the common weaknesses among all professions that need to be corrected going forward?
5. What new knowledge did you gain from this book and how could it help you to be a better professional in the area of emergency management and homeland security?

Index

Bold page references indicate tables and *italic* page references indicate figures

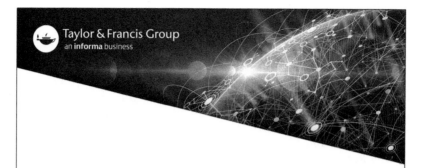

9781032396446